Turn Back
Before
BAGHDAD

Turn Back Before BAGHDAD

Original Frontline Dispatches of the Gulf War
by American and British Correspondents

Laurence Jolidon

UNIVERSITY of
NORTH GEORGIA™
UNIVERSITY PRESS

Blue Ridge | Cumming | Dahlonega | Gainesville | Oconee

This book is dedicated to the men and women of many nations who fought in the Persian Gulf War, 1990-91, and especially to those who gave their lives. May you rest in honorable peace.

Copyright © 2016 University of North Georgia Press

First Edition © 2002 Laurence Jolidon

All rights reserved. No part of this book may be reproduced in whole or in part without written permission from the publishers, except by reviewers who may quote brief excerpts in connection with a review in newspaper, magazine, or electronic publications; nor may any part of this book be reproduced, stored in a retrieval system, or transmitted in any form or by any means electronic, mechanical, photocopying, recording, or other, without written permission from the publisher.

The opinions expressed in the commentary in this book, preceding each day's chapter, are solely those of the author (LJ) and do not necessarily reflect—indeed may conflict with— the views of the correspondents whose work also is collected herein. Their work appears as originally written for the combat print pool for Desert Storm, and as it was made available with the consent of all partiesfor the use of any and all representatives of the media.

The editors of this second edition have corrected mechanical (spelling and grammar) errors. All other mistakes appear in their original form, as were the wishes of the author.

Published by:
University of North Georgia Press
Dahlonega, Georgia

Printing Support by:
Lightning Source
La Vergne, TN

Cover and book design by Corey Parson.

ISBN: 978-1-940771-19-9

Printed in the United States of America, 2016
For more information, please visit ung.edu/university-press
Or email ungpress@ung.edu

Table of Contents

Preface — xxv

Turn Back Before Baghdad: An Introduction — xxvii
    By Ron Martz

First Edition Introduction — xxxv

Part I
Desert Storm: Ultimatum to Cease-Fire Tent

Tuesday - January 15, 1991

"Racehorses That Smell the Barn"—82nd Airborne Gets Rid of Xmas Gifts, Burns Letters, Prepares to Fight — 3
    By Robert Dvorchak

Scud Alert: "If This is Another Practice, Someone Should Have Their Butt Kicked" — 4
    By Charles Richards

Wednesday - January 16, 1991

U.S. Forces Scramble to Guard Airbase from Surprise Attack: "We Thought That SOB Was Coming" — 7
    By Michael Hedges

Allied Jets Roar Overhead as Ultimatum Ticks Down; U.S. Army VII Corps Still Working Out the Kinks — 9
    By Douglas Jehl

Thursday - January 17, 1991

Air War Begins: "This is History in the Making" — 12
    By Edith Lederer and David Evans

Wild Weasels Roar Into Action: "Hey, Bud-man. Hit 'em Hard" — 12
    By Susan Sachs

Cruise Missiles Off the Wisconsin: "Man, I Never Thought It Would Come to This" — 13
    By George Rodrigue and Robert Ruby

First Allied Air Kill: "When the Airplane Blew, the Whole Sky Lit Up" — 15
    By Guy Gugliotta and Joseph Albright

A Day for Rejoicing—Catapulted Into the Sky, Fully Expecting Some Would Never Come Back — 16
    By Carol Morello

The Underground Nightmare: Gas Alert in VII Corps — 18
    By Douglas Jehl

Sourceable Information From "Western Observer"—6,600 Americans in Saudi Arabia As the War Started   20
By Mort Rosenblum and Ahmad Hamad

Friday - January 18, 1991

Stealth Fighters Pay Early-Morning Visit to Baghdad: AT&T Building Goes "Poof"   22
By Frank Bruni

Despair in a British Tornado Squadron: Two Bombers Lost in First Days of Air War; Pilots Missing   24
By Ian Henry

From Ugly Stepchild to Unlikely Darling of the Skies: The "Spectacular" Scud-Killing Patriot Missile   26
By Joseph Albright and Guy Gugliotta

These Marines Say Their Prayers. A Few Hours Later, Say Them Again. Islam "Honors Contracts"   28
By Jeff Franks

Newest U.S. Military Anti-Terrorist Squad Carries Weapons and Holy Books   29
By Gary Regenstreif

Saturday - January 19, 1991

First Iraqi Prisoners Logged by a U.S. Navy Frigate: Five Dead, 15 Captured Off Kuwait Coast   32
By George Rodrigue and Robert Ruby

12 Iraqi Prisoners Placed on Hold by U.S. Marines   33
By Jim Michaels

A Great Allied Land Convoy Moves Into Position to Strike, Little White Pills and All   34
By Laurence Jolidon

First U.S. Pilot Reported Missing off USS Saratoga: May Be Down on the Desert Floor Somewhere   36
By Neal MacFarquhar

Married Woman With Machine Gun: The Supply of Shampoo Seems Endless, Like the Desert   38
By Richard Kay

Sunday - January 20, 1991

USS Saratoga Draws a Wake of Hard Luck—2nd Plane Fails to Return From Mission Over Iraq   42
By Carol Morello

USS John F. Kennedy Uses a SLAM on a MITWI (Major Industrial Target in Western Iraq)   43
By Neal MacFarquhar

Stealth Pilot's Biochemical Electric Charge Kicks In Far Above a Lightless and Waterless Netherworld   44
By Frank Bruni

First Purple Heart: Navy Medic Hit by Shrapnel While on Kuwaiti Border Patrol   48
By Jonathan Ferziger

Another Armed Presence in the Desert: Civilians With Sidearms and Automatic Weapons   49
By Laurence Jolidon

Christian GIs Pray Hard on Front Lines of Islamic Land: "No Matter What Happens, I'm Going to Heaven"   50
By Gary Regenstreif

Monday - January 21, 1991

Secret Weapon For Navy Seizure of First Iraqi POWs on Oil Platforms: "We Snuck in and Surprised Them"   52
By George Rodrigue and Robert Ruby

At the Sight of Allied POWs on Baghdad TV, the Mighty Thunderbolts Grow Quiet   54
By Joseph Albright and Guy Gugliotta

Red Sea Aerial Armada Controls Skies With 2,000 Sorties Daily, But Allied Plane Losses Reach Double Digits   55
By Neal MacFarquhar

Tuesday - January 22, 1991

The Hardest Decision: When to Send in Ground Forces: "We Will Wait Until We Are Sure We Can Win Quickly"   58
By Philip Stephens

3rd U.S. Plane Lost From Saratoga; Reporters Kept Away   59
By Carol Morello

Air Force Pilots Pluck Navy Flier From Desert: Rescue Team "Comfortable" Working in Daylight   60
By Joseph Albright and Guy Gugliotta

7 Days Later: All in a Day's Work   61
By Gary Regenstreif

Wednesday - January 23, 1991

Modern Bedouin Warriors Wear Robes Over Their Khaki, Predict War Will Last Only 3 Weeks   63
By Leon Daniel

Iraqi Artillery Targets Marines Near Khafji, Abandoned City on the Saudi Coast   64
By Kirk Spitzer

For a Near-Good Time, Desert Disco Has Near-Beer, a Chaplain, and Near-Anonymous Women in Black   65
By Stephanie Glass

A Guard's Duty: Digging on a Rock and Waiting for the Guy Who Doesn't Know the Password   65
By Laurence Jolidon

Holy Toledo, It Was Just Going to Town, and Then 50 Iraqi Tanks Surrender . . . To the Egyptians   66
  By Charles Richards

Every New War Brings New Reasons To Throw Your (Unprintable) Teddy in a Corner   68
  By John Fullerton

Marine Fighters Make Mid-Air Pit Stops for Fuel So They Can "Mess Up Somebody's Day" in Iraq   69
  By Lara Marlowe

USS Mobile Bay on Lookout for Mines in the Sea   70
  By David Alexander

Thursday - January 24, 1991

Mystery Explosion Destroys Ammo Truck in 82nd Airborne Convoy   73
  By Robert Dvorchak

Bomb-Disposal Teams Specialize in Loud Bangs and Quiet Nerves: "They Probably Got a Missile"   75
  By Charles Richards

Allied Fighters Exploit Clear Weather Over Iraq; "A Lot of Blown-Up Stuff on the Ground Up There"   76
  By David Evans

As Bombs Fall, Marine Chaplain Hears More Confessions   77
  By Leon Daniel

Speedy Marine Artillery Already Returning Iraqi "Mail," Showing a "Half-Baked Hitler" How to Play Hardball   78
  By Kirk Spitzer

Women Marines in "Rear Area" Combat Zone: One is Worried Men Won't Have a "Clear Head" if She's There   80
  By Jim Michaels

Friday - January 25, 1991

Some Desert Inhabitants Carry Weapons, Others Offer a Perfect Future to Perfect Stranger   83
  By Mike Tharp

Royal Air Force Chief Returns Fire From U.S. General   84
  By Ian Henry

The "Half-and-Half" U.S. Division: Plenty of Officers, but Not Enough Fighting Vehicles to Train or Fight   85
  By Douglas Jehl

Ready to Draw Blood, British Armored Brigade Moves North to a New Killing Ground   86
  By Simon Clifford

As Bagpipes Skirl, Desert a Kaleidoscope Extraordinaire Where a Tank Barrel Anchors a Clothesline   88
  By Philip Stephens

Saturday - January 26, 1991

USS Ranger Determined to Wipe Out Iraqi Navy, if it Can Be Found; Ultimate Objective Full Control of Gulf — 91
   By George Rodrigue

All Quiet on the American Front, Except for Scraping of Shovels: "Every Day You Dig a Little Deeper" — 92
   By Robert Dvorchak

British Armored Unit Travels Into "Great Tank Country" on Forged Convoy Papers — 94
   By Richard Kay

Life in a U.S. Army Tent is Dusty, Cold, and Coed But Not a Problem — 95
   By Laurence Jolidon

Biggest Artillery Attack Since War Began: Marines Zero in on Iraqi Positions — 98
   By Kirk Spitzer

Mine-Clearing Class Preps Marines for Hidden Dangers, Buddies Who Could "Disappear in a Big Pink Mist" — 99
   By Patrick Bishop

The Sound of a Distant Whump Means the Patriot Heroes Are Hard at Work: "We Got It!" — 100
   By Guy Gugliotta

Sunday - January 27, 1991

U.S. Projects 10% Casualties on Front Lines: "First Time They Have to Write One Off" Will be Very Upsetting — 105
   By Douglas Jehl

Iraq Laid About a Half-Million Mines in Kuwait: "This Guy Knows What He's Doing and Likes Mines" — 106
   By Jeff Franks

U.S. Navy Pilot Spots Large Oil Slick off Coast of Kuwait; Act of Desperation or Just Despoliation? — 108
   By George Rodrigue

Huge Oil Spill Seeping from Sea Island Terminal Has Not Been Set Afire — 109
   By Susan Sachs

"Frustrated Cargo" King Creates Plywood Surplus: "If We Occupy Kuwait or Iraq, We Can Build" — 110
   By Mike Tharp

Monday - January 28, 1991

Friend or Foe? Man in Saudi Uniform Indignant at Interrogation, But Allied Soldiers Taking No Chances — 113
   By Charles Richards.

Marines Make Peace at Midnight With 80 Pounds of Powder, Bomblets That Turn Armor to Swiss Cheese — 114
   By Colin Nickerson

Kuwaiti Sailors Kiss the Liberated and Beloved but Mostly Uninhabited Sand of Tiny Qaruh Island   116
By Keith Kendrick

Missile with Camera in Nose Shows Close-Up of Targets About to Disappear, Opening Chunks of Friendly Sky   117
By George Rodrigue

Follow-On Briefing: Iraqi Resistance Crumbling, Oil Slick Shrinking   119
By George Rodrigue

Women Add Drama to U.S. Airbase: Cruising the Drag from "American Graffiti"; a Fighter Plane Named "Six"   120
By Edith M. Lederer and David Evans

Tuesday - January 29, 1991

Border Shootout Between Iraqi and Saudi Patrols: "This is Not a Drill. There are Bad Guys Out There"   125
By Gary Regenstreif

Not Much to Buy in This Empty Desert, But British Troops Get U.S. Dollars for Pocket Money   126
By Keith Dovkants

Wind Soldiers Call "The Hawk" Hangs On With Cold Claws   126
By Robert Dvorchak

High-Tech Airbase Playing Chicken With Gas Alerts: Peace Activists at Home Told Evil "Must Be Stopped"   127
By Alexander Higgins and Storer H. Rowley

After 10 Days of Bombing, Considerable Damage to Iraqis; Damage Assessment—Difficult to Impossible   129
By Susan Sachs and Gilles Trequesser

Iraqi POW From Chicago Captured; "Waiting a Long Time for America to Come Finish This Problem"   131
By Tarek Hamada

Wednesday - January 30, 1991

U.S. Marines Claim Umm al Maradim Island Off Kuwaiti Coast   133
By Tarek Hamada

At Least 4 Million Instructions on How to Surrender, If You're An Iraqi Soldier   134
By Douglas Jehl

No Gas Masks Issued, Local Drivers Desert; GIs Flown in To Keep Allied Military Trucks Moving   136
By Stephanie Glass, Tim Collie, and Peter Copeland

Iraqis Make First Move With Raids Into Kuwait: Fighting With Marines "Hellacious"   137
By Kirk Spitzer

Serious Fighting at Khafji 1st Major Battle of War—The Iraqis "Probably Ought to Call 911 Right Now"   138
By Jim Michaels

Iraqi Incursion: Khafji Seized, Armored Thrusts at Several Points on Saudi-Kuwaiti Border   139
   By Caryle Murphy

Mission Unsuccessful: A Daring Dash into Khafji to Rescue Two GIs Missing from Patrol   140
   By Jim Michaels

Thursday - January 31, 1991

Allies Take Back Part of Khafji, But Iraqi Invaders Still Control Gates of City   143
   By Jim Michaels

Behind U.S. Air and Artillery, Saudi and Qatari Troops Eject Iraqis From Khafji   144
   By Caryle Murphy

Report of Marines Killed in Iraqi Incursion Accurate, But Not in Battle for Khafji   145
   By Kirk Spitzer

Numbers Game: Many Iraqi Vehicles Escape Bombing of Khafji "Like a Close-Out Sale on Ladies' Lingerie"   146
   By Susan Sachs, Dick Thompson, and Gilles Tresquesser

Expectation of 1,000 Allied Casualties a Day Triggers Debate Over Treating the Enemy   148
   By Michael Hedges

A Gurney Too Far: Doctors Dropped at Front   150
   By Michael Hedges

Tough American Paratroopers Go Dainty, But Highly Motivated, into Battle   151
   By Gary Regenstrief

U.S. Air Chief Calls Iraqi Attack "Stupidest," Scud a "Zero Weapon" With Huge Psychological Impact   152
   By David Evans and Edith M. Lederer

Top Marine Commander in Gulf Sizes Up Khafji Battle: Bad Deal for Iraqis and Worse is Yet to Come   154
   By Caryle Murphy, Tom Ferraro, and Patrick Bishop

Friday - February 1, 1991

Friendly Fire Near-Miss Too Close for Comfort—15 Yards: "Someone Got the Wrong Lat-Long"   161
   By Jeff Franks

Death of 11 Marines in Kuwait Appears to be Friendly Fire: "In Close Battles It's a Fight For Your Life"   162
   By Kirk Spitzer

Saudi General Calls Khafji Enemy "Suicide Mission"; U.S. Liaison Officer Says 200 Iraqis Died in the Battle   163
   By Storer H. Rowley

In the Battle for Khafji, Winner is Clear, But Unanswered Questions Still Smolder   164
   By Ray Wilkinson

Donna the Army Reservist Wants Combat: "I'd Like to Bag Baghdad Betty Personally"   167
   By Laurence Jolidon

The Padre as Warrior—Stripped-Down Land Rover, Tuck and Cigarettes: "God is Not an Insurance Policy" 169
By Richard Kay

More Iraqi POWs Taken at Sea, 20 Sailors From Umm al Qasr: "Pretty Dispirited, Cold and Wet" 170
By Tarek Hamada

Saturday - February 2, 1991

50 U.S. Military Vehicles Reported Missing; A Dozen or More Palestinian Terrorists Reported Present 173
By Douglas Jehl

In the Tank Repair Shop: Kneel, Pray, and Pass the Ammunition, Padre 175
By Philip Jacobson

Iraqi Seamen Say They Were Ordered to Defect: "They Know They Cannot Fight" 177
By Tarek Hamada

Sunday - February 3, 1991

Desert Looks Peaceful, but is That a Speck on the Horizon? "If You Weren't Religious, You Are Now" 179
By Jeff Franks

The Other American Army in the Gulf, Out From Behind the Desk: "Free the Louisiana National Guard" 180
By Peter Copeland

New Mine-Clearing Weapon Works Great—While the Top Brass Are Watching 182
By Douglas Jehl

Monday - February 4, 1991

Navy Turns Guns on Kuwait; 4 Marines Die in Helicopter Crash 186
By Colin Nickerson

Graves Registration Company: "No Unknown Soldiers" 187
By Caryle Murphy

When the Wind Picked Up, Those Numerals Began Roaming Well Beyond Dorking al Hambra 189
By Simon Clifford

Shit Detail: If Nobody Wants to Do It, But Somebody Has to, It Pays to be Busy Doing Something Else 190
By John Fialka

Business is Good in a Desert Crossroads Named Rafha, Thanks to This "Stinking War" 193
By Laurence Jolidon

Tuesday - February 5, 1991

18 Saudi Troops Reported Killed, 16 Wounded in Battle for Khafji: "We Need the Americans Over Here" 197
By Paul Basken

Iraqi Patrols Slipping Through Allied Lines; "A Counter-Reconnaissance Battle" 198
By Gary Regenstreif

Cryptic Radio Messages From Baghdad Ratchet Up Terrorism Fears   199
By Keith Dovkants

Fairly Undemonstrative But Damn Proud British Write Their Boys: "I'll Stick My Finger Up His Nose"   200
By Jeffrey Ulbrich

Wednesday - February 6, 1991

These Could be the Usual Suspects, But Time is Going By, and We'll Always Have Wadi Raf, Darling   203
By Mike Tharp

Dirty, Greasy Sailors Forget Makeup: "Men Have Been Sailing for 2,000 Years and Women Can't Erase That"   204
By Kathy Evans

Combat Cameramen "Capturing Human Side of the Air War"   206
By Dave Schad

2 F-15 Pilots Down 4 Iraqi Planes Trying to Escape to Iran: "The Most Spectacular Thing I Have Ever Seen"   207
By Alexander Higgins and Storer Rowley

Pets, Bibles, Bathrooms, and The Truth: Reporter's Notebook   209
By Charles Richards

U.S. Army Graves Registration: Can't Forget the Faces   210
By Robert Dvorchak

Rachel the RAF Cargo Chief Shoulders Her Load   211
By Jeffrey Ulbrich

Thursday - February 7, 1991

Saudi Colonel Explains All: I Tricked Iraqis Into Attacking Khafji (By Withdrawing)   214
By Gerard Evans

From Commons to an Army Camp: British MP On Duty in the Gulf Knows His Duty   215
By Philip Jacobson

Don't Fall for that Tank-Sized Oil Spot: Allied Pilots Finding Few Prime Targets Left in Iraq   216
By Storer Rowley and Alexander Higgins

The Warrior Agreement: Fighting For a Ticket Home, Amid Boxes of Highly Filling Choccies   217
By Simon Clifford

Friday - February 8, 1991

British Soldier Turns 21: Touch of Brandy But A Long Way From Walsall   220
By Colin Wills

Videotapes From Home on a Flickering Screen: "Say Hello to Daddy"   222
By Douglas Jehl

The Morning the Air War Began: "The Starting Gun Goes Off and You Cross the Line"   223
By Edith Lederer and David Evans

New Moon Approaches, Illuminating the Outline of an Oncoming War   228
By Charles Richards

Last Hurrah, Last Shots Fired for USS Wisconsin: "We Just Don't Build Them Like This Anymore"   230
By George Rodrigue

Last Call for a Last Will and Testament: Leaving Everything in the World to Someone   232
By Carol Morello

A British Officer's Life: From Wrestling a Hamper to a Surfeit of Marmalade   233
By Keith Dovkants

Saturday - February 9, 1991

Ominous Shapes, Iraqi Planes Keep U.S. Ships on Alert: "Like Being in a Woodpile With a Copperhead Snake"   236
By Mort Rosenblum

Praise Be to Allah—Muslim GIs Love Saudi But Oppose the War: "I Can't Be a Part of It"   237
By Carol Morello

Sunday - February 10, 1991

A Secret Base Where Bart Gets a Ride From Cheney: "For 60 Days, Everyone Thought We Were in Turkey"   241

Col. Flowers Gives a Pep Talk: "The Wind is Blowing, It's Starting toRain, and You've Got a Bad Feeling"   244
By Carol Morello

Confusing Skirmish at Iraqi Observation Post: "This is the Stuff That is Going to Get Someone Shot"   245
By Michael Hedges

Monday - February 11, 1991

It's a Free Country. But Peaceniks Suck: "It's Not Like They're Going to Stop the War and Pull Us Back Now"   251
By Douglas Jehl

The Crowded Skies of Iraq: If You Want To Attack, Get in Line, Take a Number   252
By Stewart Powell

Gathering Intelligence Any Way You Can: Iraqis Trying "To Show Us Bomb Damage That Isn't There"   254
By Michael Hedges

Tuesday - February 12, 1991

The Bear Visits the Marines: "The Logistical Situation is Absolutely Superb"   258
By Susan Sachs, Denis Gray and Jeff Franks

Maj. James Hewitt—Future Famous Name in Uniform; The Talk Was of Horne, Cost of a Haircut at Harrod's   259
By Richard Kay

Wednesday - February 13, 1991

Amenities of Civilization: Band Music, a Bank of Telephones for Calling Home, Mascots, and Hot Meals 262
By John Mecklin

Neat Iraqi Defector Screams "Saddam!" Before Respectfully Removing His Shoes 264
By Joseph Albright

Scots Sent Youngest Recruits to the Gulf War Not Yet Old Enough for Duty in Northern Ireland 265
By Gordon Airs

Thursday - February 14, 1991

Debut of Multiple Launch Rocket Systems "Biggest Goddam Roman Candle I've Ever Seen" 268
By Colin Nickerson

Tornados Scrap Missions Over Cities to Avoid Civilians: "Professionalism Says Don't Throw Bombs Around" 269
By Ramsay Smith

Friday - February 15, 1991

Letter From a Soldier's Sister—But Not Just Any Soldier 272
By Gary Regenstreif

"Poor White Middle Class, Poor Black Kids, Hispanics from the Barrio . . . That's Who I Want to Go to War With" 272
By John Sack

Marines Move North, Stretching Horizon to Horizon on Washboard Ribbons of Road 275
By Molly Moore

Saturday - February 16, 1991

Whatever Iraqis Think They Know of Allied Plans, The Allies Assume is Based on Thin Intelligence 279
By John Fullerton

Inside a Noisy Sultan, an Echo of British Pretension: "Discipline of Blind Obedience Has to Be There" 281
By John Fullerton

Flash! War is a Dirty and Uncomfortable Shambles, Even Before it Starts 282
By Simon Clifford

Careering Out of Fingerspitzengefühl, Gulf War Gives Rise to New Jargon as Well as a Few Careers 283
By Robert Fox

Marine Log Base a Microcosm of American Society: All the Guys in the Stockade are Called "Elvis" 285
By Caryle Murphy

Sunday - February 17, 1991

Falklands or Persian Gulf, Accents Differ, Killing's the Same: Finer Techniques of Hand-to-Hand Combat 290
By Robert Fox

Supply Sergeants Live Cozily in Desert, Where Lumber is Legal Tender: War Means "Trade, Trade Your Ass Off" 292
By Carol Morello

Two 1st Infantry Soldiers Killed by Friendly Fire: Apache Crew "Well-Disciplined, Together 15 Months" 294
By Michael Hedges

Body Bags Also Good for Sleeping on Cold Nights 295
By Frank Bruni

Love Can Conquer Fear Even in Battle: "Most of the Time Things Are Screwed Up" 297
By Jim Michaels

Monday - February 18, 1991

"Turkey Shoot!"—Ugly and Ominous Apaches Stage Nighttime Assault 50 Miles Inside Iraq 300
By Robert Dvorchak

U.S. Artillery Hits Mostly Desert: Iraqi Commanders Now Have Confirmation Allies Have Moved Far West 301
By Joseph Albright

British Artillery Break Out New Multi-Barrel Guns: "I Can't Help Feeling Sorry for the Iraqis" 302
By Gordon Airs

Lionized Patriot Battery Yearns for Another Kill: "You Are the Very Best Soldier in Saudi Arabia" 303
By Dave Montgomery

Tuesday - February 19, 1991

USS Princeton, USS Tripoli Hit Mines: Sailor Sleeping in Brig Woke Up "Wondering If I Was Dead" 307
By Bill Gannon and David Alexander

Women Engineers Not in the Fight and They're Sorry—"You'd Better Come Back . . . You'd Better . . ." 309
By Carol Morello

Iraqi Troops Fake Surrender to Locate U.S. Border Positions, Pay Dearly 311
By Michael Hedges

Water Well Appears Magically in Desert: "For Those of You Who Don't Believe . . ." 313
By Phil Davison

U.S. Troops Seize Iraqi Observation Post: "They Have Given Up the Border" 314
By Gary Regenstreif

Wednesday - February 20, 1991

Raiders of the Vast Iraq: "I Thought They'd Smoked Us and Gotten Behind Us" 317
By Michael Hedges

Making Unavoidable Friendly Fire Less Likely: "I Will Not Haphazardly Engage What I Think is the Enemy" 318
By Douglas Jehl

Parakeets Beak: Too Close to Front to be Gas-Sniffers, But Marines Don't Need Birds to Smell Danger   320
  By Denis D. Gray

Over the 12-Foot Berm Lies No-Man's-Land   320
  By Philip Jacobson

Terrorist Actions to Rise When Land War Starts: "I Think We're as Ready as We're Ever Going to Be"   322
  By Tim Collie

Tales of a Marine Foxhole: Sound of a Round Entering a Chamber, "A Darkness You've Never Seen Before"   323
  By Susan Sachs

Tapline Road Fast, Furious, and Lethal: "More Traffic Than on I-20 Heading into Atlanta"   325
  By Paul Basken

Kuwait Is Burning, Cratered, and Still Conceals a Formidable Enemy: "Just Bombing Them Constantly"   327
  By Storer Rowley, Edith Lederer, and Joan Lowy

Thursday - February 21, 1991

Big Red One Takes Measure of Iraqis: "I Can Kill a Tank at 3,000 Meters," says Sgt. Tim McVeigh   330
  By Leon Daniel

Apache Commander in Friendly Fire Incident Relieved of Command   332
  By Michael Hedges

On the Eve of Battle, Last-Minute Emergencies Force Some Troops Out of the Action   332
  By Mark Mooney

Friday - February 22, 1991

Marines Plan Blitzkrieg at Any Moment: "We'll Be Laying Down as Much Metal as Possible"   335
  By Phil Davison

Long-Range Surveillance Squads Scope Iraqi Positions: "You're In Your Own World Out There"   337
  By Jeffrey Ulbrich

U.S. Pilots Begin to Pity the Enemy Troops Below; Civilian Deaths a Regrettable "Cost of Doing Business"   338
  By Storer H. Rowley, Joan Lowy, and Edith M. Lederer

Lucky-as-Hell Marines Escape Direct Hit By the Floss of Their Teeth   340
  By Susan Sachs

Taking Option 3, Spike Fell From the Sky Like a Rag Doll, as Longest Hour of his Life Waited Below   342

Big British Artillery Arrived Three Days After War Began, But Now They Can Barrage With the Best of Them   343
  By Mark Fritz

British Visitors Make Great Deal of Noise on U.S. Turf, and Boast They've Made Improvements to the Ammo   344
By Charles Richards

"They'd Better Be Quick" If They're to Stop This War; Meantime, Peace in the Morning, Firing at Night   346
By Denis Gray

Saturday - February 23, 1991

U.S. Infantry Peace Plan: Hit Iraqi Air Defense Site; "This is a Good Night to Kill Something"   349
By Dave Schad

Chemicals Detected as Marines Fight Frontier Battle; "Bodies Lying Around But We're Not Counting"   350
By Jeff Franks

Sergeant is Very Far Forward U.S. Female—"I Don't Believe There is Romance to Being a Soldier"   352
By Neal MacFarquhar

Consultant Turned Army Chemical Officer Looks at War: "It's Not Going to Be a Pretty Picture . . . It Never Is"   354
By Peter Copeland

Male Bonding Has Limits—A Love Story from 937th Engineers: "Sergeant, You Need Male Supervision"   355
By Carol Morello

Anatomy of a Friendly Fire Incident: Apache Pilot Thought He Saw Iraqi Vehicles   356
By Charles Lewis

Night Visions of the Hellstorm of Fire From Apaches: "It Looked Like Somebody Opened the Sheep Pen"   359
By John Balzar

"A Look Into Hell"—On Kuwait Side, Orange Flames; On Tiger Brigade's Side, Blue Skies, and Hell on Wheels   361
By Bill Gannon

Amphibious Commander Lists Reasons Not to Hit Kuwait Beaches; "Do Not Want to Destroy the Country"   363
By John King and David Evans

Buses Needed for Expected Torrent of Iraqi POWs: "Too Much of a Good Thing"   365
By John Pomfret

U.S. Troops Grab a Foothold in Iraq: "They Don't Know We're Here. It's an Invasion the Size of Normandy"   366
By Gary Regenstreif

Strap on Gatling Gun: Deadline for Iraqi Pullout Passes, Air Missions Shift to Help Troops in Fires Down Below   367
By Joan Lowy, Storer H. Rowley, and Edith M. Lederer

Sunday - February 24, 1991

Marines Storm Kuwait "Not to Conquer But to Drive Out Invaders and Restore the Country to its Citizens" — 370
  By Kirk Spitzer

French and Americans Throw Left Hook at Iraq: "I Think it is Beautiful and We Are Ready to Fire" — 372
  By Joseph Albright

Fighter Pilots' View of Land War: "I Can't Fathom the Size of This Operation. I Can't Grasp It. It's Enormous" — 373
  By Edith Lederer, Joan Lowy, and Storer Rowley

"If This is Your Day Off You'll Miss Half the War" — 376
  By Storer Rowley, Joan Lowy, and Edith M. Lederer

Marines and Fleet Shuffle the Deck Off Kuwait: "Can't Say I Expect Something and I Can't Say That I Don't" — 377
  By John King

A Paradox Involving an Amphibious Assault and Marines in Bunks—"I'd Just as Soon the War Ended Tomorrow" — 378
  By David Evans

Marines Take Massive Numbers of Prisoners in Kuwait — 379
  By Ray Wilkinson

Marines 25 Miles Into Kuwait on First Day: "We Went In and We Overwhelmed Them" — 381
  By Molly Moore

20 Miles in 6 Hours—Land War is Gridlock for Combat Engineers: Frisbees, Hacky-Sacks, and Racy Magazines — 383
  By Mike Tharp

101st Air Assault Takes Off Late: "We'd Walk Through the Gates of Hell if We Knew We Were Going Home" — 384
  By John Pomfret

Strategy for a Brief Occupation of Iraq: "We're Looking at Two to Three Weeks" — 385
  By Mark Mooney

Quiet First Night at Navy Fleet Hospital No. 5: "The Bronx is Worse Than This So Far" — 386
  By Jane DeLynn

Monday - February 25, 1991

Here Comes the Republican Guard—And a Farewell Scud Launched from Kuwait — 390
  By Edith Lederer, Storer H. Rowley, and Joan Lowy

Scud Missile Strikes Barracks in Dhahran, Killing U.S. Troops; Bad Weather Busts Results for "Scud-busters" — 391
  By Storer H. Rowley, Edith M. Lederer, and Joan Lowy

Dawn Battle Looms for Phantom Brigade 100 Miles Inside Iraq—But Where is the Enemy? — 393
  By Douglas Jehl

82nd Airborne's Piece of Cake—"They'd Be Coming Out of Holes Waving a White Flag All Over the Place" 395
   By Robert Dvorchak

Massive Deception—Now It Can Be Told: "They Were At the Wrong Place At the Wrong Time" 397
   By Neal MacFarquhar and Philip Shenon

Just a Shitload of POWs: "Iraq is Arab and Kuwait is Arab. I Don't Know Why We Want Kuwait" 398
   By Douglas Jehl

VII Corps' Majesty and Menace: After 2nd Armored Cav, 1st Armored, 3rd Armored, 1st Infantry, British 1st Armored 399
   By Phil Shenon

VII Corps Moving Only in Daylight—"We Will Show Up in Places the Iraqis Could Never Dream We Would Be" 401
   By Michael Hedges

French and U.S. Force Closes on Iraqi Air Base: "I Love It . . . We Know We'll Be Going Home Soon" 403
   By Joseph Albright

First Casualties Behind It, 1st Cav Feints, Feints Again, Then Joins the Charge Into Kuwait 404
   By Mark Fritz

Marines Spend Night in Underground Iraqi HQ Bunker That Somehow Escaped Weeks of Allied Bombing 406
   By Phil Davison

Barren Corner of Kuwait Still Barren, But Liberated and on 30th Anniversary of Independence from Britain 408
   By Caryle Murphy

"Yay!"—Baptism of Fire Pure Excitement for Some GIs; Earning Time-and-a-Half for Playing With Guns 409
   By John Sack

The Story of Capt. John Bushyhead 410

Tuesday - February 26, 1991

Tiger Tanks Roar North: "We Nudge Them. We Don't Want to Attack and Kill These Men Until We Have To" 412
   By Bill Gannon

Scene at Ras Al Zour: Kuwaitis in First Battle, Saudis Basking in Victory, Americans Calling in Supporting Fire 415
   By Kim Murphy

48 Hours Will Tell Fate of Republican Guard: Where Will They Go? Will Their Best Tanks Go With Them? 417
   By Neal MacFarquhar

Battlefield is Ablaze with Burning Iraqi Tanks; Marines Seal Escape Routes from Kuwait City 418
   By Denis Gray

Marines Surround Kuwait City: "Iraqis Getting Out As Fast As They Can Run"   419
By Molly Moore

Blinding Shamal Envelops Allied Offensive: "Resupply by Air is Over Until This Lifts"   422
By Kevin Cooney

A-10 Pilots Adopt Young Georgia Fan   423

The 'Loggies' Lament as Supply Effort Halts: If You're On the Heels of This War, You're Not Moving Very Fast   423
By Mark Mooney

Marine Helos Keep Iraqis in Place; "As Long As They're Watching the Coast, They're Not Engaging Our Units"   425
By John King

Wednesday - February 27, 1991

Decisive Battle Imminent: Republican Guard Must Hunker Down, Go on the Offensive or Make a Run for It   427

2nd Armored Cavalry Takes On Saddam's Finest: "Republican Guard is Hauling Ass. This Could Be It"   428
By Christopher Hanson

American Armor Routs the Vaunted Republican Guard: "These Are the Guys We Came to Get"   430
By Douglas Jehl

Nine GIs Dead as U.S. and British Armor Plow Through Iraqi Troops: "I Think They Are Desperate"   432
By Neal MacFarquhar

Tiger Brigade North of Kuwait City; Controls 2 Highway Interchanges, Surrounds Iraqi Air Base   433
By Bill Gannon

Marines Take Kuwait Airport: "Once We Got Rolling, It Was Like a Training Exercise With Live People"   437
By Kirk Spitzer

Size, Shape of the War: Allies Control Chunk of Iraq; "Virtually Empty Town Except for a Few Bedouins"   438
By Joseph Albright

2 French Soldiers Killed, 10 Wounded at Iraqi Airfield: "Either a Mine, Booby-Trap, or Unexploded Ordnance"   440
By Gary Regenstreif

7 U.S. Engineers Killed by U.S. Bomblets at Iraqi Airfield: "We'll Have to Pull Together, Like the Family We Are"   441
By Laurence Jolidon

1st Cav Joins Battle—A Thundering, Roaring Herd of Grinding, Smoke-Spewing, Gas-Guzzling Machinery   442
By Mark Fritz

Marine Recon Team Kicks Off Kuwait City Turnover: "I Was Surprised They Didn't Fight a Little Harder"   444
    By Molly Moore

Liberators Greeted in Kuwait City; Businessmen in Sleek Mercedes Join the Massive Traffic Jam   448
    By Jeff Franks

Iraqi Troops Escape Net of Allied Assault: 1ˢᵗ Marines Find at Least 400 Abandoned Tanks and Vehicles   450
    By Jim Michaels

Environmental Nightmare Left in Kuwait: Rivers of Oil, Dozens of Blazing Wellheads, Plumes of Smoke   451
    By David Alexander

U.S. Sergeant Holds 7 Iraqi POWs, Gets Kissed For His Trouble: "George Bush Good!"   452
    By Mike Tharp

U.S. Infantrymen Penetrate to Banks of Euphrates, Discover Cache of Illegal Jordanian Arms   453
    By John Pomfret

Friendly Fire Casualties Mount: American and British Inflict Toll on Each Other's Forces   454
    By Michael Hedges

Thursday - February 28, 1991

Silent Battlefield Runs Out of Gas at the Cease-Fire; Republican Guard Makes a Run for It Through Basra   458
    By Kevin Cooney

1ˢᵗ Cav Soldiers Feel Cheated: "We Came All the Way Over Here. We Should Have Done Something"   459
    By Charles Richards

"Maybe We Are the Good Guys"—U.S. Paratroopers Prepare to Return Home as Line in the Sand Fades   463
    By Robert Dvorchak

Cluster Bomb Deaths Infuriate Combat Engineers: "Remember What it Can Do if Something Goes Wrong"   464
    By Laurence Jolidon

While "Twilight Zone" Plays, Kuwaitis Tell of Kidnappings by Iraqi Troops: Made-for-TV Liberation?   466
    By George Rodrigue

March 1-6, 1991

War's Over: "Whether it Would Have Gotten Exciting Wonderful or Exciting Horrible, We Won't Know"   472
    By Douglas Jehl

Smoke, Flames Etch a Hell Along Highway of Death; Gulf War's Cease-Fire Came Too Late for Many   475
    By Tom Ferraro

War's Horrors Being Guarded: "It's Different When You See Their Faces, Blood Coming Out of Their Wounds" By William Branigin	476
Life in Iraqi Desert Bunker Under Allied Bombing: Onion Skins, Orange Peels, Empty Tin of Cheese By Mike Tharp	478
Aftermath of Scud Strike on U.S. Barracks: Grief, Shock, Terror, Bullets Whizzing Through the Chaos By Mark Mooney	479
24th Infantry Commander Returns Iraqi Fire After Cease-Fire: Civilians, Children Among the Casualties By Thomas Ferraro	481
Setting of Ceremony at Safwan in Shadow of "Scud Mountain": Water, Coffee, and Diet Pepsi By Richard Pyle	482
"Big Red One" Greets Grim-Faced Group from Baghdad By Denholm Barnetson	483
Cease-Fire Signing at Safwan Iraq: "I'm Not Here to Give Them Anything," –Gen. Norman Schwarzkopf	483
Bugler Sounds Taps for a Fallen Scout: "Don't Worry, L.T., the Way is Clear and the Road is Safe" By Douglas Jehl	485
Quick Reflexes Lead Soldier Into Danger—"We'll Probably Lose More Guys Before We Get Out of Here" By Mark Fritz	487
10 Allied POWs Released in Bahrain: Few Details on Captivity but "Seem to be in Very Good Condition" By Michael Hedges	489
U.S. POWs "Cuffed Around" by Iraqis: "None Want to be Heroes. They Don't Want to Be in the Limelight" By Carl Nolte and John Balzar	490
First Group of Iraqi POWs Released from "Brooklyn," Flown to Baghdad By Ken Fireman	492

Part II
Pencils in the Pool: Bedouins of the Press

Press Will Live With the Troops; What do Troops Want? "They Would Like to Go Deep . . . to Go to Baghdad" By Joseph Albright and David Lamb	496
4 Enemy Choppers Defecting to a U.S. Base? A Story This Good (Still) Never Dropped in This Reporter's Lap By Guy Gugliotta, Robert Jagodzinski, David Evans, and Jonathan Ferziger	498

"Gentlemen, This is No Longer an Exercise"—Brit Hacks Learn "Operation Granby" Now "Desert Storm" 498
By Philip Jacobson

An Amiable but Uninformative Chat 500
By Philip Jacobson

Desert Rose, Blonde Annie Introduce the "Hackpack" to the Sandy Joys of Life in the Sweaty Trenches 500
By John Fullerton

Free, Easy, Independent—That Was Before "Shrieking Klaxons and Fearsome Yell of 'Gas! Gas! Gas!'" 501
By Richard Kay

Battle of Red Tape Gets Off to a Blinding Start in a Windstorm and Ends in a Tent with a Few New Mates 504
By Gordon Airs

4 French Journalists Without Escorts Sent to Riyadh: Low on Fuel and "Unsure of Their Exact Location" 504
By Kirk Spitzer

Copters Will Suddenly Materialize; "Not Told to Start Taking White Pills, Which Some Say Cause Nausea" 505
By Joseph Albright

Lower-Caste Bedouins? No, It's the Press: This is Your Shovel, These are Your Blisters 507
By Denis D. Gray

Inventory for Combat: "It Would Mean a Soldier Was in Trouble and I Had the Nearest Pair of Helping Hands" 509
By Frank Bruni

Reporters May Have to Drive the Humvees for "The Doves of Warfare" 510
By Philip Davison

Part III
Casualties of the Gulf War and Later Terrorist Acts

French - Desert Storm 514

British - Desert Shield/Storm 514

British - Prisoners of War 514

United States - Prisoners of War - Desert Storm 519

Americans Killed in Car Bombing, Saudi National Guard Headquarters, Riyadh, 13 Nov. 1995 519

USAF Personnel Killed in Khobar Towers by Truck Bomb, 25 June 1996 519

U.S. Navy Personnel Killed aboard USS Cole, Aden, Yemen, 12 Oct. 2000 520

Bibliography 521

Members of Allied Coalition in Gulf War 523

Acknowledgments 525

Preface

Turn Back Before Baghdad is a collection of news reports written by American and British journalists during the Persian Gulf War. Not what one might typically consider military history, but one must keep in mind that journalism is often called the first draft of history. Here we have the raw reports out of the field depicting not only the fighting, but also the daily lives of those who served in the war. Military history is more than just battles and tactics, but every aspect of the military.

The work belongs in the Leadership and Strategic Studies series as it offers a close day-to-day view of the war from a variety of perspectives. The book also offers a glimpse of leadership from the very top levels of the war including comments by General Schwarzkopf to junior officers. Of equal importance is the perspective of the average soldier and sailor and how they viewed the officers who commanded them. This ranges not only in terms of actual military leadership, but also interactions between officers and the enlisted. Finally, another form of leadership emerges—those who pave the way for others. While women serving in combat operations remain rare at the moment, at the time of the Persian Gulf War America found itself pondering this possibility with women serving in units near the front lines as soldiers—a possibility that made many Americans uncomfortable. While American sensibilities about gender roles haven't disappeared, they continually change and these first-hand accounts truly demonstrate just how our views have shifted.

Turn Back Before Baghdad: An Introduction

By Ron Martz[1]

The 1991 Persian Gulf War was a significant turning point in the often contentious history of American military-media relations.[2] This war was the last in which journalists for print publications, often referred to as "pencils" in military parlance, by-and-large pursued their craft the old-fashioned way, the same way past generations of war correspondents had done. Those of us embedded with U.S. and coalition forces in January and February of 1991 often wrote our dispatches on portable typewriters while sitting in the back of a cramped armored personnel carrier or Humvee, or huddled in a cold and drafty tent, or squeezed into a sweaty ward room on board ship. After writing our stories we would hand the typewritten pages to a military courier, and hope that the story made it back to the censors at the Joint Information Bureau (JIB) in Dhahran, Saudi Arabia before it became old news. Much of the time, that did not happen. The updated "pony express" system set up by the U.S. military failed in a number of ways. First, there was a great lack of concern about the immediacy of the stories we were writing about this largest American military combat operation since Vietnam. Then, the speed of the war with its one hundred hours of ground combat outpaced the speed with which the military pipeline could push print stories to our newspapers and magazines and thus out to the readers.

This was an era when satellite telephones were novelties. Most were the size of small suitcases and had to be stationary while being used to better enable it to connect to a satellite, if a satellite could even be acquired amid the background electronic clutter of war-time traffic. This also was an era in which those who led America's military forces retained a dim view of the media because of the perception that the media had turned public opinion against the Vietnam War and those who fought it. Many of the general officers who led U.S. and coalition forces in the Gulf War had been young lieutenants and captains in Vietnam. Among them were Colin Powell, Norman Schwarzkopf, Fred Franks, John Yeosock, Barry McCaffrey, and Tommy Franks. Some still had a media hangover from that war and did what they could to keep the media at arm's length. For young reporters on their first war-time

---

[1] Ron Martz is a former newspaper reporter and editor who has covered seven wars and regional conflicts since 1984, including Operations Desert Shield and Desert Storm with Laurence Jolidon. He is the co-author of five books on military history.

[2] This is to acknowledge the contributions and encouragement of Mike Hedges and Don North in the preparation of this introduction. Both were close friends and colleagues of Mr. Jolidon and were instrumental in providing information about his life, his reasons for writing this book, and its significance as a primary source document that provides unusual insights into the military-media relationship that has long been ignored by scholars and critics of the media's role, especially that of print reporters, in the Persian Gulf War.

assignment, it was a particularly frustrating experience. But for old hands like Larry Jolidon of *USA Today*, it was a matter of working in and around the system that the Pentagon had set up to essentially manage all the news coming out of Saudi Arabia and later Kuwait and Iraq.

Jolidon, perhaps more so than any of the other "pencils" sent to cover the Gulf War, understood its historical significance and the changing media role in reporting it. While Vietnam is often considered the first television war, print journalists dominated much of the coverage in the early years. Television reports from Vietnam often took weeks to make it to the small screens at home. In the Gulf War, the media's satellite technology had improved significantly so that television journalists could air live broadcasts from Saudi Arabia and Iraq and Schwarzkopf's press briefings, often with titillating footage of so-called smart bombs demolishing buildings in downtown Baghdad, were seen as they occurred. Print journalism took a back seat to the immediacy of television reporting for the first time not only with the American public, but in the military-media relationship.

Jolidon knew and understood this. But he also understood that print journalists often write the first draft of history, for it is from their words that historians many times are able to get a much better sense of how and why events transpired than they are from the sometimes dramatic but usually brief television reports. So it was that as one of the veteran journalists designated to help assign various news organizations to media pools that would be embedded with the troops, Jolidon fought long and hard in the months prior to the start of the war to ensure that print journalists were well-represented in those pools. The pools were not looked on kindly by either the media or the military. They were the least-worst option, a jerry-rigged system that provided only minimal improvements on media pools created but not fully utilized during the invasions of Grenada and Panama only a few years earlier.

Still, by the time U.S. and allied forces began withdrawing from Iraq and Kuwait in early March following the February 28, 1991 cease-fire, print reporters had filed more than 1,300 dispatches.[3] Many of those reports never made it out of the JIB as events on the battlefield rendered them seemingly irrelevant or untimely. Yet, as Jolidon knew and set out to prove, that was not the case at all. Like their predecessors in wars past, the print journalists in Operation Desert Storm attempted to put a human face on combat. They wrote about America's sons and daughters in uniform. They wrote about the threat of poison gas attacks. They wrote about sailors launching Tomahawk missiles from ships at sea and pilots carrying out their missions from aircraft carriers and land bases. They wrote about the burning oil wells in Kuwait and about how America's technological superiority had convinced Iraqi soldiers by the thousands to surrender. But the public never saw most of what they wrote. The failure lay not with the journalists, but with the way the military resourced the pool system.

Even before the end of the war the pool system was being derided as one in which the military took and kept the initiative, thus preventing the American public from seeing the truth about what had actually happened. The prevailing myth is that journalists never got a front-line view of the war and therefore became lapdogs for the military's version of events. According to John Fialka of *The Wall Street Journal*, "This was a war where the military remained in control of most of the evidence and where the Army commanders' paranoid fear of the media helped bury one of the most positive Army stories since World War II."[4] The truth, as Jolidon and others knew, was quite the opposite. It wasn't so much that the war was not reported from the front as it was that the military was unable to get those stories back from the front in a timely fashion.

3   Barry E. Venable, "The Army and the Media," *Military Review*, January-February 2002, 69.
4   John Fialka, *Hotel Warriors: Covering the Gulf War*, (Washington, D.C.: The Woodrow Wilson Center Press: 1991), 59-60.

As media critics began circling the remains of the war and what had been reported, Jolidon decided to do something about what he knew then was a false impression of the reporting, especially by the print correspondents. When he returned to the JIB in early March, he found stacks of stories from print reporters that had never made it past the military gate keepers. With the help of colleague Mike Hedges of *The Washington Times*, he collected them, boxed them up, and shipped them back to himself at *USA Today*, hoping eventually to sort through them so he could tell the true story of Operation Desert Storm. Using his own money and working virtually alone, Jolidon compiled about 300 of what he considered the best from the more than 1,300 dispatches filed. And, in an era before self-publishing was economically viable, Jolidon in 2002 created his own press to print *Turn Back Before Baghdad: Original Frontline Dispatches of the Gulf War by American and British Correspondents*. The entire collection of dispatches, along with other of Jolidon's papers, is on file at the Briscoe Center for American History at the University of Texas-Austin.

The book did not receive wide circulation and was overshadowed by other works that were far more critical of the media and their role in reporting the war. Among those most critical were Jacqueline Sharkey's *Under Fire: U.S. Military Restrictions on the Media from Grenada to the Persian Gulf*, John R. MacArthur's *Second Front: Censorship and Propaganda in the Gulf War*, and Fialka's *Hotel Warriors*. But these books looked primarily at the pool system and were not a true examination of the actual work done by the dozens of veteran print reporters who went to the front and reported from there. *Turn Back Before Baghdad* shatters the myth that there was no good reporting from Operation Desert Storm. There are eyewitness accounts of friendly fire, tank engagements at such long ranges that no one was sure who was who or what was what, and the jubilation of Kuwaitis as their country was liberated. There also are unexpected nuggets that pop up from time to time, like the interview with British soldier Captain James Hewitt, who later was alleged to have been Princess Di's lover. There is also an interview with a young American soldier by the name of Timothy McVeigh, who later became better known as the man who bombed the Alfred P. Murrah Federal Building in Oklahoma City in 1995. *Turn Back Before Baghdad* is being reprinted here as an invaluable resource for military officials, historians, and journalists. It gives them an opportunity to examine and judge for themselves if the criticism of the reporting from the print correspondents who covered the Persian Gulf War was truly warranted and whether it was the reporters who failed, or the system in which they were forced to work.

The Gulf War pool system was an evolutionary step not only in how war was reported, but also in the development of the military-media relationship, a relationship that has at times been characterized as grudging tolerance for one another and at other times has been openly confrontational. The first known instance of a civilian journalist accompanying American troops into combat was during the Mexican-American War in 1846, when George Wilkins Kendall rode with General Zachary Taylor and reported for *The Picayune* of New Orleans.[5] Kendall set the standard for future reporters faced with difficulty getting their stories back from the front. He is said to have developed a courier system of riders that would carry his stories to ships waiting to sail to New Orleans, at one point spending $5,000 to charter a single ship for a story, an astronomical sum for that era.[6]

While Kendall's reporting apparently had little impact on the American public's opinion of the war or how the military conducted its operations in Mexico, the same cannot be said

---

[5] Alicia C. Shepard, *Narrowing the Gap: Military, Media and the Iraq War*, (Chicago: Robert R. McCormick Tribune Foundation, 2004), 17.
[6] Ibid.

of William Howard Russell of *The Times* of London during the Crimean War (1853-1856). Russell, a hard-drinking Irishman who had reported on several small conflicts in Europe, came into his own in the Crimea. It was Russell who wrote the first dispatch from Balaclava describing the disastrous charge of the Light Brigade from which Alfred Lord Tennyson took inspiration for his famous poem. It was Russell who "grew caustic in his criticism of the suffering the soldiers had to endure," writing frequently about "the pitiful condition of the troops and the command's lack of concern."[7] And it was Russell whose criticism of blunders by British officers eventually caused the government to recall the top commanders and Florence Nightingale to recruit volunteers to tend to the sick and wounded in the field. Russell's dispatches helped turn public opinion against the British government's handling of the war at the same time they turned military opinion against correspondents. As Phillip Knightley notes in his book *The First Casualty*, "It is clear that before the war ended the army realized that it had made a mistake in tolerating Russell and his colleagues, but by then it was too late."[8]

The American Civil War saw an explosion of correspondents eager to chronicle the fighting. An estimated five hundred journalists, both North and South, covered the war for their respective newspapers and magazines, almost as many as the more than six hundred who embedded with American military units during Operation Iraqi Freedom in 2003. The telegraph, first utilized during the Crimean War, made it easier for correspondents to get their stories back to their readers more quickly than ever. The *New York Herald* out-did all their rivals, flooding the battlefields with sixty-three reporters at a cost of about $1 million.[9] Officers on both sides found little to like about the presence of correspondents in their midst. General Robert E. Lee is widely quoted as saying after the war that "In the beginning we appointed all our worst generals to command the armies, and all our best generals to edit the newspapers."[10] Union General Irwin McDowell, perhaps only half in jest, said of the correspondents with him that "I have suggested to them they should wear a white uniform, to indicate the purity of their character."[11] And General William Tecumseh Sherman so disliked the reporters who constantly criticized him that after learning that three of them had been killed near Vicksburg, Mississippi, said: "Good! Now we'll have news from hell before breakfast."[12] Sherman even went so far as to court-martial Thomas W. Knox of the *New York Herald* as a spy. Knox was found guilty of only one of the three charges brought against him—accompanying a military unit against Sherman's orders—and his only punishment was that he was prohibited from entering Union lines.[13]

Despite the large number of reporters writing about the war, government officials in the North put severe restrictions on what newspapers could and could not print. Secretary of War Edwin M. Stanton seized newspapers that he believed revealed too much military information at the same time he was planting false stories with other papers.[14] The persistent threat of court-martial for reporters who breached security put a chilling effect on the free flow of information.[15] Passage of the Espionage Act in 1917 just after the U.S. entered World War I put even more of a damper on just how liberal correspondents could be with the

---

[7] Phillip Knightley, *The First Casualty: From the Crimea to Vietnam: The War Correspondent as Hero, Propagandist, and Myth Maker*, (New York: Harcourt Brace Jovanovich, 1975), 12.
[8] Ibid, 17.
[9] John F. Marszalek, *Sherman's Other War: The General and the Civil War Press*, (Kent, Ohio: The Kent State University Press, 1999), 51.
[10] William J. Jones, *Personal Reminiscences, Anecdotes, and Letters of Gen. Robert E. Lee*, (New York: D. Appleton and Company, 1875), 241.
[11] William Howard Russell, *My Diary North and South*, Ed. By Eugene H. Berwanger, (Baton Rouge, La.: Louisiana State University Press, 2001), 250.
[12] Marszalek, 159.
[13] Ibid, 152.
[14] Douglas Porch, "No Bad Stories: The American Media-Military Relationship," *Naval War College Review*, Winter 2002, Vol. LV, No. 1, 87.
[15] Ibid.

information they provided for public consumption. In addition, General John Pershing, commander of the American Expeditionary Forces, gave credentials to only thirty-one reporters, none of whom was allowed to report from the front lines.[16]

World War II was unique in the history of military-media relations. Correspondents were considered part of the war effort, part of the team whose mission was to defeat the Japanese and Nazi Germany. Correspondents wore the same uniforms as American soldiers and willingly submitted their stories to censors before they were passed on to their newspapers or magazines. For major operations, a small number of correspondents were selected to accompany the troops with the understanding they would share their work product with their colleagues.[17] Novelist John Steinbeck, who spent time during World War II and later in Vietnam as a correspondent, wrote that during World War II "We were all part of the war effort. We went along with it, and not only that, we abetted it. Gradually it became a part of us that the truth about anything was automatically secret and that to trifle with it was to interfere with the war effort."[18] The control and cooperation of the media were so complete that only twenty-seven reporters accompanied the D-Day invasion force on June 6, 1944.[19] But those correspondents who embedded with troops produced some of the war's most memorable stories and photographs, such as Ernie Pyle's celebrations of the average American GI, Robert Capa's stunning images of the D-Day invasion, and Joe Rosenthal's iconic photo of the flag raising on Mount Suribachi as the Marines were fighting for control of Iwo Jima.

During the Korean War, General Douglas MacArthur imposed even more draconian restrictions on the media. He "imposed formal censorship, forbidding reporters to criticize, among other things, military reverses, failures of U.S. equipment, or the South Korean government," in addition to anything critical of him or his leadership.[20] So it came as some surprise to media and military officials alike that Vietnam was just the opposite. Reporters were permitted to go where they wanted when they wanted. There was no pool system, no censorship, no government oversight on the correspondents who flocked to Southeast Asia. Vietnam stood the military-media relationship on its head because of the openness with which correspondents operated. And while print journalists dominated early on, once television got involved and nightly film of the fighting, however much it had been delayed, became commonplace, the power of those moving images had a significant and lasting impact on the American public and its view of the war.

The reporting from Vietnam often seemed in stark contrast to the rosy assessments delivered by military officials in Saigon and Washington, D.C. The Tet Offensive of 1968, particularly the attack on the U.S. Embassy in Saigon, was probably the turning point in America's perception of the war. Long led to believe the government and its assessments of military activities, the American public watching nightly news saw a completely different picture during Tet. Although Tet was a disaster for the Viet Cong from which it never fully recovered, it was even more of a public relations debacle for the American military. It was "a traumatic shock to the American public . . . Coming as it did, just before the first primaries in a presidential election year, the Tet offensive caught the administration at its weakest politically, and dealt a powerful blow to its sagging credibility."[21] Media coverage of the war

---

16 *Ibid*, 88.
17 Venable, 67.
18 John Steinbeck, *Once There Was a War*, (London: Heinemann, 1959; Corgi edition, 1961), 11-12.
19 Fialka, 4.
20 Porch, 90-91.
21 Knightley, 397.

before Tet had been largely favorable. After Tet, it became increasingly negative, creating an entire generation of Vietnam veterans and many members of the public who came to view the media, not the flawed strategy, as the reason there was no clear-cut victory. What had been a cordially adversarial relationship between the military and the media prior to Vietnam became openly hostile after it.

The Pentagon was determined after Vietnam to not allow the media such unrestricted access to the battlefield again, even if it meant infringing on the First Amendment and the public's right to know how and why their tax dollars were being spent. Planning for what became Operation Urgent Fury in Grenada in 1983 failed to include the media in any aspect of the operation. The media were to be totally excluded. "As a consequence, over six hundred disgruntled reporters were marooned in comfortable exile on Barbados while the story played out unseen and hence unreported, on Grenada."[22] Those reporters who took the initiative to try to get to Grenada by boat were intercepted by U.S. Navy vessels and were told they needed to turn back or they would be blown out of the water. But in their after-action explanation of media exclusion from Grenada, the Pentagon claimed that it occurred on such a small island at such a high tempo that the media could not be safely accommodated.[23]

Media complaints about that exclusion eventually convinced the Pentagon that it could not keep journalists from finding a way to report on combat operations in which American forces were involved. Enterprising reporters would somehow find a way to get to where fighting was taking place. Army General John Vessey, Jr., then chairman of the Joint Chiefs of Staff, commissioned a study of the problem. Chaired by retired Army Major General Winant Sidle, who had been trained as a journalist, the group included members of the media and the military and became known the "Sidle Panel." In August 1984, the panel issued its report. In his cover letter to Vessey, Sidle stated unequivocally that the panel "unanimously agreed at the outset that the U.S. media should cover U.S. military operations to the maximum degree possible consistent with mission security and the safety of U.S. forces."[24] The panel made eight recommendations as a means of preventing future Grenadas. Foremost among them was that the military and the media work together to create a standing National Media Pool that would be trained, have the proper gear, and be prepared to deploy at a moment's notice if there was a military contingency involving American forces anywhere in the world.[25] The panel put the onus on the media to have trained professional journalists in the pool. It also put the onus on the military to beef up its public affairs staff, essentially to ride herd on the media horde that would descend on any American military operation.

In theory, it seemed like a workable plan. When put into practice less than six years later during the invasion of Panama in 1989, Operation Just Cause, it proved a miserable failure. It failed not because military failed and not because the media failed, but because one government official still suffering from a post-Vietnam hangover, Secretary of Defense Dick Cheney, decided to delay deployment of the pool.[26] As a result, reporters who were not part of the pool system used their initiative to get to Panama ahead of those confined to the pool. Among them was Larry Jolidon. Jolidon flew to Costa Rica, took a taxi to the border with Panama, and then hired a boy on a motorbike to give him a ride into Panama City, getting

---

22 Porch, 94.
23 Richard K. Wright, *Assessment of the DoD Embedded Media Program*, (Alexandria, Va.: Institute for Defense Analyses Joint Advanced Warfighting Program, 2004), 1-3.
24 Major General Winant Sidle, *Report by the Chairman of the Joint Chiefs of Staff Military-Media Relations Panel*, (Washington, D.C.: Chairman of the Joint Chiefs of Staff, 1984), 2.
25 *Ibid*, 4.
26 Porch, 94-95.

there well ahead of the press pool.²⁷ Jolidon was not a fan of the pool system or the politics that went along with trying to get a spot in it. He was more of a freewheeling free spirit, ready to take chances when necessary to beat what he saw as an extremely restrictive system at its own game. So it was somewhat surprising to find Jolidon less than two years later deeply enmeshed in helping to formulate the pool system that characterized the media coverage of Operations Desert Shield and Desert Storm.

After Saddam Hussein invaded Kuwait on August 1, 1990, and President George H.W. Bush five days later ordered U.S. troops to the Middle East to stop the advance, the Pentagon once again delayed deploying the National Media Pool. Its excuses this time were that it "did not involve two of the 'essential elements' that triggered deployment of the pool—combat and the need to preserve secrecy before an operation began."²⁸ The Saudis also initially were reluctant to provide visas to members of the National Media Pool because of concerns over outside influences in the highly restrictive kingdom. But once they relented, the flood of correspondents began. At one point, more than 1,600 reporters from around the world showed up in Dhahran, the gathering spot for those who wanted to cover the troops, or in the capital Riyadh, for those who wanted the big picture from Schwarzkopf and other top commanders. Those correspondents came from the traditional newspaper and television outlets as well as organizations that seemingly had no reason to be there, among them the Disney Channel and the women's magazine Mirabella.

Whether by happenstance or design, military officials left it up to the media to decide who among them would be in what pools as Operation Desert Shield continued through the summer and fall and on into the winter of 1990. The politicking among media members was intense as reporters fought over what they considered the choice pool slots. Correspondents from larger organizations thought they should have more access than those from smaller, hometown or regional news outlets. It was "a situation akin to a prison system of inmates guarding inmates," said one critic.²⁹ Those media bosses back in the States who had fought with the Pentagon for years to come up with a workable solution "felt betrayed by what some called 'censorship by access.'"³⁰ Those who chose to work outside the pool system, the so-called unilaterals who took off across the desert in four-wheel drive vehicles in search of stories, ran the risk of being shot at by both sides, or taken prisoner, as happened to CBS News correspondent Bob Simon when he wandered too close to the border before the ground war began. U.S. Special Forces troops in the area had warned him of the dangers but he and his crew decided to chance it. After Simon's capture the soldiers re-named the road "The Bob Simon Highway."

What emerged from the chaos of the Gulf War pool system initially was not pleasing to either the military or the media. There were frustrations on both sides—the military because of their lack of resources to deal with the pool products and the unexpected number of reporters with whom they had to deal, and the media because of what many perceived as a lack of access. Despite that persistent myth, there was access, and there was thoughtful, professional reporting by many of the print reporters who got that access. It's just that not many of those reports ever saw print until *Turn Back Before Baghdad*. Within two years of the dissolution of the Gulf War pool system, technological advancements had rendered pools obsolete. By the time U.S. forces deployed to Somalia, reporters were able to file

---

27 Author's conversation with Laurence Jolidon, January 1991.
28 Jacqueline E. Sharkey, *Under Fire: U.S. Military Restrictions on the Media from Grenada to the Persian Gulf*, (Washington, D.C.: The Center for Public Integrity, 1991), 108.
29 MacArthur, 182.
30 Venable, 129.

directly through their laptop computers and satellite telephones to their news organizations without having to go through a military censor. By the wars in Iraq and Afghanistan, sending stories, photographs, and streaming video from the front, even while on the move, was commonplace for all reporters, print and television. The pool system, which never was useful to begin with, no longer was a viable option for the military or the media.

By August 2002, after the publication of *Turn Back Before Baghdad,* Jolidon had moved on. He had become the top civilian press adviser to the NATO Rapid Reaction Force in Bosnia, responsible for coordinating media strategy, talking points, and news conferences. On August 20, while out for a jog in Sarajevo, Bosnia, he suffered a heart attack and died. In a letter he sent to friends and colleagues just a few months earlier after the book was published, he wrote what perhaps was his own epitaph. "Even if this is as good as it gets," he wrote, "it's been good, and it's all been worth it in my book."[31]

Sources Cited

Fialka, John J. *Hotel Warriors: Covering the Gulf War.* Washington, D.C.: The Woodrow Wilson Center Press, 1991.

Jones, J. William. *Personal Reminiscences, Anecdotes, and Letters of Gen. Robert E. Lee.* New York: D. Appleton and Company, 1875.

Knightley, Phillip. *The First Casualty: From the Crimea to Vietnam: The War Correspondent as Hero, Propagandist, and Myth Maker.* New York: Harcourt Brace Jovanovich, 1975.

Lindner, Andrew M. "Controlling the Media In Iraq," *Contexts,* vol. 7, No. 2, pp. 32-38, Spring 2008.

MacArthur, John R. *Second Front: Censorship and Propaganda in the Gulf War.* New York: Hill and Wang, 1992.

Marszalek, John F. *Sherman's Other War: The General and the Civil War Press.* Kent, Ohio: The Kent State University Press, 1999.

Porch, Douglas. "No Bad Stories: The American Media-Military Relationship." *Naval War College Review,* Winter 2002, Vol. LV., No. 1, pp. 85-107.

Russell, William Howard. *My Diary North and South.* Ed. by Eugene H. Berwanger. Baton Rouge, La.: Louisiana State University Press, 2001.

Sharkey, Jacqueline E. *Under Fire: U.S. Military Restrictions on the Media from Grenada to the Persian Gulf.* Washington, D.C.: The Center for Public Integrity, 1991.

Shepard, Alicia C. *Narrowing the Gap: Military, Media and the Iraq War.* Chicago: Robert R. McCormick Tribune Foundation, 2004.

Steinbeck, John. *Once There Was a War.* London: Neinemann, 1959; Corgi edition, 1961.

Venable, Barry E. "The Army and the Media." *Military Review,* January-February 2002, pp. 66-71.

Wright, Richard K. *Assessment of the DoD Embedded Media Program.* Alexandria, Va.: Institute for Defense Analyses Joint Advanced Warfighting Program, 2004.

---

31   Laurence Jolidon letter promoting *Turn Back Before Baghdad,* Feb. 7, 2002.

First Edition Introduction

In the aftermath of the Sept. 11, 2001 terrorist attacks on the World Trade Center and Pentagon, some connections can be seen with greater clarity.

It is plainly apparent now that a direct line exists between the infamous acts and horrible human toll of that day and the aftermath of the Persian Gulf War, which officially ended more than a decade earlier with a ceasefire ceremony at Safwan, Iraq.

When thinking back to that day, some linger over the notion that a relatively swift and overwhelming victory over the Iraqi forces in 1991 was flawed by the failure to take the next step—to send the allied force another 100 or so miles north to oust the regime of Saddam Hussein.

Such a no-doubt-brief expedition would have addressed the very root of the problem but—and even proponents concede this—would have also brought uncertainty, a longer American military commitment, and numerous unforeseen results and repercussions.

So the allied troops, although surging with awesome, deadly, and cohesive power, were ordered to stop after seizing southern Iraq to the Euphrates River, to turn back before they reached Baghdad. By halting the one-sided fight, President George Bush and other Western leaders hoped to quiet those especially in the Arab nations that had joined the effort to liberate Kuwait who rebelled at the idea of overturning another Muslim country.

But to some Muslim true believers, the mistake was even more fundamental, and almost irreversible: the very presence of a foreign army of non-Muslim soldiers in Saudi Arabia, the land that possesses and is sworn to protect Islam's holiest shrines, had been a grave error and insult.

And with the posting of a permanent protective force of American military personnel and assets in Saudi Arabia after the Gulf War—an obvious alternative to ridding the region of Saddam Hussein in the Western mind—the mistake was made more grievous.

It was that decision that is now frequently cited as the turning point in the life of a wealthy Saudi militant, Osama bin Laden. The United States—and the Saudi regime that was responsible for inviting its uniformed infidels to remain—became his target, and the target of uncounted other Muslim extremists who are now sworn to bloody retribution and destruction.

With that cause and effect clear, the Gulf War and the part the U.S. and other Western and Arab allies played become not simply an interesting slice of history, but a vital topic of study for the present and future.

So this book—a collection of accounts by combat correspondents telling the day-to-day story of the Gulf War at the scene of the action—is offered as a bridge, a prism for today's questions, and a tool for understanding.

Many of the stories here strike the same major themes of military readiness and strategy, religious practices, chemical warfare, covert operations, collateral damage, and friendly fire that are beginning to arise once more.

They help us understand the connections between those heady days of Desert Shield and Desert Storm, days filled with glory for the U.S. military, when the old ghost of Vietnam finally seemed to lift from the shoulders of the world's most powerful army, and these darker days, when the battle has moved to America's shores, leapt into view with a fiery vengeance and shown us costs in human terms that are already unacceptably high.

As a work of journalism, this book is also an attempt to rescue the efforts of the men and women of the Gulf War print pool from a myth that has lasted too long.

After negotiations with the Washington, DC, bureau chiefs of the large media companies, the Pentagon in the winter of 1990 agreed that a pool of correspondents—chosen by the reporters in Saudi Arabia from among those who had covered the long buildup and deployment—would go into the field to live with the troops, to ships patrolling the nearby seas and to airbases while missions were being flown.

Daily accounts from these print media "pools" (a separate one was formed for television, which must work in teams of correspondents, technicians, and producers) would then be shipped back to a central office, reviewed for military security and made available to all the rest of the world's press that had gathered in Saudi Arabia who could use the stories, tapes and interviews as they saw fit.

A number of pool critics and their lawyers (a group filed suit in federal court, but failed to change the outcome) opposed the arrangement and argued for completely free access to the battlefield. They looked at the big, open desert and saw plenty of room for the press to wander from dune to dune, tank to tank, wherever their instinct led them, interviewing soldiers, taking pictures, and writing about the war. (One lawyer argued that Gen. Schwarzkopf could make his front lines even longer to accommodate more reporters.)

The Pentagon looked at the big, open desert and saw plenty of room for terrorists, saboteurs, and Iraqi agents to infiltrate allied lines and bases, steal secrets, and plant bombs. Officials promised to lift restrictions on access "when the front was mature and the battle was in progress," but meantime reporters would not be allowed to travel at will, unescorted, among the allied encampments. Having reporters and TV crews roaming the front would be dangerous for them and the troops.

The Pentagon's premise was that allied armor, artillery and infantry forces were essentially vulnerable, stationed on the periphery of Iraq and Kuwait waiting for a weeks-long bombing campaign to prepare—soften up—the future battlefield.

While the specifics of how the war should be covered were still being debated in federal courthouses and hearings on Capitol Hill, dozens of American and British correspondents were called upon to do a job that some of their colleagues demeaned—and most envied. (All reporters hate pools—except, it has to be said, the one they're in.)

The print pool members tackled an undesirable situation and made the best of it, working steadily and professionally within the rules laid down by mutual agreement to find the news and share it with their colleagues. But in the years since the Gulf War ended, a myth has obscured their work.

The myth presumes that the press was virtually barred from covering the war in the Persian Gulf. It stemmed from the intense opposition to the very idea that the Pentagon had placed limits on media access, and in addition required pool stories to be reviewed for possible violations of military security.

The myth has grown with each repetition by authors, scholars and commentators. It took various forms most readers have probably seen in print before:

- Reporters were basically not allowed to cover the ground war.
- Reporters were not allowed into the field, but had to stay in their hotels, watching CNN and attending briefings where they asked inane questions, like when will the invasion start.
- Reporters were not allowed to talk to soldiers unless a public affairs officer was present.
- Most reporters were kept on ships so they couldn't talk to troops.
- Some stories were held back until after the war ended for security reasons.
- The Pentagon quickly censored any news that reporters did manage to find, ensuring that no military mistakes, embarrassments or shortcomings were made public.

None of the above statements are true. But these and similar allegations were picked up as valid by writers and repeated unchecked until they became common folklore. By October 2001, when the new Bush administration was marshaling the military to strike at the Taliban regime that was sheltering Osama bin Laden, self-appointed defenders of freedom of the press were citing the myth in warning that the Pentagon might again try to stiff-arm the press away from the fighting. It is true that many reporters who didn't arrive in Saudi Arabia until after the bombing campaign began on Jan. 16, 1991, did not see much action. But every print reporter who had reached Saudi Arabia by Jan. 1 had a spot.

The Saudi government—which limited even large news organizations to one visa and tried to force some reporters to leave the country in mid-deployment—played a major part in press restrictions simply by virtue of control over ports of entry.

And it is true that pool stories were subjected to review for military security reasons and to ensure that reporters honored their agreement not to disclose the location or size of units or prematurely name dead or missing personnel before next-of-kin are notified.

Numbers, words, and datelines were changed in several instances, but only one story did not appear because military reviewers had determined it contained a number of facts that could jeopardize the allied effort. The reporter's editor spiked it after talking to the Pentagon.

It's in this collection. ("Gathering Intelligence Any Way You Can: Iraqis Using Deception 'To Show Us Bomb Damage that Isn't There,'" Feb. 11, by Michael Hedges.) You can decide whether the story should have run.

When the dust settled, the main difficulty pool reporters say they faced was not the security review but a land-based courier system that was supposed to ensure that all their copy reached the pool office in Dhahran in a timely manner.

That system failed miserably. Some stories were delayed for days, a few for weeks. Some reporters said they thought it was deliberate meddling by the Pentagon to keep news from reaching the public. In some cases, public affairs officers did sit on stories, either out of spite or an exaggerated sense of some threat to security.

But more often, it was simply a matter of incompetence, poor planning, broken fax machines and scarce vehicles coming face to face with one of the world's largest deserts and one of history's largest military deployments.

Despite the controversy and crippled dispatch system, from mid-January until after the cease-fire on March 3rd, the print combat pool—eventually a group of about 200 reporters from American and British newspapers, magazines and news agencies—reported daily and directly from the encampments of Marines and soldiers in the desert, from aboard ships and from the flight lines of air bases.

They covered the war from start to finish, from the minefields up and the AWACS missions down. Their stories chronicled the day-to-day lives of more than 700,000 men and women of the allied military forces as they fought, died, were wounded or went missing. More fortunate than the 150 or so U.S. service members who gave their lives in the war, the reporters all lived to tell about it.

An archive of about 1,500 stories from both the American and British pools is the source of some 300 selected for this book. Completely uncensored and raw as the day they came off a sand-choked typewriter, the stories feature fine, even insightful, writing.

Woven together in chronological order (a luxury unavailable during the war) they tell a compelling story.

And the archive itself had an interesting odyssey.

After the cease-fire, I returned from Iraq to the pool offices in the International Hotel in Dhahran where I found all our stories neatly filed away.

Believing they had some historical value, I boxed them up and brought them back to the U.S., expecting some university or foundation would want to make them available to students, scholars, and the general public. When I could find no university or foundation to take them, I put them in storage, where they remained for ten years.

In the spring of 2001, I decided to once again try to attract attention to the archive by compiling some of the most interesting and best-written stories in a collection.

While preparing the manuscript, I was fortunate enough to learn about the Center for American History at the University of Texas at Austin, and offered the archive for its new and growing media library.

The archive is now in the Center's collection.

Some might say these stories belonged there all this time.

I'm just glad they made it out of the desert.

Laurence Jolidon
Dallas
October, 2001

PART I

Desert Storm:
Ultimatum to Cease-Fire Tent

Tuesday
January 15, 1991

This date was the final deadline set by UN Security Council Resolution 678, the last opportunity for Saddam Hussein to withdraw his troops from Kuwait before the allied coalition used military force to make him comply.

The date passed without war, but war was clearly coming. Gen. Colin Powell, chairman of the U.S. Joint Chiefs of Staff, phoned Gen. H. Norman Schwarzkopf, commander of the coalition forces in the Gulf, to say that he and Defense Secretary Dick Cheney had just signed the execution order to initiate military action.

The war would officially start with an attack of allied warplanes at 3 a.m. on January 17th. In his command headquarters in Riyadh, Gen. Schwarzkopf reviewed the details of a "blood chit," military parlance for a paper (or cloth, usually silk) carried by every pilot offering a reward for his return in the case of capture. The blood chits for pilots in the Gulf were in Arabic, but were for naught. All the allied pilots captured by Iraqi forces were held until the war's end.

So many grievances had led to this pass. Both sides could recite a litany of reasons for being the injured party. Unpaid war debts. Violations of oil production quotas. Colonialist boundary lines. Marshalling of troops along borders.

But the facts were that Iraq's legions had stormed into Kuwait uninvited and remained there as an occupying army in what Saddam was choosing to call his "19th province" and the UN had voted he must remove them or suffer the consequences.

History had turned somersaults to get here. The big western nations that were now lined up against Saddam had, until very recently, been Iraq's close allies, weapons providers, trading partners, and benefactors. After the war, the CIA admitted to its oversight committees in Congress that it was exchanging secret intelligence with Iraq up until Aug. 2, 1990, the very day Iraq invaded Kuwait.

The mutual exchange of intelligence, which apparently began in 1984, was based on a common interest: countering the radical Islamic movement in Iran and throughout the region.

Efforts at diplomacy to resolve the crisis peacefully wound down as the deadline approached, Secretary General Perez de Cuellar met a last time with Hussein, then consulted yet again with one of the most active Arabist diplomats in Europe, French President François Mitterand. The Secretary General afterward declared there was no hope for a diplomatic solution. The European Union likewise threw in the diplomatic towel.

Mitterand kept pressing. He tried to keep talks afloat by proposing yet another solution in which the UN would agree to an international conference on the status of Kuwait in return for Iraq's withdrawal. But more and more, diplomacy was a sideshow to this crisis.

On the Arabian peninsula and in friendly anti-Saddam enclaves nearby, the huge buildup of American and other coalition forces was peaking. Eventually there would be close to

Tuesday - January 15, 1991

700,000 allied personnel, including more than a half-million Americans, taking on Saddam Hussein's war machine. Iraq had an army of about 1 million, half of which was reported stationed in and around Kuwait.

In this opening chapter, the famed 82nd Airborne Division, whose troops were the first U.S. forces to arrive on Saudi soil the previous August, was getting down to fighting weight. They wouldn't need their parachutes for this mission.

Scud missile alerts were just beginning. They would come to symbolize for many the frustration of trying to be prepared for anything and everything that might come screaming out of the sky from Kuwait or Iraq.

After the war, allied military and intelligence experts agreed that Saddam Hussein actually had more Scuds and Scud-launchers in his arsenal than original pre-war calculations allowed for, and had done a better job of eluding the allied efforts to destroy them than anyone had anticipated.

"Racehorses That Smell the Barn"—82nd Airborne Gets Rid of Xmas Gifts, Burns Letters, Prepares to Fight

By Robert Dvorchak

IN EASTERN SAUDI ARABIA - Apache helicopter pilot Ron Moring made final preparations for war by lightening his gear, mailing home his hand-held computer games and beach shorts.

Specialist James Cox shipped home his souvenir Arab headdress and personal keepsakes, hanging on to pictures of his wife and kids to keep with his military gear.

Specialist Mark Welsh sent back his Christmas stocking and a gift shirt because "I don't want to throw away those memories."

The Army's 82nd Airborne Division was on war-ready status Tuesday, Jan. 15, the date the world had told Saddam Hussein to quit Kuwait.

The soldiers got down to the bare essentials of military hardware in their rucksacks and kit bags, some by burning their personal letters so no one could trace the addresses.

Capt. Clint Esarey, 32, of Indianapolis, Indiana, prepared by dictating a living will to his wife on a cassette tape and giving details on funeral arrangements should the worst happen.

"If I don't make it back, I want to be buried in my military uniform," Esarey said. "I'm a soldier. It's my life. The uniform is part of me."

The mental and emotional part of preparing for battle was just as necessary as making sure weapons were cleaned and attack helicopters, sitting like angry hornets at the launch stations, were armed and loaded.

"In our minds, the war has started. Today is the day. Training is over with. The mindset is this is the real thing," said Esarey, the father of two adopted children.

"The awareness of the soldiers is definitely heightened. The mood? Somber would be a good word for it. They're mulling this stuff around in their minds," he said. "Anything you don't have to have you get rid of because you want your rucksack as light as you can get it."

The mood was businesslike at a base in central Saudi Arabia where the 82nd keeps Apache and Cobra attack helicopters, along with other assault helicopters.

Gun crews loaded each tank-killing Apache with Hellfire missiles and loaded magazines with 2.75-inch rockets.

"We're a bunch of racehorses that smell the barn right now," said Chief Warrant

Officer Ron Moring, 32, who pilots an Apache called "The Virginia Regulator." "It's time to quit the pre-game show. We're a lot more serious about we're doing. There's a little more excitement in the air."

Specialist 4 Mark Welsh, 21, of Bird Island, Minnesota, worked on a newly arrived Blackhawk utility helicopter. He had been married for a month before Iraq invaded Kuwait, and he had just sent home his treasured Christmas gifts so he wouldn't be bogged down.

"I don't want to hang on to them here, but I want to hang on to them for the future. I didn't want to throw away some memories," Welsh said.

Maj. Lee Stuart, 43, of Jonesboro, Ga., executive officer of a battalion of Apache helicopters said soldiers still prayed for peace while they grimly prepared for war.

"GIs are the last ones who want to go to war. They're the ones who have to shed their blood and give their lives. We don't want to kill nobody. (But) I want it settled and settled now. I don't want my young one to have to do it," Stuart said.

Scud Alert: "If This is Another Practice, Someone Should Have Their Butt Kicked"

By Charles Richards

It was the tins, or at least something like them.

The alert came shortly after 11 a.m. on Jan. 15, the day that had entered popular parlance as "K-Day," the deadline set by the United Nations for Iraq to withdraw from Kuwait.

Suddenly figures started scuttling across the airbase, disappearing down sandbagged entrances to underground bunkers.

"Scud alert, that's all I heard."

"That's all you need to hear."

They were a group of National Guardsmen from South Carolina, firefighters with the 264 Engineering Detachment. Down below, someone switched on a light, red for security. There were boxes of rations stacked at the back of the shelter. "Weren't supposed to be any more practices," one of them drawled, his southern accent, if not his face, clear through the gas mask and hood.

"If this is another practice, someone should have their butt kicked."

Time passed. Sweat built up inside the mask. Breathing was slow, but not hard.

The bunker was more solidly built than most, with a sealed roof supported by fresh timber pit props. It became clear why.

The roof was an Air Force loading pallet "kindly donated by another branch of the military."

The threat of attack by chemical weapons launched by Scud missiles was not what most of these Guardsmen had bargained for when they joined up. Staff Sergeant Joe Horton, 48, was an insurance salesman in civilian life from Beaufort, S.C. Normal duties were limited.

"We meet one weekend a month and two weeks annual training." They came out at the end of November after a week's notice to move. "It's necessary," Sergeant Horton said, "but I don't like it at all. Rulers like Saddam Hussein must be stopped. I really didn't think it necessary to call out the National Guard."

They discussed the numbers of times they had drilled for missile or chemical attack. "One long blast is for air attack," a sergeant declared confidently. "No," a masked speaker corrected. "One long blast is ground attack. Continuous short bursts are an air attack."

Tuesday - January 15, 1991

The confusion did not seem to matter. The sense of urgency when the siren was sounded pervaded the whole camp.

Captain James Smith, however, was not impressed. "About 40 per cent were walking around out there with nothing on. That means 40 per cent loss." He and his grizzled sergeant explained the alert procedure. The warning is meant to come by radio, then be circulated by hand-held Motorola walkie-talkies to the NCOs. This time they heard only the horn, and saw the rush for the shelters. "Someone would be on duty," the captain said. "We don't have time to knock on tin." In the event that turned out to be what had happened.

Someone had heard metal against metal. They assumed it was knocking tin for a Scud warning. They sounded the sirens. The whole elaborate alert system, from high-technology radio to beating eating dishes had been reversed.

It was all a mistake, a false alarm. The exercise, however, demonstrated the heightened sense of awareness at this critical time. After a real alert, they had two minutes until a Scud might hit. But with an average of 3½ Patriot anti-missile missiles per Scud, they were confident they were well-protected. "It takes 1½ hours to launch a Scud," said one of the sergeants. "After the first launch, the launcher is going to be pinpointed and taken out." For Sergeant Robertson, the biggest threat was not Scud missiles but terrorist infiltration. He could not rightly identify who the supposed terrorist infiltrators might be.

"If they wear a rag on their head, I don't care who they are."

Throughout the region, the armies of the U.S. led coalition are continuing their preparations. British army tank transporters take vehicles of awesome destructive power down the road: Challenger main battle tanks, Warrior armored personnel carriers, even the antiquated but much loved Ferret Scout Car.

The desert is drying out now, after two days of heavy rains. A few pools remain, but the sand quickly drains it away. From the air, puffs of white vapor from the fast evaporating moisture look like treetops in the savanna. And the army turns the rain to its advantage.

A driver had parked his 4-wheel drive before a mud pond. And as a mahout would lead his elephant to a bathing pool, he was clipping in his canteen and covering his vehicle with brown watery mud, immediately transforming his bright green NATO standard camouflage into desert khaki. There's nothing like the old methods.

Other preparations were continuing at the logistics support headquarters for the 7th Corps. Around the sand barrier on the camp's perimeter, groups of men and women soldiers were digging out small bunkers for personal protection. There were clerks and orderlies, and headquarters staff more used to filling forms than sandbags.

They attacked their task with vim and wit. Or perhaps it was that nine would be happy talking and taking pictures and maybe filling the occasional sandbag while one would be using pick and shovel. One grunt leaned on his shovel and proceeded to deliver a discourse on the ideological differences between the rival Syrian and Iraqi branches of the Baath Party. "I don't think we should stop in Kuwait. We should put him out of business. If we wait two or three years, he'll be back with nuclear bombs. The guy is dangerous."

And if elsewhere the world was looking for something different, on this Jan. 15, in the base camp, the date appeared to have no military significance. Rather, such a bright sunny day after two days of rain was a popular wash day, and they were hanging out their washing on the tent guy ropes.

Wednesday
January 16, 1991

Among other things, war is one hell of a lot of paperwork. The documents that go into recording the entire history of the Gulf War include many that are still secret, some that will probably never see the light of day, some that are already reported missing from the files and others that are basic and available for anyone to read, including the National Security Directive President Bush signed on January 15th authorizing military action.

It was transformed quickly into a written order from Secretary of Defense Dick Cheney and went, via Gen. Colin Powell, to the commander-in-chief of forces in the Gulf, Gen. Schwarzkopf. From that point on, much of the paperwork generated by this war became unavailable to all but a select few, hidden beneath the stamp of security.

The "execution order" Gen. Schwarzkopf received—on a secure fax machine in his bunker command post 80 feet below street level in downtown Riyadh—specified a date, January 17th, for the war to begin.

Without tipping his hand to Saddam Hussein or any of his pals, Gen. Schwarzkopf had to get the word out to all the countries and generals who would be part of this great enterprise, so that everyone who should know would be in the loop.

In his autobiography, "It Doesn't Take a Hero," he revealed that he was especially worried about King Fahd, a man he claims is prone to telling the many princes in his entourage all sorts of state secrets, about wars and other things.

So the general worked out a scheme in which Prince Bandar, the Saudi ambassador to Washington, would be an emissary. He would be told when the attack was to begin, and would then pass it to the king with the code words "How is my favorite uncle?" How this would prevent the king from passing on the information to unauthorized ears after he'd decoded it wasn't explained. But one hopes the king had the wit to know it meant war, and not that he wasn't simply chatting with a solicitous prince.

As the D-Day hour approached, throughout the region threatening words and behavior settled in for the long haul.

Iraq closed its border with Turkey—no surprise, really, but another act that made Saddam appear to be angry, resentful and isolated, all the qualities his enemies wanted him to have. Saddam thought he was justified. After all, the Turkish government had promised it wouldn't be part of an attack on Iraq. But in the Turkish interpretation, that didn't rule out letting the allied coalition fly bombing missions from Turkish soil, as long as the Americans didn't publicly announce they were quietly using Turkey, a NATO partner, as a convenient northern base for the big squeeze on Iraq.

On the legislative paperwork front, Greece approved the use of military bases and ports in that country to assist the allied coalition and the French Assembly voted its authorization for the use of force against Iraq, just as the U.S. Congress had done.

French forces in the Gulf eventually reached some 16,000, sent to augment both air and land deployments, and were placed under U.S. command. This was no small step for the French, who are renowned for not being willing to take orders from anyone. Their first choice was to send troops to Saudi but have them answerable only to Paris. A coalition with France as one of the members is always interesting.

Making the French chain of command even more worrisome was the position of Jean Chevènement, the French defense minister. He flatly opposed sending French troops to fight Iraq, a country with whom French companies had done a great deal of business in guns and oil. But the Assembly decided if there was to be a war between Iraq and much of the world, the choice of sides was clear.

A divisional commander, Lt. Gen. Michel Roquejeoffre, was there to lead the French light armored troops into battle. By all accounts, these two robust surnames' Roquejeoffre and Schwarzkopf—got along famously, just like Alsace and Lorraine these days.

In the desert, many American and other allied units were still in motion in this critical week, just before the first official shots were fired, not yet bedded down and, although heavily armed, vulnerable to a degree.

The first story in this chapter describes the allied command's response to a threat that Iraq would try to catch the Americans off-balance while they were massing their troops and weapons.

The threat brought reminders of when the first U.S. troops arrived. They were a small, mobile contingent dropped into a desert down-range from Iraq's huge, million-man army. Allied military commanders later spoke of how, in retrospect, Iraq missed a grand opportunity to overwhelm an American force that would only have been a speed bump for them en route to Dhahran and Bahrain. Of course the retaliation from the U.S. for that kind of behavior would have been a different story.

The second report describes the latest group of Americans to arrive, the massive VII Corps from Germany, as a unit still very wobbly from a command and control perspective.

More than a half-million American troops, divisions and regiments from more than 20 other nations, dozens of ships of every description, from hospital and supply vessels to heavily armed battleships, and thousands of allied aircraft were about to merge into one massive fist aimed at Iraq.

They would have to be able to talk to each other, quickly, constantly, and efficiently, for any plan to work. And much of their communication, by necessity, would be in written and spoken code.

Probably not, "How is my favorite uncle," but something along that line.

U.S. Forces Scramble to Guard Airbase from Surprise Attack: "We Thought That SOB Was Coming"

By Michael Hedges

WITH U.S. FORCES IN SAUDI ARABIA - Five days ago, units of the 101st Airborne and the First Cavalry Division were hurriedly shifted to a defensive line around a commercial airbase when U.S. commanders feared a preemptive strike by Saddam Hussein.

"It has been a long five days" said a colonel with the 101st. "We thought that

SOB was coming," he said. "He still might." Members of the defending unit were reluctant to talk about the specifics of the mission. "Let's just say we're the guys who were here to stop him (Saddam Hussein and his army)," said a captain with the 101st.

The hurried deployment of units of the 18th Airborne Corps here in an area where the VII Corps has been newly arriving from Germany reflected a rapid buildup of U.S. forces in frontline areas. Beginning shortly after midnight last night, Jan. 16, the air activity of U.S. warplanes in this area increased markedly. The large number of night sorties continued until about 5 a.m., then dropped off, troops here said. The soldiers said the rate of flying was extremely high compared to recent days.

Yesterday morning, a long line of U.S. M1A1 tanks and Bradley armored fighting vehicles moved along an East-West highway on lowboy trailers pulled by trucks.

Overhead, two A-10 warthogs, tank-killing aircraft, performed maneuvers over bunkers set up by the 101st on a sand hill surrounded by a junked oil tanker, crushed concrete and other debris.

Twice, sentries stopped a vehicle with pool journalists and their escorts, and told the driver that if they went further north, they would probably be stopped. The units of the 1st Armored Division, "Old Ironsides," as they are known, have been massing in this part of Saudi Arabia for the past several days. Maj. John Chapman, the executive officer for the 1st Battalion, 35th Armor of the 1st Armored Div., which has arrived here from Erlangen, Germany, regarded his surroundings and said, "This is really a good place for a tanker. We'll have no problems here, especially now that the rain has bit the dust."

As he spoke, tankers who had test-fired their weapons recently and were now on stand-down strung a clothesline from the barrel of the M1A1 to its body, and began hanging their laundry. Maj. Chapman said "He has placed us where he has very strong defenses, and there are places where he does not have very strong defenses. I am confident we will attack—if we do—where it is to our advantage."

Tank companies and platoons and Bradley units dot the desert here. In places the sand, caked by days of rain and churned by thousands of tons of heavy armor, has taken on the cratered look of a moonscape. Amidst the roaring of tank diesel engines and the thunder of the M1A1 120-mm cannons, Bedouins squat in their shabby camps.

The troops here say the nomadic Saudis have taken to living close to their units for reasons that aren't completely clear. In places the desert is littered with bottles and brown MRE wrappers discarded by U.S. troops along with the light blue grain sacks tossed by the Bedouins after feeding their sheep.

At a firing range for tanks and Bradleys, Capt. David Brown, 29, of San Jose, Cal, battalion operations officer for the 6/6 Infantry, said today was a critical day for his unit. "Today the last units in this battalion are calibrating their weapons," he said. "It is critical to zero in your guns before engaging moving targets. We are combat-ready as of today."

Staff Sgt. Courtland Pegan, of Hillsboro, Ohio when asked if he expected combat said, "Truthfully, there are all kinds of rumors floating around about how we will be used. As battalion master gunner, I'm only concerned with getting the vehicles ready to go."

Staff Sgt. Pegan's words were punctuated by the roar of tanks firing at a target about a mile away. He said, "It looks like it is getting there. There is not a person out there in his right mind who wants this to happen. This is the time you start reevaluating your life, thinking back about what you would have done differently."

Wednesday - January 16, 1991

Allied Jets Roar Overhead as Ultimatum Ticks Down; U.S. Army VII Corps Still Working Out the Kinks

By Douglas Jehl

WITH U. S. FORCES, Saudi Arabia - The roar of jets on Wednesday began long before the dawn, and soldiers in the crowded Army tent were suddenly awake, wondering if this was the way the ultimatum would expire. "That's unusual," said a tense voice in the darkness, and soon the anxious soldiers headed for the camp perimeter to stand watch in the chill pre-dawn, watching from behind a sand-walled berm until the sun came up.

The swooping jets proved to be no more than another sign of the United States showing off its military might as the deadline came and went. But here with the Army's still-arriving VII Corps, usually based in Germany, the hints of war came in some contrast to indications that the unit, centerpiece of U.S. reinforcements, is still feeling its way around the unfamiliar desert terrain.

Col. Jimmy Hitt, commander of the corps' 11th Aviation Brigade, said in an interview that one in four of the unit's attack helicopters were still at a "walking" stage in terms of their preparedness for desert combat.

And across the desert, soldiers in the corps—most of them veterans of no more than two weeks in the sand—stand out oddly in uniforms of forest green rather than the brown and tan designed for desert warfare.

A two-day visit to the units of the VII Corps, a massive combat force that includes the equivalent of four Army divisions, found American soldiers now spread across a great swath of desert that a month ago was virtually uninhabited.

Its units boast the most advanced and powerful of U.S. weapons here, including hundreds of M1-A1 tanks, six battalions of tank-killing Apache helicopters, and several batteries of multiple rocket launchers that are the Army's most potent artillery. But in interviews and conversations in several units newly established in the sand, officers and enlisted men left the clear impression of an Army still trying to work the kinks out after its sudden move from Germany.

In a joint exercise with the Air Force Tuesday, the corps' 11th Aviation Brigade hoped for the first time to rehearse the kind of joint assault that might pit Army Apache helicopters and Air Force A-10 jet fighters together in a raid on moving Iraqi tanks.

But with Air Force liaison officers assigned to the corps having only just arrived in Saudi Arabia—and the Apache units themselves in place for no more than 10 days—Hitt, the aviation brigade commander, warned: "This will be a rough experience. We know that."

Indeed, as Hitt headed with his mobile operations center to a desert vantage point, very little was to go as hoped. The Army officers found they had no way to communicate with the designated battle commander, a lieutenant colonel circling overhead in a Blackhawk helicopter from which he was to coordinate the raid.

Then, as the Apaches waited long past the scheduled rendezvous, the Air Force jets failed to show—and the Army aviation unit had no way to find out what had happened.

"The breakdown," the 44-year-old colonel summarized later for an accompanying reporter, "is no Air Force aircraft, and then we had a comm (communications) breakdown with the command and control aircraft, and the Air Force can't talk to anyone either."

Hitt, a chain-smoking Texan, appeared to take it all in stride. "The first time it always goes like this," he said. "The second time it's better. The third time, primo."

The commander said he hoped at a debriefing later in the evening to "fix what happened" to improve coordination the next time.

But with this failure taking place on the day the UN ultimatum was to expire, the colonel acknowledged that such a breakdown would likely be inevitable if war were to begin. "It's going to happen in combat," Hitt said. "If the Air Force doesn't show up, I'm going to have a plan in my head to do something else."

"It won't kill us if the Air Force doesn't show up," Hitt said. "We just won't kill as many tanks."

Thursday
January 17, 1991

For the air war to begin on time—and it would begin on time, make no mistake—the aircraft assigned to fire the first shots and the planes that would immediately follow hard on their tails, without letup for hours, needed to be in the air at the appointed time, within sight of the target and trigger-ready.

So preparations at air bases in the region and on aircraft carriers in the Red Sea went forward at a crescendo hours in advance.

While the allies were busy pulling the cork on this high-tech plan of destruction, Saddam Hussein was preparing to deliver his "mother of all battles" speech.

Whatever else he might have been, the Saddam Hussein of those days was a phrasemaker with a touch that would have earned him plaudits on Madison Avenue. For months, "mother of all" were words that preceded a slew of plural nouns, putting Saddam's toothy stamp on the language.

The stories in this chapter take the allied forces through those hours of anticipation, across the final threshold and into the elation-filled day that followed as aircraft after aircraft, sortie after sortie roared into the darkness overhead and came home hours later, all with stories of supremacy over the foe. The fixed-wing aircraft that led the attack over Iraq—the raven-black F-117 Stealth fighters and the spunkily-named "Wild Weasels" (F-4Gs)—weren't the only ones who could claim to be the first to fire at the enemy, though.

Tomahawk cruise missiles also blazed in wild arcs off the decks of U.S. warships, through the sky and along rivers to targets visible only to their computer brains.

Most of the land army was an observer as the battle kicked off from the air, but a few Army personnel also owned a piece of the opening-night action. Apache helicopters from the Army's 101st Airborne Division, flying just above the desert floor, preceded the fighter planes to attack ground radar stations inside Iraq.

With those silenced, the bomb and missiles from higher-altitude aircraft would have an even clearer path to their destinations.

The first fighter and bomber sorties came into northern Iraq virtually undetected. For months, allied pilots had sped like bandits toward the Iraqi border as though headed for an attack, causing Iraqi radar stations to activate. The allied planes would then bank away or pull up before crossing the frontier, having identified the locations of yet more Iraqi radar sites.

In response, the Iraqis stopped turning on their radar. Bad decision. This night, there was no stopping at the border. And since this was the first day for taking on Iraqi fighter pilots, one allied fighter pilot would be the first to record the shoot down of an Iraqi plane.

But there were allied losses, as well. The Navy and Air Force pilots had always assumed some colleagues wouldn't come back. Sure enough, the first report from the Red Sea fleet confirmed one F-18 didn't return to the USS Saratoga on the first morning.

In the United States, opinion polls showed overwhelming support for the Bush Administration's decision to blast Iraq out of Kuwait. In Saudi Arabia, the resident foreign community—which in a story in this chapter a western "observer" estimated at some 6,000 American civilians—would probably give similar answers. Most of them presumably would like the allies to put a stop to this war-in-the-desert business, so they could get back to helping the Saudis and Kuwaitis extract petroleum products from the vast desert.

No doubt they'd prefer to resume normal life, continue sending their children to private schools, say, without Saddam Hussein breathing down their neck.

Air War Begins: "This is History in the Making"
2:27 a.m.

By Edith Lederer and David Evans

IN CENTRAL SAUDI ARABIA - The war with Iraq began early Thursday morning as a squadron of U.S. fighter-bombers took off from the largest U.S. air base in central Saudi Arabia.

"This is history in the making," said Col. Ray Davies, 44, of Battlebrook, N.J., who watched a somber group of pilots board their aircraft, taxi down the runway and take off. The stillness of the night sky was shattered by the thunder of the jets' afterburners as they took off in pairs, disappearing in red dots that winked out as they gained altitude.

The aircraft were heavily loaded with bombs and under-wing fuel tanks for the long trip north. The F-15E fighter-bombers were also armed with cannon and air-to-air missiles for self-defense. "The first ones took off at 12:50 a.m.," said Davies, the base's chief maintenance officer. "It's absolutely awesome. I mean the ground shook and you felt it." "We've been waiting here for five months now. Now, we finally got to do what we were sent here to do," he said.

The U.S. Air Force media pool was awakened about 1 a.m. by the near-continuous thunder of the fighter-bombers taking off. When the pool arrived at the flight line shortly afterwards, the parking aprons that had been crowded only Wednesday were half-empty.

Wild Weasels Roar Into Action: "Hey, Bud-man. Hit 'em Hard"

By Susan Sachs

AN AIRBASE IN THE PERSIAN GULF - In an earth-trembling roar and eye-stinging blast of hot exhaust, more than a dozen Air Force F4-Gs, the Wild Weasels armed to knock out Iraqi air defenses, shot into the moonless night at 1:26 a.m. (local time) from this base in the vanguard of the air strike against Iraq.

An hour later, dozens of bomb-laden Marine F/A-18 fighter-attack jets, accompanied by Prowler jamming and Intruder fighter aircraft, soared off from an airstrip at the same base, lighting the night sky with white torches from after-burners that flared out from their engines as they disappeared, heading north.

"Hey, Bud-man. Hit 'em hard," shouted a commanding officer to the electronic warfare officer in the cockpit as one of the sleek Weasels turned from its spot-lit parking space into the turn that would lead it to the runway.

The crewman, crammed behind the pilot and banks of high-tech gear, learned down and raised his fist in the air, thumbs up.

As the first wave of warplanes headed into the night, Marines and Air Force personnel on this secret base scrambled into bunkers, wrestling on their chemical masks and helmets as several SCUD missile alerts were announced. No missiles had fallen on the base at filing time.

At least 30 F/A-18 fighter jets, manned by Marine airmen, rose into the sky in a continuous roar nearby over nearly an hour. After each takeoff, the cool night air became eerily silent, until the next aircraft sped off the runway. The weather was "perfect," according to a military commander—a light haze of clouds, a few stars and no moon. He described the combined air operation, called Desert Wind by the White House, represents the "greatest air armada" ever assembled in terms of power and precision.

At the base, two American flags, long kept under wraps to avoid offending the host country, flapped in the breeze, lit like the Fourth of July by utility-power spotlights.

The flags were just put up yesterday afternoon and some of the Weasel pilots saluted before heading out. At 3:35 a.m. (my time), two alerts were called, requiring seven combat pool correspondents to grab masks, gloves, flak jackets and suits and run for the sand-bag fortified underground bunkers.

Cruise Missiles Off the Wisconsin: "Man, I Never Thought It Would Come to This"

By George Rodrigue and Robert Ruby

NOTE TO CORRESPONDENTS: *Technical problems delayed transmission of original file, but backup copy was sent via helicopter to JIB Dhahran. This is supplement to that report, and will be followed by additional info Thursday night, following more interviews.*

ABOARD THE USS WISCONSIN, in the PERSIAN GULF - After initiating the allied air attack against Iraq, a naval task force in the Persian Gulf fired dozens of additional Tomahawk cruise missiles in intermittent barrages on Thursday.

The battleship Wisconsin, the ship coordinating the launches, fired missile salvos on three occasions during daylight hours. It also coordinated and participated in the initial pre-dawn attack, the first-ever use of cruise missiles in battle.

By late afternoon, the Wisconsin had fired 16 of its long-range, precision-guided cruise missiles. It can carry up to 32 of the near-supersonic, ground-hugging weapons, and its captain said further shots might be fired depending on assessments of damage to strategic and military targets in Iraq. Pool members observed several other ships firing Tomahawks near Wisconsin.

Officers said those vessels included the battleship Missouri, the Spruance-class destroyers Fife, Leftwich and Foster, and the Aegis-class guided-missile cruisers Bunker Hill and Mobile Bay.

Aboard the Wisconsin, officers and crewmen shot their pre-dawn strikes toward Baghdad in a state of combat tension. On the darkened bridge, people spoke softly and moved briskly. "Man," one sailor whispered as the Wisconsin fired its second missile, "I never thought it would come to this."

In the ship's engineering sections, the usual bantering was replaced by a somber silence. But after a handful of successful launches, and with the realization that Iraqi warplanes posed little threat to the heavily armored World War II-vintage battleship, sailors not directly involved in the launches clearly became more relaxed.

At mid-morning, with reports trickling in about damage to military targets and few or no casualties among American pilots, the attitude among many might well be described as celebratory—sort of like a long-range turkey shoot. Officers allowed sailors to stand on the main deck to watch the battleship's third barrage, beginning at 10:53 a.m. (07:53 GMT, 2:53 a.m. EST.)

One of the happiest crewmen was Lt. Guy W. Zanti, the ship's missile officer. He had hoped his missiles would destroy or confuse Iraqi air defenses, thereby saving U.S. pilots' lives. "I think that the Tomahawks maybe destroyed some things that could have hurt the airplanes," he said, smiling.

News reports for hours mentioned that targets around Baghdad had been hit by airplanes, without mentioning cruise missiles. Lt. Zanti kind of enjoyed that. "It was weird," he said. "I heard the correspondents on the radio in Baghdad saying 'I hear bombs but I do not see any planes.' And that was because there were no planes."

For the morning's final launch, below-decks workers such as the ship's engineers, up from their usual posts in the bowels of the ship, carried binoculars and cameras and wildly cheered the launchings, in which three Tomahawks roared away in two minutes. Sailors also cheered two launches from a sister ship, whose missiles could clearly be seen flying over the Wisconsin's stern.

. . . Each Tomahawk launch was a dramatic, violent marriage of sound and light almost too intense to bear. During pre-dawn launches from the ship's armored box launchers, the signal of an imminent launch was a loud electronic hum, following within a second by an explosion of light that briefly turned night into day. A fraction of a second later came a chest-rattling boom felt as much as heard, like the slamming of a metal door, a blast loud enough to make people crouch as if to find shelter from the sound.

The missile emitted a low-pitched road as it broke through the seal of its launching tube in a vast cloud of noxious white and brown smoke. For several seconds, each missile would appear almost to stop, hanging at an awkward tail-down angle in the air, horizontal, gained a small tail of intense white light and rapidly moved away from the ship in a shallow arc, spreading a halo of light that turned the water pale green beneath it. From a distance, as they were fired by the battleship's escort ships, each Tomahawk seemed to rise slowly and pause, like a giant flare.

Then the solid-fuel rocket boosters dropped away, plunging into the Persian Gulf about a mile away from the ship. The missiles themselves carried on, their wings automatically popped out, the intakes to their jet engines popped open beneath their bellies, and they left an arrow-like trail of black smoke as they arced toward Iraq.

Thursday - January 17, 1991

First Allied Air Kill: "When the Airplane Blew, the Whole Sky Lit Up"

By Guy Gugliotta and Joseph Albright

WITH U.S. FORCES, Saudi Arabia - Fighter pilot Steve Tate had never fired a guided missile in the dark, even in a drill. When he finally did it Thursday morning, he shot down an Iraqi fighter, perhaps the first air kill of Operation Desert Storm.

"When the airplane blew, the whole sky lit up," said Tate, a 28-year-old Air Force captain from Watersmeet, Mich. It continued to burn all the way to the ground, and then just blew up into a thousand pieces."

Tate, leader of a flight of four F-15 fighters, was one of the first pilots to cross into Iraqi airspace when Operation Desert Storm began just after midnight Thursday.

After in-flight refueling about one hour out of an allied airbase in eastern Saudi Arabia, Tate and his colleagues joined their "package," a group of bombers en route to targets deep inside Iraq. Tate's F-15s were assigned to "sweep" ahead of the bombers to clear the skies of enemy aircraft "We crossed the border high, with our escort a couple of miles behind us," Tate said. Once over the target, the F-15s were to conduct a "combat air patrol" above the bombers. Shortly after 3 a.m., Tate said, his flight arrived on station just outside of Baghdad. At that point, the Iraqi capital had been under allied bombardment for at least a half-hour.

"I could see the outline of Baghdad, lit up like a huge Christmas tree; the entire city was just sparkling at us," Tate said. "With them shooting the triple-A (anti-aircraft artillery) at us, you saw the concussions going off, the bombs going off and some fires."

The bombers swooped down toward their target, while Tate and the other F-15s steered security patrols to protect them. A few minutes into the mission, Tate said he picked up a radar contact leaving the ground and traveling quickly upward toward the fighters. Soon, an enemy fighter loomed on the tail of another F-15.

"My number three (the other F-15) had just turned south, and I was headed northeast on a different pattern," Tate said. "I don't know if the bogie was chasing him, but I locked him up (targeted the enemy airplane), confirmed he was a hostile and fired a missile."

... The bombers were over the target for about 15 minutes, a chaotic interval when airwaves were clogged with message traffic from wave after wave of attacking allied planes. Iraqi air defense launched no missiles but kept up a steady barrage of artillery fire, lighting up the sky like sparklers.

"You're so busy you don't have time for feelings," Tate said. The bombers finished their run at 3:30 a.m. and all of the planes were back in Saudi Arabia an hour later. The F-15s landed at their home base at 5:30 a.m.

Tate, a short, husky towhead with a mustache and a reputation for disliking reporters, climbed down from his fighter with a big grin on his face, shook hands with cheering maintenance crewmen, posed for pictures and endured interviews and questions for several hours without visible discomfort.

"I feel good. I never experienced this before," Tate said. "It's unfortunate that we've had to go to war, but I guess there was no other way."

A Day for Rejoicing—Catapulted Into the Sky, Fully Expecting Some Would Never Come Back

By Carol Morello

ABOARD THE U.S.S. JOHN F. KENNEDY IN THE RED SEA - They had been catapulted into the sky, fully expecting that some of them would never come back and each hoping it would not be him.

And so Thursday was a day for rejoicing, at times even crowing, for the pilots who flew more than 80 sorties from the Kennedy the first day of the war with Iraq. Their success was measured not just by the missiles and bombs that hit their mark.

It was that everyone returned from his mission unscathed to tell tales at turns humble and proud, daring and curious.

"Let's give them another good shot," said Capt. John P. Gay, the Kennedy's commanding officer, in an announcement that the first sortie of 41 planes had returned intact.

And that they did, two more times, in flights over western Iraq and Baghdad, where they hit airfields, hangars, a pumping station, and communications facilities.

The one bleak spot from the Red Sea battle group came from the USS Saratoga, a sister aircraft carrier that flew joint missions with the Kennedy.

An F-18 fighter and its pilot were reported missing from the very first mission flown off each ship. As of late Thursday night, not a trace had been found of the pilot or his plane.

Aboard the Kennedy, there was gratitude and even surprise that none of its planes had met the same fate—mingled with a touch of envy for the two Saratoga F-18 pilots who downed two Iraqi MiG-21 planes Thursday.

Pilots still pumped up with adrenaline hours after their missions had been completed all said the one unexpected and puzzling aspect was that they met so little resistance from the Iraqis. They told of Iraqi fighter planes disappearing from the radar screen, apparently fleeing from the American invaders.

For reasons the flyers can only surmise, the Iraqi fighter planes left an unimpeded pathway for bombing.

"We prepared for every contingency and every threat in its finest condition, and when we got in there and did our strike we found them to be less than what we anticipated," said Commander John Leenhouts, 40, of Jacksonville, FL. "We had anticipated the very worst and found it to be better for us, worse for them."

Leenhouts, who flew an A-7 attack plane on the first mission that took off at 1:20 a.m., said they had expected surface-to-air (SAM) missiles to be much more intensively and skillfully employed. "In reality, they didn't use them to any degree whatsoever," he said. "We expected them to have fighter aircraft more regimented, more uniform in their attacks, and they were truly random."

Radar picked up numerous Soviet-made MiG jets.

"They acted as if they were overwhelmed by the number of aircraft coming toward them, and they couldn't quite make up their mind which strike group to come after," he said. "It was a confused evolution, racing back and forth, and in some cases I don't think they had a very clear picture exactly who was out there."

Lt. John Klas, 27, another A-7 pilot who flew over Baghdad on the initial mission, said a red light in his cockpit signaling that someone had locked his plane on radar lit up so many times he lost count. But he never actually saw any missiles fired at him.

"Until I can see a missile launched against me, I'm not going to maneuver very drastically to avoid something like that. That's what my eyeballs are for, it's really the only way I can tell."

Some pilots were disappointed they didn't get to tangle with their Iraqi counterparts. "The Iraqi fighters were between us and our target," said Lt. Cmdr. Bud Warfield, 33, of Jacksonville, FL, who flew an F-7 on the second mission that commenced at 11:48 a.m. "We were all charged up. We thought we were going to have some fun, because we brought a lot of fighters with us. But they ran away."

A certain bravado—arguably justified—ran through the pilots' explanations for the Iraqi fighters' actions.

"They're afraid of our F-14s," said Andrew Lewis, 28, of Los Altos, CA. "If I were them, I'd turn around and run, too," said an F-14 pilot called Rake. Rake said surveillance planes described several MiG-21s in three or four different groups within 50 miles of the Americans.

"As we advanced, they fell back," he said. "They knew we were there. I don't think they wanted to die."

"We know from the way they conducted operations against the Iranians they're pretty conservative," he added. "But you'd think they'd have a change of heart. When you bomb the airfield they took off from, and you do it with impunity, you figure sooner or later they'd come back. But they just stayed away."

Others speculated that other reasons may have played a role, too.

"One is that they don't know how to use their equipment," said Leenhouts. "Their equipment is not in as good shape as we thought it was going to be. It's very possible that they were protecting their equipment and saving it for a later strike. It's hard to understand why they failed to utilize the equipment that we know them to have."

The pilots said they could have chased the Iraqi fighters but that would have been foolishly indulgent. "There's no John Wayne-ing," said Rake.

"If we'd have wanted to kill them, we could have faced them," said Dave, another F-14 pilot. "But more important was to get our guys out of there."

Those who flew on their first mission that took off and landed in darkness said they met intense anti-aircraft fire that lit the sky over Baghdad.

But the aviators simply stayed above the envelope of fire and lived to tell of its awesome, awful beauty the pilots compared to thousands of lethal fireworks shot thousands of feet into the air

"To say it was incredible would be an understatement," said Leenhouts, who flew over southwestern Iraq firing Harm missiles at Iraqi SAM missile sites to take out their ability to shoot American aircraft down. "It looks like, if you can imagine, a fireworks display over Disney World, and multiply it 100 times. Just a continual sparkling effect of white flashes that range in height, well below us, from the surface upwards of 3,000 and 4,000 feet, and it's continuous. It was well over 15 minutes of continual barrage fire."

Lt John Klas, an A-7 pilot, described Baghdad as a dome of light. "You could see the flashes from the ground firing up and a few missile launches coming from the city," he said. "The downtown was really lit up."

Lt. Mike Walsh, 31, of Virginia Beach, VA, said he saw "a terrific light show" from the window of his A-6 Intruder. "It really awed me," he said. "It was spectacular. There aren't enough wows and gollys and all that kinda good stuff to tell you what the light show looked like."

For most of the pilots, it was their first time in combat. And while they did not duel with any Iraqi pilots, they did confront their fear. Even those who flew on the afternoon mission said they slept fitfully, if at all, the night before. Dave said a fellow pilot opened his shirt to display a St. Christopher's medal on a gold chain and told him, "If I end up on the ground and I'm dead, take this off and give it to my wife."

"The butterflies in my stomach never really went away," said Klas, who estimated he flew 40 minutes over enemy territory. "It felt like there were a dozen of 'em in there. From the time the admiral came on the speaker system and announced we were going in till the time we came back in, I was pretty nervous. The butterflies never went away, but I felt safer when I flew back into friendly territory. I was listening on the radio for all the guys to check in. I was hoping everybody, it was a real sense of relief."

Rake said he felt "dry around the mouth, nervous, jittery," going in.

"Well, we practiced to do this before. But this is the first time I've ever done anything like this before," he recalled telling him. "God, please don't let me screw this up. Let me get in there, do it right, and get out in one piece. It's like a big weight off your shoulders, knowing you did your job and did it right," he added.

The first-timers said they still consider themselves rookies, not combat veterans.

"If we talk about this over a beer back in the states, I'll tell you I'm a veteran," he said. "One flight does not necessarily mean you're accomplished in combat. All it means is I've been exposed to it and I know what to expect the next time.

"The first one, there is a lot of anxiety, a misunderstanding of what to expect. Going in, you build up the threat to be larger in your mind than it is. You leave and you realize you can cope with it. You're starting to build the experience level that you need to make you a combat veteran after several missions."

More missions lie ahead. Still, the pilots said the onset of war was a needed shot of adrenaline. "We've been here four or five months," said Walsh, the son of a fighter pilot in Vietnam. "Now we feel like we're doing something to get our butts home."

The Underground Nightmare: Gas Alert in VII Corps

By Douglas Jehl

WITH U.S. FORCES - The first hint of war came at midnight, when the order was passed by senior officers: a MOPP-1 chemical alert was in effect.

Anxious soldiers and their visitors in darkened tents ripped/pulled on the heavy jacket and trousers of charcoal-lined protective suits. For the first time since the crisis began, they took a pill designed to moderate the effects of a nerve-gas attack.

Not yet required to don masks, gloves and boots, we lined them up within easy reach. And then, while rumors rose and fell about whether this was really the beginning, there was nothing to do but wait. Then at 3 a.m. came the air horns, three loud blasts in the night, over and over again to jolt this Army VII Corps camp awake. "Gas, gas, gas!" the soldiers on guard shouted in terrifying refrain, as the sleeping jumped from their cots to scramble for their gear.

For a reporter lulled to sleep by the effect of the medication, it was difficult to tell whether the call was "Gas, gas, gas!" or "Mask, mask, mask!" But it didn't matter. The surge of adrenaline was just the same, and I grabbed for my gas mask and fitted it to my face. Certain that an Iraqi missile would explode before I could get a seal around my face, I felt as if I were in slow motion, clumsy at what could be the most important time. But when I finished, I found that others still lagged behind, and I later found that in my panic, I had pulled my straps too tight.

Outside, the horn continued its urgent top alert. But inside, the sound of modern war was the sound of heavy breathing as soldiers, bug-like in their masks, gasped for air at double time and protective valves clicked reassuringly, first open and then shut.

To the light of a dim lantern and some red-filtered flashlight bulbs, we continued our preparations, now fitting clumsy galosh-like boots over our own heavy shoes.

Finally came the rubber gloves, heavy with impregnated charcoal, to complete what—we hoped, and had been assured—was a chemical-proof seal to provide shelter from any mustard, nerve, or biological agent Iraq might choose to launch.

We yanked helmets over protective hoods and headed for a nearby bunker, whose sandbags, we had been assured, could shield us should Iraq attack by air.

As we left the tent, an Army captain intercepted each of us at the door, checking straps and buckles like a paratroop jumpmaster to make sure we hadn't left a gap that could let the gas get through.

Underground we found a nightmare: the assigned bunker already crammed with soldiers from the tent next door, and no place else to go.

But someone realized the space was filled not just with bodies but extra rucksacks, loaded with food and water, and Capt. XXX Coco ordered that all baggage be passed back out.

This provided room—but barely, and just after 3:15, 19 soldiers and their visitors squeezed shoulder to shoulder in silence, packed into the gloomy chamber, a cell four-feet tall, walled with sandbags and illuminated by a single lantern.

A reassuring voice urged us all to breathe slow and deep, to purge our bodies of adrenaline.

. . . I crossed my fingers and hoped this alert might prove short-lasting, so that next time I could put my mask on right. More silence, and then another voice, giving up the attempts at humor: "It might be a good time to pray."

Then, at 4 a.m., as some began to settle down to sleep, an all-clear siren sounded dimly in the distance. A soldier was sent to investigate, and came back with welcome news: The alert was over, and the masks could come off at last

Yanking mine off, I found it dripping with perspiration, and felt the marks it had left on my face. Almost limp with relief, we went inside and, while soldiers were posted to the perimeter, we were told it might be best to sleep. No one knew what had happened, and the informal consensus was that we would have been kept underground for hours had the war really begun.

No one thought to check the radio. Then, as we stripped off the masks and gloves and boots, and climbed back upon our cots, our escort, Maj. Cook, walked back into the tent with news from the operations center.

"Gentlemen," he said, "We are now at war with Iraq. Our planes have been hitting Baghdad for the last half an hour, and there are reports of MiGs headed this way."

A full blackout was in effect, he said; only red flashlights were permitted.

We grabbed for shortwaves, and listened in shock as the President began to address the nation. . . . An hour and a half later, when we emerged again, soldiers from the unit still stood at positions along the perimeter, where they had remained on guard in full chemical protection.

The sun had dawned to gray and stormy skies. A column of armored vehicles rumbled in the distance, and the watching soldiers sought to come to grips with the fact that the United States was now at war.

"I hope too many guys didn't get killed today—on our side, anyway," said Sgt. John R. Strait, a 28-year-old intelligence officer from Houston, TX.

"Today's an opportunity to excel," Sgt. Maj. Clifford Lovejoy told a group, saying that a "100 percent alert" would continue through the morning. "Let's have fun."

Sourceable Information From "Western Observer"—6,600 Americans in Saudi Arabia As the War Started

By Mort Rosenblum and Ahmad Hamad

SOMEWHERE IN THE EASTERN HEMISPHERE - We went to a large compound flying the U.S. flag and talked with a person who said he could be identified only as a Western observer, as in an Arizona cowhand on a corral fence.

(Note, please: NOT diplomat.)

He described Al Khobar as calm, with most streets open, although a few were briefly closed by civil defense officials. Thursday markets opened as usual in the Qatif area, in southern part of province, a center of the Shiite community.

Prices have gone up.

Local Saudi officials said they felt optimistic. Things are less scary now, without the "frantic emotions" of last August. People have had five months to make up their minds about whether to stay or go. Lot of people are leaving town, however, taking advantage of long school holiday and three-day weekend at Aramco.

He had no separate information on the refinery reported hit by artillery near Khafji. But he said it was owned by Arabian Oil Company, a joint Japanese, Saudi, Kuwaiti company.

He said that the threat of terrorism would go up with the start of hostilities, but he did (not?) regard it as a serious problem. Saudis understand Saddam is a threat to them, he said, and terrorism is alien to the culture. He acknowledged that U.S. officials decided not to issue gas masks to their citizens, unlike EEC countries, but declined to discuss the reasons.

In his capacity as an American official—which usable only for stats in this paragraph —he described population pattern of U.S. citizens in Eastern Province.

Last spring, the total was estimated at 12,000. . . . Aug. 2, the total was about 7,000 because of summer holidays. By early September, the number dipped to 4,800, more or less. Then some more people left but others returned.

At end of December, the total was back to 7,000. Now, with holidays et al, he estimates the level at 6,600.

There was other stuff on which can infill if interested, but it not sourceable.

Friday
January 18, 1991

The Stealth missile hit one of the first targets—the AT&T building in downtown Baghdad—exactly as planned. And as planned, that was only the beginning. During the first day of the war, allied aircraft flew some 2,000 sorties and dropped more than 2,000 tons of bombs.

Despite achieving almost instant air superiority, allied squadrons did suffer losses. After only one day, eight coalition aircraft had been downed, their crews dead or missing. A story in this chapter tells of the reaction in the Royal Air Force squadron to the loss of two Tornado bombers over Iraq in the war's first hours.

The loss of even a fraction of the relatively small RAF contingent in Desert Storm was doubly painful because the RAF had insisted on assuming the mission of flying runs against heavily-defended Iraqi airfields with non-precision bombs, the IB 233, which had to be delivered at very low altitude to be effective. Going against Iraqi ground-based artillery, including shoulder-fired SAMs with infrared sights, at low altitude all but guaranteed losses.

Air Force Gen. Charles Horner, allied air commander in the Gulf, ordered American pilots not to fly low-level "unless they could justify it." In a post-war interview with PBS, he credited the RAF aviators with being "the bravest pilots in the Gulf War."

The British air staff weeks later in the air campaign raised the altitude at which the Tornado missions flew, but for some reason went to great pains to avoid saying it was done to save crew lives.

A squadron spokesman said the reason was that British flyers had accomplished their initial mission and were attacking a new set of targets best approached from higher altitude.

In the first heady days of the air war, while allied pilots spoke excitedly to reporters about heavy ground-to-air artillery and the general lack of response by Iraqi aircraft coming up to duke it out with them, there was a response from Baghdad.

It was a response that allied leaders had dreaded from the earliest stages of the crisis. Not long after the allied air attack began, Iraq fired several Scud missiles at targets in Saudi Arabia and Israel. Fortunately, the Patriot missile batteries the U.S. had deployed in Saudi Arabia took out one of the missiles fired in that direction

There was no such defense in Israel. Saddam Hussein's objective, obviously, was to bring Israel into the war and thus fracture the fragile alliance among the U.S. and the other western countries and the Arab states who had joined their cause.

The first Iraqi missiles to strike Israeli territory caused property damage and some injuries but, amazingly, killed no one.

But with a little practice, or by the odds, it was expected the Scuds would eventually find some victims among the Israeli populace. As always, a corollary danger was that one or more of the missiles would be armed with chemicals that would spread indiscriminate poison.

It was the beginning of the Patriot saga. The first chapter is here.

The crisis over Iraq and Kuwait was also a confrontation of religions: Muslims versus Christians and Jews, and even within the Islamic world, Shiite versus Sunni. It was a war where U.S. Marines who also happened to be Muslims got special dispensation because this war was taking place on their hallowed ground.

Mecca, the holiest site in all of Islam, was on this very same desert.

From the beginning of the U.S. deployment to Saudi Arabia, the issues of religion and religious observance among the coalition troops were hot, controversial, grab-a-camera-I-see-a-chaplain topics.

In practice, when it comes to religion at least, the Pentagon is one of the most tolerant institutions around. The U.S. military might have some difficulties with sex and gender, but whatever religious belief system you choose is fine. You don't even have to prove you practiced a particular faith, or switched every few years, or don't give a damn, just name your preference or lack of it, they will put it on your dog tags and you keep marching.

But in the Gulf, the high U.S. command was touchy to the point of being absurd about it. The obvious reason, officials said, was because the Saudis, as everyone knew, had to be asked to invite the Americans to come fight to protect them from Iraq.

The Saudis firmly prohibit the practice of any religion except Islam within their borders. And they were under no illusions that with a few exceptions, the foreign troops coming to this party weren't of the Islamic persuasion.

It's their desert, and Allah rules.

The compromise Schwarzkopf worked out was that his non-Islamic soldiers would be free to practice their non-Islamic religions, even hold services in the shadow, you might say, of Mecca, but his people wouldn't talk or make a big deal about it and the press wouldn't be allowed to cover it.

British chaplains would be referred to as "welfare officers." American chaplains would make themselves scarce when the press was around.

You might call it the Turkish air base solution.

Of course believers find a way, whether the belief is in a God or in the right to write about people who believe in a God.

In this chapter is the first of a number of stories in this collection that explore the entire subject, from a number of angles, by reporters who themselves actually may not believe in much at all, except calling things by their rightful names.

Stealth Fighters Pay Early-Morning Visit to Baghdad: AT&T Building Goes "Poof"

By Frank Bruni

SAUDI ARABIA - Slowly, as if in slow motion, the AT&T building just south of the Tigris River in Baghdad came into the view of the Stealth fighter pilot, taking his sleek black plane into the city under the cover of night.

He trained his sights on the microwave towers and antennae atop the roughly 12-story structure as he zeroed in on it. Then he let go a 2,000-pound laser-guided bomb.

Poof—the building disappeared in a thick cloud of black smoke as large chunks of debris shot hundreds of yards in each direction.

That was it.

Friday - January 18, 1991

The first strike, the bold stroke with which Operation Desert Storm began about 1 a.m. Thursday Saudi time.

A pilot's-eye view of it—and of several other strikes that followed as a squadron of Stealths claimed the skies above the Iraqi capital—was made available to a group of seven media pool members late Thursday at the air base out of which two squadrons of Stealth fighters are flying their sorties.

The videotapes, routinely taken by the aircraft as they perform their missions, previously had not been shown to anyone outside classified, high-ranking military.

They depicted the first wave of destruction to hit Baghdad and revealed a carefully planned operation, that exploited extraordinarily detailed intelligence on the locations and even floor plans of strategic buildings.

In unleashing their bombs, pilots zeroed in on particular rooms within buildings or particular towers atop buildings and hit their targets with devastating accuracy.

"You pick precisely which target you want. You can want the men's room or you can want the ladies' room," said Col. Al Whitley, commander of U.S. Air Force 37th Tactical Fighter Wing, which flies 58 F-117s, or stealth fighter, in the U.S. air fleet.

Two of the wing's three squadrons are in Saudi Arabia and ran missions early Thursday morning and overnight Thursday into early Friday morning.

Whitley said the Stealths led the allied forces' air raid on strategic structures and locations in Iraq. Their goal, he said, was to destroy communications and operations centers, hampering the Iraqi military's ability to function. Whitley said of the 400 sorties against 100 targets during the first early Thursday morning attack on Iraq, the Stealths flew 30 of the sorties against 80 of the targets. He would not say exactly how many Stealths flew.

Whitley, who flew one of the single-pilot fighters himself, said they initially entered Baghdad undetected, but that after the AT&T building was hit, intense anti-aircraft fire from the ground erupted. He said the fire did not seem targeted at specific planes but rather was an attempt simply to hit anything in the sky.

The targets were "key command and control functions" and every one that the military selected was hit/damaged, he said.

As he rolled the tapes of roughly eight different bombings and described the missions, his smile was wide, his mood buoyant. He said the mission was a spectacular success and that the pilots who flew it—most of whom had never flown in combat before—returned to base pumped up by their accomplishment. "I saw a lot of old boys become young men last night," Whitley said, who has previously flown in combat.

"I told them there would be hormones that would flow that they'd never tapped before," he said. "I told them they'd know what I meant after they came back." The tapes depicted bombings of underground military bunkers, communication towers and "sector" or area operations centers. One target shown on tape was what Whitley called a "presidential" bunker, "one of the places he calls home."

The pilot who hit it zeroed in precisely on a skylight in the roof, so that his bomb would penetrate the building and have maximum impact. The pilot hit his mark, and the structure seemed almost to implode.

Whitley did not say whether the military had expected Saddam Hussein to be there. The videotapes, eerie silent, showed the city and the structures as the Stealth pilots saw them with the center of their field of vision the cross of one vertical and one horizontal target line. Pilots clearly tried to place their targets at the intersection of those lines. Sometimes, they did it with ease. Other times they shifted their sights abruptly from top to bottom and side to side before locking in.

The pilots' field of vision was gray, with buildings forming either white or black rectangles. Around some of the buildings targeted and hit, light car traffic was visible. Whitley said as soon as the bombing began, people started fleeing the city and roads jammed. He could see it from the sky.

"I have never seen so many people leave a city," Whitley said. "It was bumper to bumper leaving the city. I don't think they were going to the Saddam rally that night."

The pilots located underground military bunker complex by spotting distinguishing characteristics. And when targeting the communications tower, they were able to aim at and hit what Whitley called the "space needle" atop it.

Whitley said the operation was not meant to wreak mass destruction but "to minimize collateral damage." He said anti-aircraft fire never seemed to lock in on any of the Stealths and that every one of the planes returned unscathed. They were out flying again late Thursday night and early Friday morning.

Stealths, which first became operational in 1982 but were not disclosed until 1988, are sleek, angular black planes designed to fly only at night and to be as undetectable as possible to radar systems. They include radar-absorbent material, and their angles deflect radar beams. The Stealths that flew over Baghdad in the initial air strike were the first planes in, and they all carried 2,000-pound laser-guided bombs, Whitley said.

Whitley said his pilots had been studying target maps far in advance so they would recognize their targets when they saw them.

The Stealths at no point were engaged by Iraqi aircraft or had to worry about defensive actions, he said. Watching one tape, Whitley described the Stealth's unobstructed movement as a "leisurely drive through Baghdad . . . the Stealths owned the skies"

"It can drive downtown undetected and deliver a bomb to the AT&T building and no one knows it's even there," Whitley said.

Although the first strike was successful and 100 targets were attacked, Whitley said he expected the bombings to continue unabated through the next several nights and maybe even longer. "I think there'll be plenty of targets for us to strike for quite some time," he said.

Despair in a British Tornado Squadron: Two Bombers Lost in First Days of Air War; Pilots Missing

By Ian Henry

They count them out. They count them coming back.

But for a squadron of Gulf-based British jet fighters, there is despair that they are not all making it back. So far two of their Tornado ground attack bombers are lost on missions to cripple Iraqi and Kuwait airfields.

Today the crews of the stricken squadron opened their hearts to tell of their emotions, their fears, and their despair as they grapple to cope with the realities of real-life warfare. One broke down in tears as he attempted to explain how he comes to terms with going airborne time and again on bombing missions knowing it could be his turn next to be shot down.

Veteran top gun fighter ace Squadron Leader Pablo Mason, 40, from Birmingham, said: "You feel guilty that you have survived and they haven't." The pilot, with 18 years with the RAF, is celebrating his 17th wedding anniversary today. After his debrief from an early morning mission, the Squadron

Leader added: "You feel very clinical, terribly clinical. There is a constant awareness that in a few seconds time you might not exist.

"When you get back and it's all over you feel relief. You can't feel more relief yet you do. I would not be doing this job if I was worried about it. You have got to control your reactions," he said, as tears began to roll down his cheeks.

After recovering his composure, the flying ace went on: "I flew helicopters in Northern Ireland as a young junior officer responsible just for myself. But I was on my own then. Now I am responsible for my whole crew. I feel the men are my responsibility." He has seven men under his command.

On the squadron's second sortie into enemy territory, an engine of one of the two-man GR1 flights caught fire and crashed. The pilot and navigator were seen to eject, and there is hope that they are safe and well.

Then early today another of the jets crashed on return from (its) bombing mission. There are fears the crew may have perished with the aircraft.

Another pilot, Flight Lieutenant Mark Paisley, 26, from Oxford, who lost friends, said: "At the moment I am going through the full range of emotions, from elation right down to dread and the fear of dying. Whatever your emotions you still fly the aircraft. We went as four crew, now we are three crew. Tomorrow there might be two or one," he added ominously. He went on: "It has just not sunk in yet that they have not come back, but I have a feeling they are still alive."

For the men of the Squadron, their job is probably the most hazardous of the entire Allied air contingent. Loaded with two 4,500 lb JP233 bombs, they fly deep into Iraq with sarcastic messages scrawled on the metalwork. The messages for Saddam include: "These are environmentally unfriendly" and "Only returnable with receipt of purchase" as well as "This is guaranteed to ruin your health."

Once over their airfield target, they race in at 600 mph at a level below 100 feet, before dispatching their deadly payload on the runways, and then sweeping up and heading back for home. The airfields are heavily fortified and they keep their fingers crossed that they escape unscathed from the battery of anti-aircraft fire leveled at them. They rarely see the craters left by their bombs, which also carry a mushroom cluster of anti-personnel mines to deter a rapid repair job.

The boss of the operational fliers, Wing Commander John Broadbent, led the first airfield bombing mission of the current conflict. He said: "You don't have to psyche yourself up. When the pressure is on you are psyched up enough. We are talking to each other all the time, making sure the attack goes successfully. Also we are looking around for hazards which we might be able to avoid on future missions."

The wing commander, whose job is to aim the bombs, added: "It is pretty serious business up there, and when you get nearer the target it gets more serious. On these particular sorties the vast majority of time we are not aware of any threat at all. It is very similar to the training sorties we do day in and day out at home.

"It is the last two minutes before reaching the target, and just afterwards, that there is the tension." Talking of the actual bomb-strike, the wing commander said:

"At night all you see are the pretty parts of it, like fireworks in a series of red lines through the sky. Your mind just thinks, 'well here we are, let's go and get it.' The triple-A looks like a roman candle. All you see are red lines shooting towards the plane. When it doesn't hit you don't mind, and when you come out the other side you know it is behind you."

His pilot, Squadron Leader Nigel Risedale, explained his feelings, saying: "It is equally dangerous, I think, to drive on the M25. There are thousands killed on the roads of Britain each year, but when one aircraft is lost it is news. People look for 100 percent success, so the loss of one aircraft is seen as a failure."

Squadron Leader Gary Stapleton, 37, from London, who as navigator is another bomb-aimer, said: "It is precision bombing. We are talking of accuracy of feet. They go where you aim them. You have a good idea whether or not you have hit the target. It is difficult to explain exactly what our job is. It is easy to explain what a salesman does, but to tell someone what it is like to fly on bombing missions is very, very difficult.

"We are fully aware of the risks, but when you lose someone it really brings it home that the risks are real. You see the flak rising from the ground but it is actually coming from the target. You can't avoid it, you are committed to doing a job. You just have to say to yourself that it is not going to hit me. You believe that because the flak doesn't appear to be aimed, but it is random, it will miss you. But there is always a risk of being hit. But when you have gone all that way to do a job you have got to do it. It has taken you one and a half hours to get there. You can't just turn 'round say, 'let's forget it.'"

The Squadron commander, Group Captain David Henderson, paid tribute to his crews, saying: "It takes a very special sort of courage to do the job they do, and go back out again knowing you have already lost some of your colleagues. I have the utmost respect for them.

"Obviously, mentally morale does take a bit of a dip and the whole detachment is very subdued. While every loss is sad, these men have the discipline to bounce back.

"We are normal human beings, and of course we have reactions like everyone else. Why we have lost two planes, and others haven't, I don't know.

"In every walk of life there is an element of luck."

From Ugly Stepchild to Unlikely Darling of the Skies: The "Spectacular" Scud-Killing Patriot Missile

By Joseph Albright and Guy Gugliotta

WITH U.S. FORCES, Saudi Arabia - The Patriot battery, ugly stepchild of one of Saudi Arabia's biggest air bases, shot down a Scud missile today and became everybody's darling.

"I'm sitting in my jet, getting ready to go," said Air Force F-15 fighter pilot 1st Lt. Steve Kirik. "I looked over at my port engine, and there it was. It was like a big, brilliant flare. It jumped off the ground, snaked back and forth a couple of times and then, boom!

"It was pretty spectacular."

Kirik, a stocky 24-year-old from Moline, Ill., was one of the few people on the base who had a pretty good idea what had happened. An inbound Iraqi surface-to-surface Scud missile had been intercepted and killed by a single rocket fired from an Army Patriot launcher.

It was the first time in history a Patriot anti-missile missile, the U.S. military's state-of-the-art air defense system, had ever been fired in anger, and the result was a spectacular fireworks display for thousands of servicemen who had donned gas masks and crouched behind bunkers in anticipation of an imminent enemy attack.

"We didn't expect it at that moment," said Patriot battalion commander Lt. Col. Leroy Neel, 42, of Houston. "It was there, we reacted properly, and it was gone."

And good riddance. As Neel finished his account, a half-dozen soldiers gathered in the base chapel clapped and gave him a rousing cheer. It was much the same elsewhere. The snazzy fighter pilots and Hollywood Air Force types who hang out here had nothing but nice things to say about the Army grunts who man the Patriot batteries: "Let's just say my respect for them rose tremendously," said Kitik. "Glad to have them here."

They are dogged, stubborn artillerymen, who wear chemical warfare suits 24 hours a day and who have been on Scud alert every minute since Operation Desert Storm began two days ago. They spend their days in a dark van full of computers watching green television screens, waiting to see the tell-tale parabola that lets them know that an enemy ballistic missile is inbound.

"I knew right away what it was," said 1st Lt. Charles McMurtrey, the 27-year-old Montgomery, AL native who was the duty officer on watch when the Scud crossed the Iraqi border a little after 4 a.m. "There's no way you can confuse it."

Friday afternoon McMurtrey and his bleary-eyed assistant, Sgt. Joe Oblinger, 26, of South Bend, IN, were standing on a bleak stretch of desert on the outskirts of the base. It was a typical Patriot launch site, close to the glamour, but not part of it.

Pieces of paper and plastic bags blew through shredded tires and junk that littered the sand. The launchers themselves, ugly dumpster shapes pointed toward the sky, completed the picture. "We alerted the command post and the battalion immediately," said battery Capt. Jim Spangler, 27, of Dayton, OH. Besides their normal alert, the Patriot team was also listening to Armed Forces radio, and had heard about the eight Scuds that had exploded in Israel moments earlier.

"Actually," Spangler said, "I don't remember when I heard about the Israel Scuds. Both things happened almost simultaneously." When McMurtrey hit the alarm the base public address system sounded a siren and announced "Condition Red, don your gas mask!"

In this war, any report of Iraqi attack raises fear of poison gas.... At 4:38 a.m., the Patriot launcher fired its missile. It arched upward, swerved once, and twice, then found the target, invisible on a moonless night. "I was standing outside my tent about three kilometers away," said Neel. "I saw the explosion, but it didn't register immediately. Then I thought, 'My God, that's one of mine.'"

Inside the van, Oblinger was making sure of the kill, insuring that he didn't need to fire a second missile. McMurtrey was looking for more targets. Neither man could spend the time to congratulate the other, because they both had too much work to do.

Eleven hours later, there was little difference. "We have yet to cool out," Spangler said. "We're always on edge. You're talking about a matter of seconds."

Neel didn't know if the Scud warhead had been high explosive or chemical, and he didn't particularly care. "A chemical team takes care of that. My people just find them and shoot them down."

These Marines Say Their Prayers. A Few Hours Later, Say Them Again. Islam "Honors Contracts"

By Jeff Franks

WITH THE U.S. MARINES IN NORTHEASTERN SAUDI ARABIA - Now that war has broken out, Lance Cpl. Harlow Fisher, like a lot of Marines, makes sure he finds time to say his prayers.

But, unlike most Marines, Fisher says his prayers five times a day while on his knees bowing toward the holy city of Mecca. Fisher is a Muslim, a rarity in the U.S. military, and this war has put him in a dilemma because he does not want to fight against his Muslim brother, Iraqi president Saddam Hussein. "I told my commanding officer I never would have come over here if I didn't have a contract. I don't agree with the war, but Islam says honor your contracts," said Fisher, 22, of Newburg, NC.

Fisher converted to Islam a year ago because he found Christianity too fraught with hypocrisy. "I found many falsities in Christianity. With Islam, I found myself and that is beautiful," he told Reuters. Now he is a devout reader of the Koran and a Marine who seriously questions what his country is doing to Iraq. "Basically, I think this thing is about a whole lot of money. People are always trying to get money," he said while sitting in a bunker filling up sandbags.

Fisher believes that President George Bush is acting on the behalf of the "aristocratic class" in the United States in launching his action against Iraq.

"If he was so concerned about fighting 'naked aggression' as he says, why didn't he send troops to South Africa when they were killing all those people down there?" asks Fisher, who is black. "If you're going to be the policeman of the world, you have to be fair about it," he insisted. Fisher said he does not agree with some of the things that Saddam has done—like gassing his own people—but believes that the Iraqi leader "had some legitimate gripes against Kuwait." "Kuwait was taking oil from Iraqi oilfields and they were producing more oil than they were supposed to."

Fisher, who is in a 2nd Marine Division supply unit positioned near the Kuwaiti border, dodged questions about whether he would take up arms against Iraq. "Will I shoot? I haven't asked myself that question yet," he said. Fisher said that there are three other Muslims in his unit, but that many Marines do not accept his religion.

"Let's just say that Islam is not widely accepted in the United States," he said. But, he said his commanding officer is open-minded about his beliefs. In front of a reporter, he asked the officer if he could go to Mecca, which is a couple of hundred miles to the west in Saudi Arabia. "Sure, you can go if they give you liberty," the officer said.

Fisher has been in the Marines two years and has another two years to go before his contract expires. He plans on getting out and going to college to study architecture and African theology. He plans on going to college, that is, if this war does not live up to his hopes. "I hope this is Armageddon so we can get it all over with," Fisher said.

Newest U.S. Military Anti-Terrorist Squad Carries Weapons and Holy Books

By Gary Regenstreif

EASTERN SAUDI ARABIA - The U. S. military hopes to root out terrorists with a tiny band of new soldiers who carry the Muslim holy book and sport "Free Kuwait" buttons on a personal mission to liberate the emirate.

About 300 Kuwaitis in exile, mostly university students who trained for eight days at Fort Dix, NJ, are expected to help identify Iraqi troops hiding in civilian clothing by recognizing their accents, detect false identification papers and interrogate Iraqi prisoners. Some, admittedly, are seeking revenge for the plundering, looting, and raping of Kuwait and its people after Iraqi troops rumbled across the border on August 2.

"I don't need this weapon," said Mohammed, his army standard issue M-16 rifle slung over his shoulder. "I can kill them with my hands. I'm usually a calm person." Mohammed, 24, a student of business information management at California State University in Fresno, does not want his full name used for fear of reprisals to family members remaining in the occupied land. Iraqi soldiers stormed into Mohammed's family's house and emptied it of food. Luckily, they left his parents and siblings untouched. "My life is much more worthy if I do this," he said.

The 300, who arrived from as far (away) as Japan and Switzerland, complement a volunteer force of about 7,000 Kuwaitis trained by Saudi and Egyptian armies, and a regular army force of about 4,500 who escaped after the invasion. These 300, though, are attached to the 82nd Airborne Division's 313th Military Intelligence Battalion. The Kuwaiti volunteers kissed and hugged each other when they first learned that allied warplanes and missiles launched a vicious air campaign against Iraqi targets.

"It's fantastic," said Jamal, 34, who holds a PhD in engineering from the University of California at Los Angeles. We were we would be home soon."

Jamal, who joined with his two brothers, is prepared to risk his life to liberate the oil-rich emirate and his family. "If it costs our life, that's fine," said Jamal, who fled Kuwait 45 days after Iraqi troops invaded. "At least our families will be free. We're willing to make the sacrifice. I'm driven to protect my country. The country gave me so much. They gave me a scholarship to the United States and medical help when I needed it."

For Khaled, 21, an engineering student at Brevard Community College in Cocoa, FL, there is also a need for revenge. "He (Iraqi president Saddam Hussein) killed many of my friends," Khaled said. But with the allied attack, "We felt powerful. We are ready to go to the front line."

The volunteers said the striking of Israeli targets muddies the Gulf situation and could complicate the alliance.

"Most Arabs don't like Israel, that's true," said Fuad, 22, a petroleum engineering student at Penn State University in State College, PA. "But I mean (in) this situation he is the one who is attacking Israel, so Israel has the right to attack him, that's for sure."

Saturday
January 19, 1991

Scud attacks on Israel continued, and the U.S. renewed its offer to ship the Israelis Patriot missile batteries to offer some protection. Israel had previously declined, but accepted this time, proving that differences that often divide even the closest of allies in this part of the world occasionally respond to a practical suggestion.

Meanwhile, using Patriots to kill Scuds in flight might make a fine display for television, but it still left a major gap in the grand design for liberating Kuwait and crushing the Iraqi military. The Americans had practiced shooting down Scuds for months prior to shipping the Patriots to the Gulf. Where was the plan to deal with those bad boys before they could be fired?

U.S. Special Operations, heirs to the famed Rangers of yesteryear, with Delta Force soldiers on alert 24/7/365, would seem ideally suited to scramble behind enemy lines to seek out and pinpoint or destroy items like Scud launchers and their mobile trailers at the source.

After the war, special operations commanders testified to Congress that they had pulled off some derring-do in the Gulf, including sending Navy Seals to set off explosions on the beaches of Kuwait near the end of the war while a Marine amphibious force floated offshore to make it appear the Marines were landing when they weren't.

But at Gen. Schwarzkopf's insistence, some special ops people later complained, they had been shut out of the Gulf War plans at the beginning. The commander had a grand plan that was resting on buttoned-down timing, coordination and deception and he didn't want any sneaky petes starting the war before he was ready.

Commandos from the Israeli military, who have done the honors in many penetration operations like the type called for in Iraq, were also straining to be unleashed. It was their cities, after all, taking the hits from those Scuds. But involvement of any kind by Israel was a double-edged sword for the allies.

Enter Lt. Gen. Sir Peter de la Billière, commander of the British contingent in Desert Storm. Sir Peter's military career was spent primarily with the SAS, the elite British commando units that carry out special ops for her Majesty.

Schwarzkopf liked Sir Peter's style.

He had already agreed (very reluctantly, Gen. de la Billière revealed in a postwar interview with PBS) to Britain's request to swap the U.K.'s original coalition assignment—supporting the Marines in their march directly into Kuwait—in favor of joining the main tank surge by VII Corps up the Wadi al Batin to take on the Republican Guard in southeastern Iraq and along the Euphrates River.

De la Billière argued that, now he could see the big picture stretched out on Gen. Schwarzkopf's briefing displays, the Marine mission was militarily ill-suited for the British contingent, or vice versa.

Britain's fast and powerful Challenger tanks would be wedged in and cramped on the short haul to Kuwait City, he worried, whereas the charge up the wadi (with three American divisions and assorted reconnaissance units) would afford more maneuver room.

He also noted the Marines were expecting extremely high casualties in their well-mined sector.

After what Sir Peter himself described as incredible civilian pressure, the famed "Desert Rats" of the British 7th Armoured Division split away from the Marines and took a new assignment with the VII Corps troops who, like most of the Brits, had shipped out from Germany for this conflict.

That decision had ripples that went beyond the briefing room. More Americans had to be called in—Tiger Brigade from Germany drew the assignment—so the Marines would have at least some heavy armor protection on their western flank as they drove north to Kuwait City.

Meanwhile, de la Billière the old guerrilla fighter had also gotten around Schwarzkopf's aversion to special ops. He explained later how he convinced the theater commander that sending SAS patrols to set up shop behind the lines in western Iraq would usefully divert attention from the allies' central effort in the east, in and around Kuwait. Oddly, even though the allied plan was to pull off a big surprise by appearing to ignore Iraq's vast western expanses and then strike hard from that direction, Schwarzkopf bought the diversion-in-the-West idea.

But de la Billière said Schwarzkopf attached one condition that clearly revealed one of his misgivings about special ops: the condition was that SAS would never have to be—or at least never ask to be—rescued. Done, said Gen. de la Billière, and the British commandos saddled up for secret duty north of the Saudi-Iraqi border.

Once Iraqi Scuds began striking Israel, there was more pressure from Washington—this time to nullify the Scud threat before Iraq provoked the Israelis into retaliating, which could torpedo the coalition.

Sir Peter came up with yet another solution, he told interviewers later. He could just change signals for the ever-flexible SAS and swap their mission from creating a diversion in western Iraq to Scud-hunting all across the enemy's territory.

Once again, Schwarzkopf agreed, and—according to Sir Peter's later interviews—thanked him for taking him off the Scud hook. The no-rescue condition apparently remained in force, however. Schwarzkopf and other allied commanders told later of how the Scud issue was an unwelcome pre-occupation, even though they had assumed from the start Iraq would use them.

Gen. Horner, the allied air commander, said Gen. Schwarzkopf grew very concerned as the Scud menace ballooned and called him often to ask what else could be done to counter them. "We were never able to shut them down," said Gen. Horner, only "suppress them."

In this chapter is a story about the first Iraqi POWs—captured at sea by the U.S. Navy, from offshore oil platforms two days after Desert Storm started.

In the air war, action continued off the American aircraft carriers. In addition to total air supremacy for this war, the allies also enjoyed something very dose to total sea supremacy.

If the Euphrates had been dredged deep enough, the Navy could have sailed the USS John F. Kennedy or some other flagship through a harbor and right up the river to within yards of Saddam's palace and saved a lot of jet fuel.

Aircraft carriers under sail, like floating, self-contained cities, were also among the first pieces to appear on the allied chessboard the previous summer.

First Iraqi Prisoners Logged by a U.S. Navy Frigate: Five Dead, 15 Captured Off Kuwait Coast

By George Rodrigue and Robert Ruby

ABOARD THE USS WISCONSIN IN THE PERSIAN GULF - The U.S. Navy guided missile frigate Nicholas (FFG-47) attacked an Iraqi oil platform about 40 miles off the Iraqi-Kuwaiti coast, killing five Iraqis and capturing 15, five of them injured, the captain of the battleship Wisconsin said Saturday.

Captain David S. Bill III said the platform had been used as an observation post by Iraqi forces, who also had fired on U.S. warplanes,

The attack occurred Friday night, several hours after the Nicholas disabled two Iraqi patrol boats, sinking at least one of them. USS Nicholas is commanded by Cdr. Dennis G. Mortal. Her home port is Charleston, SC.

Iraqi troops on the oil platform fought for approximately three hours.

They were equipped with machine guns—which would not be terribly effective against a frigate—and with shoulder-fired missile launchers, Capt. Bill said. Five of the 15 Iraqis taken prisoner were wounded, Capt. Bill said. It was not clear whether any of the Iraqis remained in custody on the Nicholas, or whether they had been taken elsewhere.

The Nicholas is capable of carrying two SH-60B Seahawk helicopters. It is equipped with a three-inch, 75-mm gun, one launcher for anti-ship and anti-aircraft missiles, and a phalanx rapid-fire gun system designed for use against aircraft or incoming missiles.

The ship, which normally has a 205-person crew, has a top speed in excess of 28 knots.

Meanwhile Saturday, the Tomahawk missile strike group coordinated by Wisconsin continued to launch cruise missiles against Iraq. Capt. Bill estimated that 20 to 30 additional Tomahawks were fired Saturday by vessels in the Persian Gulf.

Ships in the strike group received congratulatory words Saturday from naval commanders, clearly delighted by media reports indicating that all the Tomahawks' targets had been destroyed.

Navy officers had hoped to prove that the precision-guided, ground-hugging cruise missiles could effectively supplement manned bombers. Battle damage assessments so far are based on limited information, including British Broadcasting Service journalists, who reportedly are about to be expelled from Baghdad. Those limited assessments, however, indicate that the missile-firing crews "did a tremendous job," according to one Navy analyst.

The Pentagon said on Friday that 195 Tomahawks had been fired by vessels in the Persian Gulf, Red Sea, and Mediterranean Sea. Wisconsin's crew declined to state which targets its missiles had been aimed at. But, after hearing reports of massive and precise destruction of Iraqi military and strategic targets around Baghdad, Cmdr. Rod L. Sams, 40, Parkersburg, W.Va., said: "We had some of the finest targets you'd ever want to have."

After two false alarms that sent crew members to battle stations in record time on Friday, the Wisconsin on Saturday was an altogether more relaxed place. One small proof was Capt. Bill donning a short-sleeve shirt for evening dinner, instead of the long-sleeve models that are de rigeur since they offer at least a modicum of extra protection in case of chemical attack.

12 Iraqi Prisoners Placed on Hold by U.S. Marines

By Jim Michaels

WITH U.S. MARINES, SAUDI ARABIA - U.S. Marines are holding 12 Iraqi prisoners that were captured by allied raids carried out on 9 Kuwaiti oil platforms in the Persian Gulf.

The prisoners of war are the first since hostilities began and they will be interrogated and placed in a prisoner of war camp behind front lines.

A press release from U.S. Central Command said the Iraqi forces were using the platforms in the Persian Gulf to fire at allied aircraft with shoulder-held anti-air(craft) missiles. The attack was carried out by the Nicholas, a guided missile frigate, a Kuwaiti patrol boat and Army helicopters.

Saturday the captured Iraqis had been placed in a makeshift holding bunker by the Marines. Most looked in good health and were being fed U.S. field rations, Meals Ready to Eat. A Marine warrant officer, who asked not to be identified, said the prisoners would sleep in a tent tonight and would eat well. "They'll be taken better care of than the Marines guarding them tonight," he said. They will be in a dugout protected from Iraqi artillery, which has been fired sporadically in the area.

The Iraqis, viewed by a handful of reporters Saturday, were dressed in various uniforms, including camouflage fatigues and navy blue sweaters.

One bearded Iraqi sat off to the side and appeared dejected. He was slightly injured and was waiting to receive medical treatment. Wearing an olive-drab field jacket with the hood pulled over his head he ate an MRE cracker and spread peanut butter over it with the help of one of his guards.

The other 11 sat cross-legged in an open dugout, appearing scared but well-fed and healthy. Marines in sand-bagged bunkers with M-16 rifles watched over them, while other Marines walked among them and gently showed them how to open the field rations, which appeared to mystify the Iraqi prisoners.

One Marine showed a prisoner how to pour water into the dehydrated fruit in the field rations. The warrant officer said the meals had been screened for any that included ham, which is prohibited in the Islamic religion.

When a nearby mosque sounded the call for prayer, the prisoners would be allowed to pray, the Marine warrant officer said.

A Navy corpsman walked among them, inspecting the prisoners for injuries. The warrant officer said the ranks of the Iraqis had not been determined yet, but that they were generally cooperative. "We're not going to use thumbscrews and racks," the warrant officer said. "That's a thing of the past." Instead, he said humane treatment provides better results. "They're professional soldiers," he said. "We treat them as we would treat professionals."

A Great Allied Land Convoy Moves Into Position to Strike, Little White Pills and All

By Laurence Jolidon

WITH U.S. FORCES - The Great Convoy is on the move.

All of the armed might of the U.S. and its allies that has been living and training in the desert is closing its fist for a punch aimed at Iraq.

The exact locations of units are secret, but it can be no secret that the troops, tanks, artillery and transportable supplies that have poured into Saudi Arabia since last August are moving into position to strike.

Along a main highway near the Iraq-Saudi border, a virtually continuous stream of military vehicles rumbles toward the northwest.

At intervals, where a rough road meets the highway, smaller convoys feed into the main one, adding their specialty—British tanks, U.S. Army engineers, French heavy transport—to the mainstream.

At 8:30 a.m. Jan. 18, headquarters company of the 937th Army Engineers Group formed a small convoy to send its advance party to the group's new location.

The drivers and communications specialists who comprised the group got last-minute instructions from Sgt. Major Lincoln Mallisham, 47, of Enterprise, Ala. "If we're hit by hostile fire," he said, "get out of your vehicles, spread out and stay close to the ground. Get out and disperse. And don't panic."

Mallisham, a Vietnam veteran, explained his advice later. "In Vietnam, we had a lot of young kids like these, and there was panic. The highway the Great Convoy is using is known for being dangerous anyway, but mostly because of traffic accidents. The civilians who normally make it dangerous are gone, however. The military vehicles crawl at 40-45 miles per hour, keeping 50-meter intervals.

The Great Convoy moves at all deliberate speed.

The soldiers have other things to remember.

The night the war against Iraq began, they were put on alert for chemical attack. Besides donning their chemical protective suits and overshoes, they began taking small white pills, one every eight hours. The pills enhance the effectiveness of the injections of strong antidotes they must self-administer should they suffer nerve agent poisoning.

As the Great Convoy grew longer and more numerous, those in it seemed to grow quiet, thinking of what might lie ahead.

The usual herds of camels were nowhere to be seen. The Bedouins had taken a respectful step back from the mammoth display of military hardware. As the convoy passed through towns and villages, only the Saudi police in their tiny blue-and-white cruisers and Military Policemen, some wearing bright-red vests, watched them pass.

Even in the larger towns, streets were deserted. A few repair garages that face the highway were open, but business was slack. Nearly all the civilian traffic is being kept off the road. It was as though the entire region had lapsed into a prolonged silence. A soldier in a camouflage helmet stood erect, his hands on a machine gun.

Besides the big trucks hauling tanks, armored personnel carriers and pallets of ammunition and supplies, occasionally a truck would weave in and out of the convoy with crude, wooden huts strapped to the back.

On one side of the huts was painted: "Male Latrine" or "Female Latrine."

Saturday - January 19, 1991

The Great Convoy is making sure there are proper facilities for the women soldiers who will be on or near the front lines of any engagement with the Iraqis. The support roles women fill in the U.S. military have seldom been as close to combat roles as here in Operation Desert Storm.

To the left and right of the convoy, packs of dark green Apache helicopters race ahead of the slow-moving vehicles. Their skids and rockets are defined against the gray sky, barely 30 feet above the desert floor.

Soldiers in trucks that have pulled off the road to rest or re-fuel rustle through their packs for cameras and grab quick shots of the choppers. The pilots wave at them, or give a thumbs-up as they pass overhead.

The Great Convoy has been in motion for nearly two days, and the evidence is beginning to appear. There is always junk in this desert, but it is civilian junk: old, rusted cars; plastic kitchenware; bits and scraps of paper, cloth and metal; discarded tires from the big tractor-trailers and haulers of chemicals and crude.

Now there is military debris on the roadside: broken boxes of MREs, the dry packaged rations that the soldiers will begin to live on again as they move away from their stoves and mess halls, into the fields of battle.

A few hours after the 937th's section joined the convoy, Capt. Mark Menkhus, 29, of St. Louis, headquarters company commander, orders a refueling stop. The group's designated refueling site is still ahead, but Menkhus and the other 937th officers have sighted another engineer camp and decide it would be prudent to do business with them.

"It's engineers helping engineers," said Menkhus. The U.S. has one Army, but it is made up of thousands of units, each with parallel loyalties to soldiers of similar skills, jobs and traditions. . . .

The refueling takes too long for some of the enlisted men. They joke about "all those years of college" in one place, meaning a group of officers talking while the trucks refuel, and grumble that it was too soon to stop for gas.

"This will take us all day now," they say. They are right.

As the group drives back to the highway and rejoins the Great Convoy, the weather worsens. Fat drops of rain splat against the windshields. Beside the road, large puddles appear. The men and women of the 937th imagine themselves putting up cots and tents in the rain, in a virtual swamp. But they speak very little.

Some trucks in the Great Convoy travel mostly in silence.

As the 937th group passes through one village, four trucks jump in line ahead of them from the right. The first is a two-and-a-half ton truck loaded to the top with blankets and bedrolls. Standing on top of the mound is a dark-skinned soldier holding the flag of Kuwait.

The Kuwaitis have joined the Great Convoy. Everyone in the convoy is headed home eventually. The Kuwaitis will reach home first. "Hey, they've got all new trucks," says Sgt. Dave Keel, 22, of Sequim, Wash.

The Chevrolet truck Keel rides in and the Ford pickups the Kuwaitis have are the same light brown color, but the Fords are right out of the showroom and paint shop.

. . . The Great Convoy is loaded with hundreds of lethal weapons.

Even an experienced soldier like Sgt. Keel can't keep them all straight. "What kind of weapon is that?" he asks Capt. Menkhus.

"That's a Mark 19 grenade-launcher, chain gun," says Menkhus. The artillery moving in the Great Convoy will be the next punch the Iraqis will feel, after the blows struck by the fighters, bombers and Navy missile-cruisers.

. . . At 9 p.m., it had been dark for nearly four hours. The 937th pulled off the highway for the night.

The grid coordinates of its new home were not far away, somewhere on the flat, rocky plain. Sgt. Jackson and the other drivers reverted to "blackout" conditions, which means driving with only a pin of light coming from each headlight. Capt. Menkhus and the other officers got out of their vehicles and walked ahead a few feet, to avoid hitting other vehicles or obstacles.

The Great Convoy brought the 937th to its assigned location, but too slowly for some of the soldiers. "I could have driven all the way home in this amount of time," said Sgt. Jackson. "From Fort Riley (Kansas) to my doorstep in South Carolina. And that's 1,300 miles." By 10 p.m., the 937th's advance party was setting up cots and unpacking bedrolls to sleep under the stars and rainy mist.

Earlier that day, while the Great Convoy was massing the troops under his direction, Gen. H. Norman Schwarzkopf gave a briefing in Riyadh, the Saudi capital, the BBC reported. He showed video of the ferocious air assault and said U.S. B-52s had begun bombing the Republican Guard and its 5,000 tanks.

Out on the highway, the Great Convoy kept moving, bringing guns, troops and supplies to the border, closing in on the grid coordinates of war.

First U.S. Pilot Reported Missing off USS Saratoga: May Be Down on the Desert Floor Somewhere

By Neal MacFarquhar

ON BOARD THE USS SARATOGA IN THE RED SEA - There is no chivalry in the high-tech jousts with screaming jet engines and smart missiles that unfold 20,000 feet over Iraq. It's kill or be killed, and the whole thing might take a minute if you wait long enough to actually see the other guy.

When the pilots have their feet back on the carrier deck, they talk about the sheer terror in knowing a hiccup in their reflexes could mean getting blasted out of the sky.

One USS Saratoga pilot has not returned from the first strike of the war—he may be dead, or down there on the desert floor somewhere. Pilots Mark and Nick wondered if they would disappear during their encounter with two Iraqi MiG-21s. Instead, it ended with the two becoming the first F/A-18 Hornet pilots ever to down an enemy aircraft.

Before the MiG-21 silhouette was painted on their fuselages of the radar plane Saturday to mark the kill, the two related how the battle unfolded. Neither wanted their full names or hometowns used to avoid exposing their families to unwanted attention.

Four Hornets were streaking about western Iraq, each minutes away from dropping four 2,000 pound bombs—"swimming pool makers"—on their targets 30 miles north. Mark had already been in the air for hours during the first attack on Iraq early Thursday.

This second daylight attack was more dangerous because Iraqi pilots usually don't fly at night.

A call from the ship's Hawkeye radar plane floating in the area alerted them to the menace of the two Iraqi jetfighters hurtling straight at them.

Using cryptic radio contact, the four maneuvered into a straight line. Mark locked his radar on the Iraqi to the left. Nick took the one on the right.

"They were coming at us basically nose-to-nose. We took a real hard look. We took it again within basically visual range. And

Saturday - January 19, 1991

they weren't friendly," said Mark. He is 35, with short brown hair, a quiet manner and an easy smile.

Unlike most of the Navy pilots, it was not his first combat experience. He had flown intercept off Libya about five years ago. But he had never shot down a plane. "You have to be able to see the person, because there are so many allied aircraft in the area," Nick said.

Nick started flying Hornets about a year ago, and joined the squadron just before the Saratoga left its home port in Mayport, FL, on Aug. 7. Stocky and 25 years old, his fellow pilots call him Mongo after a character in the film Blazing Saddles because of his short blond hair and square head.

"It would be better not to shoot a bad guy than to shoot a good guy," said Mark.

Pilots fall in love with the $24-million Hornet because it has the agile, coordinated response of a fighter even with fully loaded bomb racks. They first checked if they themselves were targeted—but saw no incoming missiles and no telling smoke trail near the MiG's missile rails.

They knew they were probably ahead in both time and technology.

The Soviet system used by Iraq discourages independent action.

Pilots are choreographed from the ground.

And the radar system in the MiG-21 is decades old. "They are very structured in terms of telling their guys where to go, when to turn their radars on, what to do, when to shoot," said Mark.

For the U.S. Navy, rank all but disappears in the air.

"You might be a lieutenant right here on the pointy end of the spear, and there's not some guy telling you how to make a decision," he said. The independence cannot dilute the fear.

"My thoughts were, am I targeted? Am I going to be shot down?" said Mark.

The hair on Nick's neck stood up. "I was pretty scared, quite scared. . . . Initially that's how you react and then your training takes over. That's all it does for about 10 minutes of sheer terror," said Nick. That is the time it took to get the MiGs, drop the bombs and get back to the rendezvous point.

The hundreds of hours of practice meant the decision to lock on the radar and fire the Sparrow missile came automatically. Watching performance tapes later, both were surprised at their rote reactions. They remember feeling overwhelmed by the information pouring in. "We have a pea brain—you can only take in about three percent of the information that's flooding into you," said Mark.

The planes fly at each other at over 1,300 miles per hour.

Shooting at a plane coming on straight, called a "forward quarter shot," is considered the most difficult because it is done in the fleeting minutes the planes would take to pass each other.

From the initial warning to firing took about 45 seconds. Nick hit his target from a mile away. Mark from two. Nick yelled "Splash One" after the first fireball and the pilot flying next to Mark yelled "Splash two." There was no time for gloating as two more MiGs veered into sight and right back out again, Nick figures the two Iraqis knew they were being tracked and when "you see two fireballs about 15 miles downrange, you figure it's probably not a good idea to strike."

Mark and Nick again locked their radars but let them go. Their mission was to bomb. The decision caused a twinge of regret later, but there are no second thoughts about the kills. "I didn't lose any sleep last night. There's no doubt in my mind they would have been glad to do the exact same thing to me. And it was his misfortune to be in an Iraqi MiG-21," said Mark.

Back at the ship, they spent a lot of time describing it all to flight crew members. "I let them know what happened. That their efforts don't go in vain. I share it with them,"

Nick said. Their elation was bittersweet, tinged by the loss of fellow squadron pilot Lt. Michael Speicher, missing since the first strike against targets around Baghdad.

"I hope he is out in the desert right now really pissed off because his radio got lost in the ejection and he's picking sand fleas out of his shorts. I haven't given up," said Mark. "But I'm realistic . . . you have to face the fact that there are a lot of things in life you can't control and you work very hard to deal with in training those things you can control."

Accepting the risks is part of that for all pilots. "Here, you make a conscious decision. I'm gonna be scared spitless. And yet I know I have got to do what I've got to do," Mark said. After their encounter, dropping their bombs on target came easily and they believe will give them an edge during future missions. "It feels great to know that you already smoked one of them before you ever get over the target."

Married Woman With Machine Gun: The Supply of Shampoo Seems Endless, Like the Desert

By Richard Kay

WITH THE DESERT RATS, EASTERN SAUDI ARABIA - With a Sterling sub-machine gun over her shoulder and compact in her haversack, Lt. Karen Card was happy to be just one of the boys yesterday

But the pretty 23-year-old blonde who, with her 29-year-old husband Richard, a captain, are thought to be the only married couple with British desert forces—apart from medical staff—admits being a woman at the front does have its advantages. She has not had to dig her own trench yet, does not share a tent and even enjoys her own, personal, primitive desert shower.

Karen, who is administrative adjutant to the commander of the 39th Field Regiment, said: "I suppose I get spoiled because I am the only woman among 460 men, they like to look after me. They decided to put up a screen around my shower area, but it's more for their modesty than mine.

"Funnily enough when I do run out of things like shampoo, I only have to ask the men. They seem to carry stacks more of the stuff than me." Thrilled to be with the Desert Rats, her only regret is that she must see so little of the man she married last June.

Ironically, her husband, an adjutant with the 7th Tank Transport Regiment, is stationed only a few bumpy miles away across the sands. "When I last saw him I asked why he hadn't written to me and he said, "Oh, no, surely I'm not going to get nagged in the desert."

"But seriously, I feel I am luckier than many of the wives left behind in Germany because I feel closer. Of course I worry, but I worry less." So part of her duties are to write a letter with news from the Gulf back to the regimental base in Sennelager and once a fortnight send a video, too, with messages from all the men.

She met her husband in Hong Kong, three years ago, shortly before she enrolled in an officer training course at Sandhurst. And it was while they were on a delayed honeymoon back in Hong Kong, last September, that Richard was called up.

"It was all a bit of a shock, but three and a half months later I got sent out here too. Obviously, when we got married last summer I didn't think we were both going to end up spending our first Christmas in a war situation," she said.

Karen, from Staffs, and Richard, from North Wales, do not know when their next reunion will be. "I saw him a few days ago, but that was only for a few minutes. Hopefully it will be longer next time." When the Desert Rats go into action, Karen will not be at the front but in a support role. Although excited at the opportunities of serving with the forces here, she added perceptively: "Now the war has started, at least it is the beginning of the journey home."

Sunday
January 20, 1991

The flying services upstairs were monopolizing the war action in January, but also in this chapter is the story of the first Purple Heart of Desert Storm, which was handed out on land—weeks before the land war started.

The fact that it went to a corpsman hit by shrapnel while on patrol with the Marines near the Kuwaiti border was, in a way, an omen that events in the Marines' sector were not going to wait patiently for the grand allied plan to unfold.

The stories of medics in past twentieth-century wars make up a genre all their own. Whenever and wherever armies slugged it out with steel and gunpowder, there were always brave medics. "Corpsman! Corpsman!" someone would shout over the din and one would come darting across murderous fields of fire, or dive into the bloody surf to pull out shattered bodies and begin trying to remedy what war had done to them.

Medics hunched over horribly riddled comrades in full view of enemy gunners, risking their own lives to administer dressings or plasma, place a canteen of water or a cigarette against bloodied lips, whatever would save a life or make death less grim. This was not one of those legendary episodes. But the medal given in the Gulf was a flash of pain signaling that this war would soon enough have its share of burning tanks, bloody minefields, brave sagas, and Purple Hearts to pin on the chest.

A story in this chapter about armed civilians in the front lines zeros in on another unique facet of the Gulf War. Battlefield security demands were high, visibility was always changing and the possible mistakes in judgment multiplied with every kilometer of dust-blown highway.

The human terrain along the allied lines was a mix of military and civilian elements, just as in every war, but with its special look, feel and demands, simply because this was the Persian Gulf. Armies seldom have the whole battlefield to themselves, and in some deployments of the modern era—Bosnia, Somalia, Northern Ireland—civilians may even predominate in the fields of fire where the soldiers must operate.

But in the Gulf front lines, civilians were a distinct minority, and the allied military worked hard to keep it that way. As the war started, much of the U.S. press was engaged in a running argument with the Pentagon (most of the American public sided with the Pentagon) over how much access reporters, photographers, and television crews would have to the battlefield, and under what operating rules.

The Pentagon stance was that some controls were imperative, at least until the opposing armies were actually engaged in full-scale battle, given concerns about terrorism and the set-piece nature of the allied war plan.

Simply letting the international media who managed to reach Saudi Arabia (eventually something like 1,500 people from many nations, the vast majority from the United States) roam free and unrestricted wherever their instincts, creative pulses, contacts, editors, and producers drew them wasn't a viable plan in the Bush Administration's opinion.

Urging the journalists to organize themselves into distinct groups by media, the Pentagon authorized dozens of representatives (pools) to be escorted to the field to ship back reports that would be checked for security issues and then made available to all.

Every American journalist who was registered with the main press office in Dhahran on Jan. 1, plus a handful of British reporters, was assigned a spot in the combat pool. Some who came later also managed to find a spot in an expanded pool roster, a list that eventually grew to about 200.

But many of those who arrived after the bombing campaign began in mid-January, and virtually anyone who was not representing either U.S. or British media, were not able to win a pool assignment. Restricting the number and movements of reporters, photographers, and video crews on the front lines won favor in opinion polls in the U.S., but became a wedge between the military and the press, and between those in the pool and those who came later.

There were even congressional hearings on the subject while the bombing campaign was underway. And at one extreme, a group of publications and writers generally opposed to the war filed suit in federal court to overturn the Pentagon's rules, basically claiming journalists had a right to unfettered access. The case was still in court when the war ended at the end of February. But by then it was clear the court had found no basis, in U.S. law at least, for a right to accompany an army into battle.

The ever-popular religious theme is heard from again in this chapter—this time featuring born-again, hard-praying Christians.

On the aircraft carrier USS Saratoga, a story in this chapter reveals, there was a very human side to the extremely high-tech air war. The ship had lost 21 of its crew to a boating accident the previous December during a shore leave at Haifa, Israel. Now it was missing a couple of its strike planes over Iraq. U.S. officials weren't keen to have any more details than absolutely necessary made public, for the sake of both the families of the missing pilots and the loyal sailors and aviators aboard ship, the other family of the missing pilots, who waited each day for the birds to all return—or not.

Strict press ground rules governed the release of the names of the dead and missing so that families would be sure to hear of any loss first from the military, not their newspaper or television.

The stories about the Saratoga endeavored to honor those rules while sharing the most information possible about an air campaign that was going extremely well but in some dark corners was a reason to grieve.

In this chapter's slice of the air war, there is an idea of what Stealth pilots see, feel, and think while they're in the driver's seat of these powerful machines. Since they were first introduced, from behind a manufacturing curtain, the Stealth fighters have had a fearsome reputation as the ultimate warplane.

Flying this ultimate warplane, the interviews show, were some pilots who thought, perhaps logically, if they could only complete enough missions, drop enough bombs and destroy enough of the enemy's capacity to wage war, the air effort alone might be powerful enough to ultimately make a land war unnecessary.

Down below, Purple Hearts waited in their little boxes.

USS Saratoga Draws a Wake of Hard Luck—2nd Plane Fails to Return From Mission Over Iraq

By Carol Morello

(Note to pool: Includes information on A-6 crew from Saratoga who is missing—the second plane to not return to the Saratoga from strike missions since the war began. Though it has been reported by DOD that a Navy A-6 is downed, it has not been publicly tied to Saratoga. Agreement with Rear Admiral is that stuff on A-6 will not be tied to the Saratoga until the Pentagon has confirmed that families have been notified. They may already have been notified, anyway, but the admiral had not received confirmation of that. He told us this Friday night, so all should be cool by the time this arrives. But check with JIB before releasing.)

ABOARD THE USS SARATOGA IN THE RED SEA - If the Saratoga is any indication, death and loss leave a quiet wake behind them.

The aircraft carrier, one of three in the Red Sea battle force, has had a particularly rough deployment. First, 21 young sailors drowned Dec. 21 during a port visit to Haifa, Israel, when their ferry overturned.

Now, two aircraft from the carrier are missing after being downed during the first and third strikes from the ship on the first day of the U.S. attack on Iraq. There are few overt signs of tension, none of grieving. The shipboard television plays war movies like "To Hell and Back," "Full Metal Jacket," "The Sands of Iwo Jima," and "The Green Berets."

A blackboard in the helicopter pilots' lounge directs all air crews: eat, sleep, fly.

But what is most noticeable is what is missing—the air of barely-suppressed ebullience that is evident on the sister ship, the USS John F. Kennedy, where every single pilot and plane has returned without a scratch from all its missions.

Rear Adm. George Gee, head of the Saratoga battle group, characterized the mood aboard ship as very serious. "War is tragic," he said. "Human lives are lost in combat. Obviously, when there is success, there is a sense of accomplishment it was done right. It's great to see our pilots come back home in their aircraft, when they do, and know that they got the MiGs and the MiGs didn't get them. At sea in itself, there are laughs and there are tears every day of the week. And we're going to find that same thing during wartime."

Thursday, the day the war began, may turn out to have brought one of those times for tears. An F/A-18 Hornet joined more than 25 airplanes from the Saratoga on the ship's first strike over west Baghdad. The pilot, Lt. Mike Speicher, 33, of Jacksonville, was noticed missing when the strike force made a headcount at its rendezvous point over Saudi Arabia, according to Gee.

He has been declared missing in action, the first pilot downed in the war. A similar scenario happened with an A-6 Intruder on the ship's third strike operation over an Iraqi airfield early in the morning Friday. The crew's names have not been released. Search and rescue missions were launched after air bases in Saudi Arabia were checked to make sure the airplane had not simply run low on fuel and touched down. It is continuing for the A-6 crew. But to date, there has been neither contact nor sighting of either crew or plane. Gee said strike planes do not fly wing-to-wing, and so it is only when a plane fails to reach a rendezvous point that anyone would notice a pilot was missing.

Pilots may fly below the radar horizon, and fly without electronic communication to minimize the chances for detection. As a result, he said, neither the loss of a plane from a radar screen nor the lack of a radio signal is initially considered a cause for alarm.

"You can try to reconstruct what occurred," he said. "But frequently, with the loss of an aircraft in combat, it's increasingly difficult to determine what happened."

One officer on the ship said the aviators' fellow squadron members were "devastated" by what has happened. Many fighter and attack pilots say a bigger fear than death in combat is their fear of being shot down over Iraq and becoming a prisoner of war.

"I include him in my prayers every day," said an F/A-18 pilot of Speicher.

"I hope he's out in the desert right now really pissed off because his radio got lost in the ejection, and he's picking sand out of his shorts.

"I haven't given up. But I'm realistic. If there's anything that's come out of this, you have to face the fact that there are a lot of things in your life you can't control. And you work very hard to deal in training with those things you can control.

"If anything, it's been a faith-deepening experience for me. I know what my limitations are. I can live with that. Here, you make a conscious decision, I'm gonna be scared spitless. And yet I know I have got to do what I've got to do."

For many of the "blue-shirt" enlisted men in particular, the crews that never came back served to remind them of the 21 seamen who never returned from Haifa.

"I lost some friends," said Aviation Ordnance Airman Scott Morano, 20, of Cincinnati, of the drowned sailors as he loaded bombs onto an A-6 Intruder.

"I've thought about 'em a lot. Still think about 'em. But it's in the past, and I've got to look toward the future. Like I said, I keep my head in the game, do what I do."

USS John F. Kennedy Uses a SLAM on a MITWI (Major Industrial Target in Western Iraq)

By Neal MacFarquhar

ON BOARD THE USS JOHN F. KENNEDY IN THE RED SEA – The commander of the Red Sea battle force said in a weekend (Saturday) briefing that bombers have successfully used a stand-off missile for the first time and a submarine was deployed to fire a cruise missile for the first time ever in war.

Rear Adm. Riley D. Mixson told the combat pool aboard his flagship that the first use of the SLAM, or standoff land attack missile, came during an air raid against a major industrial target in western Iraq. He would not provide the details of the firing of the Tomahawk cruise missile, but noted that more than 40 had been fired by the U.S. Navy from the Red Sea since the start of the conflict.

Bombers from the carriers Kennedy and Saratoga were the first to fire the SLAMs.

The admiral said the first two fired hit "a very important target, I would classify it as a well-defended industrial-type activity." He would not give further description. But he said the missile could be used against facilities in Iraq linked to producing nuclear, biological and chemical weapons—a major goal of the U.S.-led attacks against Iraq. "We haven't seen that capability used in this war since we've started our bombing. That tells you that a good number of our targets are against those capabilities," he said.

The elite pilots of the F-117As, or Stealth fighters, say they have never known such exhilaration. And it is fueling a determination to win this war in the skies, to prevent Iraq from launching even one more missile, to spare Army and Marine troops bloody ground combat.

The spectacular video of the SLAM became an instant hit "special war channel presentation" on the carrier's in-house television channel. Like many smart weapons of the video generation, the missile was built with its own camera that provides instant footage of it hitting its target. The SLAM video gave the view from the missile's nose as it honed in on what looked like a large research and development complex. It crawled over a number of outlying structures, honing in on a large building. The ladders and windows were clearly visible as it slammed into a broad white wall and the transmission ends.

The video of the second firing two minutes later showed a cloud rising from the complex as the missile closed on the same building and then disappeared into the hole created by the first, "My eyes were like this big watching the second missile go into the first hole," said the pilot who guided both of them, holding his fingers in big circles in front of his eyes. He asked that his name not be used for security reasons.

The pilot said the A-6 Intruder and A-7 Corsair pilots went through an accelerated course in August to learn to maneuver the weapon, whose development program was sped up due to Operation Desert Shield. The A-6 fires the missile while the pilot in the A-7 has a special radar to make adjustments to the flight path programmed into the missile before it is loaded onto the plane.

Accurate use of the missile, which can be fired from up to 60 miles away, requires strong prior intelligence. U.S. officials have said previously that European firms who helped build many industrial facilities in Iraq gave them detailed ground plans after hundreds of foreign hostages were spread among them as human shields at the start of the Gulf crisis.

Kennedy Captain John P. Gay said pilots in Vietnam first asked for stand-off technology after being peppered with anti-aircraft artillery fire. "We took such a beating at low altitudes in Vietnam. That is really when the cry for a standoff attack weapon started," the veteran flier said. "You no longer have to go down to a low altitude to deliver bombs." To work, the pilots need visual contact with the target. The SLAM carries less punch than a conventional bomb, but the accuracy is seen as an acceptable trade-off. It also minimizes damage to surrounding areas where civilians live.

The pilot said the air defenses around the plant were silent until the first missile hit, and then erupted with anti-aircraft fire and surface-to-air missiles. "I don't think they knew what hit them . . . The sky erupted as the first missile impacted," he said.

Stealth Pilot's Biochemical Electric Charge Kicks In Far Above a Lightless and Waterless Netherworld

By Frank Bruni

AN AIR BASE IN SAUDI ARABIA - They all talk about the adrenaline—how it tears through them like an electric charge, obliterating the fear they feel when they first enter enemy airspace, see the bullets rising from the ground and wonder how they'll get out alive.

Sunday - January 20, 1991

Somehow they do, or at least they have so far. Their skill and the unique design of their aircraft are paying off. Their luck is holding. Bomb by painstakingly targeted bomb, they are chipping away at Iraq's war-making machine and plunging parts of Baghdad into a lightless and waterless netherworld. The elite pilots of the F-117As, Stealth fighters, say they have never known such exhilaration. And it is fueling a determination to win this war in the skies, to prevent Iraq from launching even one more missile, to spare Army and Marine troops bloody ground combat.

"We all have friends up north, close to the border, in all the different bases," said the U.S. Air Force lieutenant colonel who commands one of the two squadrons of stealth fighters here. He requested to be identified only by his first name, Greg, for he fears any terrorist reprisal directed at his family back in America, who live in the suburbs of Detroit.

"I'd like to see all my friends when I get home," said Greg, 39, a native of Roseville, MI, who is stationed near Las Vegas with the 37th Tactical Fighter Wing, which flies the Stealths. "There's a lot of Army guys out there living on the ground, and they're the ones who are going to suck up the Scuds," he said. "They're going to have to face the tanks. They're going to have to face the trenches. And they're going to have to face the chemicals.

"If we can pull off what we've been pulling off so far . . . and we can bring this regime to its knees, those guys won't have to go into battle. They won't have to die. I don't know how many lives we can save, but we can save a lot. Every damn time I drop a bomb, that might be saving 10 Army guys, that might be saving 1,000 Army guys. Every time we go through there and put a bomb right through his bedroom window, or put a bomb through his bunker, or put a bomb through his pickup truck, he knows that we know."

Greg spoke in an air base hangar just after daybreak Saturday, about two hours after returning from the third night of air raids over Baghdad. He participated in the first and the third. All the pilots alternate a night of flying with a night off. It had gone well, with everyone once again returning unharmed, but bad weather had forced some pilots to hit alternate targets or come back to the base with one or two of their laser-guided, 2,000-pound bombs still in the underbellies of their wildly-shaped, state-of-the-art planes.

The Stealths are so named because they are designed to escape detection. The nickname for Greg's squadron is the "Ghost Riders." Individual planes have monikers like "Mystic Warrior." They are painted black, so they are invisible at night, the only time they go out on missions. "It's the old vampire syndrome," said Col. Klaus J. Klause, 48, a Stealth pilot who was born and raised in Germany. "We sleep during the day, then get up at three or four in the afternoon to do our mission."

The Stealths look like giant origami birds, with sharp angles and diagonal planes designed to confuse radar. They are built at least in part of radar-absorbing material.

Stealth pilots talk about concentrating on being invisible or "small" as they sneak into enemy airspace. "You get as small as you can get," Klause said. "You sit down low in the cockpit, concentrate on the gauges and don't look out." Stealths led the first night of air raids on Baghdad, dropping the first bombs, and continue to be a lynchpin of the aerial assault. Their laser-guided bombs strike with surgical precision.

Their goal is to hit key military and communications centers but minimize civilian "collateral damage," pilots said. They will aim for and hit a communications tower, leaving unscathed all the other buildings around it. They will penetrate the skylight of a structure, maximizing the damage to the interior of the building. They will strike a particular headquarters room.

Both pilots and ground crews said their experience so far has convinced them that Iraqi radar is inferior to what was believed, and that the danger Stealths face is the random reverse hail of anti-aircraft fire coming into the sky airspace that first night.

"The adrenaline was pumping, between trying to find the target, and, 'Oh, God, they're shooting at me.' You get a little hyperactive, and your throat gets dry. Coming off target and knowing you're safe is one of the most exhilarating feelings I ever felt. It's such a feeling of relief: I made it through a spot I didn't believe I was ever going to go into. There's always what we call the golden BB—the aimed or unaimed bullet that you run into because there are so many bullets," Greg said.

The first squadron of Stealths snuck into Baghdad unnoticed the first night, but by the time the second squadron arrived last night (Greg's squadron), anti-aircraft fire was very intense. He said the intensity of the fire has decreased since then, when it lit up the sky like a spectacular fireworks display.

"They fired more bullets than I thought were ever made in the history of the world," Greg said.

"The only way that I can describe it is if you turn a room into the world's biggest popcorn popper and, you know—just popcorn going off all over the place—and try to walk from one end to the other without getting hit by a piece of popcorn. That's really what it was like. You just have to think invisible. Think 'They're not going to hit me,' and keep on going," he said.

Several Air Force service members on base said they were elated but surprised that all their planes came back the first night, and then again on subsequent nights.

Staff Sgt. Brad Bowers, 36, a native of Boston and crew chief for one of the planes, said that when crew members watched the Stealths first take off for Baghdad, "We said here we're going to lose those two everybody predicted. When they all came back, it was one big party. . . . So much for the French (*sic*) impression of what their radar is."

In fact, Bowers said, the Stealths proved so stealthy that friendly aircraft sometimes weren't aware of their presence. "During that first firefight, there were planes almost bumping into these guys, 'cause they couldn't see them. That's the biggest problem. . . . I worry about friendly fire more than the other flak that's flying."

Stealth pilots say they represent the most experienced flyers in the Air Force. While all but three here have never flown in combat before, some are in their late 30s or early 40s and have been in the Air Force for two decades. Greg said that while the average age for most fighter pilots is about 25, it's 30 to 32 for his squadron.

They have been flying Stealths, however, only a short time. The existence of the planes was not declassified and made public until 1988.

There are a total of 59 Stealths and all three squadrons that fly them—one of which is a training unit—are based in Nevada. But they spend their typical work weeks elsewhere, training in a location they cannot reveal. They see their families in the Las Vegas area only on weekends. The pilots don't expect to be rotated out of Saudi Arabia until the war is over. "There are only so many Stealth pilots in the world, and nine-tenths of them are here," Greg said.

The pilots are trim, fit men with erect postures, confident gaits, and ready smiles that usually reveal perfect orthodonture. The respect they command is evident in the awed expressions on the faces of the crew members who stand in phalanxes inside the hangars, as if on ceremony, to greet each pilot as he pulls in from a night's mission. Sometimes the crew members applaud, visibly relieved by the pilots' safe homecoming. The flights through anti-aircraft fire are dangerous. The pilots say they expected them to be, but never anticipated the intensity of the surge of adrenaline they feel.

Col. Al Whitley, commander of the 37th Tactical Fighter Wing and one of the three Stealth pilots who has flown a plane (not Stealth) in combat before, said that before the men left for their mission, he told them "it would seem a little bit like fear, perhaps a little like anxiety, but not to worry, because we are well-equipped."

Klause said time seemed to accelerate after he entered enemy airspace that first night. "The adrenaline was pumping, between trying to find the target, and, 'Oh, God, they're shooting at me.' You get a little hyperactive, and your throat gets dry." Greg said: "Coming off target and knowing you're safe is one of the most exhilarating feelings I ever felt. It's such a feeling of relief: I made it through a spot I didn't believe I was ever going to go into."

The pilots said fear jolts them when they first see the anti-aircraft fire and, being rational, they wonder whether they'll get through it.

But then they focus on the job, because they know concentration and skill are their best hopes for survival.

"In the preparation stages, there's a lot of anxiety, but there are 1,000 things going through your mind," said Lieut. Col. Barry Home, 41, a native of Irwin, N.C., near Raleigh. Home is an 18-year Air Force veteran.

All of the pilots interviewed flew the first mission over Baghdad and were taken aback by the intensity of the anti-aircraft fire. Greg said: "Thoughts go through your mind, like you see that and you say, 'God, I'm never going to get through that. Geez, this is nuts . . .' then you sit down and say, 'Hey, this is what I do. I'm going to go through that.' And then you do."

He said many of the pilots say a prayer aloud, and that you can hear those pleas—"Dear God, help me get through this"—on cockpit recordings played back later.

Thoughts can turn sentimental as well, Greg said. "Usually, you have a thought of your family—at least I did—that you love them, that you care about them, and it's time to go. You can't let that be a distraction. . . . You have to get your mind on what you're doing, because if you don't you're going to get killed, and you're not going to get your mission accomplished on top of that."

Each man flies alone, and their mission—getting from base, bombing their targets, and getting back—usually takes (deleted) hours.

They bring water with them, because the excitement often dries out their throats. Some bring candy bars.

And many bring Walkmen and tapes that they listen to before they get near enemy airspace and after they leave it. They slip the Walkman's small earplugs beneath their headsets and can still hear radio communications, Greg said.

They use the music either to build their excitement or calm them down, he said. Greg said that on the way to a mission, many pilots listen to heavy metal bands such as Van Halen. He only listens to music on the way back.

The first night, it was a tape of female country-western singers.

Military intelligence usually provides pilots with detailed maps of the areas and the targets they are seeking, and they study the information for as many as four hours in advance, Greg said. Some targets are conspicuous; others, like underground bunkers, may take several minutes to find and "lock in."

Pilots don't drop their bombs unless they can find their targets, he said.

As a squadron commander, Greg said his anxiety doesn't end immediately after he leaves enemy airspace. He listens carefully for word from other men in his squadron, checking their names off against a list on his knee. "You're just trying to compare and count that you have as many coming home as you did when you left," he said.

He added that he was surprised he didn't lose any men on his first two missions.

Greg grew up in Roseville, Mich., where his parents still live. He loves the excitement, even when it includes danger, as it does now. "It's like roller-coaster fanatics," he said. "The scarier it is, the better it is—when it's over."

He, other pilots, and ground crew said they feel they should be fighting this war because the Iraqi regime is brutal and dangerous. They said if they don't fight now, someone will have to take on a more powerful and dangerous Saddam Hussein later.

Greg said the pilots weren't told they were going to attack until about six to eight hours before they left on the mission with which the war began. The news was a relief,
 he said. "Indecision is the worst," he said. "If you know you're going, you can mentally prepare yourself for it," he said.

The first squadron came over in August. Greg's squadron joined them in early December. "Most of us have felt all along that the quickest route home would be through Baghdad," he said. At home in Las Vegas are his wife, Lucy, and two dogs. He wants to get back to them as soon as possible.

Although the pilots' missions are dangerous, he said pilot losses would never equal what the Marines and the Army will lose if they must slug it out at the front. "You could lose 100 Army guys to one artillery shell," he said. "You could lose 1,000 to one Scud attack. We have the capability to go out and do this," he said. "It's time to do the job. Not all the jobs you do are pleasant, but you've got to do them."

First Purple Heart: Navy Medic Hit by Shrapnel While on Kuwaiti Border Patrol

By Jonathan Ferziger

WITH U.S. MARINES, Saudi Arabia - A Navy medic hit by shrapnel from enemy fire while on a Marine patrol near the Kuwaiti border will receive the first Purple Heart in Operation Desert Storm, military officials said.

Navy Corpsman Clarence D. Conner, 19, of Hemet, CA, was recovering at a military hospital after doctors removed a jagged piece of metal from his right shoulder, but begged his commanders to let him return to action. "I'm damned proud of him," said Marine Brig. Gen. Thomas V. Draude. "We were standing by his bedside and he said, "Please don't send me home. I've got to get back to my unit. They're depending on me."

Maj. Gen. Mike Myatt, commander of the 1st Marine Division, said he was so moved he wanted to pin the Purple Heart upon Conner's chest while he lay in his hospital bed. Unfortunately, the Pentagon has not yet sent over to Saudi Arabia the heart-shaped medals that decorate soldiers wounded in action.

Conner, a Navy-trained medic assigned to the Marines to provide combat first-aid, was with a five-man team near the Kuwaiti border Thursday night when (the action occurred). Although the team ran for cover, shrapnel penetrated Conner's shoulder and he was evacuated from the field by helicopter. Two Marines suffered minor injuries.

Capt. Owen Lovejoy described his friend as a "happy-go-lucky fellow" with a blond flattop, who was committed to his mission. "He behaved like a Marine," said Lovejoy.

"He kept a cool head. He knew that the guys he's trained with are depending on him. I wouldn't have expected any less from him."

While several pilots who flew bombing missions over Iraq are missing, Conner was the first casualty among U.S. ground troops. Officials at the U.S. Central Command could not say when they would receive the Purple Hearts and present one to Conner.

Another Armed Presence in the Desert: Civilians With Sidearms and Automatic Weapons

By Laurence Jolidon

LOG BASE CHARLIE, Saudi Arabia - Some U.S. troops, who have had very little contact with Saudi citizens since arriving here months ago, want even less now.

The past few days have seen the appearance in some rural areas of Saudi men walking around with sidearms and automatic weapons. And it's making the GIs nervous.

They're used to being the only people around here with firearms. The outbreak of war with Iraq has apparently caused some Saudis to open up their gun collections, or start one. Capt. Mark Menkhus, 29, of St. Louis, Mo., CO of Headquarters Co., 937th Engineer Group, went into a village near his camp to make an emergency phone call home Sunday. He was startled to see several Saudi men, dressed in the customary robe and head scarves, but with guns.

"One guy had a grease gun," he said, which is a World War II-vintage machine gun, "another had a handgun in a shoulder holster. And one guy had a single-shot hunting rifle. He was also wearing a (U.S. military) gas mask, only it was strapped on so it hung down his back."

He said when he saw so many armed men, "I felt pretty worried. We're close enough to the border, you can't be sure who these people might be. It was the first time I've been here in country I've felt uncomfortable. But I sure was this time."

As he walked toward the men, who made no threatening gestures, Menkhus moved a round into the chamber of his revolver. "A military policeman came up and asked me if everything was okay. I told him, yeah, I just chambered a round. He said good. Nothing happened, though."

Spec. Eric Logan, 22, of Burbank, Il., a heavy equipment operator, works on projects close to a busy highway. He's been more nervous lately watching the few civilian cars that have been permitted since the highway has been virtually given over to military traffic.

"I look at these guys driving by in their little Toyotas," he says, "and I wonder which ones are Iraqi terrorists."

Christian GIs Pray Hard on Front Lines of Islamic Land: "No Matter What Happens, I'm Going to Heaven"

By Gary Regenstreif

EASTERN SAUDI ARABIA - Tears welled in the eyes of U. S. Army Capt. David Smith after praying in his last Sunday service before heading north for likely combat against heavily-armed Iraqi ground troops.

"No matter what happens, I'm going to heaven," said Smith, 32, an intelligence officer with 82nd Airborne Division's 2nd brigade, who was choked with emotion as he considered his fate. "If you know God is with you, that helps a lot."

On what may be the eve of a bloody ground battle, a small but devout group of regular church-goers like Smith, of Leesville, LA, are considering their spiritual preparation for war as crucial as their physical training.

"We've been getting ready spiritually and physically," said Cpl. Steven Moore, 21, of Mount Olive, NC, a mechanic.

While the U.S. military has acknowledged religious services are held in Saudi Arabia, it has banned journalists from covering them for fear of offending authorities in this cradle of Islam. After (illegible) service, which cannot be reported, three soldiers said they plan to carry their Bibles into battle.

But, concerned they may not have the opportunity to consult them, they sat together memorizing passages, especially one from Romans in the New Testament suggesting that neither danger nor sword "would separate them from their love of Christ."

"If I didn't have the assurance I would go to heaven, it would be a lot more difficult," said Staff Sgt. Timothy Alspach, 33, a medic from Groveport OH, whose church congregation sent him 91 pounds of cookies two months ago. "If our real strength doesn't come from weapons it should come from God. He gives life and can take it away."

For some, their faith has eased their fears. "I know in my heart that whatever happens it's going to be alright," said Spec. Brendan Baird, 20, a scout from Stillwater, Okla. "I know He (God) is going to be taking care of me. If I get killed, I know he's got a reason for that."

"I'm scared and I'm asking God to be my strength," said Capt. James Lin, 31, company dentist from New York City. "I'm depending on him. I have a good feeling that I'm going home in one piece. I have peace in my heart."

"We have to have faith in God that victory is already ours," said Military Police Lt. Joseph Posusney, 27, of Philadelphia. "The power up there in Baghdad is doing a lot of evil to a lot of people. We feel God's hand on us as we go there." Soldiers said they were told in what they described as a practical service not to underestimate the Iraqi troops and not be overconfident following allied successes in the air campaign against Baghdad. The soldiers said they had wrestled with the prospect of taking another life. "My job is to kill and take ground," said Baird. "It's sinful if I enjoy it, but this is for the good of people. Look at David's slaying of Goliath."

Yet another soldier has had to reconcile his feelings and his surroundings. Spec. Victor Stark, 36, a radio operator from St. Louis, quit his job as a successful real estate broker two years ago to serve his country. He is Jewish.

"I am a Jew in a world where I am not welcome," said Stark. "In certain respects I'm fighting for an Arab cause. But my duty is first to the U.S. Army. My feelings come second."

Monday
January 21, 1991

The Iraqis taken prisoner from oil platforms by the allies in the first days of the war were quickly hustled off to a secure enclosure on land and guarded by U.S. Marines. How they were captured had a fairly simple explanation, rendered in this chapter by the captain of the frigate involved, with no casualties on his side.

In keeping with the Geneva Convention, and as monitored by the International Red Cross, the Iraqis' identities were never released. The rules governing press coverage of POWs (EPWs in Pentagon-ese) tracked the Geneva Convention language and forbid having the press interview them or photograph their faces for wide public display.

It was a different story in Baghdad, where the rules were very different. Pictures of the faces of some of the allied pilots captured in the first days of the air war were displayed on Iraqi television. The TV pictures were first mentioned in a second-hand report by Jordanian businessmen who had joined the flow of refugees departing the Iraqi capital in the wake of the devastating bombing campaign.

But it was soon easy to verify from virtually any TV set. The rapid forwarding of recorded video and sharing of television signals that also gave the Gulf War its own technological signature led to an almost immediate reaction from fellow pilots waiting to suit up for another sortie and assume the risk of joining them. How they felt about seeing their buddies' faces on Iraqi TV is in this chapter.

The sortie count was jumping higher every day, to around 7,000 total, enough to bring the allied aircraft loss count to 16, a majority of them American. Some of the pilots of those downed aircraft were reported missing, but all of those missing hadn't been displayed on Iraqi TV, so there were many anxious moments.

So Iraq's flouting of the Geneva Convention wasn't even good for helping the allies check whether all of the missing pilots were alive or not. It was simply propaganda, and counter-productive propaganda at that, at least in the eyes of allied officials. What the residents of Baghdad made of it, we don't know.

Authorities in Baghdad ratcheted up the POW issue, announcing that the allied prisoners would soon be put to work as "human shields," tethered at strategic sites likely to be bombed by the allies, as was done earlier with foreign civilians who found themselves trapped in Iraq when the war broke out. The International Red Cross was quick to again point out that would be a violation of the Geneva Convention, but of course the Red Cross was not a close or respected adviser to the Iraqi leadership.

On the Scud-attack front, more of them struck Israel and wounded a number of people, but took no lives. British commandos were already at work behind enemy lines, with the objective of neutralizing the Scud menace, but—as Gen. Schwarzkopf no doubt had feared—the work wasn't going terribly well.

Some of the commandos published their own accounts after the war. They make for heart-pounding reading. One of them, Andy McNab, told his version in "Bravo Two Zero," which was the name of his eight-man patrol. Briefly, soon after they entered Iraq, McNab and his team were spotted and surrounded; their radios failed to work properly. But then they weren't supposed to need rescuing anyway. They headed for the northwest, and Jordan. Five made it back.

Secret Weapon For Navy Seizure of First Iraqi POWs on Oil Platforms: "We Snuck in and Surprised Them"

By George Rodrigue and Robert Ruby

ABOARD THE USS NICHOLAS, in the Persian Gulf - On Jan. 18, the USS Nicholas, a Navy guided-missile frigate (FFG 47) cleared 11 Iraqi oil platforms of observers who had been tracking American ships and planes and reportedly firing at U.S. warplanes.

The ship took 23 prisoners, including three seriously wounded, and killed five Iraqis. It suffered no casualties. Judging by the descriptions given by the ship's crew, the episode illustrates several strengths of U.S. operations, and several Iraqi weaknesses, ranging from weaponry to communications to supplies, Nicholas' commanding officer is Cmdr. Dennis G. Morral, 40. He and his staff said there was nothing particularly secretive about the techniques they used. "We snuck in and surprised them, and that is why we didn't take any casualties," Cmdr. Morral said.

"If you can set up the situation tactically so that you can have all the aces in your hand, that is the way to do it," said Lt. Tom Buterbaugh, 30, of Norristown, Pa., the ship's combat systems officer. According to Cmdr. Morral and his officers, the engagement went like this: On Jan. 17 and 18, Nicholas and its helicopters scouted the (illegible) oilfield, about 40 miles from the shore of occupied Kuwait. It was a Kuwaiti field until Aug. 2.

The field's 11 platforms lie along approach and departure routes used by American pilots raiding targets in Iraq. Nine platforms were believed to be occupied by Iraqi troops, who were using them to spy on ship and plane movements and to shoot at passing U.S. warplanes. They presented a major hindrance to USS Nicholas. Frigates are relatively small ships, and at the time Nicholas was the U.S. Navy vessel closest to Iraqi territory. It counted upon secrecy for survival. It and its helicopters were charged with recovering downed U.S. fliers, and anti-aircraft guns also could seriously threaten the helicopters.

Around 8 p.m. on Jan. 18, USS Nicholas crept toward the platforms from the south, masked by darkness and its total lack of telltale electronic emissions—radar, radio, lights, for instance. This condition is called emcon, for emission control. Far out of sight of the platforms, several of Nicholas's helicopters took off with their lights blacked out and their pilots relying on night-vision devices. Some swept the distant areas, looking for threats on the surface.

Others circled and approached from the northwest (the direction of Iraq) coming at the platforms from their back door, so to speak.

"The mood in the combat information center was pretty calm. I guess clinical would be a good way to describe it," said Lt. Buterbaugh.

Flying low, with sea sounds covering their engine noise, the Nicholas's helicopters were undetected until they came within missile range of their targets: two platforms believed to be heavily armed, and farthest from Nicholas's 3-inch gun.

Once they were within their weapons' range, but before they came within range of the platforms' 23-mm anti-aircraft guns, the helicopters launched a barrage of precision-guided rockets. (The precise type of rocket the Navy declined to disclose, but ships' crewmen said they were hideously destructive, sending thousands of shrapnel fragments through everything around them.)

The rockets ripped through the sandbag-and-plywood shelters erected by the Iraqis. Six soldiers scrambled from one tower into a Zodiac lifeboat below. Seconds later, the ammunition supply above them exploded, filling the night sky with sparks and flames. Having finished their targets, the helicopters withdrew, clearing the firing range for the ships.

By now USS Nicholas and a Kuwaiti patrol boat had brought the remaining platforms within range of their 76-mm guns. While the Iraqis presumably were still staring at the flaming remnants of their friends' fortifications, the three ships followed a pattern of firing three shots at each platform to set the range, followed by about 20 rounds of high-explosive shells for effect. The effect was to quickly demolish all the remaining bunkers on seven platforms. "At this point I determined that some of the Iraqis probably wanted to surrender," Cmdr. Morral said.

With no fire being returned by the platforms—indeed, it is not clear whether the Iraqis ever managed to return fire—Cmdr. Morral had to decide whether to risk American lives in order to save Iraqis. He asked his helicopters to sweep the platforms again with their heat-sensing scopes. Seeing nothing threatening, he turned his ship's sophisticated infrared eye on the platforms.

With the thermal eyes on, said Lt. Buterbaugh, "we do not have to get close to do what we call bomb-damage assessment." An Arabic-speaking crewman called out the ship's loudspeaker that anyone who wished to surrender should raise his hand.

On the black and white monitor above the Nicholas' darkened combat information center, a ghostly white infrared image showed an Iraqi party waving.

It took hours for the Nicholas to pick up all 23 of the survivors (three with serious wounds) along with five Iraqis killed in action. Teams also boarded each of the nine platforms that had been assaulted, destroyed their remaining fortifications, and seized or destroyed all remaining weapons. They found caches of shoulder-fired surface-to-air missiles, an unpleasant surprise for the helicopter pilots who had been flying near the platforms over the previous few days.

They found only one long-range radio on the platforms. Apparently the Iraqis were forced to communicate among the platforms, which are about two to three miles apart, by firing rifle shots. They also found a handful of maroon berets, evidence that some of the men on the platforms were members of the elite Republican Guards. Part of their job was apparently making sure the men did not desert.

"They were prisoners of war already," Cmdr. Morral said.

Cmdr. Morral said the great majority of the POWs appeared to be hastily-drafted reservists, forced to sit on these platforms, lacking adequate food and supplies. "I don't think that they wanted to fight," he said. "I don't think that they know how to fight. I think that they were very relieved that we were rescuing them from this situation."

The men had no clean clothes for weeks, and appeared to be fishing for their dinners by lobbing hand grenades in the water, he said. "Fish would float up and that's what they'd subsist on. Most of them put their hands up, thanked us in their own way, and cooperated."

At the Sight of Allied POWs on Baghdad TV, the Mighty Thunderbolts Grow Quiet

By Joseph Albright and Guy Gugliotta

WITH THE U.S. AIR FORCE, Saudi Arabia - Fighter pilot Scott Hill was lounging in the ready room Monday with 10 other pilots, gas masks strapped to their hips, when the television showed them the videotape of other American fighter jocks turned into Saddam Hussein war trophies.

"We were just kind of in awe, I guess," said Hill, who flew a bombing mission north of the Saudi border on Thursday.

"We didn't say much," said the 38-year-old pilot who grew up in Chagrin Falls, OH. "We all handled it in our own distinct ways. That's kind of the fighter pilot way, I guess. You know, at times we have gigantic egos and are very self-centered. At other times we just kind of sink into our own feelings."

He and the scores of other Thunderbolt pilots at this largest Thunderbolt base in the world don't have long to put their feelings in cubicles. But they are clearly trying. If the weather clears, Hill could get the call within the next 12 hours to drop a cluster bomb on a troop concentration or a Maverick TV-guided missile on a mobile Scud launcher.

Moods tend to vary with events at a fighter base. The mood here on Monday afternoon—before news spread of the pilot rescue—was far from cocky.

Pilots were frustrated because the pea-soup clouds over Iraq kept many of their low-tech A-10 Thunderbolt 11 fighters from taking off. There was also the realization that some of Saddam's Scuds were up and firing after the most destructive allied air strike since World War II. And finally, those televised images of their brother pilots.

"It puts a jab in your gut," said Capt. Pete Edgar, 28, of Littleton, NH. "It doesn't make you feel that great about what is going on up there, but I would hope he would treat them under the Geneva Convention."

Fellow Thunderbolt pilot Capt. Mike O'Dowd said he would have no trouble driving the apprehension out of his consciousness once he straps himself into the cockpit. "The fear, you just put it somewhere back there behind the adrenaline," O'Dowd said. "You let the adrenaline take over."

Maj. Hill said Saddam Hussein is wrong if he thinks the televised pilots tableau could destroy American pilots' morale. "We will hit 'em harder and make him pay for every violation of decency," he said. "I've got nothing against the average Iraqi foot soldier on the ground. He is a soldier down there doing his job, doing what he is told, and so am I."

"So when I have to attack any ground troops, it is not with any malice. I am just doing what I am told and serving my country."

Hill said pilots don't fly off to exact revenge. "When we go to war, we go to war smart," he said. "We don't go with our hair on fire and our fangs out."

When asked to describe the currents running through his persona, he said:

"A million factors. You don't want to have to kill anybody. You have never done that in your life and you roll in and you hit the button and you know people are going to die. And you say, 'Well, it's just the way it's got to be.' And you've got that emotion to worry about. And there are two emotions there suppressing each other: the thrill of the hunt, hunting for prey, the fact that the prey shoots back . . . the fact you might get hit and have to jump out and become a POW and maybe never see your family again.

"All that stuff plays into a massive flurry of emotions. And only a fighter pilot really gets to experience that."

Monday - January 21, 1991

Red Sea Aerial Armada Controls Skies With 2,000 Sorties Daily, But Allied Plane Losses Reach Double Digits

By Neal MacFarquhar

ABOARD THE USS JOHN F. KENNEDY IN THE RED SEA - Pilots will be ripping up and down the flight deck of this carrier Monday—but in running shoes, not their fighter jets.

The USS America and USS Saratoga are flying combat strikes while the Kennedy crew assesses the results of five days of bombing Iraq with little opposition.

The three carriers in the Red Sea battle force change roles every few days, with two flying combat missions while the third only flies combat air patrols or caps over the 30-ship fleet and everybody tries to relax. "It's not just the air crews. It's the guys that work on the decks as well. People forget that they have been working 18-20 hours per day," said Cmdr. Robin Jan, executive officer of a squadron of A-6 bombers.

Nearly six months at sea with constant activity have taken their toll on the carrier decks' non-skid surface. "We've had so many takeoffs and recoveries that it's slick. It down to bare metal in places," said Cmdr. Ron Jaen, 45, of Lake Tahoe, Calif., the aircraft handling officer on the Saratoga. On deck, airplanes are often moved by two tractors to prevent skidding and the entire flight deck is scrubbed every 4-5 days. Drip pans are under the aircraft to keep oil from breaking down the surface. "Pilots have to be more careful about coming up on too much power," he said.

The last two strikes from the Kennedy Sunday included their largest and longest to date. A pre-dawn attack went about 200 miles into Iraq, north of Baghdad, to knock out a chemical munitions factory, while a daytime strike with 37 aircraft destroyed a turbine electric plant and other targets in central Iraq.

Pilots noticed a slight increase in the height of the anti-aircraft fire and some additional surface-to-air missiles, but said the overall threat from Iraqi air defenses remained low. The lack of any MiG fighters or ground fire even led to a little war photography to help with battle damage assessments. Cmdr. John Leenhouts used the three seconds after he dropped his payload on a power plant to snap off a few frames of the explosions with a 35-mm camera and zoom lens. "If I had been shot at, I would have been ducking and dodging and rocking and rolling and out of there. But it just seemed like a golden opportunity," the pilot of the single-seated A-7 Corsair light attack plane said.

Even the increased number of SAM missiles, which look like a huge bottle rocket as they whiz past, proved relatively easy to evade, pilots said. "I look out over the window and watch them launch. I just sit there and wait and see where it goes. If you panic, you're probably going to get shot down," said Jan, a 38-year-old A-6 Intruder medium attack pilot from Annapolis, Md. If the beam of light created by the missile does not waver in flight, it means it is targeted at you and pilots take evasive action to break the radar lock.

Pilots believe the lack of an Iraqi challenge stems from the fear of the overwhelming number of aircraft the United States and other forces send over the border—about 2,000 daily. "I don't think we're surprising them any. We're just overwhelming them with superior weapons and technology," said Lt. Steve Bristow, 28, of Tillamook, Ore., and part of the crew of a radar-jamming plane.

"It's like Grand Central Station out there. We're all proud of ourselves because we haven't run into each other yet," said Leenhouts, of Jacksonville, Fla. Iraqi jet fighters only appear when the planes are streaking out of the country, apparently trying to pick off any stragglers. The pilots think Saddam may yet have a few surprises up his sleeve. "A lot of people say they are saving a knockout blow for us, but if they try to do that, they are going to get knocked out before they have a chance to do it," said Parsons, an F-14 Tomcat pilot.

They keep their guard up and prepare themselves for any kind of attack. "You don't expect to see a particular weapons system. You don't expect to see a particular defense. It's just whatever comes at you, you have to handle," said Jan. Added Parsons: "Every time we do a brief, they say if any of you isn't scared, then there is something wrong with you."

Part of their review process includes looking at mistakes made over the past five days such as missed radio frequencies. Flying out of position and getting separated are things that can still make the difference between life and death.

U.S. forces have lost 16 planes (I don't have latest total here. Note newspaper pool report for (illegible) losses from Red Sea carrier Saratoga.) F-14 fighter pilots admit to a certain frustration that none of the squadrons on board the Kennedy has yet to get so much as a missile off against an Iraqi plane—all staying on the ground or running out of range. "An air force on the ground is no better than having a bunch of taxicabs," said Kevin, a 31-year-old lieutenant from Trenton, N.J., who asked that his name not be used for fear of reprisals against his family. "Now the going comment around the ready room is 'this combat stuff is not all what it's kicked up to be,'" he said.

"We're all guarding against complacency. It's like sneaking in and dropping bombs and sneaking out. But it may not be that way the next time," said Lt. Cmdr. Kevin Creahan, 35, of Merced, Calif., and an A-7 pilot.

The dangers involved prevent anyone from getting a false sense of security. But the F-14 pilots wonder if the air war could end this way.

Rear Adm. Riley D. Mixson said Saturday the air war could take at least two more weeks, but perhaps longer if Iraq decides to try to preserve its 500-plus aircraft by keeping them in hardened bunkers. Navy pilots are flying up to 30 percent of all sorties.

"I dream about getting a MiG. I'd look forward to it. I don't want to say I want to run into one, but I wouldn't be disappointed," said Lt. Cmdr. Drew Brugal, a balding, 33-year-old officer from Manhasset, N.Y. Quipped Kevin: "He also dreams about growing hair."

Tuesday
January 22, 1991

Another plane lost off the carrier Saratoga. Another allied pilot interviewed on Baghdad TV, this time a British flier. Sometimes bad luck just leads to more bad luck. But in a war this big, and with hundreds of planes in the air every day, there's bound to be some good luck.

This chapter includes a good-luck story. A Navy aviator, shot down in the desert, is rescued thanks to some Air Force pilots who go looking for him.

The drama of one man in a hostile desert puts a firmer image in the mind than the daily rattling off of figures. But the figures are important, too.

To this date, the number of allied sorties flown exceeded 10,000.

In any war situation, a military organization chooses to disclose some numbers and keep others close to the flak vest. The press and public generally assume that the numbers the military chooses to reveal are those that reflect well on their actions and those they choose to hold back would make the press and public think less of them.

The fact is, numbers in war are constantly changing. A man reported dead or lost can show up at an aid station. An enemy force reported as a division at first sighting can be discovered later to have been a mere battalion. So the numbers become weapons, too. That was the case with the question of how many allied planes Iraq had shot down.

Even with occasional bad luck on the allied side, much of Iraq's aviation and air defense assets was destroyed in the first days of the air campaign. These assets were (a.) Soviet made, and (b.) mercilessly blasted night and day by allied attacks.

The conclusion could be that Soviet aviation and air defense manufacturing and training were way below par, having taken a big slide since Brezhnev's day because of a sliding economy. In fairness, no military armament could withstand the destructive power hitting Iraq at the present time, no matter who made it.

Both conclusions could be true, but the Soviets themselves offered a third: The allies were exaggerating the numbers that showed what was being destroyed in Iraq, lying about their air prowess. In fact, they said, allied aircraft had actually missed many targets, thanks to Iraq's excellent deceptive measures.

The Iraqis themselves claimed their gunners had downed far more than the 16 warplanes the allies had reported losing to date. They also claimed to have launched more Scuds than the allies reported seeing or shooting down. With both sides hurling figures, the Persian Gulf conflict had become a modern war in all respects: in the air, at sea, on land, and by the numbers.

The Hardest Decision: When to Send in Ground Forces: "We Will Wait Until We Are Sure We Can Win Quickly"

By Philip Stephens

With 1st ARMOURED DIVISION, Eastern Saudi Arabia - Timing. It is the hardest decision they will have to make. As the allies ranged against Saddam Hussein maintain the relentless aerial bombardment, the commanders of the U.S.-led ground forces camped in the Eastern Saudi Arabian desert are pondering just when to strike.

No one expects an attack within the next few days. The roads north to the border are still choked with military traffic. But by the weekend, the armies of the 17-nation coalition ranged facing Iraq are expected to be deployed in the forward positions which will provide the springboard for the battle for Kuwait.

Then the decision on when to attack will be dictated by military judgment rather than by logistics. The pressures on the army commanders come from both directions —some pointing to the need for an early strike, others suggesting that they should be ready to spend a few more weeks yet in the inhospitable Saudi desert.

For the moment, it seems that the second option is more likely. The euphoria which followed the first air strikes against Iraq and Kuwait has been followed by a more sombre, realistic assessment of the scale of the land war which most believe remains inevitable. The nightly Scud attacks on Saudi Arabia, though thwarted by U.S. Patriot missiles, have meant that the focus of allied air attacks are still on strategic targets in Iraq.

The elite Iraqi Republican Guard, based well behind the Kuwaiti front line, has been subject to heavy bombardment. But the concentrated "carpet-bombing" of Iraq's heavily fortified defenses and troop concentrations has yet to start in earnest.

Maj. Gen. Rupert Smith, the commander of Britain's 35,000-strong 1st Armoured Division, has made it clear that the waiting phase of the war could last for several weeks. Like his U.S. colleagues he refuses, for obvious reasons, to be specific, but his recent allusions to lengthy U.S. bombing campaigns during the Vietnam War have conveyed the same message. His caution has been reinforced by Brigadier Christopher Hammerbeck, the commander of the British 4th Brigade. This week he told journalists that, "There are those who think it all is going to be over in 48 hours. I don't. I think it will take us some time—a month, maybe two months—to sort out the problem. And that's assuming everything works in our favour."

The caution is shared by the Americans who are likely to assume tactical command of the British forces once the attack is launched. "There is no hurry ... we will wait until we are sure we can win quickly," a U.S. officer serving in the allies' joint command centre said.

Winning quickly is the key. Once tank and infantry engagements start, the casualty rate on the allied side may escalate rapidly, so the aim will be to cut through and outflank the Iraqi defenses as rapidly as possible.

Despite the constant reports of low morale and defections from the badly-trained Iraqi divisions on the front line, allied commanders are far from confident that the defenses will buckle during a relatively short air bombardment. The combination of powerful Soviet and South African artillery, a deep line of defensive obstacles, some 4000 tanks, and the sheer size of the Iraq army point in the opposite direction.

Allied commanders are convinced also that Iraq will use its artillery to deliver the chemical weapons which it has so far decided against using on its Scud missiles.

Even if the respirators and chemical protective clothing issued to allied troops proves effective in minimizing the number of casualties, the use of nerve and blister agents would probably slow their advance. Against that background it is hardly surprising that officers like Gen. Smith talk in terms of waiting "as long as it takes" for concentrated bombing to destroy as much as possible of the defensive line. Neither the army, nor the politicians who will have the final say, want to go into battle anticipating heavy casualties.

The approach in March of the searing Saudi summer threatens both to undermine morale and to limit the operational effectiveness of the troops. Tanks and guns do not work well when the temperature is well over 100 degrees Fahrenheit.

Officers on the ground are aware also of the political imperatives. Their political leaders certainly do not want a premature battle with massive casualties, but nor do they want an open-ended delay which might encourage fractures in the Arab coalition against President Saddam. So at some point soon—perhaps in a week but perhaps more likely in two or three—the army commanders will study their satellite photographs of Iraqi defenses and decide to strike the balance. No one can envy them their choice.

3rd U.S. Plane Lost From Saratoga; Reporters Kept Away

By Carol Morello

ABOARD USS AMERICA in the Red Sea - The Red Sea battle force has announced the loss of a third plane from the USS Saratoga during a strike mission over Iraq.

An F-14 Tomcat, a two-seater fighter jet, never returned from its Sunday night mission. Under military censorship rules, that is all the pool knows that it can report about the incident. The plane's mother ship, the USS Saratoga, has taken a heavy toll so far. Last Thursday, the first day of the war, an F/A-18 was shot down during a mission over west Baghdad. An A-6 Intruder went down during the third mission that initial day, over a western Iraqi airfield.

Crews of both planes have been listed as missing in action.

In addition, another A-6 from Saratoga has been badly damaged.

The Saratoga is the only carrier in the Red Sea that has had downed aircraft. The carrier pool has been denied permission to make a return visit to the Saratoga. The stated reason was "logistical difficulties," despite almost daily helicopter flights between ships in the Red Sea. The pool is trying to arrange a face-to-face meeting with Rear Admiral Riley D. Mixson aboard the Kennedy to appeal the decision his name was attached to. The America arrived in the Red Sea on the very day the war began.

After flying protection for the carriers the first two days, the pilots are just now returning from their first flights over Iraq. The pool talked to a bunch of them. We also got to watch them suit up, putting on their gravitational suits—tight leggings that inflate with water on takeoff, keeping the blood from their heads from draining entirely into their lower bodies, which would make them pass out.

In all their little zipper pockets, they stuffed survival equipment like land maps plotting escape routes if they go down, and a pistol with a clip holding 15 bullets to protect themselves with. During final suit checks, they turned the Rolling Stones' "I Can't Get No Satisfaction" up high on the ready room's broadcast system, and gave each other high fives and hearty slaps on the back.

Up in the air, they said later, the same old pattern of resistance continues. Lots of AAA anti-aircraft and small arms fire, some SAMs careening wildly at the planes, and Iraqi MiGs appearing on the radar screens, only to turn tail and run away when the Americans approached. Monday's daytime raid was pretty hairy for the pilots, who by the way earn $35,000 for lieutenants and $50,000 for lieutenant commanders, with an extra $110 a month thrown in for combat duty.

Air Force Pilots Pluck Navy Flier From Desert: Rescue Team "Comfortable" Working in Daylight

By Joseph Albright and Guy Gugliotta

EASTERN SAUDI ARABIA - Two U.S. Air Force fighter pilots helped rescue a downed Navy flier in the Iraqi desert Monday, flying an eight-hour mission deep into hostile territory to search for the missing man and ensure his safe recovery.

A helicopter vectored to the downed pilot, picked him up, and took him to Saudi Arabia early in the afternoon. The pilot was unhurt, Air Force authorities said. His name was not released.

"He is rather pleased to be where he is tonight," said Capt. Paul Johnson, 32, of Dresden, TN, the A-10 Thunderbolt 11 pilot who led the rescue flight. "It was a rather indescribable feeling to know that he was now on the helicopter and we were coming out of enemy territory—that we were about to pull this off."

Minutes before the helicopter flew in to make the final pickup, a large Iraqi truck drove into the area, apparently headed straight for the rescue site. "Unfortunately, the truck was in the wrong place at the wrong time," said Capt. Randy Goff, 26, of Jackson, OH, the second A-10 pilot. "We couldn't afford to have him be there."

Goff and Johnson attacked the truck with 30mm Gatling guns, stopping it on a dirt road and setting it on fire "Things are happening rapidly," explained Johnson with some regret. "We have other things to worry about."

The two pilots, assigned to the 354th Tactical Fighter Wing, of Myrtle Beach, SC, had to refuel in the air four times for a mission that lasted eight hours and 18 minutes. Johnson said they spent perhaps half that time flying over Iraq.

Johnson said he and Goff were among several A-10 pilots trained specifically in search-and-rescue operations, able to work with different kinds of aircraft from different services in a coordinated, complex and often dangerous operation.

The pair scrambled into the air and headed north, radioing ahead to arrange in-flight refueling and advise helicopters in the area to be alert for a pickup. After two refuelings and two hours in flight "we built our plan," Johnson said.

Air Force spokesmen explained that the Navy pilot had ejected after being hit with ground fire, and had parachuted into a vast, featureless expanse of Iraqi desert. In such circumstances, the spokesmen explained, a downed pilot has flares, smoke grenades and a small radio to help him communicate with would-be rescuers.

Johnson said it wasn't until midday that the two A-10 pilots, who had picked up the downed flier's radio signal, finally located the general area where his plane was believed to have gone down.

Then came the painstaking process of lining up a rescue helicopter and bringing it deep into hostile territory. The idea, said Johnson, is to get "all the key players in place," then "go in and pick up the survivor with minimum risk."

7 Days Later: All in a Day's Work

By Gary Regenstreif

NORTHERN SAUDI ARABIA - A U.S. Navy pilot whose jet fighter was downed last week was rescued by an elite military squad that flew deep into Iraq in broad daylight and plucked him into their helicopter in what members described as "a day's work." Two squad members interviewed requested their identities and some details not be revealed for fear of jeopardizing future such missions and the secrecy of branch. The force conducts special missions, often behind enemy lines, including raids, evacuation of civilians and search and rescue.

The Navy pilot (check name, date) ejected from his F-14 Tomcat after being hit by Iraqi fire. He managed to send his location by a portable survival radio.

An A-10 fighter aircraft picked up the signal and alerted the squad at 0700.

"We were told to go pick him up," said one officer who conducted the mission.

They crossed the Iraqi border by helicopter and swirled around the site where the pilot was believed to be hiding. He wasn't.

It was still unclear whether the pilot's transmitting device was damaged when he ejected or whether he moved from his initial parachute site.

It was not until the third attempt, at 1400, that the pilot was spotted in the desert with the skyline of an unidentifiable Iraqi city in the distance.

"He was laying down, trying to hide," said one mission member. But an Iraqi military truck, believed to have picked up the radio signal, was 100 yards behind the pilot and racing to catch him. "He was getting up to run because they were going after him," he added.

A nearby A-10 fighter was called in and it strafed the truck. "Fire went only one way," he said. The truck was destroyed. "We got him on board and took off in the other direction," said the crew member. "He looked a bit stressed but he was happy to see us." "We were damn glad to pick him up," said the second squad member. "We have accomplished something we have trained for six months. It's part of our job, that's all."

The squad member attributed the success of such missions, and apparent fearlessness in the face of firepower, to rigorous physical and mental training.

"We know the stuff (weaponry) they have there," said the second squad member. "But everybody is alert. If you keep your edge, there's no threat."

"You get out there and it's pretty comfortable."

Wednesday
January 23, 1991

The Kingdom of Saudi Arabia had been a close ally of the United States since President Franklin D. Roosevelt's time, but its response to the crisis brought down on its regal head by Saddam Hussein on Aug. 2, 1990 surprised even some Americans.

Gen. Schwarzkopf reported in his autobiography that he was absolutely stunned by the Saudi reaction when he and Secretary Cheney first presented a plan to let the United States of America come to the rescue by sending in a massive force of non-Islamic fighters. He said he had expected the king to take it under advisement, like a recommendation for a risky mutual fund.

Instead, as soon as the Americans completed their pitch, the king exchanged a few whispered words in Arabic with his advisers and then said basically, okay, let's do it. Get those GIs over here. In the snap of a royal cloak, American troops were on their way to Saudi, and the Saudis were putting their own army in the field. (In the past decade, historians have revealed that tough internal debate between the king's men and key religious leaders bitterly opposed to having American troops on Saudi soil actually preceded this brief meeting.) A story about the fledgling Saudi force is in this chapter. Saudi fighter pilots had emerged from the emirate's elite class by this time, but no real army capable of self-defense, not even the token force that Kuwait had by then.

The conflict over Iraq's invasion of Kuwait marked the first time Saudi Arabia had fought a war, or even helped fight one. A country should really have an army, or be ready to hire one, if it's going to do that.

Some cynics said the Saudis and the Kuwaitis did both. A Pentagon breakdown of financial pledges to offset the massive cost of the war showed Saudi Arabia and Kuwait providing the lion's share, about $16 billion each. Japan, whose main interest was in seeing that the world's oil supply still reached Japan's harbors, was the next largest donor, with $10 billion.

This chapter also brings out another aspect of the war often slighted in Western accounts, the involvement of other Arab countries, in this case the Egyptians.

But there were other Arab armies in the field, too, like the Qataris, the Kuwaitis and even Syrians. While their numbers were small in comparison to the United States and Britain, they provided absolutely vital political cover for the whole operation.

Schwarzkopf writes of what an Arabic hot potato he was handed just before he launched the land war. The Syrians told him they'd decided they couldn't participate after all because it would mean their Arab boys killing Iraq's Arab boys.

Schwarzkopf, who spent part of his youth in Iran while his father was a U.S. government official there, knew something about the Mideast mind, and knew this was no minor flap. Something like this could unravel the whole Arab seam of the coalition.

Before the problem got any worse, he did two things. He told the Syrians he understood their misgivings. And he told them they could move their troops back in the line of march and go into Kuwait behind the Egyptians. Then, if their soldiers had to fight the Iraqis it would only be after Iraqis had overrun the Egyptians and the Egyptians needed help. They would be Arabs fighting Arabs but helping Arabs.

The Syrians stayed in. They were out of the line of fire but still in the coalition against Iraq, and the Western-Arab alliance was intact. Some people think Gen. Schwarzkopf earned his pay for the whole year with that one idea.

As the air war pounded on, the mission of the midair-refueling aircraft came into sharp focus. The picture of huge gasoline-filled tankers circling Saudi airspace dispensing jet fuel to fighters and bombers so they could stay in the air longer and attack more targets wasn't glamorous. But as a story in this chapter shows, without them the air campaign would have lacked a deadly continuity.

And unlike peacetime, when U.S. aviators operate under strict gallon-limits, the sky was the limit here. Somebody would worry about how much all this jet fuel was costing later.

While tons of fuel were being burned in allied plane engines, the troops in the desert were witnesses to the great torching of the oil wells in Kuwait. There didn't seem to be much military logic to it, although the thick, black smoke created by the fires affected visibility across miles of desert and for hundreds of feet in the air, making it more difficult for allied aircraft to see their targets.

At the same time, the first real signs of a conflict at ground level appeared. Marines on the east coast began reporting incoming fire from Iraqi artillery just over the Kuwaiti border. It was plain to everyone, down to the GIs on guard duty in another story in this chapter, that the tempo was picking up.

Modern Bedouin Warriors Wear Robes Over Their Khaki, Predict War Will Last Only 3 Weeks

By Leon Daniel

WITH U.S. MARINES IN EASTERN SAUDI ARABIA - Khalid Kablan, commander of a platoon of armored vehicles dug into the sand at the head of the massive allied force facing Iraqi-occupied Kuwait, looks for all the world like a Bedouin warrior.

"Attacking will be no problem," said the 22-year-old lieutenant in the Saudi Arabian army. "When they tell me to go forward, I will go." The bearded Saudi soldiers wore Arab robes over their khakis to shield them from the chill wind whipping across the bleak desert.

They keep a sharp eye out for any movement, day or night.

Kablan and his men have spotted only a few deserters since the war erupted a week ago. The flow of refugees to the south has stopped now.

The war, for the hordes of men deployed in the vast desert, has become a waiting game. Kablan, who before the war was a university student in Riyadh, seems at home in the desert. Allied forces sometimes grumble about sudden climatic change that can turn the sun-baked sand into a sea of mud, but Kablan and his men are undaunted by the heat of the days or the chill of the nights. "This is my home," he explained.

The lieutenant predicted that when the ground war starts it will be completed in two weeks or less.

"Maybe three weeks," he amended, grinning confidently. "No more."

Iraqi Artillery Targets Marines Near Khafji, Abandoned City on the Saudi Coast

By Kirk Spitzer

TASK FORCE TARO, Northeastern Saudi Arabia - "Eight O'clock Achmed" was late last night.

It took him until almost 9:00 before he lobbed a couple of artillery rockets at U.S. Marines hunkered down just south of the border town of Khafji.

No one was hurt and the brief, daily barrage has become almost routine. But while the air war rages and ground troops elsewhere in Saudi Arabia gather for an expected offensive in the coming days or weeks, Marines of Task Force Taro have been under fire since the first day of battle.

"We're well aware that we're the first under fire. It's kind of a dubious distinction," said Col. John Admire, commander of the task force, from a well-fortified command post. The task force is composed of Marine units stationed at Kaneohe Marine Corps Air Station in Hawaii.

The Iraqis have been firing from four to eight rockets daily at the city of Khafji, a few miles from the border, and Marine positions nearby. None has caused any casualties but Khafji shows signs of the battering and the Marines have quickly swung into a war footing.

Task Force Taro's main compound is stuffed with deep, sand-bagged bunkers and heavily armed patrols range throughout the border region.

Marine artillery has begun to fire back at the Iraqis, as well.

"The first and third nights (of the war), the 'flash and bang' was just outside the perimeter. It shook the tents and everything. Everybody was pretty nervous," said Cpl. Mark Watson, 22, a radio operator from Sevierville, Tenn. He said the barrages were nicknamed "Eight O'Clock Achmed" because they usually arrived punctually in the early evenings.

. . . The Marines run frequent patrols into Khafji, to check on artillery damage and make sure Iraqis haven't moved in. The city has been abandoned since the day the war began. "It's pretty quiet up here right now," said Sgt. Bill Iiams, 28, of Burbank, CA, before a patrol Wednesday. "Nobody's here—just cats and dogs. The first couple of days (of the war) everybody lickety-split south."

The city shows the effects of the war. A huge column of black smoke hangs over the city from a burning oil refinery—a victim of the first night's barrage.

The streets are pocked with small shell holes and some buildings are scarred from shrapnel. During Wednesday's patrol, Marine scouts came across the evidence of the previous evening's barrage: the remains of four rockets that had impacted on the city's main street. Bombs and artillery frequently can be heard rumbling in the distance. Singapore Airlines' office near the port is closed.

Lance Cpl. Benton Barron, 21, of Mount Holly, NC, said he gets butterflies in the pit of his stomach before entering the city, much like a football player before the opening kickoff. "Especially when you hear the (artillery) rounds coming in—you just start paying more attention, staying alert to what's going on," he said.

Lance Cpl. Ian Lewis, 22, of Chicago, said the Marines aren't as jumpy as they were the first few days of the war. "It's not as scary as it was when the shelling first started. You get used to it somewhat. I can think of better things to be doing, though," he said.

Wednesday - January 23, 1991

For a Near-Good Time, Desert Disco Has Near-Beer, a Chaplain, and Near-Anonymous Women in Black

By Stephanie Glass

EASTERN SAUDI ARABIA - Risking the exposure of a MASH-era chic hotspot in the rough, we offer Studio 85, the 85th Evacuation Hospital's all-rank dance-club-in-a-tent, complete with disk jockey. "Near beer for a near good time," is how Capt. Ralph Otte, the unit's chaplain from Oakland, CA, describes the club's ambience.

The dance club skirts the Saudi prohibition on male-female dancing. "This is our compound. We can do that," said chief nurse Lt. Col. Linda Freeman, from Waycross, GA.

"We cover the women in black," said Lt. Col. Hudson Berry, an orthopedist. "We don't know who the women are we're dancing with," Otte said. "Stealth women."

What is a chaplain doing in a dance club? "I have to make sure the troops are behaving themselves," Otte said.

The dimly-lit club fashioned from two tents glued together over a plywood floor may not be plush but you get what you pay for: drinks are free, there is no cover, and no one is going to send you home for not wearing a jacket.

Staffers call it a place to unwind and consider it effective because there hasn't been a fight yet. Sgt. Mark Martin, the disc jockey, "spins" cassettes, some of them the Saudi bootleg variety, others brought from home. "You've got to have a really good sense of humor. Look where you are," Freeman said.

"He goes out of his way to make it a good time."

Non-alcoholic beer and munchies the staff donates from food packages from home. It sports no wall decor. Patrons would like to pass on they are looking for a spare disco ball, if one is around.

A Guard's Duty: Digging on a Rock and Waiting for the Guy Who Doesn't Know the Password

By Laurence Jolidon

WITH U.S. FORCES - In the middle of the night, in every shallow foxhole dug out of the hard rock of the Saudi desert a few kilometers from Iraq, there's a U.S. soldier waiting for somebody who doesn't know the password.

Between 3:30 and 6:30 a.m. every morning for the past week, one of those soldiers has been Pfc. Kenneth Johns, 24, of Chico, CA. He's also in that foxhole from 3:30 to 6:30 p.m. every day. But the nights "are a lot worse," he says.

"I pray every night," says Johns, a Roman Catholic, "and I hope the Lord is listening. I ask him to send a sign to their families back home that everyone over here is safe and will be home soon."

Once in a while, he looks out at the black night, into the mist that makes anything beyond 25 feet away invisible, and he thinks about his next birthday, May 2. He'll be 25, and he knows he'll still be here.

"I'm too young to die," he says. "If it's my time, there's nothing I can do about it. But it's not my time. I know it. I've got too many things to go back to, and too much love."

He's single. "That's another reason to get out of here," he says. "Get married and have kids."

Talking about his four months here, since arriving Sept. 21, his words rock back and forth between confidence and fear, between pride in taking on this dangerous work and being ready to get on with his life, beyond Saudi Arabia and Iraq.

"This is one big cat box," he says of the desert. "Nothing more, nothing less. It's like when you move into a new neighborhood, and there's a bully on the block. Iraq's the bully. We've got to knock him back."

The young trooper makes his jaw firm. "I'll stay over here as long as I have to. I don't want to come back to this place. We have to do it right this time. If he'd moved out of Kuwait, we'd have left and gone home but we'd be right back in three to four years and it would be worse, with more chemical, biological, and even nuclear weapons."

The weariness begins to show.

"I've been digging on this rock for the last four days and it's really not fun." He talks about the job he'll do when the ground war begins. "I'm on an assault team. We do reconnaissance for the artillery. We go out and direct fire for the gun battery. We stay out for a couple of days and to not get found we never stay in one spot very long."

He slips into his reasons for joining the Army.

"Good money, good solid job. Boy, was I a fool." But he catches himself.

"I'm glad I'm doing it," he said proudly "Glad I'm helping people." But his job for now is stopping people. "I don't like it out here," he says. "They can come from any direction. You can hear the jets up there. Hopefully they're ours. I just want to get this over with and get home safe and sound. I've served my country."

His enlistment is over in March 1993. He'll be in the reserves for years after that.

He figures it's not his time because back in the rear, he stopped one night by the side of the road to eat a snack and "some Arab guy" sideswiped him. The crash broke off his rear-view mirror. He feels lucky it wasn't more serious.

"I'm taking that broken mirror frame home with me in the bottom of my rucksack," he says. "It took me a week to clean all the broken glass out of it. It'll be something to help me remember all this, what I did for my country, what I did for history. I'll look at that thing and say, hey, I was really there, and I'll feel good about it."

In the middle of the night, hunkered down in the foxhole he makes a little bigger and better every day, chipping away at the hard rock, he peers into the black, and prays and thinks. "I talked to my mother an hour before we came up here," he says.

"She told me, keep my weapon beside me and my mask on my side. I told her, 'Don't worry, mom. That's exactly what I'm doing.'"

Holy Toledo, It Was Just Going to Town, and Then 50 Iraqi Tanks Surrender . . . To the Egyptians

By Charles Richards

The order to scramble came out of the blue.

It was the afternoon of Jan. 17, a few scant hours since the multinational coalition forces had unleashed its engines of war on Baghdad. And the wicked-looking Apache helicopter gunships of the U.S.

Army were to get their first test in combat of their much-vaunted killing power.

Their target: a column of tanks sighted crossing the Iraqi border into Saudi Arabia.

First up was Capt. Mike Klingele, commander of Charlie Company. Like many of these Army aviators, with his lean frame and quick intelligence, he looked and sounded more like a fighter pilot. His company has ten aircraft, a mix of Apache helicopter gunships, and OH-58C scout helicopters. "It was mid-to-late afternoon. I was talking to some of the gun pilots. I came out of their tent and was going over to mine when the S3 (operations officer) said, 'Go up onto the P, the little power engine, before you go on the big engine and contact us on battalion command.'

"I went, 'Wow.' I stuck my head through the pilots' tents. Now when I do that they all freeze. I said, 'Come up on the P (the auxiliary power unit), Company Uniform, Company Victor, Battalion Command.' I got everyone up to running speed.

"Everyone was like, boom, the activity, the fury had started. Then grabbing helmet bag, grabbing this, grabbing that. Trucks also were coming from everywhere.

"Whooah. The crew chiefs caught it right away and they were there with their trucks. Basically, we dumped our stuff there and boom, we were gone.

"As we were driving out there to the flight line, I was giving them the codes. Dropped everybody off at the aircraft. It was just going to town. It was great. I jumped in the aircraft. I started up the APU, the auxiliary power unit. The boss continued to give us information. Got everybody up to running speed. Got the word to depart.

"Right as we were departing, that's when they passed the target to us. The intelligence officer came over the net and said, there are 50 tanks at this location.

"There were some busy cockpits then, it was like, I got the map right away and whooah, plotted it. I went, 'Holy Toledo.'

"As we were up, they passed the target to us. En route when they said return to base, I think those instructions came from the brigade commander via the battalion commander. So we came back.

"But I tell you what, there was some real thrill. It all came together real fast. Everyone saw it as real, everyone thought it was real."

Later the commander of the Egyptian force in Saudi Arabia was to state that 50 Iraqi tanks had come over and given themselves up to the Egyptians.

Charlie Company is one of three companies in the 1st Battalion of the 227th Aviation Regiment with the 1st Cavalry Division. Its Apache is the most formidable anti-tank weapon in the U.S. Army. It is equipped with laser-guided Hellfire missiles, which can lock onto a target from out of sight over the horizon and fire from eight kilometers away or more.

Charlie Company was first up because in the normal rotation, it was on standby.

That day the entire battalion was ordered up. But the call to abort came as the others were still on the ground. The mission was the nearest that the battalion has had to real combat. There have been other alerts since.

On Jan. 22, there was another report of movement on the border. Another aviation unit was activated. It turned out to be 18 Iraqis defecting, without tanks.

Lessons were learnt, Mike Klingele explained. "From my standpoint, as the commander, I was really very pleased that it happened. Because first of that the plan we'd talked through and rehearsed at a slow pace now for real came to being and worked quite well.

"There were two or three minor lessons. I learnt a few things about my cockpit. But basically everything we had practiced and done went well.

"That's the biggest thing that made me happy. The only change I had made over the radio was lights. You go down your checklists. You get to lights. That's a peacetime requirement. That was one difference. I said lights. There was no need.

"There is always a little doubt in your mind. Have we trained the right way? Have we drilled the right drills? I can't believe how close the National Training Center was."

Now they are waiting, waiting to be called in for real, to attack the Iraqi tanks wherever they can find them.

Every New War Brings New Reasons To Throw Your (Unprintable) Teddy in a Corner

By John Fullerton

WITH BRITISH FORCES ON THE ALLIED FRONT LINE, Saudi Arabia - Don't throw your teddy in a corner because there aren't any sherbets in the Gulf. Have a mellow day instead. And if you don't get out of your green maggot and clean up the Rudolph Hess, I'm gonna Scud you.

British soldiers on Saudi Arabia's northern border with Iraqi-occupied Kuwait have a language all of their own. It encapsulates regimental tradition, Britain's earlier wars in Asia and Africa, and has absorbed new phrases and expressions from the Gulf War.

To Scud someone is to give him a good bashing, after the Iraqi missiles that have been fired in large numbers at targets in Saudi Arabia, Israel, and elsewhere. A depressed soldier is an unhappy teddy; his gobbing rods are his knife, fork, and spoon; and to tealeaf is to steal.

Minging or gopping means dirty, to sponge is to scrounge and a maggot, or doss-bag, is a sleeping bag. A Rudolph Hess is simply a mess. Gregory Peck is a neck. And there are several words for the one item that is never seen but greatly missed by the Desert Rats—beer.

Wets, scoobs, sherbets, bevvys and socials—the troops dream of ale in a pint glass.

A soldier's weapon is his bondook, his washing is the dhobi and the middle of nowhere, or jungle, is the ulu. The good soldier, or switched-on cooky, never gonks (sleeps) on stag (sentry duty) but stays mellow (calm and cool) even if he's been spammed or jiffed (given an unpleasant or bad task.)

Many, many terms are unprintable.

There are scores of derogatory nicknames for rival arms and services in the British armed forces, reflecting the tribal and highly-competitive instincts of the British fighting man. Soldiers call Royal Marine commandos cabbages, while members of the Royal Tank Regiment are known as clankie-tankies. Members of Guards regiments are wooden-tops.

Britain's allies are regarded with affectionate contempt. Germans are box-heads, Americans septic yanks. Shreddies are underpants, and dessies refer to desert boots worn in the Gulf. You don't wash your face, but clean your fizzog instead. And at all times in the Gulf War, a soldier never forgets his rubberface—his gas mask.

Wednesday - January 23, 1991

Marine Fighters Make Mid-Air Pit Stops for Fuel So They Can "Mess Up Somebody's Day" in Iraq

By Lara Marlowe

WITH MARINE AIR GROUP 13, 3rd MARINE AIR WING, Over the Arabian Gulf - It was the stuff that military recruitment films are made of.

As if unrelated to Scud missiles, mustard gas, and forced television confessions, four KC-130 Hercules turbo-prop tankers rose in staggered "stairway to the stars" formation over Gulf reefs and blue-green waters, breaking through the fog onto an expanse of white clouds and blue sky. Shouts of "Tally-ho" signaled each sighting of attack and fighter aircraft swarming in to suck an aggregate of 120,000 pounds of jet air fuel in three hours from the tankers' reservoirs.

The six-man crew of the "Battle Herc" did not know who or what their U.S. Marine and Navy pilot receivers, each armed with 4,000 pounds of ordnance, would target, but they delighted in today's (Wed.) clear weather and their role in stepping up the bombing. Instead of 24 scheduled refuellings, the four aircraft delivered gas to 31 aircraft, representing, the crew members said, a significant increase in damage to the Iraqis.

"The fighters are going to work real hard on messing up somebody's day," said Squadron Commander VMGR-352 Lt. Col. Arlen Rens, 43, from Escondido, Calif.

The Marine air wing's more than a dozen KC-130s are so much in demand that there is no time to repair minor mechanical failures like a leaking hose which spilled a trail of white jet fuel through the sky or a broken fuel indicator. "We just tap on the tank to see how much fuel is still in it," said Gunnery Sgt. George Leath, 38, from Orlando, Fla.

The pewter-colored tank, perhaps 20 feet long and six feet high, holds 23,000 pounds of jet air fuel and occupies most of the fuselage of the KC-130. When the tank is removed, the same area can transport 92 troops. Incredibly, a crew member smoked a cigarette just a few feet away from the airborne fuel tank.

The possession of an in-air refueling capability gives American and coalition air forces an important advantage over the Iraqi air force. "We call ourselves the force multipliers," said Col. Rens. "If we weren't here, the fighters would have to give up ordnance to carry more fuel. It's like moving the whole airbase 200 miles north. We're a team. Every scenario in this theater revolves around the tankers."

The bulk of Iraq's aircraft are now believed to be hidden in hardened hangars in northern Iraq. Without mid-air refueling it is unlikely that (illegible) in Saudi Arabia or other Gulf countries. "They have no refueling capacity that we know of," said Col. Rens. "It's one of their weaknesses."

Yet Iraqi jet fighters might be tempted by unarmed AWACs (airborne warning and control) and tanker aircraft flying within reach of the Kuwaiti and Iraqi borders. "In Soviet military doctrine, which is what the Iraqis follow, you watch the tankers to predict what the enemy is doing," said Rens. "So we observe EMCON (minimum control) or radio silence on our missions. If we can monitor radio frequencies, so can the bad guys. If we talked to the fighters, the Iraqis might know we were planning a raid."

Despite their lack of weapons, Col. Rens said his KC-130s were well protected by coalition BAR CAPS (barrier combat air patrols). "They establish a line of fighters in two sections that extends from the Gulf to the Saudi-Jordanian border," said Rens. "We've got hundreds of guys whose sole goal in life is to be an ace. You just say the word "MiG" and they're all over them like flies on sugar."

In theory, each receiving aircraft knows in advance which tanker and hose to approach for refueling. "We set up a point in space at which we meet. We give them coordinates and we give them a time. It is their job to find us," said Rens. When the operation is carried out as planned, the colonel said, "it is a thing of sheer beauty."

But radio silence, poor weather and the unexpected arrival of "stray" or battle-damaged aircraft can reduce the carefully orchestrated formations to something more reminiscent of a bar fight, Col. Rens said.

Since the war started, more than 100 aerial tankers scattered from western Saudi Arabia to the Gulf have maintained dozens of these mid-air refueling stations at all times. Below Col. Rens' 30-mile east-west track today, the British Royal Air Force refueled Tornados and Jaguars from their tankers. Above the Marine air wing's KC-130s, the Air Force's KC-10s and KC-135s could be seen refueling their own fighters. When the ground war begins, Col. Rens said, his mission will probably shift to refueling helicopters.

Allusions to natural science are almost irresistible when describing the refueling process. The 3rd Marine Air Wing's F/A-18s look like tiny hornets when they speed toward the giant tankers and hover while inserting their elephant trunk probes. The para-drogue feeder at the end of the tanker's port and starboard hoses resemble white tulips. The KC-130 crew referred to the hoses, drogues, and probes as "male" and "female" apparatus.

At the back of the tanker, radio operator Staff Sgt. Randy Reynolds, 32, from Cooper, Tex., kept a ledger of aircraft refuellings, noting the types and tail numbers of each jet which received fuel from the tanker.

The first, a U.S. Navy A6E Intruder, took 1,330 gallons. "In the States, each squadron is allocated X number of dollars," said Reynolds. "We still keep records, but no one is really concerned because it's all coming out of the Desert Storm budget. When the war is over, someone will add up all the sheets and figure out how much it cost."

USS Mobile Bay on Lookout for Mines in the Sea

By David Alexander

ABOARD THE USS MOBILE BAY, Arabian Gulf - The morning after U.S. fliers bombed an Iraqi mine-layer in the Gulf, Seaman William Huff was back in his chair, perched precariously at the front of the cruiser Mobile Bay, scanning the water ahead for any object

"It makes me happy (they sank the Iraqi ship)," said Huff, 25, of Harrison, Ark., who normally works baking bread in the galley. "I just wonder how many more they have and how many they have that we don't know about."

Huff, bundled in warm clothing against the morning chill and wearing a safety line to protect him from falling into the water, said there was little to see from his perch during the hour-long watch—just floating trash and a school of dolphins.

"Our helicopter spotted a mine yesterday (about 20 miles away), but we haven't seen anything yet," said 2nd Class Petty Officer Kevin Weimert, 25, of Houston, who manned a 50-caliber machine gun nearby and assisted in the watch. "The closest thing we have seen to a mine is a trash bag," said 2nd Class Petty Officer Andrew Hendley, 24, of Calvert Co., Md., another 50-caliber gunner looking for mines.

With the Iraq war entering its sixth day Tuesday and most of Baghdad's warplanes seemingly grounded by the allied air offensive, mines were the biggest threat to the Mobile Bay, one of the ships nearest Kuwait protecting the three U.S. aircraft carriers in the Gulf.

The discovery of an Iraqi vessel sowing mines Monday night again raised concerns about mine warfare in the Gulf, where more than two dozen of the devices have been located in recent weeks.

Aircraft from the U.S. carriers in the Gulf bombed and sank the Iraqi mine-laying ship because it was suspected of sowing mines in international waters—an act of war, said Stephen Woodall, the captain of the Mobile Bay. The planes sank a second vessel that moved into the area following the attack, causing two other ships to flee.

For Woodall, whose ship fired several Tomahawk missiles on the second day of the war and routinely checks the identity of planes returning from raids on Iraq, running into a mine is one of the dangers that have to be constantly guarded against. "The most appreciable threat to us is just hitting a mine," said Woodall. "This ship…is the most capable ship ever built to repel air threats or surface threats. We have 24-hour-a-day mine-watching," he said.

We use binoculars in the daytime and we use night-vision devices at night," so despite the Mobile Bay's high-tech weapons, including helicopters, Tomahawks and other missiles, torpedoes, and several advanced radars, the defense of the ship these days relies heavily on several pairs of human eyes. That means seamen like Kevin Weimert, Andrew Hendley, and William have to spend four often-boring hours each day scanning the horizon for floating objects.

For Huff, who grew up around his grandmother's coffee shop in Henderson listening to old-timers spin yarns about World War II and Korea, that kind of war duty is a long way from what he expected. "All we do is launch a few missiles toward the coast and watch the planes go by," said Huff, who joined the Navy to get out of Henderson and have a look at the rest of the world.

Although the 350 sailors aboard the Mobile Bay are isolated and hungry for news from the outside, the ongoing war with Iraq often comes startlingly close to home.

The second day of battle, the ship launched several Tomahawk missiles, which took off with a deafening roar. "It was early in the morning," said Weimert, who was on mine watch. "I saw several streaks of light on the horizon. I notified the bridge and they said they knew about it . . . the other ships were launching Tomahawks and to get ready to go to general quarters in 15 minutes." But sometimes the war seems a long way away for the mine-watchers at the front of the ship.

"Me and the fifty-cal guys tell jokes to stay awake," Huff said, "just watching and waiting." Mostly Huff said he'd like to get back to doing what he set out to do when he joined the Navy. "I just wanted to go to other countries to see the world," he said.

"I'd like to see more of the world. Seems like I've seen a lot of the Middle East lately."

Thursday
January 24, 1991

A truck carrying ammunition for the 82nd Airborne Division in a convoy headed north on the major highway leading north and west out of Dhahran suddenly caught fire and exploded. The blast and flashes from each different type of ammunition cascaded through the smoke and flames, from mortar shells to artillery shells, then anti-tank weapons, machine gun bullets, illumination flares. Boom. Boom, boom.

No one was hurt, but the truck and all its cargo were destroyed. It was the kind of event that demanded an explanation. When the story in this chapter was written, immediately after the event, there was no adequate explanation yet, and the buildup of allied forces in the northern Saudi desert went on unabated.

But the mysterious fire that obliterated that vehicle was one of numerous incidents that raised the possibility that saboteurs and terrorists were at work amid the massive allied buildup and long aerial campaign. This war was being fought in the terrorists' home park. There was no reason to believe they would pass up a chance to pick targets at will. Without a specific cause to point to in the case of the exploding ammo truck, the terrorist theory hung in the air, far from proven but impossible to rule out.

There were military experts in the Gulf whose job it was to know explosives, and to live and work around explosions. What they were doing with their specialty and how it tied in with the noise of Scud missiles is told in this chapter.

In Tel Aviv, where the Scuds launched by Iraq had become an almost daily menace, the odds in Iraq's calculations against Israel twirled in its favor, and the targets of the lumbering weapons were left to deal with the devastating fallout.

One of the Iraqi Scud missiles struck a suburban residential area, killing one man, injuring scores, and leaving most of a neighborhood homeless. Just the day before, in the third Scud attack launched at Israel from Iraq, one missile struck an apartment house in another part of Tel Aviv. Ninety-six people were injured, and three elderly residents died of heart attacks.

One of the Patriot missile batteries sent to Israel after the Iraqis first targeted the Jewish state managed to shoot down a Scud as it descended toward Israel's northern coast. But the ones that hit, and killed, were the ones people remembered.

In the air war, a U.S. F-16 was reported lost but the Saudi Air Force stepped up to the plate. One of its F-15s reportedly downed two Iraqi combat planes.

The air war was spectacular enough, and generated such wide coverage that smaller actions by ground forces received little attention. But a story in this chapter describing the first rounds of artillery exchanges between Iraqis and the U.S. Marines makes it clear that the ground war was evolving long before the officially set kickoff for a counter-invasion of Kuwait.

And there are also fresh looks at two long-running issues in this war: religion among allied forces and the stationing of women in units very close to, if not actually on, the front lines. In this case, it's the Marine Corps that makes use of its female warriors, and they can speak for themselves.

Back at the Pentagon, Gen. Colin Powell, chairman of the joint chiefs, gave the briefing on war developments at which he used an expression widely quoted later, often by critics who thought the general sounded too harsh, too belligerent, too warlike.

"The Iraqi army in the field," Gen. Powell said in his emphatic, measured way, "is for the most part sitting there waiting to be attacked and attacked it will be. Our strategy for dealing with this army is very simple. First we're going to cut it off, then we're going to kill it."

Gen. Powell was only engaging in the kind of speech soldiers use around each other. Actually, the military's favorite scenario was often described as cutting off "the head"—meaning the leadership or brains—of the enemy, and then methodically dismembering the rest of it.

Of course anyone who had a problem with the top American general using the word "kill" was suffering from an excess of squeamishness. In the parlance of the American military during the Gulf War era, "kill" was a verb applied to creatures with souls but just as often was applied to inanimate objects. Anything to be overcome, put out of commission, or destroyed would be "killed." From generals to privates, soldiers armed with or riding atop weapons that could obliterate an entire building described how they would "kill" a tank or any enemy target.

"Kill" the Iraqi army? Yeah, for sure, would be the reply. We're gonna kill it, even if it's one enemy soldier, one tank, one artillery battery, one radar site and one personnel carrier at a time. Fire 'em up.

Mystery Explosion Destroys Ammo Truck in 82nd Airborne Convoy

By Robert Dvorchak

WITH THE 82ND AIRBORNE DIVISION - An ammo truck moving north with the 82nd Airborne Division caught fire and exploded in a series of blasts that turned the night sky orange.

No one was injured, but the 2½ ton truck (deuce and a half) was destroyed along with its cargo of artillery shells, mortar shells, anti-tank weapons, .50-caliber machine gun rounds, and illumination flares.

The truck caught fire at about 10:30 p.m. Tuesday, Jan. 22, and burned for about an hour, blocking traffic in two directions on a civilian highway. It was among scores of trucks moving men and equipment of the division's 2nd Brigade to a tactical assembly area in northern Saudi Arabia. The explosions delayed the convoy for more an hour.

The cause of the fire is unknown and still under investigation, according to Maj. Baxter Ennis, public affairs officer for the 82nd Airborne Division.

There were reports a driver in a white Nissan pickup truck had been shadowing the convoy and sped off just before the fire was detected, but officials said there was no direct proof of terrorism. "We have nothing to support it was any type of ambush. As far as we know, it was accidental," Ennis said. "We have no proof at all it was anything other than an accidental fire."

He said the fire appeared to start on the canvas cover near the cab. The personal gear and weapons of the two soldiers in the truck were also lost. An ordnance team checked the roadway and surrounding area for any unexploded shells or mines before commercial traffic resumed. The exploding truck looked like a Roman candle in the night sky. A ball of orange flame would shoot up, followed by a blast and the whistle of exploding metal.

The headquarters of 2nd Brigade has reached its restaging area so far north in Saudi Arabia that lookouts can see the glare of Iraqi windshields across the border, its commander said Thursday (Jan. 24). Col. Ron Rokosz said scouts "were picking up windshield glints to the north." Two infantry battalions of the 2nd Brigade were deployed in front of headquarters, the exact location of which was undisclosed for security reasons.

"Put it this way, I don't smell the ocean," said Rokosz, 45, of Chicago, Ill., surveying a desolate expanse of rocky desert almost devoid of vegetation.

Some elements of the brigade were still moving north via convoys and C-130 Hercules transport planes. "The objective now is to dig in and get everybody here," Rokosz said. Moving a brigade may not be like Hannibal crossing the Alps, but it is a Herculean logistical task. It took scores of trucks and scores of flights to ferry the paratroopers to their forward fighting holes. A convoy that left at 12:30 p.m. Tuesday arrived at brigade headquarters Thursday—minus the ammo truck.

It wasn't the only unit on the move north. Elements of the 101st Airborne (air assault) Division, the 1st Cavalry Division, the 7th Army Corps, and French forces were seen. At one point, trucks filled the road as far as the eye could see to the front and the rear. The horizon-to-horizon stream of flatbeds, water bladders, and fuel trucks made the number of 18-wheelers on the Pennsylvania Turnpike seem light by comparison. "In my 14½ years in the military, I have never seen anything like this. It reminds me of that line from the movie *Patton*: 'Compared to war, all other forms of human endeavor pale by comparison,'" Ennis said.

The convoy moved through a series of truck stops set up by reserves and National Guard units for food, fuel, and bedding. Camps were named Yak, Unicorn, Vulture, Wombat, and Exxon Valdez. The Army Reserve unit 102nd Transportation Co. from Brooklyn, N.Y., decorated its camp with signs reading: "More than Just Gas. Hot Dogs. Fires. Coffee. Latrines." The camp where the 2nd Brigade had been stationed slowly evaporated into emptiness as company after company packed their rucksacks and sleeping bags for the move north.

Paratroopers showed why they are sometimes called grunts, for the last sound they make as they sling their gear on their backs. Some packs weighed 70 pounds or more; soldiers used their knees to kick them up and then threw them on their shoulders. Soldiers camouflaged their trucks by spattering them with mud and sand to cover up any patch of green. "This may be the only time a soldier gets yelled at for leaving his vehicle too clean," Rokosz said. At any rate, soldiers were happy to break camp and confront Saddam Hussein's army, still being pounded from the air.

Said Staff Sgt. Art Lambert, 26, of Madison, S.D., a squad leader for a Military Police company: "I wish he would throw some chemicals down range so we could turn Iraq into a parking lot and put up a Texaco sign: Gas, 22 cents a gallon. Hussein's a dead man."

Up at the front, Spec. 4 Spencer Kleman, 19, of Horn Lake, Miss., looked through a roll of razor wire in front of his bunker facing Iraqi positions.

"Time to earn our money," said Kleman, a grunt with 2nd Battalion of the 325th Infantry Regiment. As he spoke, someone yelled "Gas!" and everybody donned their gas masks. It was one of two alarms of the morning. "I don't worry about getting shot.

I can dodge a bullet. I can't dodge gas," Kleman said. "Chemicals just ain't fair."

Bomb-Disposal Teams Specialize in Loud Bangs and Quiet Nerves: "They Probably Got a Missile"

By Charles Richards

AN AIRBASE IN CENTRAL SAUDI ARABIA - Bomb-disposal expert Capt. Mike Spence was just explaining how his men were sifting through the wreckage of the previous night from an as-yet-unidentified missile when there was a loud bang.

An armor officer, used to such detonations, did not flinch.

But the bomb-disposal team, people with the coolest nerves in the business, ran for the bunker. Military rules for the media do not permit the identification of the precise location, to prevent the Iraqis learning the accuracy and the effectiveness of their own weapons and the defenses arrayed against them.

In the concrete bunker, the radio set was buzzing. "Six Charlie Three Zero."

"Switch base station to the Patriot."

"All here?"

"Hoffman's missing."

"I'll get him, sir."

The radio sounded again. "Six Charlie. Go ahead."

Capt. Spence speculated what it was about. "They probably got a missile. The Patriot has two modes, operational and automatic. When it's coming in, it automatically fires. One sound was a launch. One was a detonation."

A weary woman's voice came over the radio, telling units not to keep on coming across asking what had happened.

"Juliet . . . give us time to find out. We'll put it out to everybody."

Then a man's voice, patient. "All stations on this net. When we know something, we'll send it out."

"This is India Four Mike Four Eight."

Finally Capt Spence told his men and women to go back to work.

Down below, pieces of debris were laid out on neat piles on a plastic sheet under tenting. Capt. Spence, of the 71st Ordnance Disposal Unit from Wright-Patterson Air Force Base in Ohio, explained. "We've cleared up most of the wreckage. We'll go out and make sure it's safe to handle. Our mission is to identify and render safe. There are parts of rocket motor, high explosive, solid rocket fuel, and probably one of the thermal batteries right here. You see that serrated edge? That's what's leading us inconclusive—the Iraqis have entered a new phase of the high technology war.

"It leads us to believe it was not a Scud. There are not large pieces. See how they are all uniform in size?" He pointed at little squares of metal like tesserae from a Byzantine mosaic. "That's a fragmentation sleeve. We haven't ruled out it's a Scud. It could be an anti-radiation missile."

An anti-radiation missile homes in on the radar used by a missile system like the Patriot to detect targets. If the Patriot has downed such a missile, and not a Scud—and so far the evidence is inconclusive—the Iraqis have entered a new phase of the high-technology war.

Allied Fighters Exploit Clear Weather Over Iraq; "A Lot of Blown-Up Stuff on the Ground Up There"

By David Evans

IN CENTRAL SAUDI ARABIA - U.S. pilots took advantage of the dense clouds over Kuwait Thursday to pound airfields, fuel dumps and Iraq's elite Republican Guard units.

"It's a monstrously big army. Basically when you hit the ground, you're going to get the army someplace," said Capt. Jeff Gurney, 32, who flies an F-16A fighter-bomber for the South Carolina Air National Guard.

Lt. Col. John Marshall, commander of the squadron, said allied fighters had inflicted "a lot of damage" on the Republican Guards and that craters marked the landscape.

Although U.S. pilots did not encounter heavy anti-aircraft fire, Lt. Col. Denny Lombard, 44, of Syracuse, N.Y., said, "There were more (Iraqi) airplanes airborne than there ever have been."

"I don't know why. They're flying further south. There were two shot down while we were airborne today. . . . I don't know who did it," he said.

Compared to the first two days of the air war, when the Iraqis filled the skies with surface-to-air missiles and walls of anti-aircraft artillery fire, pilots returning from Thursday's raids said the Iraqi fire was sporadic.

"Now we've got to start guarding against complacency. The threat of getting blown up is plenty of incentive to keep a guy awake," said Gurney.

Taking advantage of the clearer skies over Kuwait for the second day in a row, F-16As from the 4th Tactical Fighter Wing Provisional took to the air shortly before dawn to be over target by daybreak. The fighter-bombers were able to fly some additional missions because of the good weather. Staff Sgt. Bill Zilkenat, 29, from Augusta, Ga., a weather forecaster, said Kuwait had broken out from the clouds, but central Iraq was mostly cloudy Thursday, especially over Baghdad.

"I would imagine we're a little behind due to the weather problem the first week," Gurney said. "Morale has gone up significantly . . . tenfold with the break in the weather," he said. "If you can see what your bombs are seeing, you have a lot better feeling about what you're doing as opposed to risking your behind out there on some nebulous target that is below the clouds someplace . . . that may or may not even have been hit," Gurney said.

Gurney, from West Columbia, S.C., was flying his ninth combat mission when he led several F-16As in a series of attacks on an airfield and two fuel depots Thursday morning. "I rolled in on one fuel dump and saw large fires and pillars of smoke going up to 20,000 feet," he said.

Maj. Bobby Jernigan, 37, of Columbia, S.C., also led one of five strikes by F-16As into Kuwait on Thursday. The take-offs were staggered to maintain nearly continuous pressure on the Iraqis, and the pilots also hit Republican Guard artillery concentrations, tanks and division headquarters.

Jernigan described a panorama of devastation along the Kuwaiti border where the Republican Guards are positioned. "There's a lot of blown-up stuff on the ground up there right now," he said. "We saw a bunch of bad guys on the ground. We saw tanks and artillery, troops and encampments.

"You can see the spots where B-52s came through, because B-52s carry a lot of bombs and there is a big long swath of craters," he said. "And then you can see spots where it looks like it was bigger bombs, but maybe only a couple of them, like Mark 84s (2,000-pound bombs), which we carry. Craters would be large and just two of them sitting there."

"There are areas of the earth that are just blackened circles that are 500 feet by 200 or 300 feet. That's probably where some cluster bombs went off and covered an area," Jernigan said.

"I saw some (cluster bombs) dropped yesterday (Wednesday). It looked like there was not a piece of the earth as big as this table that there was not something hitting it," he said. Jernigan was sitting in front of a 3-foot-by-4-foot table. Asked how he thought the Republican Guards were holding up, he replied, "Badly, badly."

"Looking at the ground and seeing the concentrations of troops, and the craters in amongst them—the craters really stand out when it's clear because you cannot see a depression in the earth. It's a black soot. There's a bunch of them out there, period. They extend from the border to as far north as you can go," he said.

"Everywhere you see stuff that looks like it would be a lucrative target, it looks like it's been hit," he said.

Jernigan, whose radio call sign is "Jet," said the bombing is so effective because the targets are out in the open desert. "This terrain is not like Southeast Asia. It's not like Columbia, S.C., where I'm from with the trees and stuff to hide them. There is no camouflage. No nothing. You can see them (Iraqis) very easily," recalling the problem pilots had finding pilots during the Vietnam War.

The size of the Iraqi deployment in Kuwait surprised Jernigan.

"Their formations look a lot like our formations, just concentrations and then there might be a couple of mile gaps . . . (the Iraqi) units stand out, though," he said.

"In fact, it was kind of eye-opening to see how much there was over such a big area," he said. "Hopefully, what we're doing is shortening this thing up. . . . I'd just like to see it end," he said. "This is Jet Jernigan's personal assessment. We are rapidly approaching the point where . . . I think their ability to wage war is going to deteriorate very rapidly," he said.

"It seems their leader is willing to sacrifice all of them to make a point," he said.

"I think air power is taking its toll on them," he said. "I would prefer to keep it up and let the Army guys contain the borders . . . and let us keep working. Hopefully, if . . . the Army has to go across we will have had such an effect they will meet marginal resistance at best." But Lt. Col. Lombard offered a less optimistic assessment.

"They're dug in and I just think they're trying to survive it (the bombing) until the land war starts," Lombard said. Asked about Friday's missions, he replied: "More of the same. You can't soften them up too much."

As Bombs Fall, Marine Chaplain Hears More Confessions

By Leon Daniel

WITH U.S. MARINES, Eastern Saudi Arabia - The Catholic chaplain at this desert base said Thursday that since the war began he has heard a lot more confessions from Marines.

"Since the bombing started, they have begun to understand that this is for real," said Lt. (j.g.) Timothy Koester of Buffalo, N.Y., who is known in these parts as "Father Tim."

"Fear has to be a big thing here," said the padre, a former parish priest. "The young Marines ask me if it's all right to be scared.

I tell them I worry more about those who can't acknowledge their fear."

Koester, commissioned as a Navy officer and chaplain last May, loves his job. "For me, this is what being a priest is all about," he said.

Koester is well aware that the National Conference of Bishops, as well as mainstream protestant denominations, opposed going to war. "Whether this is a just war or not is a question to be settled on a higher level," he said. "I'm just here to serve the troops."

Koester said that so far he has talked to only two Marines about their efforts to secure conscientious objector status.

"Both of those cases are still pending," he said.

As for himself, Koester said, "I'm a true non-combatant. I don't feel a need to carry a weapon. I believe that God will guide me through."

Koester travels to a dozen points in the desert to celebrate Mass and hear confessions. He said Marines have no difficulty practicing their faith in strictly Islamic Saudi Arabia.

"My experience is that the people of Saudi Arabia and the king have encouraged us to be strong in our faith," he said.

Since the Marines have no access to alcohol, Koester said, he does not have to deal with any alcohol-related problems. Perhaps more surprising, Koester said he has not had to deal with sexual problems, although women Marines live in close proximity to men in the desert. "I'm sure there's some dating," Koester said, "but I know of no problems."

It is difficult to conceive what a couple might do here on a date. Fill sandbags, perhaps? Or field-strip their weapons?

Almost a year ago, Tescha Shipp, 21, of Dallas, Ga., and her brother Jason, 21, joined the Marines and went through boot camp at Parris Island, S.C., together.

"Now I'm out here in the desert with a rifle on my shoulder and Jason is at Camp Pendleton in California playing with a computer," Tescha laughed.

"Jason wishes it was him over here instead of me," said Tescha, a private first class, "but I'm glad it's me over here instead of him." Pfc. Shipp is a "wire dog," which means she is a telephone pole climber in a communication outfit. Shipp jokes a lot but in a serious mood she can admit, "Yes, definitely I'm worried. They say their tanks could be here in about three hours."

At night, when she stands watch, Shipp can hear the bombing across the border in Iraqi-occupied Kuwait. Flashes from the fighting to the north sometimes lights up the sky. But most of the time Shipp is cheerful.

"Right now I'm just looking for a pizza and a warm bed," she said.

Speedy Marine Artillery Already Returning Iraqi "Mail," Showing a "Half-Baked Hitler" How to Play Hardball

By Kirk Spitzer

NEAR THE KUWAIT BORDER - U.S. Marines staged a daring hit-and-run artillery raid on Iraqi forces inside Kuwait late Wednesday, firing 35 rounds of high explosives from positions only miles from the Kuwait border.

The attack was designed to destroy an Iraqi rocket battery suspected of shelling the Saudi border city of Khafji and nearby Marine positions in recent days. No official estimate of damage was available but the commander of the raiding party pronounced the mission a success. "If we got a good grid (target location)—and I believe we did—then we rocked somebody's world pretty good," said Capt. Bruce Kowalski, commanding officer of the 1st Marine Division's "Fox" Battery. "What we did was send a message to Saddam that if he sends over mail, we'll return it marked 'postage due,'" said Kowalski.

There were no U.S. casualties. It was the second artillery raid by Marines since the start of the Persian Gulf War last week. On Monday, Fox Battery also fired on an Iraqi artillery battery that was sporadically shelling Marine positions near the border.

In Wednesday's raid, a battery of 155mm howitzers crept within a few miles of the border, fired 35 rounds each of long-range rocket-assisted artillery rounds at a rocket position more than 15 miles away in Kuwait, then raced away before Iraqis could return fire.

A battery typically consists of eight guns. Because of military restrictions on press coverage of the war, exact details of the raid cannot be reported. The raiding party was accompanied by members of the U.S. press pool assigned to the 1st Marine Division.

Kowalski said that because the Iraqis enjoy an advantage in the number and size of artillery pieces—the Iraqis have almost five times as many artillery pieces in and around Kuwait as the U.S. and coalition forces and many have substantially longer range—U.S. strategy will rely on speed and stealth.

"There are quite a few units that could engage us here," Kowalski said as his unit moved into position for the raid under blackout conditions late Wednesday. "The Iraqis' doctrine is to make an entire (map) grid disappear (with massed artillery fire), but as long as we're out in 20 minutes, we're good to go," he said.

A standard map grid represents an area 1,000 meters square—about the size of an average college campus. As artillerymen stood within sight of the Kuwait border under the glow of a half moon, many said they were excited but nervous. The raid took place in roughly the same area as the first raid Monday. "There is a fear factor, but it's exciting because we get to do our job. This is what we live for out here—to engage the enemy," said Lt. Anthony "Tino" Sellitto, 26, a platoon commander from Honolulu.

"I'm glad it got started, but this is a real dangerous place," said Sgt. William Beathards, 27, an artillery mechanic from Millsboro, Del. "If they hit us, we won't make it out." There were several tense moments as the unit, accompanied by heavily armed security units, moved into final position. Salvos of rockets trailing long, golden columns of fire hurtling toward the battery: the rockets passed overhead, apparently on the way to other targets and it was later learned they had been fired by a nearby Saudi unit.

After navigating a long, circuitous route through the desert, the battery finally came to its firing position. It set up in minutes, unleashed the salvo in just under 120 seconds, and was back on the move again.

Just before firing, Kowalski moved among the gun crews, offering advice, last minute instructions and an occasional pep-talk. "Don't get excited. Don't rush. We only have five rounds (per gun) we'll crank out and we'll rattle somebody's cage," he said to one crew.

To a driver unsure of the withdrawal route: "Keep the moon on your left and you'll be OK. If you go a mile and still don't find anybody, don't worry I'll come back and get you."

The brief salvo was deafening; the shells could be seen leaving the gun barrels, then appeared again high in the night sky as the rocket motors—designed to give the shells extra range—briefly flashed on. There was no return fire from the Iraqis and the battery moved out without incident. Later, Kowalski, a barrel-chested, recruiting poster Marine, said he was satisfied with the mission. "We'll show any half-baked Hitler that if he wants to play hardball, he's going to take some heavy (hits)," he said.

Fox Battery is part of the 1st Battalion, 12th Marine Regiment, stationed at Kaneohe Marine Corps Air Station.

Women Marines in "Rear Area" Combat Zone: One is Worried Men Won't Have a "Clear Head" if She's There

By Jim Michaels

EASTERN SAUDI ARABIA - Every night, Pfc. Amy Dever hears the sounds of allied bombing and wonders how close she will come to the fighting.

"When you get up at night you can see the lights and the flashes in the sky," the 20-year-old Alabama native said. "It seems to be getting closer all the time."

The 130 women Marines at this logistics outpost, which is less than 30 miles from the Kuwait border, say they are the closest females have ever been to the front lines.

The role of women in the armed forces has expanded greatly during the past decade and the Gulf War will likely expose more women to combat than any conflict in the past. As the nature of war changes, and as women take on more jobs within the services, the war here may prove the largest challenge yet to the Pentagon's ban on women in combat.

Under Pentagon regulations, women can be assigned to support units that are not directly related to combat, such as supply or maintenance. They are prohibited from flying fighter planes or serving in infantry or artillery units.

Here the argument is not an academic one. Women are living under the same austere desert conditions as men. It was two weeks after this camp was built before there were any showers. Meals are eaten outside on plywood tables while standing up.

The women here wear flak jackets and helmets and carry a rifle or pistol.

"I didn't think I was going into the combat zone," Dever said. "I didn't think women could go into the combat zone."

They can't, according to the Defense Department. But in the modern battlefield it is increasingly difficult to distinguish between the front lines and rear areas. "I don't know where it starts and where it ends," said Staff Sgt. Jacqueline Bowling, a 29-year old Marine from Nice, Calif.

Iraq's long-range Scud missiles have been aimed at air bases at Dhahran or Riyadh, not at combat units dug into the desert. There, women and men sit next to each other in bunkers as air raid sirens scream.

But women in specialties such as communications, administration and supply are also sharing the dangers and hardships of frontline units, especially in the Marine Corps, which believes in placing its logistics facilities as close to the action as possible. Because of its closeness to the front and the primitive living conditions, this logistics post is something of a field experiment in how well women can adapt to a combat environment.

"This is the furthest women have been in the combat zone," said Lance Cpl. Patricia Perez, a 20-year-old from Rochester, N.Y. "And I want everyone to know how much a part of it I was." For most it has not been an easy adjustment, but they say they now feel comfortable in these surroundings. "If I have a hot shower, I'm good to go," said Bowling, a platoon sergeant in a maintenance unit. "I don't think I have any more fears than the guys have," she said.

"I think we have the same feelings." Her husband, a Marine assigned to a nearby post here, was surprised to learn she was so close to the border. "I guess that's where that male ego kicks in," she said.

Women in the armed forces say they see a wide range of attitudes among men. "Some of them really try to help you out," Dever said. "Other guys say you're a Marine you just have to handle it. Some don't want you in the Marines."

In this part of the front, where enlisted troops spend much of the day filling and lining heavy sandbags, physical strength and endurance are important. "I'm a little more small and I have a lot of problems with the physical things," said Bowling, who is 5'1" and weighs less than 100 lbs. Others say they have no problem with physical chores. "I lift just as many sandbags as anyone else," Perez said.

Most of the women say the men they work with here are accustomed to working with females, since they have deployed with their units from the United States.

Still, there are difficulties that surface in a combat environment. Dever's job is to hook up field telephones. It can be a dangerous job, moving at night between positions.

But she finds that her supervisors would prefer to place her at the switchboard, a safer job, but one where she cannot get as much experience. Women join the military generally for the same reasons men do, for adventure or to gain skills. So they chafe under any restrictions that prevent them from gaining experience and getting ahead. "I just want to go out," Dever said, "just to learn my job better. I joined up for the adventure."

Overall, the role of women in this conflict is somewhat uncertain and still evolving. When Marines first came into Saudi Arabia, women were not brought because it was believed hostilities were imminent. But in subsequent deployments, women were sent here because the area was considered secure and because there was no one else to do their jobs. "At first they tell us we're out of artillery range, but who knows we may have to move up," Dever said. Already, rockets, which have a longer range than conventional artillery, have fallen in the area.

Perez, a chemical defense specialist, said she is capable of doing her job, but worries what effect a woman may have on the men in frontline combat units. For example, part of her job is to help frontline troops who have been contaminated by chemical weapons. "I'm pretty sure the men, after a month or two without seeing women, their loins start aching," she said. "And they see a woman and their needs aren't clear. They want to go into combat with a clear head. I feel that women in general should not be this far forward."

What ultimately may decide the fate of women in the military is the public's reaction to women dying or getting injured in battle. "The first woman to die will really cause problems," Bowling said.

"I don't think the public in general is quite ready to accept it."

Friday
January 25, 1991

For months leading up to the war in 1991, the northern Saudi desert throbbed with the sounds of a massive coalition army revving its engines, testing its weapons with live-fire exercises and cutting the mammoth desert down to size with its hives of helicopters. Information was scant about what the Iraqi troops were up to, other than persistent reports of acts of atrocity and plunder within occupied Kuwait.

For their part, the allies were carrying out a very public preparation for what was billed as a kind of Normandy invasion, with more sand in the gears but without the cliffs or flame-throwers.

By late January, the northern desert was no longer the weather-beaten, inhospitable, barely populated place it had been the previous August, before Iraqi troops seized Kuwait.

Now it was a weather-beaten, inhospitable, and thickly populated war zone. The look and sound of the future battlefield is in this chapter, in stories about soldiers who brought bagpipes to serenade the vast empty spaces, and the desert inhabitants who suddenly found themselves sharing their ancient camel trails with heavily armed newcomers.

Before the allies came, the Bedouins and camels traveled mostly off-road while those with vehicles traveled on narrow, sand-blown highways in modern sedans or white Toyota pickups. The squat, long-bed pickups were handy for giving their beasts of burden a rest, the camels looking like sullen, long-necked relief pitchers being transported to the mound. They were born to the desert and could always find their way without much signage.

Urban areas had lots of signs for motorized traffic—although U.S. information officers quickly gained an unwanted reputation for getting lost and confused while escorting busloads of press from Dhahran to military outposts—but out in the boondocks many kilometers could go by without a sign.

Yet the natives seemed able to get where they wanted to go.

The foreign army with its global positioning systems and maps and field telephones, computers, satellite dishes, and its almost obsessive need to know where everyone was going every minute also added signage—much of it no more than crude posts of wood, cardboard or metal, usually marked with a brushstroke of paint or an indelible marking pen.

Usually they were not very helpful except to the troops who stuck them there or already lived there because they shrank to near-invisibility when taken to the shoulder of the highway and poked down into the wide, swirling desert. The desert was hard on signs. It could make them disappear like gnats in a hurricane.

The U.S. Army's VII Corps, the multi-division unit comprising the allies' main attacking force for the coming land war, was still receiving supplies many days after the air war started. The supplies moved from ports and air bases thanks to continuous truck convoys, which often traveled too fast for the road and traffic conditions, but still not fast enough to meet the demands of a thirsty, hungry, beefing-up army. A story in this chapter describes the shortages that VII Corps still registered at this late date, some extremely critical to its vital mission.

Already packed with several U.S. divisions, VII Corps was due to grow even more massive. Split off from the Marine sector in the east, the British armored division was on the move, headed west to join the VII Corps.

In the original plan, the British tanks had been assigned to go directly into Kuwait with the Marines and help liberate that emirate.

But the Brits had sought be relieved of that mission.

Getting their one division to Saudi had required cannibalizing four divisions stationed in Europe. Gen. de la Billière, the top British commander, asked to be moved to a mission that might be perceived as more significant, more in keeping with the status of the Americans' main western ally: the envelopment and destruction of Saddam Hussein's elite Republican Guard.

That was the job of VII Corps.

When the British tanks finally reached their new location on the front, they would be ready to fight. But they would still need supplies, while no doubt on some maps, and some lists, the Brits would still be at their old location. Or somewhere in between, en route.

No doubt there would be more military-made signs stuck in the ground, just waiting for the desert wind and rain to go to work hiding them.

Some Desert Inhabitants Carry Weapons, Others Offer a Perfect Future to Perfect Stranger

By Mike Tharp

WITH U.S. FORCES - Up to 18 Iraqis, some carrying weapons, have been intercepted and arrested at checkpoints between Dhahran and the Iraqi border within the past week.

Local reports of the incidents were confirmed by U.S. military authorities in the area and elsewhere. However, Saudi Arabian police officials in Nuariyah, a town along one of the main highways in the region, downplayed the reports. A senior Saudi police officer attributed them to a recent investigation of a suspected Iraqi who was seen carrying a weapon in the area.

Eventually, the Saudi police officer said, the suspect was found to be a Saudi citizen with a legal weapon. He said 47 Iraqi citizens have been identified in the region since the Iraqi invasion of Kuwait, all of them Bedouin shepherds who traditionally have moved their sheep back and forth across the border without regard to diplomatic niceties.

"They are harmless," said the police officer. "To control the situation, we sent them back across the (Iraqi) border." He added that Saudi officials had given them food and tents before sending them back.

Nonetheless, U.S. military officials said they believed reports from guards at various checkpoints who had stopped Iraqis and seized at least one weapon. It wasn't immediately clear whether any of the Iraqis could be considered refugees or defectors.

Checkpoints manned by both military and civilian authorities have been erected all along major roadways leading to the Iraqi border. Many of them are choked with vehicles involved in the massive movement of troops and equipment to staging areas near the Kuwaiti and Iraqi borders with

Saudi Arabia. The buildup will support the United Nations forces ground attack to retake Kuwait whenever it occurs.

Security for the convoys clearly is a major concern, and the senior Saudi policeman said, "I'm ready to protect whatever I'm responsible for in this area to stop terrorists and spies."

ADDITIONAL DISPATCHES FROM THE FRONT:

Abu Mohammed is a man who hopes the war will pass him by.

Though legally a Saudi, the 55-to-60-year-old Bedouin is first, last, and foremost Muslim. He lives with his family—several wives, sons, daughters, and grandchildren in several tents off one of eastern Saudi Arabia's main highways.

But like all Bedouins, he and his family move across the desert with their herd of several dozen camels, sheep and goats.

Recently, he and two of his sons invited foreign visitors to sip camel's milk with them. Frothy and sweet, the milk came from a camel whose name translates as "Perfect" in English. "This means if you drink it, you will be perfect," he tells a guest.

Abu Mohammed says the only opinion he has about the war is that he is "on the side of Islam. They're all Muslims," he says of the Iraqi and Saudi combatants. "I'm just a shepherd. I pray for peace." As they depart, he offers to give his visitors a live sheep, but the offer is gratefully declined. He offers his hand and a parting comment as the foreigners walk through the ash-like sand to their vehicle.

"We have no thoughts. This is all for the governments."

(Note: His comments interpreted by an Arabic-speaking U.S. Army lieutenant.)

Royal Air Force Chief Returns Fire From U.S. General

By Ian Henry

The RAF chief who has lost three of his Tornado jets in the Gulf War hit back at criticism yesterday and fiercely defended the strike bomber he is using.

Group Captain David Henderson said he was "sick and tired" of the criticism, which was causing distress to families of the crews involved. There was no structural defect in the GR1 planes being used to attack heavily fortified Iraqi airfields, and he insisted the crews still had every confidence in their aircraft.

The group captain was angry at a retired U.S. Air Force general who described the performance of the RAF in attacking Iraq as "disappointing." He responded:

"That sort of language, I am afraid, makes me very disappointed that a senior retired officer would say things like that. Our performance is not disappointing. We have been very, very effective out here and we will carry on being effective. I don't think it is at all constructive for anybody on the Allied side to be criticizing us in this way at this time."

There had been lots of conjecture about the cause of the air losses, but the group captain said: "It is very, very wrong to speculate, and again it is distressing for the families involved that so much publicity be given to this aspect of the war."

Group Captain Henderson revealed there was still hope for another of the three crews lost from the Bahrain base. Two of the crews are in Iraqi hands, two are feared dead, and the other two remain unaccounted for. But the inactivity of the Iraqi air force remains a mystery because the Allied commanders have no clear picture if his air force is still intact or out of action. His airfields are ringed by hardened shelters which could be housing warplanes, and the fear is that Saddam may come off the ropes with a "killer punch" attack.

Group Capt. Henderson, base commander at Bahrain, said: "I think we are perhaps forcing him out a little bit more because if he doesn't get airborne soon his pilots will be very uncurrent, and the last thing you can afford to be in a war situation is to be uncurrent.

"We have given him such a pounding and shown no letup in our activities that we are well-prepared for him if he does come off the ropes. We fully expect him to do something, and we are not going to be caught unawares. But I just don't know how much longer the bombing will continue. We are given our tasks on a daily basis."

The group captain said Saddam had a lot of very well-built hardened shelters and quite excellent airfields. The desert airfields are built on 4,000-to-5,000 acre sites. "It takes time to knock out each one individually. The damage assessment can be excessively slow."

The "Half-and-Half" U.S. Division: Plenty of Officers, but Not Enough Fighting Vehicles to Train or Fight

By Douglas Jehl

WITH U.S. FORCES - Off they slogged into the mud, captains and lieutenants playing the part of an Army battalion and looking little different from a high school football team at midweek practice, pacing off a play they hoped to use in the big game.

"This is not going to be easy to do," warned Lt. Col. Stephen Smith, battalion commander ankle deep in muck Thursday morning as he walked his soldiers step by step through the fundamentals of a nighttime operation.

More than a week into the war, it is scenes like this one that remain characteristic here of preparations for a ground offensive, where Army units from Europe are still arriving in the desert and soldiers are only now beginning to maneuver in the sands.

"I'm only kind of half-and-half here," said Capt. Tracie Cleaver, one of the officers marching through the desert in the rudimentary battalion rehearsal. Of the Bradley fighting vehicles that give his infantry company combat punch, well fewer than half are now on hand. "It makes training kind of difficult," the 28-year-old captain said.

"Not having our vehicles has really put us behind," said Lt. Flip Hicks, a platoon leader in a sister company equally short of its armored vehicles. "We can train, but it takes some imagination."

On this day, Hicks' platoon was reviewing trench-clearing tactics on a sand-table, where pen-scrawled rocks represented Iraqi tanks and sugar-dappled sand served to highlight the deepest of the enemy bunkers.

The battalion is the last element in this Germany-based 1st Armored Division to reach full combat strength, with its final Bradleys and other equipment not expected to arrive in the desert until this weekend. But officers here said its still-incomplete status reflects a wider backlog that appears to have left the Army a number of days from being prepared to launch a ground offensive.

"I hope I've been the exception rather than the rule," said Smith, the mud-slogging commander, whose battalion's armored vehicles and other equipment were split among seven ships as the unit sailed from Germany after being mobilized Nov. 9, with the last vessel only now pulling into port. When some equipment landed in Saudi Arabia only to face days of delay before it could be trucked northward to the front, an exasperated Smith ordered that they simply be driven to combat positions here, a two-day roadside trek of more than 200 miles.

But other officers said that the Army unit, part of a 3rd Infantry Division brigade attached to this 1st Armored Division, remains far from alone in not yet being at full strength. Among those still awaiting key equipment, they said, was the 3rd Armored Division, another of the German-based units trained to fight the Soviet Army and added to the American buildup to give the United States some of its most formidable combat power.

"Everyone may have forgotten this with all the bombs falling and all," one Army officer said. "But we were never going to be fully up to strength by Jan. 15, and even if the war has started, we're going to need more time."

The concern over the late-arriving equipment Thursday came as officers in this unit were warned for the first time that terrorists had begun to operate behind U.S. lines near this forward-based American position. The officers decline to provide further details, but said the official alert represented a change from previous reports and assessments that had found no indication of any such terrorist operations.

Ready to Draw Blood, British Armored Brigade Moves North to a New Killing Ground

By Simon Clifford

WITH 4TH ARMOURED BRIGADE IN THE SAUDI DESERT - Traveling at regulation speed and at regulation distance apart, the convoy that is 4th Armoured Brigade sped along Saudi Arabia's super-highways to a new home somewhere close to the Kuwait border.

Everyone was aware of the risk from missile or aircraft attack—and everyone was issued with instructions on what to do: Drive off the road, scream to a halt, run from the vehicles, and then hit the deck.

In a vast ribbon of traffic stretching out of sight despite the view over the flat Saudi desert, the convoy moved out. It was leaving its training ground in eastern Saudi and was searching for a killing ground. 4th Armoured Brigade is ready to draw blood. It will link up with its sister brigade, the 7th Armoured, which moved several days ago to take up its own new strategic position.

The two brigades make up the famed Desert Rats. The 7th with its rat logo showing the tail on the ground. The 4th—in the words of its Brigadier Christopher Hammerbeck—with its tail up. Both brigades will be reunited and ready for action—but under the technical command of the U.S. forces.

The convoy moved the entire brigade, from tanks to toilet rolls, rockets to cases of non-alcoholic beers. For security reasons, I am not allowed to say where the 4th Armoured Brigade came from, when it left, which direction it took or where it is now.

What I can say is that I traveled ahead of the convoy and the hundreds of vehicles spread over a huge distance took hours to pass. And the new home is now in range of the Iraqi forces' formidable rocket systems—and some of its biggest guns.

Friday - January 25, 1991

That includes the feared RM21 rocket launcher and its Sarajeel cousin as well as artillery like the 283 and other heavy guns. After an intensive training programme finishing up with a major live-firing exercise, the 4th Armoured now knows it could come under fire night and day both from the Scud missile and artillery.

For most of today (Friday), I traveled at the head of the convoy but much of the heavy armour will travel at night—with no lights on, over desert tracks, just a tiny guide glow from the vehicle ahead.

Col. Mike Vickery, commanding officer of the 14th/20th King's Hussars, said getting the whole brigade on the road and fully "bombed up" would be a new experience.

"We have never had to do this before, so we are learning as we go along," he said.

His own regiment, with its impressive Challenger tanks, would be stronger than expected.

"We had allowed for a certain number of breakdown and losses, but we have had only a third of that number," he said. At his base there was a huge arsenal of ammunition for his Challenger and Warrior tanks laid out ready to be moved. The tanks themselves were loaded onto transporters for the long journey. Along the road the countryside changes noticeably from sand dunes, hummocks and scrub plants to a massive and uniformly flat plain.

It is vast desert. Along the verges, I saw numerous areas where new grass was springing up—a sign of the amount of rain we have seen in the past three weeks. Junk littered the side of the road, shrapnel from previous convoys along this busy highway. And there were signs too of some horrendous looking crashes.

In one place two coaches and a tank transporter had obviously hit head-on—they were smashed to pieces. Goats and camels, tended by small lads near the tented villages of the Bedouins, dotted the countryside—but the only busy areas were the roadside garages.

For owners, this war must have been a financial dream. Everyone is packed with soldiers buying anything from deodorant to radios. The people behind the tills all wear American combat uniforms, swapped for goodies inside. Restaurants are also part of the garage. Like a Little Chef in England.

One of these served me my first meal from a plate for 10 days today—chicken with rice, bread, and Pepsi—a feast. It was a little odd to see a wall-sized picture of snow on mountain tops as I ate, but that is life in the place—it is all upside down.

And as we travel along, the only attractive part of the scenery are the bright white mosques with tall minarets—and singing voices calling the faithful to worship. Troops came in anything that moves. The 1st Battalion Royal Scots started by coach, then had a plane trip and were picked up by a Chinook helicopter after that. Then they marched to wait for the arrival of the armour. Others came by coach all the way, and I spoke to some who traveled with their armoured vehicles.

As the mighty convoy passed me, names like Saddam Buster, Boom Boom Rats, and Haggar's Horribly Good Army rumbled by.

The men were all very aware of the risk from attack.

Lance Corporal David Woods, from Morecombe, said his mates were feeling a little scared. "It has brought it home to us now because we are so close to the border," he said. "We have only been exercising up to now, but this is the real thing." Others were more warlike.

"I want to get in there to smash this bloke. The British Army is on its way," said Lance Corporal Paul Leech, from Manchester. Trooper Darren Eddowes, from Barrow-in-Furness, said he was waiting for the arrival of his first child and was worried about his own safety. "We all know we can do it, but there is a risk and that is a lot bigger now we are up on the front than it was back where we trained," he said.

As unloading took place all around me, helicopters flew in and out dropping off kit and men.

The Desert Rats are back where they like it best—on the front line.

As Bagpipes Skirl, Desert a Kaleidoscope Extraordinaire Where a Tank Barrel Anchors a Clothesline

By Philip Stephens

WITH THE 1ST ARMOURED DIVISION, Eastern Saudi Arabia - The images etch themselves into your consciousness as deeply as the sand embeds itself in your hair. As America and its allies prepare for war with Iraq, they have turned the vast deserts of eastern Saudi Arabia into a kaleidoscope of the extraordinary.

It is there in the skylines filled by endless convoys of tanks, armoured troops carriers, towering trucks struggling with their loads of ammunition, food, soldiers. In the skies above, the clatter of helicopter blades competes constantly with the controlled thunder of jet engines.

At a camp carved out of the sand by the 1st Armoured Division of the British army, a general talks quietly about trench warfare 75 years ago in the fields of Flanders, about Blitzkrieg in 1940. He sees nothing strange in it. Generals never forget the lessons of history. In arid expanses stretching for scores of miles in every direction soldiers from Manchester, from Massachusetts, from Morocco prepare from their desert encampments to add another chapter to the history of modern warfare.

Shrouded in camouflage netting, the bases blend easily into the ever-shifting sand dunes, shaped and reshaped by biting night winds. It is only one step to the surreal. From the fearsome barrel of a Challenger tank a soldier has stretched a clothesline.

T-shirts and Y-fronts bought in Marks and Spencer hanging now in the Saudi desert.

Bedouin tribesmen look on bewildered at the lumbering frames of soldiers encased in chemical warfare suits, the gas masks and clumsy rubber overboots reminiscent of Hollywood's first science fiction movies. There is nothing of Hollywood, though, in the Bedouin camps—wooden and corrugated iron sheds, not flowing white tents.

The surrounding desert landscape is littered with sand-colored bus shelters; except there are no roads and no buses. They turn out to be the makeshift lavatories for 700,000 soldiers who must brave storms of flies during their daily ablutions.

It is not all ugly. In the blackness of a moonless night, the breathtaking beauty of the stars above a clear sky leave you impervious to the debris of the armies below. Miles in the distance, the gas flared from an oilfield lights a tiny corner of the desert with a warm orange glow. Sometimes you think that if you close your eyes you might open them again to the sands of the Mediterranean, not of Arabia.

But the harsh realities are never far away. At the camp of the Grenadier Guards, the young officers who will command the tank platoons storming Iraq's defences sit in the sand to listen to an army psychiatrist. He tells them how to cope with the horrors of war. They look unconvinced.

So often the ordinary is overlaid with the bizarre. In a petrol station supermarket, young soldiers push around shopping trolleys. It could be Saturday afternoon in Camberley, except for the rifles slung over their shoulders, the bayonets in their belts.

A Chinook troop-carrying helicopter flies north to the desert plains on which the battle for Kuwait will be decided. This time though it is carrying not men but haggis. It is Burns night and some things are sacrosanct even in the Saudi desert. For many—most—of the soldiers the extraordinary has become the commonplace.

There is nothing strange about the bagpipes playing almost within earshot of the Kuwaiti border. For many—most—of the soldiers the extraordinary has become the commonplace. And as they fill the daylight hours with the exhausting preparations for war, the soldiers have little time to dwell on the battle to come. But in the still of the desert nights, they too find it hard sometimes to disguise their disbelief.

Saturday
January 26, 1991

In this chapter, the story of the action in the Red Sea is raised a notch with the skipper of the USS Ranger outlining his mission to do away with the Iraqi Navy.

Given the sea power brought to bear in the region by the allies, it was a mission for which the outcome was all but certain. But that didn't mean the chances of casualties were zero. The Red Sea was a watery minefield, and mistakes had happened before when allied ships were on station there to monitor the oil tanker re-flagging operation.

For ground troops, the safest place in exposed terrain like a desert is usually a fighting position, a depression dug into the turf similar to what previous generations of American troops referred to as foxholes. A fighting position of today is definitely more elaborate than the Richard Widmark, Ernest Borgnine, or Audie Murphy models featured prominently in World War II movies. The modern versions might very well sport a portable CD player or boombox in addition to sandbags and camouflage netting.

Whatever they're called, the reporters who tackled this topic in the Gulf were all assured that two things about them haven't changed over the years. First, you'll look a long time before you find an atheist in them. Second, you can't dig them too deep.

The Scud-busters were engaged in their continuous battle with the enemy missiles, and when a Patriot succeeded in taking one out in mid-flight, it was "like a viper killing a rat," a story in this chapter says. But the Scuds weren't the only weapon in Iraq's basic arsenal. There were oil valves, for instance. From the facilities Iraqi troops had seized in Kuwait, millions of gallons of oil was pouring into the Persian Gulf, creating a massive ecological hazard and threatening the Saudi desalinization plants to the south.

Any threat to the supply of potable water in an environment like the Arabian desert had to be taken seriously. The allied army was a big army, and a very thirsty one.

The Iraqis and their sympathizers claimed the oil was set loose by allied bombing raids, but presented no evidence for their claim. The allies said their bombs had nothing to do with causing it. Some attempts were reportedly made after the spill appeared to bomb inland sources of the oil to curtail the amount that reached the water.

In the British sector, a story in this chapter tells us, some of the secrecy that armies always employ to keep their foes guessing was being practiced.

But it was no secret that the Challenger tanks the British had brought to the war were the envy of many a tanker. Saudi Arabia might prefer to think of its sandy, oil-rich homeland as the seat of the holiest site in all of Islam. Iraq might prefer to think of the land within its modern boundaries as the cradle of civilization. But there was one description of the land that was commonly heard in these parts during the Gulf War: This is great tank country, the

Saturday - January 26, 1991

military experts said. Vast, exceedingly flat, with a good surface for metal treads and plenty of room to maneuver vehicles that weigh tons and fire their guns for miles. The desert's best qualities were all in the eye of the beholder.

USS Ranger Determined to Wipe Out Iraqi Navy, if it Can Be Found; Ultimate Objective Full Control of Gulf

By George Rodrigue

SYNOPSIS: USS Ranger begins serious campaign to exterminate Iraqi navy, as American forces begin practicing huge amphibious invasion. Admiral says Iraqi AF is more active now. US pilots say weather continues to hamper them, makes their missions more dangerous as well as more difficult. Many mourn loss of colleague, but say grief can't interfere with mission. Dallas-area reservists form key part of Ranger admiral's surface warfare staff.

NOTE TO CORRESPONDENTS: Both technical problems and transmission problems delayed this file. That is to say, computer broke and we had nothing to write on. Then we borrowed a computer but were unable to send via satellite phone, because Saudis don't accept collect phone calls and Navy hadn't figured out how to make them at our expense and bill us. PAO aboard Ranger declined to use Navy message system because previous reports lacked news value. We'll try to do better this time. By the way, this dispatch quotes numerous Texans. I wasn't trying to be selfish, but they kept seeking me out and I hate to turn down an eager interviewee. Apologies to folks from lesser states. I will try to spread the wealth in the future.

ABOARD USS RANGER, in the Arabian Gulf - As American troops begin their largest amphibious landing exercises since Inchon, the U.S. Navy is stepping up its efforts to exterminate the Iraqi Navy.

Within the past week, A-6E Intruder airplanes directed by the USS Ranger have sunk at least 15 Iraqi naval vessels, mostly small patrol and utility craft.

American warplanes patrol the northern Gulf almost 24 hours a day on "armed reconnaissance," and have repeatedly attacked the Iraqi port of Urn Qasr.

Earlier this week, Rear Adm. R.J. "Zap" Zlatoper said the attacks were designed to keep open the option of an American amphibious assault. Members of his staff said the U.S. hopes in particular to sink the vessels carrying Exocet anti-ship missiles, which could threaten even relatively large U.S. warships.

Weather and the Iraqis have combined to make this difficult.

Low clouds complicate the visual identification pilots require before an attack, and the Iraqi Navy, like its air force, seems to have sought shelter more than combat.

"The Iraqis are not as aggressive as we had thought, but they are not as easy to find as we had thought, either," said Capt. Marc Liebman, a Dallas reservist who is among the leaders of Carrier Group 7's tactical information center.

EXTENT OF DANGER: Navy officers say the Iraqi boats, and the oil platforms that conceal them, pose several dangers. Straddling the routes used by American attack planes, they give early warning of bombing raids and threaten the safety of downed pilots. Some have fired at U.S. warplanes, and many of the patrol boats are believed to carry the French Exocet anti-ship missile.

"I think if you look at the ultimate objective, and that is full control of the Gulf, the FTBs, the Osas, the other patrol craft tend to introduce an element of lack or complete control over the sea here. So there is no question that we have got to take them out," said the USS Ranger's Capt. Ernest E. Christensen.

"The Exocet is what we're really worried about," said Lt. Chris Eagle, 27, of Wheaton, Md., an A-6 navigator-bombardier. "I'd hate for my stereo to get wet, and my personal computer is insured against everything but combat damage."

(ADDL POOL NOTE: Cdr. Mark Lawrence, 38, Syracuse, NY., intel officer for USS Theodore Roosevelt, said the Navy's also attacked coastal Silkworm sites. These missiles, with a range of about 50 miles, are considered a threat to allied ships. Navy has destroyed many sites, the commander says, but it cannot be sure which are actual installations (Iraq was believed to have two) and which were among Iraq's numerous dummy sites. For the sake of certainty, it will continue attacks until both dummies and live sites are obliterated)

Capt. Liebman, who has helped supervise surface-warfare planning, said that in his personal opinion, Mr. Hussein is willing to sacrifice thousands of Iraqi lives to sink a U.S. carrier, battleship or cruiser. "If he could trade his entire Navy for one major U.S. combatant, I think he would do it for the propaganda value alone," he said. "He would have wounded the Great Satan."

The Iraqis have scant chance of success, he added. "But you have got to honor the capability, keeping in mind that the Iraqis are familiar with the Exocet. . . . Once you get rid of the missile patrol boats, the rest of the Iraqi navy is basically of nuisance value."

All Quiet on the American Front, Except for Scraping of Shovels: "Every Day You Dig a Little Deeper"

By Robert Dvorchak

WITH THE 82ND AIRBORNE DIVISION - The scrape of shovels hollowing out bunkers and filling sand bags grates against the quiet on the American front lines. Every few yards, infantrymen from lowly privates to officers to chaplains pound the ground with picks and tools to gouge out havens against artillery and mortar shells.

"I'm going to dig more and more until I can't dig no more," said Pvt. Gregory White, 20, of Los Angeles, CA, who has been in Saudi Arabia only six days but is now a forward scout with the 2nd Brigade of the 82nd Airborne Division in northern Saudi Arabia. "Each shovel I scoop out means I might save an arm. The next shovel means I might save a leg. Each shovel could be a part of the body you're protecting," White said.

Dig, dig, dig. If you're lucky, an engineer can scoop you out a bunker or a fighting hole with the scoop of his backhoe. Most have to heft personal entrenching tools, flat-faced shovels and picks to do the dirty work.

The first priority of any infantryman in a new location is to dig in to make yourself less vulnerable. The first shallow hole is called a "hasty" or a "run and dive." They provide sparse protection. But each day, infantrymen improve them, scooping deeper into the rocky dirt and piling more sandbags on top. "You should keep digging until somebody can't find you," said Col. Ron Rokosz, 45, of Chicago, IL, commander of the 2nd Brigade. "It's a mental thing. It puts you in the right frame of mind."

Saturday - January 26, 1991

The brigade is camped within seeing distance of the border separating them from Iraqi positions. No one needs to be told how vital the work is. "It's a constant process. Once you dig the first one, you keep improving. It never stops," said Maj. Baxter Ennis, public affairs officer for the division. "With each passing hour, we get stronger."

Most of the brigade has been at its new home in the desolate Saudi desert for less than a week. Their Iraqi counterparts have had over five months to dig in.

Forget laser-guided bombs, satellites that can pinpoint a location within 10 meters from any point on earth, gadgets that turn night into day. The infantryman's mind is on the unglamorous task of filling bags with dirt.

"Sandbags protect your ass. We're taking no chances," said Sgt. Leo Philip, 25, of St. Croix, Virgin Islands. He and his squad stayed up till 11 p.m. one night this week, filling bags by the light of a half-moon and a dazzling array of stars. They filled 800 nylon and burlap bags, building a hootch that had four-deep layers of bags on the sides and the roof. It's not lowly work. "If it'll save my life, I'll be more than happy to fill sand bags," said Pfc. Bryan Richards, 20, of Victorville, CA.

Some people even used steel bowls to scoop and scrape dirt in the blister-inducing toils. Only a reinforced concrete pillbox can absorb a direct hit from a 200-pound artillery shell. But 18 inches of dirt can stop an AK-47 round. And officers figure it takes about 150 sandbags per infantryman to protect him from the indirect fire of artillery and mortars.

"When that incoming round is coming, how good do you want your bunker to be," said Sgt. George Johnson, 22, of Kansas City, MO, a chaplain's assistant.

The ideal bunker is dug to the depth of the armpit of the tallest man. Then four layers of bags are placed on roof beams for maximum protection.

Some bunkers get to be like home. Capt. Scott Barrington, 29, of Chester, VA, always builds an earthen shelf in his to lay his rifle and personal gear. Maj. Carl Horst, 35, operations officer for the 2nd Brigade, has two bunkers, one in the brigade area and the other on the forward lines where he does his scouting. "Infantrymen have been digging in for hundreds of years. We're continuing in the fine tradition of our brothers," Horst said.

The men dig like gophers but they act like wolves. They scrape and scratch out a shelter to protect them from their enemies, then use their dens to begin hunting in packs. "Your hole's never deep enough. The deeper you are, the better chance of surviving you have," said 1st Sgt. Jim Southerly of Delta Company, 2nd Battalion of the 325th Infantry Regiment. "In a case like this, every soldier takes the shovel in hand with a purpose. I dig this damn hole so myself and everybody around me will survive. Every day you dig a little deeper. Every day you make it harder to penetrate," Southerly said.

The only incentive people need to dig is knowing you're close to the other guy's big guns. Some paratroopers even argued over whose turn it was to use the pick. "It's like camping at the foot of a sleeping volcano," said 1st Lt. Steven Swanson, 29, of Reno, Nev.

British Armored Unit Travels Into "Great Tank Country" on Forged Convoy Papers

By Richard Kay

WITH 4th ARMOURED BRIGADE, Eastern Saudi Arabia—The map showed a thousand square kilometers without a contour.

And when the light came up it was clear the grids hadn't lied.

Bleak, flat, and as desolate a landscape as you are likely to see, the only relief coming from the Challenger tanks being disgorged by the squat low-loaders.

A tank commander, who flew in on a Chinook to rejoin his 62-ton beast, looked across the plains and declared: "Great tank country, great fighting country."

We were at the "RP," 4th Brigade's receiving point where for hours now men and machinery had been assembling as though from a never-ending conveyor belt.

The armour came by road in a logistics operation of mind-boggling dimensions, while the infantrymen dropped out of the sky in helicopters.

As I write this in a Military Police bunker, the din of that operation is all around. The huge 26-wheel transporters bring a pair of Scimitars on one, a Challenger on another. Behind is a line of Warriors with, between them, the breech-busters and giant recovery trucks or carriers. The Chinooks flutter out of the sky shuttling soldiers from a desert landing strip where they had been flown to by Hercules. Within the coming 24 hours, we shall have joined with the men of 7th Brigade to provide the heaviest division of British men and armour for 40 years.

The orders to move had come a day earlier. The instructions passed down to us by the Brigade Commander.

With such a vast convoy on the road, 5,500 men and 1,600 armoured vehicles, security was a priority. We would, they said, be a sitting target for an opportune Iraqi strike bomber. So if an air attack came we were to drive off the road, grab our gas masks and tin hats, and leap into the desert.

For reasons I cannot tell you, we traveled on forged convoy papers, so good not one security patrol doubted their veracity. But if our papers were not all they should be, our convoy discipline was perfect. We traveled at a steady 40 mph, maintaining the correct 50 metres between vehicles.

Our route took us into the afternoon sun on roads empty of civilian traffic.

On hummocks in the sand, American Humvees with their 50-calibre Browning machine guns stood sentry while helicopter gunships of the MRS, Main Route Security, patrolled the skies above us. For 45 minutes we stopped at a roadside café for a late lunch. Somebody remarked how good it was to eat off plates for a change.

But we tore the roast chicken apart with our fingers.

At a checkpoint, an MP in fluorescent vest was a shimmering mound in the sand behind his tripod-mounted general purpose machine gun. Dug into the shale around him were the black-and-white army movement signs of the kind you see dotted around any of our garrison towns. In our direction, the road was chocked with loaded supply lorries, heading the other way, empty trucks going back for more. By the time they finished, the drivers would have clocked 1,200 miles, a round circuit in the sand.

Sometime before dusk, we stop at a "rolling re-plen" where huge fuel bowsers pumped diesel into 14-ton Bedford ammunition trucks, eight at a time with 40 gallons in each. Now we were heading off

Saturday - January 26, 1991

the metalled road into the desert, where heavy rain and heavier tracks had churned the sand to the consistency of glue.

We slept beside the vehicles under a canopy of CARM, chemical agent repellent material, that we weighted down with shovelfuls of mud, mindful that a tear could expose us to the noxious poisons in Saddam's armoury.

Throughout the night, as the machinery of war roared by us, the sound of allied bombers looking for Iraqi targets thundered overhead.

Air support is everything, the cornerstone of all our hopes.

Hunkering against the bitter wind, you begin to silently wish them Godspeed.

For the infantrymen of the Royal Scots, with whom I shall be going to war, and the Fusiliers and Staffords, air attacks are the lifeline. And a comfort in all its power and precision.

By morning the mud of the previous evening has set hard; digging trenches may not be easy but now that we are within reach of Iraqi artillery, the motivation will be. The 1st Armoured Division is in place, their training complete, their supply lines secure. We now await nothing more than the signal for battle.

Life in a U.S. Army Tent is Dusty, Cold, and Coed But Not a Problem

By Laurence Jolidon

WITH U.S. FORCES - The dusty green tent I'm living and writing this story in is about the temperature of the vegetable bin in your refrigerator. Well, maybe a little colder.

I can see my breath in the light of two bare light bulbs hanging from each of the main rafter poles. I'm wearing long Johns, shirt and jeans, leather jacket, a British camouflage cotton cap, and I'm mainlining coffee and chocolate candy. If I could type with leather gloves on, I'd try that. My feet are cold inside my boots.

At 9 p.m., it's down to last night's low of 38 degrees Fahrenheit and dropping, with a stiff breeze for added wind chill. There's one floor heater for the entire tent and it's at the end of my cot, in the aisle, but I can't feel any heat from it.

I'd give $100 for the heat stroke I nearly had last August when I first arrived in Saudi Arabia to begin covering the deployment of troops. I'm sure it's even colder up north, in Iraq, where the people in this tent expect to be soon.

I'm sharing the tent with ten soldiers—men and women, officers and enlisted. They usually live in separate tents. But this is an advance party of a headquarters company. The few tents that fit in our allotted number of vehicles that brought us here from base camp must be shared until the rest of the company brings the rest of the tents and supplies.

In a week, people will be separated again—men from women, officers from enlisted personnel. But for now we're living together as though there are no difference between the sexes and few distinctions between an officer and a private first class.

We all take off our pants one leg at a time. We all get up during the night to relieve ourselves. We all talk about being homesick, or cold, or mad at something stupid one of the officers or sergeants did that day. I'm fortunate. I wear a lot of the gear and equipment the soldiers do, but I don't carry a weapon and no one orders me around. I can leave here anytime. That confuses some of the soldiers.

The two most-common questions I'm asked—in those off-guard moments when

I'm digging around in my pack for my toothpaste or deciding if I can go another day without washing some socks—are these: Did my paper order me to cover this story? And, do I get paid extra for covering a war? When I say no, they sound genuinely amazed. "Wow, man, then I'd be outta here," one will say, and I make a mental note to tell my editors how respected the American press is among the young soldiers.

Our 11 cots, made of light aluminum and canvas, rest in two rows the length of the tent. Three women—the military calls them "females"—are scattered among eight men. One woman is a sergeant. The other two are "specialists," one rank above private first class. One man is a major, one a captain; the rest are enlisted. Inside this tent, for now, we are more like a family, a coed fraternity or co-workers sharing a summer cottage than a disciplined fighting unit.

Strictly combat units are all-male. This headquarters company is about ten percent female, and could be involved in combat but is scheduled to move into areas already secured by combat troops. The women are ready to fight. They all carry M16s and wear helmets and flak jackets, of course.

We arrived at this advance site near the Iraqi border, after dark, about 10:30 p.m., so we slept the first night outside on cots or inside the vehicles. We moved in here the next afternoon, assigning ourselves a space for a cot, duffel bag, and pack.

The base camp we'd just left had hot showers and spiffy sand "sidewalks" lined with hundreds of sandbags. This camp was bare, rocky ground, damp with rain and not a bush or tree in sight for as far as we could see. The first day, the colonel in charge let women bathe in his tent. They filled plastic dishwashing pans with water and got clean. The next day, they said they appreciated it, although they often say they don't like men to defer to them.

They're anxious to be accepted as equals except in one way. Most readily admit they're not as strong as men. Instead of one carrying a big plywood plank for a tent floor, two will carry it. "Not a problem," as soldiers say.

The women prefer sleeping in mixed tents to all-female tents. "Tents with men are much better," one said. "A tent full of women is disgusting. They all want to be in charge, and they're sloppier. Everyone's on the rag (having a period) at the same time. And their language is filthy, much worse than with guys."

The sun goes down about 5:30 p.m., but work around the camp doesn't stop. Tactical briefings are held. Soldiers assigned to maintain 24-hour communications sit inside trucks to monitor message traffic. Troops from another unit nearby stand guard duty (this unit is too small to staff its own guard roster.)

Maintenance people repair vehicles and equipment using lights with red filters. "Light discipline" forbids any white light that might give away positions to the enemy.

Despite all this activity, the only noise I can hear now is a large generator about 50 yards away, whining like a race car. Some troops worked all day filling sandbags to stack around the generators to muffle the noise so the colonel wouldn't be kept awake. The camp's biggest generator is still very noisy.

. . . We're living close to the French sector, and the French have been calling most of the chemical alerts around here. Either they have more sensitive noses or their chemical detectors have hair-triggers because their alarms always go off before ours.

After a day of frequent French alerts, we heard they'd been told that allied airplanes destroyed an Iraqi chemical agent factory and winds from the north were blowing the poison our way. That made us feel better about all the alerts, which turned out to be false alarms.

Saturday - January 26, 1991

When we moved to this advance site, assigned to battalions of Army engineers, the war was already underway. Allied air squadrons were pounding Iraq and Kuwait day and night. Patriot missiles were blowing Scud missiles out of the sky. Navy warships were firing missiles at targets miles inland. The Army and Marines were moving into position for a ground assault. And we were taking little white pills three times a day. The pills are supposed to increase the effectiveness of the injections we'll have to give ourselves if we're hit by nerve gas. Inside the canvas carrying case for a chemical mask, we also have three sets of anti-nerve agent serum.

Each set has two syringes—one of atropine, the other pralidoxime chloride. The atropine is the size of a large crayon. The other one's as big as a large felt marking pencil. The little white pills are a source of some mystery and suspicion.

The six injections we're supposed to knock ourselves out with if nerve gas hits are very nasty-looking items and make people cringe when they're visualizing jabbing them into a thigh to save their lives. We all carry a syringe of Valium that only a medic or corpsman is supposed to give us after we've been hit with all the anti-nerve serum.

The soldiers have been told that the serum is so strong that after pumping that into their system, a shot of Valium will be necessary to spare them brain damage. Yet the little white pills are to make the serum work better. Military doctors say the pills have no side effects, but some soldiers complain the pills made them "wired" or tense.

Some called them "my birth control pills." One young soldier in this tent makes morose jokes about how the pills are probably untested and so "my kids will all come out looking like freaks. It's another Agent Orange deal," he says.

After a few days, we were told to stop taking the pills because a few days' worth is enough and, besides, they're in short supply "in this theater."

Not a problem.

This afternoon, our chemical alert only lasted five minutes and we were allowed to stow away our gray rubber masks.

It wasn't the French this time. Acrid smoke from the pit where our human waste is burned from the latrines had set off a nearby chemical detector. The detectors are supposed to react only to dangerous chemicals.

One officer said later the pills we'd been taking might have contained some of the chemical agents they're meant to overpower and the residue survived being flushed through our bodies, turning the smoke from the waste pit into nerve gas.

There's a lot more to learn about this chemical warfare business, if you ask me.

In the tent, someone who's worked all night is usually sleeping and another soldier is often strapping on all the battle gear—helmet, cartridge belt with canteen, ammunition, first-aid kit and handgun, flak jacket, chemical mask bag and rifle slung low over one shoulder—and striding off to work.

Everyone is polite most of the time. Those who've known each other for months make crude jokes about the others, but it's all friendly, and usually has something to do with sex or the lack of it out here in the desert deployment.

Everyone shares—candy, gripes, information, letters, music and living space.

One specialist hung a line of laundry over the cot of a sergeant across the aisle. The sergeant made jokes about it but didn't order him to move it.

A private first-class jumped on a sergeant writing a letter in his sleeping bag and tied his wrists to the bag's drawstrings. Nobody got uptight about it.

Everyone makes allowances for the fact that we're living in harsh, cramped conditions that no one would choose if they had another immediate alternative. We're all in this together. Most importantly, we share the knowledge that we're soon headed for a battle zone and we could be together longer—or more briefly—than we'd like to be.

There are few secrets in the tent. One of the women is sick. One of the men has trouble sleeping. One woman is in love with one of the men. Sometimes they quarrel.

They often stand outside the tent after dark, talking and smoking. We keep reading, typing, eating, or sleeping.

Today we were told we'd all have to be checked for a skin infection because one of the cooks had come down with "crabs" and we are all in danger of being infected.

We weren't supposed to know who the sick person is, but within minutes everyone knew. And we discussed whether the infection was a result of sex or something else.

Tomorrow, enough tents will be here from the old base camp to return to the normal segregated sleeping arrangements for this headquarters company.

But I'll be moving to another camp. It's an all-male combat engineer unit and my public affairs escort is a female, so I don't know how they'll handle the tent issue.

She prefers mixed tents. We both prefer warm tents.

So as long as there are tents, it's not a problem.

Biggest Artillery Attack Since War Began: Marines Zero in on Iraqi Positions

By Kirk Spitzer

NORTHEASTERN SAUDI ARABIA - Elements of the 1st Marine Division staged the largest artillery attack of the 16-day-old Persian Gulf War early Saturday, pounding Iraqi positions just 27 miles southwest of Kuwait City.

A battalion-sized task force of 155mm howitzers and other equipment fired on suspected Iraqi positions about six miles inside Kuwait, near the L-shaped "elbow" of the border with Saudi Arabia, according to officers at division headquarters.

Three Marines were killed and two injured in a vehicle accident related to the attack. An Iraqi vehicle was destroyed during a brief firefight along the border, but no U.S. casualties were reported as a result of combat.

Injuries to one of the Marines was described as not serious. The condition of the other was not known. At least one of the Marines was evacuated by helicopter.

The attack was staged at about 1 a.m. Saturday by an artillery task force from the 1st Marine Division, firing from a position only a few miles inside the Saudi border.

An artillery battalion typically consists of three batteries of eight guns each. Previous Marine artillery attacks have been carried out principally by a single battery. No assessment of damage was available and the type of target was not released. Because of Defense Department security regulations, exact details of the engagement cannot be reported.

Saturday - January 26, 1991

Mine-Clearing Class Preps Marines for Hidden Dangers, Buddies Who Could "Disappear in a Big Pink Mist"

By Patrick Bishop

WITH U.S. MARINES, Saudi Arabia - A bitter wind was cutting across the desert and most of the Marines looked as if they wished they were somewhere else as Staff Sergeant Rick Taylor took them through the mine-clearing procedure for the third time that morning.

"The reason for all this is so that when your buddies disappear in a big pink mist and body parts are flying, you'll know what to do," he shouted.

Sgt. Taylor is a former boot-camp drill instructor and conducts training in a hectoring parade-ground manner. Earlier he had warned "all you Rambos with the knives dangling from your gear. If you're with me and one of these things hits a mine I'm going to crawl out on my bloody stumps and choke you out."

Sgt. Taylor's methods may be undiplomatic but they bring a badly needed blast of the foul reality of war to the young men in his charge. The Marines are combat engineers, the troops who when the land war starts will be at the front of the front line, clearing away the formidable band of obstacles the Iraqis have constructed to block the coalition advance.

It is as dangerous as any task on the battlefield but with little compensating kudos.

U.S. intelligence believes that in Kuwait the Iraqis, following Soviet military doctrine, have bulldozed several concentric rings of sand "berms" and ditches, stretching from the border to Kuwait City.

Having negotiated the sand wall and moat, some possibly filled with flaming oil, advancing troops will then have to contend with minefields, razor wire, and tank traps as well as artillery and machine gun fire from the Iraqi defenders. This operation, the Marines believe, will have to be repeated several times before they reach the much more formidable defenses around the Iraqi redoubt of Kuwait City.

According to Lt. Chris Simmler, 23, from Franklin, MA, the initial fortifications should not present too difficult a task. "The troops are a conscript force and we are not expecting that much resistance," he said. "They are saying that a lot of these might surrender." In keeping with the prevailing Pentagon philosophy, the Marines are hoping that air power will do most of the work, supplemented by artillery. It is believed that the two could destroy 80-90 per cent of the mines before the combat engineers move in with line charges, which are fired forward to set off mines in their path, bulldozers and the humble hand-held mine detectors.

At Sgt. Taylor's class the Marines were taking what was billed as a refresher training on the latter. A sweeper moves through the danger area, locating the mines and marking them, followed by a prober who pinpoints them with a wooden stake and a demolition man to blow them up. The Marine chosen to lead off the hunt for a buried metal obstacle looked as if he was learning for the first time, failing to remember the elementary procedure of trailing a foot to mark your passage.

The bulldozers will be used to push aside mines and breach the berms. Only one of them on show was armoured, with improvised steel plates welded to the scoop and cabin.

Air superiority or not, Sgt. Taylor's commentary was brutally frank about the experience that might lie ahead, baldly detailing the procedures if the man ahead of you is shot down.

In their training, the Marines say they have been told to expect to be frightened. "Everybody has a little fear, but one thing the Marine Corps has taught us is to overcome that fear," said Lance Cpl. Carlos Morales, 20, one of the few Marines from New York City. "How? With morale, discipline, esprit de corps. Things like that."

Sgt. Taylor's candor, the Marine Corps admission that combat will not be the glorious business celebrated in its own anthem, is a corrective to the ersatz violence of Sylvester Stallone and Arnold Schwarzenegger films, which must have impressed themselves on the imaginations of many of the young Marines.

His vivid description of the reality of modern war, the pink mist and the flying limbs, also gives the lie to the sort of pasteurized television images that military censorship was struggling to ensure are all that are shown to the world.

The Sound of a Distant Whump Means the Patriot Heroes Are Hard at Work: "We Got It!"

By Guy Gugliotta

EASTERN SAUDI ARABIA - It begins with the alarm, a banshee scream cutting across the darkened compound like a ripsaw.

The Patriot launch team, napping fitfully, comes awake in an instant. Within seconds, scores of soldiers burrow deep into sandbag bunkers, grab their radios and prepare their ambush. "It's coming in this direction," said Sgt. William Salmon, 23, of Stillwater, Okla., the radio operator in Bravo Battery's command post. "We have inbounds. We have inbounds. Scud launch. Scud launch."

"We've got them on the scope," said Capt. Joe DeAntona, 25, of Scranton, Pa. "Here it comes." At 3:37 a.m. Saturday, Bravo and Alpha Batteries of the Second Battalion, 7th Air Defense Artillery fired Patriot anti-missile missiles at an incoming Scud rocket.

"We have launched," DeAntona said, the quiet banter of the bunker replaced by an expectant silence. Long seconds passed, then came the sound of a distant whump. Salmon ducked his head, listening hard, then put the receiver down: "We got it."

In the past eight days, 2nd Battalion has killed ten Iraqi Scud missiles over a sprawling airbase in Eastern Saudi Arabia. The battalion tracks the Scuds, locks them into a powerful set of radars and lets them come into striking range of the thin, arrow-like Patriots, flying sticks of dynamite that can travel at speeds greater than Mach 2 and generate 30 Gs of force as they twist toward their targets.

The end is quick and clean, over in a flash, like a viper killing a rat.

The Patriot battalions are the first heroes of Operation Desert Storm, protecting cities and vital installations from the Scud salvos of Iraqi president Saddam Hussein.

Patriots have had mixed luck in Israel and the Saudi Arabian capital of Riyadh, where Scuds have caused some significant damage and a few deaths. 2nd Battalion, however, has never missed, and the battalion prays that it never will.

For now, they are the most popular people at the airbase.

"After we got our first one, I called the Air Force and asked them to lend us a forklift to reload our canisters," said DeAntona, a blocky 1984 West Point graduate, whose

Saturday - January 26, 1991

senior sergeants have nicknamed him "Spanky" because that's who he looks like. "The second time, they called me and asked me if I needed the forklift. And they sent the operator."

The fame of the airbase's Patriot batteries has spread throughout Eastern Saudi Arabia. On the beachfront at a nearby town this week, townspeople were picking up little pieces of Scud debris to cherish as souvenirs.

In the lobby of the Dhahran International Hotel, a piece of Patriot bearing the inscription "We Love You" sits on a pedestal. Dozens of reporters who live there have penned love notes on its lobster-colored skin.

Friday night, Saudi soldiers in a pickup truck delivered a 12-foot-long piece of Scud fuel cell to battalion headquarters as a token of appreciation. The Air Force security patrol has sent cookies and brownies after particularly nasty nights, and Bravo Battery is hoping for pizza the next time.

Throughout all this, however, the men and women who fight the batteries remain largely anonymous, stuck off on squalid corners of the airbase, alone in a sea of desert sand, stones and windblown bits of trash. To hear DeAntona tell it, his people prefer it that way.

"The soldiers don't want to leave—this is their home," he said. "We had an opportunity to move off-site. I didn't favor it, but I put it to the kids. Not a single soldier wanted to move." And even less now. As night fell Friday, the Patriot soldiers rushed to finish a dinner of hamburgers, French fries, and strawberry cake, not wanting to waste time during the dark hours when the Scuds are most likely to fly.

The battalion canteen is only 100 yards from the Bravo Battery command post, but DeAntona became visibly impatient over a second cup of coffee.

"I went to town once in early December," he said. "I can't remember the last time I left the site. But I don't mind. A lot of my people take cots down to the command post to sleep there. Saves time."

At dark, the entire battalion was in Mission Oriented Protective Posture 2, wearing full chemical protective suit with gas masks strapped to the waist. It was to be a reasonably hectic night, busier than most, not as busy as some. The alarm shrieked a "Scud alert" for the first time shortly after 7 p.m. In seconds, DeAtona and 13 essential members of his crew ran to the Bravo Battery command bunker, a pair of concrete culverts sunk in sandbags a few steps from their sleeping quarters.

In the bunker, DeAntona every night monitors the progress of each attack from a radio telephone linked directly to his three-member fire control team, shut up in a van with the Patriot's computers.

The Patriot system selects its targets, tracks them and fires automatically, but the fire control team monitors every part of the intercept. The van is inviolable during Scud attacks. There is no time for distractions.

Minutes after the command team was in place, Salmon passed the words "Scud launch." He paused for a moment, listened: "Four launched toward Israel." "He's going to hit Israel again," Salmon said. "Son of a bitch," said a voice from the gloom. "I hope those guys in Tel Aviv are ready."

The Patriot battery receives its alerts and target information from a variety of sources, but once the Scud attack begins, the amount of information digested by the system is so complex that a single battery is unable to decipher it until its analysts have pored for hours over computer printouts. Often, said DeAntona, "the people on CNN (Cable News Network) know what has happened before we do."

Soon, a transistor radio tuned to the Armed Forces Radio and Television System was broadcasting reports from the Israeli capital: "Several missiles have landed," the radio said, and a little bit later, "from the trajectory it looked like a Patriot or a Scud."

"He's a genius," said a voice inside the Bravo command post. "Pack it up and go to Israel?" said another voice. "Let's do it. They want to play hardball? Let's do it."

After a half hour, DeAntona turned to Salmon: "I think we're in for a long night. Remember the last time. He fired at Israel, Riyadh, and then us."

Twenty minutes later the all-clear sounded. The command bunker emptied, leaving the radio behind to play Eric Clapton: "I Shot the Sheriff."

The peace and quiet lasted for about a half-hour before the alarm sounded again. This time there was no launch. Chief Warrant Officer Gerald Roberts, 49, of Fresno, Calif., Bravo Battery's leading mechanic, complained that he hadn't had time to finish a letter: "Every time I tell them nothing is happening we get hit."

And again just before 10:30 p.m. This time Salmon reported "Scud launch" and "incoming," but after a few minutes he said, "It's Riyadh, this time, so we're next."

Sunday
January 27, 1991

Even after the Iraqi invasion, it was possible to find some news from Kuwait. A small resistance movement survived, whose members produced some intelligence from within the tiny country.

Caryle Murphy, a Mideast correspondent for the Washington Post, was there when the invasion happened and managed to remain inside the occupied emirate for some weeks, hidden from Iraqi patrols by sympathetic Kuwaitis who also helped her ship her stories out. From time to time, Kuwaiti citizens who had recently left Kuwait City would show up in Saudi Arabia and give accounts of life under Iraqi authority.

For everyone fortunate enough not to be living there during the war, though, the curtain drawn around Iraq by the crisis was as opaque as a Muslim woman's veil.

All airports were on the allied target list, and no civilian air traffic moved. Land border posts were closed to all but the intrepid or foolish. Most resident foreigners had fled or were in hiding and the Iraqi media were on the shortest leash imaginable.

Some foreign reporters from CNN and the BBC and a few aid workers managed to stick around in Baghdad and broadcast from the capital, but their movements were tightly restricted by Iraqi authorities. Yet their eyewitness reports were valuable as occasional glimpses of a country rapidly going dark under the daily and nightly bombing.

A Canadian writer managed to reach Baghdad overland from Jordan while the bombing was going on, but stayed only five days, according to his own account, and most of that time was spent indoors, dodging allied shelling attacks.

On this day, the international press reported that more than 100 nurses from India who had been working in Baghdad hospitals when the first bombs fell were missing, but few details were available. Had they been arrested for suspected allied sympathies? Had their hospitals been shelled, turning them into patients too? Or had they joined the exodus trying to flee to safety?

No independent observers were allowed to pursue that kind of story. Such reports, unsubstantiated but wholly believable, simply stood for the chaos, fear, and panic that it was assumed filled the hours of those who were witnessing the allied bombing campaign at the business end of those bombs.

CBS correspondent Bob Simon and three members of his crew had gotten inside Iraq from the south—by driving north out of Dhahran and walking across the Saudi-Iraq border a few days after the bombing started.

They only made it a few yards before Iraqi soldiers took them prisoner and they were transported to Baghdad. They couldn't see much from their small isolated cells, however, and had no way to get word out anyway. So by definition, most information the public had of what was occurring in Iraq during the Gulf War was hearsay.

Even with no verifiable news out of Iraq, there could be no denying that a massive oil spill had occurred off the Kuwaiti coast, which allied officials blamed on the Iraqi troops who had taken charge there. The oil slick grew larger and more menacing every day. Stories in this chapter deal with the first sighting of the slick by a Navy pilot, and the rumor that it had somehow caught or been set on fire which at least could be checked on sight.

Without access to people and documents inside Iraq, there was no realistic way to fully investigate the oil spill, or look into why the Iraqis had caused it, if in fact it was deliberate. Perhaps it was simply more wanton destruction, as Saddam Hussein's worst critics alleged. To truly know the answers, it would be necessary to climb inside the wily Mr. Saddam's skull.

Saddam Hussein periodically announced that continuous allied bombings had killed civilians, sometimes scores of them. Clearly some civilians, perhaps even dissidents or Saddam-haters, had perished in the onslaught of bombs, bomblets, and cruise missiles. But separating fact from propaganda was impossible.

After the war, an investigator for Greenpeace International, which opposed the war, estimated that between 2,500 and 3,000 Iraqi civilians died as a direct result of the bombing campaign. He said he had been allowed to visit, unescorted, many of the sites bombed by the allies a few months after the war ended.

In addition, he and an employee of the U.S. Census Bureau estimated at least 70,000 Iraqi civilians died afterward, in the final ten months of 1991, as a result of bomb damage that drastically worsened health and medical conditions throughout Iraq. Their estimate was based on reduced life expectancy.

The allies regularly expressed great concern that civilians were dying in Iraq as a result of their bombing. But they insisted the fault lay with Saddam Hussein, who could end the bombing by getting his troops out of Kuwait.

In this chapter is a story that portrays the allied concern over casualties they assumed their own troops would suffer, once a land war began, and how some of the preparations for large numbers of dead and wounded were more than enough, others not enough. As for Iraqi military casualties, that was another hearsay topic.

Gen. Schwarzkopf and his top deputies, recalling the manipulation of "body counts" of Viet Cong and North Vietnamese troops in the Vietnam War, set a policy that estimates of Iraqi military casualties were not to be announced by the allies.

With a few exceptions, the policy was followed. But after the war, military and civilian agencies in the U.S.—not to mention a host of critics of the war—delved into the topic. Research into the subject was closely linked to various estimates of how many Iraqi troops were actually stationed in and around Kuwait, where the allies staged their land offensive.

Early in the allied deployment, western intelligence estimates said up to 500,000 Iraqi troops—half the Iraqi army, counting reserves—were in the Kuwait theater. By the time of the land invasion, the Iraqi force had been cut by death and desertion to an unknown number.

Post-war estimates of Iraqi war deaths varied widely, from 8,000 up to 80,000. So far as is known, the Iraqi government never announced its own official figure.

Sunday - January 27, 1991

U.S. Projects 10% Casualties on Front Lines: "First Time They Have to Write One Off" Will be Very Upsetting

By Douglas Jehl

WITH U.S. FORCES, Saudi Arabia - American commanders have warned Army doctors that some front-line U.S. combat units can be expected to suffer casualties of 10 percent over 30 days under current plans for a ground offensive against Iraq, according to officers familiar with the official estimate.

The prediction of battle losses remains tentative, the officers stressed, and applies only to the forward-based forces who would be expected to break through Iraqi border defenses or drive further into enemy-held territory and thus face the brunt of Iraq's resistance. But doctors at a forward-based medical unit that would provide early treatment for some of these soldiers say they have spent much of the last week unloading emergency supplies, including morphine and casualty blankets, that have been delivered to the unit in preparation for what most say they believe will be a bloody battle.

"We'll have some jumping to do when it all starts," said Maj. Paul Whittaker, commander of a medical support company in the 1st Armored Division that would operate within artillery range of enemy forces if the United States were to launch an attack.

"We get a lot of classes on trauma, trauma, trauma," said Spec. Russell Page, a 21-year-old from Greenwood, Miss., who is a medic in the unit. "They say, 'Expect a lot of blood.'" With the supplies still pouring northward and the unit fully manned, officers in the medical company said they now felt secure they were amply stocked for combat.

"War's not pretty," said Chief Warrant Officer William Gleason, a physician's assistant who would maneuver on the battlefield in an armored ambulance, "but really, I think we'll be up to snuff." Indeed, so vast has the stockpile become that some in the unit, which serves an entire brigade, said they were convinced that preparation had turned to overkill. But, Sgt. Dan Penkoff of Irvin, Calif., added after a moment's afterthought: "I guess in war you can never have too much."

With this heavy armored division still preparing for combat from an assembly area a comfortable distance from the front, the pace at the hospital unit Saturday remained that of a lazy afternoon, with empty armored ambulances parked in a wagon-wheel around the camp, and soldiers heading off for a religious service before lunch.

The few technicians hard at work were analyzing vials of urine to test for pregnancy—part of what doctors said had been a slew of such submissions from women soldiers recently arrived in Saudi Arabia.

But in war, officers said, the seven doctors could be expected to handle as many as 60 patients in a two-hour period, each of them rushed directly from the battlefield or from emergency aid stations closer to the front.

Moving forward as the armored brigade advanced, the medical company would seek to stabilize the conditions of the most severely wounded before sending them by helicopter to field hospitals further to the rear, doctors said. Those only slightly wounded would be patched up and—"so long as a soldier tells me he still knows how to shoot his gun," one doctor said—dispatched back to the front.

In describing what they imagined their work would be at the pitch of battle, the officers said they expected to see their command in frenzy, with medics used to augment trained doctors and patients treated on tarps outside tents and trauma units that could be filled to overflowing. As caretakers to an armored unit, they said they expected to treat many burns—the result of tanks lit afire by enemy projectiles. And with injuries from modern weapons likely to be severe, they said they had recently been reminded, as medic Page put it, "to save life instead of limb."

For these doctors as for most soldiers, though, combat remains an experience known only by imagination, and the one medic in the unit with extensive combat experience said Saturday he believed most of the medical staff still had "adjustments to make." "The doctors have to make the transition," said Chief Warrant Officer Jim Daly, 48, of Medford, Mass., an Army medical officer for the last 28 years, who served a long tour in Vietnam. "It's really hard. Physicians are people who have devoted their lives to taking care of each and every patient, and in war you just can't do that.... The first time they have to write one off—that's going to be pretty upsetting to some of them," Daly said.

Among particular dilemmas facing doctors in any ground war here is the prospect of soldiers severely wounded while under chemical attack, leaving them in need of time-consuming decontamination before medical treatment could begin.

"The problem," said Whittaker, the company commander who is chief of ambulatory care at Wuerzburg Army Hospital in Germany, "is that when you take a breathing tube or whatever and put it through that contaminated skin, you put that nerve or mustard agent inside the person. You're hurting them to help them."

At the same time, with any U.S. advance likely to seek to sweep across enemy territory as fast as possible, some doctors said they recognized that they may well encounter ambulances unloading wounded Iraqis as well as American soldiers.

"My personal feeling is that all things being equal, I would have a tendency to want to see the American soldiers treated first, when it actually comes down to it," said Capt. Steve Blaha, a 28-year-old Army dentist from Lincoln, Neb., who will take over triage responsibilities in the unit if the ground attack begins. Blaha added quickly: "Personal feelings aside, I will do whatever Army policy is."

Iraq Laid About a Half-Million Mines in Kuwait: "This Guy Knows What He's Doing and Likes Mines"

By Jeff Franks

WITH THE U.S. MARINES IN NORTHEASTERN SAUDI ARABIA - Iraq has laid half a million mines in Kuwait and is expected to scatter many more throughout the tiny emirate as it readies for an assault by allied ground forces, U.S. Marine officers said.

The mines are part of a formidable array of Iraqi defenses that include 12-foot tall berms, oil-filled trenches, and buried storage tanks filled with explosive butane. Most of the mines are strung in two belts just north of the Kuwait-Saudi Arabia border, but Major George Cutchall, a U.S. Marine mine expert, said that virtually all of Kuwait is likely to be mined by the time the ground war begins. "Kuwait is going to be turned into one big minefield," Cutchall said in a recent interview.

Cutchall said that 500,000 mines in the ground is a "conservative estimate" and that Iraq has as many as 20 million mines in its arsenal, many of them gifts from once-friendly countries such as the U.S., France, the Soviet Union, and even Kuwait.

The mines range in power from anti-tank charges that can blow a 60-ton M1A1 tank five feet off the ground to tiny "toe-poppers" with just enough explosives to blast the foot off a careless soldier.

Some of the mines are high-tech wonders in which computer chips are programmed to time when and how they go off. Others, like the "Bouncing Betty," are simply frightening. When stepped on, the Bouncing Betty pops four feet into the air and explodes. Marines said it has been known to cut its victims in half. "This guy (Iraq) knows what he's doing and he likes mines," Cutchall told about 100 grim-faced Marines gathered in the desert for a lecture on mines.

Cutchall said satellite photos indicated that between December 19 and January 5, Iraqi troops laid 60 kilometers of mines in a belt behind its border defenses in eastern Kuwait.

There are signs that another belt is being installed near Kuwait City, he said. Also, Cutchall said, Iraq is expected to scatter mines from the air, using helicopters and special artillery, in the rest of Kuwait.

The mine belts, more than a kilometer wide, front 12-foot-tall berms and deep trenches that the Iraqis hope will stall tank attacks. Many of the trenches are expected to be filled with burning oil once an assault begins and some have highly explosive butane-filled tanks buried in front of them, Cutchall said.

"He (Iraq) doesn't plan on losing," he warned the Marines.

Cutchall said explosives and tanks equipped with plows can clear paths through the minefields, but that there are so many mines that ground forces must move about carefully once they cross into Kuwait. He told the Marines not to charge into areas that have not been cleared. "This ain't the war to be out there playing Rambo," Cutchall said. Also, he advised the troops not to pick up war mementos because any object on the ground could be a mine or a booby-trap.

"You can't afford to souvenir-hunt in this war," he said.

Fortunately, the Iraqis have marked most of the minefields with barbed-wire fence so their own troops do not wander out into them and get blown up, Cutchall said. But those markers may come down or get knocked askew by allied bombing attacks, he said.

Also, as the allies move forward, they will have to be wary of their own mines, which will be installed around bases they set up on captured territory. Militarily, the minefields and barriers present the ground forces' most difficult problem, said Marine Lt. Col. Mitch Youngs, commanding officer of a battalion attached to the 2nd Marine Division.

They are designed to slow the advance of tanks and troops so that the Iraqis can rain artillery down on them, he said. "He basically wants to channelize us into what we call 'killing zones,'" Wilson said in an interview.

To counter the threat, ground forces have trained extensively on how to breach the barriers as quickly as possible. When they get bogged down, they either move to another location or call in air strikes from jets that will be buzzing around the battlefield waiting to hit Iraqi targets. Cutchall said that mines, as they did in Vietnam, are likely to cause the majority of American casualties. But this time it will be the mechanized units—not the infantry, as in Vietnam—that suffer most because their tanks and other vehicles will bear the burden of breaching the Iraqi defenses.

Youngs refused to speculate on how the ground war will unfold, but said that ultimately the outcome will hinge on the battle between the men, not the machines.

"In the last 300 yards, it basically comes down to that young Marine getting in his fighting hole and killing the enemy before he kills you," he said.

U.S. Navy Pilot Spots Large Oil Slick off Coast of Kuwait; Act of Desperation or Just Despoliation?

By George Rodrigue

ABOARD USS ROOSEVELT - Saddam Hussein has succeeded in flanking his troops in Kuwait with a 50-mile-long by 20-mile-wide oil slick, according to a U.S. Navy aviator who flew over the site Sunday morning.

The aviator, who asked not to be named, said the oil formed a golden slick from Kuwait City south to the Saudi Arabian border, and was growing. More oil seemed to be emerging, and the slick was being spread by 25-knot winds from the north, he said.

Videotapes the aviator shot at about 8:30 Sunday morning show large but broken patches of oil, which did not appear to significantly dampen wave motion. For that reason, the aviator said, he believed the oil was not terribly heavy. The oil does not appear to be terribly flammable, either. The aviator said a ship was ablaze amidst a slick, but the oil around the ship was not burning.

Rear Adm. Dave Frost, who commands the battle group centered around the nuclear-powered super-carrier Roosevelt, said his staff cannot determine whether the slick might impede military operations. "It seems like an act of desperation to me," he said. "I suppose he might have thought it would interfere (with) our ability to move close to his coast and to operate against his Republican Guards in Kuwait with gunfire support and an amphibious landing. Don't know yet whether it will be an interference, but other than that it seems like a desperation tactic.

"We don't know yet whether it will be an interference," he said. "We do not have lot of experience operating ships in oily waters."

Most naval vessels distill their drinking and washing water by drawing seawater, he noted. "Right now, the ships are in no danger because the oil is a long way from the ships," he added. He said he believed the U.S. could deal with the problem in various ways, including bombing raids to break the oil pipelines far from the water. "The best solution is to go in and retake Kuwait and deal with it that way," he said.

USS Roosevelt's intelligence officer, Commander Mark Lawrence, 38, of Syracuse, N.Y., said his staff believes the Iraqis cannot set the oil afire, because it disperses too quickly.

On the other hand, he said the Iraqis can continue to pump oil into the Gulf "pretty much indefinitely, from what we have been told. There are a lot of oil terminals."

OTHER ITEMS from Commander Lawrence:

Another Iraqi island surrenders. This one is called Maridum, just off the coast. An A-6E Intruder from the carrier USS Ranger was flying over the island Sunday and saw below, written with stones, the words "SOS We Serrender." CQ that spelling: Serrender.

Cmdr. Lawrence says the Iraqis had put 20 to 30 men out there as forward observers, but had not been able to supply the island for at least a week.

Neither ships nor aircraft have contacted the men directly yet, he said. "We will probably go and pick those guys up." Successful early raids against the Iraqi command and control and shore installations will allow the Navy, like the Air Force, to step up its attacks on Republican Guard and other inland Iraqi soldiers.

U.S. aircraft find few Iraqi fighters in southern part of the country, save for those protecting Scud sites and Baghdad. We shot down three MiG 23s last night, from such bases. "There are now more U.S. fighters over Iraq than Iraqi fighters."

U.S. doesn't know what to make of Iraqi air flights to Iran. Notes, however, that they are leaving without the guns and missiles needed for tactical strikes. So inclined to believe Iranian statements that the Iraqis will not be leaving before the war is over. He believes 12 Iraqi F-1s have flown to Iran.

Huge Oil Spill Seeping from Sea Island Terminal Has Not Been Set Afire

By Susan Sachs

(We were under tight restrictions on this trip. The seven pool members were accompanied by four Marine PAOs, two senior Saudi officials, two Saudi drivers, and a Saudi police officer in a marked car. In connection with the oil spill, the special ground rules are that neither the name, rank or brand of military service of our escort/interviewee at Khafji can be identified.

(He will be referred to, per JIB demands, as "a senior American officer" at the scene. We were not permitted to view the spill from any location other than the one chosen by the PAOs.

(In addition to debunking the report that the oil spill is on fire, this officer also related some interesting points on the frontline war.)

RA'AS AL-KHAFJI, Saudi Arabia - The oil slick seeping into the Persian Gulf from Iraqi-occupied Kuwait is not on fire and never was on fire, according to a senior American military officer in charge of this northern border coastal town.

In an interview today on the cold, rain-swept waterfront where a dead cormorant and oil-blackened rocks testified to the effects of the oil spill, the officer said he can easily see all the way to lights of Kuwait city at night.

"There's no oil on fire," he said. "I think people are viewing the bombing reports and now it's become a circular thing, with rumors feeding on rumors."

The officer said he was called last night—"late in the evening" (Saudi time)—by commanders who asked to verify if reports of fires were true. He said he told his callers that the oil was not on fire. Khafji is about 110 kilometers from Kuwait City and about 65 kilometers from the Sea Island terminal, the facility that U.S. and British authorities say is the source of the oil spill.

The officer said he has seen evidence of fires on sparsely-populated Failaka Island northeast of Kuwait City. He has not seen fires in Kuwait City itself and backed up the statements of U.S. military officials that the allied bombing raids did not hit oil-filled tankers at the Kuwaiti port.

The reported fires may actually be from the oil pit at Kuwait's al-Wafra oilfield, dynamited by Iraq last week, the officer said. Secondary fires are still burning from the oil terminal at Khafji, hit by Iraqi fire the first night of the war.

The particular slick of oil washing ashore at Khafji has now reached down 40 kilometers south to Ra'as Meshab, according to the officer. However, your pool was not permitted to check this out.

The officer said the slick "has taken a drastic turn for the worse in the last three days," although rough weather in the Gulf appears to be churning up the oil and dispersing it. He said the slick "appears to be one-half inch thick." He said he has seen previous oil spills in California, particularly the Santa Barbara spill, and "this is worse." "I don't know what his design is. I call it scorched ocean policy."

The oil slick poses no military threat: "Boats run fine," the officer said. "You can't light it. It doesn't foul the engines that badly. And you have filters in engines. I consider it a senseless act." He said he thinks "the valves are still open up there" at the source of the oil spill, probably Sea Island. "I base that on the fact that it keeps coming," he said.

What we saw were oil-stained rocks at the foot of the desalination plant at Khafji. The plant has been closed since a day before the war started and its workers sent south. Globs of oil clog a concrete culvert leading to the plant. There have been no efforts to erect booms or other containment devices by the closed plant, according to the officer.

He said that bringing civilian workers in to try to contain the spill "would be very dangerous. He (Saddam Hussein) can move very small mortars at will at night and take pot-shots and it would take us a while to shut them down."

However, the officer said that artillery and missile firings on multinational forces in the area have diminished since the first night of the war, when Iraqis fired 45 Astros and three Frogs. The second night, he said, they fired 28 Astros and two Frogs. The third night they had 13 Astros and then none for the next few nights.

"It's a supporting arms duel," he said. "He shoots multiple-launch rockets at night and we have air attacks 24 hours a day." He said Iraqi ground positions at the border are being hit by A-6E Intruders at night and F/A-18 Hornets, Harrier jump jets, and A-10 tank killers during the day. "Our contact with Iraqi ground troops has been line-crossers," he said. The forces have taken and sent to camps 31 POWs from the entire Kuwait-Saudi border.

Generally, they come over in the early dawn hours, "when they can escape their own officers." They come waving "a white skivvy shirt" Most have not eaten for two or three days. All claim not to be line soldiers: "We got 31 cooks," said the officer.

Although the desalination plant is big and well-known facility, the Iraqis have not been able to touch it with their fire. "The first night, we knew he'd respond with whatever he had in artillery," said the officer, "and he missed the plant and he missed us."

"Frustrated Cargo" King Creates Plywood Surplus: "If We Occupy Kuwait or Iraq, We Can Build"

By Mike Tharp

WITH U.S. FORCES IN SAUDI ARABIA - Maj. Frank Timmons of the 937th engineering Group continues a long and almost honorable military tradition. Like the legendary supply officer Milo Minderbinder in "Catch 22," whose aircraft ferried goods to all sides in World War II, or the James Garner character in "The Great Escape" who scrounged his way to freedom, Timmons gets things for his men and women.

Take plywood. You want plywood? Timmons has some, about 45,000 sheets stacked in an area of desert north of Dhahran. And not just any old plywood. Finished mahogany plywood, 1/2-inch or 3/4-inch thickness, from Brazil, Malaysia, Indonesia and Canada.

"I've swapped," says Timmons, a 42-year-old New Mexican who came to the

Sunday - January 27, 1991

Saudi desert from an assignment at Fort Riley, Kan. Swapping is of course another almost honorable military tradition. During Operation Desert Shield/Storm, it has become an operational necessity.

Because many U.S. units were ordered to Saudi Arabia quickly, many were unable to keep a steady flow of supplies once they headed for the Persian Gulf.

As a result, many units have come up short on the supply side. Often, it's not that supplies are unavailable, simply that a unit isn't plugged into the right computer or submitting the correct paperwork. Enter Maj. Timmons. In Kansas, he had been an engineering equipment and maintenance officer. In Saudi Arabia, he became a scrounger. Upon landing, he discovered that his carefully planned transfer of his unit's supply channel had disappeared into the bowels of a bureaucratic computer system. The technical term for equipment and supplies with no forwarding address is, appropriately, "frustrated cargo."

At one point, for example, more than 3,000 tents sat on the dock while field units "were screaming for them," Timmons recalls. "For awhile it was the same for concertina wire, pickets, MRE (a kind of boxed food) rations. The theater wasn't mature enough to respond to requisitions electronically."

So Timmons started trading.
Plywood for oil and air filters.
Plywood for long underwear.
Plywood for better rations for his troops.
Plywood for the use of a forklift.
Plywood for five trucks.

Timmons continued an ancient Mideast tradition: barter trade. Instead of the souks and bazaars of Araby, the supply officer did his deals throughout the Desert Shield command. Soft-spoken with a tangy southwestern twang, Timmons and his blond mustache could pass for the Marlboro Man. He would hand-carry requisition authorization forms, rather than merely submitting them through channels, then sit and schmooze with his colleagues about hunting and fishing.

Once he even stopped by the office of Maj. Gen. Gus Pagonis, director of all supply operations in the Saudi theater. "I got his signature to get some tents," says Timmons. "What was he going to do—send me to Saudi Arabia? The worst he could do was say no."

Timmons returned twice more for additional approvals.

Now Timmons and his unit are literally pulling up stakes and heading north toward the Iraqi border, preparing to support United Nations forces' ground attack on Kuwait and, if necessary, Iraq. The major, who has college degrees in engineering and geography, is leaving his precious plywood behind, under guard.

One recent evening, he stood atop a sandy berm and looked down at the stacks piled high in the desert. "What's going to happen to it? I don't know," he mused.

"It's at least $35 a sheet in the U.S. If we have to occupy Kuwait or Iraq, the lumber is here—we can build."

He paused. "It all comes down to one thing—supplying your soldiers."

Monday
January 28, 1991

Reports out of Iran said that more than 80 Iraqi military aircraft have so far escaped the allied net around the belligerent country and flown to safety across the Iraq-Iran border. The Iranian position was that the Iraqi planes had been "confiscated," but that they would be returned after the war was over.

Since both countries had long-standing mutual demands for reparations from their 1980-1988 war, that sounded suspicious. And in fact, six months after the war, British journalist Phil Davison quoted Iranian sources and British experts as saying some of Iraq's warplanes from the confiscated stash were being flown by Iranian pilots, who found the MiGs and SU2 fighters superior to their own models.

But under the circumstances (i.e., any Iraqi aircraft moved out of underground hangars was immediately targeted, with allied rockets up the tailpipe for the slowpokes) Iraq's air force preferred planes be "confiscated" rather than demolished, which is what happened to the ones that tried to get away but failed.

Iran opposed the allied war against Iraq, but not to the point of actually wanting to mix it up militarily. So when it was suggested the Iranians might use the Iraqi planes long enough to have a run at the allies from its airfields, U.S. Secretary of State James Baker said he thought that was unlikely. Such a move would obviously widen the war. The Iranians stayed out of it, and collected more than 100 Iraqi warplanes. If Iraq was counting on getting all its military aircraft back right away, it was disappointed.

In the allied air campaign, the pace was unrelenting. U.S. Navy fighter bombers off the USS Roosevelt took advantage of a break in the weather to go after a petroleum complex and a SAM site. A story in this chapter not only recounts the missions, but leads the pilots into a discussion of the collateral damage issue, and what that adds to their complex duties.

From a U.S. Air Force base in Saudi Arabia, a story develops the theme of women in air service. At the time, women were barred from flying combat missions. That would change after the Gulf War, and today women can qualify for scarce assignments in the elite ranks of fighter pilots. But the vast majority of women in the Air Force—just as the majority of men—are all assigned to the type of slots described here, jobs that keep the planes armed and flying.

Along the Kuwait border, the Marines were taking their artillery on the road, so to speak, staging raiding parties that delivered 200-pound projectiles to unsuspecting targets in Iraq. The account of a gun battery named "Peace Maker" brings the sound, the look, and the feel of these pre-ground war actions to life.

Along Turkey's border with Iraq, the mood was one of containment. The Turkish position on ground war involvement was manifested by the presence of more than 100,000 Turkish troops lined up on the frontier, ready to repel any uninvited guests.

Monday - January 28, 1991

In the constant puzzle of trying to identify people as friend or foe on the desert battlefield this chapter has a story about a man who said he was a major in the Saudi armed forces. But he was naturally asked to show his papers, and then things got a little sticky.

Another story in this chapter tells of a group of Kuwaitis celebrating. Most of Kuwait was still part of Saddam Hussein's experiment in terror, landmine-laying and oil spill-making, so their joy might have been seen as premature.

But few had faith in the allied cause to match the Kuwaitis. So when a few Kuwaiti sailors managed to find a small island claimed by Kuwait and free it, they saw a trend in the making. The liberation of Kuwait had clearly begun on the sandy spit called Qaruh. To the faithful, the rest was only a matter of time.

Friend or Foe? Man in Saudi Uniform Indignant at Interrogation, But Allied Soldiers Taking No Chances

By Charles Richards.

Major Malaiyat al-Otaiba of the Saudi border guard was not a happy man. Or at least that was who he said he was.

A burly American lieutenant in Kevlar body armour was not so sure. He was on the radio of his Humvee general purpose vehicle trying to raise someone from military intelligence who could come and interrogate him.

A low-profile Hemmit (HEMTT— Heavy Expanded Mobility Tactical Truck) truck with rockets for a Multiple Launch Rocket System stood idly by. Two American soldiers stood watch with their rifles across their arms.

"His license plate doesn't check out," the lieutenant explained. He was fairly sure that the man was who he said he was, but was not prepared to take chances that he was in fact an Iraqi saboteur infiltrated across the border.

The Arab looked forlorn. His long grey sheepskin *farwa* cloak lay on the sand in a rough bundle in front of his Toyota land cruiser.

A butterfly, a cousin of the European tortoiseshell, skipped from pebble to pebble near his feet, in one of those episodes of bright sunshine between the wintry showers.

The man was dressed in the desert uniform of the Saudi army, similar to the Americans but greyer, as though it had been washed with a dark colour that had run. His undershirt was ringed with grime around his chest. He had a wispy black beard sported by many of the Bedouin of Saudi Arabia in deference to the example of the Prophet Muhammad, despite the military advice that beards should be shaved off to ensure a close fit of a gas mask.

He pleaded for reason. He was, he said in broken English, known to the joint U.S.- Saudi liaison team down in the valley. It was his job to patrol the area. He was on the same side. If his car did not check out it was because it had recently been repainted.

Why didn't the lieutenant take him down to the police post to check him out there?

There was no point in bringing another more senior American there if he didn't know him and couldn't get him out of the mess.

For a Saudi major to be detained on his own turf was ignoble indeed. The Americans, however, are on alert. Any civilian or unknown vehicle in the region risks being shot at.

Rules of engagement are classified, but are believed to provide first for the safety of U.S. forces. American commanders, with their memories of the U.S. Marine barracks being blown up in Beirut in a suicide car bomb attack, are wary of suspicious vehicles in the vast desert plain.

They are on their guard against infiltrators and pro-Iraqi sympathizers in Saudi Arabia. Each morning before dawn, U.S. Army units stand to on the perimeters of their encampments to guard against possible attack. Passwords which change daily add to security.

The problem of identifying friend or foe is complicated by the presence of forces in the theatre of operations, the Syrians, Egyptians and the Kuwaitis, with armoured or infantry weapons or both similar to those used by the Iraqis.

A number of Iraqis have come across the border to defect. But the question remains, how many are genuine defectors? How many were sent across deliberately to lure the Americans into a false sense of security at the state of Iraqi morale?

How many others have insinuated themselves into northern Saudi Arabia, either to carry out missions of sabotage (there are no reported cases so far) or to spy on U.S. and multinational troop movements and concentrations? The Saudi authorities are taking few chances. They announced the day that hostilities commenced that the maximum penalty would be exacted upon anyone violating national security.

Marines Make Peace at Midnight With 80 Pounds of Powder, Bomblets That Turn Armor to Swiss Cheese

By Colin Nickerson

NEAR THE KUWAIT BORDER, Northeastern Saudi Arabia - 11:55 p.m. There is a purr of hydraulics as automatic loaders insert the 200-pound, anti-armor projectiles into the breeches of the hulking, 203 mm mobile howitzers of the Marine raiding party.

On Gun No. 3—which bears the improbable nickname "Peace Maker" daubed on its cannon—Cpl. Tobias Rios, 27, of Elizabeth, N.J., rams home an eight-charge: 80 pounds of black powder trussed in a canvas satchel.

Nearby, teeth chattering with cold, Pvt. Douglas J. Hanneken, 24, of Winchester, Mass., readies to relay fresh loads. Like his fellow artillerymen he is charged high with equal parts adrenaline and fear. Enemy batteries and missile launchers are near, too near. "This is what we've been training for," Hanneken said. "This is the moment we've been dreaming of and dreading."

11:57 p.m.

Breech locks snick shut. The hydraulics are growling now as the long guns adjust for the target, an Iraqi military supply depot located a few miles across the border.

The wind is bitter cold, numbing the faces and hands of the howitzer crews, bringing the tears streaming from unsorrowful eyes. "Better them than me," grunts Staff Sgt. Robert Vasquez, 30, of Waterbury, Conn. "Better them, period."

11:59 p.m. Comes the order: Stand by. Then, almost instantly, the command:

"Fire!" The howitzers boom. Tongues of flame lick the blackness. The tremendous recoil of the weapons jolts the desert floor. A rank wash of cordite fouls the air, briefly blots the moon. The gun crews feverishly reload, firing at will.

This morning's 2nd Marine Division artillery raid was the largest ground attack so far launched against Iraqis positioned in Kuwait. Basically a hit-and-run strike, it involved two fast-moving Marine batteries—one of the big 203mm M110A2 self-propelled howitzers, another of 155mm guns—backed by mobile rocket launchers and a screening force of amphibious assault vehicles and infantry.

"The purpose is to harm and harass the enemy, to keep him on his toes then knock him on his butt," said Capt. Mark Murphy, commander of the 203mm battery. "We move in quick, hit hard then boogie out of Dodge. By the time he hits back, we ain't there." Each battery unloosed 36 rounds in a matter of minutes. The outgoing shells whistle-whooped through the air, the sound fading, fading . . . then a flash on the horizon. Dozens of deadly glimmers reflected off the clouds—followed, after a few long moments, by the muffled thunder of impacting rounds.

"Dropping a load dead on target is a damn complicated science," said Cpl. Matthew Speese, 27, of Jacksonville, N.C., whose job is to jerk the firing lanyard on Gun No. 3, the Peace Maker. "You've got to factor in a hundred variables, from the temperature of the powder to the velocity of the wind. But believe me, we can drop these babies dead center into a trash can more than 10 klicks away." A "klick" is military slang for a kilometer.

Of the howitzer's nickname, Sgt. Vasquez said: "It is not meant to be funny. Saddam Hussein has created a situation where the only way the world is going to find peace is by blasting him and his war machine to kingdom come. It is sad, it is tragic. No one is laughing out here." The daring close-to-the-border raid was mounted and fired in about 15 minutes.

Prop-driven OV-10 Bronco spotter planes swooped near the targets, calling in coordinates, confirming "secondary" explosions signifying a hit. The 203s fired "dual purpose" rounds, equally lethal to men and machines. The shells, basically bombs carrying more bombs, explode before hitting earth, flinging out scores of bomblets whose bursts of shrapnel can lay waste to structures, punch holes through light armor, and generally wreak havoc upon enemy mechanized units or fixed installations. They can take out an artillery battery or missile launcher, and transform a light tank or troop carrier into something looking very much like Swiss cheese.

"It is the deadliest round this battery packs," said Hanneken. "It lays down a wicked pattern of metal spray." The 155mm howitzer battery blasted Iraqi positions with white phosphorus incendiary rounds followed by salvos of shells containing "Bouncing betty" anti-personnel grenades. These hit the ground, hop-frog into the air and explode at about stomach level. "Gut rippers," they are called, the scourge infantrymen.

"Jesus God," muttered Cpl. Lee Wolverton, 22, of Enterprise, Ala., as the howitzers barked, the orange flames plumed and the whump-boom of impacting rounds rolled back to the ears of the young men who had fired them. "Jesus God have pity on their souls." He added: "You want to damage the enemy, you want to kill him and destroy his might. But you can't help but sometimes remember those human beings under that firestorm. Damn, I hate that man Saddam for leading his country to death."

American troops are expected to launch more and more such high-powered ground raids in the days leading to a major land offensive. And the Iraqis are expected to become more proficient at striking back.

Last night, however, the enemy was unable to bring his guns and missiles to bear before the Marines made fast tracks to the south.

Within seconds after lobbing out the last rounds, the long cannon were lowered and engines coughed to life. In a loose column they churned back across the rain-soaked sands.

The withdrawal was the more dangerous part of the mission as each Marine waited fearfully for the incoming rounds that never came.

There were no serious wounds; the only injury was a bloody nose suffered by a Marine whose face was pressed too close to a sighting instrument when his cannon recoiled.

"Hey, Doc, do I get the Purple Heart for this?" he joked to the Navy corpsman peering at the gash.

"If you're lucky, Marine, you'll get a Band-Aid and if you're real lucky I'll toss in a couple of Tylenol," the medic joked back.

The mission was complete. The batteries had had their first taste of combat and come through unscathed.

There was laughter and wild boasting at the fallback point. "We came out in the night to do a job and we did it," said Sgt. Brendan Bailey, 29, of Clinton, Mass. "We didn't take casualties, and that's real good. I'm pretty psyched up. But I'm not forgetting we've got more fighting down the line."

Kuwaiti Sailors Kiss the Liberated and Beloved but Mostly Uninhabited Sand of Tiny Qaruh Island

By Keith Kendrick

Kuwaiti sailors told last night how they "kissed the sand" of their homeland for the first time since the Iraqi invasion six months ago.

"It is now only a matter of time before our country is returned to us," said a Kuwait Navy captain. The sailors were flown ashore Qaruh, the tiny island liberated by allied marines two days ago, to raise the flag of Kuwait and reclaim it for their people.

"It was a very emotional moment. It made me very happy," said a 29-year-old captain, whose name cannot be used because he fears for the safety of his wife and child still trapped in Kuwait.

"I kissed the sand and raised the flag of my homeland. We are the first Kuwaitis to return to our country since Saddam invaded, but soon many more will follow. It is a matter of time before he is forced to leave."

He added: "We have liberated the island of Qaruh and we are now looking forward to liberating the whole of Kuwait."

Shaking with excitement, the sailor said he last saw his country on Aug. 20. He joined Kuwaiti resistance fighters, but had to smuggle himself out of the country when it became too dangerous.

"The Iraqis came to look for my wife and kids and so after three nights we surrendered to them. But I could not stand it so I joined the resistance and stayed with them for two weeks, but they looked for us to kill us and I was forced to leave," he said.

He joined the Kuwaiti Navy in Bahrain, but never dreamed he would be one of the first to set foot on his liberated homeland. His commander, a Marine Corps major, said: "It was a feeling I have never felt before. I was happy, I was excited. I was so emotional that I kissed the sand.

"I still have relatives in Kuwait who I have not heard from since I left to join the Navy just after the invasion. I left the country after they killed a lot of my friends, so some of us got together and organised ourselves.

"It is now only a matter of time before I am reunited with my relatives. It will definitely happen, but exactly when I don't know."

The sailors were flown to the island by U.S. Sea King helicopter. "The Iraqis must have been preparing for a chemical attack because there were lots of gas masks and helmets lying around. I took some back as souvenirs," said another captain, aged 33, whose wife and four children are still in Kuwait.

He added: "I am very frightened for my family, but we should not be apart for much longer. It is a matter of time but we will be reunited.

"It was exciting, very exciting, to be the first Kuwaiti people to return home in six months. I am very happy and very proud. I hope the whole country will be back under our control as soon as possible."

Missile with Camera in Nose Shows Close-Up of Targets About to Disappear, Opening Chunks of Friendly Sky

By George Rodrigue

SYNOPSIS: F/A 18s knocked out an Iraqi gas-oil separator and petroleum complex and destroy a SAM (SA-2) site, thanks largely to the first good weather in days. With discussion of complexity of mission, and issue of collateral damage caused by bombs.

NOTE TO CORRESPONDENTS - Previous dispatch by this pool said NO allied planes had been lost to SAM sites. This is true, as far as official findings are concerned. But aviators here say they believe, absent official finding, that an FA/18 off Saratoga was shot down by a SAM on the second night of the war.

ABOARD THE USS ROOSEVELT - Naval fighter-bombers from USS Theodore Roosevelt, blessed with good weather at last, knocked out an oil-storage facility and two Iraqi missile sites on Monday.

Videotapes played for media pool members Monday afternoon showed pinpoint, single-bomb strikes by F/A 18 Hornets on a surface-to-air (SAM) site near Kuwait International Airport and on the petroleum complex's control center near Basra.

Naval officers said a separate raid by the carrier's A-6E Intruders knocked out a Silkworm missile site on the Kuwaiti coast.

In both Hornet raids, a camera in the nose of a television-guided Walleye bomb allowed viewers to get a bomb's eye view of the rapidly approaching target. The screen went blank after the 1,000-pound warhead exploded.

Birds scurried out of the way as the first Walleye approached the sheet-metal walls of the tank-farm control center, and a single Iraqi could be seen running away from the SAM site just before the second bomb hit near the base of the radar control center. "We've had a good day," said Rear Adm. Dave Frost, commander of USS Roosevelt's Battle Group 8. "Mostly, clear weather was the big news today."

The SAM site contained modified, Vietnam-vintage Soviet SA-2 missiles. They are thought to have a relatively primitive guidance system, but a relatively long range. Removing them should open new chunks of sky to safe flights by attack pilots. "It's been bothering our guys, and they flat took that thing out," USS Roosevelt's Capt. C.S. Abbot told his crew.

The pilot who dropped the Walleye on the SAM site said he took particular satisfaction in that mission because an Iraqi missile is believed to have shot down one of his best friends, a Hornet pilot based on the carrier Saratoga. "When this war began, I lost a good friend to a surface-to-air missile, just like this one," he said, asking not to be identified. "So for me this was my way of making things right."

The coastal Silkworm cruise-missile site blown up by A-6 pilots was designed to attack ships in the Gulf. Capt. Abbot said they "have to be moved out of our way before we move our naval forces out further in the Gulf."

Pilots who flew Monday's missions said they were made possible by good weather. The SAM site had been targeted previously but the earlier mission was cancelled because clouds obscured the views of American pilots and of the television camera guidance system in the Walleye bomb.

Pilots like the Walleye because its visual guidance system lets them bomb accurately miles away from their targets—reasonably safe even from the SAMs they are destroying.

"The Hornet pilots can drop it in the guy's back pocket," said Lt. John Clifton, USS Theodore Roosevelt's strike intelligence officer.

The tradeoff is that the bomb's visual guidance system can see no better than human beings can. It requires clear weather for best performance. Aviators said Monday's missions also demonstrated their ability to destroy many military targets without heavy bombing likely to kill civilians.

Iraq has claimed that the U.S. is bombing homes, businesses and schools. Lt Jack Rose, 27, of Pittsburgh, Pa., who dropped the Walleye on the petroleum complex control center, said he did not believe the U.S. would ever kill civilians deliberately. He said some "collateral damage" is inevitable in war. "But here there was no collateral damage. We just took the target out."

It was Lt. Rose's first trip "over the beach," and he said he found it a bit easier than he'd imagined, despite the presence of AA fire over the targets. "We got to do two missions and both were successful," he said. "You couldn't ask for a better day than that."

The A-6 attack on the Silkworm installation used standard unguided bombs, but an air officer aboard USS Roosevelt said they were delivered precisely because the pilot flew in at low level, then pulled up several miles from the coast and lofted four 2,000-pound bombs at the target. "On the way they (Iraqis) picked him up and started shooting at him all along the coast," so the pilot headed for home without waiting to see the bomb damage, Adm. Frost said. The Silkworm missiles were just behind the radar site, however, and should have been destroyed by the 4,000-foot radius of the bomb blast, he said.

LCDR Fred Buesser, 36, (did not want his city or state published) was the overall leader of the strike, which consumed more than eight hours of planning time and two hours of briefing time for pilots.

To safely get Hornet pilots in and out of Iraqi airspace, the raiding party included more than two dozen planes. About half were strike aircraft. The remainder were tankers, AWACS-type radar planes or EA-6B electronic jamming aircraft. "It was a team effort," LCDR Buesser said. He said there was no element of revenge in the raid for him. "I don't think that there is any revenge over here," he said. "The guy on the ground is just doing his job, and getting blown up. I don't think that it is any fun for him. But the mission is assigned to you, and you fly it."

Monday - January 28, 1991

Follow-On Briefing: Iraqi Resistance Crumbling, Oil Slick Shrinking

By George Rodrigue

SYNOPSIS: *Summary of pool briefing by USS Theodore Roosevelt's intelligence officer. Iraqi air resistance crumbling, sea resistance ditto. Land forces are under constant bombardment, with scant return fire. But they're not leaving. Having cleared coastal areas, U.S. wants to clear coastal minefields soon. Raid on Kuwaiti oil manifold seems to have cut once-immense flow of oil into Gulf. Potentially some news here, though we can't say what's already been released by Riyadh and Washington briefers.*

ABOARD USS THEODORE ROOSEVELT IN THE ARABIAN GULF - Iraqi resistance seems to be crumbling in the air and at sea, but dug-in ground troops show no signs of leaving Kuwait, a Navy intelligence expert said Monday.

Recent reconnaissance photos indicate that an Iraqi oil slick has been substantially reduced by Sunday's bombing of onshore facilities, he added.

Cmdr. Mark Lawrence, intelligence officer for the USS Theodore Roosevelt, said the Navy's next task will be to "move in close" to clear Iraqi minefields and maintain the option of an amphibious invasion. He said six of USS Roosevelt's aircraft struck elements of the Iraqi Republican Guard inside Iraq on Sunday, entering and leaving the area "pretty much unopposed" by either ground fire, surface-to-air missiles, or Iraqi jets. "That pretty much surprised us," he added. The Iraqi installations were still burning from a previous raid by U.S. Air Force planes, indicating that the Air Force also struck successfully, he said.

American and allied aircraft have encountered virtually no Iraqi air force resistance for the past several days, and Iraqi pilots continue to flee to Iran. Yesterday, Cmdr. Lawrence said, another 20 to 25 planes flew from Iraq to Iran, bringing the total to about 50. "Most of these are their top-of-the-line ground attack and fighter aircraft," he said. Iranian officials, who have kept their own aircraft well away from U.S. forces, have said the Iraqi planes will not be allowed to return until after the war is over.

Cmdr. Lawrence said the number of apparent defections was so large that it seemed to represent a policy decision, if not by Iraqi president Saddam Hussein then at least by some air force leaders. "It is a concerted effort by the air force to take out some of their aircraft and save them, knowing that the war is going to be lost and that everything in Iraq is going to be destroyed," he said. Cmdr. Lawrence said the widely reported downing of four MiG-23 interceptors by U.S. F-15s occurred as the MiGs were "transiting" the southern portion of Iraq, heading north. No U.S. or allied planes have been lost in the 48 hours preceding Monday morning, he said.

Of particular relief to the Navy, perhaps, are reports that Iraq has lost approximately half of the 30-40 Mirage interceptors that it had based near Kuwait, armed with sea-skimming Exocet anti-ship missiles. "It looks like the Iraqi air force is . . . probably out of the war," he said. Naval aviators on recent raids have noted steep reductions in anti-aircraft missile fire *(POOL NOTE: see accompanying feature material on EA-6B Prowlers)* and a noticeable drop in anti-aircraft fire, he added.

"The missiles . . . are way down and the anti-aircraft artillery is down from what we experienced the first week," he said. "It looks like the poor army guys have been left undefended by the air force and the anti-aircraft artillery."

He attributed this partly to previous attacks on Iraqi communications centers and on its network of early-warning observers, particularly those stationed on islands and oil platforms in the Gulf.

Asked whether any of these moves might reflect some sort of Iraqi strategy, he replied: "I don't think that there is much strategy now. I think that the air force is bugging out, to protect themselves (until) after the war. I think that the AA is low on ammunition and low on will to fight. I think that the army guys have been left to bury themselves.

"All those guys in the Republican Guard are getting bombed at will. They are just dug in, hunkered down."

There is no sign that the bombardment has broken the will of the Republican Guard, but it must be reducing morale, he said.

Good weather in coming days could provide U.S. and allied bombers with ideal strike weather. Their relative freedom to strike should give war planners greater freedom to wait before sending in ground troops.

Despite the bombardment and millions of leaflets dropped by C-130 cargo planes and F-16 fighter-bombers urging Iraqi soldiers to surrender, only about 20 ground troops are known to have defected during recent days, he said. *(POOL NOTE: This may help explain why Washington now says a ground invasion will be needed.)*

Cmdr. Lawrence said he is concerned by Iraqi president Saddam Hussein's threats to use non-conventional weapons, presumably including chemical warfare. Iraq has always threatened to use them as a last resort, he said, and Mr. Hussein may feel that he is in a desperate situation.

He said allied forces have been "moderately" successful at knocking out bridges and other communications between Baghdad and the Kuwaiti front. Perhaps 50 to 75 percent of the targets have been destroyed, he estimated. Some trains still are running between Baghdad and the KTO, he said, but they believe the Iraqis are filling them with men and hardware, not with food, water and ammunition.

To keep open the option of a Marine amphibious landing, the Navy has focused on sinking Iraq's navy and bombing its shore batteries of Silkworm anti-ship missiles. Both campaigns continue but both are going well, Cmdr. Lawrence said.

Minefields are the remaining barriers to invasion, he said. "The talk now is how and when (to remove them) and it is going to be as soon as possible . . . We have done our job of clearing the coastline and now we are going to move in close."

Women Add Drama to U.S. Airbase: Cruising the Drag from "American Graffiti"; a Fighter Plane Named "Six"

By Edith M. Lederer and David Evans

IN CENTRAL SAUDI ARABIA - Tech Sgt. Hattie Monson, the crew chief for an F-16A, lavishes loving attention on the fighter-bomber she's nicknamed Six, and agonizes every time it heads north to pound Iraqi targets.

"We're concerned about the pilots more than anything else. We really don't think about what our bombs are doing. We're thinking about our airplanes and our air crews," she said. In a small desert clearing outside the largest U.S. airbase in Saudi Arabia, Airman 1st Class Shan Rice deftly screwed a small fuse into a 500-pound bomb. As the bomb rolled down a portable assembly line, the 20-year-old paused briefly to ponder the morality of preparing weapons of war.

"I'm hoping the war will be over soon and not do any unnecessary killing," she said. "God says, 'Thou shalt not murder.' I try to live my life by God's word. I feel like I'm killing for the right of my people, my country, not for my own self-pride."

Though barred from flying combat missions, women in the U.S. Air Force are playing a bigger role than in any past war. From making and loading bombs to calibrating high-tech electronics equipment, doing combat surgery and flying cargo runs away from the front lines, women have become an integral part of the air war machine.

Men still dominate installations like the largest U.S. airbase in Saudi Arabia, which mushroomed from an isolated desert airstrip in the center of the country in just one month.

The women live in tents, heated in winter and air-conditioned in summer, on opposite sides of a dusty street which, like a scene from "American Graffiti," has become a favorite cruising spot for men on base.

Despite some persistent ribbing and occasional run-ins with their male peers and superiors, women like Monson and Rice are committed to doing their part to win the war and get home quickly. Even after 12 years in the South Carolina Guard, Monson said some of her male counterparts "are threatened by me still, but many have accepted me as a team member now."

Monson, 36, from Eastover, S.C., decided to follow in the footsteps of her brother-in-law who had been a crew chief in the early 1970s. "I could see myself in a green khaki long skirt, prowling around an airplane. Then, they dressed me like a man. I said OK." She finds it somewhat strange that all the male pilots call their planes "she." "Mine, I just call 'Six' . . . it's my lucky number. I think she's a female," Monson said. "Whenever she breaks they always say it's the wrong time of the month for my plane. They're awful! They all break the same amount."

Monson never wanted to fly but hopes that by the next war—whenever that may be—the gender gap will close and she or her successors will be waving goodbye to the first women fighter pilots. "I think it'd be great. I'd think of her as a sister," Monson said. "One female friend here works as an ordnance loader and another is also a crew chief. We've been able to talk about the same male attitude we're up against. I think it would be like that."

Rice, who joined the Air Force in October 1989 and was repairing trailers in Germany before she came to Saudi Arabia to work on bombs and missiles, has figured out how to cope with the razzing. "I'm enjoying the war because I'm getting a variety of training," she said. "I've worked in every shop, and that's not easy, being a woman."

"I've always got to try to live up to what guys say you can't do," Rice said. "They rag me: 'You can't do this! It's too heavy. You can't carry this.' I tell them I didn't come here to be babied. I can do everything you can do—maybe a little bit better if I try," she said. "I tell them I can be a better woman than they are a man. I don't think I could do it if I was married. Being single, I've learned to adapt and overcome, not become too attached to anyone. I make friends, but I move on and try to better myself as I go along."

Rice works 12 or 13 hours a day, helping turn the innocent shell of a bomb into an armed, deadly weapon. Members of her bomb-making crew move from site to site, each devoted to a different variety of Mark-84 2,000-pounders to Mark-82 500-pounders and cluster bombs.

When she saw the first F-15E fighter-bombers fly north to bomb Iraq and Kuwait early on Jan. 17, she said, "I was happy it was actually happening. The anticipation was scarier than the actual war." When the war is over, Rice hopes to start studying for a psychology degree. She had been scheduled to start courses this month.

Some women like Staff Sgt. Pam Krolewicz-Miles, 31, of Columbia, S.C., came to Saudi Arabia at great personal sacrifice after much soul-searching.

It was bad enough leaving behind her 10-month-old daughter, Rachel, and two older stepchildren, but the week before her South Carolina Air National Guard unit was put on active duty, her husband, Richard, was diagnosed as having cancer.

"I probably could have gotten out, but we both knew that wasn't what I wanted . . . so I came," she said. "I've been in the Air National Guard for 10 years and I'm like third-generation immigrant, and I just feel like I'm in the military, I'm part of America and if that's what America wants, I'm an American and I have to stand up for it. I don't know much about Middle East politics but nobody has the right to take over somebody else's . . . country, and we're going in with permission from Kuwait," she said. "Obviously, we're dealing with a madman. Anyone that wants to intentionally attack Israel has got to be mad . . . that's my opinion."

A Xerox technician back home, petite Krolewicz-Miles is a systems operator for the Air Force. "Militarily speaking, there are usually two main targets on an airbase. One, of course, is the aircraft. The other is communications.

"I'm not flying planes or out on the flight line. But I'm still in a critical field. You have to communicate to get the mission completed," she said.

The alerts for chemical attacks from Scud missiles have made the war more real, Krolewicz-Miles said, but "I haven't really been scared yet. I don't complain. It's still a hard decision, but I know my husband is enjoying his time with the baby, which he never had with his other children. It's a little sad I missed her first steps, but there's a lot more firsts I'll get to see and do with her."

The deployment to Saudi Arabia has had some unexpected side effects.

Staff Sgt. Brenda "B.J." Merrick, 36, of Jasper, Tenn., who has been a medic for 14 years and is a shift leader in the emergency room here, left her husband, an Air Force master sergeant, at home and sent their son to stay with her sister.

"I've been here 161 days today. I count. Every day is a day closer to going home," she said. "It was a relief to know they're doing something and it might end soon."

Sitting on a cot outside their tent, with half a dozen tent-mates and friends, Merrick joked, gave advice to a young woman who just learned she had an ulcer, and listened quietly to another who had a probe at work. "I'm Mother America to all of them," she said. "I enjoy it because it keeps me occupied. I haven't been scared yet because the girls look to me. If I were to panic, they would all panic. We're all one big family."

Since she arrived in the Gulf, Merrick has lost 35 pounds. "It's the best diet plan in the world," she said. "I don't recommend it for everybody. But it worked for me. When I retire, I'm going to open a fat farm over here and put everybody in camouflage uniforms and combat boots putting up tents and sandbagging. It's a guaranteed weight loss program—and I'm going to sell moisturizing lotion and chocolates on the side," Merrick said.

But it's hard to top the bonus for Staff Sgt. Dee Ann Heiderscheit, 27, of Dubuque, Iowa. During a sandstorm at a base in the Gulf, she stopped at a bus stop to ask directions and has just gotten engaged to the man who provided them, Staff Sgt. Steve Poole, 27, of Copperas Cove, Tex. "I wasn't lonely." she said. "I wanted to come over here and get something out of it personally and professionally. Little did I know this would be the personal side. I didn't come over here to find a guy and fall in love." Heiderscheit, who works in the public affairs office at the base here, and Poole, a weapons loader, are planning a spring 1992 wedding in Dubuque.

There aren't any engagement rings available in the desert, but Heiderscheit doesn't mind. "Instead, he just showers me with stuffed animals, jewelry, letters, cards and poems . . . No man's ever written a poem for me before," she said.

When it comes to happy endings from Operation Desert Shield and Desert Storm, Heiderscheit said, "I hope I'm not the only entry."

Tuesday
January 29, 1991

Saddam Hussein may have remained in power, but the Gulf War claimed at least one political casualty. French defense minister Jean-Pierre Chevènement was forced to resign over his opposition to the war.

He wasn't alone in his minority view. Anti-war demonstrations in the U.S. and other western capitals were frequent and noisy, although on a much smaller scale than those staged during the Vietnam era. Western newspapers and radio and TV were available in Saudi Arabia, so troops in the field knew there was some anti-war sentiment.

Early one January morning, in a line of combat engineers waiting to be served a lukewarm fried egg to put on a cold slice of toast, one shivering soldier mentioned that he'd heard on the news that the city council of San Francisco, or maybe it was Berkeley, where he and a sister lived, had voted to stop the war and bring the American troops home immediately. One of the cooks quietly admitted he was from Madison, Wis., and said he'd heard that the city council in his hometown had done the same thing.

The other soldiers shook their heads in sympathy. They said it was too damn bad that good, patriotic homeboys had to be even remotely associated, hometown-wise, with that type of thinking.

Another take on the reaction among the allied military ranks to anti-war arguments is found in a story in this chapter from an allied air base.

The resignation of the French defense minister, as diplomats say, had been expected. The pressure had begun the previous fall when a French light armored division reinforced with Foreign Legionnaires set up camp and began melding into the coalition.

The French contribution in the Gulf, joining the air war and leading the flanking attack on the western front, was meritorious. President Bush later awarded Gen. Roquejeoffre, the French field commander, the Legion of Merit, Commander in Chief, the highest U.S. military honor for a foreigner.

The climate of the northern Saudi desert never seemed to hit a comfortable temperature, except perhaps just when a pan of fresh baguettes emerged from the Legionnaires' excellent field bakery.

The first five months, during Desert Shield, it was hotter than blazes. Next, in November and December, came clouds, wind and rain, but it remained steamy at ground level. Then by January, it suddenly got very cold, especially after sundown.

A story in this chapter deals with the extremes of the climate on the Arabian Peninsula and how they affected life for people deployed for war, who drank out of canteens, worked outside or in canvas tents, and couldn't retreat to a cozy hotel.

There's also an account of some Iraqi prisoners, a group that apparently didn't want to fight very hard, but hoped the Americans would settle Saddam Hussein's hash. One was from Chicago. He picked the wrong time to visit his family in Iraq.

Tuesday - January 29, 1991

Allied bomber pilots, a story in this chapter says, knew their daily runs were producing large amounts of no-longer-usable military hardware across Iraq. But military after-action reports on the destruction actually achieved—called BDA, or battle damage assessment—are always expected to be more precise.

Satellite imagery is valuable in drawing conclusions about what's been damaged and what hasn't, but pilot and squadron reports are also essential. The pilots said the Iraqis were keeping much of their military hardware hidden, making damage assessment much more difficult.

Border Shootout Between Iraqi and Saudi Patrols: "This is Not a Drill. There are Bad Guys Out There"

By Gary Regenstreif

NORTHERN SAUDI ARABIA - A dozen Iraqi soldiers slipped down across the border this week and ambushed a Saudi patrol while a U.S. reconnaissance team crept up to within five kilometers of Iraqi defensive positions.

A senior U.S. military official said about 12 Iraqis came two kilometers inside the kingdom and wounded the three Saudi border patrol guards in an exchange of gunfire and rocket-propelled grenades.

One Iraqi officer was killed in Sunday night's ambush.

"They're coming across the border, which means patrolling is a lot more dangerous," said the official who asked not to be identified. "The ante is upped." The Saudis, in a vehicle armed with a 50-caliber gun, were not seriously wounded and were expected to return to duty within a month.

The injured Saudis told U.S. officials the Iraqi infiltrators improperly used a V-formation attack strategy and believed the Iraqi victim was unintentionally killed by one of his own troops. "It was not a professional ambush," said another U.S. officer.

Hours later, "scouts" of the U.S. Army's 82nd Airborne Division conducted their most northern mission yet, sliding on their bellies into a "no man's land" of as-yet-unpatrolled terrain less than five kilometers from Iraqi positions.

The scouts, their faces blackened for camouflage protection, laid a communication wire from their base camp forward in preparation for a possible assault on Iraqi ground troops. "We want to assess their strengths and weaknesses without being seen," Maj. Ralph Delosua, operations officer, whispered in the frosty night air.

Stealth is the watchword for the scouts and Monday night's mission was considered particularly dangerous because the full moon made them more visible to Iraqi soldiers.

Gunners peered through the thermal night sights of antitank TOW missiles to scan the horizon ahead of them and provide fire support if necessary. The scouts, an elite squad of hand-picked infantrymen, used a ground positioning system which tracks their exact location by sending a laser signal to a satellite. They can later retrace their position to within 30 metres in a desert devoid of landmarks.

While the U.S. reconnaissance team is better equipped than their Iraqi foes because of superior night vision equipment, soldiers said the Saudi ambush brought a war heretofore largely conducted in the air down to earth for them.

"The Saudi attack brought it to light that this is not a drill," said Delosua, of

Pemberton, N.J. "My guys know this is for real. There are bad guys out there."

"The adrenaline is pumping a little bit more," said squad leader Sgt. Joe Brewer of Zurich, Mont. "You don't know what will happen out there."

"We'll be more alert," added Spec. Hiram Sanders of Brooklyn, N.Y. "People tell me they don't envy my job. I do it for the adventure. And you think about your life, your family and the rest of the people back there who are depending on you."

Not Much to Buy in This Empty Desert, But British Troops Get U.S. Dollars for Pocket Money

By Keith Dovkants

A consignment of 5 million U.S. dollars, in small denomination bills, was being packed into ammunition boxes today ready for distribution to Britain's frontline troops.

Every man taking part in the land battle to liberate Kuwait will be given at least 60 (sixty) dollars pocket money, finance commander Lt. Col. Tom O'Donnell revealed, for cigarettes, food, drinks—even souvenirs—when the battle is over.

"We felt we would not be able to use Iraqi money and there is doubt over the viability of the Kuwaiti dinar," Lt. Col. O'Donnell said.

The money, supplied by a Saudi Arabian bank, was being held in empty canisters used to carry anti-tank rockets. An armed guard was placed on the section of the camp where the money is being stored, but—as Lt. Col. O'Donnell said—"We don't expect pilfering." Money is one of the major logistic headaches for the Army. So far paymasters have doled out £55 million in cash to soldiers deployed in the desert. Water money—the daily allowance to cover the cost of extra drinks—costs £2¼ million (2,250,000) a month. Many soldiers are seeking advances on their pay to cover life insurance premiums.

For those who did not have cover(age) when they were posted to the Gulf rates have soared. It is now virtually impossible to secure life cover(age) and where it is offered the premium can be prohibitive.

The army has arranged to pay 90 percent of additional premiums, asked to cover this deployment, but most soldiers, who do not have insurance are relying on army benefits.

Wind Soldiers Call "The Hawk" Hangs On With Cold Claws

By Robert Dvorchak

WITH THE 82ND AIRBORNE DIVISION - Paratroopers call it "The Hawk," a piercing chill that cuts through the flesh down to the bone with a talon-like grip.

The weather at the northern front has been rainy and cold the past few days, cold enough to coat sleeping blankets with a layer of frost and cold enough to freeze grape drinks into slush. "When I woke up, the water in my canteen was frozen," said 1st Lt. James Hall, 30, of Greenville, S.C. "It's definitely cruel weather." Below-freezing temperatures and colder wind chills are just one more element to endure for the 2nd Brigade of the 82nd Airborne Division, the first ground troops to arrive in August in Saudi Arabia.

Back then, paratroopers were greeted with oven-like blasts of 130-degree temperatures. Some thought they were standing in the back blasts of jet engines, only to find the whole country was hot.

Now there's another extreme for soldiers. Many are protected only by their fighting holes and sandbag covers. "If you had told me in August it would have been this cold, I'd have bet you all the money I owned you were wrong," said Sgt. 1st Class Aubrey Butts, 31, of Elizabeth City, N.J., part of the 1st Battalion, 325th Infantry Regiment.

His advice to beat the chill: "Put on everything you got. Hunker down in the holes. Sleep underground. Live like moles. This is the first time you ain't got to tell anybody to dig."

Soldiers at the front bundle up like mummies, wearing layers of long johns, sweaters and hooded parkas.

On Saturday, a frigid pelting rain came from the north, making it miserable for anyone who was out in the open. If your sleeping bag got wet (like mine did) it was like sleeping in a bucket of ice water until a sympathetic officer could find you comfort.

"It was one of those nights you just try to survive. Wait for the heat tab in the morning," said Capt. Brad Nelson, adjutant for the 2nd Brigade. "But guys adapt. The other side is going through the same thing we are," Nelson said.

Cpl. Frederick Spicer, 22, of Chicago, Ill., made his patrols with just the barest slit for his eyes. Everything else was bundled up. "From one extreme to the other. You just have to wrap yourself up," Spicer said.

Pfc. Terrence Knitter, 20, of South Haven, Mich., braved the cold behind the burlap sandbags of his guard post. "It feels like my feet are going to fall off. Got to get another set of feet," said Knitter.

The paratroopers who have it the worst are the scouts, who work all night long scoping out terrain and enemy positions. Some don't even carry sleeping bags. Their motto is: "Travel light, freeze at night." But some of them won't complain. "It's more miserable for the Iraqis. They're fair-weather soldiers," said Spec. John Rowe, 27, of Red Bank, N.J. "When it's cold, nasty and miserable, that's infantry weather. That's what we like," he said.

On a chill night going out on patrol, Rowe said: "The only thing better than it being this cold is if it would be raining."

High-Tech Airbase Playing Chicken With Gas Alerts: Peace Activists at Home Told Evil "Must Be Stopped"

By Alexander Higgins and Storer H. Rowley

AN AIRBASE IN NORTHERN SAUDI ARABIA - Under a full moon, Air Force A-10 Thunderbolt II tank-killing airplanes flew missions Monday night from this forward operating base in northern Saudi Arabia striking Iraqi targets.

After days of missions diminished by bad weather, Monday's clear skies allowed the pace of sorties to pick up again, and C-130 and C-141 transports continued to build a major support base in preparation for a ground war.

The base, which was started by the Saudis in the 1970s but little used by them, has been expanding rapidly since allied forces started building it up in early December. It is now one of the most forward operating locations for the U.S. Air Force, a medical center for battlefield casualties and a staging and logistics center for the U.S. Army.

The A-10 "Warthogs" based further south have started using this base as a refueling and re-arming platform to run 'round the clock bombing runs against Iraqi positions. Your pool arrived at 5:30 p.m. Monday as the sun was setting over this sprawling base where tent (illegible) and center here tracked and monitored the two Scud attacks late Monday at Riyadh and Israel, but called no alert for the base here when they judged it was not targeted. However, it has an interesting system for gauging whether the base has come under chemical attack: Buford, the command center chicken, who sits in his cage beside a gas-monitoring machine. The machine will sound when chemicals are present in the air.

Buford is the backup. If he's okay, we're okay. Like canaries used by miners to warn against deadly gases, the base has several chickens in boxes with chicken wire fronts scattered around at various locations.

Like the canaries, they will die before humans if exposed to poisonous gases. In fact, the base newspaper has been named after the command chicken: "Buford Talks."

"He's a very important bird. As long as Buford talks, we're in good shape," said Col. Bill Van Meter, 48, of Holyoke, Mass., commander of the 4410th Operations Support Wing, who is in charge of running the complex. "We have a bunch of live chickens around," said Van Meter, adding that after any attack on the base, one of the first things they would do would be to go out and check to see if the chickens are still alive and well.

Van Meter, a 26-year veteran of the Air Force who flew 125 missions in an F-4 Phantom fighter over Vietnam in the late 1960s, already sees a lot of differences between the two wars. "Technologically, this war is vastly superior," he said. "Our pilots are better trained. We learned a lot of lessons in the Vietnam War. And we used them to train our pilots." He said aircraft like the A-10 were developed to fill needs discovered in Vietnam combat. It is designed to protect friendly troops by attacking nearby enemy ground forces and particularly tanks and armored vehicles. Now, it is performing the role of "interdiction," the term for the attempt to cut off the Iraqi ability to re-supply their forces and wage war.

Van Meter came to Saudi Arabia from Tyndall AFB, Fla., where he has trained more than 100 F-15 fighter pilots, many of whom are flying missions against Iraq, some of whom are missing in action. Asked if he was bothered by current anti-war protests, given his Vietnam experience, Van Meter said: "A little bit, I guess . . . I don't think the protesters really bothered you that much. They do what they do because they feel the way they do. I do what I do because I love the United States of America. You know, we have different thoughts on some of those regimes, I guess. I appreciate the freedom I have been given. Some of them don't realize what they have been given."

The A-10 weapons loader on the base, however, was more disturbed about protests back home, and put his thoughts into a letter to the home front excerpted here. "I'm really not sure this war will last, but I would like for you to do something for me," said the letter by Staff Sgt. Benjamin A. Hoover, 28, of Claremore, Okla. "Say a prayer not only for us, but for the innocent warriors of Iraq. Most of them had no real idea of what kind of monster that Sad-Man Insane is. . . . For it is the old Republican Guards that deserve destruction. They are responsible for the systematic rape, slaughter, and pillaging in Kuwait. There can be no excuse for that type of behavior for many soldiers.

"So let the word go forth that we, the American soldiers, are not here to quibble about oil. We are here for Kuwait—the complete liberation of that tiny country.

"For these Americans who doubt our resolve, let them tremble at our might. For we will not be treated the way our brothers were treated at the close of the Vietnam War, the disgraceful treatment of fine, brave men and women whose only crime was to answer, instead of run from, their country's call of duty.

"We will free Kuwait regardless of the cost, the loss of both the allies' and Iraq's soldiers.

So say the prayers loudly because, until this monster is neutralized, war in this region will never end. Evil cannot be allowed to have a free hand. It must be stopped. We have heard about a lot of peace demonstrations (that) make me sick. I am ashamed to admit that these people are Americans. This is not about blood for oil, rather a small nation that has sustained a brutal attack and has tried in vain to liberate itself."

Hoover turned to a reporter after handing him the letter and said, "We've got to attack the Iraqi forces unless Saddam gives up. But he's like a tick on a dog. He won't leave."

After 10 Days of Bombing, Considerable Damage to Iraqis; Damage Assessment—Difficult to Impossible

By Susan Sachs and Gilles Trequesser

AN AIRBASE SOMEWHERE in the PERSIAN GULF - Allied bombers have been pounding Republican Guard positions in southern Iraq for 10 days, but damage assessment will probably have to wait until the well-entrenched troops emerge from their fortified positions to fight a ground war.

"We've taken out what's been visible to us and areas we think tanks have dug in," said Col. Manfred Rietsch, commander of the Marine Aircraft Group 11, a collection of F/A-18 Hornet fighters, A-6E Intruders, and EA-6B Prowlers. "They're waiting.

They've hidden their tanks. When we'll be able to destroy them in large numbers is when they bring them out and move them. A ground campaign will be the only way to find out."

Rietsch, a Hornet pilot, said Marine aircraft, as well as B-52 bombers and others, have been conducting bombing raids 24 hours a day almost since the beginning of the air war. The Guards, with tanks and armored personnel carriers, are protected by sand berm revetments and camouflage. He said the Marine aviators have been using cluster bombs, which are effective on people, vehicles and equipment that are out in the open. "They're very well dug in. We're hurting them, but it's hard to quantify how much we're hurting them," Rietsch said. "All we can do is demoralize them and take away some of their supplies and reduce their numbers somewhat."

On some bombing runs, pilots report secondary explosions, presumably from hits on ammunition storage depots. A few days ago, "by luck," he said pilots found a convoy of trucks and other vehicles on a road and dropped cluster bombs. "That was very much a fun mission because you could see the parts of the trucks flying."

The bombers came upon the convoy as the Iraqi soldiers were taking a break for Muslim prayers, leaving only a handful of troops as guards.

Rietsch said that the allies are not routinely timing their raids to prayer times. "We don't time our missions to coincide with prayer time," he said. "It was not pre-planned." Rietsch said the Republican Guards still have surface-to-air missiles and much of their armor, which remains well camouflaged and dug in. "They're a potential force, but not really a military force until they're employed—and to be employed they've got to come out of hiding," he said.

Rietsch said the constant bombing probably has a demoralizing effect on the elite troops. "I don't know what it will have done to them to have bombs rain on them 24 hours a day." Speaking generally about the air war, he said the allies have "air superiority" but not air supremacy and argued that, even though the Iraqi air force remains largely intact, it is effectively sitting out the war. Still, the air force remains a potential threat. "They just don't want to fight," he said. "We've accomplished the fact that their air force is not flying. Now we're taking on the ground forces. We're going after the ground forces day in and day out."

The ground targets are resupply points, trucks, oil barrels and armored personnel carriers that haven't dispersed.

Allied air power has knocked out most of the Iraqis' long-range SAMs and command and control centers. But much of Iraq's anti-aircraft artillery hasn't been destroyed. "What we want to do is take out the systems that threaten our ground forces," Rietsch said. "We need to take out artillery and tanks, and, in southern Kuwait, we've done a pretty good job."

In recent bombing missions, pilots are not running into as much surface-to-air missile or anti-aircraft fire as they experienced in the early days of the war. Rietsch said the SAM network appears "less coordinated" and operators don't seem to be handing off from sector to sector—an indication, he said, of the breakdown in Iraqi command and control. SAMs are being launched, but are not guided, at least among the troops that are not part of the Republican Guard. "I think the SAM operators have a certain quota to make," he said. "Most of the time the SAMs go stupid because they turn (the radar) off."

The Iraqis apparently have learned how to operate at least the radar systems of the U.S.-made Hawk anti-aircraft missile batteries, seized by Iraq from Kuwait after the invasion. Rietsch said none have been fired at planes in his aircraft group and no allied plane has been downed by Hawks, but "we've been locked on."

Marine Col. W.C. "Bill" McMullen, an F/A-18 pilot and squadron leader of the "Death Angels" returning from a bombing run this morning, said, "there are still a lot of areas that have not been bombed."

He said the Republican Guards are a key target, but "it's a large force and its a big desert. There are a lot of old revetments, new revetments, old oil wells, roads—even with all the bombing, there's still a lot of open desert."

Battle damage assessment is difficult. "When you're bombing infantry and armored brigades that can disperse across the desert, it's hard to assess," he said. "It's difficult to get feedback from the success rate."

Before they go out on their missions, the pilots pore over black-and-white satellite photos of small areas of southern Iraq and Kuwait. They are useful for showing permanent landmarks that can help pilots find their targets.

"From high up, unless you see a straight line, you usually can't tell what's there until you get close to it," said Capt. Tom Altorik, an F/A-18 pilot.

Tuesday - January 29, 1991

Iraqi POW From Chicago Captured; "Waiting a Long Time for America to Come Finish This Problem"

By Tarek Hamada

ABOARD THE USS CURTS IN THE PERSIAN GULF - Lt. Cmdr. Bill Jackson was surprised when he heard the 24-year-old Iraqi prisoner of war his ship had just captured speak fluent English.

"He was living in Chicago and was visiting his family in Iraq when he was drafted to serve in Kuwait," said Jackson, 36, of Port Arthur, TX. But that was the first of many interesting moments the young Iraqi and his 50 fellow EPWs provided their American and Kuwaiti interrogators on this missile frigate in the northern Persian Gulf.

The Iraqis were captured Jan. 24 when the Curts took over tiny Qurah Island off the coast of Kuwait and destroyed a mine-laying ship. Twenty-two Iraqis came from the ship and the rest were from the island. The POWs seemed relieved when they boarded the Curts, Capt. Glenn Montgomery said. "My estimation is that they were happy to be alive," said Montgomery, of New York City. "Their heart wasn't in the fight."

Maj. Ibrahim, a Kuwaiti naval officer who led the interrogation of the POWs, said most of them seemed to be in good spirits. "They said, 'Now, we are free,'" the major said. "All of them know they are losing the war."

During their 24-hour stay on the Curts, the POWs told of their total disillusionment with Iraqi president Saddam Hussein and his determination to keep Kuwait, the major said.

"They said Saddam is crazy and giving foolish orders," the major said.

"They said we are here by pressure. If we didn't go (into the army) they would have punished us or killed us," he said. "They said they had been waiting a long time for America to come and finish this problem."

The 24-year-old POW who lived in Chicago before the invasion of Kuwait told the major he was trapped by events. The youth, an engineering student who had lived in The Windy City with his mother for two years was visiting relatives Aug. 2 when Iraq took over Kuwait, the major said. "He was trying to get a green card before he left for Iraq," the major said.

But like most Iraqi men in their 20s, 30s, and 40s he was drafted into the army.

The Chicago resident told the major he didn't understand why he and his countrymen were in Kuwait. "He said it was foolish," the major said. "He was sorry about everything that had happened." The POW said he felt particularly ashamed that Iraq, a Muslim country, occupied Kuwait, which is also Islamic, the major said. "He said, 'We are Muslims. We shouldn't do this to each other,'" the major reported. He said the Iraqis caused a lot of problems by entering Kuwait.

The POWs also said they felt abandoned by their superiors and were rapidly running out of food, Montgomery said.

The soldiers on the island only had 20 bags of rice. The POWs clearly weren't dedicated, well-trained troops like the Iraqi army's Republican Guard, the major said, noting they feebly fought off U.S. forces before they surrendered. "They were not a gifted fighting force," he said.

The Iraqi soldiers who surrendered to the Curts apparently were in much better physical condition than other Iraqi defectors. U.S. officers said the other defectors were covered with lice, had open sores and appeared to be malnourished.

Lt. Thomas K. Moore, the ship's physician, said all but seven of the EPWs "were in very good shape. I didn't see any evidence of malnourishment or mistreatment."

Wednesday January 30, 1991

The Battle of Khafji began as part of a larger operation by Iraqi troops to send tanks boldly across the Kuwait border into Saudi Arabia at several points.

The Iraqi forces—apparently with no plan to support the incursions with either aircraft or artillery—executed at least two tank thrusts that night, perhaps three. The attacks did not come as a complete surprise, it was later learned. A big Iraqi military staff meeting had been attacked by allied air a few days before, and suspicious movements of Iraqi armor had been reported. But no one, even the Kuwaiti resistance, knew exactly what the Iraqi command had been planning.

And as the battle unfolded, no one seemed to be certain why this limited attack was coming at just this particular time. Were the Iraqis just trying to poke a stick at the allies and find out where units were located? Was it a curtain-raiser for a major confrontation or what the Brits call a "one-off," an event not likely to be repeated?

The Battle of Khafji began in confusion and then went nowhere for the Iraqis who started it, as stories in this chapter illustrate. The Marines who were the first to encounter an Iraqi tank battalion snaking into Saudi gave it to them hot and heavy. The first Iraqi probe was cut down in its tracks. But there were Marine casualties. They weren't in Khafji, and they later proved to be from friendly fire.

But contrary to first reports, there were also Marines in Khafji, and they were planning to stay awhile. A couple of Army supply truck drivers ended up in Khafji just when they shouldn't have. One truck got away, but by the time the Marines knew they were there, it was too late to help the other one.

And so it went, back and forth, Marines fighting one hellacious battle over here, mounting a rescue mission there, Saudi and Qatari troops supported by Marine air cover raking the Iraqi positions in Khafji and finally edging back in control.

At the end of the Battle of Khafji there were some answers, but most of them just raised more questions. The upshot of the battle for the air campaign was straightforward: having the Iraqis put a lot of their armor on the open road, visible from the air and headed for Saudi Arabia, simply added to a dwindling target list for allied aviators.

The first clue that something was up at Khafji came into the air command from a drone, one of hundreds of small, unmanned aircraft the allies used to collect intelligence from low altitude without risking pilots' lives. That electronic alert triggered a steady increase in sorties over the coastal road linking Saudi and Kuwait City, where most of the Iraqi strength was whittled down from the air.

The question of who was driving all the supply trucks for the allies, raised by the capture of two Army drivers at Khafji, was a good one. As a story in this chapter points out, many local drivers had quit once the bombing started and Scuds started flying.

Wednesday - January 30, 1991

For the majority of Iraqi soldiers elsewhere in Kuwait and Iraq, there was no relief from the allied air assault. Once in a while an allied plane would drop something that didn't explode and kill or maim people when it hit the ground.

On a good day, as a story in this chapter recounts, some of the big allied planes would drop a load consisting of thousands of surrender leaflets, with instructions on how to give up. Those planes were very popular.

U.S. Marines Claim Umm al Maradim Island Off Kuwaiti Coast

By Tarek Hamada

OVER UMM AL MARADIM ISLAND, Kuwait - A spectacular explosion Tuesday that produced a mushroom cloud of smoke signaled the end to Iraqi control of this spit of sand 12 miles off the coast of Kuwait.

The 13th Marine Expeditionary Unit ended its assault of Umm al Maradim by blowing up anti-aircraft weapons and artillery the Iraqis had apparently stored on the 400-by-300-meter island.

The 3:15 p.m. explosion was witnessed by U.S. reporters who were flown over the island, which is a collection of two communication towers, 13 tents, and buildings and brush.

"It's another step in the continuing effort to free Kuwait," said Capt. Michael J. Coumatos, commander of the USS Okinawa, from which the Marines deployed.

"I think every square inch of liberated Kuwait is important to the Kuwaitis."

Before the blast, two Marines climbed to the top of the shorter communications tower and planted a Kuwaiti flag.

"It looked nice up there," said Lt. Col. George Flinn, who led the Marines onto the island, "The wind was blowing. It was a clear day and it looked like it belonged there."

Umm al Maradim is the second island to be reclaimed for the Kuwaiti government by the U.S. On Jan. 24, forces from the Army and the USS Curts took over Qurah Island, a smaller stretch of sand north of Umm al Maradim.

The Marines decided to storm Umm al Maradim because they thought Iraqi soldiers might be on the island, said Col. John E. Rhodes, commander of the 13th Marine Expeditionary Unit. "We didn't know exactly what we were going to find," Rhodes said. "But you could interpret that we felt someone was on the island because the intelligence we gained (about Maradim) from the capture of Qurah and the news reports we heard about Iraqi soldiers scrawling SOS in the sand."

But unlike Qurah, no one was on the island when at least 50 Marines were flown to it at noon, and Iraqi forces stationed on the Kuwaiti mainland didn't fire at the troops, Flinn said. "In 29 minutes, we declared the island safe and we set about confiscating equipment and deciding what to destroy and what to bring back," said Flinn, 42, of Chatham, NY. "It was a quiet place." But it was also clear the Iraqis had abandoned the island "rather rapidly," he said. The Marines found a 30-inch television set, plates and other eating utensils, prayer rugs, stacks of military gear and cases of ammunition, Flinn said.

The Marines blew up the anti-aircraft guns and ammunition to prevent the Iraqis from using them against the thousands of U.S., Arab, and European jets that regularly fly up the coast of Kuwait, said Col. Rhodes.

The anti-aircraft guns and the communications towers indicated the island was used by the Iraqis to warn of upcoming air attacks, said Capt. Michael J. Coumatos, commander of Amphibious Squadron Five. The Marines were deployed from the helicopter carrier.

The U.S.-led multinational alliance will study the possibility of using the island, Coumatos added, refusing to be more specific. But Flinn and the other Marines who participated in the takeover of Umm al Maradim had vivid memories of their expedition.

Once their helicopters touched down on the island, "we moved carefully to make sure we didn't do anything foolish," Flinn said.

"You could feel the adrenaline pumping. I looked around, and I saw people focused on what they had to do. I was convinced we were ready." Cpl. Larry P. Hudson said "everybody had a scared look in their eyes. Yes, there were jitters." But once they secured Umm al Maradim, the Marines felt confident, Flinn and Hudson said. "It was a very good feeling," Hudson said, noting this was his first combat experience. "We were prepared for anything."

Although Umm al Maradim is a small island, Hudson said he felt he accomplished something big. "It made me very proud," said Hudson, 21, of Plymouth, Minn. "We took a part of Kuwait and gave it back to the Kuwaitis."

At Least 4 Million Instructions on How to Surrender, If You're An Iraqi Soldier

By Douglas Jehl

WITH U.S. FORCES, Saudi Arabia - In a bid to encourage Iraqi forces to give up without a fight, the United States has blanketed troop positions in Iraq and occupied Kuwait with at least 4 million air-dropped leaflets promising safe passage to enemy soldiers who signal their desire to surrender, American soldiers here were told Tuesday.

The one-page flyers, printed in Arabic and containing diagrammed instructions, are part of a larger U.S. effort to take advantage of what American commanders believe has been a significant deterioration of resolve among ordinary Iraqi soldiers, officers involved in the operation said. In telling U.S. soldiers about the procedures for Iraqi surrender, the officers said they hoped to avoid what one major described as the "credibility failure" that could undermine the operation if American forces mistakenly opened fire on advancing Iraqi troops.

"What we're trying to do is prevent soldiers from accidentally destroying our credibility by not allowing the opponent to surrender," said Maj. Leroy Slaughter, a psychological operations specialist now attached to the 1st Armored Division. "The idea," another officer said after one outdoor briefing, "is to make sure that someone doesn't screw the whole thing up by shooting the first two Iraqis who come across."

Some American commanders here said they understand the leaflet-dropping operation has already gained some success, with several groups of Iraqi soldiers carrying the flyers with them and following instructions precisely as they crossed in recent days into U.S. lines.

But the commanders cautioned that the number of such cases remained limited, and said it was unclear how many of the leaflets were actually reaching Iraqi troops. "It's just a drop in the bucket," one officer said.

And a senior non-commissioned officer who briefed a group of infantrymen about the operation Monday reported that the arrangements had caused confusion on American front lines where at least one unit mistakenly shot at Iraqi soldiers as they sought to turn themselves in.

"They've been firing some of these guys up," Staff Sgt. James Silkwood told members of Charlie Company, 4th Battalion, 7th Infantry Regiment. He did not provide further details. "I know it would be easy to shoot at them," Silkwood added in the outdoor briefing at the perimeter of the barren encampment, "but we can't be doing that because they'll be trying to surrender."

The massive leaflet-distribution effort, which officers said was mounted soon after the war began, continues as reports reaching field commanders here suggest that the level of discomfort among Iraqi troops is increasing as the American bombing campaign continues.

The reports suggest that frontline Iraqi troops are receiving no more than one spartan meal a day. To meet shortages of food, Iraqi supply officers last week resorted to an overland cattle drive to bring 1,000 head of cattle to military encampments near the area where Iraq, Kuwait, and Saudi Arabia meet, the American officers have been told.

As outlined in the leaflets, Iraqi soldiers who wish to surrender to American forces are to sling their weapon over their left shoulder, barrel pointed downward, and to wave the flyer or other white object from an upraised right arm.

The American officers involved in the program emphasized in the briefings that these instructions vary in significant ways from the both-hands-high stance that is a universal signal of surrender. They declined for security reasons to explain why new procedures had been adopted for Iraqi troops.

In briefings and in other conversations, U.S. officers said their Iraqi counterparts were reportedly seeking to prevent the leaflets from reaching their soldiers, ordering non-commissioned officers to collect the flyers as soon as they hit the ground. But with the operation slated to airdrop a total of 5 million leaflets, the officers expressed confidence that Iraqi soldiers would become well aware of the safe-surrender procedures.

In addition to the leaflet distribution effort, Army units here have taken a number of other visible steps to prepare for an expected influx of Iraqi prisoners, including the assignment of Arab-born U.S. soldiers to serve as interpreters in frontline combat units.

At the same time, some units on Monday were offered rudimentary Arabic-language instruction, with emphasis on phrases like "Put your hands up" and "Throw down your weapon."

Afterward, however, soldiers in Charlie Company said they had trouble remembering even the most basic phrases, and joked openly about the likelihood of mistaking a surrendering Iraqi for an attacker.

No Gas Masks Issued, Local Drivers Desert; GIs Flown in To Keep Allied Military Trucks Moving

By Stephanie Glass, Tim Collie, and Peter Copeland

NORTHERN LOGISTICS BASE NEAR THE IRAQI BORDER—The Army is flying in thousands of soldiers to take over the trucking of supplies to frontline troops because local drivers have refused to haul cargo into a combat zone.

The start of war spooked hundreds of local drivers hired since the start of the military buildup to haul supplies to U.S. forces.

"They are civilians. We predicted that we would have to bring over a couple thousand soldiers to drive vehicles and we have," said Maj. Gen. William 'Gus' Pagonis, deputy commander for logistics for Operation Desert Storm. "They've been flown in from the states able to drive any host nation trucks where the driver decides not to drive. We have over 1,000 already arrived," Pagonis said in an interview.

Some of the drivers have returned to work but they refuse to drive to northernmost logistics bases, and some officers worry that a massive walkout of the 2,000 drivers if a ground war moves south could slow the flow of supplies at a critical time in battle.

Forward battalion supplies dropped the week the war started after hundreds of panicked local drivers who truck 40 percent of supplies to troops in northern Saudi Arabia refused to take cargo, officials here said.

When the air raids began Jan. 17, drivers—mainly Pakistani, Filipino, or Indian—pulled their trucks up to the gate of the Army's central distribution depot here seeking refuge at a time when the installation was at the highest state of alert.

"They came in and tried to get into the expansion van where the computer system was," said Capt. Scott Neumiller, 27, a steelworker from Freemont, NE, and commander of the 1012th General Supply Co., of the Nebraska National Guard.

"The guard tried to get them out. They rushed the guard and he fired a shot in the air. That got them back in the trucks," Neumiller said. "We were in MOPP 4 (full chemical protective gear) gear and they're sitting across the road with nothing. Not even gas masks. They wanted to get in." Pagonis said the Army has since issued one gas mask per truck.

Local drivers are an integral part of the logistics operation that has been touted as deploying more equipment and supplies faster than any other time in military history.

Of the 5,000 drivers on Saudi highways at any one time hauling anything from beans to bullets to coalition troops, 2,000 have been hired locally, Pagonis said. They sleep in their trucks, heat tea on portable stoves, and the Muslims pull out rugs to pray by the sides of their flat beds. But officers say the drivers' refusal to go farther north, closer to frontline troops, hurts efficiency. "It would make it easier if they would directly ship from the port to the units," Neumiller said.

And should a ground war go badly and the confrontation move south, local drivers would have to be replaced by soldiers. "If the Saudis stop, the military starts, and it will slow it down," he said.

Pagonis said he understands their reluctance to drive when the country is at war.

"You have to understand they're civilians who have jobs, many of them are third-country nationals. They're without their families," Pagonis said. "I don't blame them. I don't know if there are too many other people who would want to drive into a war if you're not a combatant."

Though the army continues to study ways to work around the civilian drivers, Pagonis said the majority are still behind the wheel. "We put the U.S. soldiers in the vehicles with the best drivers. We've formed them into units with a captain in charge," Pagonis said. "They line up. I talk to them. Some of them even salute. They've almost become a paramilitary force in support of us."

Iraqis Make First Move With Raids Into Kuwait: Fighting With Marines "Hellacious"

By Kirk Spitzer

NEAR THE KUWAIT BORDER, Saudi Arabia - U.S. air and ground forces halted Iraqi raids into Saudi Arabia early today following heavy fighting along the border.

It was the first Iraqi incursion into Saudi Arabia and the first large-scale engagement between U.S. and Iraqi ground forces.

Iraqi forces crossed into Saudi Arabia at at least two points along the border with Kuwait late Tuesday and early Wednesday morning and were engaged by elements of the 1st Marine Division, Marine and Air Force aircraft, and coalition forces.

Battle reports were sketchy, but the heaviest fighting seemed to center along the north-south border between Saudi Arabia and Kuwait. Staff officers at the 1st Marine Division reported that at least 20 Iraqi T-55 battle tanks and armored personnel carriers were destroyed in fighting that began about midnight and continued as late as 9 a.m. Wednesday. There were no estimates of Iraqi casualties.

U.S. losses were placed at two armored vehicles destroyed and eight to 10 killed in action. Iraqi troops reportedly were in control of the Saudi border city of Khafji, along the gulf coast but were being fought by troops from the Gulf state of Qatar.

The Qatarian troops reportedly destroyed two Iraqi tanks and took 10 prisoners.

In the engagement involving the 1st Marine Division, about 50 Iraqi tanks were seen late Tuesday moving toward Saudi Arabia from inside Iraqi-occupied Kuwait. Some of the tanks moved into Saudi territory, but it is not clear how many.

The Iraqis were attacked by Marine ground forces operating in the area, Air Force A-10 attack planes, and Marine A-6 bombers and AH-1 Cobra helicopters.

Marine and Iraqi armored vehicles also exchanged fire across the border in fighting that Lt. Col. Cliff Myers described as "hellacious." U.S. forces did not cross into Kuwait.

Many of the Iraqi tanks and armored vehicles were destroyed by TOW missile fire. Sporadic fighting continued in the area through early Wednesday morning.

Thirteen Iraqis were reported taken prisoner.

The engagement was the first Iraqi incursion into Saudi Arabia and was the first large-scale exchange between U.S. and Iraqi ground forces. Because of the nearly four-to-one advantage Iraq holds over U.S. allied forces in tanks and armored vehicles, it is critical that U.S. forces win decisively in armored engagements

Marine officers were jubilant early Wednesday after the outcome of the evening fighting was clear. "It felt good, really good. We kicked their asses," said a weary Capt. Bill Wainwright, who spent most of the night calling in Air Force and Marine air strikes.

Wainwright, a native of Buffalo, N.Y., said Air Force attack planes accounted for about 70 percent of the vehicles destroyed by air strikes and Marine aircraft counted for the remaining 30 percent. "It was a joint operation and it worked like clockwork," said Wainwright.

Marine officers were at a loss to explain the objectives of the Iraqi attack, but theorized it was a response to recent Marine artillery and armor raids on Iraqi positions inside Kuwait. "I hope they keep attacking us, the dumb f____s," said Lt, Col. Jerry Humble.

The 1st Marine Division engagement took place in a desolate, wind-streaked section of desert marked only by a six-foot-high sand berm that stretches the length of the border. The Iraqis attacked on a bitterly cold night and under a full moon, which cast a bright but eerie glare over the desert landscape.

Serious Fighting at Khafji 1st Major Battle of War—The Iraqis "Probably Ought to Call 911 Right Now"

By Jim Michaels

WITH U.S. FORCES, Saudi Arabia - An Iraqi armored force has crossed the border into Saudi Arabia and is engaging allied forces there in the first major armored battle of the Gulf War.

A lead element of the Iraqi forces entered the city of Khafji late Tuesday night and as many as two armored Iraqi brigades were reported heading south towards the Saudi border city by Wednesday noon.

U.S. Marines, who have set up a blocking position south of the city to prevent a push farther into Saudi territory, believe that the lead element of five tanks and 100 troops are holed up in the city. They tentatively report another two battalions, totaling an estimated 4,000 troops, are on the outskirts of the town and are fighting with Saudi forces there. So far the Marines have established the blocking force and have provided artillery and aircraft support, but have not committed ground forces.

Marine Corps vehicles mounted with machine guns and anti-tank weapons rushed to the outskirts of the city where they have established positions along the road south to Dhahran, the major city in the Eastern Province.

First reports indicated that the two Iraqi battalions moving south Wednesday may have been surrendering because their turrets were turned around as they headed south. That hope was quickly dashed when they engaged Saudi forces north of the city. "It may have been a ruse," said Marine Maj. Craig Huddleston. "It may have been inaccurate information." Either way the Saudis began fighting the armored column Wednesday as Marine artillery hammered targets north of the city. "They (Saudi forces) have been engaged by them, so they are going to take them out," Huddleston said.

The battle began when U.S. Marines noticed movement on the border Tuesday night, which was cloudless with a full moon. A force of five tanks and 10 to 15 armored personnel carriers entered the city, which has been virtually abandoned since the war started. The tanks apparently moved into the city where they can hide from allied air and artillery attacks. It was not clear why they encountered little or no resistance as they entered the city. Saudi ground forces are positioned near the border and most major U.S. positions are behind them.

U.S. officials said the company-sized Iraqi armored unit simply drove down the road and entered the city. By morning U.S. Marines, which had established blocking positions and placed artillery outside the city, were confident that the small force would be expelled.

"They probably ought to call 911 right now," Huddleston said. "I expect we're going to expel them rather violently."

"It appears to us absurd," Huddleston said of the movement into the city. "We're going to spank them pretty hard."

U.S. forward observers called on Marine helicopter gunships throughout the night. Wednesday morning Marine 155-mm howitzers joined the battle and shelled targets north of the city. But by noon Wednesday the fate of Khafji was more uncertain as U.S. forces received news of two battalions moving south towards Saudi Arabia.

U.S. forces appear willing at least initially to allow forces from Saudi Arabia and Qatar, who are positioned in and around Khafji, to handle the ground fighting backed by Marine Corps artillery and air support.

Apparently U.S. offices will see how the battle goes before bringing in U.S. tanks and infantry to aid Saudi and Qatari troops north of the border town. U.S. officials do not believe the action is part of a larger push into Saudi Arabia, where Iraqi forces would encounter large concentrations of U.S. defensive positions and have to deal with air strikes. Rather they speculate the move may be an attempt to force the United States into a ground war before they are ready or simply an attempt to throw off allied planning efforts.

Iraqi Incursion: Khafji Seized, Armored Thrusts at Several Points on Saudi-Kuwaiti Border

By Caryle Murphy

NORTHEASTERN SAUDI ARABIA WITH U.S. FORCES - Iraqi troops early this morning stormed the Saudi town of Khafji and took control of it, and U.S. Marines made an unsuccessful attempt to rescue two Army soldiers who apparently strayed into the town and are now missing.

The Khafji incursion appears to be part of a much larger Iraqi ground operation that today included Iraqi armored thrusts into Saudi territory at several points along the Saudi-Kuwaiti border. Late this evening, there were unconfirmed reports from military sources of a major massing of Iraqi troops along the border apparently indicating preparations for even more ground incursions.

The Iraqi offensive actions, particularly the one north of and into Khafji, appear to have caught U.S. military planners by surprise, indicating a major failure in intelligence about the intentions of Iraqi forces inside Kuwait.

This afternoon, scores of Saudi National Guard armored personnel carriers and tanks were seen rushing to the scene of the fighting between Saudi and Qatari forces on one side and the Iraqis on the other. Military officials here were still unclear about outcome of fighting in and around Khafji by late this afternoon. However, it seems clear that the town itself is under Iraqi control.

Marine Maj. Craig Huddleston said around 4 p.m. that he couldn't be sure who controls Khafji, but added: "The battle is far from over."

The dramatic attempt to rescue two Army personnel came after four vehicles, apparently armored Humvees, drove to "the edge of town," Huddleston said. The major said that the vehicles apparently "took small arms fire" from Iraqis in the town. One vehicle escaped, but the other one "looked like he drove into the side of a wall," Wuddleston said.

"We went up and tried to rescue them, but they weren't there," said Huddleston. The car was there, but there were no occupants, he said. Another source said the personal gear of the two missing soldiers was in the car but their weapons were not.

Two Marine Cobra attack helicopters took part in the rescue attempt, and one fired its missiles at an Iraqi armored personnel carrier during the aborted rescue, military officials said.

While U.S. military officials had earlier in the day said that Saudi armored united were engaging a separate Iraqi armored incursion of about 80 vehicles, that crossed the border north of Khafji before noon, they were unable to provide any details on the outcome of that battle by the end of the day. Elements of the Qatari armed forces played a role in the fighting around Khafji itself,

but again details were not provided. Qatari tanks were in the area, one U.S. military source said.

Throughout the morning and afternoon, the sound of multiple rocket launchers and artillery could be heard in the town of Khafji and to the west and north of the town.

Saudi armored personnel carriers, tanks, several pickup trucks with mounted guns and at least two ambulances were seen heading north around 2:15 p.m.

A U.S. Marine artillery unit from the 1st Marine Division supported the coalition forces with repeated rounds of artillery fire from howitzer guns up until about 10 p.m.

The Khafji action, which was reported to U.S. forces in their rear positions behind Arab forces stationed in this area at about 10:30 p.m. Tuesday night, was first announced by Baghdad today. The Iraqi government declared that its forces had taken Khafji and that "enemy forces" had fled.

There was a Saudi military presence in Khafji before the Iraqi incursion, but it is not known how large the force was.

Mission Unsuccessful: A Daring Dash into Khafji to Rescue Two GIs Missing from Patrol

By Jim Michaels

WITH U.S. MARINES, Saudi Arabia - A Marine Corps motorized patrol led a daring mission into the embattled town of Khafji in an unsuccessful attempt to rescue two soldiers who had come under Iraqi small-arms fire.

A small motorized patrol equipped with anti-tank missiles and machine guns drove into the border city as fighting raged between allied and Iraqi forces.

The soldiers are considered missing. "We wanted to get them pretty bad," said Marine Maj. Craig Huddleston of the failed

attempt. Behind him lay the smoking ruins of an Iraqi armored personnel carrier hit by a U.S. Marine helicopter gunship during the mission.

Fighting continued Wednesday and U.S. officers on the outskirts of the town admitted they were unsure who controlled the city as the Saudis were apparently left in charge of most of the fighting. But clearly the Iraqis are moving through the city with impunity. During the attempted rescue mission, two Iraqi armored vehicles were spotted at the southern gates to the city, indicating they had met little resistance as they drove through town.

Wednesday - January 30, 1991

The job of defending the town apparently fell to Saudi forces, which are arrayed in and around the city, which has been mostly abandoned since the fighting started. The Saudis are receiving help from the well-regarded troops of Qatar and air and artillery support from nearby Marine positions.

A force of an estimated five Iraqi tanks and 100 troops drove across the border and entered the city Tuesday night.

Another two Iraqi battalions are also believed to have taken Saudi forces under attack near Khafji and elsewhere along the border between Kuwait and Saudi Arabia. Wednesday evening, dozens of Saudi armored personnel carriers drove north in an attempt to (assist) forces already engaged around Khafji.

A column of about a dozen American-made M-60 tanks belonging to the Saudis raced toward the town. Saudi tankers flashed the victory sign as they passed through a U.S. Marine position on the way to the city. But Marines said that on the night the Iraqis entered Khafji, Saudi troops manning a roadblock on the outskirts of town left it abruptly. Wednesday their tents and even a helmet remained, indicating a hasty departure.

The most dramatic chapter of the fighting so far may be the failed attempt to rescue two Army soldiers. Elements of the 1st Marine Division mounted the rescue patrol Wednesday when they learned that two U.S. soldiers were stranded in a vehicle in Khafji after they had come under Iraqi small-arms fire.

The pair were driving with another U.S. Army vehicle when they came under Iraqi fire. The vehicles had taken a wrong turn and wound up in the middle of the fighting inside Khafji. The one truck escaped, but the other apparently crashed into a wall.

The vehicles were taken under small-arms fire and one ran off the road, while the other took off to get help. The Marines hastily organized a motorized patrol to go to the outskirts of the city, where the vehicle went off the road and hit a wall. Marine officials took a reporter and camera crew along on part of the mission Wednesday afternoon.

The patrol went to a gas station on the edge of town where they made last-minute preparations and prepared to launch the patrol into the outskirts of town. As the patrol moved up the road, a pair of Marine Cobra gunships flew low alongside the road. When they arrived at the truck, Staff Sgt. Don Gallagher, a 30-year-old from Great Falls, Mont., jumped out of his vehicle and looked in the Army truck, but there was no sign of the soldiers.

The passenger door was opened and the wheels were still spinning, where it had crashed into the wall. Gallagher ran around the vehicle yelling, "U.S. Marines!" in the hope they were in the area. "There were no bloodstains and no signs of them," Huddleston said. It was then that members of the patrol saw two BMPs, Soviet made armored personnel carriers, and three Iraqi soldiers dressed in green uniforms practically across the street. "I think we were both surprised," Huddleston said.

The Marines jumped back in their vehicles and made it back to the gas station, where they checked an identification book to make sure the vehicle was a BMP and not a friendly Saudi vehicle. "This is it, sir," a patrol member told an officer, pointing a picture of the BMP. From there, the Cobras were controlled by radio as they moved slowly up the road, at the level of power lines. The Cobras fired a total of at least six TOW anti-tank missiles, but only knocked out one BMP.

A curl of thick black smoke rose from the vehicle, as the helicopter gunships banked south towards their base. Huddleston lit a cigarette and sighed: "I wish we had those soldiers."

Thursday January 31, 1991

Some countries found ways to show solidarity with the cause of ejecting Iraqi troops from Kuwait other than to ship soldiers or fighter planes to the desert.

The coalition's members around the world might contribute a hospital, a fuel-tanker, mine-detector, or cargo ship to the armada floating offshore.

Czech Republic sent a chemical detection unit, although the costs of the military unit's deployment were covered by Saudi Arabia. Gen. Khalid, the Saudi commander, wanted his own chemical/biological warfare detection capability, in addition to the U.S. Army's mobile "Fox" units that had been shipped from Germany.

The Czech unit got results. Postwar reports by the Pentagon confirmed that the Czechs detected a nerve agent near Hafar al Batin, Saudi Arabia, on Jan. 19th, and also reported finding "discolored sand" that may have been caused by chemical weapons five days later near King Khalid Military City, a massive allied base in northern Saudi Arabia.

The Pentagon report noted there was no way of independently verifying the reports, but said there was no reason to believe they weren't valid. Two more Czech reports later in January—one for mustard gas and another listing Sarin gas—were described as "indeterminate."

The Czech reports were not linked to any casualties and did not attract news attention during the war. Postwar campaigns to identify a cause or causes for the range of physical symptoms generally described as "Gulf War Syndrome," however, found much of interest in the detection reports.

Japan contributed billions of dollars and Germany also ponied up, donating $540 million to Britain to defray the costs of putting a UK division in the Gulf, aircraft in the air and all the accouterments of modern war. The Neo-Nazi movement in Germany couldn't let that move go unanswered. Its leaders said they had more than 500 volunteers ready to go to the Gulf and fight for Iraq.

In the saga of Khafji, this chapter takes the story through another day in which the picture on the ground started to clear. The episode in which 11 Marines were killed looked worse the clearer it got, however. At the end of the day, the Iraqis paid a price, losing most of the tanks on the excursion and hundreds of men killed or taken prisoner.

And for the allies, Battle of Khafji after-action reports knocked some of the superlatives off the initial assessments. As a story in this chapter relates, despite being lambasted by Marine artillery and fighters, many vehicles from the Iraqi invading force managed to escape the battle zone they had mysteriously chosen.

There was still no consensus as to why the Iraqis had sent their tanks and vehicles down across the Saudi border in the first place, especially to seize a small, abandoned and apparently non-strategic town like Khafji.

The first report from Saudi troops assigned security for that area was that some Iraqi tanks had their turrets pointed backward, which would indicate they were planning to surrender. As they got closer, however, the Iraqis apparently swung their guns around and fired, so the surrender must have been a ruse.

Could it be that some of the tank crews were, in fact, planning to surrender, however? If so, were their plans foiled by other Iraqi tankers who changed their minds at the last second and fired at the unsuspecting Saudis?

One possibility suggested later was that the Iraqi soldiers were running out of rations. The allied bombing had prevented supplies from getting to them and they were hoping the Saudis had left some edibles behind.

If they thought a few rounds would scare the Saudis off, leaving the rations for them, they were wrong. And if that was the actual reason, it was an expensive food raid.

While the fighting at Khafji was short-lived, the threat of terrorism never seemed to flag. The U.S. State Department announced it had logged 70 separate terrorism acts somewhere in the world since the war began.

Wars of the modern era are fought on a variety of battlefields, not always by professional soldiers. The murky leagues and secret cells of assassins and bombers take their share of action, too.

The uniformed armies facing off in the Gulf in 1991 could be enumerated carefully: so many corporals, privates, lieutenants, sergeants; so many soldiers in this regiment, so many trained for this weapon.

Non-uniformed fighters in the armies of terrorism were largely anonymous and never had answered roll-calls in front of a barracks. But they were tallied by the jobs they did, and the lives they took.

Casualties and medical care drew a lot of attention during the bombing campaign—not only from the Iraqi civilians killed in allied air strikes, but the casualties being forecast for the allied troops once the ground war erupted.

Once the land war broke out, the allies would be much better prepared than the Iraqis to care for casualties.

But even with modern field facilities and spotless hospital ships offshore, the coalition's trained surgeons and personnel weren't sure they could handle the numbers being projected without employing triage.

How they were going to decide those questions is explained in this chapter, along with a tale of military doctors who were way ahead of the war. They were at the front before they were needed.

Allies Take Back Part of Khafji, But Iraqi Invaders Still Control Gates of City

By Jim Michaels

WITH U.S. MARINES NEAR KHAFJI – Iraqi forces beat back several allied attempts to drive them out Wednesday night, but U.S. officials say the allied forces have gained control of at least part of the city.

The main ground attacks were carried out by armored Saudi and Qatari units, while

U.S. Marine artillery and aircraft pound Iraqi targets around the city. Saudi and Iraqi tanks clashed west and north of the city Thursday.

The Saudis have taken about 23 Iraqi prisoners and knocked out several tanks, according to U.S. officials, but the future of the city remains uncertain.

U.S. officials monitoring the battle said Thursday at 1 p.m. the city had been retaken, but a Marine armored patrol was turned back before it reached the gates of the city by Iraqi shelling. "This is doing nothing but help us whittle down his forces," Marine Lt. Col. Robert Rivers said Thursday, as he visited U.S. forces on the outskirts of the besieged city. Shortly afterwards Iraqi shelling of this position cut his conversation short as everyone scattered for cover.

The fighting was intense Thursday. At a position outside the city, Marine Corps heavy machine guns poured fire on Iraqi gun positions, and U.S. observers called in air strikes. Iraqi rockets and artillery responded by attempting to hit the U.S. position.

U.S. officers see the two-day-old battle as a "spoiling attack," an attempt by the Iraqis to upset ongoing plans by U.S. forces to attack Iraqi troops in Kuwait.

As a result the allies allowed Saudi and Qatari forces to do most of the ground fighting, backed by Marine Corps artillery and air support. Forces from the two Arab countries are deployed north of U.S. forces and are responsible for the defense of Khafji.

Lt. Col. William Grubb said the Saudi army and National Guard, which is largely untested in combat, proved itself in battle against the more experienced Iraqi forces.

Marine Col. John Admire said Saudi and Qatari forces were mopping up the southern part of the city while the Iraqis controlled the north. "They did it without American ground support," he said.

"It's not just against Iraq," said 1st Lt. Michael Ragoza, a 26-year-old from Bradley Beach, N.J. "We've got to get the Saudis involved." Ragoza was outside the city since the battle began and Thursday he continued to fire onto suspected Iraqi positions after going two nights without sleep.

Despite U.S. air and artillery help, several initial attempts by the Saudis to retake the city failed, and U.S. officers believe the Iraqis have hidden their forces inside part of the city and say Iraqis are reinforcing their forces in the northern part of the city. Marines pulled out two small American units that were trapped in the city after the fighting began. The teams were rescued early Thursday while the battle was still intense.

Marine Lance Cpl. Benton Barron was pinned down by Iraqi small-arms fire when he went in a vehicle behind a Saudi force to rescue one of the teams. "Have you ever heard a round go by your head?" he asked after making it to the edge of the city after helping the team get out.

"We were following a Saudi assault into the city," Barron said. "When we got into the city all hell broke loose."

Behind U.S. Air and Artillery, Saudi and Qatari Troops Eject Iraqis From Khafji

By Caryle Murphy

WITH U.S. FORCES IN NORTHEAST SAUDI ARABIA – Saudi and Qatari forces, backed up by U.S. air and artillery support, overcame "heavy" resistance to eject Iraqi forces from the Saudi town of Khafji in the first protracted land battle of the U.S.-led Gulf War, U.S. officials said.

Thursday - January 31, 1991

By 18:30 hours today, Saudi troops were said to be in control of the seaside town just ten miles south of the Kuwait border, but were facing "pockets of resistance" that included small-arms fire and perhaps one artillery battery still inside the town, one U.S. officer said.

The Arab forces reportedly captured 111 Iraqi soldiers, the officer said. Initial reports of casualties among the Arab forces were unclear. One Marine officer in the field said he'd been told the Saudi and Qatari forces had taken "heavy" casualties, but he could not provide numbers on dead and wounded. A more senior Marine officer said he had been told by Saudi commanders that they had wounded men, but no deaths.

There were no U.S. casualties, U.S. military officials said. But two Army soldiers, who went missing when they strayed into Khafji on Wednesday, are still unaccounted for. The soldiers, one female and one male, were attached to a Dhahran-based motor transport unit, according to one Marine officer.

He said there was no indication the two had been taken prisoner by the Iraqis, but Baghdad Radio today claimed it had captured both male and female American POWs.

The re-taking of Khafji at noon today also ended a 36-hour ordeal for 12 U.S. Marines caught in the city when the Iraqis overran it and who managed to elude the intruders by hiding in buildings.

The 12, who were on reconnaissance missions in Khafji, hid in the tops of buildings, survived on the food they had with them, burned secret codes and messages to protect them, and used encrypted radios to signal their locations and even call in U.S. artillery strikes, according to Marine Col. John Admire, commander of a 1st Marine Division Task Force.

They were relieved to see us," said Marine Capt. John Borth of Catonsville, Md., one of the Marines sent into Khafji to pick up the 12. "They looked real tired and worn out."

Report of Marines Killed in Iraqi Incursion Accurate, But Not in Battle for Khafji

By Kirk Spitzer

NOTE: *This report contains an advisory of erroneous radio and television reports regarding recent Marine combat deaths and an update on Marine combat engagement along the border of southwest Kuwait.*

ADVISORY: There have been erroneous radio and television reports that are confusing two separate combat actions.

For the record: There have been no, repeat no Marine deaths in the fighting for the city of Khafji. Further, there have been no Marine units actively involved in the fighting for Khafji, although a small Marine unit was involved in a rescue attempt.

No significant numbers of Marine ground troops are currently involved in the attempt to re-take the city, which is located in a zone controlled by Saudi forces.

The source for this information is staff officers at 1st Marine Division headquarters.

This is the latest available information: A total of 11 Marines from the 1st Marine Division were killed in fighting with Iraqi armored units along Kuwait's SOUTHWEST border with Saudi Arabia during an engagement that began late Tuesday night (Saudi time) and ended about 5 a.m.

This engagement took place in an area of open desert miles from the gulf coast.

This engagement was completely separate from the attack and subsequent fighting at Khafji, which is located on the coast.

Radio and television reports monitored here in the field have erroneously placed the Marine deaths in the Khafji area.

This is wrong. According to the staff officers with the 1st Marine Division headquarters, only small numbers of Marines have been involved in the fighting to re-take Khafji. It was preliminarily reported early Wednesday night that the number of deaths had been placed at 12. However, staff officers at headquarters of the 1st Marine Division today said the final tally is 11 Marines killed in action and two wounded.

Also, final Iraqi losses were placed at 22 tanks destroyed and an undetermined number of additional armored vehicles destroyed, compared to two Marine light armored vehicles destroyed. Marines are still jubilant over the victory, which was fought with Marine air and ground forces and Air Force A-10 attack planes. "It was a devastating fight to the enemy," said Lt. Col. Jerry Humble, division operations officer. He said some Marine and Iraqi ground forces were firing at each other from ranges of a half-mile or less.

"They (U.S. forces) fought a magnificent fight. Just look at the scoreboard—we lost two (armored vehicles), they lost 22 (tanks)."

The engagement was the first time the Marines' LAV-25 Light Armored Vehicles have been used in large-scale combat (a handful of LAV-25s were used in Operation Just Cause in Panama last year). "The LAVs fought very well. They fought to our expectations and beyond."

Numbers Game: Many Iraqi Vehicles Escape Bombing of Khafji "Like a Close-Out Sale on Ladies' Lingerie"

By Susan Sachs, Dick Thompson, and Gilles Tresquesser

U.S. AIRBASE IN NORTHEASTERN SAUDI ARABIA - While jet fighter pilots were pleased at last to have targets to bomb and strafe out in the open desert near Khafji, a large number of Iraqi vehicles were able to elude a swarm of attacking aircraft and artillery and return safely to the hidden bunkers back inside Kuwait.

According to Lt. Col. Dick Lazisky, 41, of Boston, Bronco squadron commander and the pilot flying over Khafji the night of the incursion, an estimated 80 vehicles moved into the Khafji area early Wednesday morning. To date, coalition pilots report having destroyed 20 to 25 vehicles—including tanks, armored personnel carriers and trucks—and the rest returned to Kuwait. "It was just a probing action," said Lazisky. "They were seeing what type of reaction we'd have and probably trying to draw us into a fight across the border where they are dug in."

Today, Harrier jets and other U.S. aircraft continued to pound the Iraqi vehicles in action north of Khafji and just across the Kuwait border. But one squadron commander said that there were so many aircraft in the area that it was difficult to find targets. U.S. aircraft were swarming over the area, said Lt. Col. Dick "Snake" White, commander of the Tomcat squadron of Harriers: "My biggest danger was running into another U.S. aircraft." White, 29, of Fort Smith, Ark., added: "It was almost like trying to get to the checkout during a close-out sale on ladies' lingerie."

Before White flew today, he told pool reporters that the long wait for Iraqis to come up and fight had finally come to an end.

"Now it's almost like you flipped on the light in the kitchen late at night and the cockroaches start scurrying, and we're killing them. They're moving in columns, they're moving in small groups and convoys. It's exactly what we've been looking for, and it sounds to me like he has lost his marbles. That's what we've been searching for and hoping for, for the past ten days. So they could come out and find 'em."

Before his flight, White spoke of intelligence reports according to which there were "800 to 1,000 vehicles moving now." But returning from his mission, he stressed he did not actually see a large number of vehicles today, although he did report a Harrier pilot flying minutes ahead of him reported seeing and dropping Rockeye cluster bombs (720-pounders) on six tanks. These tanks were spotted along the border northwest of Khafji and moving southeasterly.

Today, White had to circle for 20 minutes until ground control allowed him to make his runs. While he took out a line of vehicles yesterday, on two bombing and strafing runs, today White had to settle for a cluster of supply trucks. U.S. pilots, whose vision was obscured by smoke and blowing sand, didn't encounter SAM or heavy 3A fire from the ground. There were no Iraqi planes encountered in any of the missions flown since the Khafji attack began. It was difficult for the pilot to have a clear picture of the situation in and around Khafji because, said White, "the nature of the battlefield changes on an hourly basis."

"Everything we came to clean up was already smoking and burning," said Harrier pilot Glen Melin. "Today we saw 10 to 20 vehicles burning along a few miles on a highway just north of the border," said another Harrier pilot.

Midnight two days ago, Bronco pilot Lt. Col. Dick Lazisky and backseater Capt. Dave Neely of Pittsburgh, Pa., were circling low over the Khafji area when their cameras began recording a column of vehicles about ten meters off the Khafji road, on its western side, moving south toward a Marine contingent.

Heavy ground fire began and the small observer plane started taking long-range SAM missiles in clusters of threes.

From the plane, the airmen could see white explosions on the ground, red glows inside the cockpit as SAMs missed nearby, and red trackers streaming both north and south. Radio chatter indicated an advance unit or Marines was under heavy fire and retreating.

Neely said he observed a regular mechanized battalion off the side of the road and moving south. "The Marines said they were getting overrun and leaving that area," said Neely. Yesterday, White flew into the same area and found 20 to 25 vehicles parked "bumper to bumper" off the side of the road. Said White: "We rolled in and made two bombing passes and strafed with 25mm cannons and left the entire column in flames."

White, expressing his surprise at the Iraqi strategy, said: "It's a golden opportunity. We've been executing bombing raids for about two weeks. The biggest problem has been finding targets to hit. If Saddam wants to bring these tanks out and line them up on the road bumper to bumper, as he did yesterday afternoon, that's fine with us. We're killing them. It makes no sense whatsoever. If I were the military commander I might get worried that I'd be relieved of my job a la Saddam."

"What in the world are they doing?" said White. "It's opposed to all military logic. I just really don't know what to make of it. He was doing fairly well hoarding his assets, hiding them from air attack. We've had bad weather. As you can see now, the sun is shining. If he brings these vehicles out now and lines them up on the highway, it's going to be a turkey shoot."

Expectation of 1,000 Allied Casualties a Day Triggers Debate Over Treating the Enemy

By Michael Hedges

WITH THE 1ST INFANTRY DIVISION – For Dr. Steve Phillips, the "injury not the uniform" will determine who he treats first in combat, but within the same division, Dr. Bill Buchanan said, "We know how limited medical resources are, we will use them on Americans first."

Told to expect as many as 1,000 casualties a day in this division, doctors here are wrestling with life and death moral dilemmas as the U.S. attack on Iraq forces nears.

All the doctors here expect major, perhaps overwhelming casualties in the early days of the ground offensive. "We plan for the worst-case scenario," said Maj. Leroy Graham, 36, an Army doctor from Denver who is senior medical officer for the 201st Forward Support Battalion.

"Realistically, people have talked about 10 to 25 percent wounded in the attacking brigades." Army officers here expect there to be several Iraqi casualties for every American injured. Given what all doctors interviewed here agreed were limited medical supplies, that number of wounded will force doctors to make decisions very quickly on who gets treated. "It is real simple," said Dr. Graham. "A wounded man is a wounded man. We will try to give some priority to our troops if the level of injury is the same, but we gave an oath to save lives."

Capt. Eric Tunell, a doctor with the 201st from Redlands, Calif., said the Geneva Convention required military doctors to treat wounded enemy soldiers, but "it is more than that, we are doctors. It is what we are sworn to do." Capt. Tunell, 36, said, "If you want to be detached and say the Iraqis are not human beings, but that is not the way we look at it."

One of the most limited assets here will be medical evacuation helicopters, doctors believe. Capt. Phillips, 29, from Columbus, Ohio, said, "If I have an American soldier with a broken arm, and an Iraqi with a (life-threatening chest injury), the Iraqi is getting medevac-ed first." He added: "It is based on the injury, not the uniform."

Within the 701st Main Supply Battalion, 1st Infantry, doctors have struggled with the same question and reached a substantially different answer. Maj. Buchanan, of Hampton, Va., said, "We were the first group of doctors (from the division) out here. We had to scrounge for medical supplies. If Iraqis can be saved with minimal medical resources we will do that, but we are going to be very limited on medical assets."

Capt. Kevin Wall, a 31-year-old doctor from Minneapolis, Minn., said, "We are expecting a massive type of air-land battle." He said doctors were told to prepare for 1,000 casualties per day per division in VII Corps. "When I'm thinking about statistics like that, I realize our troops are going to need all we have, and even some things we don't. If I am in a situation where I'm dividing limited assets, I will conserve them for the use of our wounded."

Maj. Buchanan said, "Our supplies are limited, we only have so many blood units, so many chest packs. In the early going, when we are being overwhelmed with casualties, the priority will be Americans." Told some other doctors in the division saw the matter somewhat differently, he said, "That is certainly not what we've been told. We've been told to give priority to Americans."

Under the structure of this division, some doctors will be in armored personnel carriers close behind the attacking tank and Bradley fighting vehicle columns.

As described by some of the doctors here, medical care given at that level will have to be fast and will be necessarily basic. "Medical care as you know it in hospitals in the States doesn't even exist out here," said Dr. Tunell. "We have less resuscitative capability than a paramedic on an ambulance in the States."

Dr. Graham said, "Sophistication won't be our greatest asset. Our greatest asset is between our ears, the decisions we will make."

After doing rudimentary life-saving procedures like stopping bleeding and providing breathing passages, the most forward doctors then decide an order on having patients either airlifted, or if artillery fire from Iraqis makes that too dangerous, driven to hospitals in the rear.

This dividing of the wounded into categories, called triage, is the most important and most stressful part of the early care of the wounded, doctors said. "Triage was a system set up to give you a way not to go crazy yourself by trying to save everybody," said Dr. Wall.

There are actually two stages of triage here, one at the front lines and one at a makeshift medical facility just behind the lines. At each level, the wounded are categorized as either needing urgent care to survive, needing serious care but able to wait, needing minimal care, or just beyond being helped. Capt. Phillips is one of the doctors who will ride behind the lines in a thin-skinned armored vehicle so the wounded can be seen in minutes.

"My job is not to treat the wounded, my job is to prepare people to be evacuated. If they are in my aid station more than 15 to 20 minutes, they have been there too long," he said. Capt. Phillips said since he is traveling behind an armored column, he expected to see burn and blast injuries and traumatic amputations that require immediate attention to stop bleeding.

Maj. Graham said speed will be essential to the mission of doctors here, along with stabilizing the vital signs of the wounded. Statistics from Vietnam showed that if you could put someone on a helicopter with a stable pulse, he had a 99 percent chance for survival."

The doctors here are preparing themselves psychologically for what they believe lies ahead. "There is the potential for casualties here that none of us have ever seen before," said Maj. Graham. "In the busiest emergency room, 120 patients a day is considered a lot," said Capt. Tunell. "We will probably see that in just a few hours."

He said, "One of the things we will be affected by is sleep deprivation. I'm not expecting to sleep much in the first few days. But we're doctors, we've done lots of that."

They must also deal with the idea that they are in personal danger. "All of us had to get over that initial fear," said Maj. Graham. "All of us had that primary fear for self. But we got over that and we are working together in ways you really don't see in peacetime."

Capt. Tunell said, "We're unique officers, our enemies are disease and trauma. We don't fight the Iraqis, we're non-combatants."

Maj. Kelly Palmer, 38, of Pocatello, Idaho, is a psychiatrist with the 701st. He said he was already seeing people suffering stress and anxiety here. "I don't have boatloads, but people are coming in on a regular basis and saying this is difficult to handle."

Maj. Palmer said, "If the coming battle is something fast and victorious, there will be very few battle fatigue casualties." But he said if the attack bogged down, if units suffered defeats or if chemical attacks were made, the numbers of victims of combat fatigue would rise. "Hopefully, it will be fast and furious," he said.

Maj. Palmer said that some troops coming up from rear port areas had been shaken by Scud attacks. "I'm seeing people who saw Scuds overhead and didn't realize how they were going to handle fear. They have startled reactions to noise, trouble sleeping. In time, most are working it out."

Doctors, too, are learning to deal with alien and frightening surroundings. Capt. Phillips said he was taken by surprise when an explosive mine-clearing device was test-fired. "A sergeant saw my reaction and said, 'Hey, doc, wait until it's for real.'"

Maj. Graham said the rush of events, including an Iraqi attack which killed about a dozen Marines east of here, was "a sequential reinforcement that this is really a war." But Capt. Tunell said, "To be honest, I think what happened to the Marines was mild (compared) to what is going to happen here. When I finally see maimed and dead bodies, that will affect me."

A Gurney Too Far: Doctors Dropped at Front

By Michael Hedges

WITH THE 1ST INFANTRY DIVISION – Through an apparent mixup in orders, a group of non-combatant doctors spent the first week of the war as the most forward U.S. troops in Saudi Arabia, far ahead of the division's combat troops.

"We were in the neutral zone about 20 miles from the Iraqi lines," said Maj. Bill Buchanan, of the 701st Main Supply Battalion of 1st Infantry. "We were told later we were the most forward unit in the entire Southwestern Asia theater," he said.

"Doctors were digging foxholes, we were maintaining fighting positions." Several of the doctors said they spent about a week in the position without escort before elements of a division cavalry squadron arrived. Even then, most of the doctors weren't withdrawn. "The feeling was, we were so small the Iraqis would probably ignore us," said Capt. Kevin Wall, a 31-year-old Army doctor from Minneapolis. "I think it's a fairly good symbol of where doctors fit in the whole Army scheme of things," he said with a smile.

The doctors still aren't sure how they ended up as the forward force in a combat infantry division—if not in the entire Desert Storm deployment.

Capt. Eric Tunell, 36, a doctor from Redlands, CA, said his understanding was that the day the war started, the medical supply battalions in the division got orders to move to a spot about 90 miles north of where the division was then locate.

Apparently the division was to move at one time, but those orders were canceled, the doctor said. But by the time the division's plans changed, the doctors and their support vehicles had begun a 26-hour trek north. "It was a terrible traffic jam, and the roads up there are rocky and twisting," recalled Capt. Tunell. Once they arrived at their forward position, the doctors were surprised to find themselves alone, but quickly adjusted. One remembered Dr. Wall bending the point of a pick trying to dig a protective hole in the rocky soil.

Dr. Buchanan said, "We had a doctor who was a West Point graduate. He and a physician's assistant were out there determining defensive positions and finding fire lanes." Even after the cavalry arrived, the doctors said the situation remained a little uncomfortable. Several remembered an Iraqi lieutenant being brought into the camp by the troopers for interrogation. The doctors were never withdrawn, but were called back a few at a time to take care of the sick in the units that are still waiting to move forward.

Of their time in the neutral zone, one doctor said, "I'm just glad the Iraqis didn't decide to attack during that first week. We would have been a speed bump."

Tough American Paratroopers Go Dainty, But Highly Motivated, into Battle

By Gary Regenstrief

NORTHERN SAUDI ARABIA - Medical Sgt. Sal Garcia Jr. doffed his helmet, glanced about furtively and revealed a perfume-scented pair of women's underwear inside that he plans to carry into battle. No, Garcia and other troops in the U.S. Army's 82nd Airborne Division, one of the alliance's most elite fighting forces, will not wear them under their trousers.

Rather, the undergarments their wives and girlfriends have sent them, arouse and frustrate the soldiers after six months in the desert and, as such, provide a hefty dose of motivation to score a quick victory against Iraq and return home.

"When I put my helmet on I think of her because of the perfume," Garcia, 24, of Norwalk, Calif., said of Kelly, whom he began dating a month before he left for Saudi Arabia in early August. "It motivates me to get through another day because I know someone is there waiting for me. It's also a good luck charm."

Soldiers tuck sentimental or important belongings underneath the netting of their Kevlar, the synthetic helmet that can stop bullets, for safekeeping. It is perhaps the only place they can remain relatively clean and dry.

While most soldiers carry photographs of loved ones, some prefer to line their helmets with more personal reminders of relationships they left several thousand kilometers away.

While the garments are not one of the traditions of the 82nd Airborne, it is something of a status symbol and soldiers ask their mates to send them a special delivery.

"She was too embarrassed for two months but she finally did," said Specialist Michael Luoma, 21, a medic from Calumet, Mich. "I bugged her so much about it."

Luoma pulled out a pair of pink undergarments, trimmed with white lace, that were full of dust. "It's pretty embarrassing to wash them," he said. "Definitely, they make you think about home." After keeping them in his helmet for five months, Sgt. Christopher Bolner, an M-60 gunner at a base within sight of Iraqi defenses, sent home to his girlfriend a pair of black underwear not available in just any department store.

"I had to send them back," said Bolner, 21, of Lexington, Ky., shaking his head. "I was going nuts. You smell the perfume before you go to bed and you have great dreams." Asked for his thoughts when he smelled the perfume, Luoma said, "I don't know if you could print that."

Pvt. Spencer Klemen, 19, of Horn Lake, Miss., keeps a photograph only of the woman he has dated for six years. Even that is difficult. "I probably look at it every second day," he said. "That makes it harder. You don't know what's going to happen to you here."

U.S. Air Chief Calls Iraqi Attack "Stupidest," Scud a "Zero Weapon" With Huge Psychological Impact

By David Evans and Edith M. Lederer

This is an extra pool report from interview with Air Force Lt. Gen. Chuck Horner. We interviewed him for upcoming pool report reconstructing the start of the war and asked him about current status of air operations as well. Hence this spot story.

RIYADH, Saudi Arabia - Allied air power has devastated the Iraqi military and if the war ended tomorrow it would probably take a decade to restore the country's fighting prowess, U.S. Air Force chief Lt. Gen. Chuck Horner said Thursday.

He said the air war had pummeled the Iraqi military so relentlessly that Saddam Hussein was resorting to spoiling attacks across the border to show that Iraqi military can still seize the initiative.

"This attack at Khafji—that's stupid! That's the stupidest thing he could do!" Horner declared. "Now why is he doing that? To me, it occurs one of the answers is that he's desperate, and he sees that he's getting chewed up.

"So is he giving me intelligence that says, 'You're killing me, with your (air) attacks on the Republican Guards, and I've got to lash out?' I've got to force the action because he's losing his ass in these battles everywhere except in the papers if you count the vehicles destroyed out there and the prisoners taken.

"I didn't expect him to go on the offensive like this. Why is he doing that? Maybe he sees the sand running out on them. So, maybe I'm doing better than what I think I am. I don't know. It's the bright spot in my day. It's hard to see where he really gains a lot from this. He gets publicity. I think he sees it as sort of a Tet. I think he's fighting us in Vietnam."

Horner said that if Saddam was really serious about an attack styled on the 1968 Tet offensive that unhinged U.S. domestic support for the Vietnam War, he would have combined the ground assault with Scud missile attacks and air attacks.

The flight of nearly 100 Iraqi combat and transport aircraft to Iran doesn't make military sense, either, he said in an interview.

"It makes a certain degree of political sense if you say, 'Well, my air force can't stand up to the barbarians anyway, so they're out of there. And somehow I'm going to get a peace out of this. We're gonna get 'em. I've been watching CNN and I see them peaceniks out there, and I know they're gonna do just what they did in Vietnam. They're going to force the president to stop this thing. And then I will have that military force in sanctuary.'

"And I think what happened is that he built all of these hardened aircraft shelters... I'm sure he said, 'I'll just park my air force in there and it won't be a problem.' After about three nights of that (allied bombing) he said, 'Oh, shit, it's not working out, so I guess I'll put them in a bigger aircraft shelter called Iran,'" he said.

Two weeks after massive allied bombing attacks launched the Gulf War, Horner said the air is "a preeminent actor" in the air, land and sea operation. However, he said, "my weather guy keeps giving me this blue-sky briefing and it's been a struggle....

Secondly, I personally underestimated the political impact of the Scuds. I mean, they are a zero weapon. When you look at the damage they cause for the effort he's put into them. If we'd bought the Scud and sold that to the American taxpayer you would have a scandal that would exceed any scandal we've had. But the political impact of it has been very important. We've had to devote a very significant effort towards particularly keeping the Scuds off Israel.

"The B-52 (bomber), kind of like the Scud, has tremendous psychological impact. It is extremely useful on large-area targets," he said. He didn't know how effective the B-52s had been against dug-in Iraqi Republican Guards unit along the border.

"In war you deal with uncertainty, chaos and fog . . . you can't force some of these things," Horner said. However, he suggested that the B-52 attacks are forcing the Iraqis into rash actions, like their recent incursion into Saudi Arabia, before their forces are bombed out of existence.

Horner said the air war had been a strategic success.

"His military system is devastated. His country is not. I think the difficulty he will have postwar will be rebuilding the transportation system, and we were very careful about that. We're not just arbitrarily taking something out," he said.

"He'll have some work to do in power and fuel storage, and stuff like that.

"The only thing we're really obliterating are those things that are production of war assets. So his agriculture, his commerce . . . those are intact, basically. If the war would end tomorrow, I'd be very pleased that the war was over with. And I'd feel satisfied that we'd dealt a severe blow to his long-term ability to do dastardly things," Horner said.

"It doesn't mean we're over with. The problem can come back in 10 years, but that's if we put him in the stone age (from intensive bombing)," he said. "The problem could still come back in 10 years. There's GOT to be some sort of political solution at the end of this," he said.

"The Iraqi people," he said, live in "an oppressed society. I don't know whether they can get out of it or not; hopefully we can help them."

According to Horner, the two-week-old war has already shown both successes and needs which some people "may not want to hear." For example, Horner said, radar-evading stealth technology has "tremendous military leverage." He cited the F-17 Stealth fighters that flew precision bombing missions on the first night of the war.

Horner also said, "The B-2 (Stealth bomber) would be the single best weapon I could have in my arsenal right now. It would carry what the B-52 carries and I could take it anywhere." He was referring to the purported ability of the Stealth bomber to fly through enemy radar nets undetected.

Horner said the war also shows "we do need some sort of a regional missile defense." He explained that Patriot anti-missile missiles are working well in Saudi Arabia because the country has "clumps" of populated areas. Patriot missiles cost about $1 million each.

Regarding the actual bombs dropped on Iraq, Horner said, "I was surprised at the importance of precision munitions. That's because I'm a hardhead fighter pilot.

"I've been very impressed with the F-111s (fighter-bombers) and the F-117s (Stealth fighters) with their laser-guided bombs," he said.

He also lauded new laser-guided targeting systems on the F-15E fighter-bombers.

"There's no getting around it, (these systems) take war to a whole new level of efficiency, and war has historically been a very inefficient operation," he declared.

Top Marine Commander in Gulf Sizes Up Khafji Battle: Bad Deal for Iraqis and Worse is Yet to Come

By Caryle Murphy, Tom Ferraro, and Patrick Bishop

Interview with Lt. Gen. Walt Boomer, commander of U.S. Marines in the Gulf, conducted at Safaniya.

This thing (the incursions) unfolded exactly as we thought it would. We had indications (the Iraqis) were coming ... they came out in three areas ... they came down where the southern Kuwaiti border turns up to the west sharply. They came down south of the wafra oil fields and they came down the coast road to Khafji. One thing I promise you, one thing I'm not going to do in this war is get into numbers of bodies or rifles or tanks or equipment. I went through that bullshit in Vietnam, but I'll give you the best I have in that it gives you a sense of how the battle flowed.

We're relatively certain that they lost at least 25 vehicles in the excursion across the border to the west and the excursion down the middle, which was smaller than the one in the west.

Is that the total?

That is what we've been able to see and count. What we don't know is what aviation did to them later on and we were running air on them all night long as they moved into Kuwait so I can't tell you what the damage was after they moved back into Kuwait.

It is my belief aviation brought it (Iraqi losses) up significantly. We're beginning to get some BDA now that has to go from the pilot to the squadron and then back up, and they reported they have done well. So my sensing is that they lost more than 25 vehicles and whatever people involved.

They (Iraqis) were back into Kuwait by the morning. They stayed in Khafji, which is not in my area. But that too I don't think Khafji was evacuated when the bombing campaign started. So there was no plan as far as I know to protect Khafji as such. I think the plan there too unfolded, as was expected. That they'd be allowed to come down ... and if need be, they would push them back out. And it sounds like that's what in fact they did today.

Why do you think they did it?

I don't know. Honest to goodness I don't know why they did it. Unless they thought it would, it was something that would keep us off balance or disrupt future plans.

Do you think they could do it again?

Well, I think they're capable of attempting it again.

Do you expect it?

We're ready for it.

Were you surprised by this?

No.

What's your reading of reports that there is considerable movement or Iraqi troops across border in Kuwait? What is your understanding of this movement?

We've seen a lot of movement in the last few days, and we're watching it very carefully, to see if we can discern what it is he (Saddam) might try to do.

Have the plans for the ground war been affected?

Zero. Zero effect.

When you say movement, can you be more specific about what Iraqis are doing?

I don't want to be more specific other than that there's some movement.

What's your assessment of the way the Saudis and the Qataris have handled the Khafji episode?

As of this afternoon, I'm pleased.

You say zero, zero effect on the ground war, but what will go into your decision in deciding if and when to launch a ground war?

One, we will do it when we're ready, not when he's ready, he being Hussein. Two, I would say that it's a time for patience. In my view, the air campaign is working. I never believed that it would be over as quick as some thought it would be. It never has in the history of warfare, at least since we've been using airplanes.

At the same time, I think that our pilots on Marine side and the pilots in the Air Force side have done a great job. I'm more than satisfied with the progress we are making. We're not in a hurry.

What effect is the air campaign having on the troops along the border?

I think it's very positive. Everybody needs to sense that we're not in this alone. That there's somebody helping you. The guy on the ground needs to have confidence in the person on his right and on his left. He needs to have confidence in his leaders. And it's helpful to know there is somebody up there dropping bombs on his behalf. So I think it's a morale-builder.

What about the effect on the Iraqi troops?

Well, we haven't put tremendous pressure in terms of the air campaign on those guys right in front of us. And we've had today we're up to 400 POWs or deserters. That's just what we've picked up and the Navy has picked up . . . the Saudis I know have picked up an equal number and so my sense is that they're a little discouraged and I don't think morale is pretty good. They all tell us that morale is next to nothing, but you always have to take that with a grain of salt because he's the guy who left so we (illegible). That being said, we don't underestimate (the Iraqi soldier). I think he'll fight.

Do you feel (there) will be a need for ground movement soon just to keep the momentum going? (paraphrase)

I would only say that I think patience is called for now. I think ultimately Kuwait will have to be occupied.

Mr. Cheney suggested something would happen by the end of February. Is that how you see it?

I wouldn't speculate on it.

Do you think there is any problem with keeping the troops out in the desert for a considerable time in terms of physical conditions and morale?

Not now, because I think there is a sense on their part that something's going on. They're not simply sitting there. Well, they've never just been sitting there because they've been training their rear ends off but I think they certainly sense now it's entered a new phase. I don't foresee a problem with that. But you've been out there with them, have you not?

Yes, but what say to everyone is want to get it over with and get home.

That's not a bad sentiment.

General, has (the) oil spill caused any problems for an amphibious assault?

Based on what I know about the oil spill, and I haven't had a lot of information, you probably have more than I do although maybe you don't considering where you've been. I don't see the spill to be of any military significance. I think it's tragic that he did it. I suppose, from what I've read, it will be an ecological disaster. That's always sad. But I don't see it having any effect on us militarily.

Progress of air war—do you anticipate a protracted phase of that before any ground war?

I think those guys can expect the worst. The worst is yet to come.

Can you be more specific?

No.

Do you expect more surrenders of Iraqis when air war intensifies?

Yes.

Significantly?

I don't know. . . . I didn't expect to see it (a lot of surrenders) down where I am or where we are. But I honestly did not; in fact, I was a little surprised at the numbers that came across when the bombing campaign started, and obviously they weren't even hearing a bomb drop, because it was taking place in Baghdad. But I would think that they could, probably would, increase but I (illegible) can they get across the minefields they've put out?

Well, I think it's very difficult for a couple of reasons and this is based on what the POW reports say. They've got to come across a barrier that they've established to keep us out, and that's a fairly dangerous thing. Secondly, they're almost . . . particularly I think those infantry troops along the border are almost prisoners themselves, by the barriers, by their own officers. They will be quick to tell you that if anybody senses that they're going to desert, they are done away with.

Killed or sent to the rear?

I would say both, from the readings I've done of POW reports . . . one story from a POW said his buddy picked up a leaflet and that his officer saw he had it in his pocket, and he was sent to the brig for 15 days and had his head shaved. It's sort of interesting.

Any senior officers among the POWs so far?

We've had officers desert, yes.

Prior to the war or after?

I'm trying to think. We may have picked up one or two before and some afterwards.

Highest ranking?

This has been relatively junior officers.

Do you see U.S. ground troops going into Iraq as a military necessity at some point? And what would be the implications for the U.S. if its troops occupied an Arab country?

I really don't want to speculate on what would happen to the Republican Guard. I don't know really what the implications would be in the Arab world. I'm not going to get into future plans.

What's happened to the Republican Guard so far? What damage inflicted so far?

I haven't seen many reports that discuss what has happened to them specifically. I can only give you my sense and that's probably not worth a cup of coffee. And that is that they've been hurt. Simply because I have some feel, although I don't watch that day by day or hour by hour, for what's been done to them in terms of the number of strikes against them. I would say that they're probably smarting by now.

At what stage would you expect the Air Force to start attacking the ground force in Kuwait?

Well, we're attacking ground forces in Kuwait now.

You said the worst is yet to come for those along the border. When do you think the worst will start to come? Days, weeks?

I wouldn't put a date on that. But even with these incursions, our reaction has been to bomb along the border through the air force . . . that will certainly continue.

Has there been bombing prior to (the incursions this week)?

We've been bombing along the border all along.

Taking any steps to counter these Iraqi troop movements along the border? Any new developments?

I did some minor repositioning but I was fairly satisfied with the way we were set up, and we've done some minor repositioning just to strengthen our hand a little bit. It's sort of a natural thing as I saw it we looked at this and said, "well, let's shift over there."

What's your understanding of what Syrian troops will do in a ground assault?

I don't know.

Do you expect them to fight Iraqi soldiers?

I honestly don't know and I don't mean to cop out by saying that it's not my area, but I haven't followed it.

What's the situation on the ground in Khafji?

The Saudi commander told me that the city had been retaken and a Kuwaiti told me that they had captured 110 prisoners but I would be careful with that figure . . . that's all I know. What the Saudi commander told me and I do know that my people, my aviators, said they had destroyed 13 vehicles attempting to go back out of Khafji headed north.

At what time was the city retaken?

Must have been about noon time.

What were the vehicles?

They didn't say.

Do you (think) these past three days of Iraqi incursions has been valuable to some extent for the coalition forces and if so, how?

Probably valuable in that there's been some shakedown. There's been some fighting. People have probably gotten rid of some of their fear of the unknown. A few less cases of nerves, I would think. That always happens with any force. I'm sure it's probably what happened with mine, those who were involved have a better understanding of what goes on, a better appreciation. They know now what they sensed. Knowing Marines, I'm sure they sensed they were going to do ok. But you never really know 'til the time comes and I think what has happened is, it's confirmed that "Yeah, we can do this."

What about tactically, did you learn anything new about the Iraqis?

No. We didn't learn anything new about the Iraqis.

It was quite a bold thing to do, though, on their part, getting into Khafji, hanging on for 24 hours?

I don't know how much courage it took to stay in Khafji when there wasn't anybody there. It sure didn't take very long to have 'em exit.

Baghdad Radio has said they have taken U.S. POWs, and some of them are women.

Those two would be the only two I know of that they could have taken. They didn't take any Marines.

Boomer referred then to fighting inside Kuwait.

I'll tell you this, all my plans assume that every Iraqi up there is going to fight like hell. That's the way we plan. If it turns out not to be true, then great, but we've planned for it. It's nice to hear about this guy and that guy, or this unit and that unit is going to surrender, but we don't believe it until we see it.

Did the Iraqi troops in the latest incursions engage any Senegalese troops?

I don't think so . . . but again, I'm not certain.

What role would Republican Guards play if (they) were moved out of position to defend Kuwait City?

I don't know, would he want to risk them defending Kuwait City? Anybody who's in Kuwait City isn't going to make it out. They'll either surrender or die in Kuwait City. That would probably have to go into his equation thinking about where he's going to position his troops. Which is why he's putting infantry troops down here along the border. He doesn't care about these guys . . . one big difference between Hussein and us is that we care very deeply about all of our people, every single one of them. I don't think he gives a hoot about these soldiers that he has here along the border. But what I'm interested in is what the troops along the border think. My guess is that they feel they've probably been left to hang out (word indecipherable).

What about readiness, is everybody ready to go?

Yes, everybody is ready to go.

Think the Army is ready to go?

I think they're doing well. They had so much stuff to move, from such a long way, the move, the logistics effort has really been fantastic when you consider all the materials that's made it here in such a short period of time. My hat's off to the guys (who did it).

From your experiences in Vietnam, is there anything you see in the way this has been conducted so far or is going to be conducted that is a direct lesson from the experience?

Yes, I see some direct lessons. One I don't see any sanctuary and I think Gen. Schwarzkopf has said that, so there's no place really to hide (for the enemy).

I don't sense any micromanagement on my part from anyone. I'm not being micromanaged by CINC or from Washington ... I was a company commander and advisor for two tours in Vietnam....

I don't sense any holding back on our part except what you would expect us to do anyhow and that is protect innocent civilians to the extent we possibly can. That's reflected in the campaign in Baghdad ... there's been no bombing in Baghdad in the sense cities were for example in World War II, so that's the only thing I see that's a restriction. In terms of my ability to prosecute my piece of the campaign, I don't have any restrictions.

What about support from back home?

It's been amazing the way it's manifested itself here ... we've got so much stuff from home (referring to packages and mail) ... I've never seen anything like that in Vietnam.

I believe that our guys and the gals really feel that the U.S. is solidly behind them.

Friday
February 1, 1991

While all eyes were on the fighting that broke out after Iraqi ground forces stormed into Khafji, only to be turned back, another group of Iraqis also headed straight into the arms of the allies. A story in this chapter describes the failed exploits of a group of sailors from Umm al Qasr, who sailed more or less directly into the allied armada in total charge of the Red Sea.

Were they attacking the allied ships on a doomed suicide mission?

Were they trying to slip through the net of allied frigates and cruisers, battleships and allied carriers and reach a haven in Iran, like the Iraqi fighter pilots?

Even if they managed to sneak past all the ships the Americans, British, French, and other nations had put in their path, had they calculated the dozens of floating bombs that their own mine-layers had salted throughout the sea lanes?

Khafji. Umm al Qasr. If the Iraqi high command had a grand plan for confusing the allies with minor military moves that failed and amounted to sacrificing pawns without gaining an advantage, it wasn't working. The allies took the pawns and smiled.

The Battle of Khafji, as it turned out, was tragically costly for some Saudi troops along with the Iraqis who perished there. A story in this chapter describes the scene in the city while the battle debris was still smoking.

And in a rare lapse, a U.S. liaison officer gives an estimated body count—200—for the enemy dead. No one, including the Iraqis, questioned it. On the Saudi side, however, the top Saudi commander's estimate of friendly casualties were lower than subsequent accounts.

In the air war, the weather was good, and the sortie count soared up to 2,500. But a loss incident from the day before—an AC-130 Spectre gunship with a crew of 14—pushed the number of allied dead and missing far higher. The gunship was reportedly on a covert mission off the coast of Kuwait. No survivors have been found.

Part of the increase in the numbers of missions flown resulted from a decision by France to allow U.S. B-52 bombers, flying out of bases in England, to cross French air space while on missions in the Gulf. The decision gave the bombers a more direct path to and from their targets in Iraq, but of course also gave Saddam Hussein another stick with which to pound the table next time—presuming there would be a next time—he discussed a trade deal with the French.

Saddam had more pressing complaints to deal with. He picked up on reports that some Tomahawk missiles fired from U.S. ships in the Persian Gulf had landed on civilian neighborhoods in Baghdad, killing a number of people.

Allied spokesman gave assurances that the missiles had been aimed at military targets, but said they could have been knocked off-course by Iraqi ground fire.

The Tomahawk cruise missiles are some of the most expensive weapons employed by the U.S. military in the Gulf. Moreover, they are extremely powerful, very devastating and—for those detached enough to view them this way—thrilling and photogenic in flight.

Friday - February 1, 1991

Whether they were worth using in a war like this one, in which the enemy puts up limited resistance, was a question that allied commanders eventually answered with a no—especially if continuing to use them would give Saddam Hussein more fodder for his denunciations of civilian deaths.

Friendly Fire Near-Miss Too Close for Comfort—15 Yards: "Someone Got the Wrong Lat-Long"

By Jeff Franks

WITH THE U.S. MARINES NEAR THE KUWAITI BORDER - In a night of heavy fighting along the Saudi-Kuwaiti border, allied aircraft Thursday reportedly knocked out a convoy of Iraqi tanks and armoured personnel carriers, but also inadvertently unloaded eight cluster bombs on a unit of the 2nd Marine Division.

A Marine spokesman said that the Iraqi convoy was destroyed by bombs dropped from B-52s as the vehicles moved near the border about 40 miles west of the Persian Gulf. No further details were available, but a pall of black smoke hung over the northern front Friday morning in the aftermath of the bombing runs that lasted most of the night.

Numerous explosions and flares illuminated the horizon as the B-52s and other jet fighters launched bombs and rockets on Iraqi positions.

Shortly after midnight, two deafening blasts thundered across the desert and the sky was lit up by a giant flame that observers said appeared to be the work of either a massive cluster bomb attack or a powerful fuel-air explosive bomb. "It looked like a nuclear bomb going off," one Marine said as he knelt in his foxhole at a forward Marine base.

Iraqi forces launched at least three rocket attacks during the night, but there were no reports of allied casualties or damage.

A Marine infantry battalion narrowly escaped catastrophe when a bombing run—apparently by two U.S. jets—went awry early Friday. The jets, in attacks three minutes apart, dropped four cluster bombs each, just missing the battalion camp. The first bomb struck 700 meters from the base command post and the other 200 meters away, said Maj. Bob Weinmann, 40, of Woodbury, N.J.

"The first one got everyone's attention. The second really woke them up," said Weimann, the battalion's executive officer. He said that in the confusion caused by the bombs, it was not immediately clear if the attacks were perpetuated by Iraqi or friendly forces. "But with our air supremacy, I assume it was friendly fire," Weimann said.

The debris left by the bombs confirmed his suspicions. It clearly bore the marks of U.S. weapons. Serial numbers taken from the bomb casings were sent to Marine headquarters for investigation, he said.

Weimann said the Marines were not angry about the attack because they recognized that in the fog of war, accidents happen. "Someone got the wrong 'lat-long' (latitude and longitude)," he said, referring to the coordinates used to guide pilots to their targets. The exact location of the camp could not be disclosed because of security concerns.

The deadly bombs left two large areas of scorched sand near the camp and parts of the weapons, which come apart in mid-air to unleash hundreds of small parachuted "bomblets," were strewn throughout the area.

Some of the bomblets, landing in soft sand, did not explode on impact and were still resting partly submerged in the desert Friday morning. The Marines were awaiting arrival of explosives experts to detonate the duds, Weimann said.

Tiny bits of shrapnel from the bomblets reached to within 15 yards of where the Marines slept, but there were no casualties, Weimann said. "There were no casualties and no damage except we used a lot of toilet paper," he joked.

Sgt. Ernest Grafton, a Marine photojournalist who was visiting the camp, said the bombs looked like "a thousand sparklers all lit at once," when they detonated. Also, on Friday afternoon, a long line of Saudi armored personnel carriers and other vehicles were seen pulling out of their positions in the northern desert and heading east. A Marine spokesman said the Saudis might be reinforcing their positions at Khafji, the scene of heavy fighting the last three days.

Death of 11 Marines in Kuwait Appears to be Friendly Fire: "In Close Battles It's a Fight For Your Life"

By Kirk Spitzer

This report contains hard news of a renewal of combat along the southwest Kuwait border with Saudi Arabia; a further advisory of the location of Marine combat along the border, and investigation of possible Marine deaths by friendly fire.

WITH THE 1ST MARINE DIVISION - Fighting flared up again late Thursday along an area of the Saudi-Kuwaiti border where 11 Marines died in air and tank battles earlier this week.

At least three Iraqi tanks were destroyed in fighting Thursday with elements of the 1st Marine Division in an area of open desert near the Kuwait border town of Umm Hujul.

Marine light armored vehicles operating along the border called in artillery and air strikes but did not cross into Kuwait. Four Iraqi soldiers were taken prisoner.

No U.S. casualties were reported in the fighting Thursday.

Marines fought a fierce air and tank battle with Iraqi forces in the same general area late Tuesday and early Wednesday, destroying 22 Iraqi tanks while losing two light armored vehicles. Eleven Marines were killed and two injured in the Umm Hujul fighting on Tuesday and Wednesday. Those casualties have been erroneously attributed in some press reports to the ongoing battle of Khafji, some 50 miles away.

Marines are investigating the possibility that one of the light armored vehicles was destroyed by a missile fired from a U.S. aircraft during the battle Tuesday, said Lt. Col. Jerry Humble, operations officer for the 1st Marine Division.

He said Marine and Iraqi air and ground forces exchanged fire from as close as 25 yards during the nighttime battle. At least half the Iraqi tanks were destroyed by U.S. aircraft attacking close to the desert floor.

Humble said a four-man Marine investigation team, including a munitions expert, has been appointed to look into the incident and their findings would be known soon.

"We're saddened and disappointed," about the possibility of deaths from friendly fire, Humble said. "But historically, there's always casualties by friendly fire in close battles because it's a fight for your life."

Friday - February 1, 1991

Saudi General Calls Khafji Enemy "Suicide Mission"; U.S. Liaison Officer Says 200 Iraqis Died in the Battle

By Storer H. Rowley

KHAFJI, Saudi Arabia - Rocket fire and air strikes rumbled in the distance Thursday night as Saudi troops tried to secure this battle-torn town near the Kuwaiti border and isolated Iraqi snipers still fired sporadically.

Four Iraqi mechanized armored brigades were reported on the move north of the border, which is about six miles from Khafji, and another Iraqi attack appeared imminent, according to military officials here.

Large numbers of Saudi armored personnel carriers topped with machine guns and TOW anti-tank missiles lined the coastal highway.

Saudi Gen. Khalid Bin Sultan said his forces, backed by U.S. Marines and allied air attacks, had "cleared the whole area" of Iraqi forces by 1:45 p.m. Thursday. He described the Iraqi occupation of this deserted town 24 hours earlier as "a suicide mission."

Gen. Khalid, commander of the allied Arab and Muslim forces, briefed reporters Thursday night just inside the southern gate of darkened Khafji, outlining the battle on a map tilted against the blasted remains of an Iraqi BTR-60 armored personnel carrier. Nearby, the body of an Iraqi soldier killed in the fighting lay sprawled along the wall of a house.

In all, Khalid said, allied forces knocked out 46 enemy vehicles and tanks and captured some 350 Iraqi prisoners, while taking only light casualties in the Khafji sector. Allied forces lost four dead, eight wounded, two tanks, and six vehicles.

"They lost 90 percent of their forces," Khalid claimed, including "hundreds of casualties (and) hundreds of equipment losses." During the briefing, the horizon occasionally flashed to the north amid the sound of incoming rocket and artillery fire, but no shells fell near the town. It was accompanied by the distant, concussive pounding of Iraqi positions by periodic allied air strikes, possibly including bombing by B-52s. Battle debris was strewn all along the road into town. A large chunk had been ripped away by a shell from a metal lamppost. This section of town was blacked out, but lights twinkled from buildings further north along the coast of the Persian Gulf.

Soldiers warned one another to walk carefully because mines and booby traps are thought to have been left behind by the Iraqi forces. It was unclear whether the Saudis were preparing for another attack by Iraqi troops from occupied Kuwait, but one U.S. military officer here said Iraqi forces were "certainly capable" of crossing the border again.

U.S. Army Col. Jack Petri, a liaison officer with Saudi forces, called Khafji "pretty secure," but he said there was still "sporadic fire" coming from straggler Iraqi soldiers in some of the buildings. He said there were not enough Saudi troops on hand to clear the town building-by-building overnight Thursday.

Iraqi tanks and Soviet-made BTR-60s were in Khafji until mid-morning Thursday, when two Saudi tank companies "pushed them north" and scored "major kills" on the withdrawing Iraqi armor, Petri said. Their most effective weapon was the U.S.-made TOW, a tube-launched, optically-sighted, wire-guided anti-tank missile.

Khalid called the battle, part of the first major ground combat of the Gulf War, "the greatest accomplishment" for Saudi forces, with "tremendous" support from the U.S.

Air Force and Marine aircraft blasting Iraqi armor and ground forces.

Petri estimated the Iraqi casualties at about 200 dead and wounded. He said there was "no military purpose at all" to the Iraqi incursion, although Iraq will try to use it for political advantage. "It was an effort in futility," he added, pointing to the heavy Iraqi losses.

The sounds of rocket fire heard in Khafji were Brazilian-made Astro rockets, used by both sides, according to Marine Capt. David Rababy, another U.S. liaison officer. He said the Iraqis also had 155mm (rockets).

Saudi officials hustled reporters out of the town Thursday night amid fears over Iraqi armor movements to the north. The press pool was escorted to a location miles out into the desert of Eastern Saudi Arabia to see Iraqi prisoners of war. However, the bus broke down and the only POWs seen by reporters were about 15 scragglylooking men in green fatigues under guard in another bus passing by in the desert. They were identified by the Saudis as Iraqi officers taken captive in the siege of Khafji.

"I don't think that they fight well," Gen. Khalid said of the Iraqis. "I think they were pushed for this (by their superiors). It's a suicide mission for them. They can't gain anything except politically from that mission. This is the biggest land battle. We gained a lot," he added. "Most of them surrendered without a fight after we surrounded them."

He estimated Iraqi strength on the attack on Khafji at more than a battalion, which could mean 500 to 600 men or more.

In the Battle for Khafji, Winner is Clear, But Unanswered Questions Still Smolder

By Ray Wilkinson

KHAFJI - The badly charred skeleton of a Saudi soldier was heat-seared into the driving seat of a still-smoldering armored personnel carrier. The blackened corpse of a second soldier lay draped in death, half in, half out of the destroyed vehicle, vivid evidence of the vicious street-to-street fighting which took place between Iraqi and Arab troops for control of this abandoned seaside frontier town.

A few yards away from the Saudi vehicle, an Iraqi soldier lay wrapped in a blue-and-white blanket. His arm was draped over his face in a dramatic gesture of pain and suffering. He had apparently been wounded, rescued, and then abandoned by his fleeing colleagues and left to bleed to death where he lay.

I visited the southern suburbs of Khafji together with other correspondents on Friday for several hours. The Saudi government had announced Thursday its forces, backed by American Marine artillery, had successfully recaptured Khafji after two days of street fighting, mainly between armored vehicles. But as I entered the town Friday, there was still sporadic heavy artillery fire and heavy weapons exchanges in the city. At one point an artillery round scored a direct hit on a huge water tower which Saudi officers said the Iraqis were still using as an observation post to direct their own fire.

At that point, the fighting was still continuing in the northern sections of the town. Towards noon the firing declined in Khafji but could still be heard in the distance as the Saudis and forces from the sheikdom of Qatar chased the last pockets of Iraqis

Friday - February 1, 1991

northwards toward the frontier. Far to the west, I could hear the deep rumble of heavy allied air strikes, reportedly against Iraqi armored columns.

During the battle for Khafji the Iraqis had sent a second column of at least 100 armored personnel carriers and tanks to the west of the city. Marine commanders on the spot said repeated air strikes had "decimated" this column, knocking out large numbers of vehicles. It was continued strikes on this column that I apparently heard Friday morning though even further west along the Saudi-Kuwait frontier there were also renewed clashes between Marine units and a large force (estimated by some sources in the area as being tens of thousands of Iraqis) of Iraqis. The Marines reportedly knocked out at least three Iraqi tanks during that separate fighting.

In Khafji itself on Friday, Saudi military officers on the spot said they had taken at least 100 prisoners that same day, adding to the estimated 200 they said they took previously.

These figures could not be independently confirmed, but I saw one truckload of Iraqi POWs dressed in olive green, Saudi guards closely watching over them with loaded weapons, being moved out of the town in a gray military bus. A fleet of other buses stood by to transport other Iraqis taken in the fighting. The small group of journalists entered Khafji from the south, through rings of Marine artillery positions which had been pounding Khafji during the fighting, and Saudi troop concentrations.

At the ceremonial archway marking the entrance to the town there was a burned-out Qatari armored personnel carrier. A little further along the main highway there were two friendly armored vehicles, blackened and "dead" from direct Iraqi hits from sagger rockets.

A combined force of Qatari and Saudi troops had tried to retake Khafji under the cover of darkness late Wednesday. They entered the southern suburbs but pulled back to regroup after running into fierce Iraqi resistance. The charred armored personnel carriers I saw were apparently disabled during this attack.

At dawn Thursday, the Arab allies launched a much larger and fiercer drive into the city and eventually cleared most of the Iraqis out of Khafji.

Near the burned-out Qatari armored personnel carriers, a large U.S. Army truck had smashed into a cinder block wall. After two days its engine was still running. Its back tires were still spinning. The engine eventually died when it ran out of gasoline.

According to U.S. officials on the spot, two U.S. service people, including a woman, were in the vehicle at the time and possibly captured. They have not been seen since.

If the report is true, and there was confusion surrounding how many Americans had disappeared in Khafji and in what incidents, the woman soldier would probably be the first female prisoner-of-war the Iraqis have captured. (According to radio reports we heard later, two U.S. servicemen were later rescued in Khafji but we are unable to clear up the confusion of just who disappeared and who has been rescued.)

Several dead camels littered the main highway into Khafji. The highway was cratered by occasional artillery strikes and littered with discarded artillery shells and small arms. Two small seven-man Marine reconnaissance units played cat-and-mouse with the Iraqis in Khafji during the battle for the town. At one point, the Marines called in artillery virtually on top of themselves to protect their position and destroy nearby Iraqi armored vehicles.

Marine Cpl. Jeff Brown was slightly wounded in the leg when shrapnel from an American cluster shell, timed to explode in the air, sprayed his hiding place with deadly shards. Cpl. Brown will probably become the first American to win a Purple Heart for being wounded in the Gulf War.

After two days of hide-and-seek with the Iraqis, one team of Marines Thursday sprinted safely to allied lines through several hundred yards of no-man's-land.

The second team drove to safety in two Hummers even though the tires of one of the vehicles had been punctured by incoming shrapnel.

The two teams had entered Khafji before the battle for the town began to act as forward aerial and artillery spotters for the allies. Wednesday night they heard the Iraqi armor clanking through the deserted streets of Khafji. They said they had time to escape but stayed in place to call in air-and-artillery strikes on the Iraqis.

It was a perilous two days. At one point Cpl. Brown said Iraqi troops entered the four-story apartment complex his team was hiding in, possibly looking for the Americans. They maintained radio contact with U.S. Marines outside the town and though they transmitted only in short bursts and in code they were under no illusions that the Iraqis were picking up their broadcasts and knew they were somewhere in Khafji. "We could see their helmets bobbing up and down," Cpl. Brown said.

The Marines set up a series of Claymore mines in the stairwell of the apartment complex, ready to detonate them if the Iraqis discovered the hiding place.

"They sure would have had a rude awakening if they had come up after us," the corporal said. "We would have blown them to hell." Later the same day his team spotted a cluster of Iraqi APCs nearby. It was then they called in an artillery strike during which the Marine was slightly wounded. "We knew we had to take those vehicles out," he said. "If we hadn't, they could have caused us and everyone else a hell of a lot of trouble."

. . . Another American caught in the Khafji fighting had an amazing escape. Capt. Joe Fack (Madison, WI) entered Khafji with the King Abdul Aziz Brigade of the Saudi National Guard on Wednesday. As heavy machine gun and tank fire erupted during one street battle, Capt. Fack took cover beside his Hummer. As he crouched there, an Iraqi RPG (rocket propelled grenade) smashed into the pavement a few yards away and directly underneath the chassis of a Marine Corps mobile gun.

But the RPG then bounced out the other side without damaging either the gun or any of the sheltering allied troops. It was the first time Capt. Fack had been under fire. "I said to myself, here goes," he recalled. "If I gotta go, it looks as the time might be now." The captain vividly described the confusion of the nighttime fighting in the town. "We got bogged down as soon as we entered the city shortly after dark," he said. The Saudi units began to fire TOW anti-tank missiles.

The Iraqis replied with sagger rockets. The two sides fired heavy machine guns at each other. "There were probably three battles I saw during the night," he said. "Tanks were firing at tanks. But everything was so confusing I didn't know what unit was which and who was firing at who."

One of the Americans' worst worries has been that in the heat of battle some of its Arab allies such as the Saudis or Egyptians might be difficult to differentiate (from) the Iraqis.

Friday - February 1, 1991

Donna the Army Reservist Wants Combat: "I'd Like to Bag Baghdad Betty Personally"

By Laurence Jolidon

NEAR THE IRAQI BORDER - The U.S. Army has been trying to keep Spec. Donna Brown out of combat. She's not buying it.

"I don't like Saddam Hussein that much," she says in her soft, high-pitched voice, "and I'd like to bag Baghdad Betty personally."

While she's scared, her gun is loaded and she knows how to use it. "I always sleep with my gun (M16) beside me, everything close by. I try to always keep alert to everything that's going on." Brown, 32, volunteered to leave her San Francisco telemarketing job to fight here. She gives several reasons for wanting to remain with her Army Reserve unit—the 907th Firefighting Platoon, out of Clarkston, Wash., which is attached to a combat engineer battalion that will be in the forefront of any allied land offensive.

"I really don't (want to be in combat) but my unit's going and that's my job." She's a clerk-typist for the platoon, and the only female. The combat engineers are an all-male outfit. "I definitely feel a lot safer here with this unit," she adds, than with an engineer group headquarters company where she was sent a week ago. After proving her position with the firefighters is listed in Army regulations as one that may be filled by either a man or woman, she returned to the combat engineer compound yesterday (Thurs., 31 Jan.). "These guys have been training to go into combat. Those guys (the headquarters company) are pencil-pushers. And they're not taking this seriously. I don't want to get too serious about it, but you have to realize there's a war going on." Does she just want to take a chance? "Yeah. It'd be neat to be up there. Hopefully not dead, though."

She says she knows that's a real possibility, for her or any other soldier in a combat support unit in this war. "I want to make a stand for women's rights," she says. "I hate to see the guys always getting eighty-sixed (the military category for killed in action). Not fair."

Brown, who joined the Army reserves in 1983 and went through the same basic training and advanced infantry training all regular soldiers receive, set out to find a spot in the Desert Shield deployment last summer. When her reserve unit—the 2nd Hospital Center—was at summer camp at Fort Lewis, Wash., she heard the 907th was looking for people to fill vacancies prior to being activated for duty.

She arrived here Dec. 4. No questions were raised about her assignment until the platoon reached its current site along the Saudi-Iraqi border. The firefighting platoon is assigned to provide fire security and crash-rescue help at airstrips built or repaired by the 27th Engineer Battalion (Combat Airborne).

Like the 27th, the platoon has been deployed to Honduras before, and its high firefighting scores were noted by Army manpower officers looking for a battle-ready unit to assign the Fort Bragg-based engineers.

Once her presence was noted at this all-male camp, however, she was ordered to report to another unit slated to be farther to the rear once the ground offensive begins. Brown said her officers there told her "America's not ready for women in combat. The media will splash pictures of blown-up females across the front page and the United States can't handle that." Her reply? "I said it's 1991, and what about the females who were in Panama?"

She argued that the firefighters have always had women in their ranks. "The whole history of this unit was with females," but "now all of a sudden, war's breaking out, and you guys are saying no more females."

Her platoon commander, Capt. Steve Janzen of Moscow, Idaho, helped her prove her case. Janzen, she said, "has really stuck up for me the whole way. He was fighting when we found out they were going to move me."

Janzen said every slot in his platoon is "interchangeable"—open to either a man or woman. "I don't agree there should be female combat troops," he says, "but I have no problem with women being up there on the front lines. I dug out all the paperwork Dona needed to prove she wasn't just trying to buck the system."

"She'll be with us and doing her job," said Staff Sgt. Richard Vosler, 35, of Puyallup, Wash. (In civilian life, firefighter Vosler is a shipfitter and a steelcutter at a shipyard in Bremerton, Wash.) "She shoots as good as anybody else in the unit."

Brown said the objections raised to her staying with a front-line unit included concern that her next-of-kin might ask later why she was permitted to stay in harm's way and that commanders who permitted her could be criticized for it.

She said a captain told her, "Congress has turned their heads during peacetime, but now the real stuff is happening. Your next-of-kin could come back and say what was my daughter doing over there?"

Brown, who is single, said her family is split on the war she volunteered for.

"I love my parents," she said, "but my mom already wrote me a letter. They got that phone number to call about servicemen. So she called to complain I was the only female (in her unit), why is this happening, and will the newspapers look into it."

She said her father, a Navy veteran, supports the war, but her mother opposes it.

"She's my mother," she said. "What do you expect? Well, she's also women's lib, until it called for her daughter going off to war. She's not so upset, I think, about (my) going forward. She's really pissed that I'm the only female. And she thinks all these terrible things are happening to me, and that men are just bothering me to no end."

There are quite a few other females in other forwardly-deployed units—support units—along the border. And Brown says she hasn't been hassled by men since she got here.

"I don't have problems," she said. "These guys are all like my big brothers." Brown shares a tent with male firefighters.

A canvas shelter-half divides her area from the rest. "We say, 'Ok, Donna, we're changing pants now,' And she turns around," says Vosler. She does the same thing for us. It's just mutual respect for privacy."

Brown hopes the issue is settled, but thinks it may not be. Before she was allowed to return to her unit, there was talk that a decision may be sought from a higher echelon.

"They told me, if you get hurt, somebody else is going to get in trouble."

She was warned that her becoming a casualty could jeopardize some commander's military career. "I would hate to see that happen," she said, "but at the same time, you've got to start somewhere." If she's ordered to the rear again, she will ask to speak to the Army Inspector General's office about "sexual discrimination."

"I'm here for now," she says. "We'll see what they say." Brown is a diminutive person with brown hair and dark-rimmed glasses. On her camouflaged helmet is a strap with the words, "La Unica Mujer"— "the only woman" in Spanish. "It was so appropriate," she said, "because no one ever called me by my name" after she arrived in Saudi Arabia. "It was always, 'Well, you're the only female.'"

Her brother and sister "wonder what I'm doing" in the military, she said. "But me, I think Saddam's a jerk and trying to bully a little country. And I don't think it's just the United States. We have the French, British, everybody. It's kind of neat. We're all against the bad guy." She punctuates the last with a laugh.

Janzen said he thinks Brown's case will depend on eventual public reaction to the report that a female (soldier) is now missing. "If there's no big outcry about that," he said, "they will have no reason to force her to move back again. And I don't think there will be an adverse reaction. I think she'll stay right with us now. I hope she does."

The Padre as Warrior—Stripped-Down Land Rover, Tuck and Cigarettes: "God is Not an Insurance Policy"

By Richard Kay

The padre came bouncing across the desert in a Land Rover stripped down for warfare. He had taken a 4½ lb. hammer to the windscreen and all the other glass but he had etched the word "chaplain" on the bonnet.

With a shemagh wrapped around his head, Stephen Blakey jumped into the sand with all the enthusiasm of a battalion sergeant major about to lead his company into battle.

But the men who gathered at his feet had come looking for spiritual guidance to carry with them on the eve of conflict. He told them they had been sent by mankind to put right an evil, but one that could not be achieved without a cost.

What he was saying was that while it would be nice if, for the task ahead we prayed God could put a shield around us, a sort of thickened body armor if you like, He did not deal in insurance policies.

The padre's delivery, in the plain, blunt language of the Royal Scots who faced him, echoed across the sands. And as he spoke, I thought how easy it would be for his words to be twisted and misinterpreted back home. For this was a man of God who could see good in the right to wage war. Now, when I looked at the young faces rubbed raw by the wind and sun, I swear you could see a kind of contentment settle over them as they prayed.

We were sitting cross-legged on the ground or on bunched-up packs of webbing. And we clasped the blue order of service books of the Church of Scotland.

As a concession to the moment we had discarded our helmets, but the weapons of war lay at our feet. There were about 165 soldiers, a company's finest. Young men of extraordinary contradictions. Their language coarse and studded with profanities, but they had polished their boots for their appointment with the padre to a parade-ground shine.

With their severe cropped heads, tattooed biceps, and dark glasses, I selfishly wondered how many had turned up because padre Blakey also supplies the Desert Rats with tuck and cigarettes. But from the moment the opening bars of Highland Cathedral floated across our heads, there was a growing anticipation. This was probably the last time Bravo Company would assemble for church before they are committed to battle.

The padre had cut up a trestle table, covering it with tartan and white linen cloths. From a traveling kit of sacraments, he brought out a simple cross and silver communion cup. For bread he broke pieces of brown biscuit from a compo rations box.

Unaccompanied by music, the men sang "Fight the Good Fight," a hymn that could have been written for physical as much as spiritual conflict.

And when the padre spoke, the soldiers turned their gaze up towards him. He was saying that this could be their last chance to reach an understanding with God.

In times of war, men who would not step inside a church need to find an inner strength and comfort. And this is what is happening among the Royal Scots, (for) of all the British forces committed here, they are the ones facing the greatest dangers. Trench warriors, they will be doing the hand-to-hand fighting, their targets will not be unseen from a cockpit or tank turret but face-to-face at the end of the SA 80s.

But now we were being told we could not choose when we died on account of whether we had lived good lives or bad. "We need God for peace and courage in the days ahead, but He is not an insurance policy," the chaplain said.

"It will require all of our inner strength, more than we have ever had. People will die and have died on our side not because they lived a good or bad life, but because mankind has got us into a war because an evil has been done. We have to put that evil right and the price of it is the lives of soldiers.

"In knowing what will happen, in knowing how many of us will die, we must get ourselves right with God. This may be our last opportunity and we must do it as we prepare for war. Because He will look after our souls and give us help to make us even better soldiers than we have trained to be. So we can go into our task with glory, honor, and inner strength. For God inspires a deeper courage, a deeper strength."

When it was over, the queue for men wanting communion too was as long as that stretching from the padre's truck awaiting sweets and cigarettes. It had been a sweet moment to savour, and afterwards we stood around in knots, all reluctant to leave.

They say here that courage is like a bank balance. Today all of us, soldiers and non-combatants, received a boost to our reserves we will surely need in the days ahead.

More Iraqi POWs Taken at Sea, 20 Sailors From Umm al Qasr: "Pretty Dispirited, Cold and Wet"

By Tarek Hamada

ABOARD THE USS CURTS IN THE PERSIAN GULF - Twenty Iraqi sailors were rescued Wednesday (Jan. 30) after U.S. and British aircraft attacked the Iraqi navy in the northern Gulf.

The shivering and tired soldiers, who appeared to range in age from the mid-20s to the mid-30s, are the survivors of an attack that destroyed an amphibious vessel near the port of Umm al Qasr, Curtis Capt. Glenn Montgomery said. "These guys are pretty dispirited, cold and wet," Montgomery said. "But there were no bloody wounds."

The arrival of the POWs at the Curts was one of the most visible results of intermittent fighting between allied aircraft and Iraqi warships that began Tuesday evening, Montgomery said.

Wednesday morning, helicopter pilots from the Curts, the USS Paul F. Foster, as well as the British ships the HMS Brazen, Gloucester, and Cardiff attacked Iraqi boats in waters off the coast of Iraq. "The vessels have been hit by missiles" from the U.S. and British helicopters, said Lt. Cmdr. Michael

Pearey of the HMS Brazen. "They are taking a bit of a beating." There were divided opinions about why the Iraqi ships, which up to now had been taking a low profile, had ventured toward allied ships.

Pearey said he thinks the boats were trying to escape allied bombing of Iraqi navy bases. But Montgomery said the Iraqi navy apparently started the fighting by sending patrol boats and other small vessels toward allied positions in the Gulf.

This is a foolish move because the Iraqi navy is no match for the U.S., British and other Western navies in the Gulf, he said. Iraq, which before its takeover of Kuwait had few outlets to the Gulf, has a small navy. Montgomery said he doesn't understand why the navy made such a move, and said it might be the work of a lower-level commander who wants to prove his bravery.

A Kuwaiti naval officer on board the Curts, who would only identify himself as Major Ibrahim, said he thinks some of the sailors were trying to flee to neighboring Iran.

The Iranian government has announced it will hold the pilots and their planes until the war is concluded. "They must have wanted to go to Iran by traveling through a narrow channel" in the Gulf, said the 34-year-old major, who has served in the Kuwaiti navy for 15 years. "They probably were going out into the Gulf to escape the rockets and planes."

Although the Iraqi sailors' motivations were unclear, it was apparent they were beaten men when they arrived at the Curts Wednesday evening. The sailors were blindfolded with white scarves, handcuffed, and wrapped with pink blankets moments after they stepped off U.S. helicopters. Three other sailors had minor bumps and bruises.

One short, thin sailor in his mid-20s appeared to be dehydrated and suffering from shoulder cramps. The man needed help to walk to Curts physician Thomas K. Moore. After checking his vital signs, Moore said the man really suffered from "being cold and wet."

During their first hour on the boat, the prisoners sat in a hallway, their heads bowed in exhaustion. They were later fed box lunches of sandwiches, fruit, and milk. Kuwaiti and American interrogators interviewed some of the prisoners, hoping to gain information about Iraqi positions and plans.

This group of Iraqi prisoners was in far better shape than the 51 Iraqis captured by the Curts Jan. 24 when the U.S. took over Qurah Island off the coast of Kuwait.

"They are better fed, they are better dressed and they are in much better shape than the last batch. Unlike the other ones, they are wearing their uniforms," said medical corpsman B. R. Essary of Fort Worth, Tex. "Once they warm up, they will be fine."

Saturday
February 2, 1991

The group of more than 100 Indian nurses reported missing from hospitals in Baghdad turned up safe this week, in a refugee camp in Jordan.

Similar journeys westward out of Iraq, along roads whose origins date to the dawn of civilization, have now been made by thousands of refugees. Many of them are foreigners overwhelmed by the perilous present, like the nurses. But thousands of Iraqis also finally see no choice but to abandon their homes and escape.

Many will try to return when the war between their country and nearly 40 other declared enemies—many from this region—is over. There are already reports that Iraq's capacity to deliver basic services such as food distribution and medical care has been severely damaged by the allied bombing.

Not all the curtailed services can be blamed on the allies, however. Saddam Hussein's detractors point out that the Iraqi leader has spent much of his country's wealth on military campaigns and his own personal comfort for some time. Thanks to him, they say, the Iraqi people—especially the Kurdish minority in northern Iraq, where even chemical weapons were used to quash dissent—have suffered deprivation before.

Even Iran, which fought a vicious, bloody war with Iraq that lasted a decade, has called for Saddam to withdraw his troops from Kuwait. But the call to quit Kuwait was accompanied by a humanitarian gesture—Iran began shipping food and medicine to Iraq to help alleviate basic shortages.

Iran reiterated that Iraqi fighter aircraft reaching its territory would remain there until the war is over. This looks less and less like a war that will be decided militarily by a few dozen fighter planes, no matter who is flying them.

The number of coalition aircraft lost thus far in the conflict is still disputed between the attackers and the attacked. There is a large discrepancy in that category of the numbers war. The allies say a total of 19 of their aircraft have been lost to enemy fire since the allied bombing campaign began on Jan. 17.

Saddam Hussein's government says 180 coalition planes have been downed. Given a difference of 161 aircraft, either somebody's badly mistaken, or lying.

It's possible, but unlikely, that a few allied planes appeared to be shot down after being struck by Iraqi ground fire, but then pulled up at the last second while the Iraqi spotters wiped their brow and put a checkmark in the shootdown box. But 161 shootdowns are too many to miss. If Saddam is paying bonuses to his artillery batteries for shootdowns, he should probably demand an audit.

In this chapter, there's another development in the story of the Iraqi sailors from Umm al Qasr, in southeastern Iraq, who were stopped on their way out of Iraq. Their story was that they were ordered to defect, as a means of salvaging some part of the Iraqi navy. They were

Saturday - February 2, 1991

supposed to defect to Iran, where many Iraqi aircraft have taken refuge. They ran into the U.S. Navy first.

But at least they got out before the entire Iraqi navy was virtually wiped out by allied air strikes, some of the 2,600 flown overnight.

Iraq's air force and navy aren't the only ones bugging out. Morale among Saddam Hussein's ground forces is sagging badly—according to an increasing number of "defectors" from the Iraqi ground forces.

The issue of religion among the allied military again surfaced, in a story about British chaplains in the desert. The whole notion that religious observances by non-Islamic allied troops can be kept under a blanket has a lot of holes in it.

Saddam Hussein would like to make this a religious war—his loyal Islamic warriors against the Christian, Jewish, and atheist infidels from America, Britain, France, and elsewhere. But the British "padres" aren't preaching religious hatred. They're issuing forgiveness, a little steel for the spine, plus tack and smokes.

And as further proof that having a huge army stationed for weeks in a desert waiting to go to war can be perilous, a story in this chapter reports 50 missing U.S. military vehicles. The story hit a lot of hot buttons in the U.S. military when it appeared. Among other things, it suggested some large gaps in the U.S. battlefield security.

Doug Jehl, the reporter who wrote the story, was upbraided by the military brass for bringing the losses to light, and there was even pressure to curtail his pool privileges. Whether the vehicles were stolen by terrorists, hot-wired by car thieves, or simply driven off by allied troops, no one ever challenged Jehl's facts. He stood his ground, and stayed to report on the war until the end.

50 U.S. Military Vehicles Reported Missing; A Dozen or More Palestinian Terrorists Reported Present

By Douglas Jehl

WITH U.S. FORCES - In a rash of theft that has raised concerns about a possible terrorist attack, at least 50 American military vehicles have disappeared in the last several weeks from a forward-based facility used by the U.S. Army here, according to senior officers.

The almost nightly losses of five-ton trucks, Humvee jeeps, and other distinctive Army vehicles from within the apparently secure military compound has left the officers troubled at the prospect that terrorists might attempt to pose as U.S. soldiers in launching an attack on military camps or other facilities.

An officer said Friday that despite an extensive investigation by U.S. military police and other authorities, none of the vehicles has been found yet.

The mounting toll of vanishing vehicles assigned to units throughout the theater comes in the wake of intelligence reports issued to commanders last week warning that more than a dozen Palestinian terrorists were known to be operating in the sector now occupied by this 1st Armored Division. In response, the sentries posted on the perimeter of American camps scattered across the desert here have been warned to be extra-vigilant in watching for "foreign nationals" driving civilian vehicles and behaving in a "suspicious manner."

But with hundreds of ammunition trucks, tankers, and every other manner of military vehicles criss-crossing the barren tabletop terrain every hour, the specter of an attack launched in a U.S. vehicle has added markedly to commanders' trepidation.

Some officers have discounted the notion that the thefts are terrorist-related. They contend instead that U.S. soldiers may be stealing the vehicles in an extreme response to what remain some significant shortages of spare parts and vehicles among VII Corps units whose supplies have not yet been delivered to their desert base camps.

"Some of these guys are having trouble keeping their vehicles going," one intelligence officer said. "The way I look at it, this is cannibalization pure and simple."

"The supplies that were short are still short," another officer told colleagues recently in an epigrammatic summary of what officials say are still-inadequate stocks of a wide range of supplies, including maps and chemical protection suits for which urgent requests were submitted more than 10 days ago.

Some Army divisions here are still awaiting replacements for the chemical suits first used Jan. 17 when Iraq fired its first Scud missiles in response to the U.S. attack on its territory. Soldiers were advised before the war began that the suits would begin to lose their effectiveness two weeks after being removed from sealed pouches. With the spares not yet distributed, however, they are being told that the suits can remain effective as long as 30 days after they are opened.

But most officers here said a main theory for the raft of mysterious thefts, from a sprawling Saudi base about two hours from here and now dominated by the U.S. Army and the Air Force, remained the prospect of a well-organized prelude to a terrorist attack in what one senior officer described as a "real nightmare."

They stressed, however, that they believe adequate security measures are already in place to guard against such a raid. These steps have transformed this section of the desert, populated until 45 days ago only by local Bedouins, into a virtual American military security zone in which military police and sentries for a time were under orders to halt any "foreign national" driving through the Army division's area of operations, officers confirmed.

Those orders were modified early this week, however, after a local police officer was detained for several hours after the U.S. military police who stopped and searched his vehicle found a suitcase full of cash. The man was allowed to proceed with apologies after his identity was established, officers said, and the U.S. military security personnel are now authorized only to detain those behaving in a "suspicious manner."

The worries over terrorism here come as the night-long thud of artillery practice at nearby firing ranges and the ever-louder roar of American warplanes passing northward overhead has begun to bring the sound of war to camps still well-removed from ground skirmishes to the east.

Nevertheless, the vast gulf between current comfort and battle has raised concerns among commanders that troops might be becoming too accustomed to what for most of them remains a phony war.

"We have the potential for our soldiers and our leaders to become stale in this environment—to become camp-stale," Col. James C. Riley, commander of the 3rd Brigade, 3rd Armored Division, warned his commanders the other night. "We need to stay with it," Riley admonished. "Don't allow your soldiers to get rusty around here."

Saturday - February 2, 1991

In the Tank Repair Shop: Kneel, Pray, and Pass the Ammunition, Padre

By Philip Jacobson

WITH 7TH ARMOURED BRIGADE - Against a lowering desert sky, two British army chaplains prepare for a non-denominational church service, setting out trestle tables and half a dozen wooden benches in the middle of an immense workshop for repairing tanks.

All around is the paraphernalia of war: rifles, dugouts, a ground-to-air missile post in the middle distance. The chaplains themselves carry crucifix, chalice, and paten in boxes normally used for ammunition while the wafer and wine are tucked into an airtight medical canister.

As soldiers straggle across the sand towards us, both priests—universally "padre" to the troops—talked quietly about their mission as men of God amidst the pandemonium and suffering of the modern battlefield.

For Alun Price, ordained in the Church of Wales and built like a typical Welsh scrum half, the looming possibility of ground fighting involving British units greatly increased the need for what he described as "field counseling."

His major's crown was, he insisted, the least of his titles: "I am here to provide someone to talk to when the soldiers' thoughts begin straying to what lies ahead for them. We live in an imperfect world, as anyone with eyes can see, so it is up to me, as a representative of our Lord, to strive to bring something of the spirit of God into the madness of warfare."

In his own way, Father David Kelly, a Roman Catholic, had much the same message for us: "It is perfectly sensible to be afraid, who would not be, and I see my role as helping men come to terms with that as the likelihood of going into action approaches. For me, it is very much a question of adopting the role of listener, an ear for the fears that many soldiers may not feel able to express to their comrades."

Until very recently, the presence of army chaplains and the services they have been conducting with increasing frequency within the 7th Armoured Brigade—there are no such things as Sundays anymore, both observed—were considered a matter of huge sensitivity.

The Saudis would take great offence, it was argued: cannot risk upsetting the hosts to the allied armies. Chaplains were to be described as "welfare officers" and mention of their spiritual activities was strongly discouraged in the British press.

To one very high-ranking officer here, this was "utter bollocks," and in truth, the Saudi authorities seemed quite unconcerned about the prospect of Christian services being held, always provided due discretion was observed.

Thus, we can now report, without tying ourselves in knots to get the message over, that Alun Price and David Kelly were ministering to their flock, and that some thirty men, mostly from a REME battlefield recovery unit that can expect its fair share of danger should ground fighting take place, turned up to worship. They looked very young when their helmets were removed and laid beside weapons and chemical warfare kit: number three haircuts, which leave little more than a dusting of fluff on the skull, made them seem more vulnerable, for all the drooping mustaches and fiercely tattooed arms.

With the two priests standing before them, side by side, the service began with Hymn 42 from the beige-coloured Army Prayer Book, "Guide Me Oh Thou Great Redeemer." Echoes of a Welsh crowd singing its heart out at Cardiff Arms Park were underlined by Alun Price's wry lament about England's recent triumph there.

David Kelly, lean and crewcut and a long way from his former parish in Westminster, then read prayers in a voice that was sometimes whipped away on the gathering wind. The troops sat quietly, shivering occasionally beneath their flak jackets, not looking up as a camouflaged helicopter clattered busily past overhead.

"Some of you are probably going to see things you never dreamed of, and will never want to think about again," Alun Price told them. "Perhaps it will make you question your religion in days to come, but there is a point at which Christians need be afraid no longer because of their faith in the certainty of resurrection."

Then it was time for the 91st Psalm, and some unashamed tears on the young faces. Quite a few of the soldiers had scribbled on their helmet covers the letters "91/5," a talisman or reminder of that intensely moving section of the psalm: "Thou shalt not be afraid for the terror by night, nor for the arrow by day . . ."

When the small congregation separated into two groups for Holy Communion and Mass, a pair of the renowned American A-10 tank-busters—"Warthogs" to their many admirers in the allied ranks—flew noisily overhead in the direction of the Iraqi front line.

Business as usual, and a few minutes later we heard the crump of explosions in the distance. The two chaplains carried on packing away their kit (everything is kit in this army), ready for another service in another corner of the brigade. Before they left, we asked the stock question: are there really no atheists in the foxholes?

Both smiled and left the answer to each other: "I'd say people under fire tend to behave in a manner that might surprise them," observed Alun Price.

"The battlefield is no place for proselytizing, and in any case, a bullet near your backside concentrates the mind wonderfully," David Kelly concluded.

If fighting starts on the ground, both priests will be found in an exposed frontline medical post, comforting the wounded and the dying, helping to bury the dead with proper religious ceremony. They will also put their modest training in First Aid at the service of the medics there. Their ministrations will not be confined to Christians: both carry condensed versions of the Jewish and Muslim prayer for the dead.

"There we are at the service of any soldier who has need of us, and that includes Iraqis."

Back at our base, musing on the morning's events, we were shown a small brown booklet bearing the royal seal and containing the Gospel of Saint John, with an introduction by King George VI. Issued in September 1939, it was found on a battlefield in 1941 by a young Italian officer fighting in the western desert. Gen. Tuilio Sturchio, he had sent the prayer book to Brigadier Patrick Cordingley, commander of the 7th Armoured Brigade, "with whom we were often engaged in combat, with mutual respect, I believe."

Gen. Sturchio requested that the book should now be returned to a soldier of the brigade that was once his enemy.

Saturday - February 2, 1991

Iraqi Seamen Say They Were Ordered to Defect: "They Know They Cannot Fight"

By Tarek Hamada

ABOARD THE USS CURTS IN THE PERSIAN GULF - Thirty-five Iraqi sailors who were captured this week said they were ordered by their superiors to defect to Iran, their Kuwaiti interrogator said.

The prisoners said a courier from the "highest levels" of Iraq's navy delivered the order Tuesday night to commanders at Um al Qasr Port near the southern Iraqi city of Basra. The message specifically said that the navy units should travel to Bandar Khomeini, a port on Iraq's southwest coast, said the interrogator, who would only identify himself as Major Ibrahim. The major, a 15-year-veteran of the Kuwaiti navy who has worked with the Iraqi navy, interviewed the prisoners for hours after their arrival Wednesday and Thursday.

"They know they cannot fight and they don't have the ability to defend themselves against the aircraft," Ibrahim said, referring to the international coalition apposing Iraq's occupation of Kuwait. "They want to keep their ships in Iran until the war is over."

The Iraqi navy's leadership might have sent the message because Umm al Qasr has been devastated by air strikes, Ibrahim said. "The prisoners said many boats have been damaged," he said. Iraqi commanders also must know about the Iranian government's lenient "policy toward defectors from the Iraqi air force," Ibrahim said.

Iran's Islamic Republic News Agency announced last week that the defectors and their planes will be held until the end of the Persian Gulf war.

The sailors told Ibrahim they were happy to flee to Iran because they have no enthusiasm for president Saddam Hussein's battle to keep Kuwait. Iraq's ruling Baáth party knows of this dissatisfaction, and it has posted armed guards in Umm al Qasr to prevent Iraqi sailors from leaving the area by land, the prisoners told Ibrahim.

"There are guards everywhere in Umm al Qasr," the major said. "If they see any sailor leaving, they capture him and return him to his base."

Although the sailors were able to escape Umm al Qasr, they were quickly attacked by U.S. and British helicopters when they headed toward Iran through the northern gulf, Ibrahim said. The sailors arrived at the Curts from two separate boats that were sunk. The first group of 20 arrived Wednesday and the second group of 15 came Thursday.

All of the prisoners, who ranged in age from the late teens to the mid-30s, looked cold, tired and depressed when they stepped onto the frigate. Within minutes the sailors were blindfolded, handcuffed and wrapped with pink blankets.

While their clothes were being washed, the prisoners sat in a hallway, their heads bowed in exhaustion. They were later fed box lunches of sandwiches, milk, and fruit.

A few sailors had minor bumps and bruises from the attack on their boats. One captain lost the hearing in his left ear after it was hit by the rudder of his boat.

On Wednesday, one short, thin sailor in his mid-20s appeared to be dehydrated and suffering from shoulder cramps. The man needed help to walk to physician Thomas K. Moore. After checking his vital signs, Moore said the man really suffered from being "cold and wet."

But the biggest blows were to their pride, Ibrahim said.

A 27-year-old captain said he "didn't know why we must fight," Ibrahim said.

"He said they had to obey their orders. Their morale is way down."

Sunday
February 3, 1991

When did the land war in the desert begin? You may think you know, but you could get an argument from some of the troops who spent January and February dodging Iraqi artillery and calling in Apache gunship strikes on enemy observation posts in Iraq.

In the war to force Iraqi troops out of Kuwait, there was a valiant attempt by commanders at every level to delineate, day by day and hour by hour, one phase of fighting from the rest.

By early February there were daily bomb bursts to the north, regular artillery exchanges, line-crossers in Iraqi uniforms with their arms in the air, and furtive enemy patrols glowing green in the night-vision scopes and goggles.

In their gut, soldiers in the allied ground forces knew that the war had started when they drew live rounds and pointed their weapons in the direction of Baghdad, Basra, and Kuwait City. They had to be ready to fight from then on.

A story in this chapter lets the troops tell in their own words what was going on in their minds and their hearts in a place growing more dangerous by the day and hour. Other stories deal with two major phenomena in the Gulf War deployment: the trust, or lack of it, between officers and the enlisted ranks, and the difference between men and women wearing similar uniforms but with different types of patches—regular U.S. Army soldiers, sailors, Marines and airmen, and the National Guard and reserves.

When it was clear the U.S. government was going to expand its troop commitment on the Arabian Peninsula to historic proportions, making this the largest American military deployment since Vietnam, there were suggestions of restarting the military draft. The Bush administration said it had looked at that option and ruled it out.

But there was a massive call-up of National Guard and reserve units to augment the regular active-duty troops brought in from all over the world. How these hundreds of thousands of men and women—all with the same American flag patch on their sleeves, all who had taken an oath to defend their flag and country against all enemies foreign and domestic—had shipped in from various bases, occupations, and walks of life, then managed to coalesce into a single fighting force behind a single cause, was a story in itself.

The units in the desert waiting for the official start of the land war weren't just standing around listening to music on their portable CD players, or BBC World Service and Armed Forces Radio on their short-waves. They were imagining what it was going to be like when the shooting started. Some already knew.

The combat veterans among the American forces had gained it in Vietnam, Grenada or Panama, places with a notable lack of isthmus-sized deserts.

And new weapons were introduced even as the clock ticked toward the official hour of war. A story in this chapter tells of a case in which the latest equipment expected to give the allied ground leverage, a mine-clearing device to neutralize the thousands of land mines Iraq had laid in their path, was brought out for inspection.

But the story makes clear it was not just equipment that was being tested. So was the crucial bond between those in charge, who would order the fighting to commence at the appointed hour, and those who would then go forward in harm's way, no matter when the order came.

Desert Looks Peaceful, but is That a Speck on the Horizon? "If You Weren't Religious, You Are Now"

By Jeff Franks

NEAR THE KUWAITI BORDER - The desert here is vast, featureless—and dangerous. On barren sand—normally inhabited only by Bedouins—heavily armed allied and Iraqi forces constantly patrol their respective sides of the Saudi-Kuwait border.

At night, the sky is filled with aircraft and the sound and fury of bombs, rockets and mortar fire. In the distance to the north, the flames from burning Kuwaiti oilfields light up the horizon.

Life here has an edge sharpened by the constant threat of attack. Every loud sound, every speck on the horizon takes on added significance. Fear, fatigue, and uncertainty are the constant companions of the young Marines manning the front lines of the Gulf war. "It gets really tense sometimes," said Sgt. Richard Manwarren, 31, of Jacksonville, Fla.

Marine units in light armored vehicles patrol 24 hours a day within sight of the 12-foot-high berms constructed by Iraqi forces to defend the Kuwait border. When the allied bombs are not falling and the Iraqi rocket launchers are idle, it is quiet and eerie in the desert, they said. "It's really strange because when you're looking out there with your binoculars, you know somebody on the other side is looking right back at you," said Cpl. Thomas Kelley,

26, of Warwick, R.I. "It makes you think. If you weren't religious when you got here, you're religious now." Indeed, religious fervor appears to grow the closer one gets to the front.

At a desert camp a few kilometers from Kuwait, a Marine wanders about offering Bibles and rosary beads from a sack he carries on his back. The troops are not ordered to take them, but many do so eagerly. The danger and the fog of war—which is a reality here, not just a catchy phrase in a military textbook—play funny tricks on the Marines.

As they peer out through the smoke and dust of the battlefield, they often mistake the remains of abandoned Bedouin camps—usually rusty barrels and rotting goat corpses—for the enemy.

One night, said Staff Sgt. Sean Kevany, 25, of Temecula, Calif., his unit saw something moving in the darkness and prepared for battle. As it came closer, they recognized their would-be target had four legs.

"It was a silly camel wandering out in the middle of all this, but it really had us on edge," he said. "Out here, though, you want to take a look at every little shadow."

The ever-present threat of attack means the Marines never really let down their guard. On those nights when they get a chance to sleep, they often curl up under their ponchos so they can move quickly if necessary.

Their sleeping bags provide more warmth, but climbing out of them can cost the troops precious seconds. After days and nights on alert, fatigue becomes so deep that the troops said they sometimes find themselves falling asleep while standing up.

Despite the dangers and difficulties confronting them, the Marines said life at the front has its moments of exhilaration. They speak proudly of being the allied troops most forward in the war and eagerly tell tales of how they have been to the border berms and peeked into Iraqi-held territory.

There are actually two berms stretching all along the front—one constructed by the Saudis and another opposite, in Kuwait, by the Iraqis.

Between them is a dangerous and deserted no-man's land where few have ventured since the outbreak of the war.

Just inside the Saudi berm, in the sector patrolled by the 2nd Marine Division, two Iraqi tanks, destroyed by TOW missiles fired from a light armoured vehicle, sit as silent reminders to last week's ill-fated assault by Iraqi ground forces.

The fighting has been too hot and the fear of surprise attack too great for the Marines to go to the tanks, but they often patrol within sight of them.

Their pride in having made the kills is tempered by their understanding that the tanks could have just as easily killed them.

Fortunately, the Iraqis never got off a shot before the Marines got them.

"When we were back home, it seemed like wars were always fought by other people. Now we know what war is really like. Believe me, it's scary. We need less and less coffee to stay awake," said Kevany.

The Other American Army in the Gulf, Out From Behind the Desk: "Free the Louisiana National Guard"

By Peter Copeland

A BASE IN NORTHERN SAUDI ARABIA - Some of their faces are wrinkled and tough as leather, and they walk with the careful strides of older men.

Others are balding and comfortably middle-aged, looking like they belong in front of desks or blackboards.

With their age and experience, these men and women should be colonels or senior non-commissioned officers, but the ranks they hold make them equals to the new recruits or the squeaky-clean graduates from West Point.

They are the National Guard and Reserve soldiers—salesmen, housewives, doctors, and construction workers—who woke up one morning and found themselves wearing sand-colored fatigues in Saudi Arabia.

In "real life" Roger Baldwin, 51, lives in Calera, AL, outside of Birmingham and works as a labor relations manager for ABC Rail.

He has a wife and two children. But out here in the northern desert of Saudi Arabia, he is Lt. Col. Roger Baldwin and his job is to get tons of rockets out of the mud. Someone decided to store the U.S. rockets in a low area of the desert, which quickly filled with soupy muck after the winter rains.

Baldwin, a soft-spoken man with an Alabama drawl, won't call it a screw-up, and prefers the military's euphemistic phrase—"a lesson learned."

He commands the Alabama National Guard's 440th Ordinance Battalion from Camden, AL, which was activated on Nov. 26 and sent to Saudi Arabia on Dec. 8. "Our orders are for 180 days," Baldwin said, "but what we tend to do is count on being over here a year, and if we're released sooner, so much the better."

Construction workers, insurance agents, and school teachers from Alabama are now full-time "ammo humpers" under his command. They live in tents, eat field rations, and haven't seen a porcelain toilet in weeks.

They work 12-hour days at least six days a week, stacking, sorting, packing, and loading thousands of tons of ammunition that are bound for the front lines.

"It's different than going to summer camp for two weeks," said Baldwin, who has been in the Guard for 30 years. "That's part of the responsibility you have when you put on the uniform."

There is a sign in Ray Scott's comfy bomb shelter that reads: "Free the Louisiana National Guard." The 42-year-old commander of the 1086th Transportation Co. from Jena, La., figures he won't be free for a good while, however. "We're in uniform and we'll do it," said the tall, lean, slow-talking Guardsman from Pineville, LA. "When you're expecting 180 days and you get 360 days, you have to make some adjustments. I think the morale would drop a little if that happens, but the esprit de corps is higher than any unit I've seen."

Some consolation for these Louisiana farmers, truck drivers, teachers, and mechanics—who now haul giant canvas bladders of water to the troops—is that they don't feel so far from home. Most live within a 30-mile radius of each other, and there are three married couples (they can't sleep together), assorted brothers and cousins and three sets of fathers and sons—including Capt. Scott and his son.

Not all the Guardsmen are older, however, and 23-year-old Terry Thomson left his wife and parents running the 1,000-acre farm in Oakes, ND, when he picked up a rifle to come to Saudi Arabia. "I only volunteered for 180 days, but once we set foot over here, we're the Army's property," Spec. Thompson said, standing in the bitter cold and staring out across a bleak desert. "I came over to fight for my country," he said. "I don't like the way Saddam Hussein treated the Kuwaitis."

The boss of all these Guardsmen and women at a base not far from Iraq is Maj. Gen. William "Gus" Pagonis, the logistics chief for all of Operation Desert Storm, who says 60 percent of the people getting beans and bullets to the troops come from the Guard and Reserves. "They remind you of revolutionary days when a guy plowed the field and his country called and he dropped everything he had to go fight a battle," Pagonis said.

"If somebody wants to know if I want to go home, sure, when this is over I want to go home," Pagonis said. "But I'm a professional soldier, as they are, as the reservists are. But they also have businesses and families—talk about dedicated Americans. I've told every soldier since day one that they were going to stay for 180 days, (even) when they all thought they were staying for 90," Pagonis said. "We've told every soldier in the last four months that they are going to stay for 365."

The message has not gotten through to everyone, however, and many are counting the days before they leave Saudi Arabia. "Like all soldiers, like all human beings, they have selective hearing," Pagonis said, "and you've got to be sensitive to that."

Staff Sgt. Rodney Wiese, 34, of Freedmont, Neb., and the 1012th General Supply Company of the Nebraska National Guard figures he's got 70 days left in country and he's got a calendar in his tent to prove it. "If you push them over the 180-day mark, attitudes are going to fall to pieces. It'll be Vietnam all over again," Wiese said.

David Ramp says he will stay as long as it takes. "When we were at home, part of us was thinking, 'We don't want to be left out. We want to be part of the action.'"

Ramp, 38, joined the National Guard when he was in college. A big incentive was drawing a low number—10—for the Vietnam draft. Now he has a Ph.D. and is a captain in the Army Reserves serving as a public affairs officer in Saudi Arabia.

At home, Ramp is the assistant personnel director for the city of Raleigh, N.C. "I think every day at work—and I've got 2,400 employees—is as stressful as this environment. You really don't think about anything until a Scud goes off. Your heart beats, there's no question about it," Ramp said. "I explained to my eight-year-old son, it's like knowing you are going to be tested in spelling and you practice those words. When you go into the test, you're still nervous, but because you've practiced at the end you know you did well.

"We don't want to be hurt," Ramp said. "But there is something deep inside you that says this is important and I want to be a part of it."

New Mine-Clearing Weapon Works Great—While the Top Brass Are Watching

By Douglas Jehl

WITH U.S. FORCES, Saudi Arabia - Out on a dusty firing range more than two weeks into combat, the generals descend by helicopter, taking a break from war planning to see whether the new weapon really worked.

On display was a rocket-powered explosive used to clear minefields from a distance, a much-desired tool in an expected U.S. advance against well-fortified Iraqi positions.

But in a war certain to be a proving ground for dozens of untested weapons systems, the arrival of the men with the well-starred Kevlar helmets at the morning-long mine-clearing display underscored the gnashing of teeth that becomes almost audible in this lull before ground combat, when American commanders talk about heading into "the breach," a first probe through Iraqi lines.

Trial runs conducted last fall at the National Training Center in the Mojave Desert at Fort Irwin, Calif., have suggested that U.S. forces could suffer heavy casualties in any such crossing.

The recommended route to few losses, the mine-clearing device, is unfamiliar to many infantry and armored commanders here. Their apprehension has increased in recent weeks after combat engineers encountered chronic problems with the device in test-firings elsewhere in Saudi Arabia.

Without the mine-clearing device, commanders could be forced to rely on more primitive and far more dangerous breaching techniques that as a last resort could send soldiers armed with probing rods shoulder-to-shoulder into the open in seeking to open a path toward well-defended Iraqi positions.

"This is a make or break day for the engineers," one officer said as Maj. Gen. Ronald H. Griffith, commander of the 1st Armored Division, headed into the desert toward the test site in an armored vehicle.

Aides said the general had previously witnessed only repeated failures in attempted demonstrations of the mine-clearing line charge (MCLC) near his home base in Germany. "You always get a better feel for this stuff if you see it function," said Col. Montgomery C. Meigs, commander of the division's Third Brigade and among the many senior officers who had never seen the mine-clearing device fired, "so I thought I'd come here to do just that."

For this test, engineers from the 16th Engineer Battalion said they had spent weeks modifying the mine-clearing devices to correct what was believed to have plagued the system in the past. And this time, the test went according to plan.

As the top brass watched, a converted bridge-laying vehicle rolled forward and fired, launching what the British call the Giant Viper upward in a snakelike string that uncoiled and fell on a simulated minefield.

Within seconds the charge exploded in a massive concussion that left the earth scarred along a line that extended well forward, opening the way for a plow-equipped tank that rumbled along the path to complete the mine-clearing exercise.

A charge fired later in the morning failed to explode, a recurring malady that required engineers to climb out of their armored vehicle to detonate the device manually in what in combat would be a highly dangerous move. But equipment otherwise performed well, at least some of the morning's unease appeared to have been allayed.

"There was a lot of apprehension here this morning," said Lt. Col. Ronald H. Adkins, 41, of Rocky Mount, Va., "but I will tell you that after the demonstration here this morning, there is no apprehension at all."

Nevertheless, other officers and veteran combat engineers made clear later that no amount of technology could dispel their sense of dread in preparing for a potential path-breaking mission across well-fortified Iraqi lines. Asked his preferred tools for such an assault, Sgt. Carl Curtice, a combat engineer from Seattle with 13 years of barrier-breaching experience, replied: "Carpetbomb." "Or go around," he added later. "I don't know who's going to go through 'em, but there's going to be a lot to go through."

In confronting Iraqi minefields believed to be hundreds of meters deep, the engineers noted, they could be forced to fire several mine-clearing charges consecutively in a time-consuming operation that would prolong the time they would be vulnerable to enemy fire. At the same time, they said, the threat of chemical attack during operations conducted within easy range of Iraqi forces will almost certainly mean that U.S. forces must wear cumbersome protective suits in any barrier-breaching mission. And, in what engineers said remained their most significant concern, combat forces in the division only Sunday (cq) began to rehearse their role for such assaults. In the National Training Center mock-attacks last fall, they noted, a lack of sufficient coordination among ground, air and artillery forces had been blamed for the heavy casualties. "All this needs orchestration," said Capt. Tom Magness, operations officer for the battalion. "It's not just engineers who need to go through it."

With the quality of Iraqi fortifications believed to vary significantly along a front that now stretches hundreds of miles from the Kuwaiti coast into the interior, some officers held out the hope that U.S. forces might not have to contend with the most formidable of the barriers, which include massive berms of sand and trenches filled with piped-in oil that can quickly be set afire. "The doctrine says the best course is always to go around them," said Adkins, the engineers' commander.

In pep talks to his soldiers, Maj. Gen. Griffith, commander of this Iron Soldiers division, has also sought to dispel the impression that his massive armored force would simply lurch head-on into dug-in Iraqi defenders if it came to a U.S. ground offensive. "If we have to cross that line," Griffith told the headquarters of one battalion the other day, "we're going to be in good shape—without losing a lot of soldiers. That's going to be the goal."

The young engineers who would be asked to contend with obstacles along the way appear not altogether convinced, successful test runs and such assurances notwithstanding. At the end of the demonstration for the brass, one company commander praised his men and pointed out that Griffith had departed by the time the first misfire occurred.

"We were three for three when the general was here," the captain said. "That's what counts." There was a pause, then one soldier in the crew spoke up:

"Not really, sir."

Monday
February 4, 1991

Modern armies couldn't operate without helicopters. As a regular piece of battlefield equipment, they only date to the Korean War. But once introduced, they quickly became so integral to the American military infrastructure and then spread around the world that now it's hard to imagine a military without them.

They are vital for mundane chores like moving mail or heavy equipment and material or a visiting VIP to the most sophisticated covert or rescue mission. They're invaluable, but dangerous, even when no enemy is trying to down them.

The helicopter crashes that caused allied casualties in the Gulf began in the fall of 1990, during Operation Desert Shield, and continued until after the cease-fire when American forces on temporary occupation duty were still flying reconnaissance missions in Iraq to ensure that Saddam Hussein's legions abided by the terms of their surrender.

A story in this chapter records a regrettable, but almost predictable, tragedy among military units—four Marines killed in the crash of a helicopter on a non-combat flight. On this same day, two other soldiers were killed when their Cobra helicopter crashed while on an "escort" non-combat mission inside Saudi Arabia.

More than 2,000 miles away on the same day, a fixed-wing plane—in this case a B-52 bomber on his way back to its base on the island of Diego Garcia from a bombing run in the Persian Gulf—ditched in the Indian Ocean. The cause was reported to be mechanical. All six in the crew were rescued.

The deaths in those incidents act are typical of many flying-related tragedies written about from the Saudi desert during the Gulf War. Even when the weather was described as good, there were always risky in-flight conditions for all types of aircraft in that theater, especially those nearest the windblown, sandy ground.

For those who died, whether in combat or non-combat incidents like the helicopter crashes, the Graves Registration outfits were there and ready to fulfill their somber and sacred duties. In this chapter, the Marine graves registration unit sets the tone for the work they expected would soon come.

For the British armored division, there came the time that eventually comes to all armies—time to distribute new maps to troops, so they are well-oriented in battle, able to locate their objectives. An army without decent maps is no better off than a well-armed rabble looking for a fight but no idea where to go.

The Pentagon placed so much importance in maps that it shipped a total of 90 million, of every description, to the theater. A story in this chapter shows how putting maps in soldiers' hands when an ill wind is blowing can lead in the wrong direction.

Farther out in the desert, roughly 500 miles west of Dhahran and very close to the Iraqi border, lay a town named Rafha. The town, normally sleepy, was bustling with new customers from the French and American army encampments nearby.

But those encampments were the knuckle-edge of a large force, combining French troops and elements of the 18th Airborne Corps that Gen. Schwarzkopf hoped to use to surprise the Iraqis with a sweeping attack out of the west.

Allied military authorities didn't want the name of the town to appear in stories because it described military personnel visiting there, and they were concerned it might tip off the Iraqis. Following reporting guidelines for the pool press, "RAFHA" was scratched as the original dateline for a story in this chapter and it became "A TOWN IN NORTHERN SAUDI ARABIA."

With the constant military traffic between Dhahran and Rafha during the bombing campaign, the troops' access to international phone calls and the availability of maps in various publications indicated forces attacking Iraq from the allies' left flank, a fair question is how secret was the force around Rafha.

But there were rules, and they made military sense at the time. Gen. Schwarzkopf had briefed the plan to his top commanders in November. Sketches showing a rough equivalent of the final invasion plan were circulating in Saudi Arabia within weeks.

There were some Iraqi troops in that sector of southern Iraq across from the French light armored troops and the 18th Airborne Corps combat engineers, artillery batteries and paratroopers when the ground war came, but Saddam Hussein didn't send a lot of additional forces out there to counter them.

Perhaps the secret held and he didn't know the allies were all the way out to Rafha. Perhaps he'd heard all about some left hook option in the American and European media but thought it was a deception, the same way Hitler thought German intelligence about a landing at Normandy had picked up a hoax perpetuated by Eisenhower and Mountbatten.

Or perhaps he believed the allied troops were indeed in force out at Rafha but chose not to do anything about it. Or couldn't find more units willing to go that far on low rations. It's a question for his memoirs to answer.

Now that it's been a decade since Gen. Schwarzkopf swung his left hook, and the Legionnaires and American troops who executed it have shipped out to new posts, the name can go back in.

Navy Turns Guns on Kuwait; 4 Marines Die in Helicopter Crash

By Colin Nickerson

NEAR THE KUWAIT BORDER, Saudi Arabia - Naval guns added their chorus last night to air strikes and Marine artillery fire directed at Iraqi forces entrenched in southern Kuwait. Also yesterday, a Marine UH-1N "Huey" helicopter crashed in northeastern Saudi Arabia during a fierce sandstorm.

Four Marines were killed when the chopper went down in a war sector controlled by the 2nd Marine Division.

The cause of the crash was still unknown this morning, but a Marine spokesman said it was not the result of enemy action. Mechanical failure is suspected. Meanwhile, the American battleship USS Missouri, on station in the Persian Gulf, fired salvos at Iraqi strongholds near the Saudi border on Sunday night.

It was believed to be the first naval artillery directed against Iraqi land forces in the three-week-old war. The huge shells smashed at targets along the Persian Gulf coast, but caused Iraqis to scramble for cover dozens of miles inland. "Enemy are scurrying about out there," said Lt. Co. Jan Huly, a Marine 2nd Division spokesman.

Air strikes and Marine artillery raids continued against Iraqi forces despite a lashing sandstorm that reduced ground visibility to less than 300 meters. The stinging haze of sand added to Marine discomfort but did not affect operations.

Graves Registration Company: "No Unknown Soldiers"

By Caryle Murphy

WITH U.S. FORCES IN NORTH-EASTERN SAUDI ARABIA - Like thousands of other warriors sprawled across this barren, windswept desert, Marine Lt. Col. John Cassady and his men hope to see as little as possible of war's most unwanted stepchild: death.

But once a ground battle begins, Cassady's company knows it will see far more than its share of casualties.

For to it falls the painful task of identifying the remains of fellow Marines killed in action and readying them for evacuation home.

"If we do our job perfectly, everybody who pays the price for what we're doing would be accounted for and returned home," said Cassady, and when the Gulf War is over, "there will be no unknown soldiers."

His graves registration unit, encamped behind tall berms of desert sand just south of the Kuwaiti border, is now the most forward central collection point for the bodies of fallen comrades retrieved from the battlefield. His men work and sleep in tents burrowed into deep pits covered with camouflage netting. Refrigerated trailer vans hold the remains of Marines until they are shipped to the rear lines.

As the days before a ground assault into Kuwait dwindle, and cross-border clashes step up, Cassady's men have already received the remains of 11 Marines killed last week, at least seven of them in what the Pentagon now says was "friendly fire" from their own side.

They have also treated—in "exactly the same" way as Marines' remains—the bodies of a few Iraqis killed in skirmishes. This equal treatment is required under the international Geneva Convention governing the conduct of war. But it's also, said Cassady, "the human thing." After processing, Iraqi remains are turned over to the Saudi authorities.

Cassady and his men won't face the stark terror of face-to-face fighting, but they will be burdened with tremendous emotional and psychological pressures from their grim task. Pressures that move their commander, Brig. Gen. Chuck C. Krulak, to call Cassady's unit "the unsung heroes of this damn war."

"In a lot of ways, I think that's the truth," said Cassady. "Our guys work at all hours of the night, 24 hours. If a body comes in, the lights go on. These guys display a lot of courage. It's not facing the enemy, but I tell you, it's facing a lot of reality. They grow up fast." Cassady said he tries to emphasize to his troops, who include both active-duty Marines and reservists, "the reality of what they are going to deal with, and (to) concentrate on the process and service aspect to it, and try not to think of the reality of what's sitting in front of you."

Lance Cpl. Troy Moseley, 21, is one of the unit's handful of volunteers.

Shorty after arriving in Saudi Arabia, Moseley said he "was asked whether I wanted to be in graves registration. I said that sounds like a job I could handle . . . (even though) I didn't have any idea what it was about."

He and his fellow volunteers were given "a black book and we sat down at a table . . . we began training, doing drills, until we were ready," said the Snyder, Tenn. native. When he found out what the job entailed, Moseley said he did not ask to be reassigned. "It never crossed my mind." The toughest part of Moseley's job, he said, is waiting. "Each and every time we get a call (saying) you're going to have remains . . . it's a bad kind of anticipation."

. . . Forty-year-old Cassady, a ruddy-faced redhead from Stratford, N.J., is the senior graves registration officer for all Marines in country. He wrote the Marine Corps manual on graves registration when he was based back at Quantico, Va.

He describes the job as "a logistics function" of "identification and accountability." When remains are brought in, his men try to positively establish identification either by the dogtag on the body or by personal effects accompanying it. "These personal effects are also accounted for," Cassady said. A chaplain or a rabbi is called in for a final blessing unless this has already been done in the field.

If the remains cannot be positively identified, Cassady's staff takes fingerprints; gives the body an evacuation number and records "the circumstances of recovery of those remains," he said. When the fighting is over, his unit will scour the battlefield for those listed as missing. A top priority for Cassady's people is speed so that "the family gets the casualty back just as soon as they can." Sometimes, the remains are at their camp "as little as an hour. Sometimes we have to keep them a day."

Right now, remains are being returned to the United States, where final identification is done, in about 24 hours, he said. "The whole idea," said Krulak, "is to avoid the tragic (telephone) call of someone (to a family) saying, 'Hey, your son was killed,' when in fact he wasn't. Graves registration is just that. They, to the best of their ability, provide identification of who in fact was killed so the family at home knows this is my son, this is my husband. And it's not a case of I wonder who it was." Casualties are a sensitive topic of discussion among U.S. military here, many of whom recall how the Vietnam War's daily "body counts" and vivid television coverage of wounded servicemen helped shift American public opinion away from support of that war.

Pentagon officials have refused to give estimates of potential U.S. casualties in the Gulf war, and in a briefing shortly after hostilities broke out, Gen. H. Norman Schwarzkopf declined to offer estimates of Iraqi casualties in the allied air campaign. "And I tell you," added Schwarzkopf, "if I have anything to say about it, we're never going to get into the body count business. That's nothing more than rough, wild estimates and it's ridiculous to do that. And we couldn't do it even if we wanted to. But right now we have no estimates."

In his interview with a combat media pool, Cassady acknowledged that this official sensitivity is partly due to the military's Vietnam experience—one that could be repeated if casualties start to soar. "It's a television war," he said. "Opinion can be molded. You know that as well as I do."

The colonel also made clear, however, that he was speaking to the press with reluctance out of deference to his job. "I'm very sensitive to having you around here, to tell you the truth," he said in his desert camp. "It's not appropriate . . . (because) we deal with some very private things here . . . what we're doing is trying to take care of people and not publicize it . . . you don't go and look in a morgue in a hospital. We're not a morgue, (but) it's not appropriate for general knowledge. People could misunderstand very easily."

Cassady's men feel the same way. "I compare (my job) to going to church," said Moseley. "When you go to church, you don't laugh, cut up, play. You take off your hat. When I go in to process, I remove my cover (hat). That's just showing due respect. I treat the Marine I process just like I'd like to be treated. I treat Iraqis like I'd want to be treated."

When the Wind Picked Up, Those Numerals Began Roaming Well Beyond Dorking al Hambra

By Simon Clifford

It sounded so simple, it surely couldn't go wrong—the army was going to hand out maps to all units so they would know where to go When The Time Comes.

At the Queen's Company, the Grenadier Guards, the 19 platoon leaders and section commanders were called to receive their 45 maps each, showing the relief of various areas.

All they had to do was pick them up, check them off on a checklist and go back. A 10-minute job, nothing for a highly-organized, professional army.

I watched the first hour or so, went away for a doze and came back 30 minutes later just as it finished. For security reasons I have changed the map names and numbers—the afternoon started so well. The 19 sat, squatted, lay, or rested on elbows in the desert sand in—just for a change—scorching sun. There was a little breeze and clouds on the horizon but they were far off "We'll be finished in plenty of time," confidently predicted 2nd Capt. Greville Bibby.

Never trust a weatherman.

The 19 first had to draw a checklist grid ready to mark down the name and number of each map. When everyone had paper, then reporter Simon Clifford was called on to provide an extra 16 pens.

As the numbers were read out, there were signs of some distress, and Capt. Bibby was getting frustrated. "No, that was 3456, not 3465," he said. "That is roman numeral four after it. That's one-vee," he said. "How do you spell roman numeral?" asked Sgt. Carl Howarth, from Holton. "No, like this!" said the reddening captain. It was not sunburn.

It was all too much for Colour Sgt. Skid Dorner, who sat on his few maps and picked his teeth using the point of his bayonet. Col. Sgt. Steve Sadler was on all fours intently trying to see if he had a map covering Dorking al Hambra. "I'm sure I haven't got it," he whimpered.

Ominously, the only things moving quickly were the ends of the maps as they started to flap in the breeze. Behind the indian file of 19, three others were busy picking up pages from 45 piles—and getting confused.

Then one map was whisked away on the breeze. As the Americans on radio station Wizard 106 playing in the background would have said, "It was a footrace." The army won and now a frantic search for rocks to hold down the pages.

The wind got up—and she blew, blew, blew. Pages flapped and so did the men.

Tempers were rising and so was the temperature. Watching from under a nearby camouflaged tent was a small group—including me, having a great time.

"Look at that one go," said Sgt. Adrian Seward, as Skid was stirred from potholing in his fillings to chase map 432, which was trying its best to get home to Wadi al Stockport. Sgt. Howarth had lost his roman numeral IV anyway, so it didn't matter.

He'll just have to follow Sgt. Sadler, who was the only "cool and a cucumber" player on the pitch. Sgt. Sadler had been on all fours, holding down his pages searching for the map with Dorking al Hambra.

I have not seen a TV sitcom for weeks since coming out to the desolate desert.

Who needs it when the army can provide Charlie Chaplain and Terry and June on the same billing—and for free.

Eventually, of course, Capt. Bibby had it all sorted out. The pages were delivered, Skid found Dorking for Sgt. Sadler and they all went back to their tents for tea.

The onlookers, though, had one last chuckle.

We found a small roll of maps that should have been handed out.

"Should we tell them?" said Cpl. Steven Dunstan.

"I suppose so," Sgt. Harry Melbourne replied. "But after tea."

Shit Detail: If Nobody Wants to Do It, But Somebody Has to, It Pays to be Busy Doing Something Else

By John Fialka

NORTHERN SAUDI ARABIA - It doesn't take long during his nightly staff meetings before Capt. Neftali "Nef" Rodriguez gets around to talking trash.

Much has been written about the high technology the U.S. is bringing to bear here as armored units like this one make their final preparations for what could be a bloody ground phase of this war.

However, if history is any guide, the outcome as in wars past, will depend heavily on the skill and the discipline of small units like Capt. Rodriguez's D Company. It is a tiny slice of the Army's formidable Third Armored Division, newly-arrived here from Germany.

In combat, Capt. Rodriguez explains to his sergeants as they huddle around him on the dirt floor of his tent, seemingly minor details like trash can become life or death issues. And Capt. Rodriguez knows about details.

A former staff sergeant who has risen up through the ranks, he has been walking along the concertina wire that rings this forlorn outpost.

Instead of tumbleweed, Coke cans are blowing, rattling their way across the flat, rock-flecked desert. A motley assortment of plastic bags and field ration wrappers are impaled on the concertina wire, waving like so much dirty laundry.

It is 8 p.m. and Capt. Rodriguez is telling his sergeants:

"Anything that isn't natural, I want it up off the ground."

He explains that any hope of finding traces of terrorists or Iraqi patrols will be lost unless the sea of trash forming around D Company is cleaned up. Moreover, if the trash isn't burned properly in the morning, the residual heat from the fires could be picked up on enemy night vision equipment the following evening, neatly outlining the company's otherwise carefully blacked-out position.

At 9 p.m. the meeting breaks up. Guards are posted and Pvt. Christopher Leque, 19, of Lacrosse, Wis., is sent to one of the two tanks assigned to patrol the nearby desert

Monday - February 4, 1991

during the night, adding further protection to the few tanks and the handful of tents that are arrayed inside the wire. (Pentagon rules governing combat pools forbid descriptions of the size of units, but D Company has fewer than 100 men.)

The M1A1 is, reputedly, the most lethal tank in the world. Its whining turbine engine can propel it over 50 mph. Its computerized infrared targeting system can allocate and hit targets at night while the tank is on the move.

On this chilly night, however, the tank is simply a warm place to be for Pvt. Leque, who somehow coils his 6-foot frame into the tank's cramped driver's compartment.

Above him, where the loader and gunner sit, the only objects that show up on the ultra-sensitive targeting screen are field mice. They show up like little streaks of heat that contrast against the cold blackness of the desert.

And the tank's 120mm cannon, powerful enough to rip the hull of any other known tank, is used as a navigation aid on the patrols over the sea-like flatness. Every now and then a soldier jumps out of the tank to take a compass reading. Then the cannon is pointed to remind him of the direction where he is supposed to be headed.

Pvt. Leque, like most members of D Company, uses the quiet hours to come to grips with the idea of going into combat for the first time. As he explains to a visitor who has crawled into his tank, "There are two sides to it. I kind of look forward. I mean, it's an adventure—something that not everybody gets to do. But there is also the apprehensive side. You think I might not come out of this. I guess if it happens, it happens," he shrugs.

Before midnight there are often conversations about mortality in Capt. Rodriguez's loaf-shaped brown tent. "We sit around and talk about it," says the chunky, soft spoken, 33-year-old Shreveport, La. native.

"We'd like to think that we'll all come back, but some of us are probably not going to make it. The hardest part for us will be the moment when we take our first casualty. How well we deal with that is going to make it or break it as far as the company is concerned."

By midnight, Capt. Rodriguez is settled into the cot in his tent. He will doze, not sleep, with one ear cocked for the crackle of the radio that puts him in touch with his patrols.

He is up at 5 a.m., before the first streaks of light taint the unrelieved flatness of the horizon, and the rest of D Company is up with him preparing to man battle positions.

This is a ritual called "Stand To" and it is used in combat zones.

Dawn is considered the most likely hour for an enemy attack and any Army unit that follows the book will be ready for it.

What this means is that Pvt. Leque, having spent four hours of the night out on patrol, shuffles back out to his tank to semi-doze in the driver's seat. Above him, in the tank commander's seat, Sgt. Gary Lepelletier, 34, of Clifton, N.J., sits shrouded in an Army blanket as he fiddles with the dials that control the tank's turret.

How does he feel about going into combat? "I often think about all the things we could have trained on in peacetime and took for granted," says the 14-year Army veteran. "There are just a whole lot of little things we're going to need to know."

At 7 a.m. Stand To ends and the men come back to their tents to eat and to shave. Even shaving has a life-or-death aspect out here.

A gas mask will not make a tight seal over beard stubble. It is not just fear of Capt. Rodriguez's penchant for neatness that keeps the men of D Company clean shaven.

Most of Pvt. Daniel J. Cingel's meals come out of a series of brown plastic pouches that would be unfamiliar to veterans of past wars. They are the Army's new "Meals Ready to Eat" field rations, called MREs for short, and come in at least a dozen different variations.

The toughest part so far for Pvt. Cingel, 20, from Macedonia, Ohio, was calling his parents to tell them that D Company, normally based in Friedberg, Germany, was going to Saudi Arabia. "When I called, my father already knew it. He could tell from nervousness in my voice. He said, well, there are some things you have to do. My mother, she just started crying on the phone."

By 10 a.m., D Company's trash burning detail is in full swing.

Lt. Col. Dan A. Merritt, Capt. Rodriguez's boss, drives up in his squat High Mobility Multi-Wheeled Vehicle. (Like C-rations, the Jeep has also been replaced in this army.)

Because his units are sprawled for miles over the desert, the tobacco-chewing West Point graduate from Gladewater, Tex., spends as many as 18 hours a day bouncing over rocks in his HMMWV, which has a set of tall antennas sticking up in the back.

His back is sore.

For him, the thought of going into combat is a double-edged sword, as he puts it. "I've been preparing for this day for 23 years, counting the four I spent in the (West Point) academy. It's like practicing two times a day for the big game that's finally arrived. On the other hand, if we do this, somebody's bound to get hurt."

At 11 a.m., as the colonel's HMMWV fades into the distance and the MRE wrappers are gathered up, D Company turns to the job of tank maintenance. The sand must be cleaned from the tanks' J machine guns, a job that is frequently nullified here by sandstorms before it is finished.

Then the stage is set for a more thankless chore. The latrines are emptied and two "volunteers"—men caught by Capt. Rodriguez outside their tents without having their gas masks strapped to their hips—are given the job of burning human excrement.

An Army ritual since long before Vietnam, the "shit detail" is properly done with diesel oil, which creates the plumes of oily smoke that hang over most of the desert encampments here. It takes a long time to burn and one of the privates, eager to get the job over with, decides to pour some gasoline on the fire.

A sheet of flame erupts. The sergeants hear about this the following evening.

"Now that's one letter I do not want to write," the captain fumes. "Your son torched himself burning shit." Then the captain turns to his maps and points to D Company's next venture into the unknown—a position very near the Kuwaiti border, the final assembly point before battle. It is a place that has an Arab name, but Capt. Rodriguez stumbles over it, finally giving up. "Look, this is just outside Ali Kazam," he says. "These names, I just make them up as I go along."

Meanwhile, Capt. Rodriguez's assistant, Lt. Kurt Norem, 24, of Iowa Falls, Ia. is finishing up a chore he volunteered for. He is answering a letter D Company received from a six-year-old boy, one of many thousands that have arrived here addressed to "Any Soldier."

Lt. Norem has explained that what this war is about "is just like a gangster coming into his hometown and harming his friends. It goes beyond defending the U.S. This is a world community."

Monday - February 4, 1991

Business is Good in a Desert Crossroads Named Rafha, Thanks to This "Stinking War"

By Laurence Jolidon

RAFHA, Saudi Arabia - As the war of January 1991 drew near, a lot of people left this town near the border of Iraq.

"Most of the people moved out with their families," said Soliman Al-Khalaiwy, 34, who owns a camera store and film developing shop. "They thought the war, when it started, would cover all of this area. Now, most have come back."

A few shops along the town's rutted, cluttered main drag are still closed. The rest, like Al-Khalaiwy's, are doing better than all right. As U.S. and other coalition ground forces have taken advance positions along the Iraqi border, towns like this have flourished with business. Shoppers in the uniforms of the U.S.A., France, and Egypt, and a few nondescript foreign civilians wade in and out of the stores in groups, searching for the best buys in radios, watches, souvenirs of Saudi Arabia and winter clothes to help ward off the chilly desert nights.

Prices seem to jump every few days, but Al-Khalaiwy—who holds citizenship and a master's degree in education from the University of Tennessee—says the booming military trade hasn't affected his.

"Some people" he says, "whose heart is small or who are weak, have charged higher prices. But me, no. These people (the foreign soldiers) are helping us. Why cheat them? I want them to take a good impression of my country back with them."

Many of the shoppers are military personnel designated to buy supplies on the local market that aren't available in stock or would take too long to reach U.S. troops.

Many are Arabic-speakers. They leave puzzled looks on some store owners. Their uniforms say charge them the maximum. Their Arab speech says give me a good price.

Some items, like stoves and electrical appliances, are sold out or are in short supply, no matter the offer. Telephone booths are also very popular. GIs and other foreign troops stand in slow-moving lines for a chance to call home collect. The town's few restaurants and hotels are doing rush business. Plates of fried chicken, curried mutton, French fries, green salads, and warm pita bread are welcome breaks from the standard field rations most of the troops must eat most of the time.

Rafha has a raffish reputation among the U.S. military. Periodically, Military Police vehicles with machine guns mounted on the roof patrol the streets and parking areas, warning troops not to stay too long. On recent days, the town has been declared off-limits to some U.S. units, except for designated supply buyers. The warnings say the town's border location makes it an inviting target for Iraqi saboteurs and terrorists.

A few weeks back, U.S. visiting soldiers said they were shocked at the number of furtive-looking men in long, Arab robes and thick, wool coats carrying weapons and bandoliers. They're still around, but not so obvious.

Some U.S. officers said Rafha even has a drug trade. Al-Khalaiwy and other residents deny those troubling charges. No Iraqi spies, no terrorists, and certainly no drugs run rampant through Rafha, they say. "Rafha's clean," said Al-Khalaiwy. His American wife and young son still live in Atlanta, where he attended Georgia Tech University. She refused to move here when war was imminent.

Parked outside his crowded shop is a 1989 Mercury Grand Marquis he had shipped over from Nashville. A radar detector that plugs into the cigarette lighter is clipped to the driver's side sun visor. "I don't need it over here," he says, where Saudi drivers are notorious for high-speed highway driving virtually unhampered by The Law. "I want to go back to the U.S.," he said, "but right now my mother and the rest of my family need me here. Besides, I don't want to abandon this place now. Leave my houses? Leave my land? No, I will stay here and protect them."

The past few days, U.S. Army civil affairs soldiers have been taking a close look at Rafha. When the allied ground offensive kicks off, they expect it to be inundated with refugees fleeing the fighting. "We're the interface between the civilian government and the military," said Capt. George Cagle II, 34, using the jargon of his civilian profession—computer programmer, in Huntsville, AL.

Cagle and other members of the 489th Civil Affairs Detachment of Knoxville, TN, are some of the recent influx of reserve and active-duty civil affairs units sent to handle the chaos and confusion expected to follow the outbreak of heavy fighting.

"The war will come a lot closer to this town," said Capt. Joe Weaver, 38, an environmentalist at Oak Ridge National Laboratory, Oak Ridge, Tenn. He and the rest of the 489th arrived in late December. "I think you'll see a big influx of displaced persons."

The civil affairs specialists say the Saudi government has done an excellent job of preparing for thousands of refugees by laying in extra stores of food, water, clothing and material for building new shelters. But the civil affairs officers say even those supplies will be inadequate in the face of a refugee flood.

"You think you have enough for something like this but you never do," said Weaver. "It will go pretty fast. There'll be a shortage of foodstuffs." He said the U.S. military will arrange for more supplies so that food and water needed for fighting troops won't be diminished by the needs of civilian refugees.

The civil affairs people will also monitor public health and safety of Rafha, making sure sickness and epidemic don't threaten civilians or soldiers. "We want to minimize the start and spread of any diseases," said Weaver. "The Saudis have been planning for months and months to take care of their own," said Cagle. "I'm surprised at how much they've stocked up." The civil affairs soldiers say they've heard the rumors about terrorists in Rafha and take precautions when they are here. "You don't let anybody get under your truck," said Cagle. And the soldiers never walk through the town alone.

"There have been no terrorist incidents here and we don't want any," said Cagle. But like most of the soldiers who pass through Rafha, they wouldn't mind a store that sells U.S. newspapers—which this town of 20,000 doesn't have—or a restaurant that serves hot, sit-down meals.

"If not for this stinking war, it wouldn't be such a bad place," said 2nd Lt. Tim Higgs, 31, of Martin, TN. He and some fellow civil affairs reservists were hunting for a restaurant. "If I can get a hot meal, it's an okay place as far as I'm concerned," said Staff Sgt. Tom Webster, 40, of Chattanooga. The two of them and Spec. John Love—"Dr. of Love" inked on his helmet—24, of Anchorage, who dropped his studies at Pensacola (Fla.) Junior College to deploy to Saudi Arabia, decided on hotel fare.

With his connections back in the U.S., Al-Khalaiwy even accepts occasional personal checks from GIs for the watches, cameras and video recorders in his store. But most of the sales are for cash—Saudi riyals, U.S. dollars, or French francs.

The French soldiers have the reputation in Rafha of big spenders.

"Business is good, very, very good with the French," said one happy storekeeper as he placed a row of expensive radios on the counter for inspection by three Legionnaires.

Al-Khalaiwy said Rafha's residents—who include a few families from Kuwait expelled by the Iraqi invasion—mostly appreciate the U.S. presence and protection from a similar fate. "I'm going to name my next son Patriot," he says, in honor of the weapon that has blasted so many Iraqi Scuds out of the Saudi skies.

Tuesday
February 5, 1991

Some days during the Gulf War were tenser than others. This was a tense one. Analysis of coded radio messages broadcast from Baghdad produced one interpretation that Saddam Hussein was trying to widen the war even farther, beyond Israel, beyond the Mideast.

The coded messages appeared to summon Iraq's supporters throughout the worldwide network of terrorists to strike a blow at allied or U.S. citizens or interests that would draw blood and attract attention.

The "increased tensions" were cited in a State Department bulletin urging all U.S. citizens remaining in Jordan to leave. Jordan's King Hussein had criticized the allied effort, and despite longstanding strong ties with the U.S. was siding with Iraq in this conflict. About 4,600 Americans were reported still in Jordan.

In the air war, the latest reports said that allied bombing had destroyed a majority of Iraq's fuel-making capacity, up to 80 percent of its oil refineries. The practical effect was to halt the sale to civilians of virtually all petroleum products—gasoline, fuel oil, and cooking oil—so that the dwindling supply could go to military use.

Allied bombs were also taking a devastating toll on Iraq's military infrastructure.

A U.S. commander said that in addition to warplanes and other large weapons systems, even Iraqi military field headquarters are being moved into civilian areas in an attempt to hide them. Some headquarters units have been moved into schools or mosques, which like other civilian areas are excluded from allied target lists.

The deployment of highly sophisticated weapons, long-distance targeting and intelligence-gathering systems in the Gulf, and the open discussion of their use gave the war a kind of high-tech sheen. The Americans were credited by some with developing a new type of super-powered, arm's-length killing machine that devastated enemies while leaving the attacking forces safe from most retribution.

The American military gained a reputation for perfecting future warfare, leaving behind not only huge third-world armies like Iraq's but many of its own allies, who had not come close to matching U.S. investment in warmaking tools and techniques.

The same sophisticated warmaking techniques also produced a popular, but false, notion that the new weapons and style of war could reduce U.S. casualties—and perhaps even unintended civilian casualties in enemy territory—to near zero. But having the latest, most powerful weapons didn't prevent allied troops from being killed and wounded by their own comrades, or in combat-related mishaps.

And while the air war against Iraqi targets was certainly highly efficient, many civilians died because the military target was a facility that served both military and civilian purposes.

A military aircraft parked on a residential street could be excluded from a list of bomb targets. But no satellite imagery yet invented could look down from outer orbit and determine whether an unmarked building was occupied by students at their desks, or Iraqi soldiers planning their next mission, or both.

Another story in this chapter provides a casualty toll often overlooked in the rush of coverage of the Battle of Khafji: 18 Saudi soldiers killed and 16 wounded in the two-day struggle to regain control of that mostly-abandoned town. That's several times the number given right after the battle by a Saudi commander. But in war, all numbers are subject to later revision.

Besides the pilots who still remained unaccounted for, the U.S. count of MIAs remained at two—both soldiers, a man and a woman, captured when they missed a turn and drove into Khafji just after the Iraqis had captured it.

18 Saudi Troops Reported Killed, 16 Wounded in Battle for Khafji: "We Need the Americans Over Here"

By Paul Basken

EASTERN SAUDI ARABIA - They came into this war seen as pampered little Rodney Dangerfields. But for now they play the role of tough-talking Humphrey Bogarts.

Lying in hospital beds with various cuts, breaks and burns from their move last week to recapture the coastal town of Khafji, the Saudi soldiers speak only of getting back to the battlefield and moving on to Kuwait.

"We are ready at any time," to begin a ground attack, Sgt. Sa'ad Subahi of the Saudi border guard said while sitting up in bed at the King Abdul Aziz Airbase Hospital. "We are just waiting for the order."

Subahi, his left hand bandaged and his face covered with the red splotches of burn wounds, said he was injured in the battle to retake Khafji when Iraqi artillery destroyed the tank he was standing beside, killing the soldiers inside.

A total of 18 Saudi troops died in the battle, as they and Qatari troops went in alone on the ground, with only air support from the far larger U.S. force that's been guiding the allied war campaign. The U.S. decision to refrain from ground combat was widely seen as a political move intended to downplay their dominating role in a war the Saudis are incapable of waging by themselves.

Subahi, covered in his white hospital gown and speaking to reporters in Arabic, said the Saudis fully appreciated the U.S. role in the war but remained equally confident of their own abilities. "They came to help, but we have the expertise... and the ability to fight any enemies," he said.

Just outside his room, nurse Josie Klunder attests to the spirit of the 16 wounded Saudi soldiers the hospital received from Khafji. "They're tougher than the normal regular soldiers that we get over here" during peacetime, said Klunder, a native of Holland. "If they (other soldiers) are here when the war is not on . . . then they're complaining already about a lot of pain when they don't have any real big thing" wrong with them, she said.

"They are very good" as patients, said Kamal Shahab, the hospital's acting medical director and chairman of surgery. "They are very tough . . . They want to go back to the battlefield." Subahi also takes a tough line toward the Iraqis, with whom he stood eye-to-eye during the battle in Khafji. "Even though they are Arabs, if they behave the wrong way and they try to come into our country, we will fight them back no matter who they are," he said. And as fighters, he said of Saddam Hussein's forces, "they were actually below expectations. The way we heard about them we thought they would be much stronger, actually."

Klunder is impressed, but to a point. "Still," she said, "I think we need the Americans over here. If the Americans were not here, I was already gone."

Iraqi Patrols Slipping Through Allied Lines; "A Counter-Reconnaissance Battle"

By Gary Regenstreif

NORTHERN SAUDI ARABIA - Iraqi patrols slip into Saudi Arabia almost nightly to learn the strengths and weaknesses of allied forces in what officials describe as a "counter-reconnaissance battle" waged on the eve of all ground wars.

The Iraqis, U.S. military officials say, probe as deeply as they can into the kingdom, even to the point of drawing fire, to plan which route would be the most effective to lead an offensive. At the same time, Iraqi patrols are observing whether allied forces are moving forward to detect a possible attack on Iraqi defences.

The U.S. Army's 82nd Airborne Division, meanwhile, has been laying ambush patrols to deny the Iraqis this intelligence and, if possible, capture prisoners who may shed light on Iraq's defences and war plans. "They need to know what is the best way into here," said Maj. Ralph D'Elosua, operations officer for the 82nd Airborne 2nd Brigade. "We need to deny them the ability to (conduct) reconnaissance. It's a counter-reconnaissance battle."

The Iraqi patrols, usually numbering no more than two dozen, travel in light cargo trucks at night. While they are more familiar with the rocky terrain of northern Saudi Arabia than most of the allied forces, their night-vision equipment is considerably inferior. Last week, they ambushed a Saudi border patrol and wounded three of them before one of their own officers was killed. On Friday night, surprised Iraqi and U.S. patrols came within 65 metres of each other and exchanged anti-tank, grenade, and machine-gun fire simultaneously. No one was believed to have been injured in that skirmish.

"They know there are U.S. forces in the vicinity, but they don't know what kind of weapons systems we have here," said D'Elosua. "They want to know which positions are fortified. We want to take a look at what kind of activity the enemy plans in this vicinity." If an Iraqi patrol goes uncontested, they may feel that sector is secure for them to launch an assault. If heavily defended, they might hit that area with artillery fire to weaken allied defences but launch an assault on another zone, officials said.

Officials give the Iraqis credit for using stealth to enter the kingdom without being seen, but believe they can detect them before long. If allied night-vision goggles and sights mounted on anti-tank armaments fail to spot the infiltrators, U.S. troops use ground surveillance radar to detect human and vehicular movement by picking up their vibrations.

"We can pick up any enemy movement a long, long ways away," said surveillance systems Sergeant Michael Banditini of St. Clair Shores, Mich.

U.S. forces also use a voice intercept system that tracks signals emitted by transmitting devices and were not immediately able to determine the sources signature of a signal on a patrol Monday night that sounded like Morse Code.

On Monday, at dusk, three patrols of the 82nd Airborne Division lay waiting on their bellies in an elaborate strategy to ambush any infiltrators. They were positioned in such a way that it would have been difficult for them to avoid becoming casualties or the first patrons of an enclosure for prisoners of war built at a forward base. U.S. patrols, armed with anti-tank, grenade and machine guns, did not come in contact with Iraqis on a night when the wind chill factor pushed temperatures below zero.

U.S. Army Capt. Bill Watts said the Iraqis may be drawing fire intentionally to learn the weapons systems and force size on the other side of the border.

In Friday night's skirmish, an Iraqi soldier was believed to be holding a rocket-propelled grenade when an anti-tank missile swished by his head. Stunned, he dropped his launcher and ran. "When they get hit, that's when they know what is out there," said Watts. "They are also trying to inflict some damage, which is a morale-booster. But now they know they can come only so far.

"If they come across, we learn more," said Sgt. James Reddick, 23, of Flint, Mich., and anti-tank gunner. "If not, well, better luck next time."

Cryptic Radio Messages From Baghdad Ratchet Up Terrorism Fears

By Keith Dovkants

WITH THE 1ST ARMOURED BRIGADE - A series of cryptic radio messages from Iraq have increased fears of attacks on the allies by infiltrators and terrorists. Baghdad Radio broadcasts monitored in Saudi Arabia called upon unidentified forces to rise up against foreign armies in what appeared to be a coded call to arms.

Precautions against action by special forces have been taken by all the allies based in Saudi Arabia and security was at its maximum level today.

The 1st Armoured Division has taken extensive measures to protect personnel and materiel and ammunition dumps holding thousands of tons of missiles and shells are believed to be pretty well impregnable.

Maj. Peter Cross, in charge of security at one of the British contingent's biggest logistics bases, said that now concern over air strikes has diminished the biggest threat was likely to come from special forces. "They could operate in small patrols in the rear area, trying to target installations like this," he said.

He said Iraqi undercover commandos had operated up to 100 miles behind enemy lines in the war with Iran.

To penetrate installations holding vital spares, ordnance and vehicles, however, infiltrators would first have to breach a highly sophisticated electronic alarm system.

This is backed up by patrols using night observation devices and thermal imaging equipment to detect suspect movements.

It is known that infiltrators entered Saudi Arabia in the early days of Iraq's occupation of Kuwait. Some Iraqi agents were caught trying to slip into the country among the thousands of refugees who crossed the border in August and September. Several incidents involving attempts to spy on oil installations and troop movements during the military build-up phase confirmed suspicions that others had got through.

Note to desk: It might be worthwhile ringing the BBC monitoring unit at Caversham to see if they have detail on the radio messages.

Fairly Undemonstrative But Damn Proud British Write Their Boys: "I'll Stick My Finger Up His Nose"

By Jeffrey Ulbrich

AN AIR BASE IN THE GULF - The widow of a World War II bomber pilot, a 7-year-old boy who plays with tin soldiers, a poet from Wales.

Letters of support pour into this British air base heartening and sometimes amusing the men making war on Iraq.

Nearly every headquarters building on this Persian Gulf base has letters from home tacked to the walls. Some are addressed to the British commander here, Group Capt. David Henderson. Others are just addressed "Dear Friend," or "All Air Crews and Ground Staff."

"I think it means a lot to the men and women out here," said Henderson, boss of the Tornado, Jaguar, Buccaneer, and Victor pilots. "They can see there is tremendous support back home. Equally, I think it means a lot to the families back in the U.K. or Germany."

He added: "It takes a lot to stir the Brits up. We are a fairly undemonstrative and unemotional race. But once stirred up, we are very firm about what we believe in."

The letters are unanimous in their support of the men conducting the air war against President Saddam Hussein. They are filled with good wishes and prayers. Many are truly touching.

"I am the widow of a former Mosquito pilot who completed 75 'ops' (as we called them) in 1994," wrote a woman from Chesterfield, who sent along a package of calendars with English country scenes. "I feel close to your Tornado pilots and their wives and I wanted to write to you and them to offer what meager support I can. I salute your dedication and courage wholeheartedly. Good luck gentlemen/boys."

Deihiol Pritchard, 7½, from Gwynedd, Wales, printed: "I have been watching you on TV. When I watch the TV I play with my play mobile soldiers. I think you are very very brave boys. I think about you every night when I go to bed. And I pray for you. My daddy has got a candle lit in his church, and it is kept burning all the time until you all come home safe. I am sending you a picture to cheer you up. Love to you all. God bless you."

A Scottish housewife: "I am very proud of being British just now and especially now I think every minute of the day of everybody out in that area fighting to get rid of Hussein and his tyranny, and I pray you'll all get home safely to your loved ones. It's very difficult to say what I really want to but it may help to know that ordinary people like me do care and care very deeply about your safety and how we are all rooting for you."

Many letters referred to Henderson's recent blast at a retired American general who was said to have criticized RAF operations here after the early loss of aircraft.

"Have just read the account in the Mirror of your so-called attack on Desk Bound U.S. General Big Mouth Smith," wrote a woman from Royal Tunbridge Wells. "You tell all our boys out there they are doing a great job. We old ones know what they are going through and their feeling of loss when a plane fails to return.

"But you're British and have the courage of your forefathers. Keep the flag flying. We know you won't let us down. If it's ever my misfortune to meet Big Mouth, I'll stick my finger up his nose."

A World War II veteran from Cheshire wrote: "You have shown extraordinary bravery, courage, and skill in the awfully dangerous job you are doing. I am sure millions of British people are very proud of you all. Your Tornados are machines of great complexity and the skill of your pilots is in keeping with the great exploits in the 1939-45 war. I remember with pride and gratitude the support we in the army had from Spitfires and Hurricanes in France, Belgium, Holland and Germany.

"Dismiss with contempt any remarks made by anyone who seeks to pour scorn on you and your airplanes."

Other writers just want to be friends. "I am trusting that your squadron leader has given this to you, understanding your need for communication with the outside world," wrote a Devonshire woman named Sue.

"As a human being, my heart and my prayers go out to you and I believe you are fighting for justice and ultimately peace. My name is Sue (short for Suzanne) and I am 44 and a divorced single parent—now stop panicking—I am not looking for a partner, a boyfriend, or even a 'Dad' for my daughter, OK? I am writing to a friend whose efforts and incredible bravery will help create a more peaceful future for all our youngsters."

A young lady from the West Midlands wrote a bubbly letter full of excitement and exclamation marks. "I have been told that you can somehow arrange (or ask) one of the young pilots to write to me. I'm sure there is at least one young, free, single, and handsome lad there who wants to write to someone different. I'd like to write to one of the lads because just maybe I can brighten someone's day. So okay you Tom Cruise lookalikes—who wants to write to a 'madwoman' who tells awful jokes but loves to tell them all the same!!

"Before I start to get carried away, I've got a message from home—We love you, worry about you and are damn proud of you!!"

A woman from Wales composed a 20-line poem-prayer to "Our heroes in the Gulf," ending:

"I send this message, now to you
From mother, wife and brother,
Not as a world authority
But from one Brit—to another..."

Wednesday
February 6, 1991

At a certain level, on the deck of a Navy ship, along the noisy flight line at an allied air base or within the confines of an Anny encampment, life in the field had little relation to what was said or done in Washington, D.C., where all decisions of any great magnitude were decided.

The big headlines on this date were devoted to President Bush's news conference at the White House. He hinted that a ground war was inevitable and announced he was sending Defense Secretary Cheney and Gen. Colin Powell, chairman of the joint chiefs, to Saudi to confer with Gen. Schwarzkopf about the timing of that ground war, should it come to that.

Simultaneously, the last elements of the U.S. 3rd Armored Division reached the desert, rounding out the VII Corps, the main element of any ground-based attack on Iraqi forces. Soldiers just off the plane married up with their equipment, vehicles, and first sergeants, and fell into the routine that gives military duty its shape and sound, whether in peace, war, or somewhere in between.

Thus decisions made months earlier were laying the groundwork for decisions and crises yet to come.

An Army graves registration unit prepared for the worst, which is their mission. As casualties are inevitable, those who have seen war's worst try to train the newcomers so that the work will go according to law and custom, smoothing the way from a soldier's last moments to a family's lasting grief.

In the waters around the Persian Gulf, the USS Missouri again pounded targets in Iraq and Kuwait, continuing to help the air wings soften the resistance any ground force would inevitably face.

On and below decks, the growing presence of female sailors on U.S. ships was evident even behind an oily exterior worn by many working sailors, regardless of gender.

And the British contingent, dispatched here by that female barrier-breaker, Prime Minister Margaret Thatcher, sported its own female pacesetter, a cargo chief for the Royal Air Force.

The effort by Iraq to get its military aircraft and pilots out of harm's way continued, but faltered badly as two U.S. F-15 pilots took out four Iraqi MiGs as they raced toward safe haven in Iran.

In another wakeup call on battlefield security, Saudi authorities reported the arrest of a number of foreigners in connection with a recent incident in which an unidentified sniper fired shots at a bus in Riyadh carrying U.S. soldiers.

And at "Wadi Raf," which was a fictional name created by reporter Mike Tharp for an actual town to accommodate the military's ground rules, the intrigue of an earlier era hovered in the hushed corners of a Bogey-esque retreat.

The parallels to Casablanca were all over the place. But there were a few minor differences. Did the house decorator at Rick's, for instance, ever use pink Kleenex to adorn the place settings on the tables?

Perhaps not. But then Rick's was really fiction. Wadi Raf was real.

Wednesday - February 6, 1991

These Could be the Usual Suspects, But Time is Going By, and We'll Always Have Wadi Raf, Darling

By Mike Tharp

A SAUDI BORDER TOWN - There's no casino discreetly hidden in back, no piano in the bar, in fact, there's no bar.

No overhead ceiling fans to stir the desert air. But there is a restaurant at the Al-Sahra Hotel & Restaurant, and a veranda. And even if Bogie and Ingrid Bergman and Claude Rains never make an appearance, there's a Casablanca atmosphere at this backwater bit of civilization in this town of 20,000 near the (censored) border.

Call it, for security reasons, Wadi Raf. Founded some 37 years ago as one urban bead in a necklace of towns strung out along a major oil pipeline running from Persian Gulf refineries deep into the Saudi desert, Wadi Raf and its sister cities were built, as was the 30-inch diameter pipeline, by Aramco, the giant American-Arabian petroleum consortium.

The towns sprung up around pumping stations, spaced 150 to 300 kilometers apart, and soon acquired lives of their own, separate from the oil business.

Wadi Raf was luckier than some of the others, which became ghost towns in the mid-'80s when Aramco closed the pumping stations.

By then, Wadi Raf featured several souks, or bazaars, schools, hospitals, and a cosmopolitan population common to places at crossroads and borders.

Besides Saudis and Bedouins, Iraqis, Egyptians, Palestinians and other Middle Eastern people moved into Wadi Raf. They built or bought homes and businesses, often underwritten with loans from the town's several banks. As the town grew, other nationalities moved in—Indians, Pakistanis, Filipinos and Thais.

Even after the Aramco compound, with its incongruous but comfortable trappings of American suburbia, was abandoned, Wadi Raf prospered.

Its market was busy from dawn to dusk, as farmers trucked in their fruit and vegetables and herdsmen sold or traded their sheep, goats and camels.

Then came the war. The border was closed. Some residents moved away. Some merchants shuttered their shops. Sometimes the roar of airplanes and the throb of helicopter rotors overhead made tea-time conversation difficult. Still, says Naif Al Shammari, the fire chief, "War didn't change the town, because Saudi people have good hearts."

Throughout it all, the Al-Sahra has remained open. Abdul Rasheed, one of its managers, says business is up 50 percent since the war started. "We have no problems with the soldiers," he says. "They have been very good. The hotel is always full, and the phone lines 24 hours busy."

To accommodate the new clientele, proprietor Yasin Al-Alawi has expanded the menu to include hamburgers, steak, and French fries. The house specialties remain lamb kebab, broasted chicken, and chicken with rice.

Nighttime at the Al-Sahra reveals a kaleidoscopic mix of multinational military and civilian diners. None seems to mind the slightly seamy decor: white tile floors and walls, mirrored ceilings, glass-tiled columns, pink Kleenex on the tables with the condiments.

An embroidered script from the Koran hangs over the cash register, near a photo of King Fahd and his ministers. A large color picture of a falcon dominates one wall, and vases filled with plastic flowers adorn the windowsills.

There are Saudi men and boys in thop, the grey or white gowns, gotra, the head dress, and ogal, the band around the gotra, who sip thick coffee.

Saudi soldiers, complexions across the spectrum from black to white, soak up the last of their meals with hunks of pizza-like bread. French Foreign Legionnaires line up to use one of the three telephones, heeding the instructions in French taped to a wall that forbid collect calls.

GIs unsling their M-16s and doff their flak jackets, washing down fried chicken with bottles of non-alcoholic beer. American correspondents swap the latest war stories, table-hopping as if they were at Elaine's or the Polo Lounge.

One recent afternoon, on the blue-carpeted veranda of Al-Sahra, beneath the fading orange-and-white striped canopy, two French pilots sat with four U.S. Army women captains. Dashing and insouciant in their leather jackets, neck scarves, and jump suits, the pilots charmed the officers, who returned the favor. Across the dusty alley, at the Turkey Hotel/Restaurant, two green parrots sat on the shoulder of a mustached man. Humvee jeeps, commercial buses, and civilian cars streamed past on the road leading out of town.

As the sun settled over the traffic roundabout, it cast a golden haze over Wadi Raf.

Everyone at the patio tables knew it was time to leave, to return to the reality of a war. Finishing their tea and coffee, they sat for a final few moments as darkness gathered.

One of the captains leaned back in her chair, spread her arms wide, and regarded the flashing rainbow lights of the Al-Sahra.

"En l'enfer, c'est la paradis," she said. In Hell, this is paradise.

As they rose to go back to war, they could almost hear, from somewhere deep inside the Al-Sahra, someone playing "As Time Goes By."

Dirty, Greasy Sailors Forget Makeup: "Men Have Been Sailing for 2,000 Years and Women Can't Erase That"

By Kathy Evans

They wear dirty overalls, their hands are black with oil, jeans shiny with grease, and faces frequently bereft of makeup. They are the women of the U.S. Navy.

Hundreds are deployed in U.S. Navy and support ships in the Persian Gulf. Unlike their colleagues on the ground in Saudi Arabia, these women are out of the limelight, but the forerunners of women's service in the U.S. armed forces.

Women have now notched up nearly ten years' service at sea in the U.S. Navy, unlike their British counterparts who were allowed to serve at sea only last year.

The experiment set the pace for their growing role in the U.S. forces as a whole.

They are still barred from combat vessels, but in this conflict for the first time ever, they are manning guns aboard the supply vessels such as the Acadia, currently serving in the Gulf. The Acadia functions as a virtual floating machine shop, a factory which can repair anything from a typewriter to a nuclear reactor. Its 1,200 crew is one-third women, employed not just in the ship's administrative offices but on the shop floor.

Accommodation is strictly segregated between the sexes, and fraternization frowned on. Even so, the Acadia saw three marriages last year between their junior crew members and a rumored dozen pregnancies.

Marriage between crew members results though in immediate separation, for service by married couples aboard the same ship is at present not allowed.

21-year-old Rebecca Beck from Grants Pass in Oregon says there's still a lot of chauvinism in the Navy. On her shop floor, there's a lot of wisecracks like "why don't you mop the floor?" But Rebecca says most are just jokes, idle banter.

"You can't complain to your supervisor every time. It's still a man's world," she says. "Men have been sailing for 2,000 years, and women can't erase that."

Just a few hundred yards away on the flight deck of the USNS Spica, another supply vessel, is Melissa Paisley, 20 years old, from Conifer, Colorado, signalman and aviation mechanic. Checking the helicopter is 34-year-old aviation structure inspector Dorothy Little. Piloting the helicopter is 26-year-old Lt. Noreen O'Connell.

Colorado-born Melissa has dirty, calloused hands and sports a grease-stained jacket. Her blonde hair is pinned back haphazardly and there is not a trace of a female figure in the baggy trousers and hobnailed boots. She says while her friends back (home) complain about their boring jobs in real estate offices, she is an aviation mechanic. "It really freaks some men out when I say that, so I usually don't tell them. They really back off," she says.

The other day she met an Arab who thought she was with her husband on a U.S. Navy ship. "Can you imagine it, he thought I spent my whole day ironing," she said laughing. "I find I have nothing in common with the girls back home now. They just don't know anything about anything."

Melissa, who claims to be an old-fashioned girl, says if it wasn't for the war, she might have considered civilian life next year when her present term is up. Now, with the U.S. economy backsliding, she wonders whether she will be able to find a job at all. Her re-enlistment in the Navy for another three years seems almost certain.

"I have never regretted it though. I wanted to see the world, and I felt I needed to grow up a bit," she adds.

Military life (is) not all easy going, though, for a woman, as the aviation inspector, Dorothy Little, found out. After two years' service abroad in Diego Garcia, she returned to her husband only to find they had both completely changed. "It's only natural. After such a long time apart, it's natural that both of you change, you've had different experiences."

She is now married to a military man and hopes for better luck this time.

Noreen O'Connell, the pilot aboard the USNS Spica, is the most senior woman aboard. Noreen says she joined the Navy to get an education. "Initially I did it for the money for college, but I had lots of opportunities to quit during that time."

Lt. O'Connell says she doesn't know why the U.S. public is so concerned about the recent capture of a U.S. woman soldier by the Iraqis.

"I would have thought that you'd worry about a daughter just as much as a son."

Other women aboard the ship pointed out that according to Amnesty International, it was commonplace in the world for women to be tortured.

"Saddam made a big thing out of it because he knew our society had not completely accepted it," said Melissa Paisley.

Many of the women on the support vessels in the Gulf are hoping that their role in this conflict will pave the way for their deployment on combat ships. At present, they are strictly banned from even boarding an aircraft carrier, apart from one training carrier.

USNS Spica captain, Leroy Gill, feels the move will be inevitable.

"I don't know how they're going to stop them. The policy will change."

The only impediment will be cost, believed Capt. Gill, for it costs just as much to convert a ship to the two sexes as to build a new one.

Combat Cameramen "Capturing Human Side of the Air War"

By Dave Schad

AN AIRBASE IN EASTERN SAUDI ARABIA - In what's being called the most high-tech war in history, footage from aircraft gun cameras showing a set of crosshairs centered on exploding Iraqi targets have found favor with military briefers and the TV networks.

But three Air Force photographers have been flying in one of America's hottest fighters to bring back images that they say show the war's "human" element.

"Our footage shows the pilot," said Master Sgt. Glenn "Sky" King. "You can hear his voice and feel the emotion. We're capturing the human side of the air war."

Working out of a small flight line office on a base in eastern Saudi Arabia, the three combat cameramen assigned to Detachment 3, Operating Location Alpha, are on constant standby to document missions.

Aside from the enlisted crewmembers on B-52 bombers and certain C-130s, they are the only enlisted airmen routinely flying combat missions. When they go up, they fly in the rear of two-seat F-15 Eagles. The planes stay up for more than four hours each trip, waiting to mix it up with an Iraqi air force that seldom appears.

Detachment chief King said they are one of 15 small teams of joint combat camera teams operating in the theater. Although they are the only ones documenting fighter combat missions, all the teams share a three-part mission. King, 38, from Auburn, NY, said the teams shoot video and still photos for historical purposes, provide material for high-level briefings, and supply hard-to-get images to the news media.

None of the shooters were strangers to aerial photography when the war started. Each of them is on flight status, and they've all earned their air crew wings. Between them, they have some 1,800 hours of flight time in practically every aircraft the Air Force has.

Despite the team's experience, Tech. Sgt. David "Wolfman" McLeod said that the prospect of flying in combat was new to them. "Every time you go up, even in peacetime, you know it's a dangerous business and that you could get hurt," said McLeod, 35, from Winfield, Kan. "Going into a war, you have two chains of thought. You're excited about getting to do your job in combat—it's what separates combat cameramen from the guys who just run around with cameras around their necks. On the other side is the anxieties. You think about the combat cameramen who've been killed doing this, and you wonder if there's something you should've told your family."

The cameramen all talked about the "pucker factor" that comes with flying into combat. On his first mission, McLeod remembers hearing his F-15's call sign and being told that an enemy aircraft wasn't far away. It turned out to be nothing, but he remembers the feeling that came over him. "For a moment, I felt fear," he said.

"Then I picked up my cameras and just concentrated on doing my job." Staff Sgt. Dave "Kiwi" Vande Brake, 30, from Atlanta, GA, said that when an alarm in his F-15 went off indicating that a surface-to-air missile radar had locked in on them, he reacted much the same way as McLeod.

"I just maintained my concentration and asked the pilot to tell me which side of the plane he would fire a missile from if it became necessary," Vande Brake said. "I have total faith in those planes and the pilots—I know they're the best."

Vande Brake, who's been flying for 11 years, said he doesn't take his job for granted—"I still feel fortunate," he said.

King, who's been in for 18 years, said the excitement of flying in fighters is something that never goes away. "After you've been up in a fighter, you try and compare it to other things you've done—like a good roller-coaster ride—and nothing comes close," he said. "It ruined all my other thrilling experiences."

All three photographers talk about shooting "the image," the one picture or piece of video that will show a missile slamming into its target. But, King said, another payoff for them is knowing their images will become part of history. "We know the stuff we shoot will probably be even more valuable in the future than it is right now," he said.

---

2 F-15 Pilots Down 4 Iraqi Planes Trying to Escape to Iran: "The Most Spectacular Thing I Have Ever Seen"

By Alexander Higgins and Storer Rowley

A U.S. AIR BASE IN CENTRAL SAUDI ARABIA - Flying combat patrol in the skies east of Baghdad Wednesday, "Vegas" and "Gigs" spotted four Iraqi fighters on their radar screens sneaking toward Iran.

Within minutes the two U.S. Air Force F-15C fighter pilots closed the 60-mile distance to the Iraqi warplanes to about seven miles, rode in behind them and destroyed them with air-to-air missiles. "It was just the most spectacular thing I have ever seen," Gigs said after climbing out of his cockpit and giving Vegas an exuberant high-five on the tarmac.

The pilots, who fly daily intercept missions from the largest U.S. air base in Saudi Arabia, asked that their names not be used for security reasons, only their radio call signs. "I felt kind of cautious for starters," said Vegas. "We had to make sure there were no others around that we didn't see. I just ran on down there wondering whether we were going to get shot back at or anything like that. It was kind of nice when they didn't."

The four kills, the first for the two pilots, brought the base total to eight. They were greeted by a jubilant squadron commander and ground crew who immediately started painting two three-by-five-inch Iraqi flags below the cockpit of each of their planes.

The pilots identified the downed Soviet-made single-seat planes as two MiG-21s and two SU-25 attack planes. They said they did not see any parachutes to indicate the enemy pilots had ejected before their planes turned into fireballs.

Vegas, 30, a captain from King of Prussia, Pa., and Gigs, 26, a first lieutenant from Cincinnati, talked with reporters right after the pilots clamored down from their cockpits.

Their tired faces were still lined with the marks of their oxygen masks. They wore tiger patches on their green flight suits, a symbol of the 53rd Tactical Fighter Squadron, based in Bitsburg, Germany.

The fast-paced aerial fight involving one of the top-of-the-line fighter models in the U.S. Air Force began about 8:45 a.m. (12:45 a.m. EST) Wednesday after the pair of fighter jocks had been aloft for hours. "Our mission is to prevent these jets from leaving the Iraqi theater and that's what we did," said Gigs. "They were eastbound, obviously heading toward Iran, and we were able to push it up enough to go ahead and cut them off before they were able to make it."

About 110 Iraqi aircraft have taken refuge in Iran since the allied air war began three weeks ago. U.S military officials have said the planes are either waiting out the war or planning to come back and attack allied forces. "We saw them coming up on radar, and the big thing we tried to do was identify them, make sure they are not friendlies," said Vegas. He said a major concern was to catch up to the Iraqis before the Americans could be detected. "From there," Vegas said, "we were looking to get in there and get to them before they got to us."

Keeping watch for other fighters and anti-aircraft fire from the ground, they closed in from the side, then turned to follow from behind at sub-sonic speed and locked their missiles on the target. "We do think, however, they knew that they were under attack from indications we had on our radar," said Gigs. "It appears that they were just trying to accelerate and outrun us . . . as if they were trying to beat us to the border."

Gigs said he and Vegas "sorted out" the warplanes on their radar screens.

"I had my men, he had his guys. We took long-range shots." Next, he said, the Americans "rolled in under a visual situation for the final kills. The last two were SU-25 Frogfoot CAS (close air support) aircraft. Those were the two I shot. The two that Vegas shot were two MiG-21 Fishbeds."

After firing their missiles, the two pilots saw the flames of the downed planes, which were struck while flying very close to the ground as they tried to evade radar.

"You can't get any lower . . . less than 100 feet probably," said Gigs. "We didn't see any chutes. We saw all four fireballs."

"They started catching fire and we got the hell out of there as fast as we could after we shot them," said Vegas. The weather was clear, except for a few clouds, he said. "It was nice today," said Gigs. "They weren't shooting back for a change.

"We had a previous engagement and we learned a lot from that, and today was a lot easier. It went real well." Earlier in the war, the pilots had pursued Iraqi fighters and encountered "shooting going in both directions . . . We came away from that one with a lot more experience and knowledge, but unfortunately, no MiG kills."

On the way back to base, the pilots said they detected on their radar that a surface-to-air battery had locked its tracking radar on their planes, but they did not know if they were fired upon. "We did what we were trained to do," said Gig. "It was pretty much like clockwork. (It feels) good to be back on the ground."

"I feel great," said Vegas. "It worked the way it was supposed to. Jet worked great. Missiles worked great. Got in and out of there, no problem."

Lt. Col. Randy Bigum, squadron commander, welcomed the pilots back to Texas Stadium, the base name for the huge concrete bunker sheltering the jets. "That was great. We were cheering for you down here," he said.

Vegas and Gigs praised their ground crews for working long hours to keep the planes in top shape. "It takes a lot more than just a guy in the cockpit hitting buttons," Vegas said. His crew chief, a beaming Airman 1st Class Joe Greene, 19, of Mesa, Ariz., said, "I told him, 'come back with fewer missiles than you left with,' and he did. It's good. It's finally all paying off."

"This gets us pretty hyped up," said Airman 1st Class Michael Unroe, of Waukegan, Ill., a crew chief from a nearby F-15 who came over to help paint the Iraqi flags on Vegas's plane.

Both pilots are married. Vegas has three children. Gigs said his wife is expecting their first child next May. Vegas said there was no particular reason for his call name, but Gigs explained that the spelling of his real name gave him the nickname Giggles. "And that's not a real killer fighter pilot-type name. So it was shortened to 'Gigs.'"

Wednesday - February 6, 1991

Pets, Bibles, Bathrooms, and The Truth: Reporter's Notebook

By Charles Richards

WITH THE 1ST CAVALRY DIVISION, Northern Saudi Arabia - Pets:

Some of the units have acquired pets on the way. Bravo Troops of 1-7 Cav Squadron adopted a dog they found scavenging around their garbage dumps: a great, shaggy beast like an Arctic Huskie.

It had lost its tail in some unknown encounter and was thus christened Bob, short for Bobtail. No one knows where it came from. It was better-fed than most dogs that hang around Bedouin encampments, now long deserted. Perhaps it had been cared for by another unit earlier.

Delta Troop had a young bitch they called Sandy. Sandy, despite her name, was predominantly black. She had had all her shots. The vet gave them to her, one of the sergeants related. Vets? With the 1st Cav in the Saudi desert? But there are no longer any horses or mules with the U.S. Army. Quite so. But some of the military police have dogs, cared for by a vet.

Bibles:

Even the Bibles issued to U.S. troops are dressed in desert camouflage, and their titles printed in military-style stenciling. Is the cover design to maintain uniformity with other more lethal kit? Or as a disguise so as not to upset the sensibilities of the host nation—circumlocution for Saudi prohibition on the practice of religions other than Islam?

Many chaplains seem almost apologetic about their function. They use the bland greetings of secular humanism: "You take care," or "Have a good day." Not so the chaplain of the 1-7 Cavalry scouts, Scott Borderud.

The former Marine is open with his "God bless you," and free with his Bibles in the New International Version. Its rendering of the lesson on a Christian's duty not to deny his faith, of St. Peter's realisation that he had fulfilled the prophecy of Jesus and denied knowledge of him is as follows: "Immediately a rooster crowed. Then Peter remembered the word Jesus had spoken: 'Before the rooster crows, you will disown me three times.' And he went outside and wept bitterly." (Matthew XXVI, 74.)

Helmets:

There is no explaining why even Cavalrymen sometimes refer to the Cavalry as the Calvary. Don't search for deeper meaning. It is merely a slip of the tongue. Not so another name given the Cav. This owes its origin to the unloved disciplinarian commanding officer of 1st Cavalry Division, Brig. Gen. John H. Tilelli, Jr. His insistence that troops at all times wear their helmets of hardened laminated Kevlar gave rise to the name, "The 1st Kevlar Division."

Bathrooms:

It is always astonishing that soldiers about to kill and maim human beings in barbarism permitted in the execution of war should be so squeamish about more normal bodily functions. NCOs will talk of "the bathroom" when meaning the crude field latrines. Other conversations reveal a similar unconscious use of language when discussing human waste.

"You guys didn't bring any crappers?" a sergeant asked a mechanized infantry driver with disbelief. "When we're all loaded up with ammo we can't haul shit."

And if walls have ears, then no walls have them all the more so. It was from his neighbor in the communal latrine that photographer Steve Elfers picked up a tip about Scud wreckage at a main airbase in central Saudi Arabia.

Shaving:

Never have soldiers been so keen to obtain such a close shave as the forces serving in Operation Desert Storm. A close shave means a tighter seal on the gas mask and hood. One exception has been a female sergeant on the staff of an aviation battalion with an abnormal amount of facial hair.

Smoking:

"I only smoke after sex. And the Army fucks me all the time." Sgt. Pete Lingley, 1-7 Cav.

Truth:

"We tell the soldiers the truth at the time. But the truth changes."

A battalion commander.

Feeding POWs:

As of Feb. 4, U.S. frontline units have been ordered not to give food or water to any Iraqi defector. Up till now, the first human contacts between adversaries have resulted in U.S. troops giving the famished Iraqi soldiers some of their rations.

Now military investigators have ordered they alone can give the Iraqis food or water—giving them one more tool to extract information. Frontline troops have only to perform the five Ss: Seize, Secure, Search, Segregate and Speed back to the military investigators.

U.S. Army Graves Registration: Can't Forget the Faces

By Robert Dvorchak

IN NORTHERN SAUDI ARABIA - The faces. No matter how much time passes, the faces of the dead stay etched in the memories of those assigned the job of bagging the battlefield remains.

"Some things you see with your eyes get recorded in your brain and might stay there the rest of your life," said Spec. 4 Carlos Toro, 37, of Puerto Rico.

"I still remember the first guy I worked on. I remember his last name. Wee. It doesn't take my sleep away, but I'll never forget," Toro said.

The people who receive and identify the dead work in graves registration. Four men currently are attached to 2nd Brigade of the 82nd Airborne Division, stationed near the front lines waiting for the ground war to start. They identify the dead by dogtags, tattoos, scars or personal effects in their wallets—driver's license, Social Security number, credit cards, checkbooks, pictures. "This is the most important job in the Army," said Spec. 4 Aaron Houston, 21, of the 54th Graves Registration Co., based in Fort Lee, Va.

"We're the guys who send our soldiers home. We're the ones who get them out of here so their families can have them back again," he said. "All the parents and relatives don't accept the fact their son or daughter might be dead until they see the remains. I feel like I've done something for them and their families."

He also sends them home with a little extra, a personal prayer message.

"I ask the Lord to take care of the soldiers on their journey home, the last leg," Houston said. "I also say a prayer each and every night we don't have this war."

Before the war started, Houston worked on 40 GIs and sailors who died in accidental deaths, caring for them at the mortuary processing center in Dhahran. "We treat them as if they were unconscious," he said.

"We're going to send them home in the best condition possible."

But the faces stay with him. He can't erase the faces.

"They don't haunt me. I just remember who they are," Houston said. "It's better if you don't have personal feelings. You may just break down right there." The crew has four stretchers in their tent to receive battlefield deaths.

They have about 250 body bags. Since the bags aren't needed yet, they use them as dust covers for their sleeping bags.

Outside the tent is a refrigerated van that will store bodies until they're driven to Dhahran, then flow to Frankfurt, Germany, en route to the military mortuary in Dover, Del.

The military has paperwork for everything, even its corpses. Each body is accompanied by an olive-drab bag with a draw string called "Deceased Military Personnel, Personal Effects" bag. It is for watches, rings, money, and pictures.

"This is not the morbid side of war. It's the reality side of war. Everybody forgets people die," said Sgt. Dale Seigler, 26, of Rome, N.Y. "We kind of seem like vultures. Just waiting for someone to die," Seigler said. "You kind of build a wall."

The first priority of graves registration is reclaiming American dead, and it's a time-honored tradition in the U.S. military to not leave the dead behind. The crew will also recover bodies of allies in the coalition, civilians, and even Iraqi soldiers.

Those faces will stay with Seigler, too, just like the first body he ever worked on - an accident victim last year at Womack Hospital in Fort Bragg, N.C., home of the 82nd Airborne. "When I was driving home, every time I wasn't fully paying attention I could see that guy's face," Seigler said.

The work seems ghoulish at times, handling bodies or parts of bodies, and shipping the sum total of a soldier's life back home in a green bag. Some of the graves registration people who worked in Panama a year ago during Operation Just Cause sought psychiatric counseling, the crew said.

"It's the Army taking care of its own. Somebody has to do it," Seigler said.

Rachel the RAF Cargo Chief Shoulders Her Load

By Jeffrey Ulbrich

AN AIRBASE IN THE GULF - Rachael Berry wanted to parlay her talent for the oboe into a professional music career.

But the inevitable twists down the road of life landed her in the Royal Air Force, coordinating the loading and unloading of war cargo.

That's no mean job.

At the height of the allied buildup in the Persian Gulf, Flying Officer Berry's small crew here handled a peak of 42 C-130 Hercules aircraft a day.

That has lessened since to about three to four a day, but it's still a killing pace.

Berry is a member of the U.K. Mobile Air Movement Squadron, fondly known to the rest of the RAF as the U.K. Muppets. She describes her job as the military equivalent of a civilian handling agent, a liaison between various military detachments here. "It's one of the few jobs as an officer where you actually get your hands dirty," she says with an easy smile.

Berry is the first woman ever to serve in the squadron. News of her appointment preceded her arrival.

Stopping in Riyadh, the Saudi capital, en route to this base, she asked a senior officer there if things were busy at the loading and unloading area.

"He said they were, but then said 'with all due respect, ma'am, I don't think it's the kind of job a WRAF officer should be doing.' I said it was exactly the kind of job I would be doing and he replied, 'Oh, it's you, is it?'"

She hears the occasional passing remark that might be expected about an attractive blonde, blue-eyed woman in an operation that is overwhelmingly masculine, "but it doesn't bother me. I don't constantly think about how I can earn their respect," she says. "You have to do your job. You have to be yourself."

The task is huge. The young flying officer, with only 4½ years in the RAF, is responsible for making sure the continuous stream of transport planes get to the right place at the right time carrying the right equipment to the right unit.

Spares ordered up from the U.K. can be delivered door-to-door in as little as 36 hours. She's not afraid to pitch in with a little muscle, either. "I can use a forklift truck and haul as well as anyone," she said. "There aren't that many things that are so heavy that I can't get in there and do it. It's not a question of trying to prove myself."

The Mobile Air Movement Squadron, spread quite thin at several bases around the Gulf, has gone into a re-supply phase now. The Hercs are carrying "anything that will fit in an airplane from sleeping bags to high explosives."

Round-the-clock routine has meant precious little sleep for Berry and the five men under her command. "There hasn't been much time off since I got here," she said. "Some days the planes were coming and going 24 hours a day and it meant grabbing a couple of hours sleep on the office floor."

Indeed, stuffed under chairs and in corners of the cluttered office were several sleeping bags. "We're not that harried," she said. "We cope."

Thursday
February 7, 1991

Thin-sided decoys painted to look like armored vehicles to the naked eye. Oil splotches on the sand that looked like tanks from the air. Tanks buried under the ground over their turrets. Smaller military weapons and Republican Guard headquarters hidden in bunkers or mosques.

After 50,000 air sorties, allied attacking aircraft were beginning to think there might not be any good targets left in Iraq. But apparently that didn't mean the entire Iraqi military infrastructure was shattered or on the run.

If enough of Iraq's military muscle was now hidden from view, even though weeks of bombing have undoubtedly caused great destruction, the Iraqis may still have a formidable fighting force intact, just not one that's visible from the air.

The bombing was taking its toll, however. Interviews of Iraqi soldiers who had surrendered to the allied side indicated that more than a quarter of Saddam Hussein's regular army positions in Kuwait were unmanned, through death or desertion. Some units have severe shortages of basic supplies, especially units near the Saudi border.

In the face of such destruction and crippling of military resources, diplomatic ties seemed almost superfluous. In fact, Iraq chose this week to formally sever ties with a number of major countries that had long since put Saddam Hussein's face on their diplomatic dartboard: the United States, Britain, France, Egypt, Italy, and Saudi Arabia.

In the U.S. Congress, which is already discussing what to do with Iraq diplomatically and otherwise after the war, there was support for both the humanitarian approach—aid and assistance—and the tough approach—demanding reparations.

U.S. Secretary of State Baker allowed some will see the Iraqi leadership as more deserving than others, and that the choice should probably be determined by the political landscape—of Iraq—once the war is over. The U.S. clearly would like to see a post-war Iraq without Saddam Hussein. But exactly how that end might be achieved, other than through a general public uprising, which seems unlikely, is still pretty murky.

There are some voices for the allies to march all the way to Baghdad and see him out. But the coalition that has been forged is based and holding together on the premise of getting the Iraqi occupation forces out of Kuwait. Expanding that mission would undoubtedly require a great deal more coalition-building, just for starters.

The physical effects of the Iraqi occupation of Kuwait were described once again in catastrophic terms. The healthcare system has reportedly fallen victim to a brutal regime with health workers arrested, tortured, raped, and murdered. Such testimony tends to support the demands for reparations in the debate over postwar relationships with the rest of the world community.

In the air campaign, the allies have decided to increasingly target concentrations of Iraqi troops, if they can be located, to reduce Iraq's combat effectiveness. Allied spokesmen say they are saving some of their firepower for a final surge of destruction from on high in the days just preceding a land war.

On the Saudi side of the frontier, the British armored division, now knitted into the main attacking force under VII Corps, has its own media pool living in the same tents under the same stars and rainstorms as the British troops.

In this chapter, the pool meets a Member of Parliament who has joined up for the Gulf War, the latest in a long line of English politician-soldiers who donned the uniform to serve the Queen. He will serve as a doctor, which might come in handy considering the injuries a British reporter saw during a training exercise of Warrior fighting vehicles.

And the Saudi army, which is fighting its first war of the modem post-war era, continues to deal with its performance at the still-puzzling Battle of Khafji. In this chapter, a Saudi colonel comes up with an explanation that must have sounded good at the time.

In the Persian Gulf, a major amphibious force sailed the shallow waters, carrying a sizable assault outfit of 13,000 Marines ready to strike from the sea as soon as the curtain goes up on the allied land war. Whether the Marines will ever be ordered to hit the beaches of Kuwait, which are known to be well-defended and well-mined, is a running debate on the allied side.

The Marines, world champs at beach assaults, train more for that type of fighting than any other. So they're able to disarm and distract an enemy just by being in position to launch.

The possibility that the shipboard Marines are only assigned to act as a distraction has been suggested more than once in the Western press, and by military officials.

The debates boil down to a simple point: if a Marine feint is enough to bottle up the enemy in Kuwait and give their fellow Marines inland an open road north, the arguments for sending them in to take casualties in sandy minefields had better be very good.

Saudi Colonel Explains All: I Tricked Iraqis Into Attacking Khafji (By Withdrawing)

By Gerard Evans

A Saudi army chief claimed yesterday that Iraqi troops had been "tricked" into invading Khafji by his woeful defense of the town.

As he stood outside the charred ruins of hundreds of buildings, Col. Turki Al-Firn boasted that leaving Khafji virtually undefended was a "tactic to draw Iraqi armour into a killing zone."

"There were no civilians left in the town, so no one could get hurt. He (the enemy) came out of defensive positions and made it easy for us to kill him," said the officer whose Saudi forces eventually retook the town after three days of bitter fighting.

Sporadic gunfire still rang out in Khafji yesterday (Feb. 6) when journalists were allowed in to inspect damage and large caches of captured ammunition supplied to Iraq by Jordan. UN-backed Arab forces were scouring houses for pockets of Iraqi soldiers and advising them to surrender over loudhailers.

Artillery fire from enemy emplacements in Kuwait are a daily occurrence and several rounds were directed at journalists as they stood within view of the border, inspecting burnt-out T-55 tanks and Chinese armoured personnel carriers yesterday. Reinforcements have been drafted in to defend the town and fresh artillery and tank emplacements have been dug north of the outskirts to prevent the same "tactics" occurring again. "We are enhancing defences, but that doesn't mean we made a mistake in the first place. Of course I wasn't happy to see my country invaded, but we showed how unhappy we were by destroying them. If they come back we will do the same," said Col. Turki.

Perhaps 20 Iraqi tanks and APCs still litter the streets as tank transporters move in to remove the charred and blackened carcasses after their ordnance has been made safe. Most are 25-year-old antiquated (sic).

The Battle of Khafji marked the first time Saudi troops had ever engaged an enemy. An American army "advisor" to the national guard, Col. John Noble, said the firefight had boosted their morale and proved their aggression.

"We didn't see this town as a military objective. It was a dumb move to attack, but we now have more defense here. The Saudis had never been to war. They had heard all about Iraqi veterans with 10 years' battle experience and yet they defeated them. They surprised me, but Col. Turki told me they were Bedouins and their ancestors were warriors. He was right."

Large areas of the town have been destroyed by fire. Buildings near the shore where the fighting was fiercest are pocked with bullet holes and gaping openings in masonry where rockets struck home.

A multi-million-pound reconstruction program will be needed to restore homes, offices, shops, hotels, the telephone company, and desalination plant.

The Khafji Beach Hotel where Iraqi officers answered the phone to journalists on the night they invaded had been struck twice with rocket-propelled grenades.

At a depot on the outskirts of town, Saudi troops showed off captured munitions and equipment, which showed the Iraqi forces are not as poorly equipped as believed.

Scores of boxes of grenades, rockets, mortars, launchers, and belts of thousands of heavy machine gun rounds were stamped with "Amman, Jordan" on the side.

There were 100mm tank shells, Milan anti-tank weapons, Kalashnikov rifles and machine guns, gas masks and chemical weapons, medical packs.

Most of the munitions looked modern, but some personal weapons were old and battered. Undamaged APCs stood in line, their spartan interiors scattered with personal possessions. Bars of Imperial Leather and Camay soap, shaving brushes, and soap powder indicated that not all Iraqi troops are lice-infested and filthy.

However, there was little food on display. A few old dates rolled around one APC and some soldier had marked his name, "Karim," on his bedroll.

From Commons to an Army Camp: British MP On Duty in the Gulf Knows His Duty

By Philip Jacobson

The first serving Member of Parliament to put on British army uniform for duty in a war zone for almost half a century dropped in on the camp of the Queens Royal Irish Hussars yesterday.

Looking very much at home in his camouflage fatigues, Charles Goodson-Wickes, who represents the Conservatives in Wimbledon and is a qualified doctor, had high praise for the "miraculous" level of care available in the military hospitals now preparing for the beginning of ground fighting here. "It is a real privilege to see and be able to take part in an operation that other professionals have been putting together with such care," he observed, squinting into the bright sunlight.

Once a career officer in the Life Guards, Mr. Goodson-Wickes, aged 45, had seen service in Northern Ireland, Germany, and Cyprus before moving into politics. He volunteered for Gulf duty immediately after the appeal went out for reservists with "a military and medical background."

With his keen interest in defense—he has recently become a member of the Commons armed services committee—Mr. Goodson-Wickes reckoned he was the right man for the job and wrote to the Ministry of Defence to say so.

"My Commons duties are obviously important to me and my constituents, but I felt that I could probably be more use out here in these circumstances."

On arrival early in January, he was posted to the 200-bed 32 Field Hospital, part of Britain's First Armoured Division, where his particular skills as an occupational physician were gratefully accepted: essentially, he runs the equivalent of a casualty department, to which soldiers who are not in immediate need of surgery will be evacuated from the battlefield. "I would have preferred to be in one of the forward dressing stations, closer to the action, but I am deeply impressed by the expertise and equipment available in my present unit."

On closer inspection, Mr. Goodson-Wickes turned out to hold the rank of Lieutenant Colonel, and sported his parachute wings above the regimental color patch. In addition to his hospital responsibilities, he told us, he words in liaison with medical formations, something of a contrast, one imagines, to a peacetime post as medical advisor to Barclays Bank.

Before he was whisked away by the commanding officer of the QRIH for a tour of the tank regiment's immaculate desert encampment, the MP/Colonel recalled how he had thrown a dinner party not long before leaving for the Gulf for as many as he could locate of those who had served in the Commons and the armed forces during World War II.

Lord Hailsham was among the guests, reminiscing about the occasion when the then-prime minister, Neville Chamberlain, faced his momentous vote of confidence: after brief deliberation, Lord Hailsham observed, every man in uniform had tramped off into the "No" lobby.

NB Desks: exact circumstances of Chamberlain vote somewhat hazy this end, suggest check the record or direct with him.

Don't Fall for that Tank-Sized Oil Spot: Allied Pilots Finding Few Prime Targets Left in Iraq

By Storer Rowley and Alexander Higgins

AT A U.S. AIR BASE IN CENTRAL (Saudi Arabia) - After 50,000 sorties, allied pilots bombing and re-bombing Iraq and occupied Kuwait said Thursday they are finding it increasingly difficult to locate prime targets.

Commanders of F-15E and F-16A fighter bomber squadrons said, however, there were still plenty of targets left after three weeks of the air war against Iraq, and they believe allied planes should carry on their bombing to ease the way for an eventual allied ground attack.

Pilots flying missions against Iraq's elite Republican Guard positions insisted they have heavily damaged those shock troops, despite reports the guard is so well dug in it remains an effective fighting force.

But much of Iraq's armor remains hidden in bunkers. The commander at the largest U.S. Air Force base in Saudi Arabia said Iraqi ground forces were still using decoys to try to fool them, such as large, tank-size oil spots on the desert sand.

But when the Americans fly lower to check them out, they are usually able to discern and avoid the ploy, designed to get them to waste their bombs, the commander said. "We have fewer targets than we did when we started," said Col. Hal Hornburg, 45, of Dallas, commander of the 4th Tactical Fighter Wing Provisional. Hornburg, an F-15E Eagle pilot, has flown a number of night missions against Iraqi targets. "I would never discount the enemy's ability to fight back," said Hornburg, stressing that the allies should not get complacent about the strength of the guard despite relentless bombing by his planes and by B-52s.

"If I thought that we were going to go in there and go through them like a hot knife through butter, I think that I would be leading our people astray and setting them up for a possible disaster. So, until this is over, I'm going to think of the enemy as a formidable fighting force," he said.

The wing flight commander, Col. Steve Plummer, 45, of Earle, Ark., who flies F-16A Fighting Falcons, said it was still easy to find targets, but "finding the kinds of targets we want is becoming more difficult."

Iraqi president Saddam Hussein has buried most of his armor "making it difficult for us to locate it," said Plummer, who also is known by his radio call sign, "Ice."

"He dug in very well. The majority of his armor is dug in and concealed. He moves it as little as possible because he puts it in danger when he moves it," said Plummer.

"I think his concealment and the fact that not only does he camouflage but he also decoys quite well is something that he's doing quite advantageously right now," he said. "It is making our job a little bit more difficult."

The Warrior Agreement: Fighting For a Ticket Home, Amid Boxes of Highly Filling Choccies

By Simon Clifford

WITH 4TH ARMOURED BRIGADE, in Northeast Saudi Arabia - The lads of The Queen's Company have a new word coined in the desert for anything exciting: "gleaming," said Lance Cpl. Steve "Geordie" Gordon.

But there was nothing gleaming about a field exercise conducted over two days this week (Tues-Wed.) Stuck in the back of their Warrior armoured fighting vehicle, called Agreement after a racehorse, the crew whiled away hours at a time with only feeble light, books, and bottles of water to keep them going. It is a very basic life, supplemented by tens of chocolate bars and liberal helpings of sand.

Colour Sgt. Skid Dorney reckoned before he left England he would return from the desert bronzed, gaunt, and supremely fit. A war hero.

The reality—in his own words—is more likely to be covered with spots, white, a stone overweight, and missing all his teeth. "I have never eaten so many choccies, sweets, and biscuits in my life," he said. The reason is simple. There is nothing else to do when there are five people crammed into a space about four feet long, three feet wide, and three feet high.

Food is tinned and heated up in a kettle—the army calls it a BV or boiling vessel. After feasting on beans for breakfast, processed cheese sandwiches—the troops call it "cheese possessed" and hate it—and a warm evening meal of mash, veg, and steak with onions, the boys cram bits and pieces of sweet food all through the day.

They buy choccies by the box load—and eat them all that day. I spent 24 hours with the infantry in Agreement and shared the claustrophobic lack of space, shared the food and the inevitable brews, shared their books and sweets. And all this while wearing normal army kit plus the issued chemical suit. If I wanted to get out of the Warrior then I would have to go in chemical state Three Romeo—full chemical suits, flippers, gloves, and gas masks. Nobody looks forward to that.

Onboard we have a seat that doubles as a toilet, bottled water, and clouds of flies which have turned up almost overnight. It is uncomfortable in the extreme. People doze off, read, or smoke. All the time the tracked "wagon" rolls on over bumps and berms—not the BMX bike boys' little humps but real sand anti-tank defences.

For security reasons I cannot give details of the exercise. But it started at 5:30 a.m. and did not finish until (blank), during which time we lived in our charcoal-lined suits, knowing that on the big day the rear door will at some stage open and we shall all be spilled into trenches—and potential hand-to-hand combat. It is not a pleasant prospect. Said Col. Sgt. Steve Sadler, "You have to find something to fight for. I have got my family and that is why nothing will get in my way. I have a round-trip ticket to get back home."

Platoon commanders like 2nd Lt. Charlie White-Thomson have had heart-to-hearts with their men about the fight. Everyone now has sorted out their own personal fears.

One thing is for sure. Exercise or the real thing, it is going to be one really rough ride. During the exercise there was a series of accidents involving some quite serious casualties. In one collision between two Warriors, five men were hurt, two with serious head and neck injuries. They were flown out of the area by helicopter. Other collisions involved a reconnaissance vehicle and an anti-tank craft.

The exercise ended when the blue and maroon flag of One Platoon, 1st Grenadier Guards, flew above the captured "enemy" position.

Friday
February 8, 1991

The plunge into war from the air in the very early hours of Jan. 17th was described on the fly by reporters stationed at airbases, on board Navy ships, and at various other coalition nerve centers.

Although the bombing had been long anticipated, there was little time for reflection and no time for leisurely analysis in those first hours and days.

Some of the reports exactly fit a favorite term academics and other intellectuals often have for news stories: a first draft of history. Fortunately, with each day there's usually another draft, more refined and updated.

For example, initial reports in which the Air Force attempted to identify the pilot who scored the first kill of an Iraqi aircraft were later revised. In one postwar account, the pilot initially credited with being No. 1 was knocked down to No. 4 when after-action reports and verifications were complete.

But along with producing their daily first drafts, in the weeks that followed that blazing rush of bombs and adrenaline, a few reporters patiently went back to the start of the air campaign, interviewing and re-interviewing, searching for more detail and clarification in order to reconstruct a great panorama.

In this chapter is a reconstruction of the start of the air war in the Gulf by Edith M. Lederer and David Evans, who seemed to spend as much time among the allied aviators as crew chiefs. Call it a second draft of history.

Their story appeared at a hinge date in the war—the weekend Defense Secretary Cheney and Gen. Powell arrived in Saudi Arabia to confer with Gen. Schwarzkopf, the theater commander, and to evaluate final plans for a ground offensive. At the same time, French President François Mitterand and the top British commander in the Gulf, Gen. Sir Peter de la Billière, both said they saw a ground war as inevitable.

The allied march toward all-out war was no secret to Saddam Hussein. He monitored the travels and statements of the high coalition officials and issued an in-your-face reply, saying he was growing impatient for the ground war to start so that "tens of thousands" of American soldiers could be sent home in coffins.

Clearly he wasn't looking forward to a war that would involve military aircraft, however. At latest count, 147 Iraqi planes had reached sanctuary in Iran.

And the air war was still taking a serious toll on the ground forces already sent to the front lines near the Kuwait and Saudi borders. A total of 900 Iraqi soldiers were in Saudi custody, having gone over ("defected" in somewhat stilted allied military parlance) from front-line units. The losses from surrender had become so numerous and harmful to morale, intelligence reports said, that some Iraqi commanders had formed anti-surrender squads to hunt down and kill anyone ready to give up before they could reach allied lines.

On the seas, the USS Wisconsin, which had last fired its big guns in anger in the Korean War, opened up for the first time against targets in Iraq. The Wisconsin's post-war home would be much quieter: Hampton Roads Naval Museum in Norfolk, Va. A story in this chapter gives an account of the venerable battleship's last hurrah.

The very different flavor of the British military is also illustrated here in stories from the media pool that accompanied the UK's armored division. There are many similarities between the U.S. and British military, and a great many common values, but almost as many differences. The differences go beyond officers with hyphenated names and a chain of command that's linked to a palace. They can go all the way to hampers and marmalade.

The American Army greatly outnumbers the British, but the youth of those in uniform for both countries was visible everywhere in the Gulf, from the desert birthday parties to the solemn lines leading to the signing of a last will and testament.

The far-flung coalition military effort, which radiated out for thousands of miles from Gen. Schwarzkopf's command headquarters in Riyadh, was continuously being tested by enemies who probed for weak spots in security, and occasionally found them.

In the Turkish city of Adana, Bobbie Eugene Mozelle, 44, an American citizen employed at the U.S. airbase at Incirlik, where some allied bombing missions originated, was fatally shot on his way to work by unidentified assailants. The slaying was believed to be in retaliation for Turkey allowing its territory to be used in the war against Iraq.

The Persian Gulf War was conducted most of the time on the territory of Iraq and Kuwait. But there were days when it extended much farther.

British Soldier Turns 21: Touch of Brandy But A Long Way From Walsall

By Colin Wills

WITH THE 7TH ARMOURED BRIGADE - Alan Shadbolt, "Shaggy" to his friends, celebrated his 21st birthday a couple of days ago.

It wasn't much of a do. No booze-up, no disco, no cake, no Kiss-O-Gram, no nothing, really. But his family made sure Shaggy wasn't entirely forgotten. They sent him a miniature of brandy. It came in a box of Aramis after-shave to get around the no-alcohol laws. Love, plus a little cunning, will always find a way.

To Shaggy, every sip was nectar. He drank it alone in his little one-man shelter made out of chemical protection sheeting, gazing out on a desert night radiant with stars. By his side was his SA80 assault rifle with its armour-piercing rocket that fits on the barrel. He thought of home, but not for too long because thinking of home too much can do your brain in. So what else did he think about, on the night he became a man? He considered the question for a second or two. "I thought," he said, "that I'm a bloody long way from Walsall."

Shaggy and his mates in the Staffordshire Regiment have been in this seemingly endless desert country for nearly four months now. But they have already lost virtually all track of time. Days come and go in a monotonous procession, broken up only by stags (guard duty) and training exercises. Even taking the foul-tasting nerve gas injections—laced with whooping cough vaccine to make them take better—would be looked on as a welcome diversion if they didn't make your arm so sore.

But if you get too set in your ways, you can always think of what lies ahead and feel the familiar knot of apprehension tighten in your stomach.

Taking part in a huge divisional exercise involving tens of thousands of soldiers, it comes home to you more than ever just how much of a young man's war this is.

Young faces everywhere, fresh, apple-cheeked; one Warrior fighting vehicle has been christened by its crew of eight, "The Young Guns." In the coming land war it will be the 19-to-25-year-olds who, for the most part, will be at the sharp end. Infantrymen and their support groups, storming trenches, bayonets fixed, kill or be killed, him or me, the main targets of the artillery, the shrapnel that maims and slices.

This will be their hardest test of all, and to fail it will be fatal. "You'll never know until the time comes whether you've got the bottle," one 19-year-old said. "Can you really stick it in him? Have you got the balls to do it?"

They view the prospect stoically, and with a cheerfulness it is impossible not to mire. Open-hearted, generous, forever offering you a "brew" (tea) at the end of an all-night move, it seems so unfair somehow, so cruel, that young lads with so much their lives ahead of them should be so prematurely concerned with dying.

Reading comic books, Viz mostly, flicking through smuggled porn ("You was wiggling about in your doss bag last night looking at 'er—yes you was, don't deny it.")

Leaning against the wheels of eight-tonners with yellow Walkmen plugged into their ears, the images of this more than any other war are predominantly youthful.

The favorite listening is the American armed forces station, Wizard 106, with its dawn-to-dusk pop. The favorite laugh is a rejuvenated country-and-western artist, much played on the station, who has rushed out a gung-ho warning song to Saddam Hussein, called "Don't Give Us A Reason."

One extract will give you the flavor, pungent to say the least:
You can take that poison gas
And stick it up your sassafrass.
The desert ain't Vietnam.
You got nowhere you can run.
And we got some real Top Guns.
Don't give us a reason.

That kind of tub-thumping may be okay in a recording studio in Nashville, but out here the young soldiers know the real risks. Paul Edwards, 22, a Grenadier Guardsman from Canterbury, Kent, will help run the "rolling replen" driving through enemy fire to bring the battle groups fresh supplies of fuel and ammunition, one of the hairiest jobs going. His thoughts before his ordeal seldom stray far from his wife Karen and their little daughter Gemma, born last July. "I'm missing her growing up," he says sadly, counting up the time that has slipped away. "I missed her first Christmas. She'll be a different person when I get home." He fingers a single red rose, an early Valentine's gift from his wife. "Do you think she'll know me?"

Little private gestures of love appear everywhere during the buildup to war. I saw one guy leap down from the cab of his Army truck and sniff inside the envelope of a blue airmail letter. "I'm always doing this," he explained. "It's Opium. I bought a bottle for my wife at Christmas and she always puts a little drop in before sealing it down. Tell the truth, it takes me back to her more than anything she writes. I can see her face so clearly."

It is a very self-contained army, miles from anywhere, with little or no fraternization with the "ragheads" as they call the Arabs on account of their headdresses. Nonetheless, through the impetuousness of youth, connections are sometimes made.

Mark Soloman, 23, of the Staffords, known to all as Solly, started befriending two little Arab boys who kept hanging around the camp. A few cans of Coke later, Solly and his friends found themselves invited by the boys' family for a meal. "They were Bedouins and we went to their tent. Weekend Bedouins like, they lived in the city but liked to come out to the desert when they could. And what a meal! More like a feast, it was. Rice and a whole roast lamb. We tore bits off with our fingers.

"We all knew to watch our manners. Like only eating with our right hands and, when you're sitting cross-legged, not showing the soles of your feet. It was a fabulous place. Persian rugs worth a thousand pounds each covering the floor. I'll never go anywhere like it again." Solly treasures the moment and talks about it endlessly—a moment of delight, blotting out for awhile all imaginings of the horrors he might see.

A feast, friendship; something strange and wondrous in the middle of nowhere.

Like his mate Shaggy says, it's a bloody long way from Walsall.

Videotapes From Home on a Flickering Screen: "Say Hello to Daddy"

By Douglas Jehl

WITH U.S. FORCES - In the gloomy Army tent, a television flickered and soldiers clutching cups of coffee to ward off the morning chill huddled in the corner to watch as home came suddenly to life.

There on the screen were their wives, their kids, on sofas or on folding chairs, looking into the close-up lens and trying to find the words to tell their man how very much they missed him. It was if the soldiers could look into their living rooms, their military portraits even mounted on the wall, their wives self-conscious and children fidgety and all of it bringing lumps to throats in this dusty desert camp.

The tent became quiet as the soldiers watched intently, some of them puffing now and then on a breakfast cigarette and all savoring the video connection, however brief it was.

Letters still come rarely to the men of this 26th Support Battalion, deployed from Germany at Christmas-time and waiting in high tension almost ever since. For some of the dozen whose loved ones were first on the Army list to make these postcards by videotape, it was a long-awaited glimpse of those they had left behind.

At five minutes per family, the flickering screen brought progress reports of bills paid and dogs who missed their masters, tales from kids of movies seen and classmates befriended, assurances that school and church and work were going well.

Wives bit their lips and tried to think of what they should say next, adding admonitions to be careful, confessing sometime tears, and reminding their soldiers gently to read Bibles every night before they went to sleep.

But mostly, in this cross-section of military-family life playing unannounced this frigid morning in a supply-company meal tent, there were protestations of love and hopes, amid concern of war, for a happy reunion.

The tent became more crowded as other soldiers from the unit came in to grab a cup of coffee and stayed to watch, voyeurs of a sort, but in a way nobody minded, for all knew too well what everyone had shared.

"I'll hug you and hug you and hug you," one sergeant's wife promised her man with a fervor that left the tent quiet, "and love you and hug you, and you'll be saying, 'What's wrong with that woman?' But it's just that I love you so much."

Then mouths began to water as one young wife detailed a menu for a homecoming dinner of shrimp, cornbread, and sweet potato pie. All listened in silence as another held herself erect and sang in a haunting gospel-choir tones the hymn her husband could think of "whenever you feel alone."

And when another held her daughter close beside her and told of how difficult it was to finally take the Christmas decorations down, all seemed to be remembering their final days at home before the war began.

As static filled the void from one postcard to another, there were complements on wives and children, good-natured joking about the wife who admitted she was playing a lot of bingo.

Fathers beamed as their youngest stared blankly at their camera, legs swinging from their chairs as mothers prompted them to say hello to Daddy. They shook their heads as older children ran impatiently on and off camera to show off new toys and tell new stories.

And when one little girl sat almost in silence, singing a song to herself, they shared stories about being bashful. And then finally the static didn't go away, the videotape suddenly over. The spell broken, the soldiers tossed their coffee cups away.

They gathered their rifles, and headed back to the war.

(hand-written) Reviewed by Cpt. M.H. Wilbur. No security violations, but I could have missed something.

The Morning the Air War Began: "The Starting Gun Goes Off and You Cross the Line"

By Edith Lederer and David Evans

Editor's Note: Exact altitude figures have been changed to approximate heights at the request of the U.S. military and have been delineated in parentheses.

IN CENTRAL SAUDI ARABIA - In the early morning hours of Jan 17, a huge air armada orbited in the skies over northern Saudi Arabia, lights out, radios off, every pilot waiting for the predetermined moment to cross the border and begin the war to liberate Kuwait.

"It's almost like the starting gun goes off and you cross the line," said Capt. Alan Miller, who was leading a flight of four F-15C fighters.

Spread along the Iraqi and Kuwaiti borders were some of the most sophisticated planes in the Western military arsenal, poised to catch the Iraqis by surprise and hit key communications and military targets in one staggering blow.

The war's beginning was planned deliberately to be like the toughest air-war-game that pilots had been flying for years over the desert at Nellis Air Force Base, Nevada, called "Red Flag." Col. Hal Hornburg, commander of the 4th Tactical Fighter Wing Provisional and Miller's boss, said: "They had flown this mission before. They just hadn't flown it in Iraq."

Miller, a 32-year-old pilot from St. Louis, Missouri, was like most of the younger aviators airborne that night: he was flying his first combat mission to execute a warplan that had been honed over five months.

The arrayed air power ready to clear the skies and drop bombs literally through specific rooftops, skylights, and command post doors represented the most formidable concentration of Western military technology.

Twenty U.S. Air Force F-15C air-to-air fighters would sweep the skies while radar evading Air Force F-117 stealth fighters, F-15E and F-111F fighter bombers, Navy and Marine A-6E attack bombers, British Tornado jets and Saudi F-15s went into action against targets in Iraq and Kuwait.

The bombing would start at 3 a.m. (0000 GMT) and finish in half an hour.

"It was one massive, coordinated strike. At the start of the war, they had a time-on-target window of 30 minutes," Miller explained.

"I knew from previous planning that that first 30 minutes of the war was going to be pretty intense, as well, because it was simultaneous attacks everywhere throughout their country," Miller said.

Years of training were the key to success. "It was really very similar to Red Flag," Miller recalled. "It's just oriented north instead of west."

"You have a line. Prior to the time-on-target window, none of the offensive forces cross that line. We got our gas, came off the tanker (plane), and everybody's waiting," he said. But Miller said he knew as soon as he taxied to the end of the runway that this was not a training flight. "The arming area was full. The taxiways were full. The trail of airplanes back into their parking areas was all lined up with airplanes with their lights on. It was like a flush. It was (F-15C) Eagle after Eagle after Eagle. Between us and the F-15Es (Strike Eagles) that were launching at the same time," he said.

"Prior to us crossing the line, we thought it was going to be a food fight like none we had ever imagined. We really did expect that," Miller recalled.

AWACS radar planes had been flying continuous airborne alert, but several days earlier, the crews started making false radio calls, similar to those used for real on the night of Jan. 17th. Capt. Mark Alred, a 33-year-old F-15E pilot from Tulsa, Okla., who had been part of the U.S. Air Force war planning team and was in one of the first planes over the border that night, said the deception was crucial.

Even before the mass of planes took off, four F-15Cs from Miller's squadron were in the air protecting the AWACS that would provide crucial intelligence to air crews heading north. From airbases throughout the kingdom, aircraft began crossing the Saudi border around 1:30 a.m. (2230 GMT on Jan. 16) for the run to their targets.

U.S. Special Operations teams were some of the first across the border with the task of knocking out Iraqi radars. The first planes in were about two dozen Stealth fighters. Their high-priority job was to knock out Iraqi communications. "There's no use giving a guy a telephone in Baghdad to pick up and call out to all his places and say, 'Hey, look out for air strikes.' If we can't get all his airplanes, at least we can kill the brain," Hornburg said.

The next wave of aircraft were the F-15Cs air-superiority fighters.

"Our tasking was... right at the beginning of the war to sweep with 16 other F-15Cs in pretty much a wall across the border and up to Baghdad and come back out," Miller said. "It was to provide air superiority from the very beginning so that all the strikers could go in. The strikers that did not have the benefit of stealth. The F-117s could all go in unopposed from (Iraqi) counter-air forces.

"The amount of information we had prior to crossing the line was incredible. AWACS was telling us how many (enemy) airplanes were airborne, where those airplanes were, types of airplanes ... I was simply amazed," Miller declared.

"We had word that there were Fulcrums (MiG-23s) airborne, right at the point where we had planned to set up our Combat Air Patrol just south of Baghdad," said Capt. Scott Mason, who was Miller's wingman

Friday - February 8, 1991

that night. "The fact that there were some folks airborne kept the excitement and adrenaline going," said the 33-year-old F-15C pilot from DeKalb, Ill.

As the strike force crossed the border, Miller said, "We pushed it up (accelerated), dropped our wing (fuel) tanks because we were scared and we didn't have a whole lot of extra gas and we didn't know what to expect. We'd never dropped tanks before in our lives."

The Iraqi planes circling near Baghdad were apparently fearful of meeting the Americans head-on. "They would go out to the west and they would go out to the east, any we had our corridor and there was absolutely nobody home by the time we got up close to Baghdad," Miller said.

While the F-15Cs were flying high over the thin wisps of clouds that partially concealed the landscape below, the next wave of aircraft, 22 F-15E fighter-bombers, were screeching in at low altitude, with a pair of EF-111s along to jam Iraqi radars.

Scores of Navy Tomahawk cruise missiles launched from warships around the region added to the punch of the aerial assault.

Alred was leading the first group of six F-15Es. His squadron commander, Lt. Col. Steve Turner, 41, of Portsmouth, VA, was leading the second group of six.

"It had been planned that, to get under the EW/GCI net (early warning and ground control intercept radars), we would start out at (about 20,000 feet) and start descending down to what would be below their coverage some distance out," Turner explained. "We don't ever practice that, so here we were with a full load of bombs on an air-plane. The next thing you know you're on a roller-coaster ride down," he said.

Alred said, "The last refueling we did was (under 10,000 feet), about 150 miles south of the border. No one has said a word since we took off. Everyone moved into the pre-briefed attack formations." Armed helicopters from the U.S. Army were assigned to knock out three Iraqi early-warning radars along the border at the moment the strike force headed north. "As we approached this one radar, about 25 miles from it, I watched this thing blow up in front of me," Alred said.

Maj. Bill Polowitzer, 36, of East Hartford, Conn., was the weapons systems operator in the back seat of Alred's F-1E. "Up to that time, I was convinced. 'Are we the only ones who know this? Have we got the right day?'" he recalled.

Alred said he watched the radar still burning as he roared past at (ground-skimming altitude) and 500 miles an hour. It was at that moment that he, too, became firmly aware that they were taking part in a much larger orchestrated effort. At their extreme low altitude, Alred said, "We could see cars driving down the highways and thinking that that guy could stop and telephone somebody 150 miles away from here," alerting Iraqi defenses.

Speed, darkness, and a radio blackout by the air crews were their best protection.

"Obviously, we're doing this with every light off the airplane so . . . anybody along that road . . . they just hear a noise and have no idea where it came from or where it's going," Alred said. "It was very eerie to be flying in their country for roughly 40 minutes before we got to the target, and knowing that all this time we're in Iraq and getting ready to destroy something that belongs to Iraq," he said.

"There were three bombs that hit the ground before mine did. And those were from the Stealth fighters. They went in 5 minutes before we did," Alred said.

The first bomb to fall on Iraq demolished a key communications building near the bank of the Tigris River in downtown Baghdad. A gun-camera videotape showed the 2,000-pound laser-guided bomb hitting the roof of the building right where the pilot placed the crosshairs.

"When Bernard Shaw went off the air for CNN, the whole room exploded in cheers," said Lt. Gen. Chuck Horner, the U.S. Air Force commander who was in the operations center in Riyadh monitoring the progress of the first night's strikes.

"That was the most direct feedback we ever heard," said the 54-year-old general from Des Moines, Iowa. "It was right on the minute the bomb was supposed to hit."

Col. Alton Whitley, commander of the 37th Tactical Fighter Wing, said his Stealths also dropped bombs through the skylight of one of Saddam Hussein's command bunkers.

The target for Alred's plane was a Scud missile-launching site in western Iraq.

"Our objective was to keep Iraq from launching Scuds at Israel," he said.

Another ground radar that could have detected Alred's plane was knocked out by a Stealth fighter. "Bill and I felt like they didn't know we were there until the bombs hit the ground. We flew across the target (close to the ground) and dropped these 12 canisters of bombs. As we're pulling off the target, it's about 35-40 seconds later, we figure it's just about enough time for everybody to wake up and figure out what happened—the world just comes to light," he said.

The darkness below exploded in a cascade of anti-aircraft fire.

"We estimated somewhere in the neighborhood of 70 to 80 triple-A guns (anti-aircraft artillery) about one to two miles north of the target, and every one of them was just streaming red bullets up into the air," Alred said. The anti-aircraft fire, he recalled, was like huge "4th of July waterfalls, where sparklers are coming off in a great display, except this stuff is going up 5,000 or 6,000 feet and then coming back to the ground." The Iraqis also launched surface-to-air missiles. . . .

High overhead in his F-15C fighter, Miller also felt that the surprise was complete. "The lights of the city were all a-glow. The city was lit up underneath just like we see Riyadh when we come home," he said.

Col. Whitley, who flew one of the Stealth missions over Baghdad, said people started fleeing the city when the bombs began exploding. "It was bumper-to-bumper leaving the city. I don't think they were going to the Saddam rally that night," he quipped.

Col. Hornburg, 45, from Dallas, Texas, was in a second wave of F-15Es that followed Turner's squadron. "I crossed the border right about the time everything was starting and it was spectacular. It was panoramic. Just strikes going off all over," he said. "I couldn't see other aircraft, but I could see the results of their work. I would see an airfield with a strike going into it. Then I'd see the triple-A come up. Of course, by that time the bombs had already done their damage," he said. He, too, was impressed by the sheer volume of enemy fire. "There's so much going off around you. Kind of makes you hunker down in your cockpit a little bit," he admitted.

After the bombs were dropped, Miller and his fellow F-15C pilots still had to contend with possible enemy fighters. "On the way out we were still worried about quite a few southern airfields that we thought were populated with MiGs," Mason said. "One of the things we thought might happen is they'd let us in, and launch this big beehive back behind us and we'd have to fight our way out," he said.

However, no Iraqi planes rose to challenge the departing Americans.

As the U.S. pilots approached Saudi territory, and safety, many were low on gas and there was still the potential for a dangerous mistake. Miller said that other F-15Cs from his own squadron had started out flying combat air patrols on the Saudi side of the border and "got pushed much further north than they had planned to be."

"They were faced with that formidable task of hundreds of airplanes coming back

Friday - February 8, 1991

through them, 99.9 percent of which were expected to be friendly, but looking for that 0.1 percent that might not be," he explained.

"One of the worst nightmares of air superiority fighters is to shoot down one of our own," he shuddered. "So before we left about the only thing we talked to them about was, we said, 'We're coming out at this altitude. Please don't shoot us.' They didn't."

Turner said the fighters spent 100 miles searching for aerial tankers. "They were not where they were supposed to be," he said. "Everybody was ready for Miller time. Everybody that had participated was out of gas. We were one of hundreds, probably," Turner said.

During the anxious search for the refueling planes, Turner said the planes turned their lights on. Like a school of fish suddenly spotlighted in the ocean night, Turner said. "It was surprising to see how close you were to everybody else. All of a sudden you've got 20 airplanes around you."

Finally, they were able to find a lone refueling plane. "Some guys were lower (on fuel) than others," Turner said. "We were making sure they go on the (refueling) boom first. We had one kid who was down to about 3,000 pounds of fuel. That's low."

Even with the hasty refueling, the god of war remained fickle.

"You come off the tankers and you think you've got it made," said Turner. "And the next thing we hear the (landing) field is under condition red." Condition Red is the threat of an enemy attack.

"We wonder, 'Geez, I don't have enough gas to barely make it back. I never knew I had to keep it up this long,'" Turner said.

The actual problem was more benign. "We had an airplane that didn't drop one bomb; that one bomb stuck on the airplane," Alred said. "We've got a jettison area down 30 miles south of the field, so we went down there and dropped the stuff. Apparently, somebody saw something blow up south of the field, so they thought the airfield was being attacked by somebody," he said.

Polowitzer recalled, "They had a Scud launch alert, so we go into alarm red. And as we come out of that we got a (loud) speaker that is starting to crackle, and the cops (security police) thought it was small arms fire, and that the airfield's being attacked. As we come out of that we've got commercial airliners. They're unidentified. There's one cop thinking it's a Czechoslovakian plane, and he started to put his car in front of the nose wheel," he said, referring to an attempt to block the plane from taxiing close to the flight line. The plane, diverted from the Saudi capital of Riyadh, turned out to be a U.S. cargo jet chartered by the military. But base security personnel were worried that it was a Trojan horse full of Iraqi commandos who would burst out when the doors were opened.

Despite the last-minute chaos, all aircraft returned safely to base. "I remember climbing out of the airplane and hugging the crew chief and hugging Bill, and shaking hands with everybody around," Alred said. "It was wonderful to be back on the ground and to have everybody back with us. There was a big potential on this mission to NOT bring everybody home . . . being the first people in the country (Iraq). I was very happy that we ended up with all 22 airplanes back here," he said.

. . . At the end of the first mission, Hornburg also was anxiously counting his returning young aviators. "You know what surprised me?" he said. "It was the fact that they were all coming in, and everybody had kind of their piece of the war to talk about. Then, they hung up their stuff and they said, 'Time to go to bed,' and get ready for the next day."

For Polowitzer, the first day in combat evoked the terrors and thrills of childhood.

"I felt as high as I could get," he recalled. "I equated the feeling to being on a roller coaster when you're a kid. It's that dread of standing in a line waiting. Your father says, 'This will be great!' and you're watching people scream and everything going on, and you think, 'I don't like this, and I don't want to go on.' And I'll be fearful the whole time until when you make that first drop and your breath's taken away and everything like that. And as soon as the roller-coaster comes to a stop and you get out of it, you go, 'Geez, that was the greatest thing in the whole world! Let's do that again.'"

"It was that kind of emotional thing," Polowitzer said. "It was just a feeling that you survived this—we're someone to reckon with."

New Moon Approaches, Illuminating the Outline of an Oncoming War

By Charles Richards

IN NORTHERN SAUDI ARABIA - On a calendar hanging in a U.S. Army field tent somewhere in northern Saudi Arabia—ground rules laid down for the media by the military authorities forbid mentioning the precise location of any unit—there is a large blue circle in the square for Feb. 14.

"New moon" reads the legend. And the signs are that St. Valentine's Day or thereabouts will be G-Day, the day the U.S.-led forces launch their ground offensive to root Iraq out of Kuwait. All the commonsense, external evidence points to this date. Most important, for operational reasons, it will be a dark night. The new moon, not even a crescent slither in the Arabian sky, will give the cover of darkness to the coalition forces.

With their night-vision capability, they will have the greatest advantage over the foe. They are thermal imaging goggles, which show up on body or machine heat, and devices which magnify ambient light. The Iraqis have only limited means to see in the dark.

Secondly, the U.S. deputy commander of forces in the Gulf, Lt. Gen. Calvin Waller, announced six weeks ago, to much consternation and disbelief, that the forces that had at that point just arrived in Saudi Arabia would not be up and ready until mid-February. That time approaches.

Third, the U.S. Secretary of Defense Dick Cheney and the chairman of the Joint Chiefs of Staff Gen. Colin Powell will have completed their fact-finding visit to Saudi Arabia. They will have learnt from the U.S. commander in the Gulf, Gen. Norman Schwarzkopf, exactly what his plans are for the future conduct of the war, and reported back to President Bush.

And fourth, the air forces will have had a full four weeks to weaken and wear down—attrit, in the ghastly language of U.S. commanders—the Iraqi ability to fight.

It is an open secret that the bombing campaign has gone on longer than at first envisaged, and that proposals for a ground offensive were postponed.

Allied commanders have said that they were hindered at the beginning, after the first couple of days, by poor weather.

The skies were overcast, preventing aircraft from dropping their bombs and missiles with the accuracy desired. Many planes were coming back with their bomb racks full. In addition, Iraq's defences proved more resilient than some had thought.

It made sense then for the allied commanders to keep on bombing targets and to delay the moment when ground forces were to be committed as long as possible.

Bombing raids have continued. But these are not the massed attacks by waves of aircraft blacking out the sun. Rather,

Friday - February 8, 1991

with the naked eye you can see how the U.S. Air Force attacks its targets. The massive, old B-52 bombers tend to go in threes, their vapour trails advertising their approach long before they arrive. The A-10 tank-killers and F-15 Eagles generally fly in pairs. But each pair or trio delivers as much high explosive or "smart" munitions as an entire squadron of earlier generations of aircraft.

Military doctrine states that in advance of any ground attack, the enemy positions are softened up by artillery. Doctrine also states that artillery be massed to pound the point in the enemy's defences which the engineers and infantry are to breach.

Heavy mobile armour would then surge through the gap to exploit the opening.

The greatest concentration of U.S. firepower is to the west. Reports over the past days of the fighting around Khafji, on the coast south of Kuwait, disclosed that the U.S. forces in the area—that is, to the east—were Marines.

These are more lightly armed, with old-style M60 tanks as well as more modern, heavier, faster, bigger-gunned state-of-the-art M1A1 tanks. By contrast, the U.S. Army armoured divisions to the west deploy almost exclusively the M1A1 main battle tank.

Several plans are open to allied commanders.

The artillery barrage frontline units, mainly mechanised infantry. The fast, mobile allied forces could then sweep round and up and attack the Republican Guards at their weakest point, in the rear. At the same time, the Marines would launch a direct attack straight up into Kuwait itself.

Many uncertainties surround the likely success of the ground operation. Battlefield damage assessments can only give a partial picture of the effectiveness of allied bombing will be only when the coalition forces join battle that they will learn the extent to which the bombing has penetrated the deep bunkers of the Iraqi divisions, and broken down the psychological defences of the Iraqi troops.

If the enemy's potential is an unknown quantity, so too are the fighting abilities of the U.S. forces. Traditionally, American armies have relied on equipment and training to overcome any shortcomings in the quality of the manpower. The new American Army, however, is better educated, better trained, and with a greater sense of purpose than probably any other in American history.

One area of weakness, however, is its blind faith in technology. Many of the weapons so far deployed in combat have performed better than expectations. Others have yet to prove themselves in battle.

The MLRS, for example, which its manufacturers claim can take out a whole grid square by firing rockets each with 644 bomblets to kill personnel and destroy materiel. Will it really be as accurate as hoped?

Other anti-tank missiles—the artillery-fired Copperhead and the helicopter launched Hellfire missiles—are also both fallible.

What will happen to the morale of U.S. troops when they see the weapons on which they had relied so heavily failing to measure up to expectations?

Will they have the resilience and adaptability to make do without?

Since hostilities were joined, there have been a number of incidents of friendly fire, of U.S. aircraft hitting U.S. targets by mistake. Such incidents are likely to multiply as the battle progresses.

It has become accepted wisdom that the course and timing of the ground war will be of the allied commanders' choosing. What happens if the Iraqis launch the first strike?

How quick will allied commanders be to exploit a fast-changing situation on the battlefield? How great a threat will the massive Iraqi artillery strength really be?

What happens if the Iraqis fire chemical shells from their artillery pieces?

Once hostilities begin on the ground, units and entire divisions may change roles and missions and fall under different commands.

The 1st Cavalry Division, with its mix of heavy armour, artillery, infantry, is designed for the quick counter-punch. When it locks horns with Iraq's forces, both sides have a part of history to live down or up to. For the Cav, one unit—the 1st Squadron, 7th Cavalry Regiment—are in direct line from Custer's regiment defeated at the Little Big Horn. The squadron, now the divisional scouts, subsequently restored their battle honours in Vietnam.

Saddam Hussein seeks inspiration from the battle of the Horns of Hittin, fought on July 4—yes, July 4—1187. On this day, the Muslim leader Saleheddin al Ayubi, known in the West as Saladin, defeated the Crusader forces in northern Palestine and in effect brought an end to the Christian presence in the Holy Land.

Saladin, a Kurd, came from Saddam Hussein's own village of Takrit. Saddam, a man not noted for his religious fervour, has invoked Islam as the motive forces against this latter-day confrontation with forces from the West.

It will not be long before that confrontation takes place.

Last Hurrah, Last Shots Fired for USS Wisconsin: "We Just Don't Build Them Like This Anymore"

By George Rodrigue

ABOARD USS WISCONSIN IN THE NORTHERN ARABIAN GULF - The battleship Wisconsin attacked a dozen Iraqi artillery emplacements with her 16-inch guns early Friday, in support of a major U.S. Marine probe into occupied Kuwait.

Several senior crew members said they hoped their devastating 1,900-pound rounds also help win the battle against Defense Department budget-cutters.

"Anyone who has ever served aboard one of these ships understands their importance," said Wisconsin's commanding officer, Capt. David S. Bill.

"We just don't build them like this anymore."

But several officers and enlisted men mentioned sadly that Friday was the official decommissioning date for their sister ship, the USS New Jersey, and Capt. Bill said the Pentagon's most recent budget submission contains no funds for operating battleships.

"I quit reading after I saw that," he said, sadly but matter-of-factly.

"There has been a lot of hard work put into this ship" (which was re-fitted and re-commissioned in 1988), he told pool reporters. "That effort will not have been in vain, but to see that effort cut short by a premature decommissioning would be a great sadness, not only to this crew but to all battleship sailors and to all who understand the capability of the battleships."

Wisconsin fired 36 rounds early Friday as part of an "harassment and interdiction" mission, designed to pin down and confuse Iraqi gunners during the early morning Marine attack on Iraqi troops inland in Kuwait. The battleship fired no traditional "all-gun" broadsides, but roamed off the coast picking off a new target every few minutes.

Because this was pre-programmed shooting, based upon previous reports by ground spotters, the ship's remotely

Friday - February 8, 1991

piloted vehicle had not been launched and the ship had no direct information on the effectiveness of its fire.

(Parenthetically, shock waves from the guns did damage USS Wisconsin, as they often do. On the bridge, close by the Number Two turret, the blasts broke radar screens and loosened light fixtures. And one officer suffered a broken wrist when a gunshot's concussion wave smashed a steel door into his hand.

(Sailors had repaired most of the damage by Friday afternoon. No bridge windows were broken, because battleships learned long ago to roll them down during gun firing.)

The shooting began around 2 a.m. and involved targets more than 30,000 yards from the ship. The published range of the 16-inch diameter shells varies from 23 to 24 miles. Several pool members viewed a series of three-gun salvos from aboard USS Nicholas. They could see a massive ball of blinding orange fire, taller than the Wisconsin, and then could make out the ship's low gray outline in the dull-red afterglow.

Pool reporters aboard USS Wisconsin could learn no details of the Marine probe. But it seemed to involve massive amounts of artillery and rockets. Even more than 10 miles out to sea the cold night sky glowed orange with American (and possibly Saudi Arabian) heavy-weapons fire. For at least half an hour the low rumble of heavy bomb blasts also rolled across the calm Gulf waters.

Late Thursday night, Wisconsin also fired 50 high-explosive rounds at a marina complex on the Kuwaiti coast. (Pool note: See previous pool report, which we tried to send by wireless late Thursday night, and sent again by helicopter Friday afternoon.)

"There were some targets in southern Kuwait that were used as a staging area for small boats. Iraqi small boats that were conducting operations against the northern Saudi coast," Capt. Bill said Friday. "Our mission was to take out the base that supported those operations . . . There was a lot of floating debris after we were finished. We are up here doing what we were trained to do and what we do best," he said, "which is supporting the ground troops ashore."

. . . Television pictures from Thursday night's RPV (remotely piloted vehicle) mission indicate that there is some truth to the Riyadh briefers' statements that the ship could blow up a tennis court at more than 20 miles.

Probably, however, it would destroy a bunch of other tennis courts first.

Everything from barometric pressure to the age and temperature of the rifled gun barrel influences the range and direction of a shot, and every barrel's characteristics must be determined separately. So as a practical matter, gunners must use the time-tested method of firing several shots from each barrel to test their range, and then "firing for effect."

For example, the first round of shots fired against the marina Thursday night did not hit any boats or piers. But after turrets were sighted in with the aid of RPV television pictures, the pattern of fire grew much more devastating. And when you're shooting 1-ton projectiles you may not need direct hits. Several shots clearly ripped apart boats that were at least 20 to 30 yards from the shells' point of impact.

Gunners say that bulls-eye hits are largely a matter of mathematical odds.

Even after adjusting for each barrel's characteristics, every powder charge will differ slightly from its predecessor. So bunkers, tanks and other hardened targets, which would require nearly direct hits, will force the ship to shoot more rounds per target.

No one aboard Wisconsin doubts that they'll kill what they hit. A conservative, published estimate is that Wisconsin's armor-piercing rounds will blast through 16 inches of armored steel or 20 feet of reinforced concrete.

Master Chief Fire Controlman Stephen Skelley said soft sand absorbs the energy of shell bursts, reducing their cratering range to 10 to 15 feet diameter and 5 or 6 feet in depth. But immense damage can still be done with specialized and armor-piercing projectiles, he added. Armor-piercing rounds can penetrate at least 25 feet into the earth, he said.

Last Call for a Last Will and Testament: Leaving Everything in the World to Someone

By Carol Morello

IN EASTERN SAUDI ARABIA - A line furrowed on specialist Paul E. Frazier's smooth brow, and anyone looking into his dark brown eyes saw a man looking back older and more scared than any 20-year-old has a right to be.

Twenty-year-olds are not supposed to be concerned with writing their last will and testament. But with the ground war expected to start any day now, it is a time when, for young men like Frazier, everything becomes momentously burdened with its potential for finality—the final training exercises, the final letters home, the final disposition of a young man's few possessions and Army benefits.

And so one bright morning this week, Frazier and two of his buddies from the 27th Engineer Battalion left their camp near the (censored) border and drove to an Army lawyer for what has become a formality among adolescent men preparing for death. There, in a dusty tent where combat boots stomped over plywood floors and a field telephone jangled like castanets, they filled in their parents' names on an impersonal form with a blank for listing beneficiaries.

"I'm just trying to get all this paperwork done," said Sgt. Everett Long, 24, of Riegelwood, N.C. "Before it's too late."

"The closer it gets, the more I think about it. That's the reality of life, and it could happen. I want to make sure what few belongings I have go to my parents."

Everyone else in the battalion had already seen to the "paperwork" of wills, most before leaving their base at Fort Bragg. Not Frazier, Long or Pvt. Kelvin A. Smith, 19, of Chicago.

Initially, they were based too far from the front for death to be jogged from the rear echelons of their minds. But as they moved closer to the front, death no longer seemed to be lurking on the distant horizon, but breathing over their shoulders. "As I got closer to be border, more and more questions popped up in my mind," said Smith.

Since the air war started on Jan. 17, they have lain in their cots at night listening to the planes flying north on bombing missions, and huddled around transistor radios keeping up with reports on the approaching war that seem at odds with the calm routine of their daily lives.

And so when the last call came for will preparation, they were at long last ready. "It's gonna happen," said Long of the ground war. "It's better to be prepared for the worst and the worst doesn't happen than to get caught."

Long, the combat engineer, Smith, the rookie, and Frazier, the medic, filed in together, each a witness to the others' wills. Long and Frazier named their parents as beneficiaries, while Smith divided his assets between his parents, a son and a newborn infant so young he hasn't even had a chance to learn if he has another son or a daughter.

Like most young soldiers, they wrote blanket bequests simply willing all their assets, whatever they may be, to their beneficiaries.

"Soldiers don't have a lot really," said Capt. David Francis, 27, of Philadelphia, the Army lawyer who has drawn up about 100 wills for soldiers in Saudi Arabia during the last four months. "Maybe a car, household possessions, maybe a saving account. But they're just starting a life, so don't own much."

But with wisdom beyond their years, the young soldiers want to spare the people they love one more cause for grief.

"When I'm dead, I don't want my parents to go through the trouble of dealing with what I leave behind," said Frazier. "The death of a family member causes more problems than just the death itself. If you divide it up beforehand, that's one less problem."

Carrying their rolled-up wills into the sunlight, soldiers said they would mail them to their parents for safekeeping. None had yet figured out what he would write in an accompanying note. They hadn't expected to worry about such somber matters as wills so early in their lives, but it wasn't so hard, really, they said. Not compared to what lies ahead.

"About the only thing we can do is prepare ourselves for going to war," said Long. "But the reality is, while I can prepare a soldier to fight, I can't prepare him to face up to his friend being shot."

A British Officer's Life: From Wrestling a Hamper to a Surfeit of Marmalade

By Keith Dovkants

WITH THE 1ST ARMOURED DIVISION - The difficulties involved in attaching a Fortnum and Mason hamper to an armoured car are not to be underestimated.

Even for a cavalry officer, it presents a challenge.

Lieut. Henry Sugden succeeded in lashing his hamper to the side of his Ferret reconnaissance vehicle, but still worries about it being exposed to enemy fire.

If it lasts that long. Comrades in the 16th/15th The Queen's Royal Lancers seem determined to finish off the smoked oysters, after-dinner dark chocolate, and Gentleman's Relish long before the Iraqis hove into view.

This may be sooner rather than later. As the medium reconnaissance regiment of Britain's Gulf troops, the Lancers will be at the very tip of the spearhead. They are, as their commanding officer Lt. Col. Philip Scott said: "The eyes and ears of the division." Their job is to seek out enemy positions and direct fire onto them. This frequently involves penetrating enemy lines and working behind them in the quest for what Col. Scott calls "real-time intelligence."

Even the infantrymen regard the Lancers' task as high-risk, and it is significant that they are among those soldiers for whom body armour is standard equipment.

The lightweight, desert camouflage waistcoats have been a great success with the cavalrymen. One of Lt. Sugden's chums proudly showed me a 5-penny-sized blister on his. "Gave it a round from the 9 millimetre at 25 feet, Stopped it dead. Quite encouraging really."

In an effort to encourage them further, the commanders had the Lancers driving across the desert with live artillery shells exploding within 200 yards in an exercise aimed at hardening them to enemy fire. "It was the most exciting day we have had so far, apart from the day the rain stopped," said Lt. Sugden.

His Fortnum's hamper was sent from his home in Fulham, but before it can be allowed into strictly-Islamic Saudi Arabia alcohol and port products were exchanged for other items. It has left 24-year-old Sugden's squadron with something of a surfeit of marmalade.

The 16th/15th Lancers are currently providing the 1st Armoured Division's protective screen. Two squadrons of the regiment are deployed below the border to give early warning of any incursion by the Iraqis.

Saturday
February 9, 1991

For a very few American soldiers—GIs of the Muslim faith—shipping out to Saudi Arabia for the Gulf War could be both a startling opportunity and an affront to their conscience.

Suddenly, at their government's expense, they were on the other side of the world and in close proximity to the city of Mecca, the holiest site in all of Islam, the sacred hub where they directed their daily prayers of religious obedience.

But for at least two Muslim soldiers, being in Saudi Arabia under arms, in uniform and in an army aimed at another Arab nation subtracted from their lives more than it added. A story in this chapter deals with these two men, united by their faith but segregated from their comrades in arms, left in the rear and glad for it.

Disunity among Arabs and Muslims was evident elsewhere in the region. Sheik Tamimi, head of the Islamic Jihad (Holy War) in Jordan, announced a fatwa (death warrant) against Egyptian president Hosni Mubarak, who had contributed troops to the anti-Iraq coalition. The response from Syria, which also sent troops to the allied cause, was to ask for the death of Saddam Hussein.

Gen. Schwarzkopf told the press that he had seen reports from the field, as yet unconfirmed, that some of the Iraqi pilots fleeing to Iran tried to bomb one of Saddam Hussein's presidential palaces on their way out of the country. If so, they had to get in line behind the allied aircraft trying to do the same thing.

As Secretary Cheney and Gen. Powell visited the war zone, the coalition reported that the number of air strikes now numbered 57,000.

A closer look at that number yields some graphic averages: more than 2,400 sorties a day, for 57 days; more than 100 sorties per hour, day and night.

A Pentagon self-examination of U.S. military performance during the Gulf War, issued a year after the war ended, admitted that some of the tens of thousands of bombing missions were redundant—attacks on facilities that had already been destroyed or badly damaged. Wartime intelligence about the results of allied bombing runs was inadequate, the report said. Despite the intensive bombing, much of Iraq's nuclear weapons facilities escaped damage, however.

The Central Command reported on this date in 1991 that military equipment belonging to Iraq destroyed in these missions included 750 tanks (of an estimated 3,400-5,000 when the war began), 650 pieces of artillery (of 2,500-3,500), and 600 armored personnel carriers (of about 3,000-5,000).

Losses among the Iraqi ground forces caused by the constant bombing, due to death, wounds, and desertion, were difficult to quantify. But that didn't stop some experts from trying.

In fact the whole issue of numbers—how many soldiers, tanks, artillery pieces, aircraft, missile sites, etc. existed in the Iraqi military when the war broke out and how much survived "Instant Thunder," the military moniker for the allied air campaign—is a moving-target debates that never seems to find resolution.

The Pentagon's year-after report stated that allied forces destroyed a total of 3,847 Iraqi tanks and 2,917 artillery pieces; the figures were close to the numbers claimed immediately after the war. However the later number of Iraqi armored troop carriers destroyed—1,450—was drastically lower than the wartime estimate of 2,400.

The CIA, DIA, and other agencies working in secret cited a pre-war estimate of about 1-million Iraqi troops, with upwards of 547,000 (42 divisions) sent to Kuwait. Other experts believe no more than 350,000 Iraqi troops were ever in Kuwait and up to 20 percent were either killed or deserted before the land war began.

Saddam Hussein announced additional callups of reserves and eligible males during the air war. But how many men were subsequently pressed into military service, and whether they balanced the number lost through death and desertion, are unknown.

The allied coalition's policy was not to estimate the number of enemy troops or Iraqi civilians, for that matter—killed by their side. Opponents of the war later estimated as many as 120,000 Iraqi troops may have died in the war, but provided no hard evidence. The top allied air commander in the Gulf, Gen. Chuck Homer, said after the war he believed the figure could have been under 10,000.

In a study of Gulf War air power, commissioned by the Air Force secretary and directed by Eliot Cohen, a university professor of strategic studies and carried out by a mostly-civilian staff, the number of Iraqi troops deployed in the Kuwait theater when the ground offensive began was set at only 336,000, after accounting for deserters.

Assisted by interviews with Iraqi deserters, the air power task force concluded there were 420,000 Iraqi troops in Kuwait as the war began and of that number 84,000 had probably deserted by mid-January, when the allied attacks began, leaving only 336,000. Only a few thousand deserters were in Saudi custody by the time the land war began; others may have gone north, of course. In April 1991, the Central Command said 19,000 Iraqi troops had turned themselves in to U.S. occupation forces in southern Iraq since the war ended on Feb. 28.

By the time of the land war on Feb. 24, the task force estimated, Iraqi strength in the Kuwait theater—reduced by death, non-fatal serious wounds, and more desertions—was down to 200,000-to-222,000.

How valid were the numbers offered by Iraqi deserters, who would naturally want to please and impress their captors? How valid were the figures issued by the Pentagon a year after the war, while the despot Saddam Hussein remained in control of Iraq and the U.S. was still denied access to the ground it had attacked?

The Iraqi government never issued figures for troop or equipment losses.

Ominous Shapes, Iraqi Planes Keep U.S. Ships on Alert: "Like Being in a Woodpile With a Copperhead Snake"

By Mort Rosenblum

ABOARD THE USS R.K. TURNER IN THE PERSIAN GULF - A spotter saw that ominous black shape in the water, one spike poking upwards.

This billion-dollar missile ship, with 400 souls aboard, scrambled to alert over a garbage bag. "It's always there at the back of your mind, even if it doesn't seem like war," said Lt. Cmdr. Tim Kisley of Bristol, R.I.,

Saturday - February 9, 1991

whose job is controlling damage to the ship. Mostly, it doesn't seem like war.

As soldiers opened MREs in the sand Friday night, sailors ate barbecued chicken from a recipe Clifford Liferidge learned in South Carolina from his mama. "Feels like peace, normal times," said Liferidge, a petty officer third class from Brooklyn.

Few crewmen see much difference between Gulf duty and the canceled six-month voyage of their missile cruiser, except maybe for the missed port calls in Nice and the anguished letters from home. "I been here a month, and I don't feel no stress," said petty officer Mario Washington, of Rocky Mountain, N.C., a radioman in the ship's sophisticated communications center.

But everyone aboard the Turner, and more than 75 other allied ships in the Gulf, knows that one lucky hit from the crippled Iraqi war machine can send their self-contained world to the bottom. Petty Officer David Blake, a ship's barber, finishes up with scalps and joins the watch for mines. Along with freshly laid mines, old ones float loose from the Iran-Iraq war. "Several days ago we saw this thing, black, round, with a spoke sticking up," said Capt. James Burke, the skipper. "In the binoculars, it looked like a mine."

It was a tied-up Hefty bag. "You just can't take any chances," Burke said.

Just Thursday, the British destroyer H.M.S. Gloucester missed a mine by 15 feet. Even more, there is the phantom air force.

Iraq's deadly Super Frelon helicopters are somewhere, untracked. Radarmen look west but also to the rocky coast of Iran, where ship-killing planes shelter.

Vice Adm. Stanley Arthur, U.S. naval commander in the Gulf, worries aloud that Iraq's top-gun warplanes, French-made F-1 Mirages with Exocet missiles, are in Iran.

Promises do not reassure him. If a cluster of Iraqi planes sneak down the valleys that parallel the Gulf, they can burst into allied radar within 40 miles of ships. At Mach 1, the speed of sound, that is four minutes. "It's sort of like being in a woodpile with a copperhead snake," he said. "They give you no warning. You can play around in the woodpile a long time, and you can still get a nasty bite."

Against any eventuality, young specialists below decks sit round-the-clock in front of displays that look like video arcades gone wild. "We call this the pickle," said Wayne Kohnen, a gunner's mate from Jackson Hole, Wyo., holding up a simple metal trigger device that seems out of place among the blinking electronics. If Trackers' Alley decides a blip is malignant, Kohnen's partner, Petty Officer Bill Beaton of Lowell, Mass., fingers some keys. Kohnen fingers some more, and he squeezes the pickle.

The action happens down in the Missile House, where gunner's mate Darrell Sergeant of Sodus, N.Y., will have fitted gleaming death onto the rails.

"I can't tell you how far," he said, "but we can reach out . . ."

Praise Be to Allah—Muslim GIs Love Saudi But Oppose the War: "I Can't Be a Part of It"

By Carol Morello

IN EASTERN SAUDI ARABIA - Spec. Cheveron Scott has moved his Koran to his bunker for safekeeping.

Pvt. Jerry Walker has sealed his copy of "Islam in Focus," a primer on the principles of Islam, in a Ziplock bag tucked inside a pocket of his chemical protection suit.

Muslims whose unit was ordered to Saudi Arabia in December, the two young Atlanta men are finding that in most other aspects, Islam and the American-led war against the Muslim nation of Iraq do not so readily mesh.

They are the mirror image of the typical American soldier in Saudi Arabia, who can't stand being in this abstemious country and can't wait for the ground war to begin to oust Iraq from Kuwait so at least some of the troops can go home.

Rather, Scott and Walker love being in Saudi Arabia, with its public displays of piety that cause the country to grind to a halt five times a day for prayers. Yet, this is a war that they oppose, seeing it as a war of aggression rather than self-defense.

"It's not for the cause of God, and I can't be a part of it," Scott told his commander in the 265th Engineer's Unit when they were deciding who to send farther north to help build roads in the desert and who to leave behind in a rear support position. "If you force me to go further, I'll be no more than a liability and I will fight only in self-defense."

And when the list was drawn, they were left behind.

Walker has asked for permission to retire from his military duties or be placed on non-combat status when he returns to the U.S. "I don't want to have to put my weapon on another day longer than I have to," he said, sitting on his cot with his gas mask hanging from a hook and a red prayer rug to the side. They are not your typical conscientious objectors and they are immune to Saddam Hussein's call for Muslims worldwide to attack the U.S. and its allies through terroristic acts.

But in one way, their predicament is a common one for many GIs who find themselves caught up in something bigger than they bargained for when they joined the military.

Like many soldiers in the all-volunteer army, Scott and Walker joined the National Guard to help pay their way through college. Scott, 21 and the son of a Methodist preacher, joined the Guard two years ago, six months before he took the first steps in converting to Islam. Walker, 23, left the Baptist church for Islam four years ago, about the same time he enlisted in the Guard.

At the time, he saw no conflict between his religion and a duty he thought would call on him for nothing more dramatic than a natural disaster. Now Scott, trained as a legal specialist, and Walker, a radio telephone operator who initially was assigned to monitor the radio for Scud missile alerts, are sitting contentedly to the rear as clerk typists.

Even in their camouflage American uniforms, they are readily identifiable as Muslims. Walker wears a small green lapel pin saying "Praise be to Allah" in Arabic script. Scott has mastered enough Arabic to be able to copy from the Koran, "Praise be to Allah, the cherisher and sustainer of the world," and taped the saying to the first-aid pouch hanging from his ammunition belt.

Grocery clerks press extra food on them at the checkout counter. Worshippers at a mosque they visited for the first time last week discreetly corrected their praying position. And the operator of a gymnasium where they work out has presented them with Korans and books explaining Islam.

"Saudi Arabia is beautiful," said Scott. "Being in the holy land has helped me to grow as a person and a Muslim." Both men said the racial barriers that in the U.S. make them feel ostracized as black Americans do not exist among Muslims in Saudi Arabia.

"Muslims over here don't see color," said Walker. "There are no color or racial barriers. I feel more at home here than I do at home." Admittedly, neither has seen enough of Saudi Arabia to form an impression of the Third World nationals who form a permanent worker's underclass in Saudi society, earning meager wages and unable to leave the country at will because their employers hold their passports. "I haven't been exposed to that," each said.

But there is one Saudi custom they would not like to see exported to America—the ban on women driving. "My girlfriend drives, and I'm not going to stop her from driving," said Walker. "I don't think Allah came down and passed the word women can't drive. I think it's more a custom."

Sunday
February 10, 1991

The war in its fourth week continued to be dominated by the air campaign and international diplomacy.

In the latter, Mikhail Gorbachev, a Soviet leader of high international standing who could usually deliver even the most strident speech in a disarmingly reasonable tone, in contrast to many of his predecessors, complained that the U.S.-led coalition was going beyond the United Nations mandate in conducting the war against Saddam Hussein.

In general, a leader like Hussein could ask for no more influential a friend in a crisis than the last Communist Party chairman (we didn't know it then, of course) in the Kremlin. But the specifics of the UN mandate were not the kind of arguments likely to sway the nations pouring troops, planes and bullets into the all-out effort to get the Iraqi leader to leave Kuwait in the grace period provided.

The early February visit to the allied war command centers by the U.S. Defense Secretary and Joint Chiefs of Staff chairman was mostly business. After all, people were being killed, buildings and military equipment were being destroyed, hundreds of thousands of allied military personnel were drawing imminent danger pay, every day. But the trip had a lighter side, and it's told here.

Secretary Cheney accepted a Bart Simpson doll from an Air Force sergeant for redeployment to the Oval Office. Both men autographed bombs that were to be dropped on the enemy. That virtually guaranteed that their autographs would never be read once the bombs left the airfield, of course. The ceremonial signings drew new attention to a massive aerial warfare campaign whose origins dated back to at least the previous August, when Gen. Schwarzkopf first delegated the chore of creating a three-stage air campaign to a handful of Air Force generals.

The plan decided upon was dubbed "Instant Thunder." And it was designed to pack a big punch up front, in the first hours and days, a plan far different from "Rolling Thunder," the extended, gradualist type of campaign waged in the Vietnam War.

The strategic air campaign in the Gulf was based on massive numbers of fighters and bombers striking quickly and thoroughly, paralyzing Iraq's communications, command, and control mechanisms and focusing on a number of key "strategic centers of gravity" over a period of days, not weeks.

From mid-January on, nearly 1,800 combat aircraft from 12 countries were participating in the coalition assault from the air. The desired effect was almost immediate. The allies gained air superiority and proceeded to blind the enemy in a technical sense, making it impossible for Iraq to conduct meaningful surveillance of allied operations.

By the end of the air campaign, an estimated 90,000 tons of ordnance was dropped on Iraq and Kuwait. Under the cover of this massive bombardment, the allied forces on the ground in northern Saudi Arabia refined their plans for a land operation and prepared their soldiers and Marines for the final attack.

One field commander's preparation talk is described in this chapter. Leading a brigade of combat engineers, whose main job in this war would be to go ahead of the main force and clear a path through minefield after minefield, he addressed them on a windy Sunday afternoon at their desert camp.

The engineers were trained to arrive at the battle zone by parachute. When they went in this time, they would be in trucks and on foot. For field officers on the brink of battle, there are the orders from above to interpret and pass on, the rules of war to cite for the record and battles of the past to summon for examples of courage. The rest is largely a set of personal choices.

Each commander is expected to know his men best, from seasoned veterans to the newest addition to the squad, and to be able to find the words that will speak to them. He will seek to motivate, to gear them up to perform bravely, but not recklessly or cruelly. The difference, sadly, can sometimes be a hair's breadth.

Pushed beyond the edge, from bravery to confusion, a soldier might take a friend for a foe. That happens in every war, but in the Gulf the incidence of friendly fire would go higher than many expected or found acceptable. A story in this chapter delves into the subject from the standpoint of ground troops assigned to cooperate with helicopter pilots while involved in a border skirmish.

In the end, the objective—an Iraqi observation post—was minor. The principles involved were as basic as life and death.

A Secret Base Where Bart Gets a Ride From Cheney: "For 60 Days, Everyone Thought We Were in Turkey"

Central Command and the JIB laid on a special enlarged pool to cover the visit of Secretary Cheney and Gen. Powell to an F-117 Stealth base Sunday.

Please note: In the interest of time, this report is being given to you in the form of raw notes.

The following report was compiled by David Lamb of the L.A. Times, Chuck Lewis of Hearst, Bill Gannon of the Newark Star-Ledger, Lara Marlowe of TIME Magazine, and Phil Shenon of the New York Times. (FYI, there was a Washington-based pool on board the Cheney plane; however, that pool indicated it would not file until the plane reached Shannon Airport in Ireland to refuel about 2:30 EST.) The pool flew 2.5 hours via C-130 to a base in Saudi Arabia to await their arrival following the Riyadh news conference and en route to Washington.

AN AIRBASE IN SAUDI ARABIA - Cheney and Powell and entourage arrived at this secret base—so secret that the Americans here cannot call home, despite the fact that other GIs throughout the Arabian peninsula are making calls to the states, so secret that we aren't allowed to tell you if it's in Northern, Southern, Eastern, or Western Saudi Arabia. "For the first 60 days, everyone thought we were in Turkey," one airman said.

Cheney/Powell were met by U.S. Air Force Col. Alton C. Whitley Jr., U.S. base commander, and his Saudi counterpart, Gen. Abdul Aziz bin Khalid al-Sudairi, at the end of the stairs bringing them down from the Air Force 707. They walked beside a 28-man Saudi honor guard armed with submachine guns, shook hands with a row of junior officers, and strode on a red carpet into the airport passenger terminal.

After a closed meeting there lasting about 10 minutes, they went to a concrete revetment hangar where they addressed several hundred Air Force personnel, some of whom have been at this base since August.

Cheney, tieless and wearing black cowboy boots and a suede leather jacket, told the group that he and Powell "had spent all day yesterday with Gen. Schwarzkopf and his commanders and will meet with President Bush tomorrow." He said the purpose of his trip was to allow him "to give some thought about what comes next." He praised the U.S. effort to date and told the troops the U.S. military "has had enormous success" in the war thus far. The Air Force folks shouted their approval.

Cheney said he and Powell "have a briefing every morning in the war room and we see the tapes of what's been happening here." Cheney said he stopped at the base because he "wanted to say thanks" and tell them "the people at home are 100 percent behind you."

"There was a little debate last fall on whether we should be here (but) the president has made the right decision and Congress has approved it." (Asked whether he believed that 100 percent of Americans support the war, Airman Brian Zarycki, 25, from Cleveland, Ohio, said: "No, because I see the protestors on television." The base receives CNN.)

Powell then told the group that the U.S. military campaign has brought back "a sense of pride to America" and he told how people want to shake his hand and pat him on the back wherever he goes.

"But it's your hand they want to shake and your back they want to pat," Powell said, observing that "it's easy to be chairman in this environment." Both Cheney and Powell said they wanted to bring the war to a speedy and successful conclusion and bring the troops home. "We want to get this over with as quickly as possible in a way that leaves no doubt who won with minimum loss of life to our forces and the coalition forces," said Powell.

Cheney then asked for questions and after a couple of seconds when it appeared none were coming, Cheney thanked the troops and began his departure. Journalists were forbidden from asking the Secretary or General Powell any questions.

One of the airmen, Tech. Sgt. Mark Singleton of Sonoma, CA, asked by a pool correspondent why no one raised any questions, said: "We're very well supported here. We're doing a fantastic job. This is a good facility. Morale is good. No one had anything to complain about."

"We've been pretty isolated back here. It's kind of like a country club war," said Staff Sgt. Brian Dooley, 31, from Bedford, Virginia.

Did members of the Tactical Fighter Wing ever talk about the Iraqis being killed by the Stealth bombers? "No one here that I know of ever thinks of anything like that," said Dooley. "I'm a soldier, and we do what the government thinks we should do." Tech Sgt. Michael Battaglione, 29, from Vineland, N.J., said he hoped the President would continue to allow the Air Force to pound away at the Iraqis before "the grunts go low-tech. We're all real proud of how things are going and our role in the war so far. Maybe we should just hammer away at them until we starve 'em out," Battaglione said.

Cheney and Powell repeated their stop-and-greet-and-speak routine five minutes later at another stop on the base. Their message was essentially the same except when Cheney concluded and asked if there were any questions, an airman to one side responded: "Yes, sir. I wonder if you could tell us whether this warplane (the F-117) has performed beyond your expectations?"

Cheney responded with a long ball that's still soaring over the grandstand, the guts of which was that the plane has performed "far beyond anything anybody ever envisioned."

When Cheney asked if there were any other questions, Air Force Staff Sgt. John Pennell, standing in the front row, raised a Bart Simpson doll clothed in desert camouflage and asked whether Cheney would take it back to Bush.

Amid a general uproar of shouts and laughter among the troops, Cheney promised "it will be in the Oval Office tomorrow morning."

Pennell, 30, an air traffic controller who resides in Okinawa, bears a close physical resemblance to Bart, with his blond crewcut sticking straight up and high-wall hair on the sides. It turns out that Pennell is an amateur barber who volunteers to cut hair on the base; the more your pool looked around the crowd, the more "Bart Simpson" cuts we saw.

Pennell later told reporters the doll was a "mascot and inspiration" to the unit but was "definitely not an underachiever." Another airman said the doll had accompanied an F-117 on at least one mission.

Cheney and Powell also stopped to autograph a bomb. There was some sensitivity on their part and on the part of the public affairs officers about whether to allow reporters and cameras to record this event. Several officers even positioned airmen between the VIPs and the press to block the view of the event by your pool. However, a sanity of sorts prevailed and first Cheney, then Powell, used a black magic marker to write messages on a bomb.

Powell wrote: "To Saddam: You didn't move it and you'll lose it. Colin Powell."

Cheney wrote: "To Saddam, with affection. Dick Cheney, Secretary of Defense."

Some miscellany:

One of the fighter pilots mentioned to Cheney and Powell during a photo opportunity that his aircraft had been plagued by electronic "glitches."

Maj. Lee Gustin told Powell and Cheney his fighter was named "Christine"—the killer car of Stephen King fame, because "it's just a jinxed jet sometimes . . . we've had some unusual electrical anomalies. But we keep her flying." It should be noted "Christine" bore 11 bombing mission stencils.

The Stealth base is the only F-117 base in Saudi Arabia. The unit, the 37th tactical Fighter Wing, is based at Tonopah, Nev. We were told officially by Tech Sgt. Robeert Shelton, the base spokesman, that the planes only fly during the night.

"That's why it's a black airplane," said Shelton. He confirmed that the Stealths are still flying every night.

However, an officer later told one of your poolers that the planes fly "mostly at night," and grinned when informed that the official spokesman had said it flew only at night. "We still have targets to take out," said Shelton. "Command and control as well as supply line type targets. Bridges, railroad tracks—so they can't re-supply their troops down in Kuwait as easily. The Stealth is being used against frontline targets. We are still using 2,000-pound bombs." Shelton said the Stealth refuels en route to and on its way back from its bombing sorties. He said no Stealths had been spotted by the Iraqis. "That's how we advertised the plane—as being undetectable. Gen. Schwarzkopf and Gen. Horner are convinced now." Unlike other bombers, the radar-invisible Stealth flies unescorted by fighter planes. "They are virtually by themselves," said Shelton.

An F-117 from the base scored the first bombing raid on Baghdad the night the war started—the AT&T building. The 37th TFW's Stealths also hit a nuclear reactor in the first two days of the war.

Shelton bristled at the suggestion by one of your poolers that the Stealth had outlived its usefulness in the war against Iraq, since the Iraqis had all but shut off their air-defense systems anyway, negating the need for the Stealth's fancy talents.

Nonsense, he said. "We still have important missions to complete."

We saw two fighters up close. The side on the left of each plane, right below the canopy, was stenciled with silver-painted bombs, one for each combat mission flown by the plane. It appeared the mission count for each was between 10 and 20.

One of the planes was being loaded with a laser-guided 2,000-pound bomb designed to explode after it penetrates the target. (The Stealth also carries bombs which explode on contact.) It surprised some of your poolers to see how fast the weapon was installed inside the bomb-bay, not on the wing (this is Stealth, remember!)

Col. Flowers Gives a Pep Talk: "The Wind is Blowing, It's Starting to Rain, and You've Got a Bad Feeling"

By Carol Morello

IN EASTERN SAUDI ARABIA - Hundreds of pairs of solemn eyes, shaded from the desert sun by helmets draped in desert camouflage, stared out above mouths uniformly set in a grim line.

Col. Robert Flowers held them all. Commander of the 20th Engineer Brigade from Fort Bragg in North Carolina, he is the type of man these young combat engineers will walk through minefields for. Sunday was his day to steel them for what lies ahead.

Throughout the day, in a series of visits to his battalions to deliver a final pep talk, he told them where their mission fits into the larger battle plan with a frankness deserved by men ready to bet their lives on their training and preparation.

So still you could not even see them breathe, the soldiers sat in the sand at his feet, their M-16s resting across their knees and on their shoulders.

At the 27th Engineer Battalion, Flowers pointed to a large map of the battlefield with the point of a flagpole holding the engineers' banner, a white castle on a red field. He hooked his thumbs in his ammunition belt as he paced, his eyes scanning his soldiers spread before him so that everyone sensed he was talking to him alone.

He spoke to them of fear, as if it were a more formidable enemy than the Iraqis and only bringing it into the open one more time could help allay it. "There are going to be some very tough days ahead for you," he told them. "I won't sugarcoat it. I expect you to deal with it. It's like when you (parachute) jump, and something doesn't feel right. The wind is blowing, it's starting to rain, and you've got a bad feeling. But you fight back your fears and you do it, because you're a unit and the guys around you are doing it.

"You have to prepare yourselves collectively and individually for fear. You can't let it become panic. Panic is what causes you to fail, and it will kill you." Wild rumors will sweep through the battlefield, he warned. There will be exaggerated reports of many Iraqi tanks coming over the next hill up ahead. Don't believe them. Don't run.

"Your best opportunity to defend yourselves is from where you are. In World War II, at the Battle of the Bulge, three U.S. divisions broke and ran. One engineer battalion did not run. It stayed in place as the others streamed through. They stayed and accomplished their mission, destroying bridges over rivers in Belgium, and stopped the German advance to Antwerp. One battalion made the difference."

Then he asked them to rise and join him in prayer.

Sunday - February 10, 1991

Hundreds of helmets were lifted off heads shaved to a fraction of an inch of baldness, and they bowed their heads.

"Father, as we walk through the valley of death, we know you will be with us. I ask you to take care of my soldiers. Be with them as they walk and give them the strength they need." The helmets went back on. The lowered eyes returned again to Flowers.

"27th, I look for big things from you." Then he ended with an Airborne flourish.

"TAKE A DEEP BREATH," he commanded, and paused.

"LET IT OUT."

"AIR-BORNE" they shouted as one, their deeply resonant voices sounding full of confidence and determination.

As Flowers lit up a King Edward cigar, the men of the 27th stood in formation. Over a loudspeaker came the strains of Lee Greenwood's "God Bless the USA," the unofficial anthem of Operation Desert Storm. The song rose to the occasion:

"And I'm proud to be an American, where at least I know I'm free. And I won't forget the men who died, who gave that right to me." As the soldiers marched away, kicking up dust with their combat boots, they were led in a marching chant:

"Oh hell, oh hell, oh engineers."

"What the hell're we doing here?"

"Oh, mama, don't you cry."

"Your little boy is gonna die."

Flowers watched them parade past, these men half his age whom he will order and lead into battle.

"I'm just hoping I bring them all back," he said. "That was my commitment to their families when they left Fort Bragg. We've done a lot of work. Everyone is anxious to get it done and over with."

Confusing Skirmish at Iraqi Observation Post: "This is the Stuff That is Going to Get Someone Shot"

By Michael Hedges

WITH THE 1ST INFANTRY DIVISION - The 2.75-inch rocket fired yesterday morning from a Cobra helicopter gunship detonated in a brilliant explosion which crumpled the corner of a suspected Iraqi radar post, causing an antenna atop the building to list.

From an armored vehicle two miles away, the Cobra could be seen hosing the building with cannon fire as Apache helicopters had done the previous night.

It was the latest skirmish in a five-day contest of forces and nerves over a complex of buildings—not quite a town—straddling the border between warring armies.

So far, the Iraqis had fired few confirmed shots but, at least at night, they controlled the motley collection of sheds, houses and small mud-brick buildings. Cavalry units of the 1st Infantry Division called helicopter strikes onto the hamlet, took occasional deserters prisoner, but for apparent strategic reasons which frustrated some of the troopers they did not attack Iraqi convoys they believed would prowl the area at night.

"The last four days there has been a trend," said Capt. Michael Bills, 33, of West Springfield, Va., who commands a cavalry troop.

He said the Iraqis would move mounted troops into, or just behind, the buildings at night to monitor American positions. His radar and night-vision spotters believed as many as two-dozen Iraqi armored vehicles moved forward each night under cover of darkness.

"We are going to try to trap them with Apaches tonight," he said. Lt. Thomas Karns, 24, of Linesville, Pa., said his platoon of Bradley fighting vehicles strung out as a forward observation post had been having frequent contacts with Iraqi vehicles at night. There have even been exchanges of gunfire. "They got in between us," he said, recalling an encounter a few nights earlier. "It got pretty confusing." The lieutenant said the war entered a new dimension for him and his soldiers when they saw the streaking green tracer bullets used by the Iraqis firing past their positions. "Nothing like this had happened to any of us," he said. "It got a little hairy. We got a little nervous, scared, whatever you want to call it. I was happy when it was over."

In another skirmish a few days ago, a Bradley from Lt. Karns' platoon went into the village to take charge of a deserter captured by a Cobra crewman.

"He had gone home to Iraq and found out his whole family had been put in prison when his name appeared on a deserters' list," said Capt. Bills.

The Iraqi then returned to his unit to visit friends, only to be forced by his commander to man a forward observation post without his shoes. When U.S. helicopters flew over the village, he willingly surrendered while three armed Iraqis fled to the north, Capt. Bills said. "He said a lot of his friends, he couldn't say how many, had been killed in bombing raids," the captain said.

The thin strip of desert separating two huge armies is eerily serene by day. Large earthworks called berms shield Iraqi movement from view. Last week, the Iraqis tried to improve their berm with a bulldozer, but a TOW missile fired from a Cobra gunship disintegrated the vehicle.

On the American side of the line, the Bradleys are mostly silent sentinels by day, their crews scanning the flat, rocky plain, squinting at camels and the bushes that seem to move and shimmer when watched too long through binoculars.

On one observation post, Pvt. Brian Chavez, 18, Wagoner, Okla., and Pvt. Michael Muzik, 21, of Palos Hills, Ill., watched for movement on the Iraqi side while sitting atop a Bradley nicknamed "Bucephalus." "That name was Lt. Karns' idea," said Pvt. Muzik. "I thought he meant Bocephus, the nickname for Hank Williams Jr., but he said it was the horse of Alexander the Great. He's been to college."

Pvt. Chavez was one of the troopers who went into the village after the Iraqi deserter. His strongest recollection was of the opulence of one of the homes, and of being so full of adrenaline he and a sergeant could not get a gate open, finally giving up and going around to the rear.

The men expected to be in Southwestern Asia a long time. "There will be all new music when we get back," said Pvt. Chavez, "a new way of dancing." Pvt. Muzik said, "We will look like dorks, like we're dancing the Watusi or something."

About 100 yards west of the Bradley "Bucephalus," Sgt. Tarin Hawkins, 27, of San Antonio, Tex., and Pvt. Hugh Bohannon, 20, of Buffalo, N.Y, operated a ground surveillance radar unit from an armored personnel carrier.

Pvt. Bohannon said for the past few nights he has seen Iraqi vehicles numbering at least two dozen pull into a triangular pattern just north of the border. But when Apache helicopters are sent to attack, the pilots can't find them. The pilots are claiming the troopers are making erroneous identifications, some of the men said. "It is very frustrating," said Pvt. Bohannon. "I don't know what is wrong with the Apaches."

On a recent night, the APC of Sgt. Hawkins and Pvt. Bohannon was almost fired upon by a Bradley from another troop, they said. "It just shows you what

Sunday - February 10, 1991

it is going to be like when this kicks off. When it hits the fan there will be lots of friendly fire kills."

Sgt. Hawkins said he is concerned about Iraqi artillery. "What scares me is, some night they are going to open fire on us with their 180-mm guns," he said. "We are well within range, and they probably have a gun trained on each one of us, they just have to push a button."

But both men are most scared of chemical gas attack.

Pvt. Bohannon said, "I don't wear my flak jacket, it won't stop a bullet or a ricochet anyway, and it might slow me down getting into my chem suit." As the men speak, they suddenly pick up a line of Iraqi soldiers on a reconnaissance patrol. But after a tense few minutes, an observer identifies the blip as a line of camels.

Just before sunset, a line of four armored vehicles moved across the Bradley's front two kilometers north. Again, tense minutes followed until it was determined the vehicles were from another troop, moving without radio coordination.

"This is the kind of stuff that is going to get someone shot," said Lt. Karns. "At night, this is confusing."

In the twilight, two Apache helicopters creep in at low altitude, remarkably silent for aircraft, and settle onto the desert. They are to search for the vehicles picked up each night by the observers.

At first the Bradleys could not raise the helicopters on the radio. Lt. Karns jogged the several hundred meters to relay a radio frequency.

At dark, Iraqi flares were fired to illuminate the border in case of attack. Within an hour, the radar crews began to pick up the blips they have interpreted as Iraqi vehicles. Soon Bradley crews were on the radio link, saying they were seeing shapes through their infrared equipment they believed to be Iraqi armored cars.

The Apaches took off, but as on previous nights they didn't see any Iraqi vehicles. On the radio network, Bradley crews were unrestrained in their frustration. "If those Apaches can't find the targets, let me know and I'll shoot them myself," said one.

Pvt. Bohannon looked at the blips on his screen and said, "Every one of those is an Iraqi target. People don't have faith in the Apaches. They have the world's best helicopter and they aren't doing diddley."

The Apaches disappeared without firing. But a few hours later they returned, and shot Hellfire missiles and cannon rounds into buildings suspected of housing Iraqi electronics equipment. Shortly after that, the radar crew and some Bradleys picked up what they identified as an Iraqi drone—a pilotless aircraft that can gather and transmit radar information. One Bradley fired at the drone and missed. Then orange tracers lit up the sky as a .50-cal. machine gun joined the firing. In a post-mortem of the incident the next day, it was decided the .50-cal. probably fired at an American refueling jet several miles away.

The drone appeared to orbit the Bradley line a few times, then disappeared. Deep into the night, the Apaches returned for a second mission. Again, their missiles caused white explosions inside the village. At 10 a.m. yesterday, Cobra helicopters flew in to assess the Apache fire and to add rocket fire of their own.

But the net result of the day-night cycle is frustrating to some of the troopers.

"They still hold the town because we let them," said one trooper. "We've been begging to go forward and clean them out, but I guess the highers have their reasons. It doesn't feel like a war."

Capt. Bills said he understood the attitude of some of his troopers, but said he isn't overly concerned that the Iraqis apparently escaped a trap and performed another reconnaissance of his lines. "It is possible they are a kilometer or so further back than where the radar is picking them up. They could be hiding in a low place behind the town," he said.

But, he added, "We'll get them eventually. We are just a few days into this."

Monday
February 11, 1991

The Iraqi military earned low ratings in most categories during the Gulf War, from marshaling its weapons to motivating its troops. An exception was in the field of deception. The allies conceded that on some bombing runs, a shape that looked like a real enemy tank or building was in fact a sham. And if a report of a target's location was more than a few hours old, the target could very well not be there any more—moved to an underground shelter by the time an allied plane arrived to attack it.

The allies played the game of concealment and fakery, too, from putting a mud finish on rolling stock to broadcasting false radio traffic, or simulating the operational noise of make-believe units, or deploying fake tanks and trucks.

The latter might barely withstand a stiff wind but they could fool some of the Iraqis—from a distance—some of the time, and that was the point.

Sophisticated allied technology was of some help dealing with Iraqi decoys and submerged weapons. After dark, heat-sensing radar devices could look into the gloom and register the glow from tanks that had still not cooled from being driven during the day. Once the allied pilot gained assurance that no friendly units were in the area, they could be blasted away. At least that was the way it was always supposed to work.

Discerning real from phony enemy personnel and materiel became a many-sided mission, not just a matter of night-vision. How the U.S. forces took on this mission became a story—the only story during the entire war, as it turned out, that was censored in its entirety because of the Pentagon's system of military security review of pool stories. The Pentagon's rationale for its policy of curtailing information, and what it called "security review," was to deny the Iraqis accurate, current, and specific information that could prematurely betray allied intentions, strength, or locations, or be used to gain an edge over coalition forces in the intense military intelligence wars.

All pool reports sent in to the pool office from mid-January through the Feb. 28 cease-fire were subject to allied security review. Stories that included information a military public affairs reviewer considered in violation of the security rule were "flagged" and discussed with pool officials—all media representatives—in Dhahran, where the Pentagon's Joint Information Bureau was located.

Any dispute that couldn't be resolved at that level was forwarded to the Pentagon, which would contact the reporter's newspaper, magazine or news agency to try to resolve the issues by agreeing on what should or should not be published. Five stories—of a total of about 1,300 sent by U.S. correspondents in the pool—reached the level of a Pentagon review. In four cases the offending passages were made more general or deleted and the story released.

In the fifth story—about gathering intelligence—reporter Michael Hedges gathered the details in the field from military officials who were obviously willing to discuss the mission with a pool reporter. The Joint Information Bureau's later objections, first registered in Dhahran, were then forwarded to the Pentagon.

After an unexplained delay of a few weeks, the story in question was put to Hedges' editor in Washington, D.C. The editor sided with the Pentagon and agreed to spike the entire story. But it's all here.

Accurate intelligence was crucial in the allied air campaign.

In post-war interviews, the U.S. air commander, Air Force Gen. Charles Horner, explained that when the attacks began early on Jan. 17th, specific targets and missions were arranged only for two and a half days in advance.

From that point on, plans were made daily for two days hence. Missions for, say, Friday were drafted on Wednesday and approved by Gen. Schwarzkopf on Wednesday night. Then a final list was issued Thursday to squadrons so they could launch the required flights the following day. And so on, day after day.

After three-and-a-half weeks, the number of allied planes aloft each day en route to targets—more than 2,000, on average—was enough to cause potential mid-air collisions, as one commander warned in a story in this chapter. The allies registered their first air loss in a week.

Saddam Hussein, meanwhile, hosted another visit by an envoy from the Soviet Union, one of the few countries that remained willing to engage his government.

The Iraqi leader and a number of opponents and critics of the war effort complained that allied planes were killing an increasing numbers of civilians. Some accused the coalition of doing so intentionally to create fear and panic. Allied commanders denied this and re-stated their policy of avoiding civilian casualties to the greatest extent possible, but recognizing that some would inevitably occur.

When word of anti-war sentiment or actions reached troops in the desert, as a story in this chapter relates, soldiers weighed the hostile evidence against the support they received from home and found the anti-war side wanting. As one soldier said, "It's not like they're going to stop the war and pull us back now."

One form of war protest with a tradition dating to the earliest years of the American republic is the refusal to serve based on conscience, or religious belief.

There were no draft resisters, as during the Vietnam era, because there was no draft. But anti-war groups such as the War Resisters League claimed that about 2,500 active-duty and reserve military sought conscientious objector status during the Gulf War. Many of those must have stopped short of submitting paperwork, however. Or maybe their superiors or buddies convinced them it was a bad idea. A post-war General Accounting Office study put the figure at closer to 500.

In a total military force of more than a half-million, the number of objectors—those who refused to report for duty or board a plane when their unit left for the war—only amounted to symbolism.

On the other side, there were 300 volunteers from Afghanistan, veterans of the Mujaheddin "freedom fighters." They joined the coalition's Arab forces.

Monday - February 11, 1991

It's a Free Country. But Peaceniks Suck: "It's Not Like They're Going to Stop the War and Pull Us Back Now"

By Douglas Jehl

WITH U.S. FORCES - All the talk about peace marches back home had begun to get to Army Spec. Steve Wiersgalla.

Then came the morning when the 21-year-old could pick up a phone and talk to his folks in Minnesota. Their message to him, like that reaching thousands of young soldiers here, was nothing if not reassuring. "My father told me the silent majority had begun to speak up and put down the protesters," Wiersgalla said with a grin shortly after the call. "That really made my day."

Here deep in the desert, with American troops, faintly heard echoes of anti-war protests still stir periodic waves of unease. But with a pre-fab structure now erected to house dozens of satellite phones nearby, many have found their apprehensions quickly allayed by long-distance. As soldiers prepare for battle far from home, the war-zone to living-room link appears to have eased what could have been a traumatic adjustment to war.

With some news reports stirring fears of public hostility, the troops appear most inclined to depend on the more-comforting scenes described by parents and spouse.

"In my town, our pictures are hung up in the Wal-Mart, and stuff," says Pfc. Kenneth Eversole, a 22-year-old from Hyden, Ky. Adds. Pvt. Edgar Uriarte, 19, of Garfield, N.J., "My father told me flags are flying in every town, and there are yellow ribbons everyone. That really made me feel good." To be sure, the upbeat assessments from home have not dispelled altogether concerns that American troops might still face a bitter homecoming.

With newspapers near absent and radio reception infrequent, the depth of dissent can be difficult to gauge. There are flashes of anger from soldiers frustrated by news of mass demonstrations that seem to them a disturbing reprise of the anti-war fervor seen in Vietnam. "If they're big enough to protest," fumed Pfc. Douglas Raybourn, 22, of El Paso, TX, "then they're big enough to come over here and get shot at."

At the same time, some of those who recognize that opposition has been limited describe the protests with an increasing sense of betrayal.

"It's like a put-down because you're constantly wondering if someone you know is out there in the street protesting," said Spec. Mick Bostic, 22, of Miami. "We're here. It's too late. It's not like they're going to stop the war and pull us back now."

"A lot of us have started to realize only now what the people in Vietnam were bitching about," added Pfc. Paul Flipse, 22, of Chula Vista, Calif. "They think, 'What if I made it right through the whole thing and came back to see my family, and then there at the airport are people with signs?' It used to seem like the Army was anonymous," Flipse continued. "Now, it's like everybody has suddenly sat up and paid attention."

But in dozens of interviews across an Army armored division, soldiers for the most part exuded faith that the nation is behind them. Many said they took particular comfort in hearing from relatives that demonstrators have rarely criticized troops. "Now that people have talked to home," said Flipse, the young private, "they understand it's anti-war, but pro-soldier."

In a resuscitation of language from a previous war, soldiers put great stock in the "silent majority." They cheer news of counter-marches, rooting for pro-war activists to shout down the peaceniks. And, after nearly four weeks of war, most seem confident that there remains widespread support for what they describe as a straightforward objective. "The main reason I feel that I'm here is to kind of show that knucklehead he can't be doing that stuff," said Sgt. Richard Baird, 25, of Rock City Falls, NY, in a particularly concise summation.

At the same time, there remains a small fraction of those U.S. soldiers deployed here who side with the protestors in contending that the United States is out of its place. "I can't see where this land is worth losing American soldiers over," mused Sgt. Leonard Neuman, 33, of Beaver Pass, Wisconsin, as he scanned a horizon virtually devoid of all life. "It's just not worth all those casualties."

Most often, however, even the most outspoken critics of war here make clear that they remain somewhat mistrustful of those taking the same tack back at home.

"I was born in a war, World War II," said Chief Warrant Officer Jim Daly, a physician's assistant who has spent the last 28 years in the Army. "I had family that went to Korea. I went to Vietnam, and now I'm in Saudi Arabia.

"It doesn't work," the veteran medic said gently, referring to war. "Nobody has to do this." But Daly, who returned from Vietnam in 1967 to San Francisco International Airport and protestors who pelted him and others with spittle and food, said he would now be far less likely to follow orders to turn the other cheek.

"If I come home to that, I'm not going to listen to some colonel," the 48-year-old said fiercely. "I'm going to deck somebody."

The Crowded Skies of Iraq: If You Want To Attack, Get in Line, Take a Number

By Stewart Powell

AN AIRBASE IN CENTRAL SAUDI ARABIA - So many allied bombers and ground-attack planes are crowding the skies over Kuwait and southern Iraq that midair collisions are a growing concern, according to a senior Air Force commander.

Col. Gary A. Voellger, commander of the 552nd Airborne Warning and Control Wing of AWACS aircraft stationed here, said the increasing number of bombing missions in the Kuwait theater of operations is making air traffic control more complicated.

In a related indication of congestion, Air Force Col. Charles M. "PJ" Pettijohn, commander of 4409th Operational Support Wing (Provisional) at the base, said ground-attack planes often have to move off assigned targets with ordnance still aboard to make way for other warplanes to carry out scheduled missions. The two commanders' remarks during interviews at this air base in central Saudi Arabia underscored the shift in the air campaign from targets across Iraq to targets within a Rhode Island-sized area of the Arabian peninsula to prepare for an expected allied ground offensive.

Allied aircraft carried out 650 bombing raids over the area Sunday, with 200 sorties alone directed at the Republican Guards, a 150,000-strong force dispersed across 4,000 square miles of desert. "It's very congested up there," said Voellger, 46, whose unit is based at Tinker Air Force Base, Okla. "There are a lot of airplanes that are getting compressed into a small area."

Voellger said the risk of mid-air collisions was increasing in part because airborne command and control aircraft such as the Boeing 707 AWACS aircraft are

Monday - February 11, 1991

too busy focusing on their combat missions to serve as airborne traffic controllers.

"One of my concerns is the mid-air collision," said Voellger, who flies AWACS missions twice a week to monitor operations and spare other pilots. "The AWACS watches for problems, but we are not air traffic controllers. The number of sorties up there is overwhelming. It's a busy time for all." Added Voellger: "We have to work it real hard. It's just another challenge we have to overcome."

Streams of aircraft coupled with the likelihood of fast-moving ground combat also raises concerns about casualties from friendly fire, Voellger said.

Seven Marines died inside a six-wheeled Light Armored Vehicle when an allied aircraft of unidentified nationality fired a Maverick anti-tank missile during an intense nighttime firefight with Iraqi forces near Al Wafra on the Saudi-Kuwait border on Jan. 29.

An eighth Marine died shortly thereafter in a separate incident when an allied aircraft dropped a cluster bomb near a Marine convoy inside Saudi territory.

With a fast-moving ground campaign, "the tough part will be to cooperate to make sure we're all singing off the same sheet of music so we avoid friendly casualties," Voellger said.

Pettijohn, 46, commander of a U.S. AWACS and aerial tanker facility on a Saudi air base for the past 18 months, said large numbers of ground-attack planes are on such tight schedules that pilots occasionally have to be ordered to clear their target "kill zone" to make way for the next wave of attack aircraft.

Modified C-130 transports loaded with airborne command and control capsules cycle ground-attack aircraft through the target areas on a strict schedule, Pettijohn said. "The skies are so crowded it's like a freeway, a traffic jam, if we didn't do that," he said.

Asked about reports that A-10 Thunderbolt tank-killer aircraft waited as long as 20 minutes over Al Khafji to carry out ground attack missions during the first major land skirmish, Pettijohn said pilots can get "very frustrated."

"Sometimes we have had boys that want to play longer than their time. We have a schedule, an air-tasking order, that says you've got say ten minutes over this kill zone and you're supposed to get out of there," Pettijohn said.

Combat pilots are assigned altitudes, times over target, and other parameters to keep the flow of attacks continuing on schedule and to avoid mid-air accidents.

But pilots often complain they don't have enough time. Explains Pettijohn: "These guys say, 'Wait, I've got ordnance and there's targets down there, you can't do this to me.' So they don't want to leave." But if pilots loiter, air traffic "backs up," Pettijohn said. "It has a cumulative effect. Everything has to flow."

Pettijohn said if pilots "allow the lack of discipline to develop, then it's a tremendous problem for us in managing the air portion of the battle. We have to be kind of hard-nosed about it and say, 'You're out of there. Get out of the way and let the next guy have his turn.'"

Some pilots remain eager to stay over their targets, Pettijohn said. "In spite of the triple-A (air-defense artillery) and everything else, they're there to blow something up and they want a chance to do that," he said. "They hate leaving with ordnance. They really get frosted about this."

Air Force Capt. Ken Boykin, 32, of Wayneboro, Miss., an airborne intelligence officer attached to the 7th Airborne Command and Control Squadron from Keesler Air Force Base, Miss., said crewmen aboard the specially equipped C-130 routinely work to coordinate allied aircraft criss-crossing Kuwaiti targets. "There are a huge number of aircraft squeezing into a limited space," Boykin said. "We just try to act like an air traffic controller wherever we can." Boykin said few ground-attack pilots seemed eager to linger over targets. "No one hangs around over the enemy," Boykin said. "They get in and get out."

Brig. Gen. Richard I. Neal, deputy director of operations for U.S. Central Command and a spokesman for allied headquarters, acknowledged that air traffic over Kuwait and southern Iraq has gotten considerably more congested since air operations began to focus on Kuwait and adjacent Iraqi territory.

"It's just mind-boggling how well orchestrated it is," Neal told the daily briefing Sunday. "It's a busy place up there. It makes LAX (Los Angeles International Airport), Dallas and Atlanta combined look like kids on the block."

Neal hailed the crews of airborne command and control aircraft for orchestrating the flow of warplanes from bases to airborne tankers to target areas and back to bases. "They do a superb job as indicated by the lack of an accident rate over the battlefield," Neal said. "I don't have a concern about it (congestion). It's put into the equation as we're developing the air tasking order, so I'm very comfortable with it."

Gathering Intelligence Any Way You Can: Iraqis Trying "To Show Us Bomb Damage That Isn't There"

By Michael Hedges

WITH THE 1ST INFANTRY DIVISION - Lt. Col. Bill Moore's job is easy to define but hard to execute; take vague and contradictory information and create an accurate picture of what the Iraqis are doing, while deceiving and confusing them.

As head of a battalion of military intelligence, Col. Moore's soldiers will be "scattered left to right, front to rear. Our mission covers a lot of disciplines, a lot of territory." A short list of the battalion's duties includes interrogating Iraqi POWs, long range reconnaissance, providing a radar screen for the U.S. front line, jamming Iraqi radios and setting up dummy posts to fool the enemy.

Right now the unit is spending a lot of time assimilating information from Iraqi defectors. "I'm convinced they are telling us everything we need to know," said Col. Moore, 43, of Brownfield, Tex. "They are giving us a very accurate view of the morale of the Iraqi soldiers, their condition, and also of the psychological impact of the bombing campaign."

In the past two days more than two dozen Iraqis have crossed the border here as the Air Force moves its bombing campaign closer to the front lines. "There is a pattern all along the front, the more bombing the more desertions," he said.

To interrogate the prisoners the battalion has 44 Kuwaiti soldiers, most of whom were recently sent here from the United States. "This is the closest I've been to home in a long time," said Qassem, one of the Kuwaitis. The men prefer to be identified only by first names to protect families in Kuwait.

He said he has heard nothing from his family since late July. But despite the fact that American bombs might endanger his family and are clearly damaging his country, Qassem said he is an ardent supporter of the current campaign. "You can always rebuild the country," he said. "It was nothing as long as the Iraqis are there. They have to be gotten out."

Qassem said he was a college student in Pennsylvania when Iraq invaded Kuwait. He called the Kuwaiti embassy and volunteered for any duty that arose. Several months later he was told to report to Ft. Dix, New Jersey, for a one-week training course and then flown to northern Saudi Arabia. He said he didn't anticipate any problems handling duties as an interpreter here. "It is the same language, different accent," he said. "The principal difference is in the speed and pace of talking," he said.

Asked what reaction he had to dealing with Iraqi soldiers he said, "I wouldn't want to hold what is happening to Kuwait to Iraqi soldiers," he said. "It kind of cuts you up to think this man might have killed your father, or hurt your family, but I'm going to stick to the Geneva Convention."

Col. Moore said he feels protective of the relatively untrained Kuwaitis. "Their safety is an overriding goal. When the area is free, we'll march into their home towns and liberate them together."

The best trained troops in the battalion, at least in terms of combat expertise, are the Long Range Surveillance Detachments, the modern equivalent of the Vietnam-era LUURPS who prowl enemy territory ahead of attacking columns to gather intelligence on the movement of Iraqi forces. "Their mission will be to go in between two groups of Iraqi forces and give us information on where the next force is coming from before we fight them," said Col. Moore.

The LRSD soldiers can be parachuted or landed by helicopter behind the lines. Many of them have Ranger, sniper or other special training. "They are the best infantrymen we can find, the most fit, the most able to stand deprivation," Col. Moore said. The teams are spread along the border in friendly territory now, he said.

Also along the front lines now are several armored personnel carriers equipped with ground surveillance radar which are manned by crews reporting to Col. Moore.

The line of GSR radars are expected to give early warning of any Iraqi movement near the border. Designed in the early 1950s, the radar sometimes has trouble distinguishing between the blips that show up on its screen.

But Col. Moore said, "It is not an exact science, the point is it gives you early warning much farther than any other system. It is old technology but it works. It may give you a false alarm once in awhile, but it does give you effective warning."

The military intelligence battalion has a much more sophisticated system for pinpointing Iraqi forces and intercepting voiced radio transmissions.

Besides gathering information from the enemy, Col. Moore's battalion is charged with trying to confuse and deceive the Iraqis.

"The Iraqis use deception; they have been trained by the Soviets and they were very good at it," he said. "I think the Iraqis are using it now to show us bomb damage that isn't there. When there is an airfield that appears cratered from one end to the other, but planes are taking off, that is an example."

Col. Moore said that by looking at things through a variety of intelligence gathering equipment and technologies, it is possible to sort out Iraqi deception fairly quickly. "Our intelligence gathering is too robust to be fooled, it only takes a short time to figure it out," he said. "We have much of our total intelligence gathering capability focused here. We have systems looking at things"

The hope is that the Iraqis, with less sophisticated systems, can be fooled.

Staff Sergeant Victor Quinones, 24, of Junction city, Kansas, works in the battlefield deception company. "Our main mission is to make the enemy commit themselves to a place where we are not going to attack, or disguise a place we are going to attack."

Without satellite or consistent Air Force intelligence, the Iraqis will be relying much more on information they gather by electronic means than U.S. forces will, officers said. But for times when the Iraqis do send helicopters or jets over the lines to gather information, Sgt. Quinones said his unit has a whole arsenal of canvas and plywood toys.

With careful use of fake bunkers and camouflaged netting, the deception unit can create an entire battalion-sized camp where none exists. But the devices are not used randomly. "You have to study the enemy and know what he has that you can fool. The Iraqis started the war with some fairly sophisticated stuff. He has moved it, hasn't used some of it, but that doesn't mean he won't use it."

Col. Moore said U.S. military intelligence learned much from the Iraqi raid on Khafji. "How capable is his command and control, was he able to move his forces in an integrated way, did he integrate his artillery, those are the kinds of things we were looking at." Col. Moore said it is going to be extremely difficult to use intelligence effectively in the confusion of combat. "There is always that fog of war," he said. "We have a saying that the first report is always wrong, and that has been proven over and over again. The confusion in war is incredible," he said.

"I've tried to describe to my soldiers what the first day of war will be like, the sounds, the obscuration, the noise. . . . That is why we have multiple systems and intelligence analysts in the rear to put it all together."

Tuesday
February 12, 1991

The Gulf War attracted its share of celebrities and VIPs. During the buildup phase of Desert Shield, so many congressional delegations were popping over to the Gulf region for a whiff of desert air and a briefing at Central Command that Gen. Schwarzkopf recalled in his memoirs he had to quietly request a cutback in political sightseeing tours so he and his staff would have time to plan the war.

Most of the visits to the field by well-known entertainers (Bob Hope, Steve Martin) and just plain famous people (Prince Charles, a slew of U.S. politicians, the cast of Good Morning America) were wrapped up before the actual fighting got underway.

But the war was quite capable of creating its own roster of names that would be instantly recognizable—at least for awhile. Gen. Schwarzkopf, son of a New Jersey state police commander whose prominent role as an investigator and security chief in the Lindbergh kidnapping case had made his a household name, was well on his way to military exploits that would match or exceed his father's fame.

Gen. Walt Boomer, the top Marine in the Gulf, quickly became a media favorite, too. He was comfortable with a lot of press, having run the Corps' public affairs branch, and the Marines' long list of legendary battles automatically gives them icon status.

In this chapter, a meeting between the Bear (Gen. Schwarzkopf's nickname) and Gen. Boomer is chronicled. Some might dismiss this type of event as more show than substance. After all, in the modern era, if a military theater commander needs to exchange information or orders with one of his top generals, he can get the job done quickly and efficiently with a vast array of telephones, fax machines, computers, and lieutenants and colonels. But there must also be unspoken messages that need to pass between two large-as-headlines warriors, messages that can only be transmitted in each other's presence.

The British army, being a much smaller force than the American, has a more personalized air. In this chapter, a story about a visit with the Life Guards, a unit with a past thick with legends and famous names, features another name that would claim headlines—but not for gallantry—before the war was over.

Maj. James Hewitt, commanding the Life Guards in the Gulf, may have posted a sterling bit of service in the barren desert. But he became better known for his place in the lovelorn heart of a young mother back in London.

In his plain-spoken memoir, *Love and War*, he reveals that while he was in the Gulf he exchanged love letters constantly with Princess Diana. She signed many with an alias, and some were sent via his mother, to keep their affair secret.

At the same time, however, he told the officer who would take his command if he were to be killed about the correspondence. He had kept some letters, and didn't want them to fall into the wrong hands.

President Bush, with top military deputies Cheney and Powell back at his side in Washington, indicated that he was still not quite ready to order a ground attack. The air war would continue for awhile, he said. Of course he couldn't very well be expected to announce an attack before it was underway.

The daily rate of sorties of allied aircraft rose once again—750 a day in Kuwait alone—thanks to improved weather. In Kuwait, a coordinated attack among Marines, Saudi troops and Navy aircraft bombarded Iraqi troop concentrations causing heavy casualties among the occupation forces. These attacks on enemy ground forces were part of the overall plan to weaken the Iraqi defense before sending in the main force. Iraqi deserters reported that thousands of their comrades had been killed in such attacks.

Between allied air strikes, Iraqi troops in Kuwait set another 50 oil wells on fire, part of a widening streak of destruction aimed at the source of the emirate's wealth. The latest status report on terrorism believed linked to the campaign against Iraq was issued: 100 incidents, all aimed at American or allied interests.

The Bear Visits the Marines: "The Logistical Situation is Absolutely Superb"

By Susan Sachs, Denis Gray and Jeff Franks

NEAR THE SAUDI BORDER - Descending in a cloud of dust from his helicopter the bleak desert headquarters of the 2nd Marine Division, Army General H. Norman Schwarzkopf dismissed the latest diplomatic messages from Baghdad, huddled with top Marine field commanders and declared that the U.S.-led military coalition is ready to fight.

"I haven't heard anything in the last 24 hours to indicate that Saddam Hussein is going to get out of Kuwait," he said as he prepared to fly from the dusty outpost back to Central Command. "All he has to do is get out of Kuwait and this war is over. It's that simple."

Schwarzkopf, who has made few visits to ordinary soldiers and Marines in their desert encampments since the start of the Gulf war, met for nearly three hours with Lt. Gen. Walter F. Boomer, commander of all Marine forces here, and other Marine leaders. He said they discussed general operations, as well as amphibious operations that the Marines may conduct when a ground assault begins.

As speculation grows about the timing of a ground war, the Desert Storm commander said concerns about fighting during the Islamic holy month of Ramadan, which begins March 17, are "overblown."

Muslims, including the Saudis and members of the Arab coalition forces allied with the United States, normally refrain from eating or drinking during the daylight hours of Ramadan. But Schwarzkopf said he believes Muslim forces will fight then and that "dispensations for military operations" could be given by Islamic authorities.

As he has been since the start of the war, Schwarzkopf was upbeat about the readiness of the allied troops. The complex logistics and supply problems of the massive military deployment "are being solved every day," he said. "The logistical situation is absolutely superb. There are no logistical problems out there that will be showstoppers."

Schwarzkopf declined to give a possible date for the start of the assault, in which

Marines arrayed along the Saudi border will play a pivotal role.

The generals arrived in an airborne convoy of Sea Knight and Huey helicopters that circled over the tents and camouflage netting of the 2nd Division command post. Schwarzkopf was preceded by a handful of bodyguards dressed in civilian clothes, city shoes, bright-colored backpacks and M-16 rifles.

At one point, as they scoured the flat empty sands for intruders, Schwarzkopf climbed into a Humvee military truck and drove away to a briefing tent.

"Follow the general!" a security man shouted as the bodyguards broke into a run.

Over the northern horizon of the camp was a haze of black smoke from burning Kuwaiti oilfields. But Schwarzkopf said that the fires would not deter an allied attack.

"They (the Iraqis) talk about the smoke they're going to create, but look over there. It's overblown," he said. "Smoke really isn't that big of a problem. Whatever difficulties it's going to cause are going to be neutral, as much of a problem for them as for us."

"There was a very, very, very good reason for bombing that bridge in Baghdad," he said. He repeated that the bombing raids are targeting military, not civilian, targets.

By its own actions, he said, Iraq has shown its belief in the allied policy of attempting to avoid civilian targets. "They dispersed airplanes into residential areas, they've moved military command centers into schools, they've put guns on top of residential buildings," Schwarzkopf said, because the Iraqis don't want them bombed.

So far, he said, the allied forces haven't targeted those military centers in civilian areas, although he said they would be permitted to do so under the Geneva Conventions on warfare.

Earlier Schwarzkopf and his chief of staff, Maj. Gen. Robert Johnston, met with Boomer, 2nd Division commander Maj. Gen. William Keys, 2nd Division service support group commander Brig. Gen. Charles Krulak, 1st Marine Division commander Maj. Gen. James M. Myatt, and 1st Division service support commander Maj. Gen. James A. Brabham Jr. Before climbing into his helicopter to leave, Schwarzkopf stopped for a few minutes to shake hands and chat with a Marine standing stiffly nearby.

Then he ascended in another cloud of dust.

Maj. James Hewitt—Future Famous Name in Uniform; The Talk Was of Horne, Cost of a Haircut at Harrod's

By Richard Kay

WITH 4TH ARMOURED BRIGADE, Northern Saudi Arabia - For a moment it seemed it had to be a mirage.

Shimmering in and out of view sat a group of young officers, not on the ground but at tables and chairs, a meal spread before them. After 30 days of desert life behind you, where battle readiness must take precedence over more civilized eating habits, the unusual easily assumes that of a vision.

But when the Life Guards invite you to lunch you should be prepared for the unexpected. Somehow they had got hold of trestle tables, and we dined on a spaghetti bolognaise laced with garlic, accompanied by alcohol-free beer and conversation more reminiscent of the Cavalry Club than the Saudi desert on the edge of war.

And the only shimmering was that of A Squadron's claret-and-blue ensign which barely floated in the breathless air.

The talk was of home, of the cost of a haircut at Harrods and of friends with nicknames like Beetle, Gungy, and Dickie, who to everyone's irritation had been boasting of frontline exploits from the comfort of armchairs way back in Jubail.

You can't get much sharper than A Squadron's Challenger tanks without running into Iraqi ditches. But the only fidgeting was with the Zippo lighters that lit a ceaseless stream of cigarettes and when someone said they were three days short of a campaign medal—30 days of hostilities is the accepted norm—it simply produced a groan.

For it has almost become boring having to ask our boys about the signal for the ground forces to advance to contact.

Maj. James Hewitt, the squadron's laconic commander with the profile of a Hollywood matinee idol, was clear and direct. "They are not over-worried. Of course they do want to get the job done, but they are prepared to wait till the balance swings decisively in their favor." Flashback a few days, and the contrast could not have been greater. On a trip to a U.S. servicemen's PX, I had bumped into an American correspondent, a familiar face from pre-war days. Gripping me by the elbow, he took me to one side and asked: "Aren't all the guys fed up with the waiting, isn't it getting on their nerves?" The answer is both yes and no. A frustration at the lack of action weighted by the knowledge that every hour of every day reduces the odds of the ground battle.

There was a period when we began to hold out hope that the Iraqis could be persuaded to accept the inevitable and withdraw from Kuwait without the "mother of battles." As one intelligence officer told me: "We have given Saddam a window of opportunity. He could easily pull back now and say 'I have won, they did not dare take a step into Kuwait.' And as long as the air campaign goes on, that opportunity still exists."

In a war of this sort, with strong political overtones, the commanding officers have little chance of proving themselves great warriors like Montgomery or MacArthur. Their task is to achieve victory at the lowest possible cost. As safely as anything can be called safe in war. Which means the precision air raids aimed at the armour of the Republican Guard and their supply routes will go on.

Now there is a growing feeling among the Desert Rats that the air raids may soon reach some kind of peak. That while they can continue to wreak a clinical havoc on Iraq's machinery of war, the enemy themselves may become inured to what we can throw at them.

As the Life Guards swarmed over three tanks for a photograph that will go into the regimental scrapbook, it seemed a tragedy that any more brave men would need to die to prove that Saddam the despot is beaten. With their sleeves rolled up to the elbow, their young faces exuded confidence—the squadron's average age is 23.

The regiment is brimful with its tradition of valor. Battle honors won in all corners of the old empire. For some, like Lt. Piers German, there is a personal badge of courage to carry. For his middle name Gonville was given to him in memory of his great, great uncle whose heroism a century ago earned him a Victoria Cross. Lt. Gonville Bromhead won Britain's highest award for valor at Rorke's Drift, the epic battle of the Zulu wars. Heroism later brought alive by the actor Michael Caine in the film Zulu.

At 21, Lt. German, who followed his godfather into the Life Guards, hopes to live up to the family name. He has renamed his Challenger Bromhead and while he hopes the famous name will bring him luck, the memory is proving both an inspiration and a responsibility.

Wednesday
February 13, 1991

War on the front lines is mainly a young soldier's game and a story in this chapter deals with some of the youngest in the Gulf—17-year-old recruits from Scotland who wore their youth with bravado. But the Iraqis were not to be outdone. Baghdad, suffering troop losses daily from death and desertion caused by allied bombing, announced a lowering of the draft age for their young men—to 17.

Among the allied ground troops, the degree of harshness in living conditions varied from unit to unit, depending on a soldier's job description (in military speak, MOS—military occupational specialty), physical location in the desert, order of battle, availability of supplies and the creativity of commanders and supply sergeants.

Barbed wire and other security measures were constants. But as a story in this chapter reveals, there were amenities and options available to some units that were some distance from the front lines.

In the air war, continuing good weather cleared the way for another 2,800 allied sorties over Kuwait and Iraq. One U.S. F-117 Stealth fighter struck a target the allies would later regret including on their daily target list—an underground bunker being used as a civilian air-raid shelter. The two bombs that struck the bunker killed hundreds of people—men, women and children.

Allied commanders stressed that their new electronically-guided munitions could attack with precision even in densely populated urban areas. But in the case of the Feb. 13 bombing of the Al Firdos bunker, technical precision only made the situation worse. The bombs hit a wrong target with great accuracy.

Air Force Gen. Charles Horner and others explained later that the bunker was one of several locations identified before the war as part of the Iraqi leadership's command and control network—a legitimate target, in the allied design. However, it was not one of the prime, high-priority locations that were tagged to be struck in the first days of the bombing, but was considered a backup target location, a facility that could or would be used as a command post once primary facilities had been destroyed.

At first, some allied officials thought the scenes of civilian death and injuries at Al Firdos might be a ploy, that the carnage shown on international television was somehow rigged. But it was soon evident the scenes were real.

The bunker was in fact being used as an air-raid shelter. Allied intelligence was evidently not current enough to indicate the bunker's true role, which would have removed it from the target list. It was a prime example of the problem of scant intelligence about actual conditions on the ground in Iraq. But there wasn't much that the allies could do to correct the problem, given the state of play in the war.

White House press secretary Marlin Fitzwater suggested the Iraqis were deliberately placing civilians at military sites, but the bombing caused a storm of international controversy and lent support to opponents of the war. Many critics said it proved the "precision-guided" bombs and missiles could hit their mark, but still spread destruction and death in a wide radius that endangered innocent lives.

After the war, Greenpeace International published an unofficial list of incidents of accidental "collateral damage" to civilian areas that caused dozens of deaths. In some instances, civilian casualties were people who worked (perhaps under military coercion) at such dual-use facilities as telephone exchanges and electrical plants; others lived in residential areas very close to legitimate military targets.

The Al Firdos bombing led the allies to severely reduce targets in and around Baghdad. Gen. Horner said later that didn't greatly affect the bombing campaign since most major targets in Baghdad had been destroyed by then anyway.

Amenities of Civilization: Band Music, a Bank of Telephones for Calling Home, Mascots, and Hot Meals

By John Mecklin

NORTHERN SAUDI ARABIA - Life is becoming gradually less primitive for the men and women in the rear of the Army's 3rd Armored Division.

As they wait for a ground offensive to begin, they have found small ways to make life in the middle of the desert less stark.

That is not to say conditions are civilized. Forward elements still live what might be called a rough camp life. Even in the rear, soldiers live in tent camps enclosed by barbed wire, with nothing but sand and rocks stretching to the next camp.

One might create a reasonable mental image of life in the rear by recalling the camp in the television show M.A.S.H., subtracting all alcohol and adding huge doses of sand and desolation. Still, some distance behind the front lines, there are amenities.

This division has its own band, a 41-piece affair called the Spearhead Band to coincide with the division's own nickname, conferred because the unit often led allied forces driving across Europe toward the end of World War II.

The bandleader, Chief Warrant Officer Paul Clark, said his ensemble is quite popular with the troops, and for good reason. "We are the only (live) entertainment they have out here, except for the camels, I guess," Clark said.

The Spearhead band easily outdistances camels in entertainment value because it actually is three bands in one. There is a show band, a country and western group (known as Spearhead Country), and, Clark said, a rock combo.

Clark, 45, who does not claim a particular U.S. city as home, said the rock group plays "the tunes of today" but could not name any of them Monday morning, acknowledging rock is not among his favorite musical genres.

Day to day, the band travels to the various camps spread across the desert, often playing near mess tents or other natural groupings of soldiers, Clark said. Although there is a surreal aspect to the band's desert circuit, its performances are, according to many observers, genuinely enjoyed by the troops.

The band also provides music for chapel services, playing at five prayer sessions on Sunday alone. Key in those performances are brass and woodwind quintets, Clark said.

Wednesday - February 13, 1991

Although the desert here near the northern Saudi border is stunningly dark at night, troops hardly consider themselves confined to their own camps after sunset.

A phone bank providing service to the U.S. and Germany seems a particular draw for those prone to cross-desert driving in pitch black during the middle of a war. During one recent night ride, vehicles of all sorts could be seen jolting across the desert hardpan, on and off such roads as exist.

Night travelers are expected to use only "blackout" lights, which shine dimly perhaps ten feet in front of a driver. Some drivers navigate by way of night vision goggles, binocular-like instruments which give a sharp, green-tinted view of the night desert. Even with such aids, however, concertina, a coiled form of razor wire encircling many outposts, is a constant night danger. Once entangled under a car or truck, the wire tends to wrap around axles, noticeably impeding further travel.

Despite concertina and rutted, rocky, rolling terrain, vehicles stream through the night toward many destinations. But the phone banks draw them like light attracts moths. Outside the phone tents, the trucks and Humvees, those squat successors to the Army jeep, park in rows across the sand, occupants ready to make the call home that might be their last before ground combat starts. For now, the phones are open 24 hours a day.

Advances in technology also have provided this division and other U.S. forces with secure cellular telephone capability. The cellular telephones are part of the Mobile Subscriber Equipment (MSE) network, which can link camps within the division and, by connecting to other networks, throughout Saudi Arabia.

The cellular element of the system is expected to be a primary communications link during a ground offensive, providing instant information from the front lines to commanders. This system will be first use of cellular technology on the battlefield, said Capt. Robert Prudhomme, an operations officer for a signal battalion attached to the 3rd Armored Div.

Prudhomme, a 28-year-old from Denver, Colorado, said the MSE system also gives officers communication features usually associated with the home front. Conference calls, call forwarding, and even facsimile transmission can be accomplished from fixed and mobile battlefield phones, Prudhomme said.

Generals and colonels also have the ability to dial direct to the U.S. from their vehicles or command stations, Prudhomme said. Lower-ranking officers also can call the U.S., but must go through an operator first, he said.

Like many units, the rear area of this division has gained a mascot, a white puppy of indeterminate lineage with brown and charcoal head markings.

It is named, oddly enough, Spearhead, and is female. One female soldier seems to have become the dog's main caretaker, feeding it Army-issue milk in the morning and, at night, meat from an MRE, the much-maligned, ready-to-eat meal provided to servicemen.

Although the dog seems cute enough, its friends privately complain that officers have threatened to shoot it, on grounds it is a health hazard. The dog was both untrained in military latrine hygiene and unexamined by a veterinarian early this week.

As yet, however, there have been no confirmed attempts on Spearhead's short life, and there are plans to have the dog, acquired from Bedouins in the area, checked by a vet. There are still questions, however, about disposition of the noisy puppy when troops move forward.

There are other comforts being added to division-rear while the offensive is on hold. A small kitchen trailer provides some hot meals, giving respite from the dreaded MREs. Movies (actually, videotaped films) are shown at night. The showers have been relocated for convenience, although water for them remains an intermittent luxury. Still, a recent arrival at the tent city in the desert known as D-rear received the greeting: "Welcome to Hell."

Neat Iraqi Defector Screams "Saddam!" Before Respectfully Removing His Shoes

By Joseph Albright

WITH U.S. FORCES NEAR THE SAUDI BORDER - American Army artillery troops rushed out of their sleeping bags to maximum alert early Wednesday after an Iraqi defector crossed outer perimeter lines and appeared a few yards from a battalion headquarters screaming, "Saddam! Saddam!"

Spec. Leonard C. Holifield, 31, of Diamond Bar, Calif., said: "We cut all the lights in the Tactical Operations Center. I took a set of night-vision goggles and peeked outside. He was five feet from the entrance of the TAC. He was still screaming a lot in Arabic.

"I looked to see if I could see anybody else. When I couldn't see anybody, I rushed out and subdued him using a judo hold. I threw him to the ground. He tried to resist. I turned him on his stomach. I had him in a wrist and neck lock. He was in a good position to break his neck or his wrist. I didn't want to use deadly force but I very well could have," he said. Officers said the Iraqi, who said his name was Ali, had walked two days before he blundered onto the frontline American position.

The young, thin air defense soldier was fed an apple, which he devoured, and a half-quart of water. The prisoner later spoke by tactical phone with an American interpreter, who reported back to the unit that the Iraqi said he was terrified the Americans were going to kill him. The Iraqi was held under guard in a tent, then sent to the rear.

Soldiers remarked that the Iraqi evidently had a habit of neatness, in that he insisted on taking off his boots before entering the American tent.

The first alert to the battalion headquarters was called in moments before he started shouting by an American soldier at a perimeter guardpost. Capt. Dean Bennett, 34, of Windom, Minn., one of the ranking officers on the scene, said a full alert was called because duty officers were concerned that the Iraqis were trying to pull a surprise attack under the cover of a fake surrender like that which was apparently used in the battle of Khafji.

Around 2 a.m., while troops were still scouring their perimeter, frontline soldiers had a ringside seat to witness a U.S. Air Force bombing raid roughly 10 miles north of their position. Sgt. Heath Blackmon, 23, of Lancaster, S.C., said: The sky was illuminated by flares. These flashes were followed by bombs falling from planes. They were big explosions, the ground shook."

Asked what he thought was happening, he said: "I thought our infantry was about to get run over: I thought we would get some artillery fire. Everyone grabbed M-16s and thought this was it. That's the most serious alert we've ever had."

Pfc. Joker Williams, 19, of Los Angeles, said: "I was not really scared. We jumped down deep in the foxholes because we thought the enemy was coming."

Pfc. Daryl Debose, 25, of Miami, Fla., said he saw with night-vision goggles seven planes gathering in a convoy and then heading north near his position before the explosion. He said he saw at least five illuminated objects falling from the direction of the plane "like raindrops."

As they hit the ground, he could see the explosive impacts. "It went on for a good 10 to 15 minutes," he said. Asked what he thought, he said, "It is just the Air Force bombing again. It is just the regular thing they are doing."

The pool reporter and photographer, with an escort officer, arrived on a prescheduled troop visit six hours later. The poolers witnessed one series of about four daylight explosions on the horizon, about 25 kilometers away. Army intelligence staff officer, 1st Lt. Jeffrey L. Gaylord, said the explosions appeared to be air strikes and came from the direction where the Iraqis have observation posts near the front lines.

"They (the Air Force) are just bombing the hell out of it," said Maj. Mark Rambix, 35, of Shelburne, Ind., the operations officers of the artillery unit. Under military coverage rules, the name of the artillery unit cannot be identified.

Scots Sent Youngest Recruits to the Gulf War Not Yet Old Enough for Duty in Northern Ireland

By Gordon Airs

WITH 1ST BRITISH ARMOURED DIVISION, Northern Saudi Arabia - The Young Lions of Scotland paced the desert sand yesterday and looked somewhat nervously towards the Iraqi front lines.

Because this mini-magnificent seven are the youngest soldiers in this entire massive British division. All are only aged 17—just fresh out of recruit training camps. All are in the same B Company of the Royal Scots.

And all, amazingly enough, are old enough to fight and perhaps die in this desert war—yet too young, by a year, to serve in Northern Ireland.

So the baffling logic of Ministry of Defence regulations leave these young, hardly-shaven, fresh-faced youngsters right up in the cutting edge of the front line.

To look at them, it's difficult to believe they will be thrown in against battle-hardened Iraqi troops in formidable defences. Yet tiny Tam Rennie, of Dalkeith, Midlothian, just eight months in this man's army, will jump into enemy trenches. And as the military lingo blandly puts it, he will "post" grenades. That means he'll be face to face with highly-trained, adult killers—and he'll be throwing grenades at them.

Vincent Scott, from Edinburgh, the youngest in the British Gulf forces, will have to throw himself into the sand near Iraqi positions and take on Soviet-built tanks single-handed. With an anti-tank weapon nearly as big as he is.

Stephen Mearns, from Leith, Edinburgh, was just two weeks out of the Penicuik infantry training depot in Midlothian before being sent out here. He will fire rifle-grenades in support fire, along with Gordon Quate, from South Queensferry. And aiming lethal machine-gun fire will be Mark Foley, from Edinburgh, Darren Ferguson, from Livingston, West Lothian, and Greg Kinnison, from Alyth, near Dundee.

Mark may be young—but he will celebrate his first wedding anniversary next month, on March 24. His wife, Louise, 18, at present unemployed, lives with his mother. Said Mark: "From her letters, I have had she can't wait for me to get back home. But that's what we are trained for and I have got to do it."

How do the Young Lions get on with their elder comrades in arms? Said Tam Rennie: "We just get treated the same as everyone else. That's the best part about it. The rest of the guys are brilliant. If you need any help they give you it. If it comes to a battle we will just be the same as everyone else... scared."

"But I am confident with the guys we are working with. I'm part of an assault and fire team, 'posting' grenades. I don't know how I'll feel when I'm face to face with the enemy. We'll just have to wait and see..."

Said their company commander, Major Normal Soutar, from Kirriemuir: "These lads grow up very quickly and they have fitted in just fine. In the heat of the battle, some of these youngsters may end up doing the jobs of NCOs."

Meanwhile, the tallest and the smallest soldiers in the British Gulf forces sized each other up yesterday.

The Little and Large double act took centre stage in the Royal Scots front line.

On your left—measuring up to a towering six foot eight inches is Grenadier Guardsman Duane Ashworth, 22, from the "Scots Town" of Corby, Northawts. On your right—stretching to a full 62 inches is Private James Gourdie, 17, of the Royal Scots. And it was only an eye-to-eye confrontation when he sat on the shoulders of older brother Gordon, 21. Just to keep it in the family, their other brother Alex, 19, is over here as well. All three are in B Company of the Royal Scots and their parents live in Tweedbank near Galashiels. But having three brothers facing a land war has really worried their mum, Helen, and dad, Gordon, a post office worker who also served 10 years with the same regiment.

James is five foot two inches, Alex five foot four inches, and Gordon five foot three inches. All are privates. Said Gordon: "Our folks are not too happy about this. And I admit it's a bit worrying having my two young brothers here for a war. We more or less look after each other. But when it comes to a land battle, my first priority will be to keep a look out for them and help them if necessary."

Just days before they left, there was a double engagement. Gordon got engaged to knitwear factor worker Rosemary Capelle, 20, in Galashiels, and James did the same with hairdresser Linda McMurdo, 18, of Langlea near Gala, after a whirlwind six-month romance.

The wedding dates? "Sometime" after they get home from war.

Thursday
February 14, 1991

As Iraqi rescuers pulled nearly 300 bodies from the ruins of the Al Firdos bunker/shelter, the tragedy brought a new sensitivity to the issue of civilian deaths in the Gulf War.

In response, a special, closed-door meeting of the UN Security Council was called to discuss the Persian Gulf crisis. The U.S. might play the lead role in practical terms, but the war was officially the result of a declaration by the United Nations. So this was a council of war, so to speak, but one held at some distance from the rooms where the real decisions were made on tactics.

The World Health Organization and UNICEF announced they were sending $600 million in aid to assist Iraqi mothers and children hurt in the air war. This was the start of a flood of international aid and concern directed toward Baghdad.

In the decade after the war, civilian deaths in Iraq (especially of children) would be debated in many forums. An international movement would develop around the belief that a great many postwar deaths were due to the actions of Saddam Hussein's enemies (the massive bombing, UN trade sanctions, restricted oil sales).

Saddam's detractors would argue his decisions and methods (repression, military interventions, grandiose palace projects, costly programs for chemical, biological and even nuclear war) were to blame.

For the pilots, the bombing environment did change after the bombing of the Al Firdos bunker. A story in this chapter describes the RAF's decision to scrap two missions rather than risk adding to the list of civilian dead in Iraq.

U.S. Defense Secretary Cheney drew attention to another allied mission not completed out of concern for one of civilization's oldest treasures. Iraq had parked two of its MiG fighters next to a world archeological treasure, the ziggurat (temple) at Ur, just south of the Euphrates River. The ziggurat dated back nearly four millennia, to 2100 B.C.

Those MiGs and the ziggurat were too close for comfort, air war commanders concluded. Whether the aircraft simply ran out of fuel there, or the Iraqis intended to protect the MiGs - or the temple - or the lot - by parking the warplanes on that spot wasn't known. Again, the Iraqi regime was silent. But it worked.

There wasn't the outrage generated by "human shields" - hostages placed near critical installations in Iraq. But apparently neither the ziggurat or MiGs were hit.

The running total of allied sorties flown continued to mount, reaching 67,000 since the war began. And on the desert floor, the allied ground forces unveiled another high-powered weapon - the MLRS, or Multiple Launch Rocket System. A story in this chapter compares the affect on the desert sky to the gods switching on arc lights.

The new super-charged artillery launchers could deal a devastating blow, but not without blatantly giving away their location. That didn't faze the troops operating the big guns.

Recent defectors from the Iraqi side reported that communications from frontline trenches back to any sort of Iraqi command post were in very poor shape, and that messages could take several days to reach Baghdad.

And any Iraqi aircraft that dared emerge from hiding with an idea of mounting a counter-attack were quickly spotted by one of the AWACs flights that operated around the clock, which would then send in allied fighter planes to deal with it.

At the end of the day, there simply weren't enough ancient ziggurats in Iraq to protect all of Saddam's military hardware from destruction.

Debut of Multiple Launch Rocket Systems "Biggest Goddam Roman Candle I've Ever Seen"

By Colin Nickerson

NORTHERN SAUDI ARABIA - The night fell fast after the sun went down on the wide floor of the desert wadi.

Yet even before the sun's rays finally dissipated, and after the first 3, 4 stars had appeared, the moonlit sky was suddenly lit up. It was as though the gods had switched on the arc lights. With a gigantic woosh, rockets flew off at twice the speed of sound on their way north. It was a moment of military history: the first time in wartime that American forces unleashed one of their most lethal but untested weapons of destruction during a mass artillery raid from northern Saudi Arabia.

And it was as spectacular a baptism of fire for the MLRS or Multiple Launch Rocket System as a July 4th fireworks display. The after-burn of the rockets suddenly and eerily turned the whole desert floor white as if illuminated. Smoke trails crisscrossed the sky. "That was the biggest Goddam roman candle I've ever seen," one platoon leader said.

It was a first in other ways. It was also the first major engagement of the war for the 1st Cavalry Division out of Fort Hood, Tex., whether or not this was what the military call harassment or interdiction fire, or the prelude to a major ground offensive.

It was part of a composite plan. Elsewhere the division's engineers breached the berm sand ramparts that divide Saudi Arabia and Iraq (runs along the border).

Was this to clear lanes through an obstacle for the eventual ground assault? Or was it a feint, to draw Iraqi forces down to meet the challenge, when the real attack is intended for elsewhere? Or was it, in this complex game of bluff and double bluff, intended to appear a feint, when in fact, after all it is the real thing? Before and after the operation, yellow parachute flares floated down in the distance, as the Iraqis tried to determine what was going on. That they had to use flares showed up their lack of night-vision capability. There were great flashes on the horizon as coalition bombs hit.

For the artillery operation, the 1st Cavalry deployed their MLRS, also in service with the British Army, as close as possible to the border. It is a powerful weapon of mass destruction. Each tracked vehicle can fire 12 rockets up to 30 km. Each rocket is 298 mm. in diameter and about 13 feet long. It contains 644 bomblets or submunitions.

The exact targets of yesterday (Wednesday) evening's attack were classified. Typically, MLRS goes for saturation coverage of an area. Its bomblets are particularly aimed at artillery pieces, command posts, radar stations and lightly armoured vehicles. Manufacturers assert that a single launcher can take out a grid square.

They say that one salvo of all twelve rockets has the punch of three volleys from each of the 24 155mm howitzers of an entire battalion of conventional artillery.

1st Cavalry has only one battery of MLRS launchers - Alpha battery of the 21st Field Artillery Regiment. But the Cav can also call up MLRS from other batteries with the Corps to which the division is attached, although the exact numbers deployed in the operation cannot be revealed. Alpha battery's commander, Capt. Hampton Waite - it sounds like his address in Emporia, Virginia, but is in fact his name - was keen that whatever else he brought his men safely home.

And to him, too, it was the first time he had seen his battery fire off his rockets, so expensive are they. The MLRS crews rely on highly sophisticated navigational aids to establish their exact position for firing from. They are given their target coordinates. They fire and get out quickly, out of range of enemy counter-fire.

The Iraqi army also has rocket launchers, including the Brazilian-made Astros II, with a range of 60 km, twice that of the MLRS. But the Americans are confident that the Iraqis do not have the capability to observe targets needed for accurate counterfire. The Americans, however, have ground radar to detect enemy artillery, to trace where it was fired from, and to direct down artillery or Air Force fire.

Thirty-five minutes after the first salvo, another unit of MLRS opened fire, lighting up the sky. Were they answering Iraqi counter-fire or performing a secondary mission?

The men of Alpha battery were happy to have drawn blood at last. They had had a long wait. Most have been in-country since October, one of the longest stints of U.S. forces here.

The refrain was the same as it has been these past months. "I just want to kick some butt and go home."

Capt. Pam Keeton, a lapsed Catholic media escort officer, asked what day it was. When told it was Ash Wednesday, she placed her fingers, black from the charcoal lining of her freshly unpacked chemical warfare suit, on her forehead and made a cross under the brim of her Kevlar helmet. Now the commanders are assessing how effective yet another of these untested high-tech weapons systems was, how it can be improved, and how best it can be deployed in the future.

Tornados Scrap Missions Over Cities to Avoid Civilians: "Professionalism Says Don't Throw Bombs Around"

By Ramsay Smith

WITH THE ROYAL AIR FORCE, Saudi Arabia - An RAF bombing raid on Iraq was scrapped when Tornado crews told allied commanders that the mission threatened civilian lives, it was revealed yesterday.

And another sortie was abandoned only five seconds before the bombs were due to be dropped because airmen feared that residents living near the target were at risk.

Following the outcry over the bombing of the Baghdad bunker, Tornado crews spoke of their frustration when they have to turn back from targets. "When you put your body over enemy territory for more than an hour, you want to make it worth your while," said pilot Simon "Shifty" Young, 31. But he added: "Your professionalism says that you don't throw your bombs around. If one of our stray bombs hit a primary school or an old people's home, we would feel absolutely terrible because that is not what we would have gone out to do."

"It's a thin line now when there is a sly and callous man who is putting his military assets among civilians. That is why we need to use precision weapons."

"Shifty" was on both the missions scrubbed because of the potential danger to civilians. The first target was a fuel dump due to be hit (by) a barrage of 1000-lb. "dumb" bombs. But Wing Commander Jerry Witts, commander of 31 Squadron based in Eastern Saudi Arabia, said that questions were raised over the target because it was so near a suburban area.

"We looked at it very carefully," said the wing commander. "It was before we had the laser-guided capability and the target was on the outskirts of town. We knew we could hit it but we could not guarantee that one of us would not miss it. If it had been in the middle of the desert, that would have been all right but this was on the outskirts of a town."

When Witts alerted commanders the target was changed and later taken out by a laser-guided bomb. The wing commander also led a mission to hit a bridge in the middle of an Iraqi town. With only five seconds to go before "bombs away" the crew of the Buccaneer warplane due to pinpoint the target with a laser called the Tornado formation and voiced their fears.

Because of a thin layer of cloud, the Buccaneer crew recommended the Tornados should not drop their load. "There was a large town on one side of the bridge and a suburban area on the other," explained the wing commander. "We were certain that we had target on radar but the Buccaneer wasn't happy and we have to guarantee ourselves that we will get the job done properly before we release the bombs.

"It was very frustrating flying around and being shot at, but it is a matter of discipline and professionalism. It is as simple as that.

"Each task is a contract between the man who targets it and the guy who is going to bomb it. He will not accept the contract if there is a professional reason for not doing so."

Witts, 40, applauded the skill of the air crew involved in the controversial Baghdad bunker raid. He said: "They did not know who was in there. That should not be their concern. Obviously, it would both people afterwards but they should be proud of their ability and accuracy. We have a great deal of faith in our intelligence and if they tell me to bomb a factory in the middle of the desert because it is making chemical weapons, I will do it.

"If that turns out to be a baby milk factory then, I'm sorry, but I can't help that."

Friday
February 15, 1991

After weeks of bluster and boasting, while his air force and navy fled to Iran and his soldiers deserted or hunkered down under a constant barrage of bombs, Saddam Hussein finally announced he was ready to withdraw his occupying army from Kuwait.

This appeared to be what the world had waited for. The devil had dropped his guard. Anticipating a change in the long standoff, the Soviets hailed the breakthrough. The UN Secretary General said the Iraqi statement should be carefully studied.

Not so fast, Mr. Hussein, the allies said. Reports of Iraqi "security forces" executing Kuwaitis were on the increase. And Saddam Hussein had attached so many conditions to his offer that President Bush termed it a "cruel hoax."

So the march toward a ground war continued, leaving a deep impression that nothing would stop it now. In this chapter, the Marines pushed closer to the frontier with Kuwait. Some U.S. and other allied forces had already breached the Kuwaiti and Iraqi frontiers, but officially the coalition was still waiting for the word to attack.

And among the more than 500,000 ground troops there was certainly no slacking in preparation. This was as real as the real thing gets. Writer John Sack listened as an American colonel preparing to take his men into battle told them—as much as he could reduce it to mere words—what it was going to sound, feel, and taste like when they were thrown into combat for the first time.

Fear, said the colonel, will taste metallic, like number ten nails in their mouths.

In the Persian Gulf, the Navy brought another aircraft carrier on station. USS America was now the fourth carrier under sail in the task force, joining the Midway, the Ranger, and the Theodore Roosevelt.

In the air over Iraq, the U.S. lost its first electronic jamming and radar-detection aircraft of the war, an F-111A Raven, with two crewmen now missing.

And the allies added two new items to the menu of punishment to be delivered by air: a 10,000-pound conventional bomb, the BLU-82, known informally as the "Daisy-Cutter," and a fuel-air bomb, a type of munition that releases a flammable vapor when it explodes over a target, spreading flame and causing downward air pressure over a large area with a force great enough to crush buildings and cause secondary explosions at ground level.

Just to hear such a device explode, and feel the earth shake miles away when it hits, was a life-changing moment. It was another one of those experiences that soldiers who have been in war would try to describe, in terms of the sound it makes, the tremors it generates, the emotions it puts in the pit of the stomach. When one of those babies goes off, tongues by the thousands across the desert stop and lie soundless in the mouth, dry and sharp with a metallic taste.

It tastes lot like number ten nails.

Letter From a Soldier's Sister—But Not Just Any Soldier

By Gary Regenstreif

NORTHERN SAUDI ARABIA - U.S. Army Pvt. Michael Hoey was feeling the blues one day this week because he had received no mail from home, so he thought he would get a morale boost from a letter addressed to "Any Soldier in Saudi Arabia."

What he got was an unlikely surprise.

Tens of thousands of such letters a day flood into the Kingdom from school children, veterans, organizations of all kinds, concerned mothers, and others offering emotional support for the U.S.-led effort to drive Iraqi soldiers from Kuwait.

"I came up to get the mail for people on my shift," explained Hoey, 24, of Richmond, Indiana. "I didn't get any. Having no mail is a drag.

"I thought it would be nice to have some 'Any Soldier' mail, which is usually pretty uplifting because someone is reaching out and supporting us."

He picked one at random that had no return address. "I opened it and she said, 'My name is Jennifer Hoey.' That's my sister!" Hoey yelled. "I thought, 'Wow, this is incredible.'"

Indeed, the odds of Hoey selecting at random a letter from his 16-year-old sister in Phoenix, Arizona, is boggling. "You can't put statistics on that," said Hoey's first sergeant, Oscar Polk, 39, of Florence, Alabama. "It won't happen again in theatre."

"She said she was proud of what we were doing here and praying for us," added Hoey. "I was glad someone in my family is willing to bring somebody some happiness and put a smile on their face."

"Poor White Middle Class, Poor Black Kids, Hispanics from the Barrio . . . That's Who I Want to Go to War With"

By John Sack

From John Sack, Esquire Magazine, with a company of the First Infantry Division. NO HARD NEWS. This is a transcript of parts of an extemporaneous talk by Lt. Col. Gregory Fontenot of Eunice, Louisiana, a battalion commander in the First Infantry Division.

About 1 p.m., Tuesday, February 12, Fontenot, in desert camouflage, helmet, web gear, canteens, gas mask on his left hip, cigarette in his left hand, was standing against a Bradley on which he'd chalked a map of Jordan, Iraq, Kuwait and Saudi Arabia. In front of him, sitting, kneeling, and standing, were about 150 infantrymen, engineers and tankers and, behind them, the sun in Fontenot's face.

"Now the B-52s are doing some ugly shit. A B-52 carries 45 750-pound bombs. So like a whole bunch of Goddam bombs are falling upon them, the Iraqis, every day. And then what you're doing is, the next day they'll drop leaflets. And the leaflets say, 'Give up, asshole, 'cause we're coming tomorrow with bombs.'

"And it's starting to work, apparently. Apparently Rashid and Abdul find it demoralizing to spend 24 hours a day in bunkers, several hours of which is occupied with dodging bombs dropped by B-52s. So that seems to be going well.

Friday - February 15, 1991

"Now, the Air Force would have us believe they have destroyed 780 tanks. And every tank that isn't out there fighting us is a tank that can't hurt us.

"More important than killing tanks, though, because killing tanks is a job that we can do pretty handily, is killing artillery. And guys, we want them to kill every gun tube they can kill because the Iraqis have a lot of artillery.

"And they have killed somewhere around 400. But the point is, and the point you need to come away with is, that the bombing campaign is having a decidedly adverse effect on life for Rashid and Abdul.

"They're not getting three hots and a cot. They seem to be getting one meal a day, and it's even worse than MREs." Laughter.

"So these guys are eating rice and water once a day, and I believe the Iraqis don't mind rice, but they're getting a very small quantity of rice and it's making them crazy.

"They're coming across in our sector right now at the rate of about 10 or 15 a day. Now, you multiply that by all the sectors across the area, it turns out 75 or a hundred of them are starting to come across every day.

"Saying, 'Hey, I'm really unhappy about this shit, I'd like to give myself up to the Allied forces.' They have even given themselves up to reporters.

"Think of that. Rashid and Abdul say, 'Where can we turn ourselves in?'

"Okay, so that's what's going on in the air campaign. All right, at some juncture the air campaign obviously needs to be moved to the tactical campaign. . . .

"I want to talk about fear. You will be afraid. If you're not afraid, there's something wrong with you. Everybody went on 8913 (desert training at the National Training Center at Fort Irwin, California) put your hand up. Anyone went there last May 16? Okay.

"Now, when you go to live fire, are you kind of nervous about that? Cause artillery's falling around you? Running into bangalore torpedoes for real?

"CEV drives up, shoots 165 pounds of plastic explosives? And tankers are firing? In back of task force, rounds are passing up through the task force?

"The drone flies over, and every sonofabitch with a pistol starts shooting at it?

"Tracers are flying around your head? If that doesn't make you nervous, then you're unhealthy. The truth is, it's going to be lots more scary than that because at the NTC, normally if you get shot, and it happens, it's by accident. You know, when I was out there last time, the assistant S-3 starts pulling on my sleeve. And he's jerking on my shirt and I say, 'Well, what the hell do you want?' And he says, 'Well, look over your head.'

"And I look up, there's 50-caliber tracers passing between the two antennas. And I told him, don't bother me now, I'm busy. But I thought about that later, and I really got quite frightened about it. So it's okay to be frightened. It's natural. You're going to be scared.

"And fear is not a bad thing. It can be used to advantage.

"Let me tell you some of the physiological things that occur when you're afraid. When you're really afraid. I'm not talking a little scared. I'm talking no-shit-you-believe-you're-going-to-die afraid. It's only happened to me a couple of times. I can remember with stark clarity what it felt like.

"The first time was U.S. artillery shelling. I was real afraid. I was certain I was going to be killed. But the second time, and the more instructive of the two times, tank caught fire with combustible ammunition. My gunner said to me, 'Sir, we have a fire on board.' I looked down between my spotless shiny corcorans and discovered flames licking my toes. It wasn't a fire, it was a fucking ape-shit conflagration. We were burning to the Goddam ground. And I yelled, very carefully and casually, 'Un-ass this motherfucker!'"

Laughter. "And I stepped from the TC's seat to the top of the turret in one step. And that's not easy. But I was strong.

"Physiologically what fear does to you is it pumps adrenaline into your system. It does a couple of other things, cause it drains the capillaries of the extremities of the body: the arms, the legs. And what that does for you is, if you get shot in the arms or legs you won't bleed as much. That's good news.

"The second news is, because the adrenaline pumps, you're quite strong. I stepped from the turret in one step, assessed my situation and stepped from the turret to the ground in the second step and realized my driver is still stuck in the tank and stepped in front of the tank in the third step, and yanked him clean out of the driver's hatch.

"Really by grabbing him on the shirt, just shaking the dust out and putting him on the ground. Now I would not do that, even at that age, and I was 25 or 6, if I hadn't been afraid.

"Gentlemen, I had the strength of ten men, because I was sorely afraid. So do not be afraid of fear, rather understand it, grapple with it, and cope with it.

"You'll know when you're afraid, guys. You'll have this need to urinate, you will taste a metal taste in your mouth like you had maybe a half-dozen nails, number-ten size nails. And you will find that you cannot slam a nail up your ass with a Sledge-o-matic." Laughter.

"And if you begin to experience any of those things, you are afraid. It is going to happen. Understand it. Cope with it. Talk to each other about it.

"Understand with each other that all of you are afraid. Men don't like to admit stuff like that. That's like admitting that maybe you're not a sexual athlete. But it's okay to be afraid. Now cope with it. Talk about it. Deal with it. Face it. Take it out, look at it, examine it, and then put it in its place. And recognize it for a useful thing, but do not let it dominate your mind. Do NOT let it dominate your mind.

"If you become frozen with fear, that is when you become susceptible to bad shit happening. When you're unable to act, you're unable to hit the knee switch, loaders, Bradley gunners you're unable to change the picture from 10 to 3 magnification, then you are so afraid you're not acting at all. That's not good.

"And the best way to get over that, in the presence of the enemy—fire one round.

"As soon as you do that, it's like a release. It will come to you in a moment, you know what to do. And instinctively you will do what you've been trained to do. Which is aim, fire, advance. So don't worry about that part of it.

"I tell you this now because I know what's going on in your mind. It certainly goes on in my mind, and you got to understand that it's part of the game.

"Have faith in yourself. . . .

"I can't promise you won't get hurt. I'll do my Goddam best not to waste your life. That's the only thing I can do.

"Now let me tell you something else, some terrible shit. I'm probably going to make mistakes. You probably are too.

"The mistakes you make and the mistakes I make are going to cause some of us to be hurt. All you can do is have faith in the guys around you. I have faith in you. I know you'll do the best you can.

"Have faith in me to do my best, and if we all do our best together, everything will be fine. We're going to beat these guys. But it isn't going to be free.

"You know that song you hear, the Army song.

"'It wasn't always easy and it wasn't always fair. But once they called we were there.'

"That's who we are. Like I told you before, this is not the Izod polo-shirt, Weejuns loafers crowd. Not a whole lot of kids here whose dads are anesthesiologists or justices of the Supreme Court.

"We're the poor white middle class and the poor black kids from the block and Hispanics from the barrio. We're just as good as the fucking rest, because the honest thing is, that's who I want to go to war with, people like you. And you guys will do great."

Note: Fontenot has often spoken like this at Fort Riley, Kansas. He was not implying that a ground attack was imminent.

Marines Move North, Stretching Horizon to Horizon on Washboard Ribbons of Road

By Molly Moore

WITH U.S. TROOPS, Northern Saudi Arabia - Marine Corps commanders have begun repositioning tens of thousands of troops across northern Saudi Arabia in response to shifts in war plans for the potential ground combat against Iraqi troops entrenched in Kuwait, according to military officials.

A modern-day wagon train now rumbles northward across the Saudi desert around the clock, pushing the wares of ground combat closer to the Kuwaiti and Iraqi borders: trucks lugging missiles, tanks dangling with rucksacks, flatbeds balancing plywood latrines.

Marine forces—some of which have already moved several times in the past few weeks—have begun shifting to new locations, including the corps' largest forward supply base, which will feed, fuel and arm most of the approximately 80,000 Marines expected to move into Kuwait.

"Hopefully, this is the next to the last move until we go home," said Maj. K(aren??) Schultz, 40, assistant commandant of the Marine Corps' massive combat supply depot. "We expect the next one to be Kuwait City."

The large-scale movement of Marine forces across the northern Saudi desert has begun to rival the northward march of their more heavily armored Army counterparts, which has been underway for several weeks further to the west.

Officials said the war plans have been revised significantly in recent days and are expected to be readjusted even more before any ground combat begins.

Senior Marine and U.S. Central Command officials are continuing to debate the details of a possible amphibious assault and have made no final decision on whether to use the amphibious forces against the heavily defended Kuwaiti shoreline, according to military authorities.

Gen. H. Norman Schwarzkopf, commander of allied forces, flew to a frontline Marine base this week to discuss the war plans with senior Marine generals.

Meanwhile, in scenes reminiscent of World War II film clips and epic television war dramas, hundreds of tanks, armored personnel carriers, and amphibious attack vehicles churn the desert sand en route to their new frontline positions, partially obscured by sepia-colored clouds of sand that rise into a sky already smudged with the black smoke of burning Kuwaiti oil facilities further north.

Huge convoys of five-ton trucks, squat ammunition haulers and tanks bristling with toothy mine-breaching plows stretch from horizon to horizon on washboard ribbons of roadway carved into the desert sand.

Many camps have become military ghost towns, with troops abandoning canvas tents to the dusty desert winds. Other posts, such as the wartime supply cities that feed the U.S. military war machines, have loaded their menus of ammunition, food and fuel onto trucks joining the convoys.

The stream of war materiel seems virtually endless: flatbed trucks with carefully positioned pallets of high explosive 155 millimeter cannon shells, fusty fuel tankers, armored mine-breaching bulldozers and an assortment of chunky tracked vehicles.

Brightly colored Saudi buses, which usually carry thousands of Muslims on their holy pilgrimages, are now hauling Marine infantry troops to the front lines, their racks piled high with green duffles and sleeping bags.

Less fortunate troops sit on the hard wooden benches of open-aired military trucks, their faces sheathed in scarves and rags in a futile effort to block the choking dust.

Military chuck wagons stacked with boxes of packaged Meals Ready to Eat (MREs) follow trucks carrying wooden shower stalls which follow vehicles filled with canvas tents. In addition to their guns and cannons, tanks and other armor hang heavy with the personal possessions of warriors—bulging rucksacks, flailing blankets, shovels, and mess hall spatulas. Some Marines have poked flags from the hatches and windows of their tanks and trucks—American flags, as well as flags from home states like Texas and Tennessee.

Others have painted names and slogans on tank barrels. "No retreat, no surrender" was chalked across one barrel and the driver of one fuel hauler dubbed his vehicle "Unselfish Lover." The occupants of other trucks have taped pinups of scantily-clad buxom women to the inside doors of vehicles that have become second homes.

Much of the convoy this week has been filled with the war and warrior supplies of the Marines' support depot, which is moving to a new desert fortress, protected by miles of high sand berms. Inside the heavily bunkered compounds are the communications centers and ammunition, fuel and food supplies of war.

Nine bulldozers working 72 straight hours have eaten great chunks (of) desert, building the deep trenches that will house tents and the giant earthen berms that will protect ammunition and command centers from hostile attack. "We keep track of the bulldozers like we do airplanes from control towers because they are so valuable to this war effort," said one Marine officer.

For this war, the American troops have taken some lessons from the adversaries. Everything from sleeping tents to command centers are buried under the sand and rock of the Saudi desert. The rubble from those holes is then piled high around the U-shaped edges of the berms—the thickest walls always facing north, the direction most likely to receive Iraqi artillery rounds or rocket fire.

At ground level, the campsites look like sparsely occupied moonscapes, with only camouflage netting and a few antennas poking above the sand heaps.

For the headquarters command bunker, two bulldozers scraped bedrock for two days, breaking the metal teeth of their blades, before they were forced to give up and find a new location several yards away.

Now the command bunker, encased in the giant metal containers used to ship equipment to Saudi Arabia, is buried deep beneath the earth and bordered by a high man-made ridge of rock and sand. For miles around the center of this new supply city, thousands of uprooted residents continue to pull into their freshly dug holes, erecting tents and the other housings of war preparation.

NOTE TO WASH POST crowd and PRINT POOL coordinators. This pool begins the process of moving to a new camp today and switching over from pony express by road to pony express by helos for relaying copy, photos, and tape. Please pay particular attention to time lapses on receiving copy so we can try to correct any glitches, which are likely to occur over the next 2-3 days. ALSO, please pursue with the JIB in Riyadh AND with Pete Williams in Washington the use of satellite telephones forward when war breaks out. We are told field commanders say there is no problem in using them—the holdup seems to be Centcom. It appears the phones will be critical in getting copy back in a timely manner, especially in units such as this which will place reporters with combat units far north into Kuwait once fighting begins. MOORE.

Saturday
February 16, 1991

The mind games in the Gulf War could be serpentine.

In this chapter, a few of the serpents are taken out for inspection. An allied military official in one story seemed to tease Saddam Hussein by observing to a reporter that the Iraqis may have thought they knew where the coalition forces were located along the desert frontier, and their approximate planned line and time of attack, but their information couldn't possibly be accurate.

This is serpentine reasoning at its best. Did the allied official say that because he knew it to be true, and hoped making it public would demoralize the Iraqi command?

If your enemy is in the dark, do you tell him? Assuming he knew his observations would eventually—probably within days—be read in Baghdad, was it simply a matter of the more question marks implanted in the minds of the Iraqi government and military intelligence the better?

Another story in this chapter describes the serpent-like penchant of the modern military to let ideas and concepts shed their skins and dress them in new verbal raiment, borrowing and creating new jargon for briefings and operational reports.

The American military has long been known for its alphabet soup, forming acronyms to be used as words for almost every process and tool of warmaking. Here the latest jargon, mainly out of the mouths of the Brits, comes in complete words and phrases, but often just as obscure, and not always in the Mother Tongue.

In the aftermath of Saddam Hussein's latest trial peace balloon, the diplomatic cards were re-shuffled, yet none of the hands looked much different. Morocco, which had remained on the sidelines, said its government had been studying Iraq's latest settlement proposal and thought it saw some daylight. But the Soviets, whose stance was much more important than Morocco's, backed away from their earlier support, saying the conditions Saddam had placed on his offer made it a non-starter. They were in agreement with Bush on that score.

That was a bad sign, indeed, for Baghdad.

Iraq's military efforts, meanwhile, appeared pitiful. Two Scud missiles struck Israeli territory, but landed harmlessly. Throughout the bombing campaign, these non-precision missiles launched from Iraq or Kuwait and landing on Israel or Saudi Arabia were militarily insignificant, at least in the opinion of allied military commanders.

But the psychological effects on civilians, magnified many times by exposure in the media, were considered hugely important.

The fact that most Scuds didn't deliver much damage, whether a Patriot intercepted them or not, helped fuel a perception that the allied efforts to counter the Scuds were more successful than they were in reality. During the war, the allied command claimed the Patriot had a high kill ratio, destroying 80 percent or more of the Scuds that flew within range of their missile batteries, and said more than a dozen mobile Scud launchers were destroyed.

Later, after some detailed analysis of videotapes and missile records, the Pentagon had to admit that the Patriots managed only about 10 "warhead kills" of Scuds, out of some 86 fired during the war. Patriots that hit them a glancing blow probably knocked another two dozen or so off course.

And one post-war study asserted that the allies failed to destroy a single mobile Scud launcher in Iraq during the war. The special operations teams assigned to hunt down the launchers, and the Air Force commanders assigned to destroy them, would argue that point.

Within artillery range of Iraqi units, allied forces were deploying, maneuvering, patrolling, exercising, shaving, writing home, test-firing, and positioning themselves in a known slice of the Arabian desert.

Would it be an end run, a slant off-tackle, a feint from the sea and straight up the middle? Some combination of all three? Whatever the exact design of the allied plan, the weeks of intensive bombing and tough war talk from the U.S.-led coalition meant there would be fighting on a massive scale.

The Iraqis had peppered the way north from their border with Saudi Arabia and Kuwait with mines and other hazards, but otherwise appeared to have just dug deeper into the sand. Now, barring a miracle, the end game could not be put off much longer.

At ground level, the future battleground could appear trackless and unexplored, but in fact the area had long since been reduced to maps. But even the information on a map could cause controversy in this part of the world.

In Gen. Schwarzkopf's autobiography, he recalled how upset the Saudi royal circle was early in the deployment over some T-shirts that allied troops were selling or giving away.

The shirts featured a basic map of Saudi Arabia with a few main cities marked on it. The same data was available in libraries and bookstores around the world—even in Baghdad, presumably—and Schwarzkopf said he didn't understand the problem.

The Saudis were famously prudish, by western standards, but there were no scantily-clad women, or vulgarities on the T-shirts. Just a map. Their heartburn, Saudi officials eventually told him, was due to the fact that such basic geographical information had never been made available to the general public in Saudi Arabia.

Having all these foreign troops on Saudi soil was one thing. Having them break the seal on the secrets of the ruling families was something else altogether.

Whatever Iraqis Think They Know of Allied Plans, The Allies Assume is Based on Thin Intelligence

By John Fullerton

WITH ALLIED FORCES, Saudi Arabia - One month after war erupted in the Gulf, Iraq appears to have little idea where or how allied forces will launch their ground offensive.

"All the indications we have suggest that he (Iraqi leader Saddam Hussein) believes he knows the location of allied ground formations, but these appear to be assumptions based on thin intelligence," said one senior allied army commander.

That ground assault may be only days away, but Western military sources told Reuters that every effort will be made to keep Baghdad in the dark about allied intentions well after the battle has begun.

Lack of firm information of allied moves along Saudi Arabia's northern border appears to be Iraq's main disadvantage in trying to mount an effective defense, the sources added.

Despite a probing attack earlier this month on the northern Saudi Arabian town of Khafji—which the sources believed may have been aimed at gathering intelligence by trying to draw the allies into a premature shooting war on the ground—Baghdad has been forced to prepare an all-round defence of both Kuwait and southern Iraq.

That has proved difficult in the face of the allies' bombing campaign, but the sources said Iraq had so far shown no sign of irrational or desperate behavior in the way that it has moved divisions to counter what it perceived as the allies' plan to liberate Kuwait.

Instead, Saddam seemed to have given his commanders a free hand in directing the Iraqi armoured and infantry forces. The sources said there was a subtlety and maturity in the way his generals changed the disposition of Iraq's forces as the allied buildup in the Gulf gathered momentum over the past six months.

In the first stages of the crisis, the bulk of Iraq's ground forces were grouped in and around Kuwait, apparently to secure Iraq's grip on the emirate.

Eventually, Iraq shifted its formations farther west, extending both the first line of fixed defences and reserve units into southern Iraq. This meant positioning available forces across a wider front, reducing the depth of the defence. Iraq had tried to compensate by drawing units away from the Iraq-Iran border to plug the gaps.

With bridges, roads and communications heavily damaged by allied air power, the sources said, Iraq must now be forced to improvise by using minor routes and smaller groups of vehicles, particularly at night.

More recently, the sources said, Iraq had reinforced its first line of defence with brigades of tanks, while pulling troops along Kuwait's southern border back from the front line at a time when the winter rainstorms have turned the salt pans or "sabkas" in the area into muddy lagoons.

Iraq was also known to be using deception techniques on a large scale to try and mask its military moves from the constant watch kept by allied reconnaissance aircraft and satellites. But the constant pounding from the air—in recent days directed hourly at ground troops—meant that Iraq's ability to maneuver in response to intelligence on any allied thrust was being steadily eroded.

The sources said the allies' determination to "write down" Iraqi command headquarters and logistic support before committing ground troops would drive Iraq into a replay of the tactics it used in the Iran-Iraq war. Instead of using mobility, Iraq built lines of defence to soak up Iran's "human-wave" assaults.

Now the allies were having to re-think their own doctrine, using manouevre and the momentum of advance to bypass points of resistance and draw the best of Iraq's forces—the Republican Guards—out into the open for the coup de grâce.

Inside a Noisy Sultan, an Echo of British Pretension: "Discipline of Blind Obedience Has to Be There"

By John Fullerton

WITH BRITAIN'S 7th ARMOURED BRIGADE, Saudi Arabia - Zero Echo lurches, sways, pitches and at times flies into battle.

At every bump, spoons, gas masks, paperback books, binoculars, and pin-ups detach themselves from the low ceiling and walls and ricochet around the dust-filled interior. Three radios hiss and gurgle. Disembodied voices—Scots, Welsh, and Cockney accents mingling with languid public school inflection—crackle from headphones. It is like riding to war inside an outsize vacuum cleaner.

Every nook and cranny is crammed with the paraphernalia of soldiering—sleeping bags, grenades, saucepans, biscuits, secret code books, army manuals, and tins of sausages.

Zero Echo—otherwise known simply as "Plans"—is a thinly-armoured Sultan command vehicle at the heart of the Royal Scots Dragoon Guards battle group surging up to Saudi Arabia's northern border for the start of the allied ground offensive.

It is also home for a captain, a corporal, and two lance corporals.

In this microcosm of the British Army at war, there is no room for barrack-room discipline or spit-and-polish. Instead, there is a mutual, understated respect between officer and other ranks—a far cry from the stereotype image of the fashionable cavalry regiment and its social pretensions.

The slight figure of the bespectacled Simon Oliver perches on the top of a 250-gallon petrol tank, reading off map grid references and encoding them with the speed and precision of the single 7.62mm machinegun that provides Zero Echo with its only self-defence. Oliver's father and brother served with the regiment. His main interest outside the army is fox-hunting.

It is time for a "brew." The square teapot known as the boiling vessel or BV is steaming and it is Oliver's turn to perform the acrobatic feat of filling plastic mugs with tea, milk and sugar. "He's brilliant. He looks after us," said the radio operator, Andrew Yard, of the man he calls boss. "When we come off stag (sentry duty), he often has tea waiting for us." Oliver himself concedes that wartime breeds a more informal atmosphere. "They're good at their job. That's why things are so relaxed," he says.

But the Army is changing, albeit slowly, along with society as a whole and the Gulf war may give the armed forces another nudge.

Lieut. Col. John Sharples, commanding officer of the Royal Scots Dragoon Guards, explains that his officers are recruited largely through word of mouth and regimental connections. Nine sons of former members of the officers' mess were currently serving. "It's a network of sorts. Young men visit us in batches so we can have a look at one another. I'm looking to see if the potential officer is going to have the sort of approach respected by his soldiers and if he is going to fit in and not feel uncomfortable," he says.

Brigadier Patrick Cordingley, who commands the Desert Rats of 7th Armoured Brigade, recalls a time when Britain's army was composed largely of conscripts.

"When I joined, there was rigid discipline . . . being an all-regular Army you have a closer bond. Everyone these days, including infantry, is under armour and we're forced into proximity with one another as never before," he says.

"It's the job that matters rather than anything else."

Col. Arthur Denaro commands another prestigious cavalry regiment, the Queen's Royal Irish Hussars. "The comradeship is so tangible it's heart-warming. There always has been a relaxed but respectful relationship between men and officers and this is only earned by the officers' effectiveness," he says. "The first requirement for an officer is to lead, and do it bloody well. Care and consideration of your men are essential."

Lieut. Col. Charles Rogers, who commands the Staffordshire Regiment, joined the army as a private soldier. "There's a lessening of traditional public school dominance and an increase in other ranks' opportunities to be commissioned . . . it's a matter of the quality of the individual," he says.

The Gulf war was helping to bridge the social gap.

"There's a sense of comradeship out here. A healthy relationship grows out of shared hardships. There's no feeling of 'them' and 'us.' Bullets don't discriminate."

Flash! War is a Dirty and Uncomfortable Shambles, Even Before it Starts

By Simon Clifford

WITH 4TH ARMOURED BRIGADE - Oh! What a Lovely War.

Sweating, stinking, shouting—and a shambles. The frightening thing is the war hasn't even started yet.

For the past two days, I have lived in the near-squalor of our frontline troops, sharing their food, drink, and frustration during a massive divisional exercise involving 20,000 and more soldiers. For the boys of One Platoon, The Queen's Company, the Grenadier Guards, the exercise was a major headache. Whether the overall aim of the exercise was achieved, it was a success, or everyone at planning level was happy, I do not know. I can assure you from our little sight of what war could be like it was chaos.

A better title would have been "Stop the War. I Want to Get Off." Convoys got lost, there were collisions, and nobody at dog-soldier level had any idea what was going on. One group even thought this was the real thing and were psyched up for killing action.

Life is no fun when seven big men packed into their charcoal-lined and hot chemical suits cram their way into a Warrior vehicle that comfortably carries four and is already stuffed with weapons and ammunition.

But that is accepted, that's part of the job. What was not expected is that briefings are held at a canter, infantry are bottled up with no action for 18 hours at a time without a meal and there is no information.

For the Warrior crew (illegible), things started badly with one man feeling ill after an inoculation. Then the briefing was held in two minutes while we all got into our suits. "Mount up" and we were gone, leaving one vehicle behind, it couldn't start, losing another on the way—it got lost.

Off to a holding area, then off to our objective—Iraqi-held trenches at a place called Gold. On the way, we bumped into a huge convoy that was not supposed to be there. Three hours later it had passed.

By the time we reached Gold, it has been taken by someone else. No action.

No running around, no chance to stretch legs. Off to a new home.

Bam, roll into "gork" sleeping bags then off again three hours later.

A new objective, again no attack and a new home.

Saturday - February 16, 1991

We start digging trenches, after 30 minutes—"Mount up" and we were off again.

Another stop—coinciding with the news of a peace plan on the radio. Just long enough to cook a quick hot meal—the first since midday the day before—then off again, with food just about to be doled out. 8 p.m. Arrived at new home, dug our shallow trenches, then bed. Wake up 5:30 a.m. to be told we were moving again soon—moved 600 metres at 9 a.m., told to dig more trenches.

There are probably very good reasons for everything, every niggle, every contradiction. Unfortunately, very few of those reasons percolates its way down to the men who matter. For them it is frustrating and they know they have to put up with it.

But a lot of soldiers have said that enough is enough and they will quit the army after the war. "There are so many mistakes, nothing changes and nothing ever will," said Sgt. Harry Melbourne. After 24 hours and more in charcoal-lined suits, the men want to wash properly and clean their clothes—but there is a shortage of water so rations are about half a pint a man for personal admin, as the army calls it.

The end result is that when we go to war, the soldiers will be dirty, uncomfortable, and will probably think it is another exercise.

Careering Out of Fingerspitzengefühl, Gulf War Gives Rise to New Jargon as Well as a Few Careers

By Robert Fox

WITH 4th ARMOURED BRIGADE, 14th/20th Hussars, Eastern Desert - The news of Saddam's announcement of conditional withdrawal from Kuwait was greeted with mixed emotions by the men of the 4th Armoured Brigade.

First heard over American Forces' Radio during a lull in a major exercise, the information was soon fanned by the flames of rumour. First reaction was a mild rejoicing, and toasts were drunk in orange juice and compo tea and coffee. Elation soon turned to resignation as the full text of the Ba'ath Revolutionary Command Council's terms were relayed by the BBC. Within an hour gunners, tank drivers, signalers, Battery Commanders, and the proverbial cook and bottle washer had become an instant Middle East analyst wise in the lore of the professional orientalist.

What was up in Baghdad, they enquired? Had Saddam been overthrown? Was it all a gigantic bluff? When the time came to move on, it was business as usual and all knew that the war would go on. The B-52 bombers and F-15 Eagles traversing the sky with vapour trails underlined the point.

Information is a precious commodity out here in the desert. As with most supplies from the Quartermaster's Stores in the rear there is either too much or too little.

In wars gone by, a general might worry about how little he knew about his enemy. In this most electronic of campaigns, the general might be concerned that he knows too much about his enemy in some respects, though not enough in others. Intelligence arrives by satellite pictures, photos from reconnaissance planes like the Tornado GR1, and from the questioning of prisoners. Now planes on combat missions take their own videos and television cameras in missiles report their progress up to the moment of impact.

Overwhelming as the flow of raw data may seem, it does not lead to a complete understanding of the enemy. Information does not lead to instant understanding, and analysis of what is going on among Saddam's forces on the ground and his defences in Iraq itself seems to take days to evaluate.

Information for public consumption aims at the quantity rather than the quality market. Most of it reaches the nomad armies of the allies and their camp followers in the desert via the BBC World Service and the American Forces "Wizard 106" RZGZO FM station. It is a steady diet of fact, fiction, more or less informed comment, and some ruthless propaganda.

With the broadcasts comes a deluge of new jargon. Trickiest notion is BDA—Battle Damage Assessment. It, too, is a scarce commodity out in the desert. This should tell you what damage your bombers and artillery have actually done rather than what the pilots and gunners think they have. The toll of destruction is now called "writing down" or "degradation." Soldiers, bridges and ammunition dumps, tank parks and shelters and their human inhabitants are no longer killed or blown up, but "written down" or "degraded" in the abstractions of the allied official spokespersons.

Most gruesome is the concept of "collateral damage." In plain terms it means the bomber or gun hit something it did not intend. In other words "collateral damage" is a miss or a wild shot. Civilians are the victims of collateral damage.

The relentless round of shelling and aerial bombardment is not launched, ordered, or executed by the men in uniform but, in the words of the official U.S. spokesman in Riyadh this week, they are "choreographed." The Torville and Dean of the latest dance numbers must have been the flight of three B-52s the other evening which tastefully etched the sunset sky with an arc of trails in lurid pink.

In private the commanders have been overwhelmed by a new military lingo.

The British command has never over the years been noted for its great prowess in the finer points of academic metaphysics nor linguistics.

Now they mutter abstract tactical concepts in German; they have become the slaves of Von Clausewitz, the father of military theory of the modern era.

Favorite terms are "fingerspitzengefühl"—finger-tip control—where the commander delicately probes enemy positions with his tanks.

The outright winner of the new tactic-speak is "auftragstaktik"—even a photographer of the more popular press invoked this particular rune the other day.

The concept of "auftragstaktik" is mission-orientated orders. Every man should know enough of the overall plan to be able to use his initiative in his part of the battle, provided he does not wreck the whole enterprise.

Each level of command is given the plan that has been revealed two levels above. A Brigade commander knows what the Corps commander has been ordered; the Battalion or Regiment or Battle Group commander knows the Divisional commander's intelligence and orders; and the process goes down to level of Platoon and Troop Commander.

The Commander of the British 1st Division, Major General Rupert Smith, is said to be an aficionado of the doctrine. He has spent hours discussing concepts, plans and tactical possibilities with groups of young officers and NCOs, winning a deal of respect and admiration in the process, an assessment endorsed by American colleagues, according to several sources.

The least-publicized of the British commanders, he is emerging as the star of the show. His desire to communicate and discuss at all levels of his command may be due less to infatuation with German abstraction than to his training as a paratrooper. Because paras drop in small sticks of four men, and are liable to be distributed all over the countryside if things go wrong, the training watchword of the Parachute Regiment is that every soldier must know his task and mission.

About the encampments of the 4th Armoured Brigade, there is little evidence that the new doctrinal abstractions are turning Tommy Atkins into Prussian Guards, Pikelhauber, or Pomeranian Grenadiers of a new Bismarckian order. The formula of their tactical doctrine is still that of British arms through the ages: "muddle through," and "see what you can get off the Regimental Quartermaster when nobody's looking."

Life in the desert is now a round of Compo rations, washing infrequently, and trying to get spares ordered weeks ago. It is not that the articles have not appeared, or are missing. They are "not visible" in the euphemism of stores' jargon.

Such privations are part of the perpetual war of them and us. Faced with a defective kit for up-armouring his tank, Sergeant Major Geraghty of Command Troop, 14th/20th Hussars, lamented, "I was a deprived child, so I didn't have Meccano. Officers not only had Meccano, but they had people paid to play with it for them."

The 14th/20th pride themselves as being the "mellow" regiment, which believes in taking things calmly. Many officers and troopers admit they never expected to go to war, and are surprised to find themselves about to do so.

The hero of the regiment is the downtrodden but resourceful Baldrick, servant to the scheming Blackadder in Rowan Atkinson's TV series. Most of all it is the spirit of Baldrick in his last incarnation, the long-suffering Tommy on the Western Front, which stiffens the sinews of the Hussars.

Baldrick's catch phrase, "I have a cunning plan," drops from the lips of Colonel and Trooper alike. Some say they have adopted the ruse of their hero inscribing an item of their own ammunition, so they have the bullet with their name on it.

Sadly, videos of their role model are not seen out here. But in the rear units the uncut version of David Lean's "Lawrence of Arabia" is doing the rounds.

The antics of Peter O'Toole with his cut-glass diction and Persil-white robe seem closer to the spirit of "Carry on Camping" than past or present reality in these desolate parts.

Marine Log Base a Microcosm of American Society: All the Guys in the Stockade are Called "Elvis"

By Caryle Murphy

WITH U.S. FORCES IN NORTHERN SAUDI ARABIA - Ernilio Zuniga's do-it yourself laundromat opens at 7:15 a.m.

Attorney Robert Leas, his shingle outside his tent, is drawing up wills. And mechanic Robert Lamb complains over the blare of rock music that he's waiting for spare parts. Perhaps more than any other U.S. military outpost that has mushroomed in the Saudi desert, this giant Marine logistical supply base is a microcosm of American society—as if small-town U.S.A. had been swooped up by a Steven Spielberg back-to-the-desert machine. With its airstrip, criss-crossing dirt roads, and hundreds of tents interspersed with huge steel transport, communications, medical aid, newspapers, ammunition, rockets, cannons, water, forklifts, bulldozers, spare parts, and just about anything else a fighting force needs, to the battlefield.

The several thousand Marines working here, including more than 170 women, will not be among the hard-charging first-liners into Kuwait. Rather, they have the task of seeing to it that those up ahead have all they need to plow ahead. As such, they represent two-thirds of U.S. Marine Corps personnel: those dedicated to logistics and supply.

A two-week stint with these Marines, many of whom are performing their real lives' work of computer specialists, chaplains, truck drivers, doctors, and cops, offers a reflection of contemporary American life. And brings some discoveries as well.

The PX rakes in about $20,000 a day selling junk food and soda. A voice on the phone is still better than a letter, so the lines outside the new AT&T satellite phone tent are three hours long. And moments of privacy are more often than not spent talking to a tape cassette, playing portable video games, or listening to music on a Walkman. Here people are dying needlessly from one of the biggest killers in America: road accidents. The destruction, however, comes not from alcohol, but from the blinding swirls of desert dust whipped up by never-ending convoys of supply trucks, tanks and armored personnel carriers on their way to the front.

Here too, women Marines, or "WM's," as they are called, push the limits of newfound opportunities in the military, while feeling the tug of children left behind.

And the camp's physical fitness freaks come running out of the eastern edge of the base early each morning, when mostly everyone else is shivering from the bone piercing cold. They are led by Rick Johnson, 34, who was raised near R.F.K. Stadium and is, as he puts it, "a fine, shining example of what Washington can do when it's feeling good about itself."

In this camp also you find the American compulsion to make the complicated, simple; the strange, familiar, Thus, Cpl. Michael Urango, a military policeman, refers to his ward of Iraqi POWs as "Elvis."

"I call 'em all 'Elvis.' That's our name for 'em," said Urango, explaining how the sobriquet arose after he and his friends saw that truck drivers in Saudi Arabia, many of them expatriate workers from India and Pakistan, "all had their hair slicked back like Elvis." As to why Urango is thousands of miles from home: "We understand Saddam's doing some bad things," he says. "Nobody can treat people like that and get away with it."

On a tour of the camp laundry, supervisor Staff Sgt. Emilio Zuniga displays both an entrepreneur's pride, and one of his most basic instincts: self-protection.

Asked why those who brought in their unit's dirty clothes had to do the laundry themselves, the 29-year-old San Bernardino, Calif., native replied: "I don't want my people to be responsible if something gets lost." But for a nation whose family life is supposed to be in tatters, these Marines do an awful lot of talking about the family back home. For every dogtag out here, there are several more well-worn snapshots of children, parents, boyfriends, and girlfriends pocketed close to the hearts spread across the desert here.

As it has been for the past six months, the prevailing mood among the troops here is "Let's get going, get it over with, and get home." Few dwell much on what "getting it over with" may entail. But success is assumed as a foregone conclusion.

As one medical worker expressed it in his "Thought for the Week" on a field hospital bulletin board: "Hard Rock Cafe, Kuwait City, Opening soon."

Lt. Col. Robert Leas, who runs the Marines' Office of Staff Judge Advocate, sees many young Marines, nurtured on the culture of instant gratification, when they drop in to draw up their wills. "They're anxious to get it over with," said the Texas native. "You tell them three weeks is not a long war. Maybe by Israeli standards, but not U.S. standards."

Leas, whose office is also responsible for prosecuting criminal cases, reports that the population is also a pretty law-abiding bunch. Only one larceny, the theft of a pistol, has been reported and a Marine brig built back in the Saudi town of Jubail has yet to hold one prisoner, Leas reported.

Sgt. Bruce Richardson says he's had "only a couple" of discipline problems with people "showing disrespect." Otherwise, he says he gets little irritation from the men and women of his communications company. He does hear quite a few complaints, though. "I think that it's hard for these young Marines, being in this environment. They think it's harsh," said the 44-year-old Richardson, who spent 1967-68 in an infantry company in Vietnam. "This is paradise to me," he said. "Don't take incoming. Doesn't rain. Get two hot chows a day. What more do you want? We didn't have luxuries like this."

About the only appliance missing here is television. Yet, in an almost surreal reflection of this American staple, this camp seems surrounded by one big tv screen on which the still-distant combat of Operation Desert Storm is near enough to see and hear, but not yet close enough to hurt.

When U.S. B-52s drop their deadly payload on Iraqi troops just across the border, the rumble of the explosives roars into camp. And at night, the twinkling lights of allied jet bombers streaking north look like giant fireflies in the inky sky. On the ground, round-the-clock convoys of buses and trucks ceaselessly push supplies and U.S. troops further into the desert.

This base is commanded by Chuck C. Krulak, an effervescent brigadier general who operates out of an underground bunker that looks like a set from a World War II movie. A dark, sloping tunnel leads down from the desert surface into cramped quarters lit by naked light bulbs. The staff attends daily briefings seated on folding chairs that face a map on the wall.

Krulak makes it a point to show up regularly in almost every part of camp, one day dishing out chow himself in the mess tent; another, doing a card trick in the radio room and offering 24 hours off to anyone who can show him how he did it. (Someone did, and got the one-day vacation.)

The general, who cut his combat teeth on two tours as an infantryman in Vietnam, enthuses about his Marines with the boosterism of a loquacious mayor: "Go out and talk to them. They will blow your mind," he says. "I have one guy who was pulled out (of) the seminary to be here."

But Krulak still makes clear he is running a military installation. Word went out the other day that officers will be saluted, a practice that Marines in the field dropped during the Vietnam days, when officers were stalked by enemy snipers.

And a makeshift disco, where some Marines let off tension by dancing something called "The Gas Mask," was ordered closed after opening night. Krulak reportedly feared that front-line Marines reading of the disco in the local newspaper might think their supply troops were not taking the war effort seriously enough.

Cpl. Christian Gervasi had another Marine rule—never misplace your rifle—indelibly engraved on her mind. For five days, whenever the 25-year-old activated reservist wasn't on guard duty, she was at a very public sand berm filling sandbags. Sgt. Richardson decided that 1,000 Gervasi-filled bags would ensure that she never forgot her rifle again. "This is like a cardinal sin here," said the Bellmore, N.Y. native bending over her shovel. "You don't walk around without your equipment. It's known throughout the camp that I'm doing this and the reason I'm doing this. I'll never forget my rifle again."

Gervasi, who got her BA from (State University of New York at) Stony Brook where she studied political science, joined the Marine reserves in 1987 because she "wanted to know if I could do it." She'd hoped to go to officer training school, get her MA, and become a high school teacher.

When she got her call-up notice last November, she was unemployed, studying for the air traffic controllers' exam, and planning to work at the jewelry counter of Fortunoff's [eds: spelling] over the Christmas holidays for some extra money.

Gervasi is one of the 172 women assigned to this vast supply camp, most of them junior enlisted or activated reservists. They helped build the camp from scratch, setting up radio antennas, digging bunkers, filling sandbags, stacking sandbags, restacking sandbags, repairing computers, driving trucks, cooking, running communications.

In the tent that she shares with 11 other WM's, cots are laid out in two rows. Someone threw green Astroturf on the sand to make a sort of carpet. There's a yellow teddy bear on one bed and a Valentine's Day balloon above the cot of Sgt. Pamela Wells, who wears her blonde hair in a pony tail and red polish on her toenails.

"It's pretty neat, being over here in combat," said Lance Cpl. Sonja Scott, 20, of Shreveport, La., "Two years ago, I never would have thought I'd be here fighting a war. We have to fend for ourselves over here." But, said Lance Cpl. Ermalinda Torres, 22, of Eola, Tex., this new experience leaves some things unchanged. "When I go back, I want to wear a dress for a whole week. Just to feel like a woman," said Torres. "We use a lot of body sprays," during shower-time, she added. "If we can't look like a woman, at least we can smell like one."

Some women Marines say they are impressed with the fortitude of their younger peers. "I'm probably the oldest woman here," said 41-year-old Lt. Col. Ruthann Poole of Newport News, Va., who is the base's senior administration officer and its highest-ranking female Marine. "I've talked to lots of them, 18-19 (years old). I'm not sure I could have done it at their age." For Poole, leaving behind her four-year-old daughter was "probably the hardest thing for me . . . someday she'll understand. She thinks Mommy's gone to the field. That's all I told her. I didn't tell her anything about a war."

"We all had doubts how the women would do, I mean I'm sure the men did," said Poole. "They all had doubts about how we would handle this, especially when you started hearing the bombings . . . but the men have been very supportive."

Every woman in camp knows about Army Specialist Melissa Rathbun-Nealy, who went missing during a recent battle between allied and Iraqi forces near the Saudi town of Khafji. Though not officially listed as a POW, Rathbun is believed to have been captured by Iraqi troops and her fate weighs on these women's minds, many say.

"I can empathize with her," said Poole. "It could be me."

Sunday
February 17, 1991

The Vietnam War was a ghost in the Gulf, far in the past yet never far from mind, heart or memory. Vietnam veterans led the allies' Persian Gulf effort at many levels, from Gen. Powell and Gen. Schwarzkopf down to sergeants and reservists in the enlisted ranks.

As a new war rose up from the Arabian Desert, the American experience in Vietnam returned in many guises to act as a measuring rod, a thorn to be extracted, a salve applied so that healing could finally occur and the American military could once again stand proud. From the evidence, the operation was a success. A story in this chapter captures an example of the Vietnam theme on the eve of combat, through the eyes of a veteran officer for whom Vietnam was a promise to keep.

In the British camp, another story relates, the best available comparison with a past conflict was the Falklands War. Like the Gulf War, the war over the Falkland Islands was precipitated by someone grabbing a small chunk of territory that may have seemed of small consequence, but actually mattered to certain influential people.

A story in this chapter captures the Vietnam theme on the eve of combat, through the eyes of a veteran officer for whom Vietnam was a promise to keep.

In the British camp, another story relates, the best available comparison with a past conflict was the Falklands War. Like the Gulf War, the war over the Falkland Islands was precipitated by the grabbing of a small chunk of territory that may have seemed of small consequence to some. A British correspondent puts his analogies to work on the matchup to shed light on both conflicts.

The Gulf version of military horse-trading also visits in this chapter. Any shortage can be solved with the right amount of trading savvy, goes the military maxim. In this war, some of the traders have done so well it's easy to find their home in the desert. And it helps that the goods available for trading have expanded along with the number of female troops volunteering for active military duty.

After a solid month of the air campaign, the allies looked back on a long string of successful missions and a few failures. A British briefing showed film of an RAF mission in which a missile misfired, striking a bridge in the small, non-military town of Fallouja.

The Iraqis immediately claimed that the errant missile had killed 130 civilians. The British said they didn't think any civilians were killed in the incident. Such incidents were difficult to judge without adequate BDA (battle damage assessment), which essentially required access to the damaged area the allies didn't have. Once the ground war was launched, it was believed that battle damage assessment would improve.

Allied ground forces picked up the pace of their pre-offensive, launching seven probes by small patrols in a single day. Their purpose was to engage the enemy in a limited way, then pull back, taking the measure of Iraqi troops just across the roughly-marked front line.

They found enemy to engage. Iraqi military vehicles were destroyed; enemy troops were taken prisoner. And as a story in this chapter says, two U.S. soldiers were killed and six others wounded by friendly helicopter fire. They were the first American troops—along with 11 Marines killed in fighting in late January during an Iraqi incursion associated with the Battle of Khafjis—to fall to friendly fire in the Gulf War, a group that eventually numbered 35, of 146 U.S. combat deaths.

The high ratio of friendly fire deaths on the allied sides—which by war's end also included 11 British troops killed by mistake by a U.S. warplanes—sparked a search by the Pentagon for new methods of preventing such accidents. All allied tanks and other vehicles in the Gulf were supposed to be marked with an inverted "V" to help differentiate friend from foe. Especially in close-in fighting action, and under poor visibility conditions, that wasn't enough.

Somewhere in all the technological wizardry of the modern age, it seems fair to think there must be many smart new ways to help identify friendly troops, tanks, and other vehicles in the midst of battle.

The challenge was to find the smartest gadgets in a laboratory or on a computer screen and then factor in a few non-computer-generated hazards: such as dust storms, freezing cold, dizzying heat, blinding rain, deafening noise, wind, fog, chaos, fear, haste, minefields, smoke, confusion, fatigue, incoming fuel, pain, blood, explosions, paralysis, panic, nerves, thirst, fumbling hands, adrenaline . . .

In other words, factor in war. Then see how they work.

Falklands or Persian Gulf, Accents Differ, Killing's the Same: Finer Techniques of Hand-to-Hand Combat

By Robert Fox

WITH 4ᵀᴴ ARMOURED BRIGADE - Wars and campaigns can seem worlds apart, only the grim business of killing is the same.

In nine years, Britain has twice sent an expeditionary force to fight in some foreign part. The style and shape of the Falklands operation and the campaign in the desert involving more than 40,000 British servicemen and women now could hardly be more different.

The Falklands was very much a West Country affair. From the Navy, the Navy Air Arm and the Royal Marines, the accents of Devon and Cornwall rang clear. Even the landscape of the bare rocky islands in the South Atlantic has something of Exmoor, Dartmoor and Bodmin Moor about them.

The only aspect of the Falklands in common with the Eastern Saudi Desert is the sheer sense of remoteness, the feeling that the broad swathe of the human race has wisely decided to pass the place by.

In the Falklands, the infinite variable was the weather. Here it is the terrain, which changes in the matter of a few hundred yards from sand as liquid as water to mud pans or "sabka," and hard shale enough to block a tank's tracks at forty paces.

Here the daily round for the men in the front line is the same struggle for water, shelter, and how to make Compo field rations remotely interesting.

The accents are very different. They are those of the men of the North, Lancastrians, Northumbrians, Scots, and Irish. It is Coronation Street in uniform and Billy Connolly done up for war.

Sunday - February 17, 1991

Hardest of the bunch up here in the 4th Armoured Brigade is the Royal Scots, the "Jocks." War is their business and has been so for centuries. They have practiced the finer techniques of hand-to-hand combat in Gorbals' backstreets and Leith. They are the old and bold, the most ancient British Regiment of the Line: the Royal Regiment, the First of Foot, "Pontius' Pilate's Bodyguard."

The boys of 5 Platoon, Bravo Company, inform me through their spokesman Pvt. Stephen Gow that they are happy to be here. "Just one great big happy family," grins one, most of his front teeth the casualties of previous battles.

The Jocks live harder than any unit I encountered in the Falklands, even the ferocious Paras. They go to war in the Warrior Infantry Vehicle, with two main guns, and a steel box behind carrying seven fully-laden men who spring out once they are dumped at the edge of the enemy's trenches. To fight hard, they travel light. Five men share one rucksack with a few extra pouches for personal kit. Every spare space on the person and off is reserved for ammunition and grenades.

For weeks now, the Jocks have bristled like hedgehogs, bandoliers of tracer and grenades dangling from belt and harness, ready to be unleashed at a moment's notice.

Each man has a virtually non-existent haircut. The alternatives are short or very short. I took the short course, and my thatch has not been as brief since it was trimmed to cope with the Falklands' peat dust.

The Jock style, too, has its practical side. The scalp is thick with dust in minutes in this season of sandstorms and the hot squalls of the north wind, the "shamal."

At least the Jocks are delivered to battle by their armoured Warriors.

In the Falklands, the main conveyance was helicopter or your own two feet. It was the war of the "yomp," of belts and Bergen rucksacks.

The stars of the show out here are the massive 72-ton Challenger tanks—the heaviest main battle tank ranged on either side, and the M-109 self-propelled guns and the Warrior carriers. Each has turned out a better performer than expected.

More problematic are the older vehicles such as the Ferret Scout Car, designed in the late 1940s and has served in trouble-spots the world over, Aden, Cyprus, and last in Beirut in 1983. They are all older than the men who drive them, and in some cases twice over.

For an aspiring motor insurance agent, they are a nightmare of unreliability. The regimental Sergeant Major of the 14th/20th Hussars was heard to mutter the other day, "If my Ferret collapses once more, I am putting in for an up-armoured Skeda instead."

Mechanised war in tanks and armoured cars is short, sharp and extremely violent. But for the rest it is a matter of waiting, mending equipment and eating.

Each breakfast is the invariable compo baked bean, sausage in a sea of fat and anemic eggs acquired from the Saudis. So unrelenting is this diet that the chief of staff of 4 Brigade, Maj. Julian James, a veteran of the Paras' fight on Mount Longdon in the Falklands, declared, "I am giving up breakfasts—too much cholesterol—I don't want a coronary to get me before I can get at Saddam Hussein."

At times the prospect of closing with Saddam's armies in combat has seemed remote. For a month, the war has been the distant thunder of bombs and artillery beyond the horizon. At night the clouds light up to the flashes of direct hits.

In the day, the sky is criss-crossed by the vapour trails of the massive B-52s and tile smaller F-15s and Tornados, making no attempt to conceal their presence, so convinced are they that they rule the skies. The opening of the ground phase of the campaign seems a movable feast, and any interpretation of how close it is depends on the mood of the moment. In the meantime, business goes on as usual—most prepare for the best, but some of necessity have to prepare for the worst.

Lift the tent flap at the Regimental Aid Post of the 14th/20th Hussars, the main tank force of the 4th Brigade, and you will discover a touch of the West Country. Oilier West Country folk are hidden (in) other interesting places, too: 42 Commando provide close sup-port for the Sea King helicopter force and Lt. Col. Charlie Rogers, the commanding officer of the Staffordshire Regiment, the infantry battalion of 7th Brigade, is a Devon and Dorset in disguise.

The Regimental Aid Posts, the first line of casualty stations behind the fighting elements of the Battle Groups, are manned by bands. In all 16 bands are represented in all with the British 1st Division. The Bandmaster of the 14th/20th Hussars is Colin Hicks, 28, from Liskeard—anything east of the Tamar he considers not truly West Country.

The Hussars, he says, have always looked for bandsmen from the West. Now they are to perform their main duty in battle, to be stretcher-bearers and first aid orderlies to troops wounded in the front line. "No we haven't brought our instruments—we just wouldn't have time to play them," he explains. "Besides, the sand would wreck them."

He admits that he finds the waiting for battle hard. "It's thinking about what's come that worries me most—more for the boys than myself, as I'm still single. The best thing here is sunshine and a day when the tracked ambulances all work." To while away the time, he and the medics have a contest to make anagrams from Saddam Hussein. "The best we've had so far is unprintable: the only mentionable words are Madam Used . . ."

The other main occupation, a duty rather than a pastime, is keeping the desert tidy. It is a question of hygiene—the disease-carrying sand flies have returned—and concealing the unit's presence. A Bounty Bar wrapper can be seen a mile off.

"It's like the old piece of graffiti the Jocks used to scrawl in Germany," grumbled artilleryman. "Join the army to see the world; Join the Queen's Own Highlanders to sweep the sod."

Supply Sergeants Live Cozily in Desert, Where Lumber is Legal Tender: War Means "Trade, Trade Your Ass Off"

By Carol Morello

IN NORTHERN SAUDI ARABIA - Supply Sgt. Leona Overstreet was perplexed when her counterpart from an all-male combat engineers unit dropped by to ask if she had any female sundry kits to swap.

"There's an evac hospital down the road that has body bags, and I need body bags," he explained, "but all they need is tampons. So if you can give me some tampons, I can get my body bags, and I'll get you anything you need."

She sent him merrily on his way with a trash bag filled with tampons, and pocketed an un-cashed chit for a returned favor in the future. Swapping tampons for body bags, an hour of bulldozer time for uniforms and sheets of plywood for just about anything, a network of supply sergeants throughout Saudi Arabia has raised the art of horse-trading to a new high.

With the charm of so many good ole country boys and the tenacity of a door-to-door encyclopedia salesman, they ply the roads of Saudi Arabia in trucks swapping for their immediate needs or, if there's nothing available they need at the moment, for a rainy day.

In theory, they should be able to fill out a requisition form for supplies, and presto, within a few days or weeks it arrives down the supply pipeline. Anything outside the system is technically illegal. And, to hear the supply sergeants tell it, the only thing that makes the Army really work. "Stateside, you can try to ask the system for your needs," said Overstreet, who is with the 937th Engineers Group. "Here, maybe it works, but I haven't seen it. I've done all my supply acquisition through trading."

Even in the U.S., horse-trading is a finely honed Army tradition. But the rapid, massive, ongoing deployment of troops in Saudi Arabia has made it the grease that keeps the military machine on the move. Some even suggest U.S. troops would not be prepared to advance on Iraq were it not for all the horse-trading.

"That has been the success of all the units over here;" said Sgt. 1st Class George Boettjer of Beach Island, S.C., also with the 937th. "Those that hustle have more. This is a wartime logistical situation we've got here, which means trade, trade your ass off."

Boettjer and Maj. Tim Timmons share a small "tent" that has been made cozy as befits the kings of horse-trading. Plywood floors, walls and ceiling shut out the chill night air. A dartboard hangs on the wooden door. Reading lamps are cantilevered over the beds, which have dressing tables with drawers beside them. "I came and saw everyone else was living in the dirt, I said fooey, I'm not going to live like that."

Engineers are the acknowledged grand masters of horse-trading, largely because they possess the skills, machinery and know-how that other companies lack. And in treeless Saudi Arabia, lumber is legal tender for tents, uniforms, medical supplies, even machine guns.

"We as engineers had virtually all the lumber in the theater," said Timmons. "Everyone wanted floors. So when they came to ask for some, I said, 'We're not on the welfare system. We're on the barter system. What have you got to trade?'"

If lumber is gold, services are silver. "You'd be surprised how digging one hole will get you a lot," said Sgt. Keith Hardin, 33, of Shamokin, Pa., a medic with the 27th Engineers Battalion. "If you want something bad enough, you'll do anything to get it. You just stay within legal bounds—well, semi-legal bounds."

Working through these semi-legal bounds, Overstreet, for one, takes a day whenever she can spare one, going unit to unit "begging" for supplies she's short of. "I feel like a bag lady," she said, "going up to perfect strangers and saying, 'May I have some toilet paper?' It's like going to a store without money and saying, 'I can wash your dishes.' But by now we've got like a network going. If someone gets a desirable item, within a day I know about it, even if it's 100 miles down the road."

Machine guns for manning the perimeter came to the 937th via horse-trading, as did several thousand rounds of ammunition. Neither is officially authorized for the group, because it's a headquarters unit. "We're talking about survival here," said Overstreet.

"It's not how many requisitions you can submit. It's who you know here, and what you can do for them. We're just assisting the system, because we're spreading the wealth."

Two 1st Infantry Soldiers Killed by Friendly Fire: Apache Crew "Well-Disciplined, Together 15 Months"

By Michael Hedges

WITH THE 1ST INFANTRY DIVISION - Two soldiers from this division were killed and six others injured when an AH-64 Apache helicopter mistakenly fired into their tracked vehicles.

The deaths marked the first fatalities suffered by an Army unit while engaging the Iraqis, and the first "friendly fire" killings involving helicopters flying in close support of ground operations. According to a division spokesman, the incident occurred at about 1 a.m. this morning (Feb. 17). A division task force was conducting screening operations just inside the Iraqi border when they were intercepted by an Iraqi armored column. In the ensuing firefight, the U.S. forces fired TOW missiles and artillery, then called in Apaches to fire on enemy tanks and armored vehicles.

Through circumstances that division officials said are still not clear, one Apache mistakenly launched Hellfire missiles on an M2 Bradley fighting vehicle and an armored personnel carrier carrying a ground surveillance radar. Both vehicles were destroyed, and two crewmembers of the Bradley were killed. The six injured soldiers are not in serious condition, officials said.

During the battle, at least two Iraqi tanks were destroyed, the officials said. Iraqi forces inflicted no casualties on the U.S. troops. A statement released by the division said, "The Apache crew that fired on the friendly vehicles is a well-disciplined crew and have been flying together for 15 months."

The division continued the heavy bombardment by artillery of Iraqi positions today, firing a total of over 1,500 rounds at enemy positions from 8-inch and 155mm howitzers and multiple launch rocket systems. Over 200 of the rounds were rockets fired from the MLRS.

Neither the Apache pilot nor the U.S. ground forces engaged in the fatal attack could be reached for interviews today.

In an interview in late January, Lt. Col. Ralph Hayles, of Corpus Christi, Tex., the commander of the Apache battalion involved in the mistaken deaths, said while fratricide is always possible, the U.S.-led coalition was using a variety of methods to prevent it. "We have two methods of fire control," he said. "If we fly beyond where friendly forces are the vehicles are in enemy territory, a free-fire zone, and we see vehicles and kill them. But in close contact fighting with tanks, we must have a positive identification to fire," he said.

Methods of obtaining a positive identification varied, Col. Hayles said. One involved having one helicopter fly forward and make an identification while another remained farther back, ultimately to fire if a target proved to be the enemy.

Asked if it was easy for helicopters to get confused in battle, he said, "The Apache always knows where it is, and where the edge of the American forces are. Those are precise measurements. I have a high confidence we won't shoot coalition forces."

But on a recent visit to a cavalry unit on the border which was attempting to trap some Iraqi armor with the help of Apaches, some Bradley drivers had been less than enthusiastic about the Apache. Several Bradley crews claimed the Apache had trouble finding the Iraqis at night. Sgt. Tarin Hawkins, 27, of San Antonio, Tex., said, after listening to soldiers blast the Apache over the radio hookup, "It is true, they have very little faith in the Apache."

From the perspective of the cavalry troopers, the Apaches were failing to find Iraqi vehicles they could plainly see. "If those Apaches can't find the target, let me know and I'll shoot it," said one trooper over the radio.

"This is the most frustrating thing," said Pvt. Hugh Bohannon. "We call them in all night long, and they don't get anything. . . . This is the fourth night in a row we have seen vehicles. They got the best helicopter in the Army here, but they aren't doing diddley."

Body Bags Also Good for Sleeping on Cold Nights

By Frank Bruni

WITH THE U.S. ARMY IN NORTHERN SAUDI ARABIA - Out in the desert, soldiers take comfort wherever they can find it.

Specialist E-4 Shane Batten found it inside a body bag. That's where he slept for two weeks, using the thick nylon as an extra, waterproof shell over his sleeping bag.

Two of the other three men on his M1A1 tank also zipped themselves into the forest green death shrouds every night. They drifted off to sleep knowing that if rain fell, they'd keep dry. If the winds kicked up, they'd keep warm. Among the tank crew, only Specialist E-4 Jerry Keymon slumbered without one. He just couldn't stomach the thought. "Body bags are meant for people who don't get up," said Keymon, 20, of Brown County, Indiana. He shook his head in disgust. Then he smiled and joked about it. "I was raised that you don't get into no body bag unless you're dead," he said with a deep laugh.

This is not a story about a strange but growing trend. To the knowledge of the four men on this tank crew, only about 15 to 20 men in their troop, part of the squadron of the Third Armored Cavalry Reginlent, ever used the body bags. And they all stopped doing so a few days ago. The first sergeant in charge of the enlisted men in the troop came and took the bags away. He never really explained why, they said. He just said it was a bad idea.

Rather, this is an illustration of the way men who have lived five months in the desert, and have spent most nights stretched out atop the hard cold steel of their tank, will lose certain inhibitions, make certain accommodations.

This accommodation surprised them as much as anyone. "Some people walk into graveyards and feel weird. I'm one of those people," said Sgt. Bobby Martin, the tank's commander. He slept in a body bag. The men got the idea a little over two weeks ago, when they were driving their tank through the desert and came upon a bunch of mortar men in their troop sleeping on cots.

It was raining, and the men had scrunched their sleeping bags inside another kind of bag, green and shiny with a zipper up the middle and six strap handles spread across the length of it. The new, extra bags obviously were keeping the men dry. "I said 'Where did you get those?'" said Martin. "I'd never seen one before. After I heard it was a body bag, I said wait a minute," he said. "It was a weird feeling." Martin didn't get one just then, but Batten, who is the main gun loader, and the gunner did, going to a platoon supply area to fetch the bags. They started using them right away.

That night, it rained. Since Keymon, the tank driver, gets to sleep inside the machine, Martin was the only one in the crew to wake up wet. It felt miserable.

"After that, I seen the light, you could say," Martin said. He too got a body bag.

Batten, 21, of Washougal, Wash., (near Portland, Ore.) said each troop gets some body bags to carry with them—into battle. He said he's not sure when the bags came to his troop. But the mortar men discovered the bags—and the way in which they could make outdoors sleeping more comfortable—about three weeks ago.

No one in the troop seemed to have any objections; so long as they knew where the bags were, Batten said. The body bags were roomy enough that sleeping bags fit easily inside them. And the body bags not only kept their inhabitants warm and dry, but also kept the sleeping bags from being coated anew each night with the desert's chalky, dusty sand, which quickly turns bags' cloth from olive green to a speckled beige. "In five months, we've only gotten to wash our sleeping bags once," said Martin, explaining the appeal of the body bags. "How would you like to wash your sheets only once every five months?"

The four-man tank crew deployed to Saudi Arabia with the Third Armored Cavalry Regiment in early October. Their regiment has always been near or right at the front, so their living conditions are among the most Spartan of all service people. Their home is their tank, which now sits on a particularly rocky patch of desert with absolutely no vegetation, not even the gnarled skeleton of a scrub brush. They drive it around during the day, often hooking up with other tanks and soldiers for battle exercises.

They stop it at night and roll out their bags on its top—except for Keymon, who stretches out inside. The tank's surface is hard, but they prefer it to the desert floor, where they might well wake up covered in sand.

They get hot showers perhaps once every two weeks.

It's been rough living, they said, and it only got rougher about a month ago when the rains started and didn't let up for a week. They huddled under ponchos at night, but their sleeping bags got soaked. There was no way around it. Then they found out about the body bags. "When we got them, it was wet and cold and you couldn't keep anything clean," said Batten. The body bag helped.

"You do anything here to get more comfortable."

Martin agreed. "We have nowhere to live inside our tank. We have to live outside. So you're always looking for something to make it easier, to help you out."

Batten said he realizes that using the body bags might sound "ghoulish" to some people, but he didn't see it that way. He saw it as survival.

There was, however, one aspect of the bag that spooked him. "It's a one-way zipper," he said. "If you're inside it and it zips all the way up, you can't get out."

Batten slept with a little hole left open so he could breathe and so his hand could poke back out to work the zipper. But, he said, "I worried about what if someone plays a practical joke and zips it all the way up. I'm kind of claustrophobic. My heart races when I get stuck in a small place." The men said they'd make do without the bags now that they've been taken away, but they'd gladly have them back.

"The first sergeant had bad feelings about us sleeping in them," said Martin. "So he took them back. I understand. But if I could use them again, I would."

Pool Note - At moment, feature material is what's most available to me. Have requested to see and talk with regiment commander and others like that and am told I will get to within next few days, perhaps. Will try to get some news. Also trying to arrange which unit we'll cover (myself, photog, and TV camera) will follow into battle, so we're well positioned.

Non-pool note to Tom Fiedler and Juan Tamayo—Living/space/light conditions make it difficult to spend much time writing, so please forgive rough copy and extend apologies to eds. Doing well and liking it. Please fax copy of this to Detroit at 313-222-5981, attn. Chip Visci, as well as to D.C. Thanks, miss you guys.

Love Can Conquer Fear Even in Battle: "Most of the Time Things Are Screwed Up"

By Jim Michaels

WITH U.S. MARINES, Saudi Arabia - Here on the windswept deserts, Brig. Gen. Tom Draude is fulfilling a promise to himself that he made as a young officer in the jungles of Vietnam more than 20 years earlier.

He said then if he survived his tours in Vietnam, he would describe his combat experiences to young leaders, so they would not face the same nagging uncertainties he had when he faced battle for the first time. Before him about 50 young officers and non-commissioned officers sat squinting into the sun as Draude described the emotions of combat. "Love on the battlefield is what will overcome the effects of fear," Draude told the group of young leaders, only one of whom had seen combat.

U.S. military officers boast of fielding one of the best-trained and equipped fighting forces ever assembled. The ranks are made up of mostly high school graduates who volunteered for service, enticed by educational and job benefits.

During and after Vietnam, the services faced discipline problems so bad that duty officers would not enter some barracks unless they were armed. In today's military, a discipline problem is a private first class talking back to a corporal.

Despite the strides made in discipline and education, the services are led mostly by officers and non-commissioned officers whose only knowledge of combat comes through books and manuals. Nearly 20 years has elapsed since the end of U.S. military involvement in Vietnam. Only a dwindling number of top-ranking officers and non-commissioned officers from that era remain in the service. Grenada and Panama were short episodes that involved relatively small numbers of troops.

As frontline troops prepare for battle here, those few who have actually seen bullets fired in anger are much in demand. The young troops want to know everything from the emotions they will feel to plans for evacuating the wounded from the battlefield.

Draude, who served as a company commander in Vietnam, is a thoughtful officer who currently is reading Henry V in his tent at night, savoring the historical parallels between the scenes Shakespeare described and fielding an army in the twentieth century.

As a junior officer, he remembers the fear and anxieties associated with taking command of Marines in battle and he made a "vow to God" to help future leaders overcome some of those anxieties by talking frankly with them and allowing them to ask questions.

The assistant commander of the 1st Marine Division, Draude when possible visits units scattered throughout the desert. There he finds young officers well-read on gunnery and infantry tactics but starved for anything that will tell them how they can expect to feel and act when the bullets start to fly.

During a recent visit to an artillery unit encamped near the border of Kuwait, the general starts out talking about something as prosaic as sleep. In peacetime training, leaders have a tendency to stay up for the duration of a three- or four-day exercise to ensure it goes right.

In combat, that won't do, Draude explains, because the fighting will not end at the end of a week. Instead, get at least four hours of sleep a night and don't chew out young troops for sleeping during the day. But the core of his message is about fear and how it is overcome. It is love for the Marines in their charge that will overcome fear on the battlefield, not a desire to win a medal or fight for the country.

"The bonds that develop will be what sustain you in combat," Draude tells the group. "There is nothing comparable to the bonds . . . that develop in combat." Peacetime military leaders like to have control over matters. Forget it in combat, Draude counsels. There chaos rules and things always go wrong. "Most of the time things are screwed up."

After the talk a young officer asks about manhandling young troops who might freeze in combat. Draude uses the opportunity to talk about the "moral responsibility" of military leaders. Battle can make civilized people do uncivilized acts.

The general referred to William Manchester's *Goodbye Darkness*, a World War II memoir that described an instance where a Marine was dismembering Japanese bodies. It is the responsibility of combat leaders to make sure things like that do not happen, he said. "As soon as we abdicate our responsibilities as officers and leaders, we've lost it."

Monday
February 18, 1991

U.S. patrols ventured ever farther into enemy territory not yet fanning the bonfire of a great ground offensive, but striking sparks, lighting a tinderbox and blowing on the flame. A story in this chapter describes the aftermath of one cross border foray by Apache helicopters 50 miles inside Iraq that left one officer feeling "great to be alive."

As in other accounts throughout the conflict, the fearsome-looking Apaches appear not simply as a fast means of travel, or high-tech flying weapons, but as looming characters in the drama, leading the action and sometimes overshadowing even the soldiers who operate and depend on them.

Another story, this one about a U.S. artillery barrage aimed at Iraqi air defense positions located in a sparsely defended area, raises a persistent question about reporting on warfare: once shots are fired, giving away an attacker's position, does it violate security to report generally where the shots landed?

The enemy knows where the attack was aimed. The attacker is trained to quickly shift position before the enemy can respond. The artillery barrage in this case originated from an area west of Hafr al Batin along the Saudi-Iraqi frontier that the allies were attempting to use as a secret launching pad for a key part of their eventual ground offensive.

Would the artillery itself give away the allies' secret? Would reporting on the attack lend confirmation? Was the allied presence in the western sector really still a secret by mid-February, or had it already been given away by loose talk, media maps, and informed speculation?

The story passed through security review. Here it is for anyone to judge. The Patriot crews, those heroes of the early days when the first Scuds came flying out of Kuwait and Iraq, were still on duty. The Patriot had knocked some of the wobbly missiles akimbo, destroyed others head-on. Many had thumped harmlessly into uninhabited dunes.

The pace was slowing, but the threat was still there. The Iraqis had become very proficient at using mobile launchers that could be parked, fired, then quickly moved before the allied eyes in the sky could get a bead on them.

The British Special Air Services patrols, on covert duty deep in the Iraqi desert, might see one moving on a highway and call in an air strike. But there always seemed to be more launchers ready to pop up unexpectedly.

That meant the Patriot crews couldn't kick back yet. And as a story in this chapter points out, they remained alert and eager to hit the trigger key on their computers. The post-war assessment of this phase of the allied effort was very contentious. Making matters worse, Saddam Hussein never announced how many Scuds or Scud launchers the allies managed to destroy.

In the air war, a good day's work by a helicopter crew rescued the pilot of an American F-16 shot down over Kuwait. But in the Persian Gulf, floating mines damaged two U.S. ships—the Tripoli and the Princeton—injuring seven sailors.

"Turkey Shoot!"—Ugly and Ominous Apaches Stage Nighttime Assault 50 Miles Inside Iraq

By Robert Dvorchak

IN NORTHERN SAUDI ARABIA - U.S. Army Apache helicopters attacked Iraqi tanks and gun positions early Monday. One pilot returning from the nighttime raid called it "a turkey shoot."

The assault occurred more than 50 miles inside Iraq. The Apaches knocked out two tanks, one armored vehicle and several trucks, according to preliminary casualty reports.

Some pilots reported receiving anti-aircraft and small-arms fire, but none of the Apaches were damaged, officers said. "We dealt him some serious punishment. We caught him totally by surprise," said Maj. Lee Stuart, executive officer of an attack battalion for a paratroop division.

"The Air Force has been after them 24 hours a day. Now all of a sudden somebody's coming out of the ground after him. They probably got the fear of God put in them," said Stuart, 43, of Jonesboro, Ga. "The Apaches rule the night."

Pilots said they fired laser-guided Hellfire missiles, 2.75-inch rockets and 30-millimeter cannon at Iraqi tanks, air defense artillery and artillery positions.

The high-tech Apache, the Army's highly-touted tank killer, attacked without running lights using infrared sensors and invisible laser beams.

For many pilots, it was their first combat mission. All rated it a nerve-wracking success. "We popped the cherry. Broke the ice. We've been sitting here waiting almost seven months to do something," said Chief Warrant Officer 2 Mike Brillant, 28, a pilot from Fort Lauderdale, Fla.

"It was not a good night for the Iraqis," said Capt. Jess Farrington, 32, of Milton, Fla., a company commander. "We caught them with their shorts down. They were in their sleeping bags. It was a turkey shoot."

Capt. Robert Tuggle, also a company commander, said he saw a tank get hit and then witnessed secondary explosions from fuel tanks or munitions going off. "We got some real good hits. That thing lit up the battlefield," said Tuggle, 31, of Columbus, Ga. He also said the Iraqis were confused and disorganized when the Apaches struck without warning.

"They were running around like a bunch of goobers. They didn't know which way to run," Tuggle said. Portions of three attack companies took off shortly after midnight beneath a blanket of stars twinkling in the inky blackness. The thundering birds of prey, which resemble giant insects from another planet, thundered off without lights and headed north.

"It's ugly but it's ominous. It's a scary-looking airplane," said Capt. Stewart Hamilton, 34, of Haven, Kan., operations officer for the attack battalion.

"We did what we wanted to do the way we planned it. We were hand-delivering ordnance. He could hear us but couldn't see us. I think it scared the daylights out of him," Hamilton said. He also said the adrenaline was flowing before, during, and after the raid. Some pilots were still pumped hours after the mission. "The air smells good. The cold feels good. It's great to be alive."

Before the Apaches left, crew chiefs painted personal messages on their Hellfire missile. Pfc. Thomas Nowacki, 21, of Detroit, Mich., used colored chalk his mother had sent him to write "Camel Smoker" on one. It was his way of getting into the war. "It's just something personal. We're done messing around," Nowacki said. "They won't even hear it. It's just waste them."

Other messages on the missiles included: "When you care enough to send the very best."

"Eat this."

"Baghdad Express."

"This Bud is for You."

Some technicians expressed some tinge of regret because their high-tech weaponry gave the Iraqis no mercy. "It's almost kind of cheating. There's just no place to hide," said Staff Sgt. Michael Osborne, 37, of Monterey Park, Calif., an ordnance specialist.

And the pilots expressed supreme confidence in their high-tech gadgetry. "It sounds morbid to say it was fun. It's like playing a video game," Tuggle said.

During training, Apache Hellfires had hit all six of the targets it fired at in Saudi Arabia. The Apache is made to operate at night, under cover of darkness, to enhance the element of surprise." The idea is to come in from where they don't think you're going to come in from," said battalion commander Lt. Col. Bill Tucker, 40, of Hoanoke, Ala.

"The Apache is the Mercedes of helicopters," Tucker said. "They can't see us at night. We can see them. They can only hear us for a couple of seconds and we're gone."

Pfc. Robert Adams, 21, of Columbia, S.C., watched the assault formation rise from the ground while he was on guard duty. "I wish Saddam could see this. I'd laugh in his face," Adams said. "I'd hate to be in his shoes."

U.S. Artillery Hits Mostly Desert: Iraqi Commanders Now Have Confirmation Allies Have Moved Far West

By Joseph Albright

NOTE TO COL. MULVEY OR COL. ICENOGLE FROM JOE ALBRIGHT: I am pretty sure this doesn't violate the ground rules as they are written now. The Iraqis know what hit them and where. The fact that military is in this area is no longer a secret because of previous print and TV reports. But if you two guys feel very strongly that this should not be published, you have my permission to spike it.

WITH U.S. FORCES in Northern Saudi Arabia - The United States on Monday fired hundreds of artillery rounds into southern Iraq into a weakly defended stretch of desert south of Baghdad.

The barrage broke the stillness of the moonless early morning hours, forcing the Iraqi military command to estimate on short notice whether this is an allied feint or a prelude to an actual attack in this region.

American artillery officers said Iraqi observers near the border would have no trouble figuring out form the near-simultaneous appearance of muzzle flashes on the horizon that this was an artillery strike and not another air raid. And in the firm desert sand, the shells dig angular furrows that are unmistakable signatures of ground-fired weapons.

The artillery rounds fell into a zone of targets west of the triangular junction of the Kuwait, Iraq and Saudi borders. For months, Iraq has concentrated virtually all its more than 500,000 troops confronting the allies into a ring of tanks, minefields and artillery guns in and around Kuwait itself. For reasons that have puzzled the allied military planners, Iraq has left its own southern border to the south of its capital relatively undefended.

American Army artillerymen said minutes after firing their 155mm howitzer into Iraq that they hoped their shots would hasten the end of their service in Saudi Arabia. "It's about time," said Sgt. Gerald Moore, 22, of Perry, FL, a gunner. "Finally we are not just sitting around waiting. I'm not saying we are warmongers or anything like that. We don't want to see anyone get killed or nothing. But we came here for a mission."

The artillery strikes fell into a virtually uninhabited stretch of Iraqi desert. The terrain is gently rolling desert whose surface is hard enough for rapid movement by tanks, trucks and even four-wheel-drive civilian station wagons. In some places, there are ridgelines resembling low buttes in eastern Wyoming.

The artillery rounds rained on or near Iraqi air defense positions to facilitate a concentrated air strike in southern Iraq by American helicopter gunships.

The helicopters were thought to be hitting scattered armored units that are deployed in relatively small numbers some 30 miles back from the Iraq-Saudi frontier.

Given the overall scale of the allied air campaigns, Monday's air attack was a pinprick. The significance is that Iraqi military commanders now have painful confirmation of their earlier suspicions that the allies had moved some significant ground forces at least temporarily to a possible jumping-off point far to the west of Iraq's massed tanks and minefields inside Kuwait.

The artillery rounds landed south of Baghdad and south-southeast of the Iraqi highway that runs along the Euphrates River and has been used to carry supplies from factories near Baghdad to frontline Iraqi troops in Kuwait.

The nearest Kuwaiti border post is nearly 200 miles to the east-southeast.

Army Capt. Bill Vockery, 29, of Richmond, Ky, the commander of one of the U.S. artillery batteries that fired 155mm howitzers, said the artillery barrage into this part of Iraq is likely to put Iraqi military commanders in a military quandary.

"He's got to be getting kind of worried," said Vockery. "He got to be looking at it and saying, 'I've got all my armored forces down in Kuwait.' Because of our air superiority, he can't get much forces over here right now."

Vockery said he understands the Iraqi positions in the region where the shells fell are manned mainly by "retirees and youngsters."

British Artillery Break Out New Multi-Barrel Guns: "I Can't Help Feeling Sorry for the Iraqis"

By Gordon Airs

WITH THE 1ST BRITISH ARMOURED DIVISION, Northern Saudi Arabia - The British Army fired its first shots against Iraqi front line positions yesterday in a dramatic build-up to a land war.

And I was one of only two U.K. newspapermen present for the historic two-hour barrage only yards from the border.

Sgt. Major Ken Cummins screamed: "Stand by...FIRE!" and the army's brand-new multi-barreled rocket launchers screamed into life...causing death and destruction.

Firing ear-shattering salvos of 12, they thundered from their tracked vehicles, the rockets blasting a fiery tail high into the sky leaving streams of yellow smoke in their wake.

Their 18 targets were about 18 miles away, and U.S. A-10 recce planes immediately flashed back results: Three tanks, three gun positions and three guns destroyed.

The computerised launchers of the Royal Artillery's 39 Heavy Regiment took part in the dangerous artillery raid operation. It's known to the gunners as "shoot and scoot."

The self-propelled launchers screamed through clouds of dust and sand to set up their attack right at the front line . . . under the very noses of the enemy. The 12 launchers rapidly fired off their first salvos—then quickly packed up their gear and moved to another nearby location before any Iraqi guns could return fire.

Then again, with Union Jack flags proudly flying from the machines, they started firing once more. This was repeated several times. But although commanders feared Iraqi artillery hitting back, thankfully there was none, although ambulances and medical teams were on the scene. The launchers only came into service in the past six months, and each rocket unleashed 644 deadly bomblets in killing clusters.

After the first salvos the gunners, normally based in Germany, cheered and waved flags before moving to a safer spot. The Division's Scottish Commander Royal Artillery, Brigadier Ian Durie, carrying his ever-present five-foot long cromag walking stick, was well-pleased at the first shots in anger.

"The early battle damage results are encouraging. It shows the aim of the attack has almost certainly been achieved. There was a real threat from enemy attacks, but fortunately there were none this time.

"I hope it is because their command control systems have been degraded and they can't respond in time. Or else they may be biding their time and waiting until we attack across the border so that they don't give away more of their positions. As soon as they fire back they give their positions away. I hope it is the first and not the second, but only time will tell. Anyway, today brings the land war closer."

Lt. Col Peter Williams, CO of the 39 regiment smiled: "They fired absolutely brilliantly. This is a devastating weapon. I pity the poor blighter at the other end. The gunners are looking forward to getting on with the job now. These launchers bring down an extraordinary amount of firepower, and are remarkably accurate. If we aim at a target, we hit it.

"I must admit I didn't expect it to be so effective against tanks—that's very heartening. But I can't help feeling sorry for the Iraqis."

One of the Scots involved was gunner Billy Grace, 18, from Springburn, Glasgow, a signaler. He said: "It's bloody marvelous. This is what all the training has been about. I'm glad it's started so we can get back home as soon as possible."

Grinned Sgt. Major Cummins—who screamed the fire order because of strict radio silence: "As we say, the Royal Artillery always brings some dignity to what would otherwise be a vulgar brawl . . ." The 12 launchers and their escorts streamed back in clouds of sand, flags flying, fists clenched in salute, to their safe base out of enemy artillery range.

History had just been made—and they were proud to have been part of it.

Lionized Patriot Battery Yearns for Another Kill: "You Are the Very Best Soldier in Saudi Arabia"

By Dave Montgomery

FOXTROT PATRIOT BATTERY, Eastern Saudi Arabia - Once again, Sgt. Eric Sellers of Bossier City, La., was "watching the skies" on the circular screen inside his cramped concealed van, but once again, there were no ominous blips.

Another day without a Scud. With the persistent allied pounding of Scud missile sites, Sellers and other "button-pushers" at

Patriot missile batteries say they are beginning to feel as lonely as the Maytag repairman.

At Foxtrot, the Patriot crews yesterday were still yearning for their first kill. At Bravo battery down the road, there hadn't been a Patriot vs. Scud collision since Jan. 28. "We want some action," said Spec. 4 Kenneth Watthuber, 20, of Houston, a Scudfinder, or tactical control assistant, at Foxtrot. "We've been here for a long time and we figure we should get one. It's something you can tell your grandchildren about."

At Foxtrot and Bravo, the frenetic days of incessant alerts and round-the-clock entrenchment in sandbag bunkers have given way to a more subdued routine. At both batteries yesterday, off-duty crews tossed the basketball or watched television while on-duty crews, working 24 hours a day, in three-hour shifts, maintained their vigil at the radar screen.

But the more orderly pace by no means suggests that the famed Patriot missile units are easing off, said Lt. Col. Leroy Neel, of Houston, commander of the battalion that includes all Patriot batteries in Eastern Saudi Arabia.

"They have been trained not to let their guard down until this thing is completely over," said Neel. "When your life's at stake, you don't let your guard down."

Nor has the downturn in Scud attacks eroded any of the celebrity which began washing onto Patriot crews when their 17-foot-tall missiles first started knocking Scuds from the skies. T-shirts, goodie bags, posters, cards, letters and other tokens of appreciation continue to pour into the Patriot defenders from admirers back home. President Bush drew thunderous applause last week when he told Raytheon employees, who make the weapon, "Thank God for the Patriot missile."

"They're deciding now when they make the movie who's going to play us," joked Randy Hackaday, 39, of Fort Worth, the first sergeant of the Foxtrot battery. "I'm hoping for Tom Selleck for myself." Hackaday and other soldiers at Foxtrot have received phone calls from deejays and admiring letters from people they haven't heard from in years.

Delicia Alvarez' kindergarten class at Fort Worth's Bruce Shulkey Elementary School penned a giant letter to Hackaday with greetings and advice such as: "Don't get hurt. I hope you catch Saddam. Do you know my Uncle Wayne? I hope the war is over soon." Hackaday said his favorite was: "You are the very best soldier in Saudi Arabia."

At Bravo, the latest gift arrived yesterday from Dow Chemical employees in Freeport, Tex.—a yellow banner proclaiming "Scud Busters," with mini-versions of the U.S. flag and the Texas flag in the corners.

Neel, a graduate from the University of Texas, also has a Texas flag displayed in his room—a gift which he received last year from then-Gov. Bill Clements.

"There are quite a few Texans" in the battalion, Neel said. "I've got a lot of aggies working for me. We're always hurling insults at each other."

Neel not only approves of relaxation and light moments among his troops—he instigates them. The 19-year veteran artillery officer is constantly looking for ways to guard against burnout among his crews and consequently has adorned Bravo battery with morale-boosting creature comforts, ranging from a weight room to hot showers.

. . . Of the 67 Scud attacks throughout the Persian Gulf theater, the batteries in his battalion have downed 10, without one miss. Neel is equally proud of another statistic—of all the troops in his battalion, he said, there hasn't been a single fight.

"What you fear is a lackadaisical attitude and a soldier who thinks he's doing all the giving and you're not giving back," he said. "Three meals and pay just doesn't cut it."

His approach, he said, is aimed at "clearing the cobwebs" and providing diversion from the occupational pressures of Scud-finding and living in constant fear of attack by terrorists or chemical weapons. He compares his battalion to a sports team.

"You've got to know how the system works. You've got to know the plays. You've got to have faith in your coach, faith in the team so that you can help the whole team effort. Which, in this case, is knocking down Scuds."

Tuesday
February 19, 1991

By mid-February, the allied armada in the Persian Gulf was in total control—almost—of the sea approaches to the battle zone.

Except for the aircraft carriers launching sorties headed for targets inland, the decks were quieter now. The riveting aerial show any time a ship fired some top-of-the-line, million-bucks-a-throw Tomahawk missiles was a thing of the past. The Tomahawks were too expensive to waste, and more pedestrian missiles delivered by fighter planes were accomplishing the job. The allied sortie count had just clicked over 67,000.

But those pesky floating mines the Iraqis strewed in the water before the armada arrived were still there. Two U.S. ships—the Tripoli and the Princeton—ran into some. Another story recounts the capture of an Iraqi observation post. No enemy soldiers were at the site, but it was perched on high ground in the border region that commanded a good view of the surrounding desert.

If anyone was going to have that view, the U.S. Army wanted it to be them. The minor action represented one more step toward an all-out confrontation.

While combat units drew their straps tighter, some soldiers who had helped bring the allied force to the brink of combat were taking a step back. In the Gulf War, there were a number of women in frontline units, but females were barred from filling positions designated as ground combat.

U.S. forces in the Gulf included about 30,000 women, about six percent of the total, a larger percentage than in any previous war. In this chapter, a platoon of firefighter-reservists says goodbye to two of its own, Sharon and Diane. Everyone is brave, but not without a few tears.

While no chemical, nerve or biological agents had yet been used, the allies knew that Saddam Hussein's arsenal included some, so precautions continued. In addition to the U.S. Army's detection vehicles shipped from Germany, the Saudi commander, Gen. Khalid, had brought a 200-man Czech military chemical detection unit to the war zone to work directly for the Saudi army.

Independent television producer Don North, who directed documentary footage for Gen. Khalid during the war, said the Czechs detected traces of chemicals—mustard and sarin gas—in January near the Kuwait border they suspected were produced by allied air attacks on Iraqi chemical-weapons storage facilities.

The allied air commander, Gen. Horner, spoke in a post-war interview with PBS about the command's concern over possible fallout from air strikes aimed at—or accidentally striking—the Iraqi stores of chemical and biological weapons.

He summarized several scientific studies he consulted as warning that bombing those sites would release deadly spores and "every living person on the Saudi Arabian peninsula would have been killed."

His concerns were later allayed, he said, by advice from a U.S. Army biological warfare officer who told him spores released by attacks on the supplies of such agents would be dispersed by wind or killed by sunlight or chlorinated water.

After briefing Secretary Cheney on the major's assertions, he said, the air attacks were approved. "We struck 'em and to the best of my knowledge there was nobody died from the fallout from those attacks."

USS Princeton, USS Tripoli Hit Mines: Sailor Sleeping in Brig Woke Up "Wondering If I Was Dead"

By Bill Gannon and David Alexander

SUMMARY: USS Princeton under tow and out of action, heading to coalition Gulf state south for survey and repair. USS Tripoli slips out of minefield, damage contained but compartments still flooded and future uncertain. Tripoli captain is hopeful helicopter carrier will remain in action but awaits final damage assessment report and decision from NAVCENT-Riyadh. Corrects size of hole in hull to 16 feet in diameter instead of initial report of 16 x 25.

POOL NOTE: USS Tripoli blast damage descriptions obtained when Gannon twice donned OBA (oxygen breathing apparatus) to go below decks with Navy inspection and repair crews. UPI photographer Joe Mahoney also went below and has moved blast photos to pool.

ABOARD THE USS TRIPOLI, Northern Persian Gulf - Two American warships crippled by blasts from suspected Iraqi mines limped out of a complex minefield off the coast of Kuwait Tuesday as damage assessment teams from a repair ship in the Gulf attempted to determine how badly they were stricken after being jolted by the explosive devices.

The USS Princeton, a Tomahawk guided missile cruiser, was disabled and undertow off the Kuwaiti coast Tuesday after striking a mine Monday morning.

Her rudder control seriously damaged and aft starboard hull crinkled by the blast, the Princeton was being towed south by the USS Buford, an ocean going tug. The vessels were heading for a coalition Gulf state for extensive inspection and repairs that may require dry docking, Navy officials aboard the helicopter carrier USS Tripoli said.

The Princeton, which was protecting a minesweeping taskforce clearing a 20-mile long east-to-west sea-lane off the Kuwaiti coast, struck what is believed to have been a submerged influence mine at 7:15 a.m. Monday.

The blast cracked the aft midsection of the vessel, damaging its power plant and rudder controls, Navy officials aboard the Tripoli said.

An Iraqi influence mine contains 400 kilograms of TNT equivalent and explodes in response to the magnetic or acoustic signature of a passing vessel, according to Capt. David Grieve, commodore of the minesweeping taskforce.

As seamen aboard the disabled cruiser restored power, British and American helicopters and minesweepers completed a 10-hour survey of the waters around the Princeton, looking for additional mines.

On Monday evening, the Buford was brought alongside and placed the Princeton under tow. The vessels were led to safe sea-lanes by the minesweeper USS Adroit, according to Capt. Bruce McEwen of the

USS Tripoli. Hours before the Princeton incident and 10 miles south, the Tripoli strayed into a minefield and was rocked by a contact mine explosion that punched a 16-foot diameter hole in the forward starboard section of the carrier's hull at 4:36 a.m. Several compartments were flooded on three decks, leaving the 18,000-ton Iwo Jima class vessel adrift in the minefield.

Helicopters and minesweepers circled the crippled carrier, spotting and marking at least three mines with smoke canisters before the power was restored and the ship was safely slipped out of the minefield. It fell in behind the Princeton and the Adroit and headed south 16 hours after the blast.

Despite damage to a forward engine room, a pump room, a dry storage locker and other compartments, the captain of the Tripoli was optimistic the vessel would be able to remain in action. "The ship is capable of continuing operations at this point," said Capt. Bruce McEwen in a Monday evening interview.

"The mine hit in the forward starboard side of the ship. We have two compartments forward that are flooded. It really presents no significant problem to us . . . the ship is not in extremis," he noted.

According to one damage control officer, if the mine had struck the vessel just 20-feet aft, the results could have been much different. "I'd say it was approximately 20 feet away from the (ammunition) magazine. If it would have blown it, we wouldn't be talking right now," said Don Ingram of San Diego, Cal.

On Monday afternoon, a team of damage control experts were flown to the carrier from the USS Jason. The effects of the blast aboard the Tripoli were relatively minor with brief loss of power and rudder control, Jason repair crewmen said.

But Monday afternoon, the ship's future was less certain. Seamen and Marines at their battle stations anxiously scanned the waters below as British and American helicopter crews spotted at least three mines, dropping smoke canisters to mark the positions. "Look, another one. Damn it. We're in a minefield and no power," said Jim Walson, a 19-year-old machinist mate from San Diego on his first cruise.

"Easy, seaman. We got lots of friends out here. They'll take good care of us," added machinist mate David Waite, 36, from Chicago, Ill., and a 16-year veteran of submarines, aircraft carriers, and now, the Tripoli.

Throughout the vessel, tension was diffused by gallows humor as firefighters and damage control crews traded their first war stories before having to don oxygen-breathing apparatus (OBA) to go below decks. Prying open a buckled escape hatch, a seaman dropped a ladder into the darkness below. Wiggling down the narrow hatch, crewmen reached the bottom of the ladder, paused and listened.

The ship eerily quiet with its engines still shut down, the waters of the Persian Gulf could be heard lapping against the sides of the bulkheads.

The water was warm and knee-deep in sections and the deck underfoot was slick. The first sweep of a flashlight finds sheet metal walls buckled, thick deck floors ripped away, ladders twisted, and hatches jammed shut by the force of the explosion.

"The compartments directly below are completely flooded," yelled seaman Perry Joiner, 22, of San Diego and one of the ship's journalists through his OBA facemask.

Peering into a small area closer to the hull, the compartment is full of twisted metal wreckage, floating debris, and ankle-deep grey paint-tinted water. The paint had been stored in the now-flooded locker compartment below and took the brunt of the blast. From the hangar deck above, grey paint mixed with an oil slick on the Persian Gulf, creating a swirling two-tone hue. Back down below, moving from one small compartment into the brig section, a 2-foot gash in the deck lies directly below a wrecked bunk.

Edwin Alvarez's bunk. The 30-year-old master of arms from Carolina, Puerto Rico, had recently taken to sleeping in the brig cell, which is also used to berth crewmen.

"Privacy. It's hard to find here. When we don't have people in the brig, my partner or I sleep there sometimes," he explained in an interview in the ship medical ward later. "I was asleep and was thrown out of my rack (bunk) by the explosion right underneath me. I was pretty shaken up . . . the sound of the explosion was like a real loud boom," he recalled. "I remember wondering if I was dead. But then I could smell these strong fumes and I could see there was a fire in the paint locker in this huge hole in the deck under my rack," Alvarez said.

"I knew then I was alive and I had to find my way out. At first, I thought a plane had hit the side of the ship. Then I realized I was cut up and covered by something—but it was just paint," he added, displaying cuts and scrapes on his chest and arms.

"Some of my buddies think that maybe I'll get a Purple Heart," Alvarez said, smiling. "I have to admit that would be real nice. But the main thing is that I don't have to sleep below decks tonight. I don't want to go back down there and sleep for awhile."

Women Engineers Not in the Fight and They're Sorry— "You'd Better Come Back . . . You'd Better . . ."

By Carol Morello

IN NORTHERN SAUDI ARABIA - It had rained the day before, and as Monday dawned bright and clear, tiny sprigs of clover poked their heads through the desert floor. It was a morning that made it possible to forget, for a brief shining moment, what the day represented, even as it made a mockery of it.

For Monday was a day for partings of friends and lovers in the 467th Engineer Platoon Firefighters. They had come over together in early December, a reserve unit based in Garden City, Kan. that had never before been deployed to foreign shores. But Sgt. Diana Laskey and Sharon Marquez had been peeled away from the unit to another camp down the road when the order came that women would not go into combat.

"Every time one of you leaves, it reminds me that we have no control over the situation," one of the firefighters wrote Marquez of the four reservists who have been farmed out elsewhere.

For almost three months, the two women had managed weekly visits back to the 467th, where Laskey's husband remains. They knew that Monday was probably their last visit before the firestorm that is to come. And so Laskey and Marquez returned to their tent to shave their legs, spray each others' necks with perfume and don a little eyeliner. While they were gussying themselves up, an officer came to the tent to order them outside to pick up a new supply of anti-nerve agents injections and pills.

When they returned, Specialists Gordon Morton and Larry Coltharp had arrived to pick them up. They threw their heavy flak jackets on the women's cots, plopped down to wait, and talked about the news.

A soldier using his gas mask for a pillow had laid his head on an atropine injector stored inside, sending the drug shooting through his skull and killing him.

More bombs had been dropped overnight in Iraq. Some American soldiers had been killed in border skirmishes. Coltharp said he senses more anxiety now than on Jan. 17 when the air war began. "Everyone's a lot more scared and terrified," he said. "I just tell them, 'Let the Lord take care of you, and you do your soldiering.'"

Morton pulled out a wallet photograph of his wife, Brenda, and 3-year-old son waiting for him back in Kansas. "I remember the time we thought reservists wouldn't go," he said. "I remember the time I was playing cat and mouse with my wife, and I got the call saying we'd been activated. When I told her, she said 'Sure,' and laughed. Then we turned on the TV and heard the 467 had been activated, and she started bawling."

He paused, and looked at his picture. "Last night, I was thinking of my son drooling, looking up at me," he said, his eyes lingering on the photo.

"I've told my wife, be ready to have another baby when I get home."

The theme of getting home dominated the conversation on the five-minute drive to the 467th. Parties were planned, as if they were on a Kansas hayride instead of bouncing down a desert road with tanks and camouflage tents out the windows, having to say cods wrdsto get home.

Laskey disappeared into a tent where her husband, Brian, sleeps. They sat on a cot and embraced, their kisses interrupted by soldiers tromping through.

Their conversation was no casual lovers chat.

Rather, they talked of what Brian Laskey called "death scenarios," and how to break the news to their three children if one of them does not come home. "We have risk factors in the states," he said. "Any time you drive a truck, you're taking a risk. Well, I figure the risk factor just jumped up 10 times here for us. It's time we talk about it."

He told her gently that if one of them dies, the other should remarry, for the sake of the children. Diana shook her head in disagreement. "You should get married again, for the sake of an income," he pressed on. "We have to think of the kids first. In my situation, it wouldn't be for the income, it would be to have a mother for them." But Diana was hearing none of it. "You'd better come back, you'd better come back," she scolded him, one hand resting on his shoulder and the other waving a finger at him. "And when you do, you'd better come find me first."

Later, out of her husband's hearing, she confided how deeply his words had upset her. "I don't know why he said what he did," she said. "I thought about all that a month ago." And then she put her head in her hands and wept.

Out in the camp, the men of the 467 were packing their gear, smearing a half-inch of mud on fire trucks and washing their clothes in empty barrels of fire-fighting foam. Marquez wandered through the camp like the proverbial earth mother, as the soldiers who consider her like a sister and confidante called out using her nickname. "Hey, Munchie, c'mere," they beckoned to her, affectionately using the shortened form of Munchkin tagged to her because of her diminutive stature.

One by one, she wandered off with them to listen as they poured their hearts out, suddenly seeming older than the 20-year-old young woman who crosses off the days on a rose-colored calendar at the head of her cot and falls asleep at night clutching the teddy bear her boyfriend gave her before she left for Saudi Arabia.

First Sgt. Gilbert Cruz, a 20-year-old Colorado State student, got her attention first. He came to Saudi Arabia in the same unit as his two older brothers, Jonas, 21, and Phillip, 23. The Army had been willing to separate them and spread them around

Saudi Arabia, to make sure that at least one of Jenny Cruz' only three children make it home from the war alive.

The three brothers had shut themselves in a room to talk it out. Gilbert and Philip, both bachelors, had wanted Jonas, who got married just last summer, to stay. But ultimately, they had decided that they had grown up together and so they would go to war together—and come back home together.

On Sunday, the decision had begun haunting Gilbert. "In fact, if this was a prolonged conflict, I think I'd be scared of that closeness. Losing friends, I feel such a responsibility for them. I worry about that, how I'll handle it if I lose some.

"That's my biggest fear. Not going up, not being in Iraq. My biggest fear is losing someone. What if something happens to one of the Cruz brothers? What if something happens to Brian? If it does, I don't want anybody else to tell Diana. Yet I realize it would be somebody else, if we're up forward."

As the afternoon wore on, Marquez wandered over to where Spec. Ken Fresquez, 26, of Denver, was sitting on a stack of MRE boxes. In his Kevlar helmet, he carries a little stuffed bunny she gave him for good luck. On Monday, she also gave him the rosary that she has not taken off for two years since her boyfriend gave it to her with the admonition to come home safely. "Someone I care for very much gave this to me," she said, "and now I want to give it to someone I care for."

"My mother mailed me some Noxema here, and I gave it to a woman I met on Valentine's Day who was sad because she hadn't received any Valentines," said Fresquez. "She was so happy she almost hugged me. I guess little things mean a lot here." He paused, then leaned over to pat Marquez' boot. "Like friends," he said.

That night, the soldiers of the 467 stood in a circle holding hands while Gilbert Cruz said a prayer of coming home. The men to either side of Marquez gripped her hands so tightly that her hands turned numb.

And off to the side of the camp, just beyond the perimeter berm, a line of tanks roared past.

Iraqi Troops Fake Surrender to Locate U.S. Border Positions, Pay Dearly

By Michael Hedges

WITH THE 1ST INFANTRY DIVISION - For four tense hours tonight soldiers from this division played cat and mouse with an Iraqi reconnaissance patrol that apparently faked surrender in an effort to find U.S. positions.

Finally, the soldiers fired machine guns into the Iraqi patrol, hitting at least one of the enemy soldiers. The small firefight illustrated the growing contact between opposing armies here as evidence grows that a ground offensive may be imminent.

Throughout the day, U.S. forward battalions fired on Iraqi positions with an array of weapons. From a location near the Saudi-Iraq border, the soft thump of mortar rounds was occasionally overridden by the deeper boom of 155-mm and 8-inch howitzers.

A-10 Warthogs, used to kill Iraqi armor, passed over to drop their bombs just beyond the line of sight. Lt. Col. Dan Magee, a brigade executive officer of the 1st Infantry Division, said that in addition to artillery raids against pre-set targets, the brigade was firing at Iraqi armored and foot patrols bumping into U.S. lines. "They will fire, then displace, fire and move again," he said. "Right now we are still in a defensive posture. But it is an aggressive defense."

High-ranking division officers said they have not been told a precise time when the outfit would go from a defensive to an offensive posture. Until then, the unit's most forward detachments are continuing to engage in a nerve-stretching game of trying to locate Iraqi positions while keeping enemy eyes off U.S. deployments.

Lt. Col. Skip Baker, 45, of Odessa, Tex., commands the 5th Battalion, 16th Infantry, the Devil's Rangers, a mixed task force of M1A1 tanks and Bradley fighting vehicles. Shortly after midnight tonight, he said, the Iraqis started sending small patrols his way. "We started picking them up in ones and twos through our thermal sights," he said.

The leader of one Iraqi patrol would stand up and wave what looked like a small staff or flag as if he wanted to attract the attention of U.S. soldiers.

"We couldn't really tell what he was holding, it was pitch black," said Col. Baker. "We tried to coax them in by flashing lights and putting up illumination rounds."

The Iraqis would appear to move forward as if to surrender, then disappear down small defiles, popping up at other locations.

Col. Baker, who was a company commander in Vietnam, said he determined the tactic was Iraqi deception. "I won't know for sure until I ask their commander, and I intend to do that," he said. "Like any good recon, they kept pushing until they hit the wall of jello," he said. At about 4 a.m., the lieutenant colonel said he decided the Iraqis had been given ample opportunity to surrender.

He ordered machine guns to fire on either side of them. When that didn't precipitate their surrender, "we fired them up," he said.

One of those firing into the Iraqis was Capt. Rick Orth, 30, of Port Jefferson, N.Y. "We know we hit one, we could see a pool of blood in the thermal sights," he said. The sights also picked up what appeared to be a body lying in a narrow gulley.

Capt. Orth said he was torn in his mind about ordering his men to shoot at the prone form. "I thought about ordering another burst into the body, but I didn't," he said. "If I had it to do over again, I probably should have."

Capt. Orth appeared to be going through the mental and emotional transition many of these men face to become combat veterans.

"I noticed when the shooting was over, I didn't call them (the Iraqis) soldiers. I called them dismounts," he said. "I guess that is part of the dehumanizing process." He marveled that his baptism of fire had passed so effortlessly. "I'd wondered what it would be like," he said when asked about shooting at Iraqis. "But I didn't have any problem with it."

Capt. Orth said his company behaved with discipline when confronted by the Iraqi patrols. "You'd expect when the firing started to have a mad minute," he said. "But only the two I ordered to do so fired. We didn't shoot indiscriminately."

Col. Baker said he waited to fire at the patrol in hopes of gathering prisoners who could provide the division with updated intelligence. "I tell my soldiers that every live prisoner is worth 100 dead guys," he said. "But I can't allow them to remain in my sector indefinitely," Col. Baker said. Asked what the Iraqis might have accomplished with their reconnaissance, he said, "I don't know what he learned except if he gets too close I'll shoot him up."

A patrol sent out by the Americans to search for Iraqi wounded or bodies had not returned by late morning. Some of the soldiers felt the terrain, cut by dry stream beds and small rises, would allow the Iraqis to move their wounded back undetected.

"It'll be like Vietnam," said a sergeant who served there. "We won't find anything."

While waiting for the patrol to return, the battalion underwent what is becoming an increasingly common ritual, a rehearsal of its battle plans with all officers. Later in the day, senior battalion officers would go through the same exercise on a brigade level. As the captains and lieutenants gathered, they passed around some of the leaflets dropped by coalition planes on Iraqi troops in an effort to induce them to surrender.

On the front of the leaflets are cartoon drawings. A black-and-white version has two panels, one showing Iraqi soldiers eating heartily while kneeling beside a fruit basket while an Arabic-looking soldier looks on.

The second panel shows an Iraqi soldier with his gun slung over his left arm presenting a leaflet to the Arabic soldier. The color leaflet shows an Iraqi soldier with an idea balloon over his head surrendering to a man wearing a U.N. armband. In the thought balloon, the Iraqi is imagining himself with his wife and two children.

An American soldier who said he had the Arabic writing on the back of the pamphlets interpreted by a Kuwaiti said a paraphrase of the message would be, "You fought well for your homeland, but now it is time to give it up and get something to eat or you will meet your doom and never see your family again."

Water Well Appears Magically in Desert: "For Those of You Who Don't Believe . . ."

By Phil Davison

WITH THE U.S. MARINES NEAR IRAQI FRONT LINES - Cynics may say it has the ring of morale-boosting propaganda.

But U.S. Marine Gen. Charles "Chuck" Krulak is nothing if not sincere. When he says it was a miracle, it is hard not to go along with him. The way the general tells it, the "gift from God" arrived last Sunday, just at the right place and the right time. It left the U.S. Marines "ready to go" should President Bush order an assault on Kuwait. Gen. Krulak is the man responsible for pushing through vital fuel, ammunition and supplies to the Marines' assault force if it thrusts toward Kuwait. He commands the massive logistics operation the Marines need to do their job.

Out here in the parched, dusty northeastern Saudi desert, his main concern was providing water. Until Sunday, water was being shipped up to frontline Marines on tanker lorries on a drive of several hours from bases in the rear. If the Marines were to push forward, water supplies were always going to be crucial.

After he helped set up the Marines' final forward logistics base a week ago, according to the amiable Gen. Krulak, he literally prayed every day that the Marines might find an oasis, an underground aquifer that would help sustain any military assault.

Drilling teams from what the Americans call the SeaBees—mobile construction battalions from the U.S. Navy—started drilling around the logistics base but were several hundred feet down without hitting water.

On Sunday (Feb. 17), one of the general's men was driving close to the base. "I swear we must have passed that place 600 times and noticed nothing," the general told reporters tonight (Tuesday) in his bustling, heavily-fortified bunker beneath blackened camouflage netting in the desert. He just came to me and said, 'Sir, I've just found a well.' I went out there and sure enough, there it was. A well already there, with brand-new engine, brand-new batteries. Some of it still had the plastic on it. It even had fuel in it."

"When I got out there, I saw a big cross-like thing that hangs down. You know, like the old-fashioned trains used to have, those things that swing out. It's got two of those. There was a button that said 'Start' and a button that said 'Stop.' I pressed the button that said 'Start' and . . . vroooom."

The 40-year-old general said he had no idea who had built the well. I put it to him it might have been Iraqi army troops, before the Marines ventured here. Earlier in the day, a Navy geologist drilling a new well in the search for water told me he had heard the Iraqis pushed this far into Saudi Arabia during land skirmishes with the Marines last month.

That was before the Marines moved forward to set up their big logistics base. The idea that the Iraqis may have built the well that will help supply any Marine offensive amused the general, but he laughed it off. He preferred the miracle scenario and, with what he may be about to face, who would blame him?

The truth may be that the Saudis themselves, or even American contractors, may have built the well and abandoned it when the Iraqis took over Kuwait.

Whatever the case, its discovery a stone's throw from the Marines' key supply base smacked of either divine intervention or gross negligence by previous passers-by. Just in case, the water was carefully tested and no trace of poison was found. Convinced of his miracle, Gen. Krulak went straight to a private Marine church service within his base and told the congregation what had happened.

"For those of you who don't believe the Lord is behind us, this is what happened . . ." is how he started.

Gen. Krulak left no doubt that the Marines would not underestimate Saddam Hussein's forces. "This guy is good. He's done a great job with his defences. My hat's off to him." He described the Iraqi defences as the classic Soviet type, with two main defence lines which the Iraqis would use to create a "firesack," or killing zone, to trap allied forces under artillery fire. Expressing confidence in the Marines' own close-air support, he described any potential Marine assault as "almost like a dance, it's very orchestrated."

It was time to leave the general to his maps and preparations. One last question. How did he feel, deep inside, in the run-up to what could be horrific combat?

"I'm feeling a little like I did when I first went to Vietnam. I will be honest. I'm a little bit scared. I have the same feeling I had as a rifle company commander. You are in command of American men and American women. I think I've done everything in my power. I'll tell them, 'Go with Godspeed. Do what you have to do.'"

U.S. Troops Seize Iraqi Observation Post: "They Have Given Up the Border"

By Gary Regenstreif

NORTHERN SAUDI ARABIA - U.S. Army forces have seized an Iraqi observation post its soldiers abandoned after being bombed by allied aircraft in a move that officials said would facilitate part of the impending offensive to liberate Kuwait.

The post was considered a significant obstacle to allied forces because it is perched on high ground that is difficult to navigate and because it could easily detect an allied advance. While only a handful of Iraqi troops were ever spotted at one time at the position just across the Saudi border, they would have time to alert rear divisions of the offensive.

"It appears as though they have given up the border," said Army Maj. Karl Horst, a battalion operations officer. "We were expecting to fight to cross it. It makes it easy for us when we roll across. It's one less fight we have to do." The U.S. division had observed soldiers at the post with binoculars for weeks and spied Iraqi troops building defense berms and several "hasty" fighting positions for one or two troops each. The U.S. Air Force bombed the area with what Army officials believed were 500-pound explosives, whose concussions alone flattened pre-fabricated buildings at the post.

"The Air Force came and effectively eliminated the target area," said Horst, of Wenatchee, Wash., 35. "The main building was leveled. We had estimated it to be 12 meters high and the Air Force reduced it to one metre. It was impressive."

The explosions, designed to soften Iraqi positions ahead of a likely ground war, also left craters three metres deep and four metres wide in the sand.

A U.S. rifle platoon moved in Monday and found nothing but documents that had still not been translated from Arabic, old Iraqi uniforms and shell casings from AK-47 machine guns. No soldiers, alive or dead, were found.

"If we would not have blown that building away, they would have used those fighting positions," said Horst. The Army believed other such posts had been hammered by allied aircraft in recent days and were also likely abandoned.

The Army has noticed a decrease in the frequency of Iraqi reconnaissance patrols slipping into the kingdom since the bombing began, and less movement north of the Saudi border. "They're not doing anything at all," said Horst. "They're not interested in getting too close."

Staff Sgt. Lester McLaney said he believed the Iraqis erred by abandoning the post. "It's a key piece of terrain. They could have bottlenecked us if they tried," said McLaney, 41, of Fayetteville, N.C. "It was nice," he added. "I had never been across the border before. When I go back I want to make sure we finish all of this." Soldiers who visited the site said no Iraqi troops could be spotted for kilometres.

"You can see forever there," said Spec. Mike Krussow, 20, of Hood River, Ore. "It kind of surprised me. But I think we're going to come across and see a lot of areas like that."

The Iraqis fled the post, but their frightened dogs remained.

"Whenever they hear jets overhead, they bark and head for cover," said Horst. "It must have been traumatic for poor Rover."

Wednesday
February 20, 1991

The largest U.S. raid yet into Iraq put a large dent in the enemy's front line, which had steadily pulled back as allied troops continued to punch forward with probing patrols, Apache raids and artillery barrages.

American soldiers rounded up about 500 Iraqi POWs and shipped them south to enclosures in Saudi Arabia. All enemy prisoners taken by coalition forces were eventually placed in Saudi custody. The Saudis then would deal with the Iraqis when it came to exchanging or releasing them.

A story in this chapter describes a typical cross-border raid. The fever of the hunt for enemy troops was tempered by knowledge that diplomatic talks continued and, at least theoretically, a settlement could bring the entire allied military effort to a stop before the ground invasion started.

On the diplomatic front, President Bush issued yet another ultimatum: within four days, Iraq must leave Kuwait, release all coalition POWs and account for hundreds of thousands of mines placed in the occupied emirate by the invaders. The chances that Saddam Hussein would, or could, comply with this rigorous set of demands were slight.

Was the U.S. really interested in a settlement without a ground war? Much post-war analysis was devoted to proving that once the U.S. declared it would send more than a half-million troops to Saudi Arabia, the die was cast, and there was no chance all those troops and tanks would be brought home without a fight.

The phrase "nightmare scenario" in fact was widely used in Washington to describe the possibility that Saddam Hussein would concede to the UN demand and withdraw from Kuwait before the allies could send in an army to boot him out. If that happened, in some sense he would have gotten away with his thievery.

He would have a chance to rebuild his military from just the punishment that had been dealt him so far. That damage wasn't minor—a story in this chapter describes Iraqi-occupied Kuwait as burning and cratered—but it was still several degrees of magnitude short of what a ground offensive would leave.

And a pre-invasion Iraqi pullout would leave the Americans and their allies on the defensive in Saudi Arabia, which from the beginning wasn't keen to have large numbers of foreign troops in residence for longer than absolutely necessary.

Another story in this chapter takes up the recurring issue of friendly fire, this time from the perspective that accidents are probably unavoidable, given enough troops, enough fighting, and enough confusion. But even inevitability doesn't relieve individual soldiers and commanders of the obligation to do their utmost to prevent it.

Besides friendly fire, another accidental killer was loose on the periphery of the battle zone: highway fatalities on Tapline Road, the main highway used by the allies to get troops into position far to the west along Iraq's borders and keep them fed, watered and fueled up.

Tapline Road wasn't an allied creation. It was already in place when the troops arrived, having long been a necessary part of the Saudi oil-economy infrastructure linking far-flung desert towns with the refineries and cities.

During the war, it was transformed into a vital land artery of a massive force stretching 500 miles from east to northwest, Dhahran to Rafha. A story in this chapter describes what Tapline Road became once the Saudi civilian traffic was forced to share the narrow strip with thousands of allied trucks, tanks and Humvees, all in a big hurry. What it became was damned dangerous.

Raiders of the Vast Iraq: "I Thought They'd Smoked Us and Gotten Behind Us"

By Michael Hedges

WITH THE 1ST INFANTRY DIVISION - Companies from this division are raiding and reconnoitering into Iraq, charting a path for a possible ground offensive, according to officers and soldiers participating.

The units moving into Iraq have exchanged fire with the enemy but have taken no casualties to date, the officers said. The soldiers have found evidence of fairly substantial Iraqi positions, and have taken weapons and equipment abandoned by Iraqi soldiers.

Other division battalions have moved up to a disputed piece of territory between Saudi Arabia and Iraq and are having frequent contacts with Iraqi forces.

For soldiers on the edge of the battle line, there have been frightening nights and frustrating days recently.

Staff Sgt. Ronald Cline, 27, of Shepherd, Mich., was watching into Iraq late last night when a cloud of vapor rolled out of the clear night and enveloped his Bradley fighting vehicle. "It came from due north, and it was moving real fast," he said.

He told his crew, Sgt. Samuel A. Johnson, 25, of Columbus, Ga., and Spec. James W. Thomas, 18, of San Clemente, Cal., to put on their chemical suits in case the cloud was an Iraqi poison gas attack.

As the men were spreading the alarm of possible gas attack, two heavy artillery rounds from Iraqi guns exploded a few hundred meters ahead of them.

"It was just Boom, Boom, Boom, and a big old wind hit me in the face," said Sgt. Cline. "I was scared," said Sgt. Johnson. "You couldn't see anything because of the mist. It was the first time I've been scared out here. I thought they had smoked us and had gotten behind us."

Spec. Thomas said he was convinced for a few dreadful seconds that his recurring nightmare of getting caught in a gas attack had come true. "That is the only thing I've been afraid of, and here it was happening," he said. The men said after testing the mist with a chemical detector they determined it was a freakish fog bank that came out of the clear night and soon dissipated without a trace.

They still haven't decided if the Iraqis fired artillery under cover of the fog, or if the timing of the rounds was a coincidence. Like many of the troops on the forward line here, Sgt. Cline's crew is frustrated at holding tight inside Iraqi artillery range, without moving to attack. "I don't understand why they aren't wailing on us," said Sgt. Johnson. "We are well within range, why aren't they kicking our butt?" Sgt. Cline said, "We'd like to go further than this line. It is frustrating being here. You see something, then it isn't there."

The men believe part of the reason they aren't moving forward has to do with an attempted peace initiative by the Soviet Union. "We'll be more than happy to help Saddam get out of Kuwait right now," said Sgt. Johnson. "If we don't, we can do it in five years when he has better equipment. He won't make the same mistake twice."

But soldiers here have seen enough of the Iraqis ahead of them to know an attack will be difficult. "There are a lot of people who think this will be a cakewalk, but I don't see it," said Sgt. Cline. "It'll be a big ol' boom when it goes down."

The commanding officer of the armored task force the men are part of shared their assessment of the Iraqi forces. "Those guys are organized well, and their patrols are run intelligently," said Lt. Col. Greg Fontenot, 41, of Eunice, La. "They are not the pushover, head-lice, starving guys I've been reading about."

Col. Fontenot's battalion has had brief, inconclusive firefights with Iraqi elements. Some have involved Iraqis that seem to want to surrender, then back off, as seen in other sectors of the division's line. "We are giving them a chance to surrender, not shooting to kill on the first burst. But that is alerting them, and they are getting away."

Col. Fontenot's troops have swept out ahead of their positions, surveying the Iraqi lines. "They are working up to their forward recon positions through a trail network they have been developing for eight months," he said. "They have a well-designed bunker system. The whole place is infested with fighting holes placed in a way that shows they know what they are doing."

Troops from this task force have found several Iraqi RPG-7s, a shoulder-fired rocket bought from the Soviet Union that can knock out tanks and Bradleys. They have also found food, including potatoes and onions. "They appear to have more than adequate food," he said. Maj. Brian Zahn, a staff officer with another task force in the division's 1st Brigade, said he saw evidence two nights ago that the Iraqis have a formidable line. "Through night sights we saw the sky fill with tracers," said Maj. Zahn, 37, of Bottineau, ND.

He said the Iraqis apparently fired at a pilot-less drone aircraft sent over their lines to gather intelligence.

Making Unavoidable Friendly Fire Less Likely: "I Will Not Haphazardly Engage What I Think is the Enemy"

By Douglas Jehl

WITH U.S. FORCES, Saudi Arabia - Amid new concerns about the threat to U.S. troops posed by friendly fire, Army aviation and armored units here have assigned high priority to steps designed to minimize such fratricide in an expected ground offensive, according to officers here.

The redoubled effort includes the use of new gun-camera footage to help helicopter pilots learn to recognize American vehicles from the air and plans to tighten battlefield coordination between air and ground commanders. Other steps may include the introduction of unspecified new recognition devices designed to make frontline U.S. tanks and armored vehicles more recognizable to attack aircraft seeking to strike at Iraqi forces. The new attention here to the problems of friendly fire comes after Army attack helicopters flying missions in border skirmishes this week have found unexpected challenges in distinguishing friend from foe. "What we've found is that when you have two opposing forces intertwined, it's very difficult to separate the friendlies from the enemy," said Lt. Col. Bill Hatch, commander of an Apache battalion in this 1st Armored Division, which has not yet been involved in combat. "It's just exceedingly difficult."

In one incident, an Apache helicopter from the 1st Infantry Division was reported to have mistakenly launched a Hellfire missile at what turned out to be an American Bradley fighting vehicle, killing two infantrymen and wounding six others. Officers here said the accident occurred in an attack that has been severely criticized within the military by theater commander Gen. H. Norman Schwarzkopf, who described the raid in a stern message to subordinates as an example of excessive use of firepower.

At least 100 laser-guided Hellfires, designed for use against heavily armored tanks, were launched against what proved to be trucks, observation posts and scattered infantrymen, according to officers familiar with the 1st Infantry Division incident. The high-tech missiles are so expensive that few Apache pilots had been permitted to test-fire them in training before the war began.

Schwarzkopf, who has insisted on close adherence to rules of engagement, restricting the use of destructive weapons against lightly armed targets, was said by officers to be "not too happy" about the border salvo.

A brigade commander here, Col. James Riley, cited the message from commander-in-chief to reinforce an order to infantry officers not to squander their most lethal tank-killing ammunition on second-tier Iraqi forces. "You use a flyswatter on a fly," Riley said Tuesday. "You save your best ammo for the appropriate target." There was no indication that the large number of Hellfire missiles fired during the border skirmish had contributed to the Bradley-killing incident, ground officers cautioned.

But they said the apparent lack of discrimination in the Apache attack had underscored the recognition that friendly fire—from the Army helicopter and an Air Force warplane—has claimed more ground troops' lives than have Iraqi attacks since the war began. In seeking to avoid such mishaps in this division, helicopter pilots began Tuesday night to use gun cameras to (take) aerial night-time photographs of some ground units to aid in identification in the low-light conditions when vehicles can be most difficult to distinguish.

The new film is to be used to augment an extensive array of daylight videotapes and photographs of both American and Iraqi vehicles and equipment that pilots have already sought to commit to memory. But with the sophisticated Apache helicopters able to fire missiles from distances at which visual recognition can be troublesome, Hatch, the aviation commander, said the most important step in minimizing friendly fire would be to make clear where American forces ended and enemy troops began.

"The crucial thing in the avoidance of fratricide is for the aviation guy to get face-to-face with the ground commander," said the veteran pilot, who commands the 1st Aviation Regiment. "That in itself goes a long way." To minimize the risk of same-side casualties when this division joins in the combat, Hatch said in an interview his Apache pilots would prefer to attack enemy forces well beyond American units at points where the attack helicopters "can take the load off your back by reaching out beyond the front lines."

He emphasized that Army pilots were trained to ensure that they were aiming at hostile targets before launching their missiles. "I will not haphazardly engage what I think is the enemy out here," the lieutenant colonel said.

But the Apache commander warned that the mission could become far more dangerous if attack helicopters were used to support a close-in fight—a mission the commander made clear he would prefer to avoid. The risks of such an operation could become so great that the lieutenant colonel said his obligation would be to make clear to others that the use of helicopters could make fratricide inevitable.

"It's very difficult right now," Hatch said he would warn ground commanders, "and if I start shooting, I'm going to take out some friendlies."

Parakeets Beak: Too Close to Front to be Gas-Sniffers, But Marines Don't Need Birds to Smell Danger

By Denis D. Gray

WITH THE 2ND MARINE DIVISION, Near the Kuwaiti Border - In ancient Rome, geese were kept to warn of approaching enemies. In Saudi Arabia, they're using parakeets. The geese were supposed to honk; the birds are supposed to drop dead.

A sizable number of parakeets were farmed out to the 2nd Marine Division as sensitive sniffers of the lethal gases Iraqi forces could use against it in event of a ground war. The division's G-1, or administrative, section acquired two, which it named Ike and Tina after the American pop singers. The sex of each, however, has yet to be determined.

Endowed with a quicker metabolism than humans, the parakeets will theoretically expire before soldiers in event of a gas attack. But Cpl. Michael Nedigh, displaying Ike and Tina in a cage well-stocked with feed, said the division is probably too close to the frontline and source of danger for the birds to be really effective. "The gas will get to us as soon as it gets to the birds," said the Bellefonte, Pa., native. "They've become pets."

Once the war is over, another Marine in the section hopes to take the pair back to the United States to add to her existing menagerie of cats, chicken, and doves.

If gas is hurled at the Marines, an animal of another stripe will probably prove more effective. The "Fox" is a German-made laboratory-on-wheels which can rapidly monitor and analyze hundreds of gases in the surrounding environment. It has yet to be tested in combat, while parakeets have a long history as gas detectors in mines and tunnels.

Over the 12-Foot Berm Lies No-Man's-Land

By Philip Jacobson

OVERLOOKING NO-MAN'S-LAND - In a fold of ground behind a solid sand berm, a team of U.S. Army scouts are relaxing after another long, occasionally tense night of watching the barren stretch of land between their position and the enemy front line.

By their reckoning, less than a kilometer separates the two sides, and though this sector has been fairly quiet. The four lightly-armed scouts are uneasily aware that full-scale hostilities may not be far away.

Wednesday - February 20, 1991

As they begin preparing the ritual tea for visitors, a heavy artillery battery not far away fires off a salvo of rocket-assisted shells aimed at Iraqi targets deep behind the front line: the boosters break away with a puff of white smoke that lingers for a moment in the bright blue sky.

For Specialist Keith Flash, a piratical-looking figure in his khaki bandana, the shelling is a sight for sore eyes. A slim, handsome black man from New York, he is serving his last few months in the Army and wants "to get this damn thing settled" as swiftly as possible. He is disarmingly nonchalant about the risks of the job for which he volunteered, noting with satisfaction that while his team has every sort of night vision aid at hand, the Iraqi patrols that venture out from their own high berm are often without radio communication, let alone infra-red equipment.

"It's just a matter of keeping your cool and thinking sensibly," he observes, as another heavy rumble marks more artillery attacks further down the line.

Driving up to the front, we had seen two of the American multiple launch rocket systems in action, sending a stream of bright fire arcing out above us, then heard the deep thud of distant explosions. The rockets are apparently accurate to a terrifying degree for those on the receiving end, fully justifying their reputation as "grid-square removal kits."

Their normal tactics are to fire a salvo or two, then move on before the Iraqis considerable ability to bring down counter-battery fire within a short space of time is tested. On this occasion, however, there were no shells coming our way, conceivably because the enemy gunners have learned the bitter lesson that opening up virtually guarantees detection by allied observation posts and another hail of incoming artillery.

Encouraged by Flash and friends, we scrambled to the top of their protective berm, feeling exposed but enjoying a clear view out towards the forward Iraqi positions. Nothing moved beneath the baking midday sun, and the scouts did not expect their repose to be disturbed in daylight. "After dark we sometimes see a flash of light over there, and last night someone started sweeping the dead zone with a big beam," said the team leader, Sgt. Bruce Culper. "Kinda crazy thing to do, because we called that straight into the artillery and they soon had it back to normal."

According to Sgt. Culper, almost twenty years in the Army, scouting is the game to keep you feeling young at heart.

When we set off back towards the allied lines, a sudden series of muzzle flashes signaled another salvo from the big guns astride a nearby ridge.

From there, we gazed out over a vast assembly of troops, armour and more guns, stretching as far as the eye could see on sands dotted with spiny thorn bushes.

Coming up, we had seen a majestic eagle swooping and rising over the inhospitable terrain, one still wet from a furious storm the night before.

At every allied encampment, sodden sleeping bags were hung out to dry on tent poles, like some weird crop of fruit. Most of the troops we passed were taking it easy, under orders to get plenty of rest in case the ground attack begins. Some energetic souls were punting a football around, one player sporting a Glasgow Rangers jersey.

A trio of B-52 bombers appeared in our sector, trailing long white tails of vapour as they flew an almost leisurely approach to their bombing run. The hollow crumps followed shortly, then they wheeled away and set course for base.

The night before we arrived, two gigantic "daisy-cutter" bombs of 15,000 pounds apiece had been tipped out of a U.S. warplane onto the Iraqi front line, the explosions not quite swallowed by a tremendous thunderstorm that raged for several hours.

Evidence of previous visits from the bombers lay all around us, leaflets dropped by the tens of thousands in an attempt to persuade Iraqi troops to desert.

The most common showed a weary-looking soldier with a think bubble depicting his wife and children back home. Alongside was a picture showing how he should approach allied forces, with rifle slung barrel-down over the left shoulder, leaflet aloft in the right hand, if he wanted to give up. The Arabic text emphasized the message—why fight on for Saddam Hussein and face certain defeat, possible death?

Although nobody has yet surrendered in the stretch (of desert) under the surveillance of the American scouts we encountered, they had heard of desperately tired, almost broken Iraqis coming across not far away.

All told harrowing stories of ceaseless bombing, of corpses piling up unburied because men would not leave their bunkers, of frantic voices calling on the radio network for medical aid that rarely arrived in time.

"I don't hate those guys over there," Keith Speed observed, gesturing across the no-man's-land. "I have pity in my heart for them because we have a fair idea of what they are suffering, but still, there is a job to be done."

Terrorist Actions to Rise When Land War Starts: "I Think We're as Ready as We're Ever Going to Be"

By Tim Collie

Synopsis: Terrorist attacks against Patriot missile systems and other strategic targets are expected right before G-day or soon afterwards. U.S. military intelligence experts believe that Iraqi and Palestinian commandos are already in Hafr Al Batn waiting and watching. Based largely on one source who is a key intelligence aide to military commanders. His views are based on intelligence shared among U.S. commanders.

WITH U.S. TROOPS, Saudi Arabia - U.S. military commanders are expecting terrorist attacks against Patriot anti-missile batteries and other strategic targets inside Saudi Arabia shortly after a ground war begins, according to a U.S. military intelligence source.

The attacks may come as soon as one day before G-Day—the date when a ground war begins—to soon afterwards, said the source, posted with a frontline military unit.

Military analysts believe that Iraqi spies are good enough to determine when G-Day will occur two or three days beforehand.

"I don't think we're adequately prepared" to defend against terrorist strikes, the source said. "But I think we're as ready as we're ever going to be."

U.S. commanders—relying on classified intelligence—believe that Iraqi special forces and several Palestinian groups have set up working three and four man cells just behind allied lines, the source said.

They are particularly concerned with Hafr Al Batn, a northern Saudi city with a large Bedouin population near the Iraqi border. Spies probably are posing as Bedouins, nomadic tribesmen with little national identity and family and tribal loyalties on both sides of the border.

The current thinking is that terrorist cells in the area are holding back while gathering intelligence, choosing targets and stockpiling weapons, the source said. "It would be stupid now for them to try anything and blow their cover—unless they screwed up and revealed themselves," the source said. "They're waiting for a ground war to start before they do anything. That will be the best time—when everybody's concerned with the ground war."

Patriot anti-missile batteries and their crews are high priority targets, the source said. "One of their primary targets is going to be the Patriots. They've made his (Saddam Hussein) missiles the laughing stock of the Middle East.

"But it doesn't have to be a big target," he said. "It can be psychological. It could be something as simple as slipping up to a tent in the middle of the night and slitting someone's throat. Then you've put an entire unit on edge for days."

"A Patriot battery would be considered such a necessary target that it would be more than a few lives to get to," he said. "To a degree, a logistics center is a soft target—it wouldn't be as difficult. A roadblock, checkpoint, guard post—they would be soft targets," he said. "A Kuwaiti refugee center would be a very soft target."

U.S. intelligence experts believe that Iraqi special forces and Palestinian terrorist groups are sharing information but running largely different organizations.

But even if the Iraqi command structure is destroyed and agents are left hanging, Palestinian terrorist attack plans would remain intact, other military sources said. "They (the Palestinians) may tell the Iraqis they're going to take out a target," the source said. "The Iraqis may say yea or nay, but the Palestinians are going to make their own decisions."

But Palestinians are at a disadvantage over the Iraqis because their distinct Arabic dialect and their lack of knowledge of Bedouin tribes make it more difficult for them to blend in. The Iraqis are believed to have been schooling agents in Bedouin culture and language for more than two decades, the source said.

The source—whose expertise before Operation Desert Storm was in Soviet and Eastern European spy organizations—said that Iraqi special forces commandos are trained as well as any Warsaw Pact force. They are the elite of the elite, specially picked from the ranks of Iraq's well-trained Republican Guards.

U.S. commanders expect that Iraqi spies will be able to determine G-Day two or three days beforehand based on their expert observations of troop movements and formations. For U.S. troops, vigilance will be the best defense, "As corny as it sounds, common sense is what's going to save us," the source said.

"Keeping guards awake, keeping sentries on their toes. Stressing to them not to blow off something if it looks strange, no matter how silly it may seem."

Tales of a Marine Foxhole: Sound of a Round Entering a Chamber, "A Darkness You've Never Seen Before"

By Susan Sachs

NEAR THE KUWAITI BORDER - Night at the front lines means mice in the foxholes, cold glutinous food, the crack of artillery fire and a sparkling canopy of stars and warplanes passing overhead in formation.

"Nights are when you feel real edgy," said Marine Lace Cpl. Joseph Edmond, a machine gunner from Uniondale, Long Island. "Nights are when you pray a lot."

Talk of peace proposals in faraway capitals rarely reaches the Marines, as they burrow into final assault positions with only rumors and occasional letters from home for news of the outside world. Their world is the sand and the noise of bombing and the long, long night. Bomb drops from B-52s rumble through the cold air. Passwords are demanded by sentries. An occasional red dot of light from someone's flashlight penetrates the darkness.

War seems all the closer as night envelops the lonely outposts near the border. At an abandoned lookout station near the sand berm that stands between the enemy in Kuwait and safety, a handful of Marines shiver in the night as they watch for intruders. "I dread when the nightfall comes and I pray for the sun to come back up because the nights here get kind of eerie," said Lance Cpl. Anthony Laparco, New York.

"In the desert, when it's cloudy, it's a darkness that you've never seen before," he added from his perch at the edge of a no-man's-land between Saudi Arabia and Kuwait.

"On a clear night, you can see to the horizon. You can see flashes of the bombs in the distance. A lot of the time, you don't see it but you feel it." Another sound cuts through the night sometimes—the sound of psychological warfare. To undermine Iraqi morale and encourage defections, the military broadcasts over concert-sized loudspeakers to the Iraqi troops over the border. Incongruously in this country of conservative mores and traditions, they use heavy metal rock music, blasting into the empty desert, before cajoling in Arabic. "Dear Soldier," the American message says. "If you desire a hot meal, better treatment and your personal safety, give yourself up to the American armed forces."

The other night, a dozen Iraqi soldiers appeared out of the night in front of a company of Marines near the border. The sight so unnerved the men that they forgot the slips of paper given them by their commander with the phonetic spellings of a few handy Arabic phrases like "hands up," "surrender" and "stop or I'll shoot."

"The guys got jumpy and locked and loaded their weapons," said Capt. Douglas Simmang, 31, of Dallas, Tex. "Out here at night, you can hear that sound cracking a long way. They turned and ran." Most nights, a British Royal Navy chaplain with a Union Jack patch sewn to his flak vest conducts prayer meetings and Bible study classes for the Marines who live, dirty and bored, in holes scraped from the chalky sand.

Gordon Craig, a 47-year-old "sober Scot Presbyterian," is on loan to the Marines, sent out to the desert front lines to minister as best he can to boys about to go to war. He finds the Americans refreshingly open about their religious needs. They don't seem to mind that the communion wafer is soggy packaged bread from cold ration packs, and the wine is sugary grape drink mix dissolved in canteen water.

Night brought a furry surprise to the chaplain. A mouse—some in the field say the pudgy rodents are closer to rats—wandered into his wind-whipped hootch. Being a Scot, as well as a reflective man, Craig transformed the visit into a moment of poetry for the nights before he must minister to the dying among his desert flock.

"You start getting philosophical when you see a rat late at night," he said. "It made me think of Robert Burns. You've heard the poem, 'The best laid plans of mice and men...'"

On the perimeter of the Marine camps, night-vision goggles turn the black night electric red for the Marines standing guard duty. Their nightly routine: three hours of watchfulness, four hours of sleep.

The young men of the Marine Barracks of Washington, D.C., the "Eighth and I," live in holes 300 feet apart on the farthest edge of the 2nd Division command post. Back home, these spit-and-polish Marines, the straight-backed honor guards at official functions and VIP funerals. The Eighth and

I, named for the intersection where their barracks are located, were last deployed in 1906, to subdue a Seminole Indian uprising.

Coming to Saudi Arabia, facing combat, took most of these young fresh-faced Marines by surprise. From dress inspection three times a day at home they've come to twice-a-month showers, washing from a canteen cup, sand in their food and a vast empty horizon to scan for enemies. "You do what you can do. You put some polish on your boots when you can," said Lance Cpl. Robert Brandolino of Albany, N.Y., as he cleaned his gun at the lip of his foxhole. The night is cold, with a wind that cuts through the cotton uniform right through to long johns underneath. His world is his hole. "We don't go away from our hole," Brandolino said. "You put on what you have and after that you just got to live with it."

The darkness of the desert just before battle also distorts space and time. Bedtime is at 8 p.m. for many at administrative command posts. But the active bulldozers and humming generators turn night into day at the 2nd Marine Division supply center, a vast collection of tents buried between man-made sand walls that sprang from the flat dusty plain only two weeks ago.

Here, the night has its rituals, although the tension of the front lines is missing. A carload of journalists passing through a sentry point was stopped by a guard one recent night. "Has anyone shown you any kindness today?" the sentry asked. The coded phrase required a set response—the password for the night.

The sergeant driving the car was unfazed. "Sorry, devil dog," he drawled, using the universal Marine nickname. "I don't know the password."

"Okay, sir," the guard replied, waving the car on through. "Have a safe night."

Tapline Road Fast, Furious, and Lethal: "More Traffic Than on I-20 Heading into Atlanta"

By Paul Basken

NORTHERN SAUDI ARABIA - The single leading killer of U.S. servicemen so far in the Gulf War isn't Iraqi Scud missiles, their long-range artillery, or even the nightmare of so-called "friendly fire."

Far more low-tech and closer to earth, it's a daily threat with which all Americans are intimately familiar: their highways.

Just like their civilian counterparts, the dirt roadways cut throughout northern Saudi Arabia are both a deadly, and an essential, part of everyday life.

The roads run from one horizon to the next, marked by Spartan borders of foothigh plowed dirt and an occasional cardboard marker on a wooden post. They tie together row upon row of bunkered military camps that dot the dry dusty landscape like huge anthills.

There's no time in the rush of war for pavement. Almost no road signs. And no thought of street lights, lane markers or cops. Constantly running their hours-long routes is an army, literally, of highly energetic and anxious young men rushing to fill their camps with food, tents, machinery and weapons.

At least one result is quite predictable. After some six months of operations Desert Shield and Desert Storm, a total of 117 service members had died as of Tuesday. Accidents accounted for 88 of those, and the single largest group—a total of 33—were vehicular.

"It tells me that the guys need to slow down," said Navy Master Chief Jack Mitchell, 45, who heads up a team of construction workers known as Seabees who work from scratch to build and maintain the roads and almost all of the other infrastructure that forms the ground level of a modern war machine.

The Seabees are among the least glamorous of America's fighting men, consisting mostly of older members of the armed forces with expertise in construction back home. But their work is crucial to all the rest, and their assignment in Kuwait could be just as dangerous as any, since they could well be called upon to open an airstrip or site a helicopter pad when ground troops first push into Kuwait City. In their few short weeks of work along Saudi Arabia's northern border, the Seabees have built a main east-west supply road known as the MGR and hundreds of miles of feeder routes that are the supply lifelines for a half-million-man army.

At times, the roads appear as nothing but scraped-out paths worn into the fuzzy thin grass of the desert floor by the weight of an endless train of multi-ton tanks, troops and ammunition. But to Mitchell and his fellow Seabees, there is an art and a labor to building a road in the desert to keep units up front in touch with their supplies in the rear.

Most of the road surface, for instance, is made by grating the top layer and mixing the dirt with a harder rock found several inches underground. "In the U.S., where I'm from," said the Alabama native, "it'd be red clay. Here it's a mixture of sand and marble. You move 100 miles and the soil changes," he said. "It all looks like sand to most people, but it's not."

Their proud product—a surface almost as hard as pavement in some places but suddenly absent in others—creates a traffic flow as individual as the vehicle being driven.

Eighteen-wheelers and other large trucks generally stay in single-file convoys, plodding along at about 30 to 40 mph. Faster four-wheel drive jeeps zip through their blinding clouds of dust, passing on the road if there's room and spinning through treacherous sand piles to get around them if not. Adding to the danger is the habit of drivers routinely forging their own paths alongside the road, or choosing the clearest path regardless of whether it happens to be to the right, center, or far left.

Most regular users can tell at least one story of a close call, or worse. Marine Cpl. Clayton Ervin, who drives the standard military 18-wheeler known as an LVS, said his close call came with a Saudi 18-wheeler that headed straight for him, apparently either not seeing him ahead or not caring. "I came to a complete stop," said Ervin, 26, of Baltimore. "He never got out of my lane. I got over to the side, but he just kept coming, and he slapped my (side) mirror as he went by. He didn't even slow down."

A friend told him of one of the fatals, when an officer riding in the basic military jeep known as a Humvee slammed into a 5-ton truck. "A lot of the Humvees, they zig-zag in between everybody, and with all the dust you don't see them," Ervin said.

The established speed limit is 25 miles per hour, but drivers routinely reach double that. "It's very dangerous," said Mitchell, "because there's so much heavy machinery, so much heavy equipment, and it's moving day and night."

"You get out there and start counting traffic and you see there's more traffic there than there is on I-20 heading into Atlanta," Mitchell says in a distinct southern drawl.

"Five hundred thousand people are here, and virtually all their supplies are traveling up and down that road."

Wednesday - February 20, 1991

Kuwait Is Burning, Cratered, and Still Conceals a Formidable Enemy: "Just Bombing Them Constantly"

By Storer Rowley, Edith Lederer, and Joan Lowy

AT AN AIRBASE IN SOUTHWESTERN SAUDI ARABIA - U.S. pilots pounding Iraqi targets said Wednesday that Kuwait is already a burning, cratered battlefield, but allied forces still face a formidable, dug-in army with plenty of tanks.

F-111 pilots who have been flying round-the-clock bombing missions to prepare the battlefield in Iraq and Kuwait for a ground offensive said that the allies have destroyed a significant part of the Iraqi war machine.

"The whole military establishment is burning," said Capt. Bradley Seipel, 34, of Virginia Beach, Va., the weapons system officer of an F-111F fighter-bomber who has directed some of the bombs that started the fires. Seipel and other airmen at this desert airbase for U.S. Air Force F-111 strike aircraft gave a birds-eye view of what the battlefield will look like to allied troops moving forward in a ground war. "It is amazing flying up there. You look at Kuwait, that whole area, just fire," said Seipel.

"It's like constant explosions, constant fires," said Capt. Mike Russell, 33, of Bradenton, Fla., the pilot on Seipel's jet. "It's just awe-inspiring night after night how we ripped them up."

The airmen with the 48th Tactical Fighter Wing (Provisional), who fly nightly missions against Iraqi troops in Kuwait and Iraq, have been concentrating their fire on tanks, artillery and Iraqi army reserves. "This is a war, and we're beating them bad," Russell said.

Russell and Seipel are (a) dynamic duo who have already flown 100 hours dropping precision-guided bombs on some of the most important strategic targets of the Persian Gulf War. They include Iraqi leader Saddam Hussein's summer palace in his hometown of Takrit, halting the oil flow into the gulf from an Iraq-sabotaged offshore oil terminal near Kuwait City and two buildings on the docks in Kuwait City stacked with Iraqi ammunition.

"We're one small part of the picture and there are so many other people that have missions in there that are just bombing them constantly," said Russell.

But pilots said the Iraqi army is by no means defenseless. "It seems to me it's still a very target-rich environment, and I don't think we've come close to exhausting all the possible targets," said Lt. Troy Stone, 25, of Hemlock, Mich., an F-111F weapons system officer. "I still see that they're going to be able to put together a great ground defense or offense," he said. "They're still able to move their goods. They're still able to produce those goods and get them to their army."

In basic military strategy, an attacking army needs far greater numbers than a defending army, Stone said. Even though the Iraqi army isn't as well-trained and doesn't have as sophisticated equipment as the allies, he said, "They still have a heck of a lot of soldiers down there, and we don't have near as many tanks as they do, even after we've been bombing them. And they're dug in so well, they've got (so) many minefields," he added.

Stone dismissed the notion that Iraq is less technologically advanced, saying they have the "second-best weapons" in the world, which they bought from the Soviet Union.

Capt. Brad Roberts, 29, of Boise, Idaho, who pilots Stone's plane, said taking on an entrenched enemy is "the worst position you want to be in" but he added that superior allied armor "is going to help us a lot."

None of the pilots said they believe allied military forces can simply roll into Kuwait despite the pounding the Republican Guards, Saddam's crack reserve corps, has received. "Anyone who thinks it's going to be two days, or three days or five days, I think is crazy, just because of sheer numbers of people. I just can't imagine it happening like that. It's kind of like the people saying the air war would last five days," Seipel said.

Several pilots said they favored delaying the ground war in order to save American lives by taking out more targets. "I think if you just spoke on pure military basis that the generals would want to hold off on a ground attack. Why not?" Roberts said. "We're taking relatively few losses and we're able to inflict a lot of damage and the longer you wait, the better it's going to be for the ground guys."

"When you look down at Kuwait, there's just stacks of military," said Russell, referring to the way Iraqi forces have entrenched themselves in echelons of concrete bunkers across the desert.

Kuwait City, where 90 percent of the population is centered, "is all lit up" when the pilots pass over at night, said Seipel. "But most of the cities in Iraq are actually blacked out. "And when you go up near the border of Iran, you can see their cities just fine," he added, indicating their lights are on. "So you know where not to go."

The airmen said Iraqi cities are not blacked out to ward off bombers but because allied bombers have knocked out most of Iraq's power plants, but have not targeted power or desalination plants in Kuwait.

Asked about oil fires reportedly set by Iraqi forces, Seipel said, "When you fly over, there are fires everywhere. We don't know an oil fire from any other fire."

Thursday
February 21, 1991

The allied forces in the Gulf were prepared for both conventional and unconventional war. And they got some of both.

As G-Day drew nearer—the day on which the allies would launch a ground attack—warnings grew louder that the Iraqis and their friends were planning to strike back in unconventional ways, using stealth and terrorism.

By mid-February, the warnings were clearer and followed those mentioned in the last chapter that were delivered over radio, in code, from Baghdad. More than 100 terrorist incidents directed at U.S. or allied interests had been logged since the war started.

The incidents had affected a few uniformed personnel—a sniper attacked a busload of American troops in Riyadh—and at least one U.S. civilian, an employee at a U.S. military air base in Turkey, gunned down on his way to work.

But they were only the first, small indications of what the terrorists had in store for America and her friends. In the decade following the war, the terrorists made good on their pledges to extract payment in blood for the presence of so many allied troops, particularly Americans, in this region.

The mere presence of these foreign troops in the home of the most sacred Islamic sites was bad enough. But even worse, they were there to wage war against Muslims.

The American officials who flew to Riyadh in the days following the Iraqi invasion of Kuwait to offer American military help to protect Saudi Arabia were surprised at the haste with which their offer was accepted.

But in fact their meeting with the Saudi royals was preceded by intense discussions between the Saudi royal family and various important Muslim officials bitterly opposed to the western military plan. In private, the fundamentalist religious leaders had won assurances that the foreign troops would not remain a day longer than necessary to accomplish the liberation of Kuwait.

Even with those assurances, academic experts in Saudi politics report that dissident Muslim leaders continued to speak out and issue sermons throughout the allied deployment attacking the western military presence and denouncing the Saudi leaders for permitting it.

Even as the American and other allied soldiers prepared to risk their lives in the kingdom's defense, they were reviled as undesirables.

In November 1995 came the first audacious mass slaying meant as a message that fundamentalist anger over the American troops continued to seethe. An explosion at the headquarters of a military training center for the Saudi national guard, operated by the U.S. military and one of its contract companies, killed seven people including six American citizens, one a U.S. Army sergeant.

The following year, in June 1996, a huge truck bomb exploded outside the entrance to a U.S. military housing complex in Khobar Towers, in a suburb of Dhahran. The price paid there was 19 lives, all active-duty U.S. Air Force personnel.

After several more years of careful planning came the suicide bombing of the USS Cole, while in port at Aden, Yemen, on October 12, 2000. Seventeen American sailors were killed and 39 wounded in that attack.

And finally, on Sept. 11, 2001, came the most horrific attack of all—hijacked commercial airliners, Islamic terrorists at the controls, crashed into both tower of the World Trade Center in New York and the Pentagon, killing all aboard and thousands of innocent workers and tourists in the buildings and many firemen, police and rescuers.

After the troops returned from the Gulf War there were also incidents of terrorism within the United States that rivaled any abroad.

An interview in this chapter bridges both worlds, the war and terror: a reporter's brief encounter with Sgt. Timothy McVeigh, then a gunner in a Bradley fighting vehicle crew, part of the 1st Infantry Div. When veteran war correspondent Leon Daniel visited McVeigh's unit, the stern-faced sergeant drew little attention, blending in with tough soldier's talk as part of a squad of tank-killers.

Just three years later, McVeigh had gone full circle, from a soldier sworn to defend freedom to a homegrown terrorist practicing violence against his government and shedding the blood of many innocent civilians as a measure of his skills. In an interview in prison while he awaited execution, McVeigh said he didn't fear death. "I came to terms with my mortality."

In the ground war, one of the first friendly fire incidents of the conflict had become a more complex case. A story in this chapter says the Apache pilot involved, a battalion commander, was relieved of duty, but not just because his firing may have caused the deaths of two GIs. Apparently, he had also violated a division order forbidding unit commanders to personally fly missions and engage the enemy.

Big Red One Takes Measure of Iraqis: "I Can Kill a Tank at 3,000 Meters," says Sgt. Tim McVeigh

By Leon Daniel

WITH THE 1ST INFANTRY DIVISION - "I fired from 400 meters," 2nd Lt. Jesus Aguirre said Thursday, describing how his tank crewmen destroyed an Iraqi truck.

The truck was in a bombed-out Iraqi village just across the border between Saudi Arabia and Iraq. The tankers had suspected the truck was being used as an outpost.

Aguirre, of El Paso, Tex., said the crew of his M1 tank fired two 105mm high-explosive rounds to destroy it.

Capt. Tony Schwam, of Atlanta, commander of the Iron Horse company, said his men had been given the mission of clearing a zone along the border when the suspicious truck was spotted. "We identified the truck," the captain said. "After we determined they were using it as an outpost we destroyed it."

An occasional rocket round whooshes northward toward the Iraqis on this sector of the line, where soldiers of the Big Red One are waiting to launch a ground offensive against the heavily fortified enemy.

At night, the sky over the Iraqi positions is brightly lit by allied air strikes. The

Thursday - February 21, 1991

ground, quite literally, shakes on this side of the border when warplanes, including B-52s, pound the dug-in Iraqis. But at times there is not much for soldiers of the famed First to do but watch haircuts.

The Iron Horse barber is Staff Sgt. Robert Morphis, 29, of Jonesboro, Ark. Morphis is an Army engineer on duty with the tankers. Morphis is a lot better at clearing mines, which is his real job, than he is at cutting hair. The haircuts Morphis has so far mastered are the "high and tight," "Mohawk" and the "basic training special," which features a completely bald pate.

Pfc. Timothy Newman, of San Diego, requested a "civilian special," which turned out much like a short crewcut. When the ground war starts, Morphis will lay aside his barber shears and start clearing mines. "Hopefully, this will all be over soon, either peacefully or we'll go in and get them," said Morphis, who left a wife and two children back at Fort Riley, Kan., home of the Big Red One.

Lance Bombardier Simon Allan of the British 7th Armored Brigade, the famed Desert Rats of World War II, is dug in near the Americans. "They're a good bunch of blokes," said Allan, 23, of Morpeth, Newcastle, who joined the army at 16. "We like to trade food rations with them."

Staff Sgt. Lester Robinson, of Live Oak, Calif., acknowledged the men in his Bradley fighting vehicle have developed a fondness for steak and kidney pie.

Robinson's men are the "dismount squad," which means in battle they take on the toughest jobs, such as blowing up a bunker or knocking out a rocket position.

"We're grunts and we're proud of it," Robinson said proudly.

Sgt. Tim McVeigh is the squad's gunner on the Bradley's 25mm cannon.

"I can kill a tank at 3,000 meters," said McVeigh, of Lockport, NY.

Spec. Jason Smith, 21, of Glendora, Calif., drives the Bradley. He is a third-generation soldier of the Big Red One. "My father was in this division in World War II and my grandfather was in the Big Red One in the First World War," Smith said.

A cheer went up from the squad when a soldier arrived packing an orange bag marked U.S. Mail. Robinson, opening a letter from home, professed to like desert duty. "This is a grunt's paradise," the sergeant joked. Some of the grunts admit to apprehension. "You're sitting here," Smith explained, "and you know those Iraqi eyes are watching you." Robinson chipped in: "Yeah, this ain't Kansas no more. This is the real deal."

Nearby, Sgt. James Weaver, 30, of Cleveland, Ohio, said, "I don't want to have to come back over here in five years and do this job again." Weaver commands a vehicle that fires a TOW missile that can knock out any tank the Iraqis have.

But the M901 Improved TOW Vehicle can be killed, too. Asked if it had enough protective armor, Weaver said, "In all seriousness, no." He pointed at a gas tank and at three-quarter-inch aluminum protection on the sides of the M901. Because the M901 is vulnerable, Weaver explained, it usually operates well behind the tanks.

Spec. Joel Rubalcaba, 31, of Amarillo, Tex., was a driller for an independent oil company until the economy hit the skids in the Oil Belt and he joined the Army. He thinks oil "has something to do with why we're here but it's not the only reason."

Rubalcaba is the gunner who fires the TOW missile. "I have to keep the crosshairs on the target," he explained. "The missile is wire-guided."

To fire the TOW, he flips a toggle switch and pushes a button. If all goes well, a tank is killed. But all tankers, on this side of the border and on the Iraqi side, fight with the knowledge that killing tanks also kills tankers.

Apache Commander in Friendly Fire Incident Relieved of Command

By Michael Hedges

WITH THE 1ST INFANTRY DIVISION - Lt. Col. Ralph Hayles was relieved of command of a battalion of Apache helicopters this week after he mistakenly fired into two U.S. armored vehicles, killing two soldiers.

The friendly-fire incident was announced earlier this week. Lt. Col. Hayles, of Corpus Christi, Tex., had been flying the Apache with the same crewman for 15 months.

The reason for the dismissal was not announced. Officers in the division said that in addition to the accidental firing into American vehicles, Col. Hayles had violated guidelines by division commander Maj. Gen. Thomas Rhame that commanding officers were not to personally engage enemy forces.

In an interview in late January, Lt. Col. Hayles talked about using the Apaches aggressively as a way to reduce ultimate battlefield casualties for American forces.

"I think opportunities exist to use the Apache right from the start," he said. "I think we have a big license to go out there and maximize our technological advantages to minimize casualties." He said, "I'd like to see some bold use of the Apaches."

Lt. Col. Hayles said he had been involved in "aviation modernization for 12 years" while in the Army. He said he had great confidence in the Apache.

"I'll tell you right now, I'd not want to be out there with anything else."

On the Eve of Battle, Last-Minute Emergencies Force Some Troops Out of the Action

By Mark Mooney

NEAR THE NORTHERN SAUDI ARABIAN BORDER - Sgt. James Fleming yesterday was caught between Iraq and a heartbreak.

After training in the desert as a gunner in an M1A1 tank for six months, he was evacuated out of the country because his mother had a stroke.

Fleming, 32, of Knox, Pa., did not want to leave on what could be the eve of the largest desert battle in history. "I'm kind of pissed off that I'm going right now, but if I don't and my mother dies, I'll feel worse," he said.

Fleming was one of about 25 people a day who board C-130 transport planes at a makeshift airbase a few miles from the enemy for an emergency trip home.

They head for the plane, their feet kicking up sprays of dust as if splashing through puddles, with mixed emotions. They are leaving Saudi Arabia, but a brother must be buried, or a mother is dying, or a child is in critical condition.

"This is probably saving a few lives," mused a staff sergeant who mans the small tent that serves as a sort of terminal for Landing Zone 82.

Fleming, his face and neck leathery from six months in the sun and wind, is not so sure about saving lives. "I don't see it saving anybody's life but Iraqis," he said.

"I see a couple of Iraqi tanks living because I'm gone." Fleming is the gunner in a state-of-the-art tank named after his son, Bubba. But now somebody else will be in charge of Bubba's big gun if a ground war erupts.

"I know one guy just dying to get my spot," Fleming said grimly. Fleming does not expect the flurry of peace talk to prevent the attack. "I just don't see it happening. The only way to take care of this problem is to go in there and wipe it out," he said.

Fleming moved unhappily from the tent to the runway, not a long walk. The tent is so close to the runway that the shadow of the plane's wing passes over the tent lines when it taxis to a stop, and with each takeoff the tent is filled with dust so fine the air turns yellow.

And the airstrip is so close to the war that the Hercules landing every 10 to 15 minutes keep their engines roaring as they unload, then take off on a commandeered road and bank away from Iraqi lines to avoid exposing themselves to the enemy.

Specialist Freddie Twiggs, 19, of Live Oak, Fla., boarded a C-130 yesterday because his mom was diagnosed to be dying of cancer. If an attack occurs, his supply unit will stay right on the tail of the 24th Mechanized Infantry, a key unit in the expected invasion.

"Wherever they go, we go," Twiggs said. "I'm unhappy about leaving, but when Mom is diagnosed as dying . . ." he said, leaving the sentenced unfinished.

Not everyone is sorry to go. Spec. Gala Hall, 25, of Monroe, La., climbed in and escaped the sand because of a medical diagnosis that she did not want to discuss. She has refueled her last Apache, Blackhawk, and Cobra helicopter for a while.

"I've been here since Sept. 1 and I'm excited about going home," Hall said.

"I'm ready to go. They can have it," she said, and happily climbed on board.

Friday
February 22, 1991

The fires of Kuwait burned ever brighter. U.S. military officials said more than 140 oil wells in Kuwait had been set ablaze by Iraqi troops in the past 24 hours.

Oil that properly belonged in the ground, or in pipelines, barrels, furnaces, refineries, or crankcases was going up in smoke and lying thick on the surface of the Persian Gulf. The large, amorphous slick, also blamed on Iraq's occupying forces, now consisted of three million barrels, according to Saudi official estimates.

The withdrawal proposal Soviet leader Gorbachev had been refining for many days in hopes of staving off an allied ground invasion was finally made public and sent to Baghdad for the government—or more precisely, Saddam Hussein—to consider. In a swap for the allies holding their fire, it called for Iraq to start pulling its occupation forces from Kuwait within one day after a cease-fire and to be completely out in three weeks.

All UN resolutions having to do with embargoes and reparations demanded of Iraq would be "rescinded." The offer might have appeared reasonable, but the UN Security Council was taking no chances on making a wrong move at the last minute. It took no position on the Soviet proposal.

Gorbachev and his Iraqi friends were dealing not only with the burden of an untrustworthy reputation (Saddam Hussein's) but a ground offensive planned to begin within hours. The selection of Feb. 24th as G-Day was all but locked in at the White House and in Gen. Schwarzkopf's command bunker.

The old tennis player, President Bush, slammed the ball back at Gorbachev hard and deep. The latest U.S. ultimatum demanded that Iraq complete an unconditional withdrawal in one week, that all his troops be out of Kuwait City in 48 hours, and that the withdrawal begin at noon on Feb. 23, which would be midnight in the Gulf—24 hours from when the President spoke.

The Iraqi government called the Bush statement "desperate." Baghdad Radio called Bush a "madman." Perhaps in the knowledge that there was little point, at this juncture, in talking or trading more deadlines or proposals, Saddam Hussein called the American ultimatum "shameful."

It was one of his lesser epithets.

The countdown toward a ground war was evident in other ways. Allied planes preempted any Iraqi plans to hinder the allied assault with oil-filled trenches by dropping napalm on the oil-filled trenches just inside the Iraqi border, which was intended to ignite and burn off the oil before any large movement of troops.

Another story in this chapter sets the stage for the ground war by describing the missions of a long-range surveillance detachment.

In the Marine-filled trenches, stories in this chapter show spirits high and attack plans being unfolded at every meeting.

Friday - February 22, 1991

The war came too close to some Marines, who counted themselves fortunate to have returned at all from a shootout with the Iraqis inside Kuwait. They returned, but without their Humvee.

The war stories some would live to tell had begun to rise out of the desert.

Marines Plan Blitzkrieg at Any Moment: "We'll Be Laying Down as Much Metal as Possible"

By Phil Davison

Urgent attention Rosemary, British pool desk. Pls ensure gets to Indy on Sunday on time. Tks cigars. ProCathcart. Re yr query. Without doubt tis either one for Mike Stent or Mandela situation like last time. Fyi I may be out of contact for while but comms set-up looks good. Will get message to you soonest thereafter. Pls tell Harv will be ass-busting to get copy to him next week as often as poss and gtfl ensure tis smoothly handled in pipeline. This means keeping in close touch with Rosemary on Brit pool desk, who is doing great job.

Spot (This report was subjected to US military censorship)

(Britain. This is Mike Stent material for reasons can't divulge).

WITH THE U.S. MARINES CLOSE TO IRAQI FRONT LINES - A huge U.S. Marine ground task force, backed by tanks of Patton's "Hell on Wheels" 2nd Armored Division, was poised last night (Saturday) to launch what its commanders call a "Blitzkrieg" on Iraqi forces.

It could come at any moment.

Senior Marine officers told me the force, spearheaded by a mine-clearing "breach team," was "ready to go" should President Bush press the button for what is widely described here as G-Day, or the start of a ground war.

Reconnaissance teams are already operating beyond the border. Detailed information on which Marine division would move first, and where, is classified. But I have been given details of the Marines' plans and The Independent on Sunday will be the only British newspaper to go forward with the first Marine assault team to breach Iraqi defences if the order is given.

It could be the first allied assault of the entire front line. I can say only that the land-based Marines have taken up assault positions in two major areas. Commanders cannot yet reveal their precise objectives but there seems little doubt, in the personal opinion of this correspondent, that any thrust would be in the general direction of Kuwait City. No one here expects it to be easy.

But for the sake of understanding the geographical layout, it is worth noting that the Marines' tanks, without obstacles, could easily reach Kuwait City within an hour.

In fact, unless the Iraqis surrender en masse, the Marines would aim for specific individual objectives on the way to liberating Kuwait and may stop on the outskirts to allow Kuwait and Saudi forces to make the final symbolic entry into the capital.

The first specific objective has been revealed to correspondents moving with the Marines. According to classic breach tactics, the initial objective would be to establish an unassailable "beachhead", pausing to consolidate, before pushing on.

The likely scenario will be for one expanded Marine division to punch through first, led by a force of M60 tanks with mine-clearing blades and ploughs, bulldozers and heavily-armored, but fast-moving amphibious assault vehicles, to create a breach perhaps no wider, initially, than a set of football goalposts.

I am not privy to such information, but (it) is widely believed a Marine assault would also take place from ships in the Gulf, probably soon after the land thrust, and that U.S. Army troops and Great Britain's 1st Armoured Division, farther west from us, would forge through Iraqi lines after studying the initial Marines' success. Further breach lanes would be created as soon as possible to allow infantrymen and tanks to swarm forward. Next would come "back breaches," or cutback lanes, to allow empty logistics vehicles to return to bases within Saudi Arabia to restock with food, water, ammunition, and other supplies.

The Marines' readiness was helped by what they now call "the miracle well," an existing water well suddenly discovered close to their main logistics base and likely to pump out 6,000 gallons of water an hour. The danger to the Marines is that Iraqi artillery, as well as Soviet-made Hind or Hips attack helicopters, trap them in a "firesack," or killing zone.

But Marine commanders believe any Iraqi artillery pieces, that would have to emerge from hiding, or helicopters would quickly be destroyed by the Marines' own air power—Harrier and F-18 fighter-bombers and Cobra attack helicopters. "Never has there been a battle in which we had so much precise information on the enemy," a Marine colonel told me. "In Vietnam, we were in a vacuum. We were in his backyard, waiting for him to act so we could react."

Any Marine thrust would be preceded by an air and artillery barrage far more intense than anything that has so far hit the Iraqi frontline troops. According to Marine commanders, that would include waves of B-52 bombers, gigantic 15,000 BLU-82 bombs that each destroy an area the size of a football field, and tens of thousands of artillery rounds in the first hours.

"We'll be laying down as much metal as possible. When there's blood coming out of their orifices from bombardment, that's the best time to go in," a Marine colonel told me. The Iraqis would be hit in so many ways that they would not know which move to make, he said. "It will be a Blitzkrieg, a tremendous shock effect," the Marine colonel said in a bunker near the front lines. The rocky (illegible) in his encampment trembled sporadically as allied bombers released their ordnance on Iraqi positions beyond the border.

The colonel's view of the likely Iraqi response was refreshingly realistic after daily upbeat reports of "demoralized" Iraqi troops coming out of military briefings in the rear. "I don't see anything to suggest they're going to fold. I don't believe the speculation that they will not fight. But even if they fight tough, we'll still roll them over," he said. "Saddam has one shot. He is like a salmon swimming upstream. He will do his damnedest to inflict maximum casualties. In modern warfare, the first round hit percentage is amazing. It's a 'shoot first and win' sort of a battlefield."

Marine officers are wary of talking of potential casualties. They leave no doubt that the figures could be horrific, particularly during any initial breach, but are anxious not to alarm families in the U.S. To allay such fears, helicopter pilots of the Marine Air Wing will risk their own lives to evacuate casualties contaminated by chemical weapons. "Our pilots will medevac contaminated casualties and keep doing so until we decontaminate aircraft and crew," Col. Mike Williams, an Air Wing group commander, told me.

One man likely to be seen in his jeep not far behind the assault forces is Marine Gen. Charles "Chuck" Krulak, in charge of forward logistical supplies. Above his

Friday - February 22, 1991

bunker fly the U.S. and Kuwaiti flags, a rare splash of colour in this barren wasteland. The latter was given to him by a Kuwaiti army lieutenant. Since Krulak's son Todd went to school in Washington, D.C., with the son of the Kuwaiti ambassador to the U.S., Saud Nasser al-Sabah, Krulak plans to carry the Kuwaiti flag across the border, plant it somewhere on Kuwaiti soil, then frame it as a gift to the ambassador.

Long-Range Surveillance Squads Scope Iraqi Positions: "You're In Your Own World Out There"

By Jeffrey Ulbrich

IN NORTHERN SAUDI ARABIA - It takes a special kind of man to lie in a shallow hole in the desert up to 200 kilometers behind enemy lines, watching for the movement of troops or equipment.

SFC Robert Kramer calls that kind of man "mellow." "The majority of the people here are very mellow," says Kramer. "The majority of them are aggressive, but they have learned to cool that aggressiveness down to do this mission."

The mission of the 522nd Long Range Surveillance Detachment of the 519th Military Intelligence Battalion is to be the eyes of the commander on the ground. They report back about enemy troops, their numbers, their types, their equipment, their movements. "Their mission is totally passive," says Kramer. If they have to fire their weapons, that means they have blown their mission. They are not sufficiently armed to fight and don't have enough men to engage in any kind of battle.

The LRS people, the "Lurss," work in teams of six. They are dropped into their positions by helicopter and usually left for three or four days, five maximum without re-supply. Each division also has a LRS element for its own needs.

Because the guys of the 522nd are attached to a corps, they are required to go deeper in their surveillance. "We look for road intersections," says Kramer. "Roads can tell a lot. Is the enemy traveling or just re-supplying? What size is the unit?"

LRS units sometimes are also given an added mission of damage assessment.

Asked the hardest thing he has to do, Kramer answers in one word: "Sit."

"At any time, you may have just been spotted. The hardest thing is to tell whether you have been seen. You are sitting there, watching. Do I call a bird to get extracted? That's a nerve-wracking position."

Hiding in this northern Saudi Arabian desert, mostly flat with little variety in the terrain, is difficult. The heat also can be unbearable. LRS men may scoop out a shallow hole and cover it over with a poncho or other material to protect themselves. How close do they have to get? "As far away as you can get and still do the mission," says Spec. 4 Raul Luevano.

They are aided by special observation equipment for day and night. In some cases, they move in closer to their objective by night and back away in the daytime.

"But generally, moving is not something they want to do too much of. It takes a lot of discipline to do something like this," says Kramer.

The helicopter part of the surveillance teams includes both transport craft for the Lurss folks and attack helicopters flying in support. "Here, it's a different story from the line grunts," said Luevano. "You're on your own, you're in your own world out there."

Lurss teams don't like to change personnel. It's a very personal business. Team members like to know each other's habits. "I think it is important to have the same people all the time," said Luevano. "You bond. We all know each other, our wives names, kids' names. You get tight."

In this kind of business, the nod of a team leader's head, a look, a single muttered word, may be enough of a signal to take action. It has to be the right kind of group to stay two, three, four, or even five days in tight, unmoving confines together.

All of these guys have done this many times in training. Now, with the Iraqi border just a jump away, the time has come for testing.

"This is the ultimate test," says Sgt. Richard Morcelo.

U.S. Pilots Begin to Pity the Enemy Troops Below; Civilian Deaths a Regrettable "Cost of Doing Business"

By Storer H. Rowley, Joan Lowy, and Edith M. Lederer

AT AN AIRBASE IN SOUTHWESTERN SAUDI ARABIA - U.S. fliers pity the Republican Guard troops they pound with bombs night after night and regret any civilian casualties they may inflict.

But they believe that is the price of war and it is not too high a price if it means stopping Iraqi leader Saddam Hussein and saving American lives in the expected ground war.

"War is not a pretty occupation," said Col. Tom Lennon, commander of the 48th Tactical Fighter Wing (Provisional), whose squadron of F-111F fighter-bombers drop the most sophisticated bombs of the Persian Gulf War.

"And I know that is why if you talk to a military man, for the most part, we're the last ones who want to go to war," he said. "But war is war, and people die in war."

However, Lennon, an F-111F pilot who has flown missions over Iraq and occupied Kuwait, argued that every mission undertaken by allied bombers diminishes Saddam's war machine and may save the lives of American soldiers on the battlefield.

"How many American servicemen do you want to lose?" asked Lennon in an interview this week at this secret desert base for F-111F and EF-111A Raven radar-jamming aircraft.

Asked about occasional unintended damage to civilian structures near military targets and the horrific scene of hundreds of dead civilians carried from a smashed shelter near Baghdad, Lennon replied: "That's the cost of doing business."

"Do I like it? No, I don't like it. Do I have sympathy for them? You're damn right I do. Hopefully, these people understand Saddam is massacring them," he said.

Capt. Brad Robert, 29, of Boise, Idaho, F-111F pilot, bristled at the public outcry over civilian casualties. "We've completely gotten away from the Kuwait issue and what is being done to the citizens of Kuwait who are living in Kuwait City right now and what they went through," Robert said. "Right now it seems like people are worrying too much about who might be dying on the Iraqi side and they don't even care any more about the atrocities that are still taking place in Kuwait City."

Pilots often bring up the report that Iraqi soldiers who invaded Kuwait have bayoneted pregnant women, taken babies from their incubators, and shot unarmed teenagers in front of their parents for distributing leaflets.

Robert's flying partner, weapon systems officer Lt. Troy Stone, 25, of Hemlock, Mich., pointed out that while allied bombers go out of their way not to hit civilians, Saddam has been lobbing Scud missiles at civilian targets in Israel and Saudi Arabia.

"Why is it that on our newscasts we can sit and complain and say how wrong we were for bombing that bomb shelter . . . but nightly he chucked Scuds into a city that has absolutely no military (significance)," said Stone, referring to Tel Aviv. "They aren't even combatants in this war, and he's chucking Scuds in there," he said.

Col. John Tindall, 56, of Kissimmee, Fla., the wing's flight surgeon, said pilots are always aware that their precision-guided bombs can occasionally stray off target.

"There was a great feeling of relief that this was not one of our missions," Tindall said of the ill-fated February attack by allied bombers on the Baghdad bomb shelter that allied forces said was also a command and control bunker. "Even with all the care we take (not to hit civilians), they realize that one can go awry," he said.

Tindall compared the necessity for the air war with President Harry Truman's decision to drop two atomic bombs on Japanese cities in World War II, saying it averted an invasion of Japan's main islands that would have cost far more lives.

"Nobody has any doubts about why it was necessary," Tindall said.

Maj. Larry Spitser, 39, of Pawnee City, Neb., an EF-111A pilot, acknowledged "it bothers me if innocent people are killed on either side." But, he said, "I've pretty much got ice water running through my veins anyway. As far as the job I'm going to do, it's just not going to affect me in any way whatsoever other than the fact that it's very unfortunate. I hate to hear something like that happen, no matter where the blame is," Spitser said. Capt. Brent Brandon, 30, of Austin, Tex., the electronic warfare officer on Spitser's plane, said, "The way I see it is, it is war, and there are going to be some deaths in war. And it's tragic. But there's one guy who really can call the shots and stop all this, and we all know who that is."

The fliers also made the point that sophisticated precision-guided bombs that have been highly perfected since their use in Vietnam have given them a greater degree of confidence than ever before that they can avoid civilians. "You have a 99.9 percent warm, fuzzy (feeling) inside of you that your bombs are going to hit where you want them to," Stone said. "We have rules of engagement, and if you are bombing something that is near civilian targets, you are not able to drop unless you have positively identified the target, and that's something we are able to do in this war that we have never been able to do before."

Lt. Dave Bristol, 26, of Flint, Mich., who flies an F-111F fighter-bomber, his voice rising in anger, said, "If you can't find your target, we're not dropping because we do not want collateral damage and civilian casualties. It can be ended by one person changing his mind and doing what he should have done months ago."

So accurate are the bombs blasting tanks and bunkers of the Republican Guard and other Iraqi troops that American fliers facing less and less anti-aircraft resistance are starting to pity their enemy. "This is sometimes like a duck shoot," said Capt. Bradley Seipel, 34, an F-111F weapons systems officer from Virginia Beach, Va.

"Sometimes they're fighting back, but we took out their air defense systems pretty quick. I feel sorry for the military on the ground, not just the civilian casualties, because we're just pounding the hell out of them," Seipel said. "Obviously a lot of them are bad guys for what they did in Kuwait, but a lot of them are just army soldiers and we're hitting them night after night. A lot of time they don't hear us until after the bombs fall. I think it will pay off.

"Try to imagine, those guys have been sitting in holes being bombed around the clock, day and night. It's got to be so demoralizing. They are not even fighting back."

Added Capt. Mike Russell, 33, of Bradenton, Fla., the pilot of Seipel's F-111F, "It's just a shame that their leadership doesn't stop this, because they're going to lose anyway.

"It's like shooting ducks in a barrel," he said. "I sometimes feel sorry for them, but it doesn't offend my sense of fair play. This is a war, and we're beating them badly, and that's exactly what we want to do."

Tindall, their flight surgeon, said the fliers "handle it the same way a surgeon does going after cancer, concentrating on the disease and not the individual he's cutting." When tanks show up on the infrared night-vision sights of the F-111F against the cold desert sand, the fliers dropping 500-pound bombs know that "somebody is likely to be inside it," said Tindall. "I think they'll see the necessity of doing that and have no problem," he said. "That's not to say they're going to like it, but psychologically you tend to look at the positive.

"One of the ways you deal with it is by not dwelling on it too much, and you don't hear the guys talking about it in the squadron room."

Lucky-as-Hell Marines Escape Direct Hit By the Floss of Their Teeth

By Susan Sachs

NEAR THE KUWAIT BORDER, Saudi Arabia - Soon after his first day of combat, with his Humvee truck a smoldering ruin from a well-placed enemy mortar, 21-year-old Robert Grady borrowed a pen and wrote his new nickname on the front of his helmet: "Lucky as Hell."

The Marine lance corporal and his buddy survived a direct Iraqi hit yesterday (Feb. 21) on their missile-toting vehicle, just at the start of a daylong battle between Iraqi troops and Marine artillery and warplanes.

The fighting in the flat desert no-man's-land between Kuwait and Saudi Arabia was the fiercest yet for the 2nd Marine Division. Hours after Grady escaped death by only a few feet, two other Marines were wounded by Iraqi artillery and evacuated from the battle area.

Division (spokesman) Lt. Col. Jan Huly could give no further details on the extent of their injuries this morning. He said the Iraqi force suffered "many" casualties in the fighting and Marines had captured 81 Iraqis. "It looked like infantry operating with tanks and support and after the tanks were destroyed, they (the Iraqi soldiers) lost the will to resist," Huly said.

Commanders in the field reported that their artillery, combined with bombing from Marine Harrier jump jets, F/A-18 Hornets and A-6 Intruders, destroyed at least two Iraqi tanks, four ammunition trucks, and an artillery battery.

This morning, constant kettle-drum booms of U.S. artillery reverberated through the chilly air as sporadic fighting continued a few miles outside the 12-foot-high sand berm erected by the Saudis at their border with Kuwait.

Meanwhile, Marines were ordered to start taking Pyridostigmine tablets, a drug that is supposed to enhance the effectiveness of nerve-gas antidotes. The last time troops were ordered to start the drug regimen, a precaution against possible Iraqi use of chemical and biological weapons, was the day before the air war against Iraq.

The Marine probe north of the berm was aimed at measuring the Iraqi force arrayed beyond the U.S.-led military coalition. Marine and Army units have pushed repeatedly beyond the border in such probes in recent weeks, as have Iraqi troops in southerly movements.

In the latest engagement, the first since the Marines moved into their final assault positions for a ground war, Huly said, "We weren't surprised but we're interested they responded so aggressively." The Iraqi response "tells us some are going to fight very strongly to the end, some will desert and go the other way and some won't fight very hard and then will surrender to us," he added.

The weather in the northern Gulf region remained clear and sunny today after a spate of heavy thunderstorms, as commanders in the field continued preparations for a ground assault, despite signs of a possible diplomatic solution to the Gulf crisis. The 2nd Marine Division's border battle began just before noon Thursday, when a convoy of light-armored vehicles crossed through newly carved cuts in the sand wall along the Saudi border. Grady and his driver, Lance Cpl. William Noland, traveling in the middle of the convoy, suddenly saw clouds of smoke and dust billow up in front of them from three Iraqi shells.

They said there was no time to swerve their Humvee or take evasive action before the fourth shell slammed into the rear of their truck, throwing them against the windshield and igniting four of the Stinger anti-aircraft missiles loaded in the back. Knowing each of the shoulder-launched missiles carries the explosive power of a half-pound of TNT, the two Marines leaped from the truck and dove for the ground. A light-armored vehicle picked them up as the truck was engulfed in flames.

"What we went in there for was to find out how close they (the Iraqis) were," said Noland, 25, of Memphis, Tenn. "We were only a few miles from the berm when we began receiving fire. So we learned they are not as weak as everybody is making them out to be. They've still got a pretty good force."

The lucky survivors of the attack on the Humvee, the military's all-purpose canvas-sided truck, lost everything they had with them but were still exhilarated hours after their close call. "There are a lot of people who have been over here a lot longer than us," said Grady, who arrived in January. "So we really feel good that we got into combat first."

Grady lost all his mementos, including pictures of his girlfriend back home in Madison, N.C., and a picture of his Marine father. He also bemoaned the loss of his dental floss. "That's our home," he said of the wrecked Humvee. "We sleep in it, we live in it, everything we own is in that vehicle."

The two young Marines hoped to get a replacement vehicle to go back into the fray. "All we want is another vehicle so we can get back into action for some payback," Noland said.

Taking Option 3, Spike Fell From the Sky Like a Rag Doll, as Longest Hour of his Life Waited Below

(no byline)

Interview with Capt. Scott "Spike" Thomas, 27, who was rescued last Sunday after he jettisoned inside Iraq following an engine failure.

He was returning from a successful bombing mission with his wingman, Lt. Eric "Neck" Dodson just before night fell. Both are from the 33rd Squadron of 363rd Tactical Fighter Wing based at Shaw Air Force Base in South Carolina. The wing is currently deployed "somewhere in southern Arabian peninsula."

Spike and Neck are good fiends since their years at the Air Force Academy, but last Sunday's flight was their first combat mission together.

Spike had his survival kit with him (which included water, food, radio, life raft, and a 9mm pistol) when he ejected. He has some stitches under his chin, probably caused by the parachute harness. Has not flown any mission since the incident but says he is looking forward for one.

As he waited on the ground for around two hours he collected stones as souvenirs and gave some of them to the members of the search and rescue team who snatched him out of the enemy territory.

SPIKE: We were returning from the target and are about 100 miles north of the Saudi border in Iraq when I experienced trouble with my engine. Neck was on my wing at that time.

I noticed a loss of thrust in my engine and he noticed leaking. Then everything literally went downhill. We feared I had three options. One is to make it across the border and land at an airbase; second to cross the border and jettison. And third and worst is to jump out in Iraqi territory.

You talk about these things, you train for them and never expect them to happen to you. And when they do some kind of big hand takes over for you and you start doing things without realizing.

Q: How does it feel to eject?

SPIKE: It is not that bad, actually. I have played football at college, and I have taken worse kicks on Saturday afternoons. I was lucky because I was only doing 150 knots. I was flying at 12,000 feet. The actual ejection was not too violent. The jet flew for about eight more miles and got away from me and did not draw attention to me. It is an amazing sight to jump out there to see a flaming F-16 flying out between your legs.

NECK: It looks more violent looking at it. I was flying 500 feet away when he made a radio call that he was getting out and I told him he was on fire. Next thing I saw his cockpit turn orange and see the canopy come behind him and his head right behind the canopy. He looked like a rag doll.

I circled to look, I hoped he did not break his arms and legs flying all around.

SPIKE: I reckoned it took me five minutes to get to the ground. It is a long time. Your first thought about your checklist, which became automatic, be sure my parachute was good, check all my equipment, then my next thought was, it is kind of cold as I was passing through the clouds.

Then I thought, where are the bad guys? How can I avoid them? You can steer the parachute somehow and I was trying to find a good place to land. It was still daylight. I was able to see probably five miles radius around. I could not see any Iraqi guys around me.

Next thing coming down I saw Neck circling all around taking care of me. Once I hit the ground, I contacted Neck and asked if I should move. We decided that I stayed put. Next thing I did was start to set up a camp. In this whole time, Neck was coordinating search and rescue for me.

We gave them a general area and where to start looking.

I noticed a thunderstorm was coming my way. I was worried that the night will be cold and did not want to get wet. So I made a shelter with my raft, propping it up with two bushes.

Q: *How long it took them to pick you up?*

SPIKE: It took two hours. First hour passed pretty quickly, but the second was the longest in my life. I was listening on the radio but was not talking.

I had no clue the search and rescue teams were coming until I saw the helicopter. I heard the air support. In fact, the whole time, let's say 30 percent of the time I heard fighters passing, which gave you a great deal of security.

The guys who picked me up were the most professional capable guys I have ever seen, I have complete confidence in them. In fact, what I found out when I came back was that I had only one hour left, Iraqis were coming from two directions to get me and they were within two miles.

I heard the helicopter passing by me. I was then screaming on the radio that "Hey, guys, you've passed me up! I'm on the left!"

Then for three minutes I have not heard nothing. I still knew they were coming back. The next thing I saw this helicopter right in front of my face. It puts down and they send out a guy to get me. He was like a self-contained army and his most effective weapon was his arms. He had these huge arms.

He grabbed me and shuffled me into the helicopter. The first thing he asked me was, "Are you all right?" I said, "Yes, I'm all right. Let's get out of here." I learned later the helicopter was fired upon by Iraqis on the way back but nothing happened.

Big British Artillery Arrived Three Days After War Began, But Now They Can Barrage With the Best of Them

By Mark Fritz

IN NORTHERN SAUDI ARABIA - Even as they fire round after deadly round into Iraqi positions, British soldiers are eager to draw a line from the great battles of the past to today's high-tech war.

The 16th Artillery Battery now hammering Iraqi targets with 155mm Howitzers, for example, fired the first cannon shots at Waterloo, says Lt. Col. Mark Corbet-Burcher, commander of the 26th Field Regiment, the "Sussex Gunners" which encompasses the 16th.

"They can bore you endlessly about their history," says Corbet-Burcher, 41, of Sussex. His unit was among three British artillery battalions that fired from positions Friday occupied by the U.S. Army's 1st Cavalry Division, the second day of coordinated attacks by the two armies.

It was the latest in a week of heavy barrages aimed at knocking out Iraqi artillery and mortar positions to pave the way for a ground offensive.

"I'm particularly interested in high-pay-off targets, especially field artillery" that could be a problem for coalition ground forces, said Col. Jim Gass, 49, of Carney,

Okla., head of the 1st Cavalry's artillery units who watched Friday's massive attack.

Two battalions of .155 and .203 Howitzers and one battalion of Multiple Launch Rocket System launchers—high-tech rockets that each scatter 644 "bomblets" on impact—shook the desert with ear-popping blasts for 20 minutes before "bugging out" to avoid Iraqi return fire, as Corbet-Burcher put it. "They give us the targets," Corbet-Burcher said of the Americans. "We're just firing at the targets they asked us to fire at." Gass, however, said the targets come from an intelligence pool compiled by the nations in the multinational force.

Gen. Joshua Robles, assistant division commander for supply and support and a former artillery commander, also observed Friday's barrage. "You can't get the smell of gunpowder out of an artilleryman's nostrils," he said as the thud of rockets and shells slamming into the sand echoed n the distance. Robles said there are numerous similarities between American and British soldiers, their terminology and regimentation.

"I find working with the Americans very enjoyable," said Corbet-Burcher. "So many of the (military) expressions are the same." But he pointed out that he thought the British-made shells being fired by the American-built Howitzers were more explosive and had more deadly fragmentation than their American counterparts.

British soldiers in general say their 35,000-member force in the Persian Gulf probably has it better than the American force that is more than 15 times larger, a logistical behemoth. "The British get their mail in about five days," said Sgt. Clive Gaughan, 32, of Edinburgh, Scotland. "The Americans get theirs in about five weeks. They're very jealous of our system."

Lt. Mark Thornhill, 24, of London, said he hears envious comments from Americans still wearing jungle fatigues. He said all of the British have the beige-on-beige desert camouflage. "We've got the desert camouflage, they've still got a lot of green," said Thornhill. "They're very jealous of that.... We do hear of supply problems, but the only reason has got to be the size of their operation," he said.

Howard Campbell, 26, of Londonderry, Northern Ireland, pointed out that even though the British artillery battalions arrived on Jan. 5, delays kept their guns from arriving until Jan. 20, three days after war began.

The British also admitted a fondness for American rations—the much-ridiculed Meals Ready to Eat—and U.S. sleeping cots, both items heavily traded for on the unofficial multinational military market-place. Even Gaughan, a 14-year veteran who believes British troops have more discipline, higher morale, and a higher degree of professionalism than their American counterparts, expressed a fondness for U.S. rations.

"I swap my (rations) for MREs every day," he said.

British Visitors Make Great Deal of Noise on U.S. Turf, and Boast They've Made Improvements to the Ammo

By Charles Richards

IN NORTHERN SAUDI ARABIA - It was visitors' day in northern Saudi Arabia.

It was the 1st Cavalry Division's turf—if the shingly desert sand can be called turf.

But the guns were British, invited in an atmosphere of cooperation between the two friendly nations to share in the shooting.

Friday - February 22, 1991

The British had fired with the Americans twice before, but this was the first time that the Cav had played host.

It was a beautiful day. The sun blazed down through a cloudless, blue sky. The great machines of war stood arrayed in their dun coloured desert camouflage like huts on a beach. To complete the impression, the heat haze created a mirage of water in the near distance.

A half moon hung in the sky.

Seconds after the one o'clock firing time, the first rocket from the multiple launchers thrust upwards in a ball of light. It left behind a trail of white smoke. Then another went off. Then another, until all twelve rockets were fired. At almost the same time, the shouted instructions of the gunners prepared the old-fashioned self-propelled guns. Then the order came: "Fire."

And with a sharp pop, six guns of the 16 Field Battery of the 26 Field Regiment of Royal Artillery (the "Sussex Gunners" who opened the fire on Napoleon's army at the 1815 Battle of Waterloo) cast their munitions of steel and high explosive northwards.

Another battery fired in virtual unison to the left, a third to the right. More MLRS rockets rose into the sky. After each firing, the massive guns recoiled, then swung round as they were re-sighted. The loaders moved languidly, one tossing the spent 155mm shell cases out to the right as another bent round behind him to the stacks behind him in the sand to untie the blue and purple bags of propellant.

Then one carried the new round for placing in the breach. Salvo followed salvo, until the bad-egg smell of cordite permeated the clean desert air. Then the order for cease-fire was given, and the loaders all of a sudden moved with quiet urgency.

One sprinted to gather up the red and white striped aiming posts. Then they were off, moving on their tracks out of range of any Iraqi artillery in the unlikely event—judging from past experience—of Iraqi counterfire.

As the British set off back in a column to the south, the sun caught on their goggles. They had different vehicles from the Americans too: Land Rovers, and 500cc Armstrong motorbikes. Many of the men wore chequered *shamaag* headscarves round their necks and tattoos on their arms. Lt. Col. Mark Corbet-Burcher had a paisley design scarf inside his goggles on his helmet. The British, almost the last to arrive, looked wan beside the Cavalry officers, weather-beaten by five months in the desert.

It was of course not real sport. It was entirely one-sided, more a turkey shoot than a big game hunt, with no risk of a wounded but still dangerous beast turning on the hunter. "What we're firing at today is about 12 to 25 kilometers away," said Corbet-Burcher. The barrage would have rained down on the Iraqi positions shortly after the end of the main Islamic religious occasion of the week, Friday noonday prayers. Who knows what prayers and imprecations were offered up by the Iraqi soldiers minutes before this massive barrage descended on them from the heavens.

For both the British and American commanders, it was a fruitful exercise in cooperation. Lt. Col. Corbet-Burcher, the battalion commander of 26 Field Regiment (artillery battalions are called regiments in the British army) aged 41, from Camberly in Sussex, said much had to do with past NATO training.

"We speak the same language. It's very enjoyable and amazingly easy."

Col. Corbet-Burcher said that three regiments of the divisional artillery of the British 1st Armoured Division were firing: 26 Field Regiment, with M109 guns; 32 Heavy Regiment, with M110 eight-inch (203mm) guns; and 39 Regiment with MLRS rocket launchers.

The equipment itself was cooperative. The M109 and M110 are both U.S. made, and the MLRS was a multinational development, led by the U.S.

Col. Corbet-Burcher however made assertions of British improvements. "The M109 is an American gun, but the ammunition is British. It is superior in three ways. The L15 first has more high explosive; two, in a gory fashion, it produces more fragments, and three, it has a multi-role fuse which bursts at different heights."

Col. Jim Gass, who lives in Killeen, Texas, the commander of the 1st Cavalry Division's artillery, concurred. "We've just a particular opportunity to work with them. Our schools of thought, our standards, are out of the same cradle. Our doctrines are very similar. It was a useful opportunity to work together." Senior officers of both forces came in their helicopters to watch the performance: Brigadier Ian Durie, the British divisional artillery commander, and a U.S. one-star general, Brigadier Gen. Robles.

"It's a good chance for them to come in and do some shooting with us," Brigadier Robles, the assistant divisional commander (ADC in U.S. military jargon) explained.

And for both forces, the more artillery rained down before the land offensive now deemed imminent, the better.

"They'd Better Be Quick" If They're to Stop This War; Meantime, Peace in the Morning, Firing at Night

By Denis Gray

WITH THE U.S. MARINES NEAR THE KUWAIT BORDER - They're sighting howitzers and passing out the anti-agent pills but there is still a flicker of hope on the front lines that peace may come—in the words of one U.S. officer—"at the 12th hour."

"We're cocked and ready, but let's hope we don't have to pull the trigger," said Capt. Ed Hughes, an artilleryman married shortly before being ordered to Saudi Arabia and whose wife is expecting a child at the end of May.

In the windswept foxholes, the command posts and computer-stocked artillery centers there is a palpable sense that the ground war is imminent, and that many may not see the end of it. But soldiers are also glued to hourly news broadcasts which tell of peace initiatives proposed one day only to be spurned the next. "I can't take this emotional roller-coaster ride," said one Marine sergeant as the radio announced yet another turn in the diplomatic brinkmanship. "It's peace in the morning and war at night."

"They'd better be quick," is often heard and refers to the would-be peacemakers racing the clock to avert "G-Day," the time the allied armies move forward into combat. The assistant commander of the 2nd U.S. Marine Division, Brig. Gen. Russ Sutton, said that walking this emotional tightrope was "a psychological thing we have to cope with" but claimed it was not having any serious effect on the troops.

"Emotions are running too high to be able to pin hopes on something we can't control," said Col. Les Palm, a 25-year Marine veteran from Marysville, Calif.

Sutton rejected the notion that many were itching for ground combat, not wanting to be robbed of possible glory and not wanting the pilots—who have to date conducted most of the combat operations—take home the laurels. "I don't think anyone who's experienced war is hoping for it.

Of those who are, it's nothing more than bravado," said the general, who lost his left eye in one of his two Vietnam War tours.

But most in the 2nd Division and other combat units ranged along the Kuwaiti border have never experienced battle and some say they are eager to do so. Others see it as a shortcut to home, preferable to more waiting in one of the world's harshest environments.

"I'd be pissed off if we didn't go in and kick his butt out of Kuwait," said a combat engineer who had already seen action in the fight for the Saudi Arabian town of Khafji. Two lance corporals—Robert Grady and William Noland—talked both of avenging what they called Iraq's rape of Kuwait and the exhilaration of combat after narrowly escaping death when a mortar round slammed into their light vehicle Thursday. "We've got so much stuff over here in Saudi Arabia we've got to go in," said Gunnery Sgt. Steve Lanners, echoing opinion that the campaign has gathered too great a momentum to be easily halted.

While commanders may have one ear cocked to the political news out of Moscow, Washington, and Baghdad, they say they must act on the assumption that a land offensive will take place. There is an intense focus on day-to-day tactics and a fixation on Target Kuwait.

In minds and on map overlays, defenses are already being cut, bunkers stormed and key ground seized en route to downtown Kuwait City.

"We're pretty much good to go," said Lt. Col. Arnie Fields when Sutton visited his motorized infantry unit. "I know where to go, generally what to do — just tell me when."

"See you at the Kuwait Hilton," the colonel, rigged in battle gear, shouted when Sutton was leaving. As the general crisscrossed the desert, reports of the division's fiercest engagement so far crackled over the radio in his light vehicle. Artillery salvos were being fired and prisoners of war taken. A single rocket streaked comet-like across the sky and from not so far away came the deep, rumbling bass of B-52 bombs exploding.

Stopping at several units of the division, Sutton delved into the minutia of battle and asked if the troops had all been issued pills to counter the effects of nerve gas and anthrax, a deadly disease the allies say Iraqi forces may attempt to spread in event of a ground war. "You've got to be ready to lay down that fire as fast as you can," Sutton told Lt. Col. Joe Stewart, commander of an artillery unit that would be providing vital support for advancing ground soldiers.

Stewart and other artillery officers assured him they could fire off the first rounds 90 seconds after getting the fix on an Iraqi target—and if the fix was accurate the fire would be lethal. "All of us are alike, all of us want to go home and have peace, but the party line is that we are ready to go to war," Stewart, of Birmingham, Ala., told this reporter.

"These are scary and exciting times. Regardless of what happens we'll be changed people, whether we shoot or not."

Saturday
February 23, 1991

The air wing of the allied force had the battlefield mostly to itself for 38 days. On the 38th day, nearly 3,000 sorties were flown in a final burst of attacks that concentrated on frontline troops along the border in southern Iraq and Kuwait.

In this chapter, the skies over Kuwait on the eve of the long-awaited ground war are described as the most dangerous place in the world. The aircraft that will be flying close-support missions, riding in just over the shoulders of the invading troops, strap on their Gatling guns for good measure.

The allies were stepping up their cross-border raids to pinpoint and distract the enemy, prepping their armored divisions for a speedy dash across the sandy plains and, in the case of a brigade from the 82nd Airborne Division, taking a foothold in enemy territory hours before the official start of the offensive.

One of the allied raids finds a trace of chemicals—believed in this case fallout from an air strike on a chemical weapons storage site, not from Iraqi weapons.

The U.S. had warned Saddam Hussein that delving into chemical warfare would bring extremely serious counter-measures. So far, the allies had not spelled out exactly what they would do, and he had not taken the dare. Every man and woman going into Kuwait and Iraq in this war would wear protective clothing over their uniform and carry a mask to cope with just such an attack.

But an open question was how much peril the allies put their own troops in by simply trying to destroy Iraq's store of chemical and biological weapons.

Detecting traces of chemicals was only the beginning. Learning their origin, the consequences of being near them when destroyed, and dealing with the long-term effects of even minor exposure would last well beyond the shooting war.

Another look at the ground-level effects of high-tech warfare in this chapter comes in a story about a video from an attack on an Iraqi position days earlier by Apache helicopters. The lethal helicopter's gun-camera video, showing the raid through a night-vision lens from the perspective of the attackers, was graphic evidence of the plight of whoever might be on the receiving end.

As the Apache's guns opened up, the enemy scattered in terrible fright. Some died instantly. Others escaped briefly, then were cut down. Their faces were not visible, only their helplessness, their dying, and the Apache's relentless pursuit.

Just reading a story about the video was too hard on some.

The allies had been taking prisoners by the hundreds for several weeks, in raids and probes across the border. So it was assumed there would be plenty more where they came from. But there were so many that even the large transport buses described in this chapter would not be enough to handle the torrent.

Saturday - February 23, 1991

As the midnight deadline approached, one facet of the allied effort was much debated. There were still about 13,000 Marines aboard ships in the Persian Gulf, armed, primed, and ready to hit the beaches.

In this chapter, their commander spells out the many reasons not to order them ashore. One very important one had been mentioned earlier: just having them sitting offshore was keeping about six Iraqi divisions pinned down along the Kuwaiti shoreline.

And the topic of females serving in the front lines is raised again in this chapter. Women in the U.S. military were restricted from assignment to frontline combat units in 1991, but some found themselves in the front row anyway, where the shooting would be.

U.S. Infantry Peace Plan: Hit Iraqi Air Defense Site; "This is a Good Night to Kill Something"

By Dave Schad

NORTHERN SAUDI ARABIA - While the United Nations brooded over the latest Middle East peace plan, a task force from the 197th Infantry Brigade drove nearly 20 miles into enemy territory and attacked an Iraqi air defense site.

The night-long raid, which involved some 200 soldiers and more than 30 vehicles, is believed to be the largest and deepest foray yet into enemy territory.

A few days before Friday night's mission, Lt. Col. Edwin Chamberlain sent his battalion's scout section across the border to see what his unit faced.

The scouts, the first soldiers from the 197th to go into enemy territory, spotted a vehicle near an obscure road before having to withdraw before sunrise. The road looked promising, so a second, larger patrol was planned.

For that one, Chamberlain put together a task force that included two mechanized infantry platoons, one tank platoon, his scout platoon, and a number of other armored support vehicles.

While the battalion commander moved across the border with the force, he stopped 10 miles inside the border with his command post and the support tracks. He left the fighting to Capt. Steve Banach, one of his company commanders.

"I picked Banach's company especially for this," said Chamberlain, sitting in the back of his M-113 Armored Personnel Carrier a few hours before the mission. "All of my companies are good, but Steve is the guy, and his company is the one for this mission."

The task force entered enemy territory just after sunset. Less than 10 minutes later, they made their first "contact"—a string of communications wire paralleling a road a few hundred meters across the border. They decided to chop out a chunk of the wire on the way home. Although the find wasn't much, Maj. Gene Kamena, the battalion's operations officer, took the discovery of the wire as a positive omen.

"This is a good night to kill something," said Kamena, 35, from Montgomery, Ala., as his M-113 bounced along inside enemy territory. "We think we may catch something up north tonight. That road's a resupply route, and we know the Iraqis like to move things at night." After leaving the command and support vehicles halfway to the objective, Banach's troops moved on.

As the group moved, they reported seeing a number of lights and flares. Nothing much developed until around 11 p.m., when the group spotted three bursts of anti-aircraft fire not far from their formation. From his spot with the command post, Kamena picked up his radio handset and advised Banach to send his M1A1 Abrams tanks to engage the guns and keep the thin-skinned M-113s in the rear.

"If it is anti-aircraft fire, those guns can tear up our personnel carriers," Kamena explained. "We'll have to lead with our tanks, and we'll need the element of surprise. If we lose that, it could be a real mess."

At that point, a one-sided game of cat and mouse ensued as Banach's tank platoon maneuvered to identify and fire at the site without being spotted. Besides the presence of the air defense gun, the force began seeing other targets around the site.

As the tanks crept across the desert floor, their platoon leader, 2nd Lt. David Oste, 24, from Swansea, Mass., kept the command post appraised of their progress. Inside his M-113, battalion commander Chamberlain listened to his lieutenant's radio reports and offered his opinion of the young officer. "He's about five-foot-two, a great American, and he's got balls bigger than all the outdoors," growled Chamberlain, 40, from LaPlata, Md.

Because the anti-aircraft site sat in a depression, Oste eventually decided that his tanks wouldn't be able to get a good shot without moving up to the edge of the hole.

"The only way we can get at those bastards is to go in and dig them out—it just ain't worth it," Chamberlain said. At that point, the battalion called for a barrage from a Multiple Launch Rocket System that was already standing by.

Before backing off with the rest of the task force, Oste decided to have his tanks hose down the target with their tank's 7.62 coaxial machine guns. The tankers reported that they started a large fire and hit several Iraqis and a vehicle. Around 1:20 a.m., the sky to the south of the task force lit up as seven rockets headed toward the air defense site. Their impact lit up the horizon and resulted in a large secondary explosion that could be felt 10 miles away. As the sounds of the impact died away, the battalion commander called Banach.

"Now comes the hard part," Chamberlain said. "I want you to take your two mech platoons and go back in there and see what it was we just blew the hell out of."

Banach moved back to within a half-mile of the site, but ran out of time before he could assess the damage. Based on the size of the secondary explosion and later assessment, the battalion believes that the site was destroyed.

A few minutes after six the next morning, the battalion returned to Saudi territory. After an after-action review, Banach said his task force had done pretty well on its first combat mission. "They stayed cool, and I didn't have to tell anybody to do anything twice," said Banach, 32, from Port Jervis, N.Y. "They knew this wasn't training."

Chemicals Detected as Marines Fight Frontier Battle; "Bodies Lying Around But We're Not Counting"

By Jeff Franks

WITH THE U.S. MARINES NEAR THE KUWAITI BORDER - Traces of a substance used in chemical weapons were found near the site of a continuing border clash between Iraqi troops and U.S. Marines, a Marine spokesman said Saturday.

The type of substance was not disclosed,

Saturday - February 23, 1991

but 2nd Marine Division Lt. Col. Jan Huly said it may have been released as a result of allied artillery and air strikes. "Probably we hit a chemical storage site and traces were released into the air," said Huly.

"From our best knowledge, we were not the subject of a chemical attack," he told reporters during a briefing at a forward command base. A Fox chemical detection vehicle found the substance Friday just inside the Saudi border, Huly said. Only a very small amount was present. "It is not thought to be a threat," he said.

The discovery was the first hard evidence that the Iraqis have chemical weapons along this sector of the border. Huly refused to comment when asked if Iraqi prisoners of war had disclosed more about their military's chemical arsenal in Kuwait.

Meanwhile, fighting that broke out Thursday along the Saudi-Kuwaiti border continued to rage Saturday with little evidence that peace talks elsewhere were slowing down either side. Marine artillery and rocket batteries could be heard—and in some cases seen—pounding away at Iraqi positions inside Kuwait. Huly said that the Marines have destroyed 18 Iraqi T-62 tanks and 15 other military vehicles in the fighting. An Iraqi soldier taken prisoner said that more than 100 Iraqis had been killed, Huly said.

"Our troops have seen bodies lying around, but we're not counting," Huly said. Only three Marines have been wounded in what Huly called "the skirmish of Um Qadar," Two of the troops were sent by helicopter to a rear hospital for treatment where their conditions were not known. The other was treated and sent back to his unit, Huly said.

The Marines have taken 90 prisoners of war in the fighting, Huly said. The battle broke out Thursday when Iraqi troops attacked a light armored infantry unit with small-arms fire, artillery, and mortars.

The Marines, who were operating in the no-man's-land beyond the defensive berm along the Saudi border, fled back into Saudi Arabia, then returned to take on the Iraqis.

As of Saturday morning, the Marines had launched 60 artillery and eight multiple launch rocket system raids, combined with numerous air attacks, on the Iraqis, Huly said. Despite the Marines' reluctance to acknowledge that they have been fighting inside Kuwait, the Marines have gotten close enough to peer into Iraqi bunkers and trenches. Huly said that the Marines reported finding well-established—and well-stocked—defenses.

"They appear to have large quantities of ammunition and numerous weapons systems. It looks like they've had five, six, or seven months to position themselves," he said. Still, Huly said that prisoners of war report that allied bombing of supply lines has been "very effective." The skirmish of Um Qadar goes on against a background of continued allied preparation for a ground assault on Kuwait. Huly said that elements of the 2nd and 1st Marine Divisions had moved into attack positions along the border Friday.

This forward command base was a beehive of activity Saturday as nearby units packed up and moved to within spitting distance of the border.

As the sun went down Friday, the northern horizon virtually exploded with an orange glow from burning oil wells in Kuwait. The burning wells have been visible intermittently since this base moved to within a few kilometers of the border last week, but never to such an extent as Friday night. At least 25 separate flames could be seen from here, but a television crew that went near the border for some night shooting said they could see more than 40 wells aflame.

Accompanying the flames was an ugly cloud of black smoke that Huly acknowledged could hamper an assault on Kuwait. He said the smoke would cut visibility and force the allies to take precautions against noxious fumes. Also, "the intense heat may cause us to steer around" the wells, he said.

A Marine weather forecaster said that visibility inside the Kuwaiti border could be cut to one mile by the smoke and that night-time fog could exacerbate the problem. Huly also said that one Marine was killed and three injured Friday when a hand grenade exploded in a non-combat accident. The condition of the three injured was not known.

Sergeant is Very Far Forward U.S. Female—"I Don't Believe There is Romance to Being a Soldier"

By Neal MacFarquhar

ON THE SAUDI BORDER - There are no women closer to the front lines than Sgt. Theresa Lynn Treloar.

"I could have turned it down. But I had no hesitation at all," she said, running chipped nails covered in clear polish through shoulder-length blonde hair about to get its first washing in a week. "I'm really excited about it. It's not every day you have a war." It is also rare to find a woman attached to a unit like the 2nd Armored Cavalry Regiment. It is the most forward eyes and ears of the heavily armored VII Corps, expected to play the central role in any ground offensive against Iraqi forces.

Military security rules preclude saying exactly how close to the border the headquarters camp is, or describing Treloar's exact job. She works for the kind of unit that has insignia on its desert camouflage uniforms, if they wear them. It is also the kind of unit that knows that the nearest woman soldier is 20 to 50 kilometers (12 to 30 miles) back.

Some officers objected to her presence, suggesting she should move back when the fighting starts and the unit has to cross the border. But Treloar's battalion commander and her commanding officer, Capt. Michael Mendell, wanted her to stay. "She's just like any other soldier, she's just a little better in her field," said Mendell, 40, of Park City, Utah. His missions have kept him from getting a mailbox in two weeks.

Treloar, a French-speaking specialist in African affairs, searches carefully for the words to describe her special qualifications. "To communicate effectively with cultures other than your own you have to be able to step into their shoes and hear what they will hear and think what they will think," she said.

In her nine years in the military, she has found her authority challenged by junior men who take an I'll-get-to-it-when-I-can attitude to her orders. She has found that yelling like a male officer at any soldier after repeated offenses does not work.

"There's nothing wrong with a man raising his voice, but God help you if you are a woman. Then you are being emotional," said the 32-year-old from Napa, Calif.

She adapted by keeping a certain distance from the men under her command at all times. She succeeded to the point that the men called her Ice Lady—a nickname she only found out about after her marriage when her husband let it slip.

They do exactly the same work in different units.

The sergeant said she is not fighting a path for all the women back home, but it is inevitable that "any female in an all-male unit is cutting a path."

Saturday - February 23, 1991

Treloar thinks gender should not affect the decision of who goes into combat. She will not be fighting, but no special precautions have been taken for her at this forward unit. She thinks men will just have to get used to the idea. "The Army is learning its lesson about women. It's going to take time," she said. She thinks it may change when the current crop of junior officers trained with women start becoming generals.

Treloar is avoiding becoming an officer, despite the encouragement of her superiors. She said she does not want to shut herself off in planning operations. "I like pushing troops, I like dealing with troops."

She has not been in combat before, but does not expect to fall to pieces. "I don't believe there is any romance to being a soldier. I don't have any illusions," she said.

As soon as Iraq invaded Kuwait Aug. 2, Treloar started reading books on the area and supports the war completely. "It's the political connection between our and the rest of the world's requirement for energy. From a political standpoint, if Saddam Hussein was allowed full reign, it endangers our country. It endangers our friends."

She sees the emir of Kuwait and other area rulers the U.S. is supporting as limiting the freedom of their people, but says it is accepted locally and they are not attacking their neighbors. Still, she nicknamed her speckled pet lizard King Fahd.

She has a good working relationship with her unit's current Saudi liaison officer, but it has not always been easy. The first one saw her giving orders to her men while erecting a tent and told her: "You shouldn't speak. I'll speak for you." It was a bit of a shock to her five-foot-three-inch frame. "First, I said, 'I don't think so.' Then I got angry and said, 'No, I don't f____ think so.'" The suggestion was not repeated.

Although she has had limited exposure to Saudi women since being deployed here from Fort Bragg, N.C., on Jan. 16, she thinks the news that American women are helping their military will encourage Saudi women to demand change.

While stopped at a roadside store, she watched a Saudi husband bring out shoes to his veiled wife sitting in the car. She would try one pair on and then he would go back for another. "I couldn't imagine living like that," she said.

Her own husband, Sgt. Charles Barbour III, 26, is now just down the line from this camp. She said he is scared for her safety, and constantly admonishes her to be careful. She does not get to see him often.

A nightgown she brought along just in case was among the personal items including a bikini that got shipped back from the front to lighten the load.

The harsh conditions demanded other concessions. She takes sponge baths behind a poncho strung in the tent she shares with Mendell. Her bathroom is a two-seated latrine in full view of the camp and open to the surrounding desert.

"At first it was difficult. I still don't go to the bathroom in front of my husband. I don't think it's being female. It's just being human," she said.

Mendell said she accepted it faster than some of the men.

A hysterectomy took care of menstrual problems, but she still finds her uniform needs to be changed more often than the men's. She also wears a cheap substitute wedding band, but found she could not ship the real one away.

Treloar gently admonishes the men if they go too many days without shaving, and rebukes them for the macho habit of letting their hands crack and bleed to the point they can't do their work. The men in her unit don't like her five Mozart tapes, but some admitted they like having a woman's face around.

She bursts out laughing at the thought she might be a Florence Nightingale-like figure bringing comfort in the event of battle. "I'm not a combat life-saver," she said.

She also demurs on the title of being the farthest-forward woman. "As I understand it, there is a woman POW in Iraq," she said, referring to Melissa Rathbun-Healey. This is her second stint with the Army. She says she is in it to stay.

She dropped out in 1980 after four years as an air traffic controller to go back to junior college. After the birth of her daughter Tiffany, now 8, and a failed marriage, she wanted to return to the military. She said she missed the combination of teamwork and discipline. It also seemed the best place to apply her studies in psychology, sociology, and analysis. She was eight credit hours away from getting her B.A. when her current assignment came up.

She was determined not to be left out of this conflict. She was not allowed to go to Panama in December 1989 because she was married to a fellow soldier. At the time, she had a showdown with her battalion commander, with all due respect.

"I was so angry. I spoke to him at length about the color of my uniform. I said I would get a divorce if that happened again and we would live together."

The hardest part was leaving Tiffany with a cousin in California, but her daughter supported her fully. She just wanted to know what weapons each side had.

Treloar skipped Iraq's chemical arsenal. She is sure her daughter will be taken care of if she is killed. She does not support the legislation that would allow parents to be given the option of going to war. "If your family prevents you from doing your job then get out of the Army or get rid of the family," she said.

Consultant Turned Army Chemical Officer Looks at War: "It's Not Going to Be a Pretty Picture . . . It Never Is"

By Peter Copeland

WITH U.S. FORCES, Saudi Arabia - If Vivian Tio were any closer to enemy lines, she would be sitting in an Iraqi foxhole.

As the chemical weapons officer for the 42nd Field Artillery, Lt. Tio, 30, of San Juan, Puerto Rico, is the brigade commander's chief advisor on how to defend against Iraq's chemical threat. Every day at 7 a.m. and 7 p.m., Tio briefs the commanders on intelligence reports, how the weather might affect a chemical battle, and on the ability of the U.S. troops to protect themselves.

She is one of the few women on the front, and the only female staff officer in this brigade. "I don't have a problem going forward," Tio said, adding with a laugh, "If I were a commander out here, I'd like to take my chemical officer."

She lives in a ring of tents surrounding a few trailers that form the tactical operations center. The showers are cold, the toilets are wooden boxes with two seats, and there is almost no privacy. Her only comment was: "I'm saving money on makeup."

Just two years ago, Tio, who has a master's degree in clinical psychology, was working as a consultant in Boston. On July 25, 1988, she joined the U.S. Army.

"I joined out of a sense of patriotism," she said, her curly black hair bouncing in the biting wind that blew across the empty desert. "The United States government gave me a lot when I was growing up and for my education. I wanted to give something back."

Asked if the sacrifice was worth it, Tio said, "Oh, God, yes. If we don't take care of this now, it's going to be a major problem in the future.

Saturday - February 23, 1991

"I believe that this is where I want to be, and I have no regrets about having left my private practice and civilian life," she said. "I think the focus people need to keep out here is that it's war. There's nothing glamorous about it. It's just something that unfortunately needs to be done sometimes, and if you learn to accept that reality, it is easier," she said. "It is out of your hands as an individual and you become part of something bigger. That's why we keep such a close eye on morale."

Her Army skills—known as NBC for nuclear, biological, and chemical—are valued more than ever by the troops, who fear chemical weapons more than bombs and bullets. "Back in Germany, it was a big joke," Tio said. "Everybody said NBC stood for 'nobody cares,' but now everybody cares."

Her big worry is convincing her fiancée, John Killoran, that she is safe. He also served in Saudi Arabia, but he recently was sent back to Germany because he is leaving the Army in April. "I told him, I know you are going to worry." He came out here in September and I came in December. I understand exactly what he was saying because when he was here and I was in Germany, I was scared for him.

"I pretty much have in my mind what we should expect," she said. "It's not going to be a pretty picture, though. It never is."

Male Bonding Has Limits—A Love Story from 937th Engineers: "Sergeant, You Need Male Supervision"

By Carol Morello

IN NORTHERN SAUDI ARABIA - Somehow, amid war and fear and a military regime that leaves little time or room for courtship, love has bloomed out in the arid Saudi desert.

Sgt. Liane Overstreet and Spec. Morgan Barnett, both assigned to the 937th Engineer Group, fell in love over long, lingering mess hall dinners, snatched truck rides together to procure supplies, and smoldering eye contact over a desert tarmac.

It hasn't been easy. Fact is, they've bended a rule or two that stood in the way of love, like a prohibition against superiors fraternizing with subordinate soldiers. They're planning to marry when they return to the U.S.

But all's fair, as they say. And as a small footnote to Operation Desert Storm, the imminence of a ground war has led to the relaxation of some rules that somehow seem irrelevant and even cruel when men and women may be about to risk their lives in war.

"I think it's good for morale," a superior officer told his driver of the handful of love affairs that have started at the 937th, where 14 women are based as clerks, cooks, and other jobs.

Overstreet and Barnett met in October back at Fort Riley, Kan., where she processed him into the unit. Their mutual attraction was immediate and, initially, shyly coy. Overstreet found herself staring at Barnett as he loaded equipment and supplies onto pallets for shipment to Saudi Arabia.

"I don't know what it was that appealed to me," said Overstreet, 34, who was born in Idar-Oberstein, Germany, and came to America with her first husband, an American soldier she met in Germany. "His eyes, I think. They look so sad most of the time."

Barnett, for his part, kept returning to Overstreet to ask her for military-issue items, even those she had issued to him two days in a row before that.

"Is something wrong with you?" she asked him, not realizing her attraction to him was reciprocated. "You need a lot of female supervision."

On the flight to Saudi Arabia, seeing her pale with fear of flying, he said, "Sergeant, you need some male supervision." When they arrived in Saudi Arabia late the night of Oct. 27, they were standing on an airfield tarmac and they made eye contact. The serious kind.

As these things go, one thing led to another. But because they are in the military, there were obstacles to the course of true love.

They ate their meals together, until a superior "advised" them to eat alone. They went together on trips to procure supplies, until another superior arranged their schedules so it was no longer possible. And they found private time together only when he visited the tent she shares with 13 other women, where male visitors must be out by 10 p.m.

"We've got to be kind of discreet, because she kinda outranks me," said Barnett, 22, of Aurora, Colo. "So we can't do things like hold hands, that we could in civilian life." Indeed, under Army regulations, Overstreet could face disciplinary action that could include a loss of pay or even court-martial.

But with a ground war on the horizon, no one seems to mind so long as they remain discreet. "If I hugged and kissed him in public," said Overstreet, "I'd be given a Field Grade Article 15. They'd make me an E5. If we were at Fort Riley, I'd be busted, or at least counseled in writing. Like everyone else in the theater, they long for the simple domestic pleasures that spell home. "Valentine's Day, I couldn't find a card, a box of candy, flowers, nothing," said Barnett. "The only thing on the market is heaters, wicks, and stuff like that. So I went around all day long saying Happy Valentine's Day to her."

Overstreet wishes she could cook for her man, "instead of having the mess hall make our decisions." But finding love at war has been a great comfort, they said. "It helps to find someone I can be comfortable with," said Barnett. "I'm tired of all this male bonding stuff. It's nice to have a female to love."

They profess no guilt at finding happiness while virtually everyone else around them is filled with loneliness. "This is a war," said Overstreet. "We all have to fend for ourselves. We have to be a team when it comes to fighting, but not when it comes to loving."

Anatomy of a Friendly Fire Incident: Apache Pilot Thought He Saw Iraqi Vehicles

By Charles Lewis

NORTHERN SAUDI ARABIA - The mission of the Army task force was clear-cut: breach the 12-foot-high sand berm on the northern border and identify and destroy any Iraqi forces nearby.

By the time the task force had returned from its weekend work, the mission had been accomplished and hundreds of young GIs had experienced their first combat.

A week later, they were still sorting through the explosion of emotions triggered by being shot at with bullets, rockets, artillery, and grenades and by seeing two fellow soldiers killed by "friendly fire" and six others wounded.

Saturday - February 23, 1991

They were proud of the courage of those GIs who rescued their wounded colleagues from a burning ammo-laden armored vehicle that was spewing exploding bullets in all directions.

And they said they were more confident that they could handle war and that the training and teamwork that carried them through their initiation would get them through whatever lies ahead and get them safely back home.

The task force under Lt. Col. James Hillman combined elements of the 2nd Armored Division and the 1st Infantry Division and included 1,000 Army troops, approximately 30 M1A1 Abrams tanks and about the same number of Bradley fighting vehicles carrying infantry troops.

They were supposed to arrive at the sand berm around 6 a.m., Friday, Feb. 15. The berm, which had been built by the Saudis, rises at a steep 75-degree angle. Its 12-foot height is accentuated by the 9-foot-deep ditch dug along the bottom of the south wall. The five-foot-wide trench was designed to stop any tanks that managed to make it over the berm while heading southward. Little footholds had been chiseled in the wall so that you can stand and peek over the top of the berm with only your forehead showing.

One company of U.S. troops, commanded by Capt. Michael Sanders, 28, of Bakersfield, Calif., arrived at the berm right on schedule. Sanders asked his sniper specialist, Sgt. Marshall Howard, 21, of Sandy Hook, Ky., to use his high-power rifle-mounted sniper scope to look over the top.

Howard said he climbed up on the footholds and swung his rifle across the horizon, looking through the scope at the desert wasteland that stretched all around him. The other side of the berm looked pretty much like his side, Howard recalled, except that the north side—the Iraqi side—was pockmarked with sand revetments big enough to conceal a vehicle.

They were empty.

Having reached the berm, Sanders assigned 2nd Lt. Danny Strickland, 29, of Glennville, Ga., to take some troops and check out two nearby buildings where U.S. observers had previously seen Iraqi scouts and communications antennas, usually at night when Iraqi troops regularly probed south of the border.

"We first did a reconnaissance by fire," Sanders recalled, referring to the technique of laying down intense fire to find out if anyone was inside. There was no response.

Strickland and his squads then entered the two-story block building, part of a now-vacant Saudi border outpost. "We found some RPGs (rocket-propelled grenades), AK-47s (Soviet-made automatic rifles), and some fuel," Strickland recalled of his inspection.

They also found a Soviet-made grenade rigged by a wire to an inside window ledge, Strickland said. Higher authorities, concerned that the structure might hold more booby traps, ordered them out of the building and the unit turned its concentration on the first goal of the mission: to punch 10 holes in the berm wide enough to get the tanks and personnel carriers through.

First, the unit's five bulldozers had to fill in the anti-tank ditch so they could get to the berm. That was quickly done and, after the dozers had carved the openings, the unit poured through to the other side of the border.

It was noon, Day 1. They were right on time. A unit of engineers headed by Sgt. Ricky Adair, 36, of Warsaw, Mo., went forward and checked for mines. They found none, even in one area where they had suspected the Iraqis had planted some.

The task force moved forward and spent the night about three miles north of the berm. Any doubt that they had been spotted vanished the next morning, Saturday, Feb. 16.

Sanders ordered his troops to make a "survivability shift," a move just for the sake of changing positions in case Iraqi gunners had figured out where they were. "Right after we moved, our former position got hit by four rounds (of Iraqi artillery)," Sanders said.

That night, the unit was checked out by Iraqi tanks, armored personnel carriers, and infantry. Further back behind both lines, artillery from both sides exchanged fire. Rocket-firing Apache helicopters joined the fray, hunting for three Iraqi tanks and an armored personnel carrier that the unit had spotted through their night-vision instruments.

Around 1 a.m. on Sunday, Feb. 17, an Apache fired at what it thought were Iraqi vehicles. Actually, the targets were an American Bradley fighting vehicle carrying a scouting party and an armored personnel carrier with ground surveillance radar. Both vehicles were hit by the fire, which included an anti-tank Hellfire missile.

The fire quickly spread throughout the Bradley and its cache of ammunition started exploding, randomly sending shells and shrapnel in all directions.

Sanders said the nearby U.S. forces at first thought they were being attacked by rocket-propelled grenades fired by Iraqi "stay-behinds," concealed infantrymen who hid out while U.S. forces advanced past their positions. "Stay-behinds" can be used to collect intelligence on advancing forces or they can be used to attack from the rear.

Only later did they find out that the attack came from an Apache.

Sanders ordered two combat teams to the area where the two American vehicles burned. Strickland pulled two wound victims into his Bradley fighting vehicle, drove them to the armored personnel carrier directed by the unit's medic, Sgt. William "Doc" Rost, 26, of Columbus, Ohio. Rost got hit in the chin by a piece of shrapnel, presumably from the exploding Bradley vehicle, but continued to give first aid while the vehicle's driver, Pfc. Kevin Kennerly, 19, of Akron, Ohio, raced back to a medical unit just to the rear.

Others in the unit also raced to the rescue.

Lt. Roger Palmateer, 34, of Brownwood, Tx., and Spec. Gregory Bateham, 21, of Key West, Fl., drove their armored personnel carrier to the scene and started looking for survivors. Both men peeled off their armored vests and placed them on two wound victims, carried them to their Bradley and drove back to Rost's site.

Rost took the two victims and ferried them back to the medical unit.

There were still four soldiers unaccounted for.

Strickland, Palmateer and Bateham continued the search around the two burning vehicles and eventually found two others, accounting for six wounded men. Two others were found inside the Bradley, dead, the next day.

There was heroism even among the victims. Spec, Khiem Quang Ta, a crewman aboard the Bradley, leaped free of the burning vehicle only to realize that the platoon sergeant, Sgt. 1st Class Richard Miller, was still aboard.

According to Sanders, in his recommendation that Ta be awarded the Bronze star. Miller was unable to get out of the tank-like vehicle because he was suffering from a broken ankle and third-degree burns, Ta "pulled Miller from the burning hull as the ammunition onboard continued to explode admist (sic) the continuous disorder and confusion," Sanders wrote.

Sanders put in Bateham for a Bronze star medal for his role in rescuing four of the wounded. He also recommended the Army commendation medal for Rost, Strickland, and Palmateer.

"I was in the wrong place at the wrong time," Bateham said. "I was pretty scared."

Bateham and others in the unit returned to the berm to get some rest and, after daylight, returned to the destroyed Bradley and the radar vehicle. They found the two dead men. "I was pretty shaken up," Bateham said, adding that he sought counseling from the unit's chaplain.

For Bateham, the Persian Gulf war has disrupted long-held personal plans.

"I joined the Army in 1987 for three years so I could make some money to go to college," Bateham said. His separation date was December 1990 and Bateham had been accepted at Florida State University in Tallahassee to start in January.

But the Army froze all departures and retirements when President Bush ordered the massive military buildup in response to Iraq's invasion of Kuwait.

Instead of starting his freshman year at FSU, Bateham found himself still on active duty. Instead of duty in Germany where the 2nd Armored Division had been stationed, Bateham found himself in Saudi Arabia. "I want to get back safely to Germany, get out of the Army, and get into college," Bateham said, reflecting on his new future plans.

Sanders praised Bateham and the others for their rescue work in the aftermath of the "friendly fire" episode. "As a result of what they did, our KIA (killed in action) was less than it would have been," he said.

For his part, Sanders said he had "a lot of mixed emotions" about his first combat encounter. "At one point when we got back, I was standing in my turret and my leg was shaking uncontrollably," he said. "My emotions ran the gamut—anger, grief, relief. And I was happy that I was able to do what I had been training for so long.

"Now that I'm here, I want to do the job. We have confidence and we have experience. We did our mission despite our losses," he said. Sanders said his experience led him to conclude that the Iraqis are "competent, professional soldiers who seemed to know what they were doing."

Sanders, a 1984 ROTC graduate of the University of California at Los Angeles, also said the taste of combat had bolstered his confidence. "We've been training for a long time for this kind of situation," Sanders said. "But no one knows how they'll react in a crisis. In this crisis, they reacted the way they should have."

The "friendly fire" casualties were not the only ones during the mission.

The next day, on Monday, Feb. 18, as the U.S. forces were heading south near the berm, an Iraqi artillery shell hit between two U.S. tanks.

A gunner on one tank, Sgt. Tony Applegate, 28, of Portsmouth, Ohio, was standing with his head above the turret's hatch when he got hit in the back of the head by three small pieces of shrapnel. The wounds required 12 stitches.

"It gives us a lot of confidence in the tank and its survivability," Applegate said. "We went through it and we came out okay."

Night Visions of the Hellstorm of Fire From Apaches: "It Looked Like Somebody Opened the Sheep Pen"

By John Balzar

THE NORTHERN SAUDI BORDER - Through the powerful night vision gunsights they looked like ghostly sheep, flushed from a pen—Iraqi infantry soldiers bewildered and terrified, harried from sleep and fleeing their bunkers under a hellstorm of fire.

One by one, they were cut down by attackers they couldn't see or understand.

Some were literally blown to bits by bursts of 30mm shells. One man dropped, writhed on the ground and struggled to his feet.

Another burst tore him apart. A compatriot twice emerged standing from bursts. As if in pity, the American Army attackers turned and let him live. For the men and women of the Army 18th Airborne Corps, the ground war has already begun. It is carried straight to the enemy in the blackness of night at 50-feet above the sand by the Army's longest punch, the fast, deadly, and controversial AH-64 Apache attack helicopter. And then upon the Apaches' return to forward attack bases like here with the 5th Squadron of the 6th Cavalry, the Knight Raiders, the evidence of this early ground war is displayed in startlingly sharp and intensely violent tapes from gun cameras.

The $10 million-plus Apaches are night-fighters and tank-killers, their pilots guided by an infrared optical system that turns blackness into a bright phosphorescent daylight where you can all but read the expressions of shock on the faces of Iraqi soldiers as they are ground up by 30mm cannon rounds and an ugly sampler of rockets.

For those who try to stay in bunkers, laser-guided Hellfire missiles are launched to an altitude of a half-mile, where they then arc almost straight down onto the target. In the 5/6 briefing tent, the officers play the tapes and a hush falls over the room. Even hardened soldiers hold their breath as the Iraqi soldiers, as big as football players on the TV screen, run with nowhere to hide. These are not bridges exploding or airplane hangars.

They are men.

"We're out there to kill their tanks and trucks, to harass and demoralize their troops," said Squadron Commander Lt. Col. Randy Tieszen, of Rapid City, S.D. "We've been here since August; we've waited a long time for this."

Tieszen rides in the front seat of the Apache, working an arcade of weaponry and directing his squadron attack. Behind him, peering over his helmet, sits the pilot, Chief Warrant Officer 4 Ron Balak, of Beemer, Neb.

The next phase of the Persian Gulf War may be the greatest tank battle in a half-century. But the soldiers who fly the Apaches believe it is they, hovering low and off in the distance, who will kill half the Iraqi tanks.

With readiness reported at high levels for the complicated and often doubted Apache, their pilots are increasingly confident.

Pilot Balak, sitting in his flight suit, the zipper shiny from wear, a .38-cal. revolver slung over his shoulder, described his first combat mission in a 20-year flying career:

"For almost five months we've been leaning forward to do this job . . . You always envision some scenario how combat will be. But I just didn't quite envision going up there and shooting the hell out of everything in the dark and have them not know what the hell hit them . . . A truck blows up to the right, the ground blows up to the left. They had no idea where we were or what was hitting them.

"When we got back, I sat there on the wing and I was laughing. I wasn't laughing at the Iraqis. I was thinking of the training, the anticipation . . . I was probably laughing at myself. . . . I laid there in bed and said, 'Okay, I'm tired, I've got to get to sleep.' And then I'd think about sneaking up there and blowing this up, and blowing that up.

"Afterward a guy came up to me, and we were slapping each other on the back and all that stuff, and he said, "By God, I thought we had shot into a damn farm. It looked like somebody had opened the sheep pen."

Prior to the war, the Apache was high on the "troubled" list of American weapons programs. Its reliability was so frequently challenged that even some of its pilots said they had their doubts. But now, with

Saturday - February 23, 1991

round-the-clock maintenance availability and a so-far limited combat role, the Apache is slowly gaining respect.

As designed, the gunship represents not just advanced technology but a complete reversal of Army ground tactics. In Vietnam, the U.S. fought during the day and went home or holed up later. For the nights belonged to the enemy.

But beginning in the late 1970s and accelerating into the mid-1980s, Army doctrine emphasized night-fighting. Originally the idea was that a smaller American force with night-fighting capability could hold off a larger Soviet foe in the event of a European war.

Now, in the Persian Gulf, the American army believes its advantage is greater because the Iraqis have almost no sophisticated means of carrying the battle past sunset.

So the low-slung, wasp-like Apaches wait out the sunlight hours on the ground spread wide and far across the hardpan desert here along the front.

Their crews live nocturnal lives, too.

With the moon, the men, most of them young warrant officers—the top of their flight classes, for this is the elite of Army aviation—spring to life, heading north in their machines of death.

"A Look Into Hell"—On Kuwait Side, Orange Flames; On Tiger Brigade's Side, Blue Skies, and Hell on Wheels

By Bill Gannon

WITH THE TIGER BRIGADE, On the Kuwaiti Border - Towering orange pillars of flame shoot out of the burning oil wells of Kuwait, defining the falling ground beneath it.

Approaching the border battlefield, more than 20 such pillars stand in a line, spewing their jets of burning oil 75 feet high.

The ignited oil turns to a thick black curtain of smoke that defines the skies over Kuwait as the men of Tiger Brigade of the Army's 2nd Armored Division and some 2nd Division Marines nearby take a break from their reconnaissance chores to snap off some photographs.

"This here is a Kodak moment," said Cpl. Rick Rushart, 19, of Piano, Tex. as he digs inside his flak vest for his camera to record the view from his Humvee. "This is like a movie or a *Twilight Zone* show. It's a look into Hell," added Cpl. Randy Davis, 20, of Camden, N.J.

It is a scene both surreal and spectacular.

Beneath the burning oil wells shooting flames into the sky and the billowing smoke stand the charred wreckage of Iraqi T-55 tanks and an unrecognizable jumble of other vehicles, burning oil barrels and discarded TOW missile tubes and ammunition casings.

A rocket bursts and Tiger Brigade artillery falls on the Iraqi side with a thunderous roar. Farther away, the B-52 bombs fall with a flash and a thud.

On the American side of the border, meanwhile, all is comparatively orderly. Even the skies over the American positions are clear blue, free of smoke blowing east toward Kuwait City. Fluttering along the ground are thousands of 3 x 5-inch paper pamphlets asking, in Arabic, for the Iraqis to surrender. On the Saudi side, the pamphlets promise, the Iraqis will be fed and clothed and safely returned to their families.

Somewhere on the other side of the sand berms and the defensive fortifications that stretch back into Kuwait is the enemy. This was where two days of sporadic but fierce fighting took place between the Marines and Iraq,

Tiger Brigade took 97 enemy prisoners of war while the Marines destroyed 9 tanks and an unknown number of other pieces of equipment and an unknown number of Iraqi soldiers. There were three American casualties—all minor wounds.

Getting home for the men of Tiger Brigade and the Marines they support with their heavy armor means heading north.

With the possibility of war near, crossing into Kuwait both scares and excites them. "I'm ready to go and Tiger Brigade is ready to go," said Col. John Sylvester, the 45-year-old commander of the brigade.

The brigade, an element of the Army's 2nd Armored Division, was formed in the early days of World War II by then Lt. Col. George S. Patton. Watching the division perform on maneuvers in Louisiana before heading to Europe for World War II, Patton declared that "when this division meets the enemy, it's going to be hell on wheels." The motto stuck, and is now worn on the patches of the men of the 2nd Armored Division. In World War II, the division won battle honors at Kasarene Pass in North Africa and made landings in Sicily and was later responsible for the famous D-Day breakout, when the division broke through the defensive German hedgerow fortifications to race toward Germany where it was the first armored division to enter Berlin. Last year, the division was ordered inactivated as a result of the latest arms talks with the Soviet Union. Halfway through that inactivation, Iraq invaded Kuwait and what was left of the division was ordered to the Middle East.

Yesterday, as he made his final battle preparations, Sylvester said both he personally and his brigade of M1A1 Abrams tanks, Bradley fighting vehicles, armored personnel carriers, TOW anti-tank teams and multiple launch rockets, were ready for whatever lay north. "I've been preparing for this moment all my life. This is my heart and soul on the line here. Like a lot of men here I'm sure I've got the same pangs in my gut as everybody else does," he said.

"Yesterday (Friday), I walked each and every commander through a terrain board. They and we all know what we are to do. Going through the breach has been practiced and well-rehearsed and we are capable of moving through very well and very fast."

"What Tiger Brigade does well—better than anybody in the Army—is move very quickly," he said, explaining that in REFORGER—a massive NATO military exercise in which hundreds of kilometers had to be crossed in simulated battlefield conditions—the Tiger Brigade crossed 145 kilometers in less than 15 hours. Here, Sylvester hopes to be able to move 75 kilometers in six hours.

"At the outset we have a clear objective. We will move toward that first objective and get there and then await orders to take a new objective," he said.

Saturday will be spent getting the Tiger Battle Team, as Sylvester likes to call his unit, ready to pour through the breach. He said he is encouraged that "every single EPW we have taken says his unit is only at 15 or 20 percent strength." "I'm not saying it's going to be easy. But it is clear that his forces are going to be demoralized," the commander said.

"We have verified information that we have destroyed in air missions some 1,600 tanks and hundreds of artillery tubes and other vehicles. That's encouraging," he said.

"Right now we're all waiting for him (Saddam Hussein). He's been given one last ultimatum to immediately start moving his crap out," Sylvester noted. "I don't think he's going to do it—to get out. I think we're gonna have to go in there and make him eat it," he added. He agreed that the Iraqis are using a scorched earth policy in Kuwait. "There were 23 well-head fires visible when we came in here. There are now 44 visible and we have not set them off with bombs or artillery," he explained. "When the time comes to go in, we'll go in with chemical protective boots and over-garments on and have the gloves and mask ready to put on.

"We'll button up and go right in. We're going to charge right on through it," the colonel said. He said all of the Iraqi defectors and most EPWs said that chemical weapons will be used when the ground war begins. "They have all told us that chemical weapons will be used and we believe them ... But we're good to go," he said.

He was quick to note that the most recent two-day border clash just across the border in Kuwait showed that Iraqi troops "haven't lost the will to fight," explaining Iraqi ground forces used RPGs (rocket-propelled grenades) and some artillery against a recon force of several hundred Marines.

The fight was quickly silenced by a combination of Tiger artillery, MLRS and Marine aviation air strikes. He added that the bulk of the 97 EPWs taken were reservists—members of an infantry brigade put into the Iraqi trip-wire positions sometime last month.

"An interpreter said they referred to themselves as cannon fodder," Sylvester said, rejecting any comparisons to Vietnam when it came to enemy morale or resourcefulness.

Asked how long he expected the ground war to last if all diplomatic efforts fail, Sylvester estimated a week. "It all depends on what he (Saddam Hussein) does. If he would start moving his stuff out now, that would be fine with me."

"Nothing would please me more than to drive toward Kuwait utterly aghast at the devastation caused by our Air Force," he said.

"If that happens, I'll try to buy every Air Force guy I meet a drink."

Amphibious Commander Lists Reasons Not to Hit Kuwait Beaches; "Do Not Want to Destroy the Country"

By John King and David Evans

PERSIAN GULF - The Commander of Marine Amphibious Forces in the Gulf said Wednesday he would try to avoid a direct attack on Iraqi defenses in a risky assault on the beaches of Kuwait and said an amphibious landing would likely cause substantial damage to civilian property on the coastline.

"We wouldn't go straight at anything," said Maj. Gen. Harry Jenkins. He said many Iraqi units have been drawn to the coast of Kuwait to defend against a Marine landing. However, he said much of the coastline is urbanized and these buildings, many of which have been fortified by Iraqi troops, would be targets for naval gunfire and air strikes before Marines hit the beach.

"If we land into a built-up area, there will be collateral damage, but obviously we do not want to destroy the country," he said. Jenkins commands a 17,000-man marine landing force at sea the past six months. He said possible operations for his men include a include a full-scale landing, one or more limited operations, or even a decoy assault, or feint, to tie down Iraqi coast defense troops while allied ground forces launched attacks.

"We've seen more and more of them along the coast. We've drawn them there," Jenkins told reporters aboard his ship, the USS Nassau.

If an amphibious landing is ordered as part of an allied offensive, Jenkins said he expected to meet stiff resistance. "The Iraqi army is not down and out by any stretch of the imagination," said the 52-year-old general from San Jose, Calif.

"They're hurting, no doubt about that, but I don't count them out."

If Marines did land their M-60 tanks, light armored vehicles, and other assault forces to dislodge Iraqi defenders, Jenkins said the swirling maelstrom of close-in combat would carry a high risk of friendly-fire casualties. "You hope not, but the potential for that is high. The jets are going so damn fast," he said. "Telling friend from foe can really be a problem if you have 12 vehicles out there and a pilot coming into that fireball," Jenkins said.

To guard against friendly-fire, which killed several Marines in fighting earlier this month, Jenkins explained that brightly-colored panels and other markers would be placed atop vehicles and tanks so pilots would know they were friendly.

That's the only way you can tell from the air, he said.

Jenkins recalls that the Israelis used such a system in the 1973 war.

In addition, he said Marine pilots have been trained to recognize silhouettes of U.S. and Iraqi vehicles most of which are Soviet-built. However, the differences in silhouettes may not be much help if Marine pilots have to fly missions to support Egyptian or Syrian units, because they are equipped with Soviet-built weaponry also. Jenkins said an amphibious force of about 30 ships moved into the Persian Gulf in the past two weeks after conducting five major exercises that rehearsed a possible landing in Kuwait.

If a landing is ordered, the Marines would have the support of strike aircraft from four carriers, the heavy 16-inch gunfire from two battleships, their own Harrier close-air support jets and Cobra attack helicopters, as well as sorties from land-based U.S. Air Force planes. Marine Harrier jets flew combat missions from an amphibious assault ship for the first time Wednesday. The air and naval gunfire support is designed not only to provide cover for the vulnerable landing force, but also to drive entrenched Iraqis out into the open.

So far, Iraqi forces have stayed in the bunkers prepared in the five-month run-up to the war. "He's not moving out of the holes now," Jenkins declared. "Despite all the bombs that have been dropped." Jenkins cautioned that it takes a direct hit to destroy dug-in troops and armor. "There's a lot of smoke when a bomb explodes, but in many cases all you've done is give him a headache. He can still fight," Jenkins said, recalling his experience from the Vietnam War. Marine, Navy and Air Force planes and naval guns have been methodically hitting targets in Kuwait to soften up the battlefield for a possible landing.

"I suppose enough is when you can go through without taking any (enemy) fire," he said. However, Jenkins acknowledged that a thoroughly sanitized battlefield is not realistic. "Enough is never enough, but I'll take all the support I can get," he said.

The Nassau rocked back and forth throughout the session with Jenkins, who said the unpredictable weather this time of year could upset landing plans.

After a day of rain, the Nassau ploughed through the 12-foot waves and 35-knot winds. Jenkins said the sea conditions tend to be calmer near the shore. If the Marines make the landing, their amphibious transports will not come close to shore, within sight of enemy guns, as was the practice in World War II. For a landing in Kuwait, the ships could remain some 20 miles at sea, out of sight, sending Marines ashore in helicopters and air-cushion landing craft that can travel across the water at speeds of 40 miles per hour.

Saturday - February 23, 1991

Buses Needed for Expected Torrent of Iraqi POWs: "Too Much of a Good Thing"

By John Pomfret

WITH THE U.S. ARMY IN NORTHERN SAUDI ARABIA - When the Screaming Eagles (101st Airborne Division) captured more than 450 Iraqi soldiers last week, an attacking helicopter pilot joked on his radio, "Bring some buses to move these guys out."

But if U.S. Military Police projections prove accurate, buses will be exactly what U.S. forces will need. American officers say they are worried that the increasing flow of Iraqi prisoners of war could turn into a torrent and stretch the resources of the allied fighting machine.

On assaults deep into enemy territory, officers said that Iraqi soldiers may be disarmed and forced to walk south to Saudi Arabia under armed guard if the numbers run too high. "The flow's been brisk, it's going to get huge," said Major Rex Forney, the deputy provost marshal of the military police for the 101st Airborne Division in northern Saudi Arabia.

Officers pointed out that in two separate strikes last week the 101st Airborne captured more than 500 prisoners. They had to be moved out in several helicopter trips.

A final trip on Thursday yielded an additional 14 Iraqi soldiers as well as a Soviet-made ZPU-4 air defense weapon.

Forney said that units planning to strike deep into enemy territory would be accompanied by one company (98 men) of Military Police ready to deal with prisoners of war.

The prisoners will be put in cages at the forward base and held for "a minimum of 24 hours," he said. They will be moved back into Saudi territory.

Behind Forney, four double-decker passenger buses sat in the brown desert sand.

"Those are my babies," he said. Soldiers have been given special training in bus driving so they can bus the prisoners out, he said. Wounded prisoners could be evacuated by helicopter, Forney said, "if the assets are available."

If Iraqi forces counter-attack allied positions in enemy territory, then the prisoners will have to walk south, Forney said.

"If we're taking Iraqi rounds, then we really don't have any other choice," he said. "It's either that or let them get possibly killed by their own friendly fire."

Allied forces so far have captured more than 3,000 Iraqi soldiers. Although initial reports said many were dirty, hungry and demoralized, Forney said his latest batch, which included a major, seemed to be reasonably well-fed.

"When we attacked them, they were setting down to a lunch of potatoes, dates, and onions," said the Gadsden, Ala., native. "I don't know if they think that's a good lunch, but I'll stick to what they give me here."

Forney said that interrogation of the prisoners has shown that they understand they will receive decent treatment at the hands of the Americans.

"Some of them say that their commanders have told them we will torture and even kill them," he said. "But they say they don't believe that."

If troops do have to walk Iraqi prisoners back, Forney said, it would stretch the resources of the military police. As such, National Guard details are standing by to assist.

Forney said that the goal of his operation is to keep captured Iraqis for no longer than

24 hours in enemy territory before sending them back - either on foot, by truck or bus or in a helicopter. "It's a big system," he said.

One of Forney's worries is the tendency of the Iraqis to surrender.

In the assault last week, attacking helicopter pilots turned on speakers over one Iraqi position asking them to give up. Out walked 473 well-armed men.

"They're scared of helicopters," said one captain.

"That's a good thing," said Forney. "But too many Iraqi prisoners could be too much of a good thing."

U.S. Troops Grab a Foothold in Iraq: "They Don't Know We're Here. It's an Invasion the Size of Normandy"

By Gary Regenstreif

WITH U.S. TROOPS IN IRAQ - U.S. forces rumbled into Iraq on Saturday to secure a foothold from which to launch a ground offensive to liberate Kuwait and met no initial resistance.

A U.S. Army light infantry brigade moved a "short distance" inside Iraq at 11:30 local time (0830 GMT), hours before Washington's deadline for Iraqi troops to begin withdrawing from the conquered emirate.

"We're finally here after looking at this on the map for almost seven months," said a senior U.S. commander, who picked up as a souvenir an abandoned Iraqi helmet. "Odds are, they don't even know we're here. It's an invasion the size of Normandy."

Dust clouds could be seen kilometers away from atop a high vantage point as battalions moved across the Saudi border into Iraq across the rocky desert. The brigade moved its artillery pieces, Sheridan armoured reconnaissance vehicles, anti-tank TOW missiles and a variety of mortars with them as they set up their foothold to launch the offensive. "You always have butterflies in your stomach when the enemy is on the other side," said Maj. Mark Siemer, 38, a brigade operations officer from Sparta, N.J. "But we had no resistance as we moved up. There's a sense of relief we didn't have to lose anybody."

"You get an awful lot of adrenaline in the body. You get geared up, you anticipate the worst and you move on."

No Iraqi soldiers were in sight as soldiers dug "hasty" fighting positions in the ground in case enemy troops came south for reconnaissance patrols they have mounted several times a week into Saudi Arabia.

The senior commander, who requested anonymity, stressed that "we're not going to conquer Iraq," but rather the drive was designed to oust its troops from Kuwait.

"He (Saddam) better get out or we'll annihilate his ass," the officer said. "The indications are positive. Whenever we approach them in force, they're surrendering. We hope that's what's going to happen."

U.S. troops moved a "short distance" officials said, without specifying for fear of revealing their location. Officials insisted they would exercise the utmost caution not to harm civilians or to wreak damage to religious sites in Iraq.

The commander early Friday delivered a pep speech to his troops before they headed off in a serpentine convoy into southern Iraq. "It's a very historic moment," he told them. "Let's do it. We've got to finish it."

As they moved, engineers moved with them, preparing to plough roads north.

Officials did not reveal what their objective was in days to come, how far they expected to travel or how long they expected it to take.

Troops, after sitting as long as six months in the desert in preparation for war, believed they were finally a step closer to home. "It feels very exciting to be in enemy territory," said Spec. DeWayne McGuire, 32, of Washington, D.C., a machine gunner. "Just to be in the same place they were and left makes me feel victorious already. It makes me realize we'll be home soon."

Iraqi troops had begun building up defenses in this sector more than a month ago but recently abandoned it for no apparent reason. U.S. troops engaged Iraqi troops several times in firefights when they slipped into the kingdom at night. On Friday night, officials said, two Iraqis were killed and a third was wounded and taken captive by U.S. forces who had set up an ambush patrol for them in Saudi Arabia.

American troops fired a TOW missile at the Iraqis and four of them fled on foot. There was no indication the Iraqis had returned fire and there were no American casualties. On Saturday, soldiers hollered as they moved north. "It's just great," said Spec. William Jungblom, 24, an engineer from Lafayette, Ind. "I've waited seven months for this day."

"The jamboree has begun," added Spec. Jerry Ellis, 22, a medic from Tampa, Fla. "We're glad to be getting this over with. I don't think we'll have a lot of casualties. We have the firepower." Spec. Richard Ashak, a Dragon anti-tank gunner from Moanaloa Valley, Hawaii, said coming across the border felt like no more than a field exercise.

"There's been no shooting yet," said Ashak, 23, a member of the 2nd platoon's "Nasty Boys." "Once the rounds start flying, we'll get serious."

His weapon, the Dragon, he said, would breathe fire soon.

NOTE: If permitted, the brigade is (part of the) 82nd Airborne Division, a rapid deployment force. A sign on-Iraqi side of border saying "Compliments of 2nd brigade, 82nd Airborne Division" was posted days ago by Apache attack chopper pilots.

Strap on Gatling Gun: Deadline for Iraqi Pullout Passes, Air Missions Shift to Help Troops in Fires Down Below

By Joan Lowy, Storer H. Rowley, and Edith M. Lederer

A U.S. AIR BASE, Central Saudi Arabia - Flying over a Kuwait set ablaze by oil well fires, Air Force F-15E fighter-bombers pounded Iraqi tanks Saturday night, through President Bush's deadline for Iraqi capitulation.

The F-15E Strike Eagles, along with F-16A and F/A-16 Fighting Falcons from the 4th tactical Fighter Wing (Provisional) continued to fly round-the-clock bombing missions against Iraqi targets in preparation for an expected allied ground offensive.

A squadron of F/A-16s at this desert base now being used as fighter-bombers may be converted back to their unique attack mission to provide close air support for ground troops if the allies launch an invasion of Kuwait.

This would be done by mounting a 30mm Gatling gun under the fuselage to pound Iraqi armor and soldiers just ahead of the allies.

Col. Hal Hornburg, 45, of Dallas, wing commander, said the F-15E and F-16A fighter-bombers and F-150 fighter-interceptors at this base would continue their current missions in a ground war.

As Hornburg prepared for a mission Saturday evening that would keep him aloft through the deadline, he described the hellish landscape that the Iraqi leader's army has ignited in occupied Kuwait. "Kuwait is on fire," Hornburg said. "Southern Kuwait looks like what hell must look like. If Saddam Hussein says he has not set that country on fire and torched it off, don't be misled. He has."

Southern Iraq is darkened, Hornburg added, and there are no lights on the ground, in contrast to the first nights of the war when cities were illuminated and flyers could see the headlights of vehicles on the road. "The only way we can tell where we are now (over Iraq) is by looking at our instruments," he said.

But over Kuwait, the night sky is ablaze from substantially increasing numbers of oil wells set on fire by Saddam's legions. "I was up there two nights ago and it was unbelievable," said Hornburg.

He said allied bombers had not touched off the fires. "I attribute 100 percent of them to (Saddam Hussein's forces) torching off those oil wells," he said. "You could see it from 100 miles away," Hornburg said, noting that he wondered to himself: "What's on fire up there? I looked at the instruments to see if we were closer to the border than I thought we were. It was just such an immense fire it appeared to be 30 miles ahead instead of 100."

Asked if it was militarily valuable to Iraq to set Kuwait on fire, Hornburg said, "I have no idea why they'd be setting the fires. The only thing I can conceive of is (Saddam) says, 'If I can't have it, no one will.' Other than that, I have no idea why he'd be setting those fires." Hornburg said the fires have had no effect on the allied bombing missions hitting their targets, because their radar and infrared-guided bombs can see through the dense smoke that blankets the blazing terrain.

Despite 38 days of allied bombings and more than 90,000 sorties, Hornburg said, "We are still in a target-rich environment. As the Iraqis move around our guys find them, and there's plenty up there every night."

In recent weeks, squadrons from this base have been concentrating their bombs on hitting Saddam's tanks, armor, and Republican Guard positions, and Hornburg said they are having "excellent success" preparing the battlefield ahead. "We do find that he puts his armor in clusters. Once we find a cluster, it's not very difficult with precision-guided munitions to do the job," Hornburg said. "We went up the other night and found a cluster of these things. And we un-clustered it for him. We had very good results."

"I don't know how many were in the cluster, but on the radar it was a perfect circle. We started putting precision bombs on individual targets. We dropped 14 bombs, and when we went back and looked at the (bomb-sight) film, we found 11 confirmed tank kills, plus one damaged tank and one artillery piece. We know how many we got with one hour's work with two airplanes. It was a real good payback."

Besides targeting the Republican Guard and Iraqi armor, Hornburg said, his wing has also been seeking out and destroying as many Scud missiles and their mobile launchers on the ground in Iraq as possible.

The wing is also working with a new type of spotting aircraft called JSTARS, or Joint Strategic Target Acquisition Radar System. The new planes use a unique radar-mapping capability to identify "significant targets" such as armor and bunker complexes in Kuwait and Iraq and pass their locations along to fighter-bombers, Hornburg said.

"I think we have been fairly successful," he said.

Sunday
February 24, 1991

In the first dull light of a desert morning about 700,000 allied troops, rising up as though out of a fighter's crouch, stormed toward Kuwait and southern Iraq where a dispirited but still well-armed, dangerous and fanatically-led enemy awaited.

In the east, two divisions of Marines and a complementary Army tank outfit, Tiger Brigade, formed a solid right. The Marines followed in the tracks of earlier patrols that had picked and dug across minefields and defensive berms in the preceding days.

The stories in this chapter don't usually specify the allied units' interim objectives. Though the U.S.-led force was clearly on the move, avoiding the use of specific place names was still the rule for reporters. The enemy was not to be given information, via the press, that might help him thwart the allied campaign.

But the ultimate objective for the troops headed up the eastern coast was never in doubt: Kuwait City—stopping only when necessary to reload or to let the Kuwaitis catch up so they could carry the flag of victory into their homeland.

Another obstacle to the Marines' rapid advance was soon evident: thousands of Iraqi soldiers who wanted to surrender. Out west, in what could be called the ground war's left hook, French and American troops were charging north toward an airfield at As Salman in southern Iraq. Their objective was to seize the field and convert it into a supply hub for the allies as they continued their advance toward the Euphrates River.

The Legionnaires, combat engineers, and other advance troops set off a few hours early, on Saturday night, so they could be just across the border and checking their GPS (Global Positioning System) readings at dawn's early light.

Between the Marines and the French Foreign Legion was the main body of the allied plan, U.S. and British armored, air assault, and infantry divisions carrying out a series of powerful, staggered penetrations.

Later in the day, out of their cockpit windows, allied flyers saw the coalition ground troops moving in tandem, moving at flank speed once clear of the berms and other obstacles, spread out across a wide, dusty vista.

The aviators found the panorama stretched their vocabulary. In a dictionary with pictures beside every word this one could easily go with awesome. In the Persian Gulf, the Marine amphibious group was still in reserve, doing its job—holding fast. The Marines' task had clearly boiled down to patience, holding the attention of the Iraqis in Kuwait until allied troops farther west could come north and swing around to cut them off at the pass.

Apparently the Iraqis weren't the only ones convinced the Marines would come ashore, though. A BBC announcer, a story in this chapter reports, issued a bulletin about a landing that never happened, and the report was repeated by other media.

By the end of Day One, the Marines inland were well on their way across the burning oilfields to their objective by the sea, with amazingly low casualties.

The troops on the western flank had also run into burdensome numbers of Iraqi troops eager to give up. Supply convoys headed north and buses packed with enemy POWs headed south clogged the roads in both directions.

Allied civil affairs officials quoted in this chapter were planning for a "brief" stay of a few weeks in Iraq as an occupation force. In the end, however, American units were there much longer, helping care for the thousands of Iraqi refugees who migrated toward allied lines as the fighting ended. The last American troops left southern Iraq in May, several months after the cease-fire.

On the first night of the land war in a Naval hospital, the hallways were mostly quiet. A full day of fighting had passed and the staff was dealing with only a trickle of patients.

Earlier predictions of massive allied casualties, especially among frontline units, were looking worse all the time—like gloriously lost bets.

Marines Storm Kuwait "Not to Conquer But to Drive Out Invaders and Restore the Country to its Citizens"

By Kirk Spitzer

AT 1ST MARINE DIVISION COMMAND POST, Near Kuwait Border - Troops of the 1st Marine Division spearheaded the long-awaited offensive to liberate Kuwait early Sunday, attacking heavily fortified Iraqi positions northwest of the Al-Wafra oilfields.

Up to 20,000 Marines backed by aircraft and artillery launched an attack against a double line of Iraqi defensive belts that run roughly parallel to Kuwait's southwest border with Saudi Arabia. The major part of the assault was launched at approximately 6 a.m., Saudi Arabian time. The first U.S. troops were through the first obstacle belt by 6:45 a.m.

Late Saturday and early Sunday, several thousand Marines slipped across the border and began working their way through the barrier by foot. They were followed by a coordinated attack by armored and mechanized infantry units at about dawn. The first obstacle belt is located about 12 miles from the L-shaped "heel" of Kuwait's southwest border with Saudi Arabia.

Marine and Air Force attack planes and bombers—including B-52s—flew hundreds of sorties over the battlefield just before and during the attack. Visibility was hampered by light rains and heavy clouds of thick, black smoke from burning oilfields in Kuwait.

The Marines were reported making good progress during the initial stage of the attack with light casualties. Iraqi resistance also was reported light, with more than 120 Iraqis surrendering to Marines late Saturday. Col. John Stennick, division chief of staff, said the assault was on schedule and held the key to liberating Kuwait. "We feel very good about things right now," said Stennick. "If we can punch through those two obstacle belts and keep moving, it's the gateway to Kuwait."

The attack appeared to catch Iraqi defenders by surprise. No significant Iraqi troop movements were reported near the obstacle belts or in southern or central Kuwait during the 24 hours preceding the attack. More than 120 Iraqi soldiers were taken

Sunday - February 24, 1991

prisoner without a fight by Marines advancing toward the obstacle belts late Saturday.

The initial assault was launched against a section of a lightly defended but heavily fortified obstacle belt northwest of the Al Wafra oilfields in southern Kuwait. The belt is more than a half-mile deep, with multiple rows of anti-personnel and anti-tank minefields, barbed wire fences, infantry fighting positions, and pre-targeted artillery "kill zones."

A second, parallel obstacle belt is located approximately five miles east. It is believed to be backed by large numbers of infantry troops and could be the scene of bitter trench fighting and close combat.

The Marines will have to pass through both belts to reach the interior of Kuwait, where as many as 200,000 Iraqi troops are stationed. None of the Iraqi units belong to the elite Republican Guard, but many are equipped with modern, Soviet-built T-72 tanks, which are bigger, faster and more heavily armed than the Marines' M-60 tanks.

In accordance with Defense Department press guidelines, the objectives of the Marine attack and other details of the operation cannot be reported at this time.

The attack came on a windy, rainy morning. Bombs and artillery fire boomed all along the border area. Heavy black clouds hung overhead from Kuwait's burning oilfields. The oilfields were set afire days after the Gulf War began to obscure the visibility of U.S. and coalition air pilots.

Marine officers have said air power will play a crucial role in the ground offensive, particularly as the Marines attempt to pass through the obstacle belts.

Iraq has a better than 5-to-1 advantage in artillery over U.S. forces and much of that artillery has been massed to fire on troops as they struggle through the minefields and barriers. It will be up to U.S. aircraft to spot and destroy artillery before it can slow or stop the Marine advance.

As preparations for the attack moved into the final stage late Saturday, Lt. Gen. Walter Boomer, Marine commander in the Saudi Arabian theater, sent a message to the troops. "After months of preparation, we are on the eve of liberating Kuwait, a small, peaceful country that was brutally attacked and subsequently pillaged by Iraq.

"Now we will attack into Kuwait, not to conquer but to drive out the invaders and restore the country to its citizens. In doing so, you not only return a nation to its people, but you will destroy the war machine of a ruthless dictator," Boomer said. The message was posted at the 1st Marine Division command near the Kuwait border.

The countdown for "G-Day," as the invasion date is known, began Feb. 10, when a 1st Marine Division reconnaissance team crept across the Kuwait border to take prisoners and seize documents from an Iraqi observation post. It was the first time U.S. ground troops had entered Kuwait.

Preparations continued the following week when several task forces belonging to the 1st Marine Division began moving to assembly and staging areas near the "heel" of the Kuwait-Saudi border, west of the Al Wafra oilfields.

Later, more reconnaissance teams crept into Iraqi territory in Kuwait, this time remaining for three days and recording details of the obstacle belt.

One team was nearly discovered when one Marine stepped on what turned out to be the roof of an underground Iraqi bunker; the Marine quickly stepped back when he heard Iraqi soldiers moving underneath, according to a Marine staff officer. Several days ago, Marine engineers began cutting more than 100 pathways through the six-foot-high earthen berms that run parallel to the border, about a mile inside Saudi territory.

On Friday, several thousand Marines moved across the border into Kuwait and after darkness Saturday they began slipping through the minefields, barbed wire and barriers of the first obstacle belt.

In a reminder that war is not always a high-tech struggle of missiles and computerized weapons, the Marines were issued simple, 24-inch plastic pointers, which they were to use to probe for mines buried beneath the sand of the obstacle belts.

In the weeks preceding the G-Day operation, the Marines' movements were masked by a series of artillery and combined arms raids along the border and inside Kuwait.

The purpose of the raids was to mask the location of the division and to entice Iraqi artillery batteries to fire on targets inside Saudi Arabia; once the batteries opened fire, they were knocked out by Marine or Air Force attack planes patrolling overhead.

French and Americans Throw Left Hook at Iraq: "I Think it is Beautiful and We Are Ready to Fire"

By Joseph Albright

Filed 2/24 7:15 a.m. with Maj. Pat Hermanson from a place about 1 KM inside the Iraqi border. Please backstop me on what I understand—but can't see—going on to the northeast.

WITH THE U.S. ARMY INSIDE SOUTHERN IRAQ - A fast column of American and French soldiers drove northeastward Sunday, threatening to cut Saddam Hussein's military off from the northern two-thirds of Iraq.

"I think I'm doing something good," said artilleryman Spec. Sandy Adkins, 21, of Fayetteville, N.C., "I really believe that. I believe I am part of history."

Adkins was part of a heavy howitzer battalion that rumbled into Iraq in a cloud of dust two hours before the expiration of President Bush's ultimatum. Four hours later they were ordered to don their chemical protective suits as a precaution. They were also told to begin taking pills to enhance their recovery if they are hit by nerve gas. But by dawn Sunday, Capt. Karl Stebbins, 33, of Bradenton, Fla., a battery commander, said he had heard no reports from his headquarters about allied troops getting hit by chemicals.

Just before 1 a.m., cheers went up from a howitzer gun crew when word came down on the gun's radio set that their guns had been assigned a target. Moments later, the dusty ground heaved under one 155mm howitzer. A flash shot out of the muzzle. There was a heavy thud, and the ground responded to a shock wave. The gun crew was coated with a dust puff kicked up by the 65-inch recoil of the cannon.

The ground shook 25 yards away. This and dozens of other cannons fired toward the northeast, part of a coordinated air and ground barrage aimed at clearing a path through Iraqi forces. At this gun line, anyway, there was no hint of Iraqi resistance in the first hours of ground combat. After firing, the artillerymen packed their trucks and prepared to move forward.

The American and French forces drove their trucks, guns, and light tanks across the rock-strewn desert nearly 200 miles east of the main Iraqi troop concentrations in and near Kuwait. It was a classic flanking maneuver of the kind military historians have been studying since the Peloponnesian Wars of ancient Greece.

Brig. Gen. Nick Halley, 51, of Koskiusco, Miss., whose 18th Corps Artillery from Fort Bragg, N.C. was among the first units into Iraq, said before the attack that the United

Sunday - February 24, 1991

States rapidly and secretly moved a large portion of its combat forces to the West starting in late January to make the flanking move possible.

"I think it will probably go down in history as one of the most amazing logistical moves there's ever been," Halley said in an interview. "We moved a whole corps of over 100,000 people over 200 miles. Mostly along one road, the Tapline Road, and we did that in 16 days, with all the combat service support, all the logistics, all the ammunition." He attributed the success of the westward shift before the invasion to the efficiency with which the allied air forces have kept the Iraqi air force from striking into Saudi Arabia.

From the point of attack, the Americans and French would have to cover about 150 miles of hard-packed desert before reaching the Euphrates River, the ancient lifeline that forms the storied Fertile Crescent as it flows south out of Syria to join the Tigris River.

Only a few scattered towns and police posts punctuated the path chosen by the allies. The Iraqis have also moved a sizable infantry force roughly 50 miles into Iraq. In recent weeks, that complex has been pounded day and night by B-52s, F-16s, and Navy attack jets. A week ago, frontline units received intelligence reports that the Iraqis had moved Soviet-made MI-8 Hind helicopters to an airfield under construction, posing the risk of an Iraqi counterstrike from heliborne troops. Since then, the airstrip is believed to have been attacked repeatedly to cut down on that risk.

The allies penetrated the Iraqi frontier many miles due south of Baghdad. By striking close to Saddam's capital, Gen. Norman Schwarzkopf, the allied commander-in-chief, forced the Iraqi command to make an emergency calculation whether the Americans might have in mind capturing the capital or whether they intend to veer east and south with a view of encircling the half-million Iraqi troops in and around Kuwait

It is the allies' goal to cut the Iraqis' supply links. Just getting inside Iraq was enough to excite the young American troops of this artillery unit.

Spec. Michael Barnes, 22, of Battle Creek, Mich., looked out over the rock-strewn flat dust patch just at sunrise Sunday and said: "I see a lot of artillery pieces. I think it is beautiful, and we are ready to fire. It's definitely an exhilarating day. It's kind of like before the game starts. There is a lot of excitement. I am sure there is fear, but it is covered up by the excitement."

Fighter Pilots' View of Land War: "I Can't Fathom the Size of This Operation. I Can't Grasp It. It's Enormous"

By Edith Lederer, Joan Lowy, and Storer Rowley

AN AIR BASE IN CENTRAL SAUDI ARABIA - Columns of allied tanks meeting light resistance rolled more than 12 miles into Iraq and tore up five miles of the Kuwaiti desert in just five minutes in the early hours of the ground war, fighter pilots flying missions over the battlefield said Sunday.

U.S. F-16A fighter-bombers pounded Iraqi artillery positions in western Iraq which had been firing at the advancing allied force, in one case leaving five out of six batteries burning, the pilots said. "The lights of Kuwait City are still on," said Capt. Randy Garrett, 37, of Rome, Ga., an F-15E fighter-bomber pilot who attacked mobile rocket launchers in north-central Kuwait in a pre-dawn raid. "You can see occasional flashes from the ground fire that was going on—and it was happening both east and west of us."

The advance across an estimated 300-mile front from the Persian Gulf deep into Iraq appeared to follow pre-battle scenarios for the air-land campaign to breach Saddam Hussein's wall of bunkers in Kuwait and flank his army from the west in the Iraqi desert.

Lt. Col. Randy Bigum, 41, of Springfield, Va., described flying over a broad front of allied tanks and armored units moving more than 12 miles north into the vast, open desert of western Iraq. "They were in groups. I had expected to see a continuous line, you know kind of like a kickoff return, but it wasn't like that at all," said the F-15C fighter pilot, who is the commander of the 53rd Tactical Fighter Squadron, based in Bitburg, Germany.

"There were armored vehicles. To be honest with you, it was less dense than I thought. I expected in my mind's eye this cavalry charge. But I think modern ground combat is more sophisticated now," he said. "I can't fathom the size of this operation. I can't grasp it. It's enormous," Bigum said after returning to the largest U.S. air base in Saudi Arabia. "You have heard people talk about the enormity of this air power... This (air power) pales in comparison."

Col. David Hamlin, 47, an F-16A pilot from East Bloomfield, N.Y, flew a close-air-support mission against Iraqi artillery for Army troops he said were advancing 10-15 miles inside Iraq from the Saudi border. He said there was no sign of Iraqi tanks or armor moving in the desert but that F-15E Strike Eagles and F-16A Fighting Falcons from this airbase were flying continuous missions in support of the allied offensive, which was launched at 4 a.m.

"We got spectacular results," said Hamlin, a farmer and Vietnam veteran who commands a squadron of F-16s from the 138th Tactical Fighter Squadron, an Air National Guard unit based in Syracuse, N.Y.

Hamlin zeroed in with two other F-16s on six artillery batteries that had been shelling the U.S. soldiers and dropped Rockeye anti-armor cluster bombs and 500-pound bombs on the targets. "We left five out of six artillery positions on fire, so we were quite pleased," said Hamlin, who flew his morning raid along a 15-mile front. Other formations of F-16s were also bombing artillery batteries ahead of the advance line.

Army units were advancing quickly, firing artillery barrages before them, he said, and spotters in the air and on the ground guided the F-16s to the coordinates of the Iraqi batteries. Unlike Kuwait, where Iraqi forces are heavily concentrated, the Iraqi battlefield west of the Kuwait-Saudi border was thinly defended by Saddam Hussein's forces, Hamlin said. "Obviously, it's all sand, and the sand is only marked by trails or roads," said Hamlin, describing his bird's-eye view. "And at this juncture, those trails and roads are all over the place. Armor has been rolling all over."

While the allied lines were well-delineated, he said, "I didn't see an Iraqi front line. Only an artillery position. You can see their positions and storage areas. I would assume that the main (Iraqi) forces are in Kuwait. I'd say they're much heavier in southern Kuwait and further up at the Kuwaiti-Iraq border, where Republican Guard is."

Practically every pilot interviewed at this base in the first hours of the ground war said they had used extreme caution to positively identify Iraqi targets so as not to hit allied forces. Special care was ordered by commanders because many of the U.S. casualties during the last months were caused by U.S. pilots who accidentally bombed their own troops.

Pilots flying Sunday had to run a gantlet of communications, passing through four

Sunday - February 24, 1991

air controllers on their way to pick up by radio with Army ground-spotters and forward air control spotters to locate their targets. "We anticipate a real fluid situation in the next couple of days, and lines of battle are going to change constantly," said Lt. Col. George Patrick, 39, a South Carolina Air National Guardsman who flew an F-16 mission Sunday.

"The desert battlefield is going to get a lot tougher. There will be a lot of smoke and dust," said Patrick, who bombed armored vehicles in central Iraq that appeared ready to leave their bunkers. "We have to be a lot more careful," he said, noting that pilots were under orders not to bomb their targets if they had any doubts.

Garrett said the allied force was advancing so fast that the line at which its artillery shells stopped falling, called the FSCL—that is, Fire Support Coordination Line—moved about five miles in five minutes. He said he and his backseat weapon systems officer, Capt. Ed Koslow, 27, of Alexandria, Va., were given a target just as they were about to cross the border into Kuwait and "not five minutes later . . . they came back and said it's (the FSCL) moved five miles."

"When they told us the FSCL had moved north, we knew it (the ground war) was definitely on," Garrett said. "Anything going north is a good sign."

At 4:30 a.m., just as their F-15E broke through clouds heading north after climbing through some bad weather, Garrett said they saw the orange flame of an Iraqi scud launched "some distance north" toward Saudi Arabia. "I at first thought it was a SAM (surface-to-air missile) until it kept going," he said.

Bigum said that the U.S. military chose the 4 a.m. kickoff time for the ground offensive for a good reason: they wanted to make sure it was as dark as possible. "The moon went over the horizon at 3:11 a.m. in Iraq," he said. "I watched it go over the horizon and said, 'It won't be long now.'"

At exactly 4 a.m., Bigum added, one of the air controllers handling his mission said, "Time hack! Time hack!" That is the military code for the strike of the hour, but Bigum said it meant something different on Sunday. "It was his way of telling me the gun went off."

Bigum, who had been flying combat air patrols protecting bombers hitting Iraqi targets, said, "My worst nightmare is that they get some MiGs (Iraqi fighters) together and get something through, and drop chemical weapons on those Army guys. I'll do anything to keep that from happening."

Capt. Steve Bills, 28, of Apple Valley, Calif., a weapons system officer aboard an F-15 bombing mission Saturday night, said bad weather hampered some bombing runs, forcing massive numbers of allied aircraft to gather in the skies on either side of the weather front. "Actually, most of the time we were well south of the (Kuwaiti) border waiting to get in," Bills said. "We were just trying not to run into each other."

"The problem is, with the weather the way it was, it's going to force people to either of two places, and that's out of the weather, it gets a little crowded," Bills said.

Other pilots said the weather started clearing later Sunday morning. Bills said he wasn't told before talking off on his mission when the ground war would start, but he deduced while aloft that it may have begun because of the tremendous volume of messages being passed over radio frequencies. "Nobody would shut up on the (frequency) we were using," Bills said.

Bigum said, "These are exciting times. They are also scary times and I wish the Army the best of luck. The ball's in their court now. The Air Force has done all it can do."

"If This is Your Day Off You'll Miss Half the War"

By Storer Rowley, Joan Lowy, and Edith M. Lederer

A U. S. AIR BASE IN CENTRAL SAUDI ARABIA - With lightning speed, allied forces surged across the Saudi border and raced north toward the outskirts of Kuwait City Sunday night as Iraqi resistance crumbled, fighter pilots flying missions over the battlefield said.

Army helicopter gunships and scouts roamed some 50 miles into the desert of central Iraq, leading columns of allied armor and ground troops across a wide battlefront, the pilots said. "They could certainly be on Main Street in Kuwait City by lunchtime tomorrow," said Maj. Keith Coln, 38, of Columbia, S.C., and F-16A fighter-bomber pilot, just after returning from a tank-killing mission south of the city.

Billowing black clouds of smoke in Kuwait and central Iraq were hampering pilots flying from this largest U.S. air base in Saudi Arabia, but didn't slow the advance.

Astounded at the unexpected speed at which allied armor and mechanized units were churning through the desert, U.S. pilots spoke of targets and missions being changed at the last minute because the front was advancing so quickly.

"Some guys had said if this is your day off, you're going to miss half the war," said Capt. Gordon Spooner, 40, of North Syracuse, N.Y., another F-16A pilot who returned at mid-afternoon from a tank-busting mission deep inside Iraq.

F-16 pilots joked with each other that things were going so well they might be landing in Kuwait City Monday. "Maybe we'll do a few touch-and-goes at Kuwait City International Airport between missions," said Coln.

"I'll see you at the lounge at Concourse C," shot back Capt. Thorne Ambrose, 36, of Columbia, S.C., both former commercial airline pilots. Asked how far allied troops had driven north, Ambrose said, "Let's just say that some of the targets we attacked before the ground war are now being controlled by the good guys."

Pilots described rapidly moving allied columns kicking up a great dust storm in their wake. "You could see them in columns," said Capt. John (Smiley) Sizemore, 34, of Columbia, S.C. "They look like little ants in a row coming from a peanut butter and jelly sandwich somebody left on the ground, just lots of them down there."

The ground war is progressing "about ten times better than I would have ever imagined," Sizemore said. "If they are advancing as fast as they are, it is that much sooner that we can get Kuwait back for the Kuwaitis and that much sooner we can get on back to our families."

Coin said, "There is a lot of troop movement going north. There are not a lot of defined borders anymore. The artillery fire line is changing rapidly, probably hourly."

Four South Carolina Air National Guard pilots described the skies over Kuwait as a thick blanket of black smoke, which forced them to change altitude to attack armor the Iraqis had tried to conceal under the sand. They said they dropped eight 2,000-pound bombs and destroyed six or seven Iraqi tanks.

Even though flying at lower altitude makes the F-15A pilots more vulnerable to Iraqi anti-aircraft fire and missiles, the South Carolinians said they encountered no resistance.

Pilots said that the immense cloud of smoke caused by the oil fires lit by Saddam Hussein's troops, supposedly to mask their movements, have backfired.

The smoke is obscuring much of Kuwait and is blowing northward toward Iraq, said

Sunday - February 24, 1991

Coln. "As a matter of fact, if you drew a line from southern Kuwait to Baghdad, that's about the direction the smoke has taken."

A new swath of smoke 60 miles long has appeared over central Iraq, forcing some F-16A pilots to divert from bombing missions they were flying in that area, said Capt. John Richardson, 35, an American Airlines pilot flying with the South Carolina guard.

"I think they're burning something in western Iraq to hide the whole country up there," said Richardson, who is from Chapel Hill, N.C.

After Richardson turned back, forward air controllers supporting U.S. Army troops advancing into Iraq diverted his formation of F-16s to a close-air support mission ahead of allied troops.

At the same time, mid-afternoon, Richardson said U.S. Army helicopters moving ahead of the allies were "sweeping ahead of the troops, bypassing pockets of resistance." He said they were approximately 50 miles into Iraq.

The walls of smoke "make it more difficult, but not impossible" to find targets, Coln said. "We were unstoppable," he said.

Marines and Fleet Shuffle the Deck Off Kuwait: "Can't Say I Expect Something and I Can't Say That I Don't"

By John King

ABOARD THE USS NASSAU IN THE NORTHERN PERSIAN GULF   Marines rushed tank-fighting vehicles and other equipment ashore Sunday to help land-based Marines and other allied forces in their attack on Iraqi forces in southern Kuwait.

At the same time, about a dozen ships that had been in the central Persian Gulf steamed north to hook up with the forward elements of a Marine amphibious landing force.

The shuffling of resources took place hours after President Bush ordered the full-scale offensive to expel Iraqi forces from Kuwait. Marine spokesmen declined to provide the destination of the ships heading for shore, or say whether Marines were being sent along with the equipment. Also, Harrier jets assigned to the Marine force afloat in the Gulf shifted their mission from bombing runs to close-air support of ground-based allied forces now on the offensive. Rainy weather and smoke clouds over Kuwait, however, forced the cancellation of some sorties.

Rear Adm. John B. Laplante, the commander of the amphibious task force carrying the Marine assault force, said he was awaiting orders from the U.S. command. "We're poised," he said. When asked if the sea-based troops were likely to see combat soon, Laplante was non-committal. "I can't say that I expect something and I can't say that I don't," he said. Laplante said mine-clearing operations in the northern Gulf continued. Also operating in the northern Gulf were naval battleships, using their 18-inch guns to pelt Iraqi forces in Kuwait.

Whether or not the Marine landing force is sent into combat, Laplante said its mission was to "fix certain Iraqi divisions in place so that they are unable to move out to the flank of the (land-based) Marines or the flank of the Army forces."

The commander of the Marine landing force, Maj. Gen. Harry Jenkins, shuttled from the Nassau command ship to another vessel to meet with his ground commanders. Laplante said the naval forces were at full alert for a possible chemical, missile, naval or air attack. He described the step as a routine precaution taken at the commencement of ground hostilities.

Laplante, interviewed on the flag deck of the Nassau at 10 a.m., 11 a.m. local time, said radio reports (BBC) that Marine amphibious forces had landed on a Kuwaiti island were erroneous.

A Paradox Involving an Amphibious Assault and Marines in Bunks—"I'd Just as Soon the War Ended Tomorrow"

By David Evans

ABOARD USS GUNSTON HALL, in the Persian Gulf - For Marines aboard amphibious ships in the Persian Gulf, the beginning of the ground war was a moment of sublime paradox.

They were just rising from their bunks when the BBC announced a victorious U.S. Marine amphibious assault on the island of Failaka. "I didn't believe it," said 1st Lt. Bob Wondra, of Staplehurst, Neb. "There's no way it could have been taken without us," said the 25-year-old leader of a platoon of 28 Marines and four light armored vehicles.

Lance Cpl. Steven Sanders, 22, of Chicago, Ill., groused. "Half of us are huddled around radios trying to find out what's going on."

Failaka is a three-by-ten-mile island located about 20 miles off the coast of Kuwait City. The Iraqis have fortified the island.

In an amphibious assault, Wondra said, his unit "would be in the second wave, right behind the infantry. They would secure the beachhead and we would punch out to set up stingray operations inland," Wondra said.

In a stingray operation, Wondra explained that his platoon would scout for Iraqi forces and call in artillery, naval gunfire, and air strikes "to destroy them before they could get to the main body."

Wondra reacted to the unconfirmed report of Failaka's fall with a mixture of resentment and lost opportunity. "I'd be very disappointed, to be among the first ones out here, to be on the first ship to sail from Moorhead City (N.C.), and not do anything," he said.

Wondra and about 500 other Marines are embarked on the Gunston Hall, an amphibious assault ship that arrived in the Persian Gulf Sept. 14, 1990. Except for a few practice landings, their ship has been steaming in circles in a 15-square-mile "box" in the Persian Gulf ever since.

The Marines have been fighting boredom while waiting for the chance to fight Iraqis, and many regarded Failaka as their main chance to get in on the action.

The captain of the Gunston Hall, Cmdr. William Marshall, said "Failaka is the closest target to us right now. It's about five hours away." Since Failaka is one of a number of possible landing sites, Marshall reacted skeptically to the announcement of its seizure by Marines. "I heard it on the BBC also, and I was surprised. I asked the watch standers, 'Didn't you guys call me when the assault took place?'" he chuckled. Despite the premature report, Americans are likely to hear about a real amphibious operation in the near future. "We'll do something, there's no doubt about it," predicted Marshall.

On Saturday, Feb. 23rd, Harrier jets from the assault ship Nassau launched 40 bombing strikes on Failaka. "The Iraqis have around 4,000 troops there," Marshall said. He added that "the Iraqis have emplaced both Exocet and Silkworm anti-ship missiles on the island, as well as quite a bit of artillery that can reach the mainland."

"The Harriers were bombing those artillery positions on Saturday, while carrier jets attacked Silkworm launching sites," Marshall said.

In Iraqi hands, Failaka is a fortified bastion that dominates the Bay of Kuwait and Kuwait City. "A situation could develop where our troops are in Kuwait within range of his artillery pieces. That's one thing that makes that island a lucrative target," Marshall said. On the other hand, U.S. Marine artillery on the island could shell Iraqi positions in Kuwait City. "Seizing the island may be far less costly than a more direct assault on the coast of Kuwait," Rear Adm. James Laplante, commander of the amphibious task force in the gulf, said. "The Kuwaiti coastline has been transformed into a formidable barrier."

"The coastline near Kuwait City is much easier to fortify against an amphibious assault because of what's there," he said. "Most of the assault beaches are urban areas that are heavily built up. There are two, three and four-story concrete structures along the beaches. All of these structures can hide tanks. They can hide riflemen. They can hide surface-to-surface missiles. Those missiles could hit ships or landing craft offshore."

Marshall said the coastal buildings have been quote "bricked up" with small gunports. "In the past couple weeks the Iraqis have moved reinforcements along any areas they think we might be able to launch an amphibious assault," he said.

While Failaka appears to be an easier target, Marshall said "we'd like to go with an 80 percent probability there are no mines in the area."

Two Navy warships, the cruiser Princeton and the amphibious ship Tripoli, have struck mines recently. Tripoli is still on station, but the mine blew a 20 by 30-foot hole in her side. The forward diesel space is flooded. A lot of shoring is supporting bulkheads, Marshall said. The mine that holed Tripoli was estimated to contain 500 pounds of TNT, Marshall estimated. He said mines are particularly effective in the shallow waters of the Gulf because the blast bounces up from the bottom with much greater force than an explosion in deep water.

For all the risks involved, Marshall has mixed emotions about an amphibious assault. "We've been here for six months training and preparing, and if we never got to do anything I'd be disappointed," he said.

"Then again, if we did an assault, there would be casualties. If I had my druthers, I'd just as soon the war ended tomorrow and not have to expend those lives," he said.

Marines Take Massive Numbers of Prisoners in Kuwait

By Ray Wilkinson

WITH U.S. MARINES IN KUWAIT - Suddenly they were all over the battlefield. Some came in ones and twos. And then in the dozens. Then around 500 Iraqis waving handkerchiefs, scarves, and white flags surrendered to advancing American Marines.

Only hours after allied troops launched a devastating ground war to drive the Iraqi army out of Kuwait, Marines who blitzkrieged into the occupied emirate at dawn had scored a devastating victory—and virtually without firing a shot in anger or suffering any friendly casualties. The mass

Iraqi surrender came at noon local time as a fleet of Marine tanks, amphibious assault vehicles, artillery and light anti-tank towed vehicles approached the main Iraqi defensive positions which Saddam Hussein's troops had built along the Saudi-Kuwait border during their six months of occupation.

The Marines had smashed unopposed through the forward Iraqi positions along the so-called Saddam line without opposition. Iraqi troops had fled long ago.

Ten miles further into Kuwait the Marines expected tougher opposition from Iraqi troops defending a formidable defensive line of minefields, trenches, and concertina wire. Marine tanks, aircraft and Cobra gunships bombarded the area for several hours, underlining the allies' determination to keep friendly casualties at a minimum even if the timetable for an advance began to slip.

But as infantry troops mounted in Amtracs and the Marines' amphibious assault troops carriers began to move through the Iraqi positions, the battlefield was transformed into a bizarre theater of surrender.

A small group of Iraqis, several without boots, stumbled from their foxholes, hands in the air in surrender. None then or later carried any weapons. A little further, a knot of 20 Iraqis dressed in dark olive green sat huddled in a bunker waving a large white flag as the Marines drove by.

The landscape of desert sand stretching for miles unchangingly into the distance was transformed into one of the most remarkable scenes this reporter has ever seen in covering nearly 20 wars.

Iraqis appeared from all points of the compass. One group of around 500 surrendered to the awed Marines. Most were well-dressed in green olive or field jackets and appeared well-fed and groomed despite days of grueling allied air and artillery attacks.

Many appeared happy their ordeal was over. They threw their wool tank caps into the air and abandoned them as they walked into captivity. Many were smiling, probably out of apprehension, fear, and sheer relief. The Marines shooed them to the rear and continued their assault into the heart of Kuwait.

For months, allied intelligence had suggested the Saddam line was so formidable it resembled the famed Maginot line and other historical defensive positions. However, the portion breached by the Marines was virtually undefended and flimsy. Combat engineers had blasted their way through a sand wall even before the main attack began.

The minefield and surrounding fortifications were around 140 yards in depth rather than an anticipated 2,000 yards. The initial attacking tank units captured a couple dozen Iraqi defenders but otherwise the first defensive line was undefended.

The Marines stormed the line in chemical outfits but there was no counter Iraqi artillery, either conventional or chemical, and no indication of chemical mines in the ill-tended minefield. The minefield itself appeared totally unattended and derelict, marked only by an occasional strand of barbed wire or concertina wire.

There were several dummy Iraqi tanks manufactured from sheet metal and painted gray, but hardly likely to fool anyone since they were only half-size.

There were few bunkers, fighting holes or other defensive networks. The few bunkers were either totally open to the sky or protected by a sheet of tin roofing and one layer of sandbags. We crossed two tarmac roads which the Iraqis had constructed in the region to aid the movement of their troops, but the roads were already heavily chewed up.

There was very little war debris or indeed few signs of any human activity at all in the region. I saw one rusting, upturned bicycle, incongruously abandoned in the middle of nowhere and a rotting sofa in a bunker which had suffered a direct hit.

Sunday - February 24, 1991

There was a flimsy metal watchtower, which looked across the minefield, south toward Saudi Arabia. Otherwise there was no other sign of life. After successfully smashing through the first perimeter, the Marines halted briefly to regroup before tackling a second and more heavily defended line of fortifications.

Marines 25 Miles Into Kuwait on First Day: "We Went In and We Overwhelmed Them"

By Molly Moore

WITH U.S. TROOPS, Near Saudi Border - Allied ground forces surged across the Saudi border before dawn today in a barrage of artillery fire and by nightfall had pushed 25 miles into Kuwait with one Marine reported killed and thousands of Iraqi forces surrendering to invading troops, according to senior U.S. Marine commanders.

American commanders, conceding that some of the toughest ground battles could lie ahead for allied forces, said Marine and Arab troops had encountered surprisingly little resistance from Iraqi troops during the first day of ground combat and engaged in only two significant firefights.

"We had a tremendous success," said one senior U.S. Marine Corps commander. "After worrying about things for days and sleepless nights, we had no heavy artillery, no chemicals and no injuries going through the minefields."

The commander said he believes it is "not a matter of days, but hours" before allied forces subdue most of the Iraqi troops inside Kuwait. "If we'd had another 12 hours of daylight, most of the forces inside of Kuwait would have given up."

The commander added: "We went in and we overwhelmed them." Allied forces, however, still face a formidable mission of routing Iraqi Republican Guard forces entrenched inside of Iraq along the Kuwaiti border.

"You've always got to be alert to him striking out in some way," said one Marine official. "As soon as you become comfortable, you get hurt. That's why you're not seeing us real jubilant. It's not over 'til it's over."

Several senior commanders described as "remarkable" the days' American casualty figures of one Marine reported killed and about two-dozen listed as injured. Officials said, however, the reports were preliminary and noted that fighting was continuing into the night.

After field commanders reported on the day's combat and the casualty figures, Lt. Gen. Walt Boomer, commander of Marine forces, told his generals, "I'm sorry you've had any (losses), but that's remarkable considering where you've been and what you've done today."

Commanders attributed the relatively weak Iraqi resistance to the weeks of aerial pounding and a lack of will by Iraqi soldiers to fight. "We made the Republican Guard into something it wasn't, we made the barriers something they weren't," said one senior commander.

After a daylong push through Kuwait, that began with a 4 a.m. H-hour, commanders said one of their greatest concerns were the thousands of surrendering Iraqi troops.

Senior Marine commanders made repeated appeals to headquarters command posts tonight for assistance in handling the thousands of Iraqi troops that have been surrendering throughout the day.

Military officials said preliminary reports indicated that as many as X,700 Iraqi troops may have surrendered after the fiercest firefight of the day in which a Marine mechanized infantry unit came under heavy tank fire from Iraqi tanks. Officials said several thousand other Iraqi troops were reported surrendering as a result of other actions.

Military officials said one mechanized infantry task force was slowed in its effort to cross a breach through second-tier minefields because as many as 1,000 Iraqi troops were attempting to surrender south through the same lanes. "We all need a lot of help with those POWs," one commander pleaded. "I have a couple thousand. We can't take care of them."

"We've got every available truck we can find to go up there and pull them out," said one Marine official.

One Marine Cobra pilot reported that as he circled one area, he described "thousands of troops waiting to give up." Commanders said darkness fell before the report could be verified.

Military commanders said air strikes on the battlefield "built to a peak" in the final nighttime hours before the attack. From command posts inside Saudi Arabia, B-52 bombing raids and other pounding could be heard throughout the night. Marine artillery forces then moved across the Saudi border under the cover of darkness and began pummeling frontline Iraqi troops across the minefields designed to slow attacking forces.

At daybreak, with infantry forces providing protection on their flanks, mine-breaching teams moved into the fields and began clearing six lanes. "We had the lanes open very fast and right behind them came the combat power," said one Marine commander. "We were through the minefield before they (Iraqi forces) had recovered from the pounding."

Senior American military officials said they don't know why Iraqi forces have not used chemical weapons against the advancing troops. Officials said several reports of chemical attacks were received throughout the day that proved either false or could not be substantiated.

Marine forces encountered sporadic artillery fire after breaching the first barrier. As the forces pushed into Kuwait, "we bypassed as many (Iraqi) troops as we could," said one official. "They're still out there—we're outnumbered." Officials said, however, those forces appeared to be showing no signs of offering resistance. As the U.S. forces attempted to cross a second-tier minefield deep inside Kuwait, they encountered heavy tank and artillery fire in the fiercest battle of the first day of land combat, Marine officials said.

The Marines' Task Force Ripper pushed through the first minefields with only sporadic fire, but at the second breach further north "they started taking a lot of heavy artillery fire on the east and north flanks," said Col. Jim Majchrzak, plans officer for the 1st Marine Expeditionary Force.

Two Marine tanks were destroyed and three Marines wounded in the hour-long tank battle involving the Task Force Ripper and Iraqi tank forces, officials said.

American forces summoned Cobra gunships and Marine attack planes to suppress the Iraqi fire against Task Force Ripper and ended the assault taking an estimated 4,766 Iraqi prisoners, according to initial reports. The American forces "surged a lot of air," calling Cobra helicopter gunships, F/A18, Harrier AV-85 and some A-6 attack planes to counter the Iraqi fire, Majchrzak said.

Meanwhile, officials said Saudi forces were also progressing well in their push through southeastern Kuwait. Saudi and other Arab forces reported capturing about 1,000 additional prisoners in southeastern

Kuwait, U.S. officials said. Saudi officials also reported "a good number" of Iraqi troops fleeing northward in the same area, Marine officials said.

Artillery and tank fire from Iraqi troops intensified throughout the day and allied aircraft attacked several Iraqi tank columns that began rumbling from central Kuwait toward the Marine forces invading from the south, the operations officer said.

Although Marine officials were optimistic about the progress of the ground forces in the first 18 hours of combat, they said allied troops have just began engaging Iraq's tougher second-echelon forces behind the frontline troops.

NOTE TO WASH POST CORRESPONDENTS: Please incorporate quotes and details from previous two reports in this file if those files—as I suspect—did not arrive in time to use. First report was filed at 6 a.m. Saudi time Feb. 24 but was not released by Riyadh Jib until about 5:30 p.m. Will be on the road tomorrow, possibly may not be able to file depending on communications links, but will certainly try.

20 Miles in 6 Hours—Land War is Gridlock for Combat Engineers: Frisbees, Hacky-Sacks, and Racy Magazines

By Mike Tharp

AT THE IRAQI BORDER - Day One of the Ground War was almost a day at the beach for the 37th Engineer Battalion.

Convoy traffic of combat units streaming into southwest Iraq was so congested that it created what battalion commander Lt. Col. Robert Holcombe called "gridlock" for units like the 37th waiting for their place in line. As a result, it was "hurry up and wait," the venerable military custom of racing to a site, then sitting or standing until new orders came down. Taking advantage of tradition, and the traffic jam, nearly 600 combat engineers kicked back near their 200 vehicles lined up along the main supply route leading into Iraq.

They tossed footballs and Frisbees, kicked hacky-sacks around a circle, read books, dozed, and played cards on field tables. Surrounded by thousands of square miles of sand, the engineers needed only an ocean to complete the temporarily idyllic picture.

Behind their relaxed exterior, however, they knew the reality hanging like the Saudi sun over their staging area only three miles south of the Iraqi border.

Sure enough, 1st Lt. Hans Scheer, the battalion's liaison with nearby French forces, pulled up in his Humvee vehicle to announce the battalion would head north in an hour. The 37th would move out nearly 24 hours after coalition troops, led by French infantry and armor divisions, along with troops from the 82nd Airborne Division, staged a lightning attack across the Saudi-Iraqi border near the Saudi town of Rafha.

Their blitzkrieg followed several hours of artillery bombardment by other coalition units intended to drive back any Iraqi defenders. Early reports passed on to the engineers indicated that the so-called maneuver units had met little initial resistance in their effort to establish an airhead, the paratroopers' equivalent of a beachhead, several miles inside Iraq.

Darkness was falling as the 37th moved out. Several trucks were decorated with "wanted" posters of Saddam Hussein. One sign read "War." Another "Somewhere."

Over the next six hours, however, the drama of entering the war became diluted, as three convoys at once converged on one pass leading into Iraq. The result was a monumental traffic jam which caused the 37th to spend six hours traveling less than 20 miles. French forces holding operational command over that section of the theater ordered the battalion and several other U.S. units to pull off road in a secure area to spend the night. Ahead, French troops, including Foreign Legionnaires, were still forging northward into Iraqi territory.

And although nearly all the 37th's engineers are paratroopers and combat-trained, their heaviest equipment is bulldozers and road-graders, not tanks and artillery pieces.

The battalion camped near a French supply unit, and after the sun came up dozens of deals began to be made between French and American soldiers. Berets were swapped, food rations exchanged, unit pins traded.

One of the more colorful transactions involved a French soldier named Chasseuil and several combat engineers comparing and contrasting each other's racy magazines. Finally, in the early afternoon, the French gave the go-ahead.

The 37th pulled out again. Again, the north-south road was clogged with traffic, traveling only eight miles the first hour. A drizzle began as the procession passed scores of vehicles parked in the rain containing troops from the 82nd Airborne Division.

A French re-supply convoy passed the 37th on the left side of the highway, which had traffic running almost only one way, north. Even so, progress was tedious.

Shortly after nightfall, with winds blowing strong enough to blow a portable toilet off of one of the trucks, Lt. Col. Robert Holcombe, battalion commander, radioed to his four company commanders to pull off on the shoulder for the night.

An hour after daybreak, the convoy was on the road again, plowing deeper into Iraq. Their part of the war had yet to begin.

Earlier, at the assembly area on the Saudi Arabian side of the border, executive officer Maj. Randy Riggins had observed, as the 37th moved out, "Military people don't sit around and wait for war. We think about wives, families, jobs, ambitions, just like anybody else. We don't wait for war." So far, however, that's what the combat engineers were doing—waiting for their part of the war.

101st Air Assault Takes Off Late: "We'd Walk Through the Gates of Hell if We Knew We Were Going Home"

By John Pomfret

WITH THE 101ST AIRBORNE DIVISION IN IRAQ - More than 100 attack helicopters blasted deep into Iraqi territory Sunday in what one major described as a "bold, bodacious action" to cut Saddam Hussein's supply lines and head for the Euphrates River.

In an invasion officers have compared to the 101st Airborne Division's landings at Normandy in 1944, more than 2,000 men were airlifted scores of miles into Iraq.

The start of the invasion came just after dawn from 13 strike zones in the forbidding desert of northern Saudi Arabia. In the dark, the whoop-whoop of helicopter blades sounded like a communal heartbeat. Dust from the Chinooks, Blackhawks and Hueys turned the sky purple. One by one in six air corridors, the black birds roared into Iraq.

"We'd walk through the gates of hell if we knew we were going home," said Sgt. Mike Southall, 34, of Galveston, Tex. Southall then boarded a Chinook that was to carry him into Iraq. Below, the bird slung two Humvees, the

Sunday - February 24, 1991

Army's new version of a jeep. Southall and other members of the "Screaming Eagles" said they were anxious to begin the ground war.

"I'd hate to sound like a warmonger, but it's time to do it," he said. "We've been practicing new and better ways to kill people. Let's get it over with."

Weather delayed the assault, which had been scheduled to begin at 5:25 a.m. The attack marks the first time the Army has put into practice its doctrine of air-land battle. Unlike in the past, where territory was considered the key, the new doctrine focuses the weight of the Army's firepower on destroying enemy troops.

Apache assault helicopters led the attack, which was backed up to the west by a strike by French troops. The Apaches flew in low, less than 50 feet off the ground, carrying Hellfire anti-tank missiles. "They're sagebrush brushing," said Maj. Dan Grigson, a spokesman for the 101st Division. "This is a bold, bodacious action."

Behind them scores of Blackhawks carried men and Chinooks lugged Humvees and artillery into enemy territory. Officers said the invasion evoked the storming of Normandy beach of June 1944. The flying time of less than an hour was about the same, the 101st Airborne Division's contribution of men was similar. "The only difference," said Maj. Robin Sellers, commander of the logistics wing of one battalion, "there's no water and we're moving in helicopters, not gliders."

By (blank), the American attack force had established its "Forward Base Cobra," from where Iraqi supply lines could be cut. Like the Normandy assault, one concern was landing on the targeted area. "It's a big desert out there," said Sellers. "There's a lot of room for error."

Mother Nature was also a concern. Officers said they worried that dust would be high in Iraq, a problem for helicopter pilots. . . . The attack was preceded by about one week of "aggressive reconnaissance." Soldiers from the 101st Division were airlifted behind enemy lines. With only radios and "20/20" vision, they staked out Forward Base Cobra, supplying up-to-the-minute details on the situation on the ground.

In addition to being one of the largest air assaults in history, the invasion Sunday also marked the first time women flew helicopters on an air assault into enemy territory. The 101st Division has 22 female pilots, although not all of them flew into Iraq.

Near sunset Saturday, a vicious wind kicked up swirling clouds of dust. Helicopters, looking like giant insects, disappeared and then re-appeared behind the dust clouds.

Soldiers leaned against tires, stretched out in the helicopters, their faces wrapped in green and brown scarves. "I'm just trying to spend a little time with myself," said 20-year-old Anthony Baquera, from Brooklyn, N.Y.

The gunner on a Chinook helicopter said he needed some time to pray. "I hope the Lord looks kindly on us," he said. Behind, in front of and above him the roar and beat of helicopter engines continued.

Strategy for a Brief Occupation of Iraq: "We're Looking at Two to Three Weeks"

By Mark Mooney

ON THE IRAQI BORDER - Army units intend to hold Iraqi territory for up to three weeks—hopefully no longer—and will either confine Iraqis to their homes or convince them to flee north.

The first objective after the combat troops sweep through enemy lines will be to safeguard water supplies in the Iraqi part of the desert. The fast-moving troops will also "requisition" any food or vehicles from Iraqi civilians that commanders feel they need. Directly behind the armored fist of the attacking brigades will be Lt. Col. Kenneth Biser, a civil affairs officer who has planned the administration of the occupied areas.

"I certainly don't expect to be treated like a liberator," said Biser, of Thorpe, Wis., who is assigned to the corps' support command. But he added, "I really don't see our presence will be that long. Let's say we're looking at two to three weeks. Let's say we're hoping for two to three weeks."

The Army, which will be rolling through a desert marked by numerous hills, ledges and other potential sniper sites, hopes to deal with as few Iraqis in civilian clothes as possible. Many of the roaming Bedouins and residents of the dusty towns have already left the region.

Those who stayed behind will be under strict Army orders to stay away from U.S. troops. "We will encourage civilians to stay in their homes, don't come out and don't come near U.S. equipment," he said.

Even better, Biser said, he will urge them to flee north, "to get out of the area." Water will be as vital as security. Hundreds of trucks are already loaded with huge bladders of water and ready to go. But Biser said, "The number one resource we are looking for is water, the water wells."

The Army will also take over whatever it feels it needs to fuel a drive into Iraq. "If we find a warehouse of food, we would requisition it from the owner," he said. The requisition would be a description and photo of the property with a notice nailed to a door or left under a nearby rock.

"It's basically an IOU," Biser said.

There will be no haggling over price and, like the Godfather, the Army will not take no for an answer. "We'll say, 'I'm sorry, you have no choice,'" the colonel said. Biser said the detailed description and photo were required after some expensive and non-military items were requisitioned during the Panama invasion.

"So it's not a license to steal, although some people are calling it that," Biser said. "But let's face it, they started it."

Iraqis are expected to drift back into occupied areas after a week or more to check on their homes and property. At that point, the allies may have to enlist Iraqis to help administer the population and key facilities.

The military has no provisions to pay Iraqis, except food and cigarettes. "If they're hungry enough, they'll work," he said. "There's the good old trick to feed them. That's one attention-getter."

"Or cigarettes," he added. "But a couple cartons of cigarettes and take them up there, and I'm sure for a couple packs a day you can get all sorts of stuff done."

Quiet First Night at Navy Fleet Hospital No. 5: "The Bronx is Worse Than This So Far"

By Jane DeLynn

NAVY FLEET HOSPITAL No. 5 - Under cold and cloudy skies, the Arabian Gulf glowed a pale Caribbean green.

Two men jogged in sweats on the asphalt as a Blackhawk slowly settled on the helipad of Navy Fleet Hospital #5 for routine maintenance. Down by Aldew An, the 24-hour concession stand where almost 1,000 hamburgers, French fries and Pepsis are sold each day, sailors and Marines ate and chatted at big wooden tables.

A flock of seagulls flew overhead, and of course there was the occasional plane. Only a Third Country National, angrily stopped from chasing another around the tables by a Marine, gave even a hint of war. One of a group of three female Marines, looking at the barefooted and barechested TCN, said it was "the most fighting we've seen since we got here."

They had all volunteered to move closer to the front. It was a quiet night in the empty Casualty Receiving Ward as five medical corpsmen played Pictionary; others drove to the canteen to buy some candy and soda but it was closed.

Down at the pharmacy, one woman leafed through a January issue of Rolling Stone; another, when issuing a routine anti-depressant, complained how boring her job was.

The Casualty Receiving Ward perked up a little at 11—partly because it was time for "mid rats" (midnight rations, actually consumed a good half-hour early), and partly because the helicopter from the Airhead would soon arrive.

Although the copies of Stars and Stripes and Space News Roundup at the hospital entrance were dated Feb. 16, it was Feb. 24, almost the end of the first day of the ground war, and Navy Fleet Hospital #5 out of Portmouth, Va., had yet to receive its first patient.

This changed at 11:35 (p.m.), when the Casualty Receiving Ward welcomed its first two of seven patients that had been flown in to the airhead, but it was an astonishingly quiet first 20 hours for this 500-bed evac hospital.

The first two patients—a Marine who had his arm smashed in a firefight and a convalescee from appendectomy who had developed pneumonia—took a ten-minute helicopter ride from the Airhead to the fleet hospital's helipad, while the remaining five rode a more leisurely 45-minute ride on the ambulance bus.

None of them seemed any the worse for the unexplained two-and-a-half hour delay in the transportation chain that had taken them from battalion aid station to a C-130 transport to the naval hospital. In fact, they seemed remarkably cheerful.

"I feel good," said a Marine whose arm had been smashed in the early hours of the attack. "The IVs hurt more" than being wounded, said another, who had been hit in the shoulder and grazed in the neck.

A Marine with shrapnel wounds and a punctured eardrum said "I could get up and run right now." He described what it was like being hit. "I thought I was dead. Then I heard everybody talking, and I tried moving my arms."

He was not in much pain, and said that what bothered him most was the bumpy ambulance ride. "I want to get back to my unit," he said.

The lack of casualties did not much surprise Lt. Cmdr. John Halpern, who said that he had counted on the military to keep casualties down—although even he was surprised at the very low numbers. "The Bronx is worse than this so far," he said.

The emergency room specialist did his residency in Lincoln Hospital in the Bronx, one of the worst areas in New York City.

Although the nurses and corpsmen at the hospital do not wish for casualties, they clearly became stimulated as the moment for the arrival of casualties approached. They set up IV bags, laid out containers for blood samples, checked their cardiac monitors, and slipped on long gloves. "It's feast or famine," said a warrant officer. A corpsman flexed his muscles behind his T-shirt. "I'm pumped," he said. "My adrenaline is up," said another.

Warrant Officer Marsha Delavan, 41, said she envied the younger corpsmen.

"This is what they train for. This is the best there is. And they'll probably never have this experience again." She paused, then added: "I hope."

This was her second war. "The wounded are always the same. They're scared and they're hurt. You always tell them they're going to make it. Then they start to share, because they know they've already made it." She said that the wounded in this war had an advantage over the Vietnam veterans in that they knew they'd be welcome when they returned home.

Only Dr. Halpern seemed as relaxed as he had been earlier. "I've been in the Bronx too long," he said.

By one o'clock most of the patients had been sent on to X-Ray, pre-op or the various ICU and acute-care wards, and the three treatment teams settled down for the remainder of their 12-hour shift. "I've cried here. I hope I don't ever stop crying," a female on one of the treatment teams confessed earlier in the evening.

But for this night at least, at Navy Fleet Hospital #5, where no one had died or even suffered a life-threatening injury, tears weren't necessary.

Monday
February 25, 1991

There weren't enough buses for all the thousands of Iraqi prisoners.

The rough count of EPWs (enemy prisoners of war) on the first day alone was 10,000. Among them were many Iraqi troops who walked up and surrendered to surprised coalition troops who disarmed and frisked them, then told them to keep walking toward the rear where someone else would direct them to a camp.

All across the wide attacking front, prisoners by the bunkerful, by the dozens, sometimes by the company or battalion waved surrender leaflets or scarves and held out their hands to be cinched with plastic cuffs. There weren't enough plastic cuffs, either. Some allied troops broke out barbed wire, uncoiled it into a circle and sat the prisoners down inside it.

In the east, the Marines met only light resistance on their dash north to the Kuwaiti capital. Just being back inside Kuwait was a joy to the natives who had been forced to flee months before. They knew their homes would soon be in sight.

On the second day of the land war, some of the top allied generals and commanders began speaking openly of the design of the historic attack, saying it had been mainly based on a "massive deception" that kept the Iraqis guessing about where most of those 700,000 allied troops were stashed. Some pieces of the deception were still in progress, however. On the western front, the French and U.S. left flank had nearly reached their first objective and were making steady progress.

The Marine amphibious force on the ships was still aboard the ships.

The 1st Cavalry Division, assigned a reserve spot in the main plan, was still carrying out its secondary role of running a "feint" maneuver on the Saudi side of the border to confuse any Iraqis watching the rear of the allied attack. Any kind of secondary role was a wound to the pride of an outfit like the 1st Cav, and its soldiers began to worry that the war would be over before they would have the chance to join it.

From reports streaming into Gen. Schwarzkopf's command post, the tightly coordinated attack into the deep heart of southern Iraq had gone much faster than anticipated for the first day, but then appeared to wobble.

The Iraqi lines were so easily overcome that Gen. Schwarzkopf ordered the VII Corps, the main attacking force, and the remaining elements of the 18th Airborne Corps, farther west along the Iraqi border, to go in early—the afternoon of the first day instead of dawn of the second day as scheduled.

The two large components embarked within hours, but that night VII Corps seemed to stall just inside Iraq. Instead of exploiting the obvious weakness in the Iraqi defenses, and heading for the heart of the enemy's elite divisions, the VII Corps was moving cautiously, as though it might get hit at any moment.

As a story in this chapter says, commanders were under orders to move only by daylight. Moving only by daylight was smart, perhaps, given the possibilities for one coalition unit to get tangled with another friendly unit in the dark, or for tanks to dash too far ahead of their fuel supplies, or for panic to erupt amidst a mass nighttime movement through the ranks of another outfit, across territory that was probably mined. But it was cautious.

Meantime, the Iraqi Republican Guard appeared to be stirring, raising the possibility that its top-of-the-line T-72 Soviet-made tanks might succeed in blocking the main allied force long enough to let the reserve forces retreating from Kuwait escape.

The land war was only a few days old, and all the deception that had been carefully inserted in the allied plan was rapidly leaking out. And besides that, where were the allies going to put all these prisoners?

Here Comes the Republican Guard—And a Farewell Scud Launched from Kuwait

By Edith Lederer, Storer H. Rowley, and Joan Lowy

AT A U.S. AIR BASE IN CENTRAL SAUDI ARABIA - Rousted from their bunkers by an allied offensive, about 80 tanks from Iraq's crack Republic Guard were rumbling south early Monday toward advancing coalition forces, pilots flying over the battlefield said.

U.S. troops firing artillery had advanced some 30 miles into Iraq, pummeling the Iraqi forces, who offered little resistance, the pilots said early Monday. Army helicopters roamed 20 miles further ahead of the advancing force. "I think it's going exactly the way we thought it was going to go," said Lt. Col. Steve Turner, 41, of Portsmouth, Va., who commands a squadron of F-15E fighter-bombers at the largest U.S. air base in Saudi Arabia.

The Scud missile attack launched at the Saudi capital of Riyadh on Sunday night originated in central Kuwait, in a rare departure from traditional launch sites in western Iraq, Turner said. Along the Saudi border with western Kuwait and eastern Iraq, an intricate system of zig-zag-shaped ditches filled with fuel has been set ablaze and is billowing smoke, he said.

So quick and successful was the allied advance that Army reserve units originally slated to be held back for the first 24 hours were committed 12 hours into the offensive, he said. He said the long months of economic embargo, combined with the relentless bombing of the nearly 40-day air war, weakened Iraq in advance of the offensive, but hadn't dislodged its dug-in troops.

The start of the ground assault early Sunday, which brought allied troops racing across the border, at last started bringing the Iraqis up from their bunkers, including the Republican Guard reserves in northern Kuwait and southern Iraq. "They're finally flushing," said Turner. "They've got to do something—either that, or get killed in their holes. This is the group we've been beating on for the last couple of weeks, and they finally started moving," added Turner. He estimated there were "around 80 tanks or so moving southeast and southwest."

Allied aircraft have been pounding Republican Guard positions for weeks because coalition commanders expect a counter-attack would be mounted by Iraqi leader Saddam Hussein's loyal presidential guard. "The tanks and stuff I saw were probably . . . 25-35 miles north of the border," said Capt. Mark Alred, 33, of Tulsa, Okla., who flew an F-15E mission Sunday night to lay mines on a bridge near Basra. Other F-15E fighter-bombers were hitting bridges in that area of southern Iraq.

Alred also flew above the forward line of advancing allied forces in Iraq, where he saw U.S. artillery barrages sending shells north toward Iraqi positions.

"I didn't see anything being shot to the south. Not until I got to Basra," said Alred. "Basra got a new load of bullets last night." He said his plane was fired on by roughly 15 or 20 batteries of anti-aircraft artillery and sustained ground fire. He also thought he saw the Scud attack being launched Sunday night.

Alred painted a picture of Kuwait in flames.

For the first time Sunday night, he said, he saw 30 or 40 oil wells in the disputed Rumallah oil field in northern Kuwait, in addition to the burning oil wells across south-central Kuwait and west of Kuwait City. Along the western Saudi-Kuwaiti border and in the tri-border area with Iraq, Alred said, "all the tank ditches are on fire. Fifteen or 20 ditches and there are some roaring fires up there. What that's created— there's a black cloud" that runs northwest in straight, parallel, ribbon-like strips carried by the wind and stretching 80-100 miles into Iraq, he said.

Scud Missile Strikes Barracks in Dhahran, Killing U.S. Troops; Bad Weather Busts Results for "Scud-busters"

By Storer H. Rowley, Edith M. Lederer, and Joan Lowy

This report contains hard news about Iraq use of bad weather to conceal Scud launchers, and stepped-up allied efforts to find and destroy launch sites.

A U.S. AIRBASE, CENTRAL SAUDI ARABIA - Iraq deliberately chose an overcast night Monday to launch a deadly Scud missile attack on Saudi Arabia knowing that the allies' best Scud-busting fighters are blinded by bad weather, U.S. pilots said. The pilots who fly F-15E fighter-bombers, the prime Scud-hunting force, increased their Scud-hunting hours starting Tuesday morning, but expressed growing frustration over their inability to completely wipe out Iraq's Scud arsenal.

"The weather is a problem for us tonight (Monday night)," said Col. Dave Baker, 44, of Phoenix, deputy commander for air operations at the largest U.S. air base in Saudi Arabia. Baker oversees two squadrons of F-15E Strike Eagles responsible for nightly Scud patrols. "The weather precludes us from seeing where they actually launch the Scuds, which is really frustrating for the guys who go on station out there," Baker said early Tuesday.

At least 12 U.S. service personnel were killed and more than 50 injured Monday night in a Scud missile attack on a barracks in Dhahran in Eastern Saudi Arabia. There was another Scud alert early Tuesday on the Saudi capital of Riyadh.

Iraq has launched more than 60 Scud missiles at Saudi Arabia and Israel since the Persian Gulf War began on Jan. 17.

"Most of the launches have been when the weather was so lousy that we couldn't get underneath it, and they knew that and they shot it," said Lt. Col. Steve Turner, 41, of Portsmouth, Va., commander of the 236th Tactical Fighter Squadron.

"Pilots risk being hit by aircraft artillery when they descend to lower altitudes to get under cloud cover, said Turner, who was on Scud patrol Monday night in an F15E in western Iraq. He didn't find any targets and bombed a bridge and railroad car instead.

"One almost hit one of our guys (several weeks ago). It came rocketing up through the clouds," Turner recalls. "If we saw it, we could go in and bomb it."

"We have found a number of them. We are out there working and have blown them up. I think we have pretty well beaten up on known (launch) sites. Usually the ones that we don't get are the mobile ones, and they seem to just pop up," Turner said. Baker said, "We've depleted not only a lot of his support capabilities, but the actual Scuds themselves." He noted that the 335th and 336th Tactical Fighter Squadrons had destroyed a total of between 15 and 25 Scud missiles.

"It's frustrating until you find something, and then it's very rewarding, because like fishing and you get a big strike, you get that adrenaline rush and you've got something and it becomes very, very fruitful," Baker said.

Capt. Rich Horan, 32, of Walnut Creek, Calif., a weapons systems officer aboard an F-15E, said, "There has been more than one time when we brought bombs back from going on a Scud-hunting mission because there wasn't anything to bomb, or we weren't sure about it. We're trying to find a vehicle in a large area of space . . . We're talking about a small space and you're looking for a truck . . . It's just not easy," he said just before leaving on a Scud-hunting mission early Tuesday.

Despite fighter reconnaissance and information from AWACS planes, and satellite imagery, Horan said most of the time pilots are roaming over a large area without a specific Scud target. "Iraq has its mobile Scud launchers about the size of a semi-tractor trailer truck, under bridges and other structures.

"By comparison, targeting tanks or other military vehicles is a lot easier," he said. "A tank is part of a brigade or division. It's easy to track the movement. They don't just randomly move one tank. If we were just looking for one purple tank we'd probably never find it," Horan said.

"There hasn't been a night since the war started that I can remember that we haven't been out looking for Scuds," he said. "It's a lot more frustrating than most sorties because I think our element (a pair of F-15Es) has gotten maybe one or two Scuds in a couple of dozen sorties." Baker said the F-15E squadron started increasing their "time on station" Tuesday morning. "We are going to keep our people up there longer and keep our presence right there," he said. "We're the Scud-busters. And that's the way it's going to remain."

F-15Es have been concentrating their Scud searches in western Iraq along the Syrian and Jordanian borders, which pilots call "Scudville." Monday's attack came from the area near Basra in Iraq, a stronghold of the Republican Guard.

"This one that hit Dhahran tonight is a real tragedy. It's the first time he's really done some damage," Baker said. "One thing it will do is it will prick a little bit of hope in everybody's heart who is over here trying to end this damn thing, that's for sure."

"What kind of scenario do you paint when we re-take Kuwait and he is still lobbing Scuds into Saudi Arabia and towards Israel? That is a question that needs to be addressed. I don't want my sons to have to come out here and finish what we didn't finish 10 or 15 years from now," Baker said. He said the Iraqis have learned to use bad weather as protective cover when launching their missiles. "They are kind of stupid, but they are not real stupid. They know we're there, they take advantage of the weather like anybody would, I guess," said Baker, who also pilots F-15Es on Scud-killing missions.

Horan said commanders vary the mission of pilots hunting Scuds with other targets, because Scud patrol is longer and more tiring. They go 600 or 700 miles a mission, refueling several times along the way, which can amount to more than five hours. "The lengths of the Scud missions are so long that they are really draining on you physically. Every time he launches a Scud, it upsets me," Horan said.

"It's Saddam versus the world. It's just pretty sickening the things they've done."

Dawn Battle Looms for Phantom Brigade 100 Miles Inside Iraq—But Where is the Enemy?

By Douglas Jehl

NEAR AL BUSSAIYA, Iraq - A massive American armored force has roared deep within Iraq after rumbling virtually unopposed across miles of empty desert in an overland assault slowed only by need to round up the Iraqi troops who have surrendered in its path.

But the Army offensive nearly 100 miles into enemy territory is now almost certain to be confronted by the elite Republican Guard forces held in reserve by Iraq against such an assault against its territory. The looming battle could pit two entire U.S. Army corps, including this 1st Armored Division, against what remains of the four main Republican Guard divisions.

In a prelude to that anticipated fight, this division began Monday night to fire a heavy barrage of rocket artillery at a well-defended Iraqi outpost here at a strategic position well to the west of the Kuwaiti border. If this enormous Army force succeeds in capturing its objective near here, the commander of this division's lead brigade said he believed it could present a fait accompli to the Iraqi army and could force its surrender. But the commander, Col. James Riley, said he could not be confident that the Iraqi leader, Saddam Hussein, would bow to such military logic.

"That's where my vision of the future turns cloudy," Riley said.

This division closed in on this crossroads town late Monday after a 26-hour charge across Iraq that saw its tanks and armored vehicles stretched out in a flying wedge battle-formation across miles of enemy territory.

To each side was another Army division, with cavalry units to the north, on a rumbling charge that created a dust storm of its own as the armor headed northward.

But in this division, the attack slowed significantly as this lead brigade confronted enemy positions that provided almost no opposition but offered up mass surrenders that took much of the afternoon to be rounded up.

"You've been victimized by success," the division commander, Maj. Gen. Ronald H. Griffith, assured his subordinates by radio. But the slowdown clearly proved frustrating to American commanders whose prisoner collection resources were quickly overwhelmed.

There were reports elsewhere in the division of resistance that led to skirmishes against Iraqi forces. But this lead brigade faced no enemy fire in continuing a northward charge that began Sunday afternoon, and did not find a need to lock-and-load its weapons until more than 50 miles inside Iraq.

In its only engagement until the artillery bombardment tonight, the brigade opened fire with artillery, mortar and tanks at an Iraqi military training camp believed to shelter a small resistance force. But the facility had been deserted, as its defenders fled into the desert and then turned themselves over to American troops. By nightfall, the brigade had taken nearly 400 prisoners, about half of them believed to have come from the compound.

The brigade had launched into Iraq at 4:30 p.m. Sunday, roaring through pre-exploded holes in an Iraqi border berm in a wide-flank armored attack in which commanders were so confident of encountering no immediate opposition that all headed into battle with hatches open to the sky. The unit, known as the Phantom Brigade and attached here from the 3rd Infantry Division, served as the advance guard for the 1st Armored Division in the centerpiece of the VII Corps attack.

The massive Army overland assault, from a position well to the west of Kuwait, was launched some 12 hours after the U.S. ground offensive began in what was to be the main American strike force in a bid to penetrate deep within Iraq.

"The soldiers know this is the way home," said Maj. Roy Adams, the brigade operations officer, as thousands of tanks, armored personnel carriers, and other vehicles began to head north in a battle formation that stretched across the horizon.

"And it's the right thing to do."

Soldiers wore chemical protective suits and had taken pills designed to ward off the effects of nerve gas. But with intelligence reports showing no enemy forces immediately in front of the Army forces, the probe across the eight-foot-tall, double-walled border berm was launched with little apprehension.

Instead, commanders have long focused their attention on what they would encounter after reaching this northern city, not far from the positions where Republican Guard divisions have established set defenses.

The initial attack came on a gusty, gritty day that turned the desert dusky with blowing sand, most helicopters were grounded and tanks rumbled in vast formations across the desert with no forward guard. But Griffith, the division commander, hovered at the border to watch as the division's hundreds of tanks and armored vehicles crossed into Iraq. A gunner held up a sign that said "Welcome to Iraq" and the brigade commander, Col. James Riley, came on a radio network to remind his men—attached to this division that they were about to qualify for the combat-duty patch that soldiers wear on their right side.

"When we cross that line," he said, "shift that Marne patch from the left side of your helmet to the right, because that's where it will belong."

Earlier, on the eve of battle, Lt. Gen. Frederick Franks, commander of the VII Corps, had told commanders here in an emotional pep talk that "the only way to get him out of Kuwait is to destroy the Iraqi army. I wish you luck," he said.

The division encountered no enemy resistance in its first hours of battle, and suffered its only casualties in a minor auto accident and the explosion of a dud artillery shell that left three soldiers wounded.

Indeed, despite concerns about possible enemy minefields, the principal threat to the U.S. advance in those first hours of the attack came from unexploded ordnance, believed to have been left over from an earlier American bombardment. Some units had to pick their way through areas where bombs and shells lay scattered on the ground; later, terrain that proved unexpectedly difficult to negotiate also slowed the Army advance.

The Sunday afternoon launch of this VII Corps attack represented a last-minute acceleration of a plan that had initially called for the main Army assault to come early Monday morning. Commanders said the change of schedule was apparently a response to successes elsewhere along the front, where Marines and Arab forces made better than expected progress in the early hours of the American ground offensive.

The absence of opposition—at least in the initial forward surge—came as a relief to officers here whose units had begun to spot Iraqi drones flying over massed U.S. positions south of the border in surveillance missions some feared would cause Iraq to shore up its defenses. Instead, as the division charged its first 30 miles into Iraq, its forward elements found terrain as barren as that of northern Saudi Arabia, with only rusty oil drums and the remains of observation posts to suggest that Iraq had ever maintained a military presence.

A first night in the desert Sunday was as peaceful as any south of the border, with only an extra-strict blackout an indication that the unit was in enemy territory.

But the skirmishes Monday afternoon, and then the artillery bombardment Monday night, brought the sound of war home.

"It'd pay everybody to get a little rest tonight," Riley advised as a rainstorm tore across the desert, and commanders plotted the battle that was to begin at dawn.

82nd Airborne's Piece of Cake—"They'd Be Coming Out of Holes Waving a White Flag All Over the Place"

By Robert Dvorchak

IN SOUTHERN IRAQ - The 2nd Brigade of the 82nd Airborne Division took thousands of prisoners and suffered "not one man scratched" in casualties during a deep thrust inside Iraq on the first day of the ground war.

"I think it's going to be a piece of cake," said Maj. Robert Pinson, the brigade's executive officer. The Iraqi army crumbled en masse, offering virtually no resistance to an onslaught of artillery and infantry from U.S. and French forces advancing on the western flank of Sunday's invasion.

Everywhere across a wide front, Iraqis abandoned their tanks, guns and bunkers dug into the rocky desert. In one startling scene, 42 Iraqis marched single file without guards through American lines. Some held safe-passage leaflets dropped from airplanes, flashed V for victory signs with the fingers, smiled and mugged for cameras.

The flood of POWs bogged down the assault.

Soldiers were running short of the plastic flexi-cuffs used to tie POWs hands, and engineers ran short of explosive because they blew up so many bunkers.

"We could have gone a lot farther except we had so many POWs," said Col. Ron Rokosz, brigade commander. "It actually slowed down the attack."

"You'd come over the ridges and they'd be coming out of their holes waving a white flag all over the place. It was the most incredible thing I have ever seen," Rokosz said.

The brigade, the first U.S. forces to enter Iraq, expected to face two brigades of enemy soldiers—about 2,000 men—plus tanks. But the ground campaign was as successful as the air war. Artillery batteries and high-tech multiple-launch rocket systems lobbed deadly fire from long distance. Then infantrymen in 5-ton trucks, a motorized version of mounted cavalry, charged across the rocky desert to find the Iraqis disintegrating.

By the end of the day, just the sight of coalition forces was enough to make the Iraqis give up. "As soon as we got within sight, boom, the white flags went up," Rokosz said. "Their morale is shot. They don't want to fight."

"There's no way I thought we could have done it, not in a million years," said Rokosz, 45, of Chicago, Ill. "To take that much terrain, that much equipment and that many prisoners and we have not had a single soldier scratched so far."

The battlefield was littered with Iraqi discards—abandoned tanks, abandoned anti-aircraft guns, recoilless rifles, mortars, AK-47 assault rifles, gas masks, bullets and bunkers. There were pairs of combat boots tossed along a road behind fleeing Iraqis.

The assault started from a foothold inside Iraq at 4 a.m. You could see the rockets riding a tail of flame and smoke heading toward Iraqi targets. The ear-splitting blasts from 155mm howitzers were enough to slap the canvas against the side of a Humvee,

By early afternoon, two Iraqis could be seen with their hands up in the desert, walking to American forces. The trickle soon turned into a flood.

"No better way to fight a war," said Lt. Mark Shepard, 29, of Lewisburg, Ohio, who serves with the 4th Battalion. "The infantry's just throwing up their arms. We're bogged down with so many prisoners." His group was searching about 100 prisoners. POWs sat silently in the sand, their hands over their heads, waiting to be searched and transported.

"We're running out of flexi-cuffs to tie their hands," said Lt. Michael Bottiglieri, 23, of San Antonio, Tex. "I thought we were supposed to fight a war, not run a processing center," said one trooper, overwhelmed by the flood of prisoners.

Down the road, a line of 42 POWs walked in file to the south. The amazing thing was they didn't even have U.S. guards escorting them as they walked to the rear. "When's the last time the world saw something like that," said Capt. Clint Esarey, a public affairs officer.

Officers were almost giddy at the way things were going.

"I think we just overwhelmed them," Pinson said. "By cutting this deep, we're cutting his logistics lines. Without supplies, he's going to wither on the vine."

Amazingly, no U.S. forces were injured. "The biggest hazard now is being trampled by the EPWs," said Maj. Carl Horst, operations officer for the 2nd Battalion.

Spec. 4 Arthur Hiscox, 21, of Downer's Grove, Ill., helped capture a group of about 15 prisoners. He yelled at them to "Raise your hands" in Arabic, and the group complied willingly, being herded like Bedouin goats.

"They were sweating big time. They were freaking out. We have too much firepower," said Hiscox. "There will be less deaths this way. Peace will come quicker."

The American forces attacked wearing charcoal-lined suits to protect them from chemical attack. No chemicals were detected, but the suits became hot and sweaty as the day wore on.

One of the busiest crews were the 307th Combat Engineer Battalion, which destroyed bunkers and leftover weapons with satchel charges. They blew up about eight bunkers, four ammunition sites and two artillery pieces. At dusk, they were busy making more explosives. "It's a cakewalk. I thought it'd be a lot harder than this, but it ain't over yet," said Staff Sgt. Kenneth Nobles, 29, an engineer from Meridian, Miss.

The paratroopers had reached their objective called Rochambeau by dusk. At 5:30 a.m. today, they renewed their assault with more artillery and rocket blasts.

Monday - February 25, 1991

Massive Deception—Now It Can Be Told: "They Were At the Wrong Place At the Wrong Time"

By Neal MacFarquhar and Philip Shenon

WITH THE VII CORPS IN IRAQ - A massive deception plan involving the largest movement of tanks since World War II fooled the Iraqi army into leaving a mammoth hole that allowed allied forces to move more than 75 kilometers into Iraq on the first day of the ground war, military officials said Monday.

By concentrating its initial buildup and attacks along the Saudi border with Kuwait, American forces tricked the Iraqis into moving what reinforcements they had into a valley that runs along the border between Iraq and Kuwait—far from the allied points of entry along the Saudi border with Iraq.

"They bought it," said one Army captain who spent today monitoring Iraqi troop movement along the border. "They were at the wrong place, wrong time."

The deception began as soon as the VII Corps arrived here in mid-December from its headquarters in Germany and concentrated its training and maneuvers in the Saudi desert south of Kuwait. It only moved its forces, including thousands of tanks and tens of thousands of troops, to the Iraqi border 10 days before the ground war began.

Col. Johnnie B. Hitt, commander of VII Corps aviation, said moving three divisions up to the border was just as difficult as bringing them to Saudi Arabia from Germany. "Moving three divisions through the desert has not been done since World War II," he said.

To further confuse the Iraqis about American intentions, the Army's 1st Cavalry Division was put into position near the Kuwait border and repeatedly charged against Iraqi troops, including the weak reinforcement that Iraq had put in place. The idea, officials said, was to convince the Iraqis that the main American thrust would come close to the Kuwaiti border, more than 100 miles east of the actual point of entry.

The weak reinforcements indicated that Iraq's army was stretched thin, they said.

When the American forces moved into Iraq, the expected resistance from an Iraqi division north of the border with Iraq never materialized.

There was so little resistance that the American forces quickly revised their battle plan to move their main armored divisions north 10 hours earlier than planned. "We had to totally revise the ground plan," Col. Hitt said. "There was enemy right over the border, but they were not fighting."

There was some concern today that the Iraqis might be laying a trap for allied armor, by moving them (ed.—inducing the allies to move) without sufficient reinforcements into the vicinity of the Republican Guard, the elite Iraqi forces concentrated just above Kuwait. Capt. David Clark, a VII Corps intelligence officer, said, "We're monitoring this closely and we think we can keep our forces out of the way of the bad guys."

Officers also said the speed of the advance north into Iraq had actually been slowed overnight out of fear that they would overextend their supply lines.

The 2nd Armored Cavalry Regiment, which led the VII Corps into Iraq on Sunday, had moved more than 75 kilometers in one day and was stopped to give heavy armored units the chance to catch up. "You don't want to move too quickly, you'll lose more men by being too quick, moving too hard, than in receiving fire," Col. Hitt said. Hitt, trying to move 80,000 (pounds) of aviation fuel north with one of the armored units, was amazed Sunday as he discovered that division after division had crossed the border hours ahead of schedule.

"Golly," the 44-year-old colonel said in the twang of his native Wills Point, Tex., after discovering that another armored division had already picked up and moved before his trucks had the chance to reach it.

"It's a problem, how do you keep up with success?" he said.

American military officials hoped that the sudden, violent thrusts into Iraq will prompt the Republican Guard to leave their dug-in positions in southern Iraq to confront the American forces, leaving their tanks exposed to aerial attacks.

On Sunday, American officials said, one unit of the guards moved to preestablished revetments toward Kuwait, apparently in response to the coalition invasion into Kuwait, but that there was not initial movement toward the west.

Allied commanders cautioned that a large battle was still expected between the Guard and the armored forces of the VII Corps, as well as Britain's 1st Armored Division.

Capt Clark, the military intelligence officer, said he expected the armor battle soon. "It will be short but bloody," he said. "Either they will come out or the others will come in and push them out," Col. Hitt said.

Just a Shitload of POWs: "Iraq is Arab and Kuwait is Arab. I Don't Know Why We Want Kuwait"

By Douglas Jehl

WITH THE PHANTOM BRIGADE, Iraq - They seemed to come from everywhere and nowhere, prisoners materializing in the desert, white flags suddenly visible across the sand.

Tattered, thin, and hungry, many had fled a remote Iraqi training camp as it was taken under fire by this advancing Army brigade, and now were coming forth from all directions to tender their surrender.

Others said they had been walking for days, headed south from their military posts and the horror of the allied air bombardment and toward the promised generosity of the American invaders. Some still carried the leaflets dropped as part of a U.S. psychological warfare campaign, each one depicting a crude caricature of a forlorn Iraqi soldier encircled by American battle tanks. And as this 1st Armored Division (moved) northward over little-defended terrain, its armored tanks and personnel carriers in a flying wedge across the desert, it seemed for most of the afternoon as if that cartoon had become reality.

"Iraq is Arab, and Kuwait is Arab," one apologetic Iraqi soldier told his Army captors. "I don't know why we want Kuwait."

U.S. officers in this brigade, which took its first three prisoners early Monday afternoon, started off according to a grand plan that called for military police to escort each small group toward interrogators at the rear.

But the numbers soon swelled beyond imagination as they Army continued its northward march, more white flags and handkerchiefs waving every mile, and soon the task of taking prisoners had become almost overwhelming.

Tanks and armored vehicles waited in their tracks, an entire division halted in its advance, as soldiers scurried to round up the Iraqis who made clear long before a shot was fired that they would rather quit than fight.

"What does Saddam do?" asked one stunned American soldier, a driver in a Bradley fighting vehicle. "Just take people off the streets and give them guns?"

"Ain't going (to be) nobody left to fight," grumbled his commander, Maj. Roy Adams, only half in jest as he stood grime-faced in the turret, where as the brigade operations officer he had become a director of the roundup.

A few miles forward, a Cobra attack helicopter was herding from a hover as two-dozen prisoners marched obediently south, having flagged down the chopper as it patrolled the desert in their haste to surrender. Another Cobra fired a few shots at an Iraqi armored vehicle before its passengers and crew piled out, in haste, waving the white flags they seemed to have set aside for the occasion.

But more typical as the prisoner tally for this brigade alone climbed from the scores into the hundreds, were the Iraqis who walked toward advancing armored vehicles, unarmed and their uniforms almost unrecognizable, often carrying little but a canteen and a rudimentary gas mask. First there would be two or three, appearing in the middle of the desert.

And then, as the brigade moved in to attack the training camp, they came in groups of 20, 30 or even more, having scattered in four directions as the Americans rumbled north.

By nightfall, what began as a novelty had clearly become a burden.

Asked how many prisoners he had gathered in what was perhaps his battalion's fifteenth roundup of the afternoon, Lt. Col. Pat Egan had given up his careful count.

"I got a shitload of 'em," he said.

VII Corps' Majesty and Menace: After 2nd Armored Cav, 1st Armored, 3rd Armored, 1st Infantry, British 1st Armored

By Phil Shenon

WITH THE U.S. VII CORPS IN IRAQ - From the air over the scrub-covered Iraqi desert, it was a scene today both of majesty and of utter menace—more than 100,000 American fighting men and their machines, stretched from the border of Saudi Arabia north into the dusty horizon, deep into the core of enemy territory.

Military officers described this massive convoy as the single largest American troop movement since WW II. Everywhere, desert sands that had been marked until yesterday morning only with the hoof prints of camels and the footprints of their Bedouin masters had become a frantic thoroughfare for the day-old northward push of American troops, weapons and equipment from the Army's VII Corps.

The men and their heavy armor, which included thousands of tanks, stretched as far north and south as the eye could see beneath darkly overcast skies.

During a helicopter trip with corps officials today deep inside Iraq, it was possible to make out individual American soldiers as they peered into the distance, their faces a picture of exhilaration to have penetrated so far behind the Iraqi border, and apprehension at what may lay just beyond. "When you looked down, almost every soldier would give you a thumbs-up or wave a small flag," said Sgt. Major Martin Shupe, 44, of Palm Springs, Calif. who traveled aboard the helicopter at dawn this morning to photograph the convoy. "You see it, and there's a pride in being an American and being involved in something so historic."

One set of the softly undulating sand-swept hills 25 miles into Iraqi territory was littered with burned-out American rocket pods. The deadly rocket had apparently been fired only hours earlier against Iraqi troop positions to the North. Nearby were the shells of several and a small crater created by the explosion. The VII Corps, which forms the leading edge of the American-led ground assault on Iraq, first crossed the mine-studded border from Saudi Arabia early Sunday morning.

By Monday afternoon, the corps' chief scouts, the men of the Army's 2nd Armored Cavalry Regiment, were reported to have reached more than 70 miles north and east into Iraq, leading a modern day wagon trail of men and heavy armor.

As the most powerful American military unit deployed in the war against Iraq, the VII Corps, which is based in Germany, has been assigned arguably the most important mission of the land campaign; destroying the Republican Guard, Iraq's most formidable military force.

American military officials have reported only light resistance so far to the assault into Iraq, and thousands of Iraqi soldiers have been taken prisoner in the first two days of the ground war. At the front of the trail snaking into Iraq today were heavily armored scouting vehicles of the 2nd Armored Cavalry, an elite, largely self-contained squadron that also led Patton's Third Army into battle in Europe during World War II.

Behind the 2nd Armored Cavalry came the vast forces of the Army's First Armored Division, the Third Armored Division, The First Infantry Division, as well as the British First Armored Division. A gargantuan Union Jack was perched atop an armored communications vehicle that led British troops into Iraq this morning.

For the allied generals here, it was an emotional reunion for three of the divisions —the 1st Armored, the 1st Infantry, and the British—which had last fought together in the North African campaigns of World War II. "When you see a moving armored division, it's awesome," said Lt. Col. James. W. Gleisberg of the VII Corps Central Command. "It takes 30 minutes to go by. There are moving vehicles as far as you can see in both directions."

Today's convoy included every sort of vehicle and ground weapon. There were tanks, troop carriers, ammunition carriers, mobile rocket launchers, self-propelled howitzers, communication vans, fire trucks, ambulances, civilian buses to transport Iraqi prisoners of war, as well as flatbed trucks laden with rubber bladders of water and fuel. The skies along the convoy were thick with the black exhaust of the tanks and trucks, and the massive clouds of dust they had kicked up in their wake.

A two-hour helicopter tour organized by the VII Corps began with a rise south of the Saudi border where large military camps had been abandoned by American troops only hours before.

The desert has already begun to reclaim the camps, the sand and dust covering over the oil-stained helicopter landing zones and the endless mounds of empty blue drinking water bottles left behind by soldiers.

In a dramatic sweep north, the Army helicopter then crossed over the man-made ridge known to American soldiers simply as The Berm that had marked the border between Iraq and Saudi Arabia. The 12-foot high ridge had been breached at several points for troops and their heavy equipment to make the crossing into Iraq.

Monday - February 25, 1991

VII Corps Moving Only in Daylight—"We Will Show Up in Places the Iraqis Could Never Dream We Would Be"

By Michael Hedges

SOUTHEASTERN IRAQ - The two Iraqi captains looked scared and the American combat engineers planting demolition charges in what they thought was an empty bunker were shocked, but both groups recovered in time to transact a routine surrender.

The small drama was one of hundreds that occurred today as five coalition divisions streamed through a breech of Iraqi lines against light opposition, taking scores of prisoners.

The American VII Corps, reinforced by the U.S. 1st Cavalry and the British 1st U.K. Division drove toward objectives that would put them dozens of miles into Iraq and on the right flank of Saddam Hussein's army.

Today the British division, consisting of two brigades of "Desert Rats," passed through the breach made by the 1st Infantry yesterday, and marched on an Iraqi force to the northeast. The British trucks and armored vehicles, many flying colorful, historic battle flags, stretched on for miles down several lanes cut by American engineers.

While commanders here are pleased with the progress of the attack, the rate of advance had been slowed by a decision to move only during the day. That decision was made because of a number of friendly fire incidents before the start of the ground war, some officers said. But in the daylight, broad lines of American M1A1 heavy tanks cut across the desert at speeds approaching 50 miles per hour. "We will show up in places the Iraqis could never dream we'd be," a tank commander had said shortly before the ground war started.

Soldiers in the 1st Infantry Division conducted a nerve-wracking search of dozens of bunkers, some interlocked in vast systems, but surprisingly few Iraqis chose to fight.

Spec. Kevin Keller of the 9th Combat Engineers was part of a small group wiring charges in a bunker when suddenly two Iraqis emerged, one holding a sidearm over his head. "Damn, this is crazy," said Spec. Keller. "We were ready to blow the thing, and the squad leader hears them talking inside."

As the Iraqi captains stumbled outside, blinking against the light, they were gestured to the ground. For an uneasy minute, American soldiers were reluctant to approach them, aware that Iraqis elsewhere had blown themselves up on capture. But the men were soon frisked, their money and other pocket paraphernalia put in plastic bags, and their hands fixed with plastic binders. "This is pretty risky business," said Lt. Curtis Palmer, of Douglasville, Ga. "It is kind of scary when you go popping through those bunker doorways in the dark."

Earlier today, Bradley fighting vehicles full of troopers and Cobra attack helicopters assaulted a huge bunker complex on a small hill behind the main Iraqi line. Artillery blasted the hill, and the Cobras laced the hill with cannon and rocket fire.

But as has almost always been the case so far in this assault, the Iraqis fled without mounting a defense. Private Reuben Perez, of La Puente, Calif., said his Bradley platoon had cleared out a number of bunkers without being fired upon.

But the platoon did engage in a couple brief firefights last night. "We picked up some dismounts coming out of their holes and running to another hole, and we fired them this morning," he said. "That included 11 officers, the highest ranked one was a colonel. They were just coming out of the bunkers like crazy."

American troops who had heard accounts of starving, threadbare Iraqi soldiers before the ground war commenced have been astonished at the things they are finding in bunkers. Pvt. Perez said he cleared a bunker with a large velour sofa, a television powered by a generator, a small refrigerator, and large amounts of food and weaponry.

Lt. Palmer saw a command bunker with a shower stall complete with concrete floor, overstuffed chairs, fresh eggs, and fruit, and a VCR with the taped movie "Scruples" inside.

At the site where engineers were destroying Iraqi bunkers, soldiers also ruined hundreds of Soviet-made AK-47 rifles and RPG-7 rocket launchers. One soldier pulled a large supply of new, unopened olive green uniform shirts from a bunker. Large numbers of packs, canteens, and helmets littered the field, most in good condition. All the bunker locations had dumps littered with canned foods, mostly fruits and vegetables, as well as packs of Sumer cigarettes. "They've been living pretty well," said Lt. Palmer.

Across the front where the Iraqi line was breached, dozens of trucks smoldered, some many hours since they'd been demolished in air strikes. At one location, three twin-barreled anti-aircraft guns had been twisted into unnatural postures by bomb blasts.

The aim of the artillery and air strikes seemed good. Ugly chunks of shrapnel littered hills where bunker complexes were arrayed. Multiple Launch Rocket System rocket tubes protruded from the earth like giant cigar stubs. One huge chunk of a 2,000-pound bomb lay just a few feet from a massive bunker.

But soldiers excavating the Iraqi lines have found few dead or wounded enemy. And most of the bunkers had withstood the pounding without collapsing.

"The bombing didn't do as much as I expected," said Lt. Palmer. "Trucks, arty, anything above ground, it got that, but the bunkers are unharmed."

Still, the lack of evidence that Iraqis could be bombed out of bunkers seemed of small consequence, at least so far. More than a thousand enemy soldiers have surrendered to the 1st Infantry Division alone.

Division casualties were believed to be less than a dozen injured and only one fatality as of early afternoon today. And most of those casualties, including the death, were caused by soldiers triggering unexploded ordnance from U.S. bombing and artillery raids.

Throughout the day, artillery could be seen peppering targets on the horizon. Occasionally, the hollow crack of Bradley 25mm guns or the louder thump of M1A1 120mm cannons could be heard, but there were no sustained armored battles involving 1st Infantry troops.

The success of the early days of the campaign into Iraq has created a mood of confidence and excitement in the U.S. troops, but few expect the honeymoon to last.

"We are moving forward soon, and where we're going we expect him (Saddam Hussein) to have Republican Guards," said 1st Lt. Dan Connella of Flagstaff, Ariz., a trooper with the 4th Squadron, 7th Cavalry. "We have reports he is moving them to meet us. It took him awhile to figure this out, but I think he finally knows we're here."

Monday - February 25, 1991

French and U.S. Force Closes on Iraqi Air Base: "I Love It ... We Know We'll Be Going Home Soon"

By Joseph Albright

WITH THE U.S. ARMY (deleted) MILES INSIDE IRAQ - French and American ground troops closed in on a key Iraqi airbase (deleted) south of Baghdad Monday as they continued wheeling northeast.

"Hopefully we will be there in a few hours," said American artillery Maj. Mark Rambis, 35, of Shelburn, Ind. He was talking about one of several recently-built Iraqi military airfields that used to help guard the southern reaches of the empty border desert. Six months ago the airfield was a busy hub for Iraqi fighter-bombers, but since the air war began, it has been hit repeatedly and knocked out of service.

Some troops were said to be holding out in bunkers, but hundreds of other troops on the main access road to the base could be seen sitting cross-legged behind rolled barbed wire barricades in makeshift allied prisoner-of-war camps.

An allied caravan numbering thousands of vehicles streamed across the hard-packed desert toward the airbase. The main northwest artery, a well-maintained Iraqi two-lane highway, was packed with every imaginable size and shape of allied military vehicle, from heavy tanks and towed cannons to earthmovers, semi-trailers carrying ammunition, French desert wheeled-personnel carriers and troop carriers packed with extra food and cots.

This main supply route, code-named Texas, was virtually solid with northbound traffic for the 30 miles just north of the border. The traffic is broken down into convoys, with each one assigned a priority for movement toward the front. Further north, as the road approaches the Iraqi town (name censored) adjacent to the airbase, the traffic thins out and only tanks, artillery and other weaponry was heading north. Every few miles, clumps of Iraqi prisoners sat by the highway cross-legged, their hands bound behind their backs while American GIs stood guard with M-16s.

At one point, south of (name deleted) the airbase, two Iraqi soldiers sat by the road waiting to surrender. They gave up to a CBS camera crew. Further on, two groups of green-garbed Iraqis walked beside the road waiting to surrender, but there were no military police available to capture them. They kept walking south through the grey, drizzly day, sometimes dashing out onto the pavement when a passing soldier tossed out a food packet from their MRE packs. Some prisoners carried leaflets dropped by the Americans calling for their surrender. One Iraqi soldier, who said his name was Saad, told me as he walked south on the two-lane highway: "Saddam Hussein is ruining Iraq just like Hitler did in 1945. He is foolish. There is no food, no water. The Iraqi women don't want war."

(NOTE: Saad was not, repeat not, a prisoner when he gave this interview. Note to the JIB. This should be okay under the ground rules.)

As the prisoners walked down Main Supply Route Texas, their hands over their heads, they passed a truck full of American artillerymen moving forward to bombard the final defenses of the airbase ahead.

"I love it," said Spec. Terry Douglas, 20, of Gibson, N.C., when he saw the Iraqis walking south to surrender. "It makes us feel good. We know we'll be going home soon."

An hour earlier, artillerymen had been given tentative orders to lay another rain of cannon fire on artillery bunkers in the area where the surrendering soldiers came into view. Officers said the fire mission was cancelled at the last moment when word came from the front that the bunker-dwellers had decided to surrender.

Maj. Rambis, the operations officer of an artillery battalion, said the influx of prisoners heading south has slowed the progress of the American and French column.

"It is a little slower than we the artillery were expecting," he said. "There are little pockets of resistance that we have to take care of slowly." From the convoy route north, there is little physical evidence of the violence wrought by the American air and ground campaign. Only one corpse has been visible over the last two days.

Off to the sides of the road, half a dozen wrecked tanks and trucks have been seen, some still burning and scores of bunkers have been crushed along the roadside, their occupants having fled or been buried in the rubble.

Ahead on the horizon, a black cloud of smoke arises from (name of town deleted) what was once an Iraqi town of seven thousand inhabitants.

U.S. military officers said that its civilian population evacuated about ten days ago, leaving the town in the hands of Iraqi army reservists and militiamen.

Just over a rise were the remnants of five Iraqi military trucks, one of them on fire.

First Casualties Behind It, 1st Cav Feints, Feints Again, Then Joins the Charge Into Kuwait

By Mark Fritz

WITH THE WOLFPACK IN SOUTHERN IRAQ - Dave Francavilla looked down the deepening hole his armored unit was helping punch into Iraq on Monday and saw empty bunkers and abandoned positions.

Lead armor units of the US. Army's 1st Cavalry Division's 2nd Brigade rolled north behind a line of heavy U.S. artillery fire. They encountered only sporadic return artillery fire and scores of Iraqi prisoners.

"What we're encountering now is a lot of abandoned positions," said Francavilla, 32, commander of Charlie Company of the brigade's 1st Battalion, 5th Cavalry Regiment. "I don't know if they deserted or if they're destroyed or what, but we're being very careful."

Francavilla's company, nicknamed "The Wolfpack," of Bradley fighting vehicles and other platoons of Bradleys and M1A1 tanks maneuvered through two minefields, one about 250 meters deep, and fired precautionary shots at abandoned bunkers.

The 1st Cavalry initially had a few routes of advance to consider, but the apparent lack of Iraqi resistance prompted military commanders to attack north into Kuwait. One danger of such a fast plunge into opposing positions is the chance that ground units will get ahead of air and artillery cover, causing so-called "friendly fire" casualties.

Charlie Company radio chatter included several warnings about the artillery fire thundering behind them. Allied artillery fired white phosphorous shells to create a smoke shield for the advancing armor. Apache attack helicopters hung low on the periphery to provide air support. Black billows of smoke drifted into overcast skies from burning trenches filled with oil, the much-publicized Iraqi defense against an allied armored invasion. Francavilla said A-10 Thunderbolts fired tracer rounds into the oil the night before so it would ignite and burn out.

Charlie Company troops caught snippets of news from elsewhere on the front and were cautious but jubilant that the agonizingly anticipated ground war was, in its earliest stages, decidedly one-sided. "This is more like an exercise than a war," said Francavilla, of Colorado Springs, Colo. He did not rule out a trap.

"They liked to sucker the Iranians by lying back and suckering them in," he said. "But we keep passing trench line after trench line."

The early ease of the operation did much to uncoil the tightly wound 1st Battalion, which absorbed its first casualties of the war on Feb. 20.

A scout patrol with armored elements from Charlie Company and Alpha Company was hit by Iraqi mortar fire in an area that U.S. troops passed with ease on Monday. The patrol had taken an Iraqi bunker and seven prisoners when it was hit.

Three soldiers were killed and nine were wounded. When the first casualties were brought back, it left other troops a little afraid, a little angrier and a lot better prepared to deal with what might lay ahead.

As the battalion pressed deeper into Iraq, soldier after soldier reached back to Feb. 20 as a moment of truth before an hour of reckoning. "It was a heart-rending day," said Maj. Jim Noel, 37, a pediatrician from Eustis, Fla., who decided to return to active from reserve duty just before Iraq invaded Kuwait on Aug. 2. "It was a day they all grew up a little bit, a day they got a renewed sense of dedication," he said.

Noel, commander of a mobile medical unit that is the battalion's northern most, said he treated the casualties, including one who later died after he was evacuated to a field hospital at the rear. Noel performed three hours of surgery in the desert and gave the soldier 18 pints of blood.

"He had no blood pressure when he came in, but he had one when he went out," Noel said. "You hate to lose a patient anytime, but you hate to lose one of these guys. They're the heroes. They're fighting for me. To see purposely mutilated flesh that man did to man, it's hard to believe," he said.

"It was a feeling you'd never forget," said Master Sgt. Jonathan Shockley of Cleveland, 39, a chief medic the troops call "Doc Shock."

"To see a human life like that snuffed out—you've got to keep moving, keep functioning and rely on your training to do your job. War injuries are so, so . . . the velocity of the weapons dismembers so nastily."

As he barreled past Iraqi positions, Bradley driver Gary Valentine recounted the series of twists the war had given his life in the past few months.

One week after he was married, he was sent to Saudi Arabia, and just 23 days after he would have completed his commitment to the Army, he was invading Iraq. In the interim, he became close friends with a young soldier from Charlie Company who died in the mortar attack on Feb. 20. "It brought a lot of reality into the situation," said Valentine, 24, of San Jose, Calif. "I had a lot of plans that had to be postponed because of this."

Francavilla, also, had to reconcile his own personal ironies. As a Jew defending Saudi Arabia and fighting to liberate Kuwait, he was urged by his parents to change the religious affiliation on his dogtags in case of capture by Iraqis.

"Now is not the time to deny my God," said Francavilla, who said he knows a Jewish pilot in the battalion who changed the religion on his dogtags to Protestant.

"I'm fighting for the interests of the United States, and if the liberation of Kuwait is in the best interest of the United States, then so be it."

One part of the United States that Francavilla said he is most interested in right now is Dardanelle, Ark., which has adopted the Wolfpack and showered unit members with gifts, food, and letters.

Marines Spend Night in Underground Iraqi HQ Bunker That Somehow Escaped Weeks of Allied Bombing

By Phil Davison

Attention U.S. pool desk: PAO and field commanders are rushing out our material fast as poss. Gtfl ensure it is moving through interim points at same speed. Since material now being choppered from front lines, there is no reason for it to surface more than a few hours later. Note times of writing, for checking transmission speed.

WITH U.S. MARINES IN KUWAIT - The U.S. 2nd Marine Division moved forward towards its second objective on Monday after capturing and spending the night at a major Iraqi field headquarters.

The division stumbled on the underground desert HQ almost by chance within one mile of their original first day's assault objective and captured its commander, a major general. The regiment leading the division's assault spent the night blocking what officers called "piecemeal" attempts to counter-attack by Iraqi brigades. They exchanged mortar, artillery and heavy machine-gun fire throughout the night.

The commander of our unit, Lt. Col. David Whittle, said field reports he had compiled so far, though still sketchy, suggested more than 10,000 Iraqis captured by the Marines' 1st and 2nd Divisions. He knew of only six injuries serious enough for helicopter evacuation, including the crewman of an amphibious assault vehicle whose hand got trapped in its hatch.

Comments by Marine officers near the front lines suggested the Marine thrust into Kuwait was a preliminary punch, with other allied forces likely to follow through in other border areas on Monday.

We spent Sunday night crammed into our Humvee jeep-like vehicle at the underground HQ where Iraqi forces had slept in tiny, reinforced bunkers only the night before. The extent of the underground bunker system, including a command and control center, surprised Marine officers.

It was all but undetectable from above ground, where there were no buildings, no other sign of life, only electricity pylons cutting across the desert through Kuwait. Nor was there any sign of craters from allied bombs. It appeared the allies had been unaware of the field HQ despite its importance, according to Capt. David Fournier.

The Iraqis had lived in the most cramped conditions, two men to a six-by-eight-foot hole, only four feet high but reinforced by pipes, corrugated iron and cinder blocks. A colour TV set and VCR were found in the command center along with documents, according to Lt. Col. Wittle, that gave the Marines information on other Iraqi forces in the area.

The Marines captured about 100 automatic rifles, a 14.5mm anti-aircraft gun, mortars, explosives, and ammunition at the field HQ alone.

We were shown crates carrying 82mm high-explosive mortar rounds, with labels saying "GHQ Jordan Armed Forces, Dir of Plng and Org, Amman, Jordan." The initials appeared to refer to the Director of Planning and Organization.

Two rusting, sand-filled Soviet-made tanks stood half-buried in sand ditches near the HQ, clearly used as decoys by the Iraqis. The Marines did not immediately know the tanks' type but said they were unusable and probably more than 30 years old.

Sunday night, after congratulating the young men of his unit for a successful first day of combat, Lt. Col. Wittle made an informal but touching sunset speech.

Monday - February 25, 1991

Calling his men to gather round close because of incoming mortar rounds, he told them: "It was a good day for the Marine Corps and a major success for this unit."

Offering himself up for questions, he was asked "How long are we staying here, sir?"

"We're moving on," he replied. "This place sucks, we're movin'."

Lt. Col. Wittle played the cassette carrying his combat log. "Incoming snowstorm," he said at one point, speaking as his men went through Iraqi minefields. He was referring to incoming artillery or mortar fire, the nearest of which landed 75 yards left of his own vehicle.

Most incoming rounds were around 2,000 meters off-target, giving the Marines confidence that Saddam Hussein's artillery may not be a great threat as the assault continues.

After we snatched a few hours' sleep, still fully clad in chemical weapons suits, above our flak jackets, with rubber boots but without gas masks, we pieced together the events of Sunday. We had moved across one of several breaches, in a massive convoy of the 2nd Marine Division. After leaving our previous camp in Saudi Arabia at sunset, we had edged towards Kuwait in the night, then moved close to the border under cover of dark after the moon set at two a.m.

Moving through the several breaches, across two minefields, took almost five hours for the entire convoy. Maj. Charles J. Clarke, with our unit, explained to me Monday that the delays had been caused by the explosion of several mines containing mustard gas and, ironically, unexploded bombs apparently dropped by allied planes in recent air raids.

The vehicle carrying myself and three American newsmen was diverted from one breach lane to another when it was blocked off by the mustard gas alarm.

But tests revealed that the amount released was not of grave danger to human beings. An eight-inch oil pipeline also slowed the convoy down, after one vehicle caught its transmission on the pipe. It was eventually covered over with sand and we moved ahead.

"We were kinda sitting ducks right then," Maj. Clarke said Monday. But no Iraqi aircraft appeared and incoming artillery was way off target. "For two months you worry about that first hurdle. You worry that you're going to live through it," he said.

When we arrived at what turned out to be the Iraqi field HQ, infantrymen were already capturing large numbers of Iraqis. Even Marines forming part of logistics backup units joined in the search, moving around foxholes and themselves captured 27 prisoners.

Among them was the major general, taken prisoner by a delighted motor maintenance man called Lance Cpl. Steve Hotaling (from New York).

The Iraqi prisoners were poorly dressed in an assortment of uniforms but appeared reasonably well-fed. They flinched noticeably as allied warplanes screamed overhead, a sign of what they had been through for more than five weeks.

They were well-treated by the Americans and looked somewhat shocked to see the extent of the Marines' equipment. The Marines, in a few hours, had built greater fortifications at their new position than the Iraqis had done since the invasion of Kuwait.

As a few Marines listened to the BBC World Service on shortwave near the front lines Monday, they let out whoops when they heard reports that 14,000 Iraqis may have been taken prisoner. "We're going to liberate Kuwait today," said one Marine.

Barren Corner of Kuwait Still Barren, But Liberated and on 30th Anniversary of Independence from Britain

By Caryle Murphy

RAS AL ZOUR, Kuwait - The gas station is blown to bits. Electric power lines lay broken and tangled. Hidden mines are still a deadly menace and the six-lane highway has been torn up into chunks.

But for the Saudi and Kuwaiti troops massed in the desert here, this destruction is less important than the fact that they are here. Two days after Operation Desert Storm's ground war began, this barren corner of Kuwait, stretching 15 miles north from the Saudi border, is now in allied hands. For Kuwaitis it was a significant victory. But for most of them the real victory will not come until the liberation of the capital, Kuwait City, where most of them have homes and family members who have lived through the occupation.

It was not that hard to retake, according to Saudi Col. Belal al Jihani, who was among the first to enter Kuwait in the early hours of Sunday morning.

His troops met no resistance from the Iraqi troops who had occupied this area since their invasion of Kuwait six months ago. "I thought those two days would be the difficult days," Jihani said today. "But there was nothing from the Iraqis."

As he spoke, Saudi artillery was sporadically pounding Iraqi positions located north and west of the main highway here in what Jihani called a "protective" mode. It was not clear how much further up the road the Saudi troops, with their Kuwaiti allies behind them, had advanced today. The Iraqis were responding with some of their own artillery, and U.S. Marines, who had accompanied the Arab move into Kuwait Sunday, were still on the scene, calling in F-18s for air strikes on the Iraqi positions.

"We didn't see any bad guys," Maj. Robert Schoenwetter, of Long Beach, Calif., recalled when asked what the first allied troops into Kuwait encountered. "I thought we'd see a lot more. We keep waiting for the other shoe to fall."

The Kuwaitis, whose 5,000-strong army is one of the smallest in Operation Desert Storm's coalition, are integrated with Saudi forces. So far, Schoenwetter said, they have not participated in any fighting, "But I'm sure we will eventually," he added, not blinking an eye at the plural pronoun.

Kuwaiti armored personnel carriers, some flying the flags of Kuwait and the United States, moved up the highway today among the Saudi forces. And late this afternoon, long convoys of trucks were moving supplies to the Arab forces further north.

Another sign of how the tables had turned in this part of Kuwait came this afternoon with the arrival here of more than 100 Iraqi prisoners of war.

Subdued and apprehensive, they squatted in the middle of the road, surrounded by their Saudi captors who were taking down their names.

One of them, a reservist from Basra, (name deleted) was eager to talk when approached by a Kuwaiti TV crew. "I want to send a message to my mother and father and family and then I have some advice for the Iraqi army," Abbas said.

The talkative reservist, who stood up to address his Kuwaiti interviewers, said he was captured by "Saudis and Americans together. As soon as they came, we just raised our arms and we told them we didn't want to fight . . . and they welcomed us."

These POWs, like the 20,000 others taken so far since Operation Desert Storm began Jan. 17, will be held in camps by the Saudis until the end of the war. The much-vaunted Iraqi defenses of 12-foot-high sand berms, minefields and oil-filled trenches they could set afire proved to be easily surmounted obstacles to the allied troops that moved into Kuwait.

But these defenses have left swaths of destruction across the desert.

For the first few miles north of the Saudi border, the Iraqis dug huge holes in the asphalt highway so that it could not be passed.

Hundreds of pipes that used to bring in the oil to fill the trenches lay scattered over the ground. The burned-out hulks of Iraqi trucks and tanks, hit during the earlier intensive air bombardment of their positions, blocked the road at several places.

Jihani, the Saudi colonel, expressed the mood of most of the Arab troops here, who said they expect this to be a very short war. "Three days," he responded, when asked how long it would be before Kuwait City would be entered and freed.

Wael al Walayati, the Kuwaiti television cameraman who was with the other reporters today, said that when he entered his homeland for the first time since leaving after the occupation, "I prayed, and kissed the land. It's the best kiss I did in my life. It had a special taste." Walayati also noted something else special about today:

It is the 30th anniversary of Kuwait's independence from Britain.

"Yay!"—Baptism of Fire Pure Excitement for Some GIs; Earning Time-and-a-Half for Playing With Guns

By John Sack

WITH A U.S. ARMY PLATOON INSIDE IRAQ - For many soldiers who lived it, their baptism of fire was more like a hooting and hollering Baptist revival.

Until yesterday, U.S. Army tank commander Staff Sgt. Ron Shaffer, 26, of Albion, Mich., and his gunner, Spec. Greg Gilliam, 22, of Chattanooga, Tenn., had never fired their guns except on make-believe training exercises.

But when their platoon led the way into Iraq yesterday and Shaffer and Gilliam spotted scores of Iraqi soldiers on a ridgeline, the two started shouting excitedly.

And when Shaffer fired his 50-caliber machine gun—a gun whose bullets are as big as human thumbs—at the Iraqis, Gilliam shouted, "Yay!" and gave him a high-five, the two soldiers said today.

At least two hundred Iraqi soldiers surrendered to their company, while no Americans in the company—which received rifle and artillery fire—was even scratched.

This morning, even as Iraqi small-arms fire whizzed by a few hundred feet away, Shaffer and Gilliam reminisced about the day they may someday tell their grandchildren about. "This is fun," said Gilliam, a good-looking blond whose face, today, was as black as a chimney sweep's from the charcoal fibers in the gas-protection clothing that he had been wearing since yesterday morning. "We get paid time-and-a-half to play with guns."

He referred to the "imminent danger" pay of $110 per month that all the soldiers in Saudi Arabia get. Shaffer echoed him. "If it keeps up like this, I'm glad I came," the easy-going sergeant said. "We got more prisoners than Sergeant York."

The two were comparing the war with Iraq to the Detroit Pistons playing a high-school basketball team when their platoon leader, 1st Lt. David Russell of San Antonio, Tex., walked up. "It's not over yet," Russell reminded them.

The Story of Capt. John Bushyhead

WITH THE U.S. ARMY INSIDE IRAQ - Women would laugh when they met him. Men would get angry, assuming that he was putting them on. And everybody would tell him, "No, what's your *real* name?"

At last the wide-smiling man who today led the raid inside of Iraq had to start introducing himself.

"I'm John Bushyhead. That is my real name. I'm of American Indian descent."

If questioned further—and Bushyhead always was—he'd report that his great-grandfather was chief of the Cherokees and his great-great-grandfather, the Rev. Jess Bushyhead, was the man who led eight hundred tribesmen along the "Trail of Tears" during the presidency of Andrew Jackson.

Jackson, "who's not one of my favorite people," says Bushyhead, had his federal troops round up the Cherokees, mostly old men, women and children, in Kentucky and Tennessee and, in the dead of winter, march them to Oklahoma, a name that is Cherokee language for Land of the Red Men.

Many of the Indians died along the way.

It's ironic, says Capt. Bushyhead, who for twelve years has worn his hair "high and tight," meaning almost bald, that he's now a federal troop himself.

He's one-eighth Indian. But his big-boned, big-toothed, dark-skinned face and his whooping, hollering personality—on his first reconnaissance trip into Iraq, on Sunday, he "ordered" his fellow officers to pose for a snapshot there—as well as his predispositions seem practically full-blooded.

"I can really identify with my Indian descent," says Bushyhead, "but I can't hold the whites responsible for mistakes made in the past. Today even full-blooded whites seem empathetic about the Indians."

Bushyhead, 31, was born at Fort Lewis, Wash., the son of an Army officer who later commanded a company of Cobra helicopters in Vietnam and who retired as a full colonel. In his teens, Bushyhead went to Leesville High School near Fort Polk, La., and Miami Killian High School in Miami, Fla., running the mile in 4.28 and winning a second-degree black belt in Tang So Do, a kind of Korean karate.

He then earned a B.A. in international affairs at Florida State and an M.A. in business from Central Michigan.

He was married and divorced, and his ten-year-old son, J.R., is living with his mother and step-father now in Oklahoma City, Bushyhead's own home town.

Bushyhead and his infantry company came from Fort Riley, Kan., to Saudi Arabia over New Year's. He notes with regret that after the war the Army intends to cut back 125,000 men, meaning that he might have to retire.

If that happens, Bushyhead plans to work on a Cherokee reservation. "There but for the grace of God go I," Bushyhead says. "I could be that alcoholic Indian making $800 a year. Because that's what the average male Indian makes today."

What would the captain do among the Cherokees? The same thing he's doing now, Bushyhead says. "I have a lot of love and compassion for my soldiers. I literally look at them as my sons.

"If I could give that part of me to the disadvantaged Indian on the reservation, we'd all get something out of it. Me, the Cherokee Indians, and America."

Tuesday
February 26, 1991

On Day Three of the land war, military action on the eastern front was coming to a rapid conclusion.

As Iraqi troops fled Kuwait in force, Marines raced to the outskirts of Kuwait through the oily soot produced by hundreds of oil well fires. In coordinated blocking moves with Tiger Brigade, the Marines maneuvered to cut off all means of escape for the Iraqi occupation troops.

Preceded into the city by special operations teams that seized and ran up flags at the U.S., British, and French embassies, the main Marine elements reached the capital about the same time that Saddam Hussein announced a formal withdrawal over Baghdad Radio. It was, in most respects, only a formality. It wouldn't affect the allied offensive, and most Iraqi troops in Kuwait had already figured out for themselves that this "19th province of Iraq" notion was a lost cause.

The allies—including Arab troops from Kuwait, Saudi Arabia, Syria, and Egypt—advanced rapidly northward, but not fast enough to prevent all the enemy troops from bugging out. Some refugees said the occupation troops had begun fleeing on Sunday, with the first shots of the land offensive.

The smoking, battered, burning Kuwait the liberators looked upon was a bleak sight. Besides the massive physical damage to the environment and the looting of stores, houses, and museums, a U.S. Army civil affairs official estimated that 25 percent of the people living in Kuwait when the Iraqis invaded were very possibly dead, many the victims of Iraqi kangaroo courts and execution squads.

Allied war casualties reported on the third day were extremely light—only four dead and about 20 wounded, according to interim battlefield figures. Some Iraqi troops had put up a fight, but any who did were quickly overwhelmed by allied firepower.

The big numbers were in the POW column—an estimated 25,000 Iraqis so far had given up the fight and turned themselves over to allied forces. All across the allied front a constant flow of POWs that required searching and processing slowed the columns of tanks and convoys of troops and supplies.

Also slowing operations was the weather, which turned foul, boiling up a *shamal*, or strong wind, that made land travel difficult and helicopter flying virtually impossible.

The main attacking force of the VII Corps had picked up steam, headed finally for the pocket north of Kuwait between the Kuwait border and Basra, where a major confrontation with the Republican Guard was now expected—the big, all-out battle that the allies predicted would settle accounts for good, and leave Saddam Hussein's military in even worse shape than after the long war with Iran.

With so few casualties on the front lines, the next shock to the coalition forces hit with even greater impact. A Scud missile landed on a makeshift barracks in the city of Dhahran, far behind the forward lines, killing 28 American soldiers and injuring 100 more.

A story in this chapter reports that the effects of the blast were made worse by the presence of new stores of ammunition that had recently been issued to the soldiers in the barracks. In the shock and confusion that followed the tragedy—the greatest single loss of allied lives in the Gulf War—false explanations circulated and, through repetition, gained credence.

Some witnesses said the Iraqi missile appeared to be on a trajectory that would overshoot the barracks, but in the last seconds of flight a Patriot missile struck it.

The Patriot, it was said, only damaged the Scud, breaking it apart and causing large pieces of debris to strike the barracks, exploding and setting it afire.

That explanation appeared in many of the first stories about the explosion. Similar types of glancing-strikes that caused damage and injuries directly below where Scuds and Patriots had intersected had been reported out of Israel. Central Command the next day dismissed that theory, saying that no Patriot missile had been fired to intercept the Scud. The military's explanation was that the Iraqi bomb had simply disintegrated. The missile, it was said, broke into pieces by itself on its descent, and so was never identified as a threat.

The world was expected to believe that all those American casualties were somehow the fault of poor workmanship at the Scud factory. Months later, the Pentagon admitted that both of these early explanations were wrong. The most obvious explanation was the correct one: the Scud struck the barracks unimpeded, at full force.

No Patriot missile was ever fired at the Scud. A computer programming error caused the Patriot battery that should have detected the Scud to shut down minutes before it emerged over Dhahran. The computer malfunction reportedly occurred because the Patriot battery had been operating for 100 continuous hours, longer than it should have, without rebooting.

At first, the Army said it had known of the flaw in the Patriot's software only five days before the attack. But a General Accounting Office investigation, and dogged pursuit of the story by the Associated Press, established that the Army had known of the flaw for a full two weeks before the attack. Patriot programmers had responded to the warning by revising the software but a corrected version wasn't delivered to the Patriot batteries in Saudi Arabia in time to prevent the incident.

A corrected program arrived the day after the Scud landed.

Tiger Tanks Roar North: "We Nudge Them. We Don't Want to Attack and Kill These Men Until We Have To"

By Bill Gannon

NEWS SUMMARY: Tiger Brigade sweeps north in massive armored attack force—meets limited resistance and kills 20 T-55, T-62 tanks and scares crews out of 8 others. Brigade takes minimum of 2,200 enemy prisoners of war—including two complete brigades who surrender behind their commander officer. Iraqi artillery also destroyed.

POOL NOTE: An entire brigade of Iraqi soldiers surrendered to Tiger Brigade M1A1 tank crews behind an Iraqi soldier holding a hand-made American flag on a white sheet. See pool photos by Ernie Cox of the Chicago Tribune.

WITH THE TIGER BRIGADE IN OCCUPIED KUWAIT - Attacking with main tank guns and TOW missiles, the heavy armor of this Army brigade destroyed 20 tanks, intimidated 8 others out of commission, and took more than 2,200 prisoners in the second day Monday of the ground campaign to liberate the emirate.

Stretching two miles wide and a mile deep, hundreds of M1A1 Abrams battle tanks, Bradley Fighting Vehicles, and armored troop carriers rolled north in a triple-wedge attack formation that stretched across the horizon.

The first Iraqi tank was destroyed, or killed, as the tankers like to say, before 7 am when a TOW missile fired from a Bradley Fighting Vehicle from the 341st Mechanized Infantry Regiment hit a Soviet-model T-55 tank dug in gun-turret deep in the sand.

Other T-55 and T-62 tanks, many similarly dug in so that only their gun turrets shown, followed throughout the day until past sundown with the last confirmed kill made at 7:30 p.m. by an M1A1 tank using its 120mm main gun.

In other engagements, the Tigers needed only to have the M1A1s demonstrate the destructive power of its 120mm main tank gun to intimidate 8 other T-55 and T-62 tank crews into surrendering.

Several times the surrender of the Iraqi tanks came after the Tigers killed one of several tanks in a formation—Iraqi tank crews would leap out of their tanks and walk hands held high toward the advancing armor of Tiger Brigade.

There were no Soviet-model T-72 tanks, considered to be the Iraqis' best battle tank, sighted by Tiger Brigade Monday.

Resistance was limited to artillery and mortar shells and small-arms fire.

Rolling in formation across a desert plain pockmarked by bomb craters, spent TOW missile tubes, used tank shells, and bomb casings, the armor sped beneath burning oil wells, stopping only to confirm a target and destroy it. The wells roared as the oil spewed forth in great geysers of flame and curtains of black smoke that drifted across the battlefield.

The smell of cordite from the tank guns was thick in the air as the armor groaned and creaked, firing its main guns and rail-machine guns at suspected Iraqi positions.

Most of the time, that was all it took to nudge the Iraqis into surrendering. The second day of the ground war for this element of the Army's 2nd Armored Division working in support of the 2nd Marine Division was marked by mass surrenders.

In other engagements, the tanks would fire their guns into the sand near suspected Iraq defensive bunkers. A few rounds later and the Iraqis would begin to surrender in droves. It was a sight that military commanders here say probably has not been seen since the North African campaigns of World War II—formations of hundreds of tanks rolling past hundreds of surrendering troops.

The largest waves of surrendering Iraqis came on three separate engagements. The Tigers would growl, firing tank guns and Bradley rail-machine guns. Miles away, white flags of every size and description would begin to flutter in the distance.

Perhaps the most memorable such surrender came when an Iraqi soldier came out with a group of several hundred, marching toward the Americans holding up a white sheet with a crude American flag drawn on it.

Tiger commander Col. John Sylvester twice accepted the surrender of two Iraqi majors, both brigade commanders, who surrendered with their entire units.

"They've got no fight left in them. They have lost the will and spirit, and we don't want to kill unless we have to," Sylvester said.

"One of the surrendering Iraqi majors said, 'It is not our cause . . . we only want peace.' And I told him I only wanted peace too, and accepted his surrender," said Sylvester, 45, of Brownsville, Tex. "He gave us a great deal of information and I showed him the respect due my counterpart. He was also very grateful for the medical help we extended to his wounded," the colonel explained.

There were several dozen EPWs who needed medical help. Several had to be moved by armored troop carrier ambulance to the rear for more treatment.

In one surrender, an Iraqi private began walking and then started running toward a waiting Army military policeman, who waved him on to another MP.

The scene was repeated until the Iraqi reached the fourth MP. There the Iraqi came to a halt, smartly surrendered, and then offered his hand. Even from a distance, it was obvious the MP was startled by the offer of a handshake.

After a moment's pause, he reached out and shook the Iraqi's hand. They stood facing each other for a moment until the MP ordered him to the ground and began searching him for weapons.

Other surrenders more resembled banner day at the local ballpark than a war.

Holding sheets four across, the Iraqis marched and sang songs as they headed for the Americans of Tiger Brigade. In the face of the relatively easy going, Sylvester warned his Tigers not to get over-confident, taking to the radio to warn them to concentrate and confirm a target before firing.

Once Monday, the commander grew concerned that an advancing Arab coalition partner-nation, Syria, had come too close to his western flank and that his men might get a Syrian T-55 tank in their sights by mistake. He radioed in to the 2nd Marine Division to request the Syrians be warned to stay clear of his sector.

Working with the Marines also took some getting used to. Marines, by their training and mission, are not used to move hundreds of kilometers per day like this heavy armored brigade. Where the Army moves and attacks when necessary, the Marines are accustomed to storming beaches and fortifications. They would move and stop to attack bunkers regularly.

The Tigers, by comparison, would stand off at several thousand meters and fire off a few tank rounds to get them to come forward. "We nudge them. We don't want to attack and kill these men until we have to," said Sgt. Maj. Thomas Calkins, 43, from Novato, Calif. "Looking at a couple hundred tanks will sure make you think twice about fighting. But it's pretty obvious these men don't want to fight and we don't want to risk our men trying to attack unless we have to," Calkins said.

News that Baghdad Radio has told Iraqis in Kuwait to retreat north has this fast-moving armored brigade preparing to race 25 to 40 kilometers north to block the Iraqi retreat. "We're still awaiting permission to go forth. I have told my superiors that with some re-positioning of forces, we can move into position within hours," said Col. Sylvester.

So far, the brigade has moved slowly, taking care not to leave the Marines they support too far behind. Sylvester said Gen. Norman Schwarzkopf instructed him to "move slowly, fix the enemy, and minimize casualties, and we have done all these things while heading for our objective." But if the Iraqis, who have been surrendering by the brigades to Sylvester's battalions of M1A1 tanks and Bradley Fighting Vehicles, are retreating north, Sylvester stressed the importance of blocking any such move.

By 7 a.m. the brigade was ready to roll north in a massive, non-stop assault. It was unclear, however, if the orders to roll would be given.

Tuesday - February 26, 1991

Scene at Ras Al Zour: Kuwaitis in First Battle, Saudis Basking in Victory, Americans Calling in Supporting Fire

By Kim Murphy

RAS AL ZOUR - The sign at the main border checkpoint into Kuwait says "Welcome," but it tilts crazily to one side, and beyond it stretches newly liberated Kuwait.

On the coastal desert plains that frame the main highway from Saudi Arabia to Kuwait City, an occasional donkey grazes amid the blown-out wreckage of tanks and supply trucks. The road itself is in long stretches little more than a pile of asphalt chunks, churned up by Iraqi forces before they fled north from advancing allied forces. Government buildings and way stations have been reduced to rubble over weeks of allied bombing raids; stinking oil trenches line the dugouts where Iraqi tanks crouched before falling back to the north; and roaring triumphantly across the battered landscape, hooting and waving, are dozens of Kuwaiti and Saudi soldiers straddling battle tanks still unbowed by war.

In this odd, turned-upside-down landscape where a wealthy oil emirate looks like parts of the South Bronx and a warm afternoon sun breaks occasionally through the impermeable smoke haze of dozens of burning oil wells, even the prisoners of war looked dazed but relatively cheerful, wheedling cigarettes from Saudi soldiers and greeting visiting journalists with uncertain grins. "Ahlan wa sahlan," said one beaming Iraqi, crouched with several dozen other prisoners near the entrance to this onetime Persian Gulf resort. Welcome again. But who's welcoming whom?

War has advanced like an express train through this part of southern Kuwait, with Arab forces encountering little resistance in their advance that was expected to put them in Mina Abdullah, some 40 miles into Kuwait, by sometime today (Tuesday.) Yet in a theater in which Saudi, Qatari, Kuwaiti, and other Gulf forces are operating in discrete pockets, the idea of a battlefront is an evolving concept. "I would say you could draw a line in the sand and you'd find it," said a U.S. liaison officer working with Kuwaiti troops, admitting it was difficult even for commanders in the field to keep score.

"It's like a chess game where you've got a blanket stretched across the board."

By Monday, Kuwaiti forces had advanced about 20 miles north of the Saudi border to an area just north of Ras al Zour and were undergoing their first real engagement of the war, a barrage of indirect artillery fire from Iraqi forces further north. Allied troops responded with a steady boom of artillery that rattled the desert floor for most of the morning. Hundreds of Iraqi prisoners were flooding by the busload into transition areas along the coast before being transported to permanent Saudi detention camps, and Saudi authorities reported that the number of prisoners Monday had grown to 25,000.

Many of them appeared to be ill-fed, demoralized by the allied bombing barrage and apparently not overly troubled about being in the hands of their Saudi captors. "God willing, Saddam will fall and this problem will finish," said one young Iraqi reservist from Basra, being temporarily held at Ras al Zour, in a rare interview with Western and Arab reporters.

"If Saddam doesn't fall, this Middle East problem will continue. I want to have a special message to Saddam Hussein: He should give up everything, let's live in peace."

Iraqi soldiers, he admitted, have engaged in looting in Kuwait. "We went inside houses, we broke the houses, we stole everything. It happened," he said.

But the army, he said, has been without food, water and cigarettes for some time. "What he (Saddam) told us, that Arab countries were going to invade us and take our sisters and mothers and families, it's not true," the man complained. "We hope the victor will be the Saudis. It's senseless that our young people are going to get killed."

The man was one of a reported 1,000 Iraqis taken captive Monday in the southern coastal region, according to a Saudi commander. Though battlefield officials could provide few concrete details of the conflict, they agreed that most of the surrenders had occurred without fighting, and the account of the prisoner in the Ras al Zour compound concurred with that account.

"As soon as they came, we just raised our arms and we told them we didn't want to fight," he said. "As soon as we raised our hands, they welcomed us . . . I was captured by our brother Saudis."

Several commanders said they were surprised, in fact, at the lack of resistance they have encountered so far in their march through southern Kuwait.

"I thought these two days would be the difficult days, but there is nothing from the Iraqi soldiers," said Saudi Col. Belal al Johani. "In the beginning they fight, but then they surrender, gave up."

Maj. Robert Schoenwetter, a Long Beach, Calif.-based U.S. military adviser to Kuwaiti forces, agreed: "I was surprised. I thought we'd see more (resistance)," he said. "We keep waiting for the boom, for the other shoe to drop." Most of what Arab forces have encountered from the Iraqis has been small arms fire, hand grenades, and some artillery, he said.

Monday morning, Kuwaiti troops were undergoing artillery hits from an unknown Iraqi source location and were calling urgently to U.S. advisers further back, who were seeking to direct U.S. F/A-18s to take out the Iraqi artillery batteries. Schoenwetter and other U.S. advisers were unable to make themselves heard on the radio, and there was an air of tenseness both in the Kuwaiti radio operator's voice in the field and in that of the American advisers seeking to help. "Thirty-four Bravo, Thirty-four Alpha, come in, over," the Americans said repeatedly.

Schoenwetter shrugged. "I got some young kid yelling over the radio. I couldn't tell you what he was thinking or feeling or seeing." Saudi officials, he added, now believe they could be in Kuwait City in the next three days—this estimate in advance of Baghdad's announcement early today (Tues.) it was withdrawing from Kuwait.

"The morale is going down," Johani said. "Today, no resistance. All of the fighters gave up without resistance. Yesterday also, no resistance . . . Right now, he (Saddam) has lost everything. He's lost his troops, he's lost his morale, he's lost his friends in all the countries, he's lost everything."

But U.S. officials were not quite so optimistic. Schoenwetter, before jumping into his Humvee to race south in hope of setting up a better radio connection, was asked who owned Kuwait City. "The Iraqis," he said curtly as he snapped shut the door.

Tuesday - February 26, 1991

48 Hours Will Tell Fate of Republican Guard: Where Will They Go? Will Their Best Tanks Go With Them?

By Neal MacFarquhar

WITH THE VII CORPS - The Republican Guard stirred Tuesday but the blizzard of political developments left VII Corps officers trying to determine whether the three divisions hunkered down north of Kuwait would remain in place, go on the offensive or make a run for central Iraq.

Officers said there had been no sign that the guards, the core of Iraqi leader Saddam Hussein's military, were prepared to walk away from the T-72 tanks and other top-of-the-line equipment in order to comply with the surrender procedures outlined by the coalition forces.

"We still have a lot of bad guys up there who haven't thrown up their hands and said 'Chiu hoy,'" said Col. Johnnie B. Hitt, using the Vietnamese term for "I surrender."

The Apache helicopters in the VII Corps aviation brigade that Hitt commands specialize in killing tanks on the move. The men that fly the surveillance planes said that no coherent plan had emerged in the Iraqi movements, but some tanks were definitely coming out of their revetments.

"We are seeing movers out there," said Capt. Gary Stahlkut, 34, of Cleveland, Ohio, from the Corps' 2nd Military Intelligence Battalion. "The best estimates were that the Iraqis are trying to conduct some kind of strategic withdrawal," said Hitt.

It was unclear if the Republican Guard had been ordered to withdraw or whether such an order would come in by Tuesday evening. The most common estimate for the battle with the guard was that it would last about 48 hours. "They can either come out or get overrun. You can't just call someone to get out with a logistics tail in a short time," said Lt. Col. Michael Lustig, 40, from Queens, N.Y., of the intelligence battalion.

But it was still possible they would come forward to try to engage the three American divisions of the VII Corps, joined by Britain's 1st Armored Division, whose lead elements were over 50 miles from the border. The main VII Corps divisions are the 3rd Armored Division, the 1st Armored Division, and the 3rd Infantry Division, as well as the corps' combined arms force, the 3rd Armored Cavalry Regiment.

Much of the elite Republican Guard was believed destroyed by the over month-long Air Force bombing campaign and it was unclear how much is left to come out of the ground. When at full strength, Republican Guard divisions are slightly smaller than American divisions—they have up to 12,000 men and 350 tanks.

Officers said 80 tanks that moved south from the Tawaklna Division, the farthest east, were among the hundreds announced destroyed by military briefers in the first days of the war. The two other divisions near the Kuwaiti border are the Medina and Al-Fao Divisions and officers said there were also signs of movement in the Medina Division, which is farther east along the Kuwaiti border. Three more divisions are (in) dug in positions further northeast toward Basra.

The air superiority established over the past six weeks has assured the coalition forces control over ground movements. "The way things are going, if it moves, it dies," said Lustig.

The intelligence battalion has been putting Mohawk and RC-12 surveillance planes in the air around the clock to help attract ground movements between 100 and 200 kilometers beyond the front lines of the

U.S. forces. Lustig said U.S. pilots have been sickened by what happened to Kuwait over the past two weeks with oil wells, storage facilities and ports all destroyed. "It looks like the Iraqis have just wasted the country of Kuwait in the past two weeks," Lustig said.

Battlefield is Ablaze with Burning Iraqi Tanks; Marines Seal Escape Routes from Kuwait City

By Denis Gray

WITH THE U.S. MARINES NEAR KUWAIT CITY - U.S. Marines knifed through Iraq's last defenses Tuesday, sealing off all major escape routes from Kuwait City and leaving scores of Baghdad's tanks ablaze in the desert behind them.

By late afternoon, the Marines had positioned a powerful blocking force along an arc running from northwest of the capital towards the southeast.

Marine tanks had seized an escarpment commanding a major crossroads in the northwest and were strung across the highways between Kuwait City and Iraq along which Iraqi troops would have to move to reach their homeland.

Marine officers said abandoned military and civilian vehicles jammed the exit roads, but it was unclear whether large numbers of Iraqi troops were still inside the city or had managed to flee before the U.S. forces tightened the noose. Lt. Col. Jan Huly, spokesman of the 2nd Marine Division, said the Marines had covered up to 30 kilometers in three hours, beginning their final thrust at noon.

Huly said the assault force had suffered some casualties, describing them as light but giving no additional details.

Before the attack began, the 2nd Division had lost only three dead while another 33 were wounded in two days of combat in the southern reaches of Kuwait. "They lost count of how many tanks they killed," Huly said of the attacking force which sped over open desert and patches of higher ground en route to the outskirts of the capital.

Tank fire and wire-guided TOW missiles, Huly said, destroyed Iraq's Soviet-made T-62 and top-of-the-line T-72 tanks that appeared in the path of the Marines. Air strikes may also have been called against the tanks, some of which may have been abandoned before the attack.

As night fell, the battlefield was set alight by the burning hulks of tanks, their turrets often decapitated. Some lay in the open, others inside protective pits scooped into the desert floor. Many were gutted just ahead and along a ridge near a rock quarry and the Kuwait City garbage dump. One T-72, set inside a charred pit, had been ripped open and a fire was eating away its insides.

Corpses were not seen, but Huly said some dead were believed to be inside the destroyed tanks.

Along the path of the blitzkrieg-style American advance, remnants of a shattered Iraqi army were dearly evident. White flags fluttered in the wind next to empty foxholes and bunkers where the fleeing or surrendering defenders had left behind cooking pots, blankets, even boots and sandals.

A single file of 15 Iraqi soldiers trudged slowly southwards across the desert towards Saudi Arabia. Whenever an American vehicle passed by or an airplane flew overhead, the soldiers would rapidly snap both hands behind their heads in the U.S. prescribed gesture of surrender.

For the 2nd Division, the third day of the ground war began with violent action and ended in relative quiet except for a howling wind and rain sweeping through their block-and-wait positions. But artillery fire continued sporadically, the bulk of it from the American lines although the Iraqis threw back a few rounds. After sunset, two shells fired by Marine howitzers burst in the air, showering the earth below with flaming orange shrapnel.

A half-hour artillery barrage pounded Iraqi positions before the final attack. Rain fell from a sky in which lead-grey clouds mixed with thick smoke burning from oil fields, covering troops and vehicles with a film of black. "Our reports are that Iraqi troops are sacking the city and trying to withdraw," Huly said before H-hour. He said the Marines expected to meet stiff resistance from Iraqi units trying to protect the retreat from Kuwait.

"I think they're starting to retreat and we want to destroy as much of his equipment as possible. But we're not going to shoot anybody who gives up," said Maj. Gen. William Keys, the 2nd Division commander.

Thousands of Iraqi soldiers had been surrendering to the advancing forces, sometimes abandoning all their weapons and equipment and giving up as complete units. "I thought they would fight harder than they did," Keys said. The big-framed, highly decorated Vietnam War veteran said two Iraqi soldiers had even tried to surrender to him. Huly said assault troops in the final push would not secure prisoners, but simply disarm them, give them some food and "point them south" in the direction of Saudi Arabia. Caring for prisoners has been a major problem of the ground war for the allies.

Food, water and blankets have had to be ferried—sometimes by helicopter—to the frontlines for the captives who are kept in temporary holding areas before being sent to Saudi Arabia.

Keys said the so-called EPWs—enemy prisoners of war—were "as much a problem as anything" in the three-day ground war which has seen incredibly low allied casualties.

Marine commanders agreed that allied air strikes preceding the ground war had taken a great toll on both Iraqi war-making capability and troop morale.

"They had no fight in them," said Capt. Matt Lagadon of Jacksonville, N.C., as he looked over a group of 15 Iraqis. "They talked about the American bombing and complained about having been thrown to the wolves."

Marines Surround Kuwait City: "Iraqis Getting Out As Fast As They Can Run"

By Molly Moore

WITH U.S. FORCES, On the Outskirts of Kuwait City - U.S. Marine forces today surrounded Kuwait City and the international airport, blocking Iraqi troops from escaping and preparing the way for Arab forces on Wednesday to reclaim the city that has been under Iraqi siege for the past six months, according to the senior Marine Corps commander.

After a three-day push through southern Kuwait, in which Iraqi forces surrendered by the thousands and abandoned their posts after only sporadic fighting, two Marine divisions sealed the city perimeters tonight, a day ahead of the commanders' original war plan. U.S. Marine Corps commander Lt. Gen. Walt Boomer said today that, unless

Iraqi forces inside the international airport compound show unexpected tenacity, "our part of the mission is complete."

Field commanders reported that Marines encountered some of their toughest fighting of the campaign during their attempts to surround the airfield and said they destroyed more than 100 Iraqi tanks. Marine forces captured a key highway intersection that controls major traffic movement between Kuwait and Iraq, and moved other troops around the southern side of the city.

While the Marines were nearing the end of their operation, the Army was expected to begin its efforts to rout Republican Guard forces from their entrenchments inside Iraq along the Kuwaiti border, military officials said.

Marine officials said two Marines have been killed and about 59 are in hospitals from injuries sustained in fighting or accidents over the last three days.

But today, the military lanes from the Kuwait border to the edge of Kuwait City are littered with the spoils of war: burning tanks, exploding artillery pieces, and bunkers abandoned so hastily that the Iraqi troops left them littered with food, clothes, and maps. Two plastic chairs and a table with a bag of what appeared to be food sat next to one smoking tank shell.

Craters pocked the desert sand where bombs and mines had exploded and the hundreds of unexploded bombs were splattered across the battlefield. Iraqi infantry bunkers, reinforced with corrugated sheet metal and sandbags had been crumped by bombing raids and artillery fire.

Along the horizon, dozens of burning oil well heads, ignited by Iraqi troops, belched orange flames and black smoke, turning the sky an oily gray-black. At times, the noon sky looked as dark as dusk.

Early Tuesday morning, with intelligence reports that "Iraqis are getting out of Kuwait City as fast as they can run," senior Marine commanders gathered at an austere mobile desert command post and, bending over large crumpled maps laid across the sand, plotted strategy for the day-long march toward Kuwait City.

"We want to stop as many from retreating as possible and to destroy as much of his equipment as possible," said Marine 2nd Division commander Maj. Gen. Bill Keys, after the planning session.

With Marine forces surrounding the city, Kuwait, Saudi and other Arab forces will move through the Marine lines and reclaim the occupied city, according to Marine commanders who said the liberation of the city could come as early as Wednesday.

Saudi and other Arab forces were still pushing northward today along the eastern coast of Kuwait and Egyptian forces were moving toward Kuwait City from the southwest, U.S. officials said.

Both Marine and Army forces have escalated operational plans to push through Kuwait as a result of weak Iraqi resistance and the surrender of thousands of Iraqi forces.

"Their heart wasn't in this fight," said Boomer. "They were some place they didn't want to be, about to die for something they didn't want to die for."

"I thought if we were going to have a real fight, it would be in and around Kuwait City," Boomer said, noting the only significant opposition was around the international airfield, which earlier in the invasion had been used as a headquarters base for Iraqi forces.

Marine forces encountered scattered resistance (from) Iraqi forces as they moved toward Kuwait City, some of whom crept out of hiding places in a large oilfield that had been bypassed by American troops in the first day of fighting, officials said.

During one firefight this morning, Marine tanks, TOW anti-tank weapons and Cobra helicopter gunships fired dozens of rounds at Iraqi artillery and tank positions in one battle, with fiery explosions lighting the sky. Some Iraqi bunkers exploded several times as ordnance stored nearby exploded in a spray of sparks and secondary explosions.

Marine forces regrouped Tuesday morning after virtually stopping their northward movement Monday night as a result of the inky darkness created partially by the thick layer of smoke and oil from dozens of burning oil well heads and the thousands of Iraqi troops surrendering across the war-fighting areas, according to Marine officials.

"We had so many Iraqi troops surrendering we couldn't get across the battlefield," said one field commander.

A group of about 24 Iraqi infantry soldiers crawled out of their bunkers near a main military roadway and surrendered to a command-and-control convoy led by Lt. Gen. Boomer.

More than 3,500 Iraqi prisoners were corralled at one makeshift encampment surrounded by two thick rows of concertina wire deep inside Kuwait. Military police said the troops said they had not eaten in three or four days and dozens of them began trying to climb through the razor-sharp wire when they saw U.S. forces approaching with containers of water, according to Capt. Rick Glaim, a military police officer overseeing the camp.

So many of the troops had given up that military police were requesting emergency airlifts of food, water, and blankets to the outposts. The numbers overwhelmed the availability of transportation, forcing the military to begin marching the prisoners to larger staging areas.

While many of the prisoners wore heavy coats, others had covered their shoeless feet in sandbags and wrapped their heads in towels. One prisoner in a group marching through the desert under heavy guard carried a Christian Bible under his arm.

"It looks like the old movie scenes of World War II with prisoners marching through Germany," said Boomer, watching a group of about 100 Iraqi troops shuffling down one supply road, guarded by armed Marine vehicles.

Boomer said Marine commanders changed their attack plan "a lot before we kicked off" but made no major alterations once the campaign began.

"We certainly thought it was going to be (a) hard proposition for us because he had so many people down there," said Boomer. He said the two Marine divisions of about 40,000 men were outnumbered by 11 Iraqi divisions. The Marines did not intend to use an amphibious assault, with the almost 30,000 Marines stationed offshore as a diversionary tactic designed to keep the Iraqi forces off-guard, Marine officials said.

During the night, Marine radars detected artillery fire from Iraqi troops directed at one Marine unit. While the first rounds fell short of the unit, operators yelled "Snow storm!" indicating incoming fire. Army multiple-launch rocket systems pounded the Iraqi artillery with 48 rockets.

"We never heard anything more from them," said Col. Les Palm, commander of one Marine artillery regiment.

NOTE TO POST CORRESPONDENTS; Having difficulty filing because we are moving so fast in mobile command center, may be shut out again for the next 20 hours or so, but am desperately trying to find ways to file out. Problem is, we are too far away from all other command posts.

Blinding Shamal Envelops Allied Offensive: "Resupply by Air is Over Until This Lifts"

By Kevin Cooney

ON THE NORTHERN SAUDI BORDER - Two days of rain and heavy winds have turned the Iraqi desert into a quagmire and slowed the race to the Euphrates River by American airborne soldiers.

Dawn broke on Tuesday with the hundred helicopters of the 18th Aviation Brigade, which is supplying the advance, trapped on the ground as clouds and fog cut visibility in some places to as little as an eighth of a mile, military spokesmen said.

Winds were blowing at 30 knots, said Staff Sgt. Michael Sincere, of Fairfax, Va., an Air Force weatherman. "This is pretty significant about what's going on out there," he said.

The 82nd and 101st Airborne Divisions had been moving rapidly through the desert toward the river on the banks of which civilization is said to have been born.

When they reach the Euphrates they will stand between Saddam Hussein's capital, Baghdad, and his elite fighting force, the 150,000 men of the Republican Guard. "Resupply by air is over until this lifts," said Maj. Ed Parrish of Fort Sheridan, Ill., a brigade spokesman.

The 18th Aviation (Brigade) had been ferrying men and supplies in a constant stream of helicopters since the 101st, the 82nd, and French forces sped halfway to the Euphrates on the first day of ground war.

"There is a chance of a small reprieve later in the day," Sgt. Sincore said. He said the rain could let up, though winds were expected to continue blowing strongly. "But we could go down again," he said. "It could get a little worse before it gets better."

He added that the desert would "dry out amazingly quickly" once the clouds lifted. The weatherman said the wind and rain were forecast before the battle was commenced. "We saw this coming but not to this degree," he said.

He made the point that the Iraqis were having to deal with the same weather, and Maj. Parrish said: "We still have the advantage because at least we (have) airplanes that will be able to fly once the weather clears." At the base camp of the 18th, frustrated pilots and crews worked by their useless Chinooks, securing them against the gusting wind.

Soldiers laboriously moved into the wind carrying sandbags to hold their tents onto the ground. Large mallets were brought out to drive tent stakes deeper into the mud. The efforts came too late for some tents, which went flapping across the ground. Portable latrines were knocked over and American flags wrapped around their poles so that only the stripes were showing.

One of the tents that collapsed was the chaplain's place of worship, the white cross painted on the canvas was wrapped, unwrapped and wrapped again.

Tuesday - February 26, 1991

A-10 Pilots Adopt Young Georgia Fan

NOTES AND QUOTES from a quick-reaction Air Force pool, written by Mark Prendergast, NY Daily News, Bruce Alpert, New Orleans Times-Picayune, and Alexander G. Higgins, AP, and reviewed by Capt. Becky Colaw.

It is about a letter and photograph of a slain 15-year-old boy, John Matthew Gay, who had wanted to be an A-10 pilot. The letter from his mother, Sylvia Gay, of Centerville, Ga., was received on Tuesday, Feb. 26, by the 76th Tactical Fighter Squadron of the 23rd Tactical Fighter Wing. A copy was given to reporters later in the day.

Lt. Col Gene Renuart, 41, of Miami, said one pilot took the photo up immediately for missions Tuesday. "John's picture's going to fly with us every day until the war ends. And we're putting his name on one of our missiles each day when we fly. We just want his family to know that we received her letter and that we're going to do that for him."

Text of the letter:

Dear Sir,

I am writing to you to let you know of a fine young man that flies with you in spirit. His name is John Matthew Gay, and he was my son. He was murdered this summer eight days after his fifteenth birthday.

My son's most sincere dream was to graduate from the Air Force academy and fly A-10s. He had studied your craft and could discuss it in great and accurate detail. It was his goal, his life. There was no doubt that he would attain his dream.

As I watch the news reports, I think of him each time I see an A-10 in flight. I know that he is there in spirit with you and each of the other pilots.

You would have enjoyed knowing my son. He was a bright, sensitive young man with the highest moral fiber. An honor student with the promise of a wonderful Air Force career. His death was a great and senseless tragedy.

I am enclosing a small picture of John taken shortly before his death. I hope that you can take it up with you on one of your missions. It would mean a great deal to me. Unless there are A-10s in heaven, which I hope there are, this would be his only chance to fly. You are in my heart and prayers as you go about the business of war. I pray for your safe and speedy return to your home and family. Thank you for taking the time to read this.

Sincerely,
Sylvia Gay

The 'Loggies' Lament as Supply Effort Halts: If You're On the Heels of This War, You're Not Moving Very Fast

By Mark Mooney

ON THE IRAQI BORDER - "So now we know what it's like if they gave a war and nobody showed," said a captain left in Saudi Arabia by the easy invasion—so far—of Iraq. While 45,000 combat troops from the 18th Airborne Corps search for enemy to fight, another 65,000 support and re-supply troops wrestle with mixed feelings about being left out of the war. "I'm kind of elated and kind of sad," said Spec. Keith Turgeon, a combat photographer who was to head to the front on G-Day plus one and stay on the heels of the battle.

Turgeon, who photographed the bullet-riddled limousine of Manuel Noriega during the invasion of Panama, was not rooting for slaughter.

His mixed emotions come from months of waiting, standing guard on frigid nights, filling sandbags, and preparing mentally for the worst—mustard gas, anthrax, Scuds, T-2 tanks, flaming ditches, Bouncing Betty land mines, Republican Guards. Instead, they got hit with a rainstorm that turned their war into a battle to keep mud and rain out of their tents and to keep their footing in muck as slippery as an oil spot.

For months they drove trucks packed with ammo and supplies to the point of exhaustion, assembled miles of trucks to rush into Iraq, nervously pushed (along) roads over the Iraqi border, and steeled themselves for the final job of driving fuel and ammo through a hail of Iraqi artillery.

Instead, thousands of trucks remain in Saudi Arabian marshaling areas because the battalions do not need the ammunition and the tanks are moving so fast that the logistic generals do not know where they will stop. "We 'loggies' never have fun," said Col. Garrett.

Garrett said elaborate plans to set up and defend two supply bases in hostile territory have now been scrapped since only one will be needed.

And his command may not even move, said Garrett, who has been preparing for this move for 192 days. Nevertheless, the military mind follows orders. Soldiers are ordered to continue taking their anti-biological warfare pills and GIs were still tearing up their gloves stringing concertina wire around camps they do not feel are in danger of being hit with surprise attacks.

Signs of a physical letdown are also evident. After so many days of growing anticipation—and then nothing—a captain and a major were found snoring in their tent in the middle of the day on G-plus one. It was the first afternoon in weeks they had not been busy. "We expected to be cranked up," the captain said sheepishly.

The biggest logistics headache so far has been finding enough buses to carry all the POWs away from the front.

TV crews were also frustrated. An NBC team returned to the Saudi side of the border after traveling 40 miles inside Iraq without finding any trace of war.

But they were jealous. They heard a CBS crew had found a single destroyed bunker. Troops idling in the rear began speculating how soon they would go home, which units would get to leave first, and whether the 82nd Airborne will return home by parachuting into Fort Bragg as they did after Panama.

But most GIs left behind in the mud had more immediate and less glorious concerns. Take Sgt. Jason Hosking, a 22-year-old red-headed reservist who was called up out of North Carolina's Pembroke College. He is nowhere near the battle, and he is nowhere near going home. Instead, he is living in a leaky tent waiting for orders to begin the biggest packing job of his life.

"Mud dripped all over my pillow last night. It's drenched," he said with a laugh.

Hosking laughed because he knows it's not the sort of war story that movies are made of, but then never really wanted to be under fire.

Tuesday - February 26, 1991

Marine Helos Keep Iraqis in Place; "As Long As They're Watching the Coast, They're Not Engaging Our Units"

By John King

ABOARD THE USS NASSAU IN THE NORTHERN PERSIAN GULF — Marine helicopters steamed toward the Kuwait shoreline overnight on reconnaissance missions also designed to appear as if an amphibious assault was underway.

Marine sources said the helicopters returned with word that most Iraqi forces deployed along the coast appeared to be holding their positions, encouraging news for allied commanders who want to keep those Iraqis from dropping down to engage Marines approaching Kuwait City by land.

"As long as they are watching the coast, they are not engaging our units in Kuwait and farther west," said Maj. Gen. Harry Jenkins, commander of the Marine landing force afloat in the northern Persian Gulf.

For now, the Marine amphibious force remains at sea, awaiting word on whether it will be needed to help the advancing land troops or perhaps assault Iraqi positions north of Kuwait City.

Asked if the successful first day of the allied ground offensive made it less likely there would be a Marine amphibious landing, Jenkins said no, and said developments in the next day or two would have a far greater impact on his forces, which could be rushed ashore to flank Iraqi forces engaging the advancing allied ground troops.

"It's still possible" for a landing, Jenkins told pool reporters aboard the USS Nassau, the command ship for the amphibious force. "We're going to work right along the coast doing preparatory work."

The Marines plan a number of actions to keep the Iraqis guessing about their intentions while awaiting word on whether they will be called on to conduct a landing.

"The key is to keep him off balance," Jenkins said.

Marine sources, speaking on the condition of anonymity, said the helicopter operation overnight was conducted to determine whether the five to six Iraqi divisions deployed against an amphibious landing had held their positions during the first day of the ground offensive. "He's still there, waiting for us to come," one of the sources said. "Maybe we will, maybe we won't."

This source said flying the helicopters toward the coast would itself add to the Iraqi confusion over the intentions of the amphibious force. A major obstacle to a Marine landing is the heavy concentration of mines along the Kuwaiti coastline and around two major islands off the Kuwait coast, Bubiyan and Faylakah. Jenkins said mine-clearing continued and that some lanes have been cut through in case a landing is ordered. The Iraqi troops on the islands are believed to have some missile batteries that could be directed against allied naval vessels.

Jenkins said those forces have been subjected to heavy bombing and were isolated from supplies. One source, speaking on the condition of anonymity, said Faylakah, at the entrance to Kuwait Bay, had been hit with 16-inch gunfire from a U.S. battleship in the past 48 hours as well as bombing from U.S. jets and even B-52s.

Wednesday
February 27, 1991

The vaunted U.S. 1st Cavalry Division, held in reserve since Sunday, didn't do much to write home about the first three days of the land war. But on the fourth day, when this shootout in the desert seemed to be a one-sided affair but with something left in it, they got their chance.

Turning north, where the Republican Guard was supposed to be unlimbering their Soviet-made tanks, the Cavalry drove eagerly to the hunt. Their main fear was they were too late.

In Kuwait, it was liberation day. All Iraqi resistance was squelched and most of the firing was celebratory—Kuwaiti resistance fighters squeezing off bursts into the air in a display of joy and wild bullets.

The 24th Mechanized Infantry Division, the armored muscle of the 18th Airborne Corps, drove headlong into southeastern Iraq, seizing airfields at Tallil and Jaliba. Huge stores of munitions and parked aircraft were confiscated and, as operational orders dictated, the U.S. troops began methodically destroying them.

Explosions ripped the air for hours, but when the task threatened to occupy the division indefinitely, the destroyers moved on, headed east down Highway 8 toward Basra to join the anticipated decisive battle with the Republican Guard.

Once again, however, much of the battle was out far ahead of even the racing allied forces. The 2nd Armored Cavalry Regiment had hit pay dirt the night before, and along with other elements of the VII Corps were already engaging Saddam Hussein's elite tankers. The allied armor swung to the attack and, mowing down division after division, routed the best the Iraqis had to offer. The outcome was never in doubt.

Deep inside Iraq, the 101st Airborne Division was in search of the Republican Guard. But Maj. Rhonda Cornum, a battalion flight surgeon in the division's aviation brigade, was on a much more limited mission. She had lifted off with a party of rescuers looking for an injured F-16 pilot.

Air Force Capt. Bill Anderson had been shot down that morning. He was in radio contact with his squadron. One of his legs was broken. He had to be rescued before the Iraqis found him.

Maj. Cornum and a team of Army Pathfinders scrambled on a Blackhawk helicopter equipped for medical rescue from their camp near the town of Rafha, with two Apache helicopters flying escort. As they approached Capt. Anderson's location, however, Iraqi artillery fire slammed into the Blackhawk, sending it crashing to the desert in a ball of flame. The helicopter was destroyed but Maj. Cornum and two of the Pathfinders, Sgt. Troy Dunlap and Sgt. Daniel Stamaris, survived and were captured by Iraqi troops.

A few hours later, the allies would declare a ceasefire. The three rescue team survivors and Capt. Andrews, the pilot, were transferred to Baghdad. They were the last of the 21 Americans taken prisoner in the war.

In the west of occupied Iraq, the greatest danger was from all the unexploded ordnance still on the ground. Weeks of air attacks on military sites like the airfield at As Salman had left cluster bombs lying around by the hundreds. Clearing them was one of the missions for the troops arriving at this objective.

The only fatalities among French troops happened at As Salman. Two soldiers from the 6th light Armored Division were killed, and perhaps ten others were injured, by unexploded ordnance.

This place turned out to be one of the most dangerous objectives of the war.

The same day, seven U.S. soldiers were killed at the same airfield, clearing the same types of munitions. Their deaths weren't officially termed friendly fire, but in a sense they were.

American or other coalition air strikes had dropped the bombs there, spreading their lethal contents across a wide swath. Americans and other friendly troops were passing through, clearing a path.

Friendly fire casualties mounted all along the allied front in the war's final hours. In this chapter, a couple of reporters tell of another two, recorded when they happened upon the scene of a horrible incident from the previous day: nine British soldiers killed in their armored scout vehicle by missiles fired from an American warplane.

A few miles away, some Americans were also killed by friendly forces.

Asked about these incidents at his first press conference since the ground offensive began, the top allied commander said any death like that is a terrible tragedy.

Gen. Schwarzkopf had served two tours in Vietnam and he'd seen friendly fire in that war, too. It happens in every war. You never get used to it.

Decisive Battle Imminent: Republican Guard Must Hunker Down, Go on the Offensive or Make a Run for It

12:05 a.m.

This is a report from a pool at VII Corps Headquarters by Neil MacFarquhar. It was reviewed by Sgt. 1st Class Tegtneier. It is flagged on the issue of whether the battle has been started or not. If started, no flags.

WITH THE U.S. VII CORPS IN SAUDI ARABIA - U.S. military officials said the decisive armor battle against the Republican Guard, the sinewy heart of the Iraqi military, could develop soon in the rugged desert plain west of the city of Basra.

The VII Corps, the heavy armor of the U.S. military, joined by Britain's 1st Armored Division to create the largest ground force deployed since World War II, has lined up facing the Guard's dug-in position west of the southern port city.

The officials said some Guard units have moved from big divisions around the border between Iraq and Kuwait, as well as from inside the occupied emirate to form a heavy defensive line west of Basra. The allied forces are poised to sweep down through Iraq, reaching the entire length of the Kuwait border. The Guard cannot move north, and any escape east would be difficult because the allied air campaign has severed bridges across the Euphrates.

Military officers said the Republican Guard has three choices: to remain hunkered down and force the coalition armor to dig them out, to go on the offensive, or to make a run toward Basra.

They are not sure which the elite troops will choose, but they are prepared for any of them. To destroy the Guard would undermine Saddam's military power base.

"They are the center of gravity," said Capt. David F. Clark, 30, of Hagerstown, Md., an intelligence officer with the 11th Aviation Brigade.

Most of their commanders come from the area around Saddam's home village of Tikrit, and unlike other forces, he has not purged their ranks with executions.

They are given the best armaments, equipment, food and clothing. They have unparalleled discipline, as many are recruited as adolescents or even younger for the corps. "They are more or less the golden children," said Clark.

During the 1980-88 war with Iran, Saddam repeatedly used the Guard to spearhead important offensive operations and then withdrew them to allow the regular army to actually hold the land. The same pattern was repeated with the occupation of Kuwait. Their central disadvantage in battle is that they follow the Soviet model of centralized control. "They are kept on a tight leash because he was afraid of losing them," Clark said. At the same time, their absolute loyalty to Saddam means wholesale surrenders are unlikely.

The destruction rained on the guards over the past month means they have little fuel, ammunition or spare parts, and officers said their best chance for survival could be to sit in their holes and fight.

U.S. forces control both the skies and the night, although the high wind, rain and lightning that swept through the area on Tuesday made flying difficult.

But if they come out, Apache helicopters (with) Hellfire and other missiles could combine (with) U.S. Air Force A-10 Warthogs to pick them off.

2nd Armored Cavalry Takes On Saddam's Finest: "Republican Guard is Hauling Ass. This Could Be It"

By Christopher Hanson

WITH THE 2ND ARMORED CAVALRY REGIMENT IN SOUTHERN IRAQ - This is an account of how confusion fogged the desert on Feb. 26 as the 2nd Armored Cavalry Regiment became locked in battle with Iraq's vaunted Republican Guards.

The Regimental headquarters detachment had paused that afternoon, as the 2nd's tanks and Bradley fighting vehicles probed ahead.

Advance scouts made contact with Iraqi tank units, with some skirmishing.

Word in early afternoon was that the Iraqis seemed to be trying to slip away and escape into northern Iraq. The regiment's scouting units kept them in sight, however.

With skies darkly overcast and 70 mph winds blowing up sandstorms, the afternoon dragged on. You couldn't see anything very distinctly.

Armored columns moving just a quarter-mile away were dark blurs. A newcomer could have had no idea what they were.

Information reaching Regimental headquarters by radio was equally hard to make out. It was now unclear whether the Iraqis up ahead were trying to escape or were simply shifting positions, with the aim of blocking the advancing Americans, allowing other Iraqi units to slip to safety from Kuwait. Only one thing seemed clear: the units up ahead were Saddam Hussein's best, the battle-tested, relatively well-equipped and well-trained Republican Guard.

Wednesday - February 27, 1991

More waiting.

Capt. Bob Dobson, the spokesman for the 2nd, returned to his vehicle in a hurry. "We're about to jump (cavalry slang for move forward)," he said. "The Republican Guard is hauling ass. This could be it." And off the headquarters column rolled.

The regiment's assignment now was to catch the Guard and engage them in battle until heavier American units could move up to finish them off.

The sky had cleared, but the wind was still blowing hard. The column moved single-file along a rutted path, across a desert that seemed as flat as the ocean.

Speed was 10-15 mph. At 5:35, after about 45 minutes on the move, the regiment's flying command center—a UH-60 Blackhawk helicopter—landed beside the column which halted. A couple of minutes later, the vehicles began making 180-degree turns and heading off in the direction they had come.

What was going on? There was a report—or was it a rumor?—that Iraqi tanks were heading in their direction.

The headquarters detachment was traveling with no heavy armor. An encounter with Iraqi tanks could have been devastating. Better safe than sorry.

Fragmentary information coming in over the radio was that at least one other support unit, following behind the regiment's main attacking forces, had been shot up with one fatality.

What was going on?

As the headquarters column pulled back, two lone American scouts were left on lookout, standing beside an (blank) searching for the Iraqi armor. They disappeared beyond the horizon in the direction where the tanks were supposed to be. Evidently finding none, they reappeared and flew off to search in another direction.

Had the rumored tank threat been false?

After a minute or two, a column of tanks appeared in the distance, coming in their general direction. There was a tense moment until an inspection with binoculars showed they were American M1s.

Later, back at the headquarters detachment, which had circled its vehicles for the night, word was that a major Republican Guard counter-attack was building.

Soldiers began digging foxholes on the perimeter. A sergeant made the rounds passing the order that the perimeter was to be pulled 50 meters further in.

The vehicles pulled back and the soldiers began digging more holes. Then the order was evidently rescinded and the soldiers resumed their original positions, well-illuminated under a three-quarter moon.

In the distance, the flash of artillery lit up the sky—first the initial burst of light at ground level, then a second flash as the light bounced off the clouds.

The regiment was engaged in a battle with the Republican Guards along a 40 kilometer front. Flares lit up the sky. Balls of flame from America's Multiple Launch Rocket System shot skyward, bringing hundreds of bomblets down on the heads of the Iraqis.

And the artillery continued, flash after flash.

Then in the darkness off beyond the perimeter came the clanking sound of tracked vehicles—possibly tanks.

It grew louder, producing a queasy feeling for some of us inside the perimeter. Soldiers in foxholes reached for their weapons. The vehicles grew closer and closer and finally into sight.

They were American. Next morning came the news that the regiment, and a heavy American armored division, had thrashed the Iraqis, destroying an entire Republican Guard division.

The American handiwork was evident as the headquarters group moved forward—there were abandoned Iraqi tanks, a burned-out armored personnel carrier, and hundreds of abandoned Iraqi fighting positions.

"The mood is jubilant," said Dobson. A high-ranking Iraqi officer captured in the battle told interrogators that the Republican Guard's assignment had been to block the Americans, letting other Iraqi units escape, but that the 2nd Armored Cavalry had hit them 12 hours before they had expected an attack.

The battle had been confusing, but the victory was clear.

American Armor Routs the Vaunted Republican Guard: "These Are the Guys We Came to Get"

By Douglas Jehl

WITH U.S. FORCES, Iraq - It started in a rush, a quick dash to cut off the Iraqi road.

But with the first exchange of fire it quickly became clear that this would be no ordinary battle. There on the other side of the asphalt strip marched a column of top-of-the-line Iraqi T-72 tanks that could mean only one thing: The American Army had at last come face-to-face with the Republican Guard.

Near the front of the American advance, Lt. Col. Thomas Goedkoop looked through the sight of his M1A1 tank at a battlefield so ripe with targets that even after his third kill, he still wasn't sure what his battalion had bumped into.

In the chaos of combat, all he could discern was "flashin' and firin'."

But along the American battle line, in an armored division that had struck deep into enemy (territory) in an attack bent on the destruction of the elite Iraqi force, there was the exultant sense that the beginning of the end had come.

"This is the seventh game of the World Series," exhorted the division commander, Maj. Gen. Ronald H. Griffith, as the battle took its shape, speaking over the radio channel used to direct the battle pitting the 1st Armored Division against a reinforced brigade from Republican Guard's Medinah Division.

"These are the guys we came to get."

The major battle that erupted here just after noon on Wednesday came after advancing American Army units headed into Iraq wheeled sharply toward Kuwait to cut off an Iraqi escape route and force the long-planned confrontation against the Republican Guard.

American officers offering a preliminary assessment of the battle, which continued into the evening, said scores of Iraqi tanks and armored vehicles were destroyed in what they described as a rout.

No U.S. tank or armored vehicle was hit by a single Iraqi round, U.S. casualties were scant, with only one American, an Air Force pilot, missing and feared dead.

The clash began (with) a simple exchange of fire between armor arrayed along the front, tank against tank, Bradley fighting vehicle against Russian-made BDM in a deadly duel in which the U.S. forces, fighting according to a plan, methodically destroyed the Iraqi units while never venturing into their range.

The strain on those who sat and squeezed the trigger as tanks approached just 2,000 meters away was nevertheless considerable. At the height of battle, Goedkoop, asked how he was doing, said only: "I gotta change my drawers."

But as more armor joined the battle and the exchange of fire became a cacophony along the front, the war grew ever more intense as the Americans sought to press home their advantage and Iraqi forces sought to rescue what had already become a dismal prospect.

First came artillery, a thunderous accompaniment to already stormy skies that for a time threatened all three American brigades slugging it out along the front lines and sent support units cowering for cover as shells were lobbed well beyond the battlefield.

But then, after communications problems and other complications delayed the American return of fire, the responding salvo began to light the sky with multiple-launch rockets and advanced-tactical missiles, silencing the Iraqi barrage as they sailed across the sky in slow and deadly arcs.

By late afternoon, the battle had long since become a rout, with Apache helicopters and A-10 attack planes shooting Iraqi armor at will. Those soldiers not in the fight themselves watched it from a distance, standing on their vehicles like spectators on the Fourth of July to watch as enemy tanks and ammunition dumps exploded to light the horizon in flame.

At dusk, smoke hung over the battlefield, darkening an already slate-gray sky, and as the sun peered through a gap in the clouds it was almost orange in the battle-haze.

"On a day like this," said Riley, commander of this division's 1st Brigade, "there is nothing prettier than the sight of a burning Iraqi tank."

Indeed, the division learned early Thursday of the cease-fire that was to begin at 8 a.m.

But in an attack that was to last until the final minute, artillery guns rained their most furious bombardment yet on enemy positions, and the division launched a three-brigades-abreast attack on Republican Guard units still trying to make their escape.

"We'll attack until 8:00," said Col. Riley, the brigade commander. "And if we're still engaged at that time, we will continue to fight those fights."

The American rush to close the circle around the Iraqi army, which even before the battle Wednesday had left tongues thick from lack of sleep, began Tuesday afternoon and continued with a night-long fighting charge across the desert as U.S. forces sought to exploit the vulnerability of Iraqi forces that had turned suddenly to flight.

"It looks like the Republican Guards are cutting and running," Griffith had said as his division began its eastward race to cut off the Iraqi escape to the north out of Kuwait.

"Our mission is to press them to the wall."

In what proved to be the climax of that effort Wednesday, this division moved out three brigades abreast to take up positions along a small Iraqi highway just outside the Kuwaiti border reported to be heavy with northward-bound military traffic in an area in which the Republican Guards had long been hunkered down.

But it was not until reports of enemy contact began to mount and then to multiply that officers directing the battle from a mobile command post just outside direct-fire range knew that the search-and-destroy mission had finally hit its mark.

"Now we've got a tank war," said Riley, the Phantom Brigade commander, as the distinctive rapid-fire thuds from tank main guns sent tremors through the air, and the smoke from burning Iraqi armor began to rise up in the air.

The fierce firefight came in marked contrast to the half-hearted resistance with which the advancing Americans had been met so far.

In the eastward rush toward the Republican Guard, this division has since early Monday fought its way through lesser Iraqi forces in an almost nonstop series of battles preceded by aerial bombardment and artillery barrages so intense that the armored vehicles near the front of this

American battle-wedge are rocked by the tremor of the launch.

The intense softening-up efforts have so far left this division with little more than cleanup work, with most enemy vehicles already destroyed or abandoned as the M1A1 tanks and Bradley fighting vehicles advancing in close formation, sometimes three brigades abreast.

In one Air Force raid in advance of an attack against an Iraqi infantry brigade, two A-10s and some six F-16s together destroyed some 27 enemy tanks, leaving only a paltry force behind to fend off this armored division.

The result Tuesday morning when the attack finally began saw a battlefield nearly empty of the enemy but littered with burning armor, some of it set alight by the Air Force strikes and some ignited as the U.S. ground forces advanced in a line of fire, completing a path of destruction designed to ensure that no Iraqi military vehicle can be left to fight again.

Those Iraqi soldiers who had not already fled were almost pitiful in their surrender, emerging from squalid trenches and some pleading in tears in begging their captors that they not be shot. "There is nothing more helpless than an army that is running," said Lt. Col. Michael Leahy, the artillery battalion commander for this division's lead brigade, sharing his quarters with a reporter in the cramped rear of an armored command and control vehicle as it bounced across the desert in the midst of the all-night fight.

The transition to a battle posture here brought a welcome sense of the hunt to officers and soldiers in an armored division whose first 24 hours in Iraqi territory had seen a northward drive remarkable for its peacefulness.

But beginning Monday morning, when the division found determined pockets of resistance in its attack on a military outpost in the crossroads town of Al Bussayah, the battle has become a series of sprints across the sand interspersed with anxious lulls as artillery thunders over the heads of frontline combat units, its multiple-launch rockets intense streaks of light that soar on a low trajectory across the sky.

And (in) what Col. Riley the brigade commander, called a mission of "exploitation," the division destroyed what was left of the Iraqi's Adnon brigade and has fought preliminary skirmishes on the way toward what is expected to be a major battle with what is left of the Medinah division, one of the elite Republican Guard units.

"Boy, if there ever was a place for a tank war, this is it," said Maj. Roy Adams, the brigade operations officer, as he surveyed from the turret of his Bradley a desert as flat and vast as could ever be imagined.

Nine GIs Dead as U.S. and British Armor Plow Through Iraqi Troops: "I Think They Are Desperate"

By Neal MacFarquhar

WITH THE VII CORPS IN IRAQ - The heavy armor of the American and British forces left scores of smoldering tanks and thousands of POWs in its wake Wednesday as it rolled down toward Kuwait, encountering some stiff resistance from the Republican Guard divisions in its path.

Interviews with troops behind the front line in three of the four American divisions indicated the largest ground offensive since World War II was rolling steadily forward,

Wednesday - February 27, 1991

but the forces had to fight their way through each division of the top Iraqi troops. By early Wednesday, nine Americans had died, but the overall casualty figure was not available.

Soldiers at the 3rd Armored Division said they suffered four killed and seven wounded in the first fighting Tuesday night, but they did not know the toll for Wednesday. VII Corps officers said one Iraqi division that had been deployed west of the northern Iraqi-Kuwaiti border had been destroyed. They said elements of the VII Corps were fighting their way through another division right above Kuwait, and seen some move of a third division deployed nearer the Gulf, southeast of the port city of Basra.

There are signs that one division was destroying some of their equipment as they move back to consolidate their positions around Basra. Officers said the American battle plan, which started with a broad sweep north before turning back to south toward Kuwait, could roll up most opposition from the Guard by late Thursday. The British 1st Armored Division and the American 1st Infantry Division moved into southern Iraq from Kuwait at Wadi al-Batin without resistance.

"We're going to keep pushing until we've eliminated this man's cotton-pickin' ability to make war," said Staff Sgt. Franklin Lott, 32, Winston-Salem, N.C.

He described the battle that started late Tuesday night and continued through Wednesday as "a good, heavy-duty battle with the Republican Guard."

Troops were all wearing their suits against chemical weapons, but not their gas masks. They were told to put the suits on Wednesday just before noon out of fear that Iraq would turn to desperate methods as the frontline pushed forward.

"I think they are desperate. I'm sure they may try it. It's like a rattlesnake. It's going to strike before it runs," said Pfc. Charles Biltz, of Culver, Ind.

Tiger Brigade North of Kuwait City; Controls 2 Highway Interchanges, Surrounds Iraqi Air Base

By Bill Gannon

SUMMARY: Augmented Tiger Brigade pushes north 50 to 60 kilometers across the desert, cutting off Iraqi retreat north and west out of Kuwait City.

Tigers seize control of two major highways and two cloverleafs in Al Jahra area just outside Kuwait City, trapping miles of Iraqi tanks, vehicles and troops backed up into Kuwait City.

One killed and at least two wounded by snipers clearing Kuwait City suburb bunker zone Tuesday evening. Ali Al Saleem Air Base surrounded with assault by Marines expected first light Wednesday.

Brigade battles Iraqi tanks and records at least 76 tank kills—including T-72 tanks—destroys artillery guns and trucks and armored troop carriers and captures or accepts surrender of estimated 3,500 enemy prisoners of war.

WITH TIGER BRIGADE OUTSIDE KUWAIT CITY—Attacking as they raced 50 to 60 kilometers north across the desert, this heavy armored unit cut off the Iraqi retreat from Kuwait City late Tuesday afternoon and closed the northern and western exits from the city.

By nightfall Tuesday, the men of Tiger Brigade controlled two cloverleaf highway interchanges and had sealed off the most direct route between the capital city and Iraq in the suburb of Al Jahra.

Military commanders here also said there were intelligence reports of several miles of jammed military and civilian traffic leaving Kuwait City four-lanes wide before they were trapped by the American forces Tuesday afternoon at 4:20 p.m.

The brigade spent the evening and night cleaning out enemy bunkers and sporadically engaging enemy troops in the suburbs of the city.

With the Saudi and Kuwaiti coalition forces pushing up (to) the north, Kuwait City was now surrounded, said Col. John Sylvester, 45, of Brownsville, Tex., who is commander of the heavy armored unit supporting the 2nd Marine Division. "The bad guys are cut off. We moved quickly. I guess we could have moved quicker, but I wanted us to be careful and kill more stuff on the way," Sylvester said, lighting up a Cuban cigar to celebrate. Sylvester said he had spoken to Marine Gen. Walter Boomer about the push north and Boomer passed along a message from allied commander Gen. H. Norman Schwarzkopf "not to let anybody or anything out of Kuwait City."

"I'm just glad most of them didn't fight because then I would have had to kill them all and that is unnecessary," Sylvester said.

Sylvester's Tigers controlled not only the two largest highway interchanges, but had also surrounded the Ali Al Saleem Air Force base.

The highway heading east from Al Jahra into Kuwait City some 10 kilometers away, meanwhile, was littered with stripped and wrecked cars, looted stores, and demolished buildings. American tank commanders and others were told to look for members of the Kuwaiti resistance, who would be wearing red or pink armbands.

Along the four-lane highway, the cars lay on their back or junked on their wheel rims. Iraqi troops had stolen the tires to be resold in Baghdad at a profit months ago. The bunkers in the heights overlooking the air base and surrounding the western exit from the city were empty of Iraqi soldiers but still protected by an extensive network of minefields.

Hundreds of AK-47 assault rifles, small artillery guns and other weapons were abandoned by the fleeing troops and found by the occupying Tigers.

Bunkers toured were well-stocked with food and made comfortable with furnishings—some merchandise still in their original store wrappers.

A similar complex protecting the northern cloverleaf and highway, however, was protected by at least one team of snipers who shot and killed one soldier and wounded at least two others. The dead soldier, whose name and other information cannot be released under Pentagon reporting rules for Operation Desert Storm, died of massive blood loss while waiting for a helicopter med-evac flight.

According to Sylvester, the soldier was shot and lay bleeding as his condition was evaluated and a med-evac helicopter was summoned. The first helicopter suffered a mechanical breakdown. By the time the second helicopter was airborne some 20 minutes later, the soldier (had) died.

The circumstances surrounding the death of the soldier, who was clearing out bunkers when he was shot, stunned the Tiger Brigade soldiers and officers. Several of the soldiers said they were angry that a med-evac helicopter was not attached to, and moving with, their unit, but had to be called in from the rear. Sylvester expressed both grief and a sense of remorse at the loss of life in an operation marked by few casualties.

There was no information available on the condition of the wounded.

The drive to Kuwait City began at 5 a.m. Tuesday when Sylvester woke and learned that Baghdad Radio was calling for the immediate "withdrawal" of Iraqi forces in occupied Kuwait. By 9:53 a.m., he had orders to lighten his load of slower-moving

Wednesday - February 27, 1991

Marines and push forward with additional fast-moving units to cross the desert, destroy as many enemy weapons and capture as many soldiers as possible and, above all, to block any retreat from the city.

At exactly noon, Operation Tiger Storm—the name given by Sylvester to the drive—began to creak and grind its way toward occupied Kuwait City.

Now consisting of two tank battalions, one mechanized infantry battalion, a battalion of light armored Marine infantry, a signal battalion, a service and support battalion, two Marine reconnaissance companies and (a) Marine howitzer artillery battery to augment its own, Tiger Brigade rolled north some 5,500-men strong.

Positioned in a dual axis attack formation with a third force kept in the rear to be used to counter any Iraqi counter-attack, Tiger Brigade moved out in a massive display of military might unseen since World War II.

Sylvester spread out his hundreds of armored tracked vehicles along a 12kilometer-wide and 15-kilometer-deep multiple-wedge attack formation and set out to cover the 40-to-60 kilometers in three-and-a-half hours.

It was a remarkable and stirring sight.

Everywhere you looked there were tanks and assorted armored vehicles, Humvees and re-supply trucks. The moving armor stretched to the horizon.

Their iron treads clicking and engines groaning, the Tigers kicked up a chalk-like sand dust that hung in the air like a fog for hours and was visible from miles away.

Moving forward through layer after layer of Iraqi-built defensive bunkers and trenches, the lead M1A1 Abrams tanks or Bradley fighting vehicles would "nudge them" by firing 50-cal. machine-gun rounds into the sand walls nearby.

Most of the time, the nudge was answered with a frantic waving of a white rag or bandage and the now-familiar sight of frightened men raising their hands in surrender to the passing Tigers. Most of the soldiers would smile, wave whatever white they had, and begin walking toward the tanks and armored troops carriers holding hands and waving their greetings.

A little white-and-black dog was spotted running on the battlefield as if driven mad by the armor and gunfire. The dog constantly changed direction as machine-gun fire frightened it one way and then another before it disappeared from sight.

An Iraqi soldier called after it when it ran by him, but quickly raised his hands as he tried to flag down a passing troop carrier to give himself over.

But with many kilometers of desert to cross to make their objective, the surrendering soldiers were simply waved to the rear by the Tiger Brigade. Some threw their fallen counterparts a bottle of water or a pre-packaged meal ready to eat (MRE) since they knew the MPs (Military Police) were still miles and possibly hours behind.

An hour into the drive, 20 Iraqi T-72 tanks were spotted and immediately attacked and destroyed.

Unlike the second day of the ground war (Monday) in which Sylvester worried about Syrians on his left flank and approved firing orders, Tuesday was a fire-at-will day. Even with only two or three feet of tank turret showing above their sand nests, the Tiger tank and TOW missile crews had no difficulties hitting their target.

In one moment in the day's initial tank battle, an Iraqi T-72 tank fired several rounds at the lead Tiger line of M1A1 tanks.

The Iraqi tank flashed and fired a few rounds in a thunderous but distant thud.

A nearby Tiger tank used its firing range advantage well, standing back and allowing the incoming shell to fall short before firing at the Iraqi tank from some 3,000 meters away.

The M1A1's 120mm main gun rose as the round left the tank at the rate of one mile per second with an ear-splitting report that subtly shifted the air pressure.

Moments later, it struck the tank turret in an explosion and immediate fireball.

White smoke turned black as the tank began to burn and the M1A1 found a new target and fired once more, killing another tank.

"It's just like in training. We get a target, confirm it, and fire on it," said Sgt. Tom Cavanaugh, 28, of Passaic, N.J., an M1A1 tank gunner. "Killing an enemy tank is something of a letdown. I just never thought it would be this easy," he added.

"I got two kills today and it was just like we trained for—stand back and shoot and kill it dead," he laughed.

In one TOW engagement witnessed, a Bradley fighting vehicle sighted a T-62 tank moving across the desert floor more than 2,000 meters away. The tank was sighted and the missile launched. It struck the tank dead center, punching a hole in it.

Even through binoculars from a distance of two kilometers, the Iraqi tank was noticeably lifted off its treads by the force of the TOW slamming into it.

"It was target right killed, target left killed," said Spec. Dwayne Morrit, a Bradley fighting vehicle TOW missile officer.

The 23-year-old Detroit native said he felt like he was back "pretending" in a simulator in Killeen, Tex., home to the Tiger Brigade's 2nd Armored Division.

Such scenes were repeated across the line of advance more than 76 times Tuesday afternoon as the Tigers went on the prowl, attacking every vehicle, tank, and artillery position they sighted. The brigade had recorded 76 kills, according to Sylvester.

In return, the Tigers took tank and ground fire, some mortar fire, and a few rounds of artillery. No damage was reported.

An overwhelming majority of the tanks killed were abandoned, Sylvester said. Those tank crews that did fight back did so poorly, the commander said, explaining that they seemed poorly trained.

Several of the tanks fired at the advancing American armor but no hits were made, Sylvester said. A series of tank battles and smaller engagements followed for the remainder of the day, he added. "This is my war trophy," said Sylvester, holding a white bandage used by many Iraqi soldiers to surrender to his tanks and armored vehicles.

Sylvester is not the only one to collect a memento of his war service.

Nearly every member of Tiger Brigade seems to have something taken from a surrendering Iraqi soldier or taken from a bunker. AK-47 assault rifles and Soviet-made 9mm pistols have become the souvenir of choice, even as soldiers admit they will probably never be able to get them home through customs or the watchful eye of their superiors.

It is against both military and national law to import either weapon without filing the necessary legal documents. Bringing home a fully-automatic combat rifle would be nearly impossible as it is against federal law barring the possession of automatic weapons, the soldiers said. But they still wanted them and began scheming on how they could try to get them back. Other popular souvenirs include bayonets, hats, helmets, and gas mask bags.

All EPWs must remove hats and drop surrender flags and all other belongings when searched by military policemen for processing into EPW holding camps. Troops pick them up. Most of the war trophies so far have been found in bunkers—a fact that leaves commanders here uneasy, given the possibility of booby-traps.

Night had already fallen and many of the soldiers had dug in for the night when across the command network radio, permission is given a Bradley fighting vehicle driver to keep something he found on the battlefield—a small black-and-white dog he has named "Tigerbait."

Wednesday - February 27, 1991

Marines Take Kuwait Airport: "Once We Got Rolling, It Was Like a Training Exercise With Live People"

By Kirk Spitzer

KUWAIT CITY - Troops of the 1st Marine Division captured Kuwait International Airport after a brief firefight early Wednesday and apparently ended all organized Iraqi resistance in Kuwait City.

The Marines remained in the southern and western sections of the city and left occupation and formal liberation of the remainder of the city—including most of the downtown district—to troops from Kuwait, Saudi Arabia, Egypt and other Arab countries. A Marine reconnaissance unit remained at the U.S. Embassy, where it had slipped in just before troops of the 1st Marine Division shot their way into the city late Tuesday.

The Marines cleared a large section of the city surrounding Kuwait International Airport late Tuesday then occupied (it) in the pre-dawn darkness. There was little resistance and Marine armored vehicles—festooned with American flags and Marine Corps banners—lined the taxiways and parking aprons later in the day.

The rattle of small-arms fire could be heard occasionally in parts of the city as troops mopped up. Much of the Iraqi forces had surrendered or retreated long before the Marines reached the city. Except for one brief tank battle in which a dozen Iraqi vehicles were destroyed, there appeared to be little organized resistance.

The Marines suffered no casualties during the fighting.

Sgt. Mark McDonnell, commander of a Light Armored Vehicle, said 34 Iraqis surrendered to his unit shortly after the Marines rolled into the western suburbs Tuesday night. "There was a lot of white flags. They were in pretty bad shape. One guy didn't have any boots—just rags on his feet," said McDonnell, 32, of Columbia, Mo.

He said Kuwaiti citizens poured out of their homes waving and cheering as the Marine armored vehicles rolled into attack positions. "I was pretty surprised to see them riding around on the roads, hanging out of their cars, while there was an attack on," he said.

Despite the dramatic nature of the Marines' victory during the lightning three-day campaign, there was little celebration.

Many Marines said the campaign had been shorter and easier than many expected. Marine commanders had expected casualties in the thousands, but only six Marines had been reported killed in combat through late Tuesday.

The 1st Marine Division fought all or part of seven Iraqi infantry, armored, and mechanized divisions during its advance from the southwest "heel" of Kuwait to the capital city. A typical Marine division has from 15,000 to 20,000 combat troops, while Iraqi divisions normally have about 10,000 troops each.

The Marine division destroyed hundreds of Iraqi tanks and armored vehicles and captured more than 15,000 Iraqi soldiers. Many more are expected to be taken prisoner during mopping-up operations. "It was easy. There were moments when it was intense, but not nearly as intense as it could have been," said Capt. Kelvin Davis, 34, of Louisville, Ky., the assistant operations officer for a battalion of light armored vehicles. "I hate to say it, but once we got rolling, it was like a training exercise with live people running around. Our training exercises are a lot harder," said Davis.

Sgt. Mark Mansour, 23, of Seattle, Wash., a member of a special Army unit attached to the Marine division, said he enjoyed the three-day battle. "It was exciting. You get to do what you're taught."

Size, Shape of the War: Allies Control Chunk of Iraq; "Virtually Empty Town Except for a Few Bedouins"

By Joseph Albright

AS SALMAN, ALLIED-OCCUPIED IRAQ - The allies on Wednesday had taken at least 10,000 square miles of southern Iraq and had captured this once-thriving trading town, leaving its ever-present Saddam Hussein portraits pockmarked to stare down at the deserted streets.

At a police station overlooking As Salman, journalists accompanying American forces found military maps still on the wall, with green thumbtacks representing Iraqi defenses and red tacks standing for those of forces of the American-led coalition.

The map room was littered with shattered glass from the windows. Out in the parking lot, spent cluster grenades littered the gravel like olive-drab orange peels. They were the leftovers from a CBU-58 duster bomb whose casing rested on the curb across the highway.

Two unexploded cluster bomblets of the kind that shattered the police posts' window still lay in the parking lot, a hazard to the French and American soldiers working to secure the first town the allies had captured inside Iraq.

At a gas station a few miles out of As Salman, either a bomb or an artillery shell had collapsed the concrete structure and blown in half the big illuminated Saddam Hussein poster that used to decorate the intersection 200 miles south of Baghdad and 60 miles from the Saudi border.

Staff Sgt. Herman Brown, 32, of Austin, Tex., looked out of his armored vehicle and said, "He's got to go."

The French and Americans have now secured a parallelogram-shaped wedge of barren, rocky land in southern Iraq that runs from As Salman southwest to the Saudi border near Rafha on the west; to the Euphrates River northeast of Salaman, southeast along the river and back southwest to Saudi Arabia.

The exact delineation of the allied-occupied zone, especially on the east, could not be ascertained with certainty. But the figure of 10,000 square miles of captured territory was a reporter's estimate based on progress reports received from several allied units involved in the surprise westward flanking strike into Iraq 200 miles west of the Kuwaiti border.

Already, the allies have taken a piece of Iraq larger than Kuwait itself. The captured Iraqi territory contains few if any of Iraq's oilfields and an insignificant fraction of Iraq's population and agriculture.

The town of As Salman, which had a pre-1991 population of about 7,000 traders, Bedouins, petty officials and their families, was captured without a fight after French and American forces surrounded the town and broadcast demands for its surrender on microphone trucks.

Army Capt. Scott Halasz, 32, of Ohatchee, Ala., a civil affairs officer, stood along with several hundred French and a handful of American soldiers and said, "Virtually it is an empty town except for a few Bedouins."

Halasz said the allies would probably place the town in the hands of a temporary allied military governor because all the town's Iraqi civil authorities have fled north.

He said the only Iraqis left when the French pushed into the town Tuesday morning were about a dozen civilian townspeople and about 15 men in the military who were taken prisoner.

Pool reporters accompanying some of the first troops into As Salman Tuesday

Wednesday - February 27, 1991

found two Iraqi civilians being escorted into an abandoned Iraqi municipal building by a dozen French troops. One French officer said the two middle-aged men in Arab headdress and one boy of about ten wearing a jacket would be allowed to reclaim their own houses after officers had searched them for weapons.

At a small hospital in the middle of town, reporters found an operating room which had been abandoned with a half-full bag of intravenous solution still hanging on its rack next to what had apparently been an operating table. The table was gone, but several olive-drab stretchers were stacked in a corner.

In one former office near the operating room, two brown military uniforms labeled "Made in Romania" hung on a coat-rack. Boots, calendars, and packages of cigarettes lay scattered on the floor. In one room, a metal dish contained the remains of a rice and onions meal. Outside, a Kuwaiti translator serving with the U.S. Army looked with disgust at the towering Saddam Hussein portrait painted on the outside of the hospital.

The translator, Masser Al-Ajmy, 22, who spent eight weeks at Fort Dix, N.J., learning basic American military skills, said "Saddam killed the good men of Iraq. It's crazy. Our job is to do something about this crazy man."

A tour through the abandoned town and its outskirts was a lesson in how much Iraq has depended on imported products to sustain its standard of living, which thanks to oil is well above Third World levels.

The brand new generator at the destroyed gasoline station was a Lister diesel from Great Britain. The mechanism for the gas pump was made by Toshiba in Japan.

The empty can of powdered milk was a leftover from the days when the United States got rid of excess farm commodities by selling billions of dollars worth to Iraq. The label said "Exported by Luxor California Exports Corp.—USA. Imported by state company for foodstuffs trading, Iraq."

At the hospital, stacks of saline intravenous fluid carried labels from Thailand.

In the first wave of troops into Iraq, nearly all of the soldiers have been males. But in the middle of As Salman, a soldier in charge of guarding one of the downtown buildings was Sgt. 1st Class Luann Lusardi, 30, of Belmar, NJ. "We were pretty excited to get here," she said. "I want to get busy and get these buildings secure."

When she heard about the big Saddam posters painted on the outside of the school and the hospital, she said "it makes me sick."

After leaving As Salman, pool journalists attached to an artillery (unit) joined a convoy numbering thousands of American military vehicles that inched in the moonlight about 50 miles to the east. The artillery unit pulled out of the convoy and set up a temporary headquarters at 2:30 a.m. on a flat, featureless desert roughly 50 miles southwest of the Euphrates River.

Officers said that the stretch of Iraq both north and south of the convoy had been secured from the Saudi border to the Euphrates.

The fact that a convoy could travel with no hint of Iraqi resistance 110 miles from the Americans' point of entry near Rafha, Saudi Arabia, was a further demonstration of how widespread was the collapse of the world's fifth-biggest army (desk check fifth, from my memory) just days into the ground offensive.

2 French Soldiers Killed, 10 Wounded at Iraqi Airfield: "Either a Mine, Booby-Trap, or Unexploded Ordnance"

By Gary Regenstreif

AS SALMAN, Iraq - Two French soldiers were killed and 10 others wounded on Tuesday by an explosion of unknown origin in this abandoned southern Iraqi town they had entered to search for enemy troops, U.S. officials said.

The casualties, believed to be France's first victims of combat in the Gulf War, were part of the allied drive north and then east into Iraq to cut supply lines to Iraqi soldiers in Kuwait. "It was either a mine or booby-trap or unexploded ordnance," said Col. Ron Rokosz, commander of the U.S. Army 82nd Airborne Division's 2nd Brigade.

The Iraqi military is believed to have forced the 3,000 citizens of As Salman out and set up the command center for 6,000 members of their 45th Infantry Division at a school, according to U.S. intelligence.

The division, specially trained in guerilla warfare, fought Iraq's own Kurds during its eight-year war with Iran.

Allied bombers hit this sector in recent days and helicopters dropped leaflets urging Iraqi surrender. When French forces rolled in on Tuesday, the only subjects of President Saddam Hussein, smiling down from posters and painted murals everywhere, were some stray sheep and dogs.

Iraqi soldiers, in the town only two days earlier, had fled.

Food was left unfinished on table tops in As Salman's buildings and uniforms were left behind. "They obviously left in a hurry," said Capt. Keith Bax, 28, of St. Petersburg, Fla., a civil affairs officer. "They knew we were coming. Now it's a ghost town."

However, unexploded bomblets dropped from the sky were still scattered around the town and officials were trying to determine if one of them was responsible for the French casualties.

Commanders said they expected the 45th to put up stiff resistance but 2,000 of them, perhaps more, surrendered without a fight and the rest moved north.

As Salman perhaps best symbolizes the ease with which allied forces have pushed north in the four-day-old ground war. "It's a rout," said Rokosz, of Chicago. "I never thought we could do that. It's the greatest feeling in the world."

The 82nd Airborne has suffered no casualties in their mission, which took them east beginning Tuesday toward the bulk of the Iraqi forces.

Perhaps the biggest challenge to commanders in this sector of Iraq, they acknowledge, was to handle the flood of Iraqi soldiers pouring from the rocky desert to surrender.

Later Tuesday, about a dozen residents of As Salman returned to their town to discover their buildings dusty, the shelves largely bare. Their own homes were searched by French troops, who questioned them. Foxholes had been dug around the town.

Masser Al-Ajmy, a Kuwaiti volunteer with U.S. forces in the town, found some bittersweet irony in invading the nation that invaded his own.

"Our job is to take care of this crazy man," said Al-Ajmy, 20, an interpreter for U.S. forces, who looked up at the smiling visage of Saddam painted on a hospital wall.

"I want to hit him but I can't. I'm happy I'm here but it's too bad there has been so much damage because of him."

Wednesday - February 27, 1991

7 U.S. Engineers Killed by U.S. Bomblets at Iraqi Airfield: "We'll Have to Pull Together, Like the Family We Are"

By Laurence Jolidon

WITH THE U.S. ARMY - Seven members of an Army combat engineer company were killed Tuesday afternoon (26 Feb.) when a pile of unexpended U.S. cluster bombs dropped during the allied air campaign exploded as the soldiers were preparing to dispose of them.

Names of the dead soldiers were being withheld pending notification of next of kin. The accident occurred at a major military airbase near the town of As Salman in southern Iraq that had been seized and occupied hours before by French and American troops.

The engineer troops, from the 27th Engineer Battalion (Combat Airborne) of Fort Bragg, N.C., were clearing the southeast end of the base runways of unexploded bombs and destroying them by attaching a demolition charge.

Lt. Col. Ron Stewart, commander of the 27th, said the incident is under investigation, but some questions will be difficult to answer "because the guys I'd need to talk to are no longer around. But we're trying to provide all the answers we can."

In the ground offensive, the 27th was given the task of seeing that the airbase's runways were usable by allied aircraft. The field was to be used to re-supply and support units on the offensive's western flank. Bunkers and command posts around the large airfield suffered major damage in the bombing campaign that preceded the ground war. But except for unexploded cluster bombs that littered the field, the airfield was usable almost from the time the engineers arrived early Tuesday.

Only a few craters marred the field's two 8,000-meter runways.

Loud explosions rocked the airfield during the day, as the U.S. troops assisted the French regiments that were in control of the base in destroying the scattered ordnance.

When they first arrived, both French and American troops walked on foot over much of the base, searching for booby-traps and live ammunition that could endanger those using the field.

The death toll, one of the highest in a single incident since the beginning of the U.S. deployment six months ago, struck the engineer battalion hard.

The engineers had seen virtually no fighting, only packs of Iraqi deserters and POWs, on their two-day convoy north to their objective. Their runway repair services were needed only marginally.

Pfc. Tony Auxier, 20, of Walla Walla, Wash., waited with the rest of his company while the platoon that suffered the most casualties in the accident huddled in a separate group around their road-graders and dump trucks.

U.S. flags flew at half-mast from two of the battalion's vehicle radio antennas.

"We'll just have to pull together, like the family we are," he said. "We've had personality conflicts, like any unit does, but when something like this happens, those become unimportant.

"You know somebody for awhile, and see him, like he laughs all the time. Next thing you know, he's not there. It's hard to understand." His eyes were filled with tears.

Sgt. Thomas Tennant, 30, of Waynesburg, Pa., said, "I know one thing. Those seven people will not be forgotten. They can't be."

"Their platoon is devastated, we all are," said Spec. Daniel Bartz, 21, of Sheboygan, Wis. "Best friends are gone, your dad is gone, your buddy, your brother. One guy was going to be best man at one of our weddings. Another one's wife is just about to have a baby. I can't believe it."

Word of the deaths flashed quickly around the airfield, where the 27th's companies were parked, awaiting their next mission in the fast-moving ground offensive.

The first logistics base they had been scheduled to create in the desert of southern Iraq was now unneeded.

The rout of the Iraqi forces was so rapid, the entire western flank was being ordered to move east, toward the Euphrates River and Kuwait. Early Wednesday morning, less than 24 hours after reaching their airbase objective, the men of the 27th Engineer Battalion moved on, joining a long convoy of troops, tanks and equipment headed east.

The airbase apparently was no longer a priority.

The accident was such a difficult thing to believe, "some people thought it was a sick joke at first," said Sgt. Matthew Coulter, 30, of Pittsburgh.

"The mission has been so easy, up to now. This will wake everybody up, bring them back to reality. We'll all be a lot more careful now. It's just too bad it takes something like this to remind us to do that."

1st Cav Joins Battle—A Thundering, Roaring Herd of Grinding, Smoke-Spewing, Gas-Guzzling Machinery

By Mark Fritz

WITH THE WOLFPACK IN SOUTHEASTERN IRAQ - It was the terrible calm, the hours before battle, the molasses minutes that give you enough time to shut your eyes or chew a ration, but hardly enough peace to sleep or swallow. Gary Valentine sat on the turret of his Bradley fighting vehicle and peered into the black pitch of night.

About 70 kilometers to the northeast sat the Soviet-built T-72 tanks of the Hammurabi, an armor unit of the crack Republican Guard. Officers told soldiers that the guard units in this region were cornered, desperate, deadly, maybe willing to make the last stand and probably equipped with chemical weapons or nerve agents.

The two bridges to Basra in the northeast were gone.

Kuwait, the 19th province, was severed and lost.

An allied armada of armor was coming to fight them.

Included in that armada was the U.S. Army's 1st Cavalry Division, which includes the 1st Battalion-5th Cavalry Regiment, which encompasses Charlie Company, which goes by the name "The Wolfpack" on the radio.

Manning the guns on one of the Wolfpack's 14 Bradleys is Sgt. Gary Valentine, 24, of San Jose, Calif. "It's like an athlete before a big game," Valentine said softly in the pre-dawn darkness Wednesday morning. "You get butterflies. I definitely have butterflies. If you're not worried, you're probably too confident and probably not prepared."

Valentine, a handsome kid with an Elvis grin and curly black hair that probably tests regulations, carries a picture of the impossibly pretty woman he married one week before he was sent to Saudi Arabia in October. The couple had to postpone a big wedding celebration.

"We had to postpone a lot of plans," he said.

Not the least of which was getting out of the Army and starting college, which (he) was supposed to do on Feb. 2, before President Bush indefinitely extended the terms of service for everyone who was deployed in the Persian Gulf.

Also in the same boat was Valentine's buddy, Sgt. Ron Randazzo.

Randazzo was still around when his company was sent out on a recon patrol behind Iraqi lines on Feb. 20. The company came under fire, and Randazzo was killed. "You've got to take this stuff seriously," he said. "Lot of guys, they goof around. You have to be ready."

The 1st Division pushed northeast into Iraq, close to the Kuwaiti border, and encountered only minimal resistance from apparently fleeing Republican Guards. Some Iraqi tanks were reported hit by 2nd Armored Cavalry Division.

Col. Michael Parker, commander of the 1st Battalion-5th Cavalry, said Wednesday afternoon, "The general feeling is this thing may be over soon." He said 1st Cavalry was keying on moving Republican Guard units, but that mass surrenders did not eliminate the chance of serious fighting. "There may be six guys waving a white flag but four willing to put up a pretty good fight," said Parker, 42, of Dallas.

The 1st Cavalry Division knifed into central Iraq late Tuesday night after spending more than a week as a decoy, a red herring meant to fool Saddam Hussein into thinking the division would lead the land assault from an entirely different location.

The 1st Cavalry had been massed just south of Iraq's southeast corner, along a dry desert gulch called the Wadi al Batin that runs parallel to the Iraq-Kuwait border.

Troops for days had been pouring massive amounts of artillery and sending scout patrols into that area to give the impression that coalition forces were focusing on the area to clear a path for the spearhead of the invasion.

Senior military officials said Iraq began beefing up troops in the area, apparently moving in units from further west where in fact the real allied invasion was planned.

"I think it was a total success," said Capt. David Francavilla, 32, of Colorado Springs, Colo. "If the enemy thought anything was coming at all, they thought it was coming up the Wadi al Batin." Francavilla, commander of a company in the 1st Cavalry's 1st Battalion-5th Cavalry Regiment, took part in the patrols, reconnaissance missions, and feints behind Iraqi lines that were meant to deceive Iraqi troops, including a patrol on Feb. 20 that frightened and demoralized many 1st Cavalry troops.

Two companies came under heavy artillery and mortar fire, and three men were killed and seven wounded behind Iraqi lines.

The casualties were brought back to the battalion base, and for days afterward soldiers talked about the nightmarish encounter of "the 20th," when the division suffered its first deaths, when men lost friends for the first time in combat, when the 1st Cavalry had its first real contact with the tragic, gruesome consequences of war.

The attack came just as the patrol had taken an Iraqi bunker and nine prisoners.

"I think mentally that really prepared me," said Capt. Dana Milner, 27, of Houston. "Coming back with the prisoners, the casualties . . . it made the war real for the first time."

When the land war began on Sunday and other allied armor units poured in from further west, the 1st Cavalry staged one more feint up the Wadi al Batin, its deepest yet into what were believed to be one of the heaviest concentrations of forces. Several companies of M1A1 tanks and Bradley fighting vehicles plunged about 20 kilometers into Iraq, but encountered only sporadic machine gun and distant artillery fire.

Some Iraqi troops ran up and ignited trenches filled with oil to create obstacles and smokescreens. Scores of others surrendered. A mine damaged one tank, but there were no casualties. A Bradley fired a round at what was believed to be an Iraqi truck, but in fact turned out to be a paper bag blowing across the desert.

Some thought was given to continuing the push up the Wadi al Batin, but military commanders decided to send the 1st Cavalry west, into central Iraq through a breach in the border already opened by the U.S. Army's 1st Infantry Division, so the cavalry could head off a Republican Guard armored division.

As the various elements of the 1st Cavalry came together for the push north, at one point the entire 2nd Brigade was speeding in concert across the flat desert plain, a vast arena filled with thousands of tanks, trucks, mobile missile launchers, and other rolling weaponry, rushing forward in tandem, a spectacle that stretched to all horizons, a thundering, roaring herd of grinding, smoke-spewing, gas-guzzling machinery that churned up clouds of dust even on a desert soaked and matted with two days of seasonal rain.

As the brigade barreled within a few kilometers of the border, it merged into giant columns that stretched from one side of the sky to the other.

Tuesday evening, as the convoy prepared to cross the border, word spread that the Republican Guard was laying down their weapons and that Saddam Hussein had personally ordered a pullout from Kuwait.

Moments later, the line stopped for refueling. Soldiers shook hands, took pictures of the amazing scene around them.

A lot of them played hand-held Nintendo games. Some could not believe the war might be ending. "I guess it seems like it's being too easy after we've been here so long," said Valentine, a gunner in a Bradley. Some did not want to believe it.

"We're ready to go in there and shoot his ass up," said Staff Sgt. Anthony Small, 25, of Fayetteville, Ark. "Disappointed? Hell, yes. I haven't even fired my gun yet." Some wanted very much to believe it.

"I feel good," said Sgt. Billy Nelson, 27, of Union, Ore. "I got three kids and another one due in April. I got my fingers crossed. I'm hoping to be there."

Marine Recon Team Kicks Off Kuwait City Turnover: "I Was Surprised They Didn't Fight a Little Harder"

By Molly Moore

KUWAIT CITY - The streets of battered Kuwait City exploded in an emotional demonstration by jubilant, flag-waving citizens today as allied forces freed the city after six months of Iraqi occupation and three days of ground war.

U.S. Marine divisions surrounded the capital city late Tuesday night in several fierce firefights, crumpling Iraqi military forces and opening the paths for Arab troops to reclaim the ravaged town just after daybreak this morning.

At mid-afternoon today, the first American military convoy to rumble into the city was besieged by hundreds of cheering men, women and children, many in tears, screaming "tank you, tank you!" The roads were lined with gleeful young girls in skirts sewn from Kuwaiti flags, sobbing women in black abayas, and young men flashing victory signs and clenched fists.

Others danced on the rooftops of buildings waving green, white and red Kuwaiti flags and banners at the troops below. One crowd raced toward the convoy and unknowingly tossed a Kuwaiti flag to Marine Corps commander Lt. Gen. Walt Boomer who had directed the

Wednesday - February 27, 1991

attack on Iraqi troops for the past three days from a mobile command center that ended its cross-desert military odyssey Wednesday amidst the frenzied city celebration.

"It was a once-in-a-lifetime experience," said the three-star general who rode through the city atop the amphibious landing vehicle that had served as the nerve center of the Marine operation. "There are some things worth fighting for. When you see them regain their freedom and their joy at seeing them (Iraqis) leave, it is quite a feeling. I'm glad we could be part of returning it back to them."

Military officials said that by the time Arab forces rolled into the city at dawn this morning, there were few Iraqis left inside and virtually no resistance.

As the troops were moving into some areas near the city, special operations forces flying in helicopters with loudspeakers asked Kuwaiti citizens to report locations of any Iraqi troops left in the city. In 72 hours, Marine forces snaked along narrow lanes cut through minefields, fanned their forces and began a steady push toward Kuwait City that was met with only sporadic resistance and occasionally was hampered by massive numbers of surrendering Iraqis.

Military officials said an estimated 20,000 to 30,000 Iraqi troops have surrendered and are being held by allied forces. Most field commanders were stunned that Iraqi forces initially considered formidable by many because of their huge size and experience in fighting their eight-year war with Iran, fled their tanks and bunkers so quickly as the Marines and Arab forces swept northward.

"The heart wasn't in this fight," said Boomer. "They were someplace they didn't want to be and about to die for something they didn't want to die for." He added, "However, I was surprised they didn't fight a little harder."

Military officials also said that they began learning through reconnaissance teams and other intelligence sources in the final weeks before the land offensive that Iraqi defenses were far less daunting than originally believed. "The magic defensive line that was the marvel of the century did not exist," said Boomer.

"Whatever they planned to do, we unnerved them," said Maj. Gen. Mike Myatt, who commands the 1st Marine Division.

"There were one hundred things that could have gone wrong," said Boomer. "It really did go as planned. We certainly thought it was going to be a hard proposal for us because he had so many people down there."

Boomer said the two Marine divisions faced 11 Iraqi divisions.

Marine commanders also staged numerous feinting attacks in an effort to keep Iraqi troops off-balance. Although more than 30,000 Marine troops floated off the Kuwait coast, commanders didn't intend to launch a dangerous and potentially high-casualty amphibious landing, but rather, used the threat of the attack to force Iraqi troops to divert massive efforts to defending the shoreline for such an assault.

Commanders learned today that the deception worked.

Across the street from the U.S. Embassy in Kuwait City, Special Forces teams discovered an elaborate sand table model of the Iraqi military plan for the defense of Kuwait City. Four huge red arrows from the sea pointed at the coastline of Kuwait City and the huge defensive effort positioned there.

Small fences of concertina wire marked the shoreline and models of artillery pieces lined the shore area. Throughout the city were plastic models of other artillery and air defense positions, while thin red-painted strips of board designated supply routes and main highways. "This is a gold mine," marveled one Marine commander as he paced around the edges of the map in a large spare room apparently used to teach the defensive tactics to Iraqi field commanders.

But while Marine forces were ending their operation, the Army was just beginning its attacks on Republican Guard forces entrenched in Iraq along the Kuwaiti border.

Although Army forces were reported to be suffering more casualties than Marines—about 58 deaths so far—military officials said the Republican Guard was also collapsing under the Army attacks. Five Marines were killed and 48 wounded in the three days of fighting, Marine officials said.

The military avenues across the desert from the Saudi border to Kuwait city are now littered with the wreckage of war: smoldering tank carcasses, twisted and charred artillery guns, infantry troops. Iraqi troops left one tank so quickly that a bag of what appeared to be food was still sitting on a makeshift table between two unmarred chairs only a few feet away from the black hulk of a burning tank.

"We just went through a whole field of burning tanks," Boomer reported to a former tanker, Gen. H. Norman Schwarzkopf, commander of U.S. forces, during one report from his mobile command center. "It would have done an old tanker's heart good."

The desert is pocked with bomb craters and splattered with shells of unexploded bombs dropped by allied warplanes on virtually every horizon in Kuwait, tongues of fire shoot from burning well heads belching thick, acrid smoke into the dark sky.

The sandy plain surrounding Kuwait City is a graveyard of abandoned trucks, collapsing bunkers and the jagged metal skeletons of military weaponry.

The oilfields outside of Kuwait City have been turned into a hellish inferno of dozens of orange blazes and black oily smoke from wellheads exploded by departing Iraqi forces. Marines encountered one of the fiercest firefights of the campaign as Iraqi troops hiding in the oilfields launched a surprise counter-attack through the haze of smoke and fire.

Early Tuesday morning, senior Marine generals gathered at an austere mobile desert outpost to plot the strategy for their final push to isolate Kuwait City.

Bending over a large map spread across the sand, the commanders prepared for the toughest battles they were to face in the brief campaign.

In the final hours, they speeded the operation in an effort to sever escape lanes from Kuwait City after hundreds of Iraqi vehicles and troops were reported fleeing the city. Marine commanders hoped to destroy as much of the equipment as they could before the forces returned to Iraq.

As the 1st Marine Division edged nearer the city, commanders heard reports of two developing counter-attacks by Iraqi forces.

"We fired on the two gathering points and it wasn't thirty minutes before we scattered them like rabbits out of the bush," said Myatt, the division commander. "The Cobras (helicopter gunships) and the LAVs (light armored vehicles) had a field day" as a "hunter-killer package" to search out and destroy Iraqi equipment.

In one battle, aging Marine M60 tanks destroyed about 100 Iraqi tanks and armor, including about 50 top-of-the-line Soviet T-72 tanks, the commander said.

Late Tuesday and into the night some of the battle intensified as Marine forces surrounded the heavily defended Kuwaiti International Airport. U.S. Navy battleships offshore in the Persian Gulf pounded the airport hangars, terminals and other buildings, leaving them a shambles of twisted metal and blackened concrete in an effort to rout Iraqi forces from the field.

Marine commanders said that cameras in remotely piloted vehicles that flew above the ground and monitored the bombings showed Iraqis "literally jumping out of the tanks."

After the Marines commandeered the critical airfield today, Special Forces teams arrived to counter snipers and other pockets of resistance that remained entrenched around the large airfield complex.

While the Marine assault through Kuwait went so smoothly that it worried commanders

Wednesday - February 27, 1991

on the first day, the operation was not without some problems. Weather and the thick blanket of smoke created by the oil fires slowed some operations. One commander said the skies were so dark one day that he was forced to use a flashlight to read his maps at high noon. On Tuesday night, the Marines stopped most of their movement because the night was so inky black.

But one of the most pervasive problems was the thousands of surrendering Iraqi troops. A field commander said that at one point he faced so many surrendering troops that they were hampering his ability to push his forces through the battlefield. Another commander said Iraqi forces began attacking his troops as a wave of fellow Iraqi soldiers were surrendering ahead of the fire.

The large number of prisoners overwhelmed military efforts to provide food and water for troops, many of whom said they had not eaten in three or four days. At one desert location, American forces rounded up 3,500 prisoners inside two fences of concertina wire. When U.S. military police officers arrived with the first jugs of water, they said the Iraqis were so desperate that they began trying to climb over the razor-sharp wire.

Many of the new prisoners were forced to march through the desert in convoys because the military couldn't provide enough trucks to carry them all. While many of the Iraqi troops wore heavy winter coats needed for protection against the chill desert nights, many others draped towels over their shoulders and wore sandbags tied to their feet.

Confusion among some Arab coalition forces created a few last-minute problems before their entrance into the city, which was delayed until after daybreak to avoid the possibility of accidental casualties as Arab forces moved through Marine lines. Although Arab forces, for political consideration, were allowed to move into Kuwait City first, a Marine reconnaissance of about a dozen men sneaked into the U.S. Embassy at about 7 p.m. Tuesday night, according to one of the Marines involved. He said members of the Kuwaiti resistance helped guide the Marines to the embassy, which appeared untouched by the Iraqi occupation forces.

An American flag fluttered atop the flagpole and the grounds appeared unkempt, but otherwise unmarred by Iraqi efforts to devastate other parts of the city. Throughout the city, devastation was spotty. Windows of some stores, such as jewelry and watch shops, were smashed and the contents looted.

Many others were left untouched. The French-owned Meridien Hotel in downtown Kuwait was blackened with smoke, its first floors in shambles and the front walls blasted away from some rooms on the higher floors.

Overall, however, most buildings throughout the city remained undisturbed.

But throughout the day, hundreds of Kuwaiti citizens began emerging from underground basements and other hiding places where they had been encouraged to take cover during the war, flying and waving hundreds of flags around the city. Elderly men stood in their yards, blowing kisses at American troops that passed on the street.

A small girl wrapped in a Kuwaiti flag waved from her doorstep. A man drove alongside the American military convoy in his car and shouted, "Thank you—really." He pressed his hands to his heart.

Young children beamed at the passing Marines and waved small Kuwaiti flags enthusiastically. Groups of women tossed candy into the trucks and atop the military vehicles driven by the American troops.

"I have never seen people so happy," said Maj. Chris Weldon as he watched the passing scene. "What a feeling of accomplishment."

Liberators Greeted in Kuwait City; Businessmen in Sleek Mercedes Join the Massive Traffic Jam

By Jeff Franks

KUWAIT CITY - Thousands of jubilant Kuwaitis shouted "Thank you!" and "Welcome!" to the commanding general of the U.S. Marines in the Gulf War just hours after his troops swept occupying Iraqi forces from their capital.

In scenes reminiscent of the liberation of Paris in World War II, the Kuwaitis, waving Kuwaiti and American flags and blowing kisses, hung out of windows and stood by rubble-strewn streets and highways to cheer Lt. Gen. Walter Boomer as he led a small convoy of Marines through Kuwait City.

Boomer waved and flashed "V" for victory signs at the Kuwaitis from atop his brown light armored vehicle. The emotional welcome of the grateful Kuwaitis made all the blood, sweat, and tears of the Gulf War worth it, Boomer said. "There are some things worth fighting for, which you can understand when you see the people and their happiness at being free. It was quite a feeling, wasn't it?" he said.

The Kuwaitis drove through the streets honking horns and shouting "Welcome, my friends" and "God bless Bush" as the Marines passed. Some on the sidewalks applauded, while others jumped up and down and waved their arms. Kuwaiti flags hung from many buildings. "At last, you did it," one man shouted, capturing the sense of relief and happiness that gripped this modern, wealthy city.

"Please tell the world that we want peace for everybody, not just Kuwait," said another. Still others chanted, "USA, USA" and "Thank you, thank you."

Kuwaiti resistance fighters appeared to be trying to keep the crowds out of the streets so that traffic could flow, but they were only mildly successful. As the day went on, more and more people poured out onto the streets and large traffic jams began to form.

Traffic lights were not working because the city has no electricity, so there were more than a few near-accidents as drivers sped to catch a glimpse of the first American troops to enter their seaside capital. The resistance fighters carried rifles, which they shot in the air frequently. The sound of gunfire could be heard throughout the city, but for the first time since the Iraqis invaded on Aug. 2, only for celebration, not war.

Boomer's tour took him from the bombed-out Kuwaiti International Airport, which was captured by Marines just four hours before he arrived, through the center of the war-torn city. He also stopped at the now-closed U.S. Embassy where diplomats lived for many weeks after the invasion in a steadfast show of support for Kuwait's sovereignty.

Damage was most extensive in Kuwait City's deserted shopping district. The streets there were filled with broken glass from the many windows broken out during what the Kuwaitis said was looting by the Iraqi army. "From the first day they stole everything. It was not an army of soldiers, it was an army of thieves," said Kuwaiti banker Essam Al-Nosuf.

Many of the modernistic buildings in the city had been turned into blackened hulks by Iraqi artillery. Some buildings, including Kuwait's main water desalination plant, were still smoking Wednesday, which the Kuwaitis said was the result of a final campaign of destruction by the Iraqis as they left the city days ago.

The streets were filled with stones and damaged cars that were used by the Iraqis for traffic barricades. Along overpasses and on top of the buildings located at strategic points, the Iraqis had constructed sturdy concrete bunkers that the happy Kuwaitis draped with flags and pictures of the Kuwaiti royal family.

The jubilation of the Kuwaitis crossed all boundaries.

Men and women, young and old, workers in banged-up cars and affluent businessmen in sleek Mercedes took to the streets on this first day of liberation. Some found it a religious experience and stood screaming, "Allah Akbar!"

The scene on the outskirts of Kuwait City was one of total devastation.

Burned-out Iraqi tanks and armored personnel vehicles littered the bleak desert. Few buildings were left standing. To the south of the city was a field of flames, a veritable Dante's *Inferno* of burning oil wells. At least 100 wells, set afire by the Iraqis, sent angry swirls of brilliant orange flames 100 feet into the sky.

Ugly black smoke from the wells mixed with rain to coat everything in an oily soot. Marines, who Wednesday morning captured the nearby airport after vicious fighting with Iraqi T-72 tank battalions, were black-faced and grimy because of the soot.

As the sun went down, the flames lit up the southern horizon.

Many of the buildings at the airport were little more than rubble, but Boomer said it was fire from U.S. Navy ships, not Iraqi bombs, that devastated them. Despite the destruction, Marine engineers reported the runways were in good shape and needed only to be cleared of barricades and blown-up cars to allow aircraft to land.

A large painted portrait of Iraqi president Saddam Hussein, dressed in traditional Arab clothing and wearing a placid smile, stood at the airport's main exit to welcome visitors.

Marines setting up a command post at the airport uncovered large caches of Iraqi weapons, including Kalashnikoff and sniper rifles, grenades and grenade launchers. They scoured the area for mines and booby traps, but found only a few of the latter.

"I found some wired grenades, but there weren't as many booby traps as we were expecting," said Cpl. Billy Jones, 24, of Marsihill, N.C.

Boomer, during a visit with the 1st Marine Division, told the Marines, "I'm really proud of what you guys did." He said Gen. Norman Schwarzkopf, commander in chief of the Gulf forces, said the liberation of Kuwait was "another glorious chapter in the history of the Marine Corps." He described Schwarzkopf as "just ecstatic" about the victory over Iraq.

"It's the first time I've heard him laugh in days," Boomer said.

Boomer took a quick walk through the tree-shaded U.S. Embassy compound in downtown Kuwait City and seemed pleased by what he saw. He said he expected the Iraqis to ransack the place after the diplomats left, but except for a couple of broken windows, it was untouched. The garden the diplomats grew for food appeared to be in full bloom.

A line of Iraqi prisoners of war, the last holdouts in the battle against the allies, sat glumly against the embassy wall, watched over by a stern-faced Marine.

From the embassy, Boomer strode across the street to a building the Iraqis used to plan their defenses. A 200-square-foot mockup of Kuwait City, complete with a detailed map of Iraqi defenses, sat on the floor. The model showed that the Iraqis expected an amphibious assault by Marine forces in the Arabian Gulf right into the heart of Kuwait City.

Their defenses included a formidable array of underwater obstacles, land mines on the beaches (no sea mines were indicated), gun placements, and troop positions.

"The best-laid plans . . ." Boomer joked after closely studying the model.

Boomer said the allies were able to eject the Iraqis from Kuwait in just three days because "they (Iraqis) were simply overwhelmed." The Iraqis were worn down by allied bombing runs and poor food supplies, he said. "I don't think their heart was in it," he said.

Many of the Iraqi defensive positions were shoddily built, but some appeared to be carefully prepared, he said. "If they had all been that good, the outcome of the war would have been the same, but it would have been a lot tougher," Boomer said.

He said the Iraqis had training and equipment for chemical warfare, but chose not to use them for unknown reasons.

After the thrashing by the allies, the Iraqi army was "dead," Boomer said.

"By the time it's over, his (Saddam's) army will be finished—and deservedly so when you see the destruction here," he said. The sight of the burning oil wells particularly angered him. "Wasting that oilfield like that is just tragic. It makes you feel good about destroying the guy who's responsible." he said.

Boomer said he was concerned about the environmental effects of the burning wells and that he would recommend that oil well fire-fighting teams be called in as soon as possible. "I'm glad we could be a part of returning Kuwait back to its people," he said.

Al-Nosuf shared his feelings. "We are very happy to Americans in our country. I was shaking when I saw the Marines today," he said. But, he added, "Our happiness is not complete yet. They took thousands of hostages three days ago, so we are very worried about them."

There is, too, the problem of rebuilding war-torn Kuwait.

"We know it will take a very long time," Al-Nosuf said.

Iraqi Troops Escape Net of Allied Assault: 1st Marines Find at Least 400 Abandoned Tanks and Vehicles

By Jim Michaels

KUWAIT CITY - Under plumes of black smoke that blotted out the sun, U.S. Marines entered the outskirts of this city today as Iraqi forces fled north.

Evidence of a rapid Iraqi retreat was everywhere and Marines only met minor resistance on their push north to the badly damaged city.

Tanks, armored personnel carriers and trucks, many unharmed, were everywhere and combat engineers blew many of them up as they moved north.

Elements of the Camp Pendleton-based 1st Marine Division had been on their way to the Kuwait International Airport, where they would seal the city off for a triumphant return of coalition Arab forces.

But on the way north, Marine officers ordered their mechanized forces to set up a blocking position to the north of the city in the hopes of destroying forces fleeing north to Iraq. They were too late. 1st Marine Division alone found at least 400 abandoned tanks and vehicles, many still had ammunition and uniform items in them

On Wednesday morning, coalition Arab forces passed through the defensive positions set up by U.S. Marines who had reached the outskirts of the city Tuesday night and entered Kuwait City.

Under drizzly skies, made even blacker by plumes of inky smoke, Marines were dirty and tired, but jubilant that the offensive had gone so well. "Men, I don't think the Iraqis are what they are cracked up to be," Lt. Doug McCann told some troops in an armored vehicle preparing to enter the outskirts of the city.

Mechanized vehicles from Task Force Ripper, made up of forces from Camp Pendleton and Twenty-nine Palms, drove through what appeared to be a graveyard of Soviet-built armor as they approached an abandoned quarry outside Kuwait City. Scores of Iraqi vehicles, now twisted wreckage, lay everywhere, the victim of allied air raids. Well dug-in positions were hastily abandoned and crumpled leaflets dropped by allied planes blew up against a broken mesh fence. The leaflets explained how Iraqi forces should surrender. The positions, almost invisible from a distance, were much better prepared than positions closer to the Saudi border, where the Iraqis placed their lower-quality soldiers.

On the road into Kuwait City, the Marines encountered still more Iraqi soldiers trying to surrender. But unwilling to be slowed in their advance, Marines used interpreters to tell them to continue to walk south on the road with their hands held high. They would be taken by other advancing forces. Marines met only minor resistance on their push towards Kuwait. In a tank battle Monday night, Marine Corps tanks killed four Iraqi tanks and took the surrender of another seven.

Environmental Nightmare Left in Kuwait: Rivers of Oil, Dozens of Blazing Wellheads, Plumes of Smoke

By David Alexander

WITH U.S. FORCES IN AL WAFRA, Kuwait - Iraqi forces driven from southern Kuwait left behind an environmental nightmare, with rivers of oil covering a vast stretch of the sandy flatlands and dozens of blazing wellheads pumping black smoke into the sky.

At the oil-producing city of al Wafra, hundreds of pumping-jacks across the huge oil field were idle. Iraqi forces apparently had destroyed a number of oil installations before being overrun by allied troops. Rivers of oil covered a wide stretch of the area around al Wafra. Three or four wellheads were ablaze, sending fingers of fire and plumes of smoke into the air.

At al Burqan, a large oil field north of al Wafra, more than 30 wellheads lined up in neat rows were aflame. Fire shot into the air from each wellhead and a dense cloud of black smoke hung over the area. The two oilfields apparently were destroyed in what allied military officials described as a scorched-earth policy that began shortly before the ground war started. There also were signs of the recent fighting in the area. In the vicinity of al Qurayn, just south of al Wafra, more than 30 Iraqi tanks and armored personnel carriers had been destroyed, their burned-out hulls littering the desert floor.

Along the Saudi-Kuwaiti border, the sand berm or hill that divides the two countries had been bulldozed in several places to create a path for allied tanks crossing into Kuwait. Several skeletons of Iraqi armored vehicles littered the area. Thousands of Iraqi prisoners of war continued to flow into temporary camps in northern Saudi Arabia. Convoys comprised of dozens of trucks, buses and flatbeds hauled the prisoners south to more permanent prisoner-of-war camps.

At the 1611th Air Medical Evacuation hospital, Marines handed out blankets to keep the prisoners warm. The captured Iraqi soldiers also were given meals of rice and beans. At the 1611th Air Medical

Evacuation hospital, Maj. Kathy Higgins of Fayetteville, N.C., said all U.S. and prisoner-of-war casualties had passed through her camp.

She declined to say exactly how many people they had treated, except that it was less than 100, including both Iraqis and Americans.

U.S. Sergeant Holds 7 Iraqi POWs, Gets Kissed For His Trouble: "George Bush Good!"

By Mike Tharp

WITH U.S. FORCES IN IRAQ - Yesterday, there were 30,000 Iraqi prisoners of war. Without Sgt. Gary Mills, there would have been 29,993.

The North Pole, Alaska, truck driver handed over seven EPWs (enemy prisoners of war) he single-handedly had captured in the Iraqi desert. After he presented an astonished group of medical evacuation helicopter crews with the seven EPWs, Mills, a 31-year-old six-year Army veteran, hitched a ride with Lt. Col. Robert Holcombe, the battalion commander of the 37th Engineers, who quickly adopted the soldier into his unit.

Mills had been with the 299th Engineers when he and two other members of the unit were driving a truck carrying a bulldozer across southern Iraq.

After a heavy rain and heavier sandstorm, the trio decided to pull off the road until visibility improved. But the shoulder of the two-lane highway was so soft that their truck overturned, tipping the dozer onto the ground.

The soldiers were unhurt, and two of them hitched a ride to seek help, leaving Mills to guard their vehicle and equipment. Mills spent the night alone with the truck, but as dawn broke he decided to move away from it in case it was struck by another vehicle. He found what appeared to be an Iraqi foxhole, hunkered down and watched his truck. Then he heard something.

"You know how people sound when they're trying to talk when they're running?" he asked. "I saw these seven guys coming by my position. At first, I was just gonna let 'em go by—there was seven of them and one of me. But then I thought, what the hell." Mills shouted the only Arabic word he knew—"Qif!" (Halt!)—and they did. He gestured with his M-16 rifle that they should throw down their weapons, which included AK-47 rifles. They did.

He ordered them with words and gestures to kneel down. They did. Then followed a two-way pantomime session in which the Iraqis revealed to Mills that they had been told they would face a firing squad if they surrendered. Mills said at one point one of the Iraqi soldiers came up to him and, while the barrel of Mills's gun was pointed at the soldier's stomach, told him, "George Bush good!"

"That was the only English they knew," Mills recalled. "Then they said, 'Saddam Hussein,' and made a slitting motion across their throats." Mills, in something of a Keystone Kops routine, eventually forced the Iraqis back to his truck. He gave them food (U.S. Army meals ready to eat, the MRE) and water. "Then they really cheered up," Mills said.

"I thought, 'Hell, you guys are on vacation, and I'm still out here.' I taught 'em a lot of English." Mills heard the helicopters landing and marched the seven EPWs over to them. The medevac crews didn't know quite what to make of the tiny parade emerging from behind the dunes. It was eminently logical to Mills. "I'm droppin' 'em off," said Mills. "There are more of you than me. One person can keep seven people occupied only so long."

As he started to return to his truck, ultimately to be rescued by Lt. Col. Holcombe, Mills raised his M-16 in one hand and his other arm into the air, as if signaling a touchdown. "I wanted 'em (the EPWs) to know they were my prisoners but now I was handin' 'em over," he said.

But before he could leave, one of the Iraqis came up to him.

"He kissed me on both cheeks," said Mills.

U.S. Infantrymen Penetrate to Banks of Euphrates, Discover Cache of Illegal Jordanian Arms

By John Pomfret

WITH U.S. ARMY IN IRAQ - U.S. military intelligence officers deep inside Iraqi territory have discovered caches of Jordanian weapons shipped to Iraq long after the United Nations ordered a weapons embargo on that nation.

On Tuesday, a reporter saw a large batch of six rocket-propelled grenade launchers, hundreds of grenades and more than a dozen 120mm mortars along with numerous mortar rounds which had been found inside a bunker more than 100 miles north of the Saudi Arabian border along the banks of the Euphrates River. The boxes said in English that they were from the General Military Command, Amman, Jordan, and also bore the Arabic symbol of the Hashimite Kingdom in Arabic with the shipment date of January 1991.

Military intelligence officers said documents in Arabic found in the boxes indicated that the weapons had been shipped directly by the Jordanian military to Iraq. The discovery was the first solid indication that countries have broken the arms embargo imposed in August following Iraq's invasion of Kuwait, military intelligence officers said, speaking on condition of anonymity. They spoke on the same day that Jordan accused the United States of unnecessarily destroying Iraq.

The cache of Jordanian arms was one of several captured during the past three days by intelligence officers participating in the 101st Airborne Division's assault near the Euphrates. The assault has brought more than 8,000 American infantrymen into Iraq. At least 2,000 of them are now less than 100 miles from Baghdad.

Officers with the 101st said they believed Jordan was not the only country breaking the embargo. They said most of the equipment contained food and electrical equipment at first, but there were no indications the shipments held weapons.

American military officials in Iraq said the Jordanian equipment came directly from Jordan. In addition to the grenades and mortars, officers also found hundreds of rounds of automatic weapons ammunition that they said came from Jordan after the embargo began.

"We've got bags and bags of Jordanian ammo," said one officer, speaking at a U.S. military command post in Iraq. "That stuff's awfully fresh."

On Tuesday, U.S. troops captured an Iraqi carrying about 200 pounds of weapons and ammunition near the Euphrates. The weapons—AK-47 rifles, grenades and ammunition clips—all originated in Jordan and were brand new.

Friendly Fire Casualties Mount: American and British Inflict Toll on Each Other's Forces

By Michael Hedges

SOUTHEASTERN IRAQ - As four American units and a British division made a right turn in Iraq and raced towards Kuwait, they passed scenes of terrible devastation rendered by air and artillery bombardments.

Iraqi resistance stiffened here, but many of the allied casualties continued to be caused by friendly fire. In the lane between the British 1st UK Division and an American division, where the ground was uncut by the treads of allied armored vehicles, the Iraqis had abandoned miles of well-fortified trench lines supported by strong bunkers. It appeared as if air strikes alone had driven off large numbers of Iraqi soldiers. The trench lines were littered with abandoned AK-47 rifles, shoulder-launched RPG-7 rockets, helmets and other military gear. In places, entire companies of Iraqi tanks had been blasted inside their dugouts. Bomb casings from American bombers lay near the exploded vehicles. The tanks, Iraqi T-54s and T-55s, had been pierced by explosives and gutted.

In one vast field dotted by bunkers, about 30 Iraqi armored personnel carriers had been blown apart by air strikes. Some of the vehicles had received direct hits and huge chunks of iron ripped from them, leaving the main body of the large tracked carriers blackened hulls.

But not all the destruction on a vast battlefield stretching for many kilometers was to Iraqi forces. A British officer said that jets from that country's air force had mistakenly destroyed as many as four U.S. heavy tanks, inflicting unknown casualties.

Another British soldier said that as of late this afternoon, 16 British soldiers had been killed, some believed to be victims of friendly fire. At one grisly scene, two British armored personnel carriers sat end to end, apparently blown apart by air strikes.

The APCs were on the edge of a battery of Iraqi 152-mm artillery pieces which were well-concealed inside earthen bunkers. The guns had also been destroyed by aerial bombs, but it appeared their gun crews had abandoned them before the raid.

The soldiers in the British vehicles were not as lucky. Bloody pieces of scalp, bone and tissue had been thrown in a wide arc from the rear APC. One flak jacket lay near the vehicle, soaked in blood. A driver's helmet was on the other side of the vehicle, a two-inch hole blown through the front.

The personal effects of the soldiers had been scattered.

A roll of toilet paper, embossed with the words Merry Christmas and a drawing of Santa Claus, lay in nearly perfect condition several feet from the rear APC.

A letter in a feminine handwriting was nearby.

After three days of breezing through southeastern Iraq against negligible resistance, a change seemed to come over soldiers here today. At one point, two American journalists and their military escort bumped into a British light vehicle, an Iraqi prisoner laying across its hood with his hands behind his back.

The British soldiers driving the vehicle approached the journalists with guns loaded and held in a ready position. One soldier refused at first to believe the identity of a reporter. He appeared grim and nervous. He finally let the American party pass with a warning to "Be careful." At a nearby British camp, soldiers had herded a small knot of enemy prisoners into a tight circle. One man guarded them with an assault rifle.

The rapid pace of the allied advance here—about 125 kilometers in the first few days of the war—created pockets in the rear of Iraqis cut off from their lines of retreat. Most appeared eager to surrender when encountering American or British soldiers, but as dusk arrived, units just behind the lines which were sometimes isolated far from support became jittery.

Master Sgt. Bill Bottoms, from a National Guard unit from Arkansas, said, "The British turned loose about 800 prisoners in this area this morning because they had no one to guard them. It has made it kind of spooky."

The Arkansas guardsmen were aware that the area where they were bedding down was near an intricate line of Iraqi trenches and bunkers which had been bypassed during the initial attack. "We came through minefields today and the Iraqis were walking up with their hands up saying, 'we surrender, we surrender,' and we told them we didn't have time to fool with them," said Sgt. Bottoms.

The pace of the allied advance, and its eastward curve, made it difficult to tell the front from the rear. Supply trains of hundreds of heavy trucks snaked along on courses discernible only to the drivers in the vehicles.

Swarms of Apache attack helicopters, sometimes as many as a dozen per flight, streaked across the battlefield, presumably to pound Iraqi armored cars and tanks with their Hellfire missiles.

The allied tanks advanced in lanes across an Iraqi landscape slightly more rolling than northern Saudi Arabia and covered with scraggly bushes.

In between those lanes were eerie Iraqi camps, marked with the burned-out skeletons of supply trucks and fuel tankers hit from the air. Well-protected bunker systems, connected with a chest-deep trench, were empty, soldiers simply dropping their weapons and disappearing.

It looked as if the Iraqis had fled without firing. Heavy artillery pieces with supplies of live rounds sat in firing position, but with covers over their muzzles. While many tanks were shattered by air strikes, others seemed to have been abandoned unscathed.

Several U.S. soldiers—including a majority of the casualties taken in some brigades—have been killed or injured by American artillery rounds that did not explode until jarred by advancing troops.

Near the Iraqi bunker complexes there appeared to be unexploded shells.

Many of the Iraqi soldiers who fled the ghost camps filtered into makeshift EPW—enemy prisoner of war—compounds set up by American military police behind the lines.

At one such camp, which was little more than a large circle of concertina wire with a thick layer of discarded plastic water bottles and MRE packages around its edges, 222 forlorn looking Iraqis stood or squatted.

"They are very happy to be here," said one of the guards. "They throw their gas masks up against the fence and say, 'no good, no good.'"

Sgt. Keith Sullivan, 25, of Carthage, Miss., said the prisoners who could speak some English said they hadn't eaten in about two weeks. "They have clearly lost a lot of weight," he said. "They looked healthy in their ID photos, but they look sick now."

Pfc. Thomas Robichaud, 19, of Dewey, N.H., said he was surprised at the number of teenagers and men past their prime in the group. "They look like a bunch of farmer types they threw a weapon to and sent to the front lines."

While Iraqis are surrendering in droves, some soldiers who have passed through the battlefield in or close to the edge of the attack have noted that despite signs of massive air and artillery bombardments, there are very few signs of Iraqis killed or wounded.

Those guarding groups of prisoners said several have been unhealthy, but a small percentage have been wounded in combat. "I was in Vietnam, and I expected the area where they breached the line to be a lot different than it was," said Sgt. Bottoms. "I expected to see bodies laying around, inside the trenches, but I didn't see any, or any signs of wounded.

"It is strange, I can't figure it out."

Thursday
February 28, 1991

The big set-piece battle between the Iraqi Republican Guard and the finest tanks and infantry the coalition could muster was played out on a grand scale, much as the allied command had anticipated. And the outcome was the one they had desired, and expected, from the beginning.

The American Abrams tanks and the British Challengers rumbled into the ring of fire, took aim from a distance the Iraqis couldn't match, and blasted away. The battle reminded them of practice maneuvers, some of the tank drivers observed. In fact, some said they'd been on tougher practice maneuvers.

The political aims of the war had been achieved, and that would be enough to settle this war. President Bush declared a cease-fire to take effect at 8 a.m., Persian Gulf time, on this date. Kuwait was liberated—although as this chapter points out, many Kuwaiti men had disappeared—and the hated Iraqi occupiers were routed or captured.

So the war was a great, undeniable success for the allied forces. But in the end the overwhelming victory in 100 hours over a slack-willed opponent lacked the clear finality at least some of the military commanders had sought.

As military men, desiring to render their enemy militarily unable to resume the fight any time soon, they had to settle for watching a few divisions, or parts of divisions, slink unharmed back across the Euphrates River.

On closer inspection, the number of Iraqi tanks and armored personnel carriers destroyed by the allies would shrink. Gen. Colin Powell had said the allies were going to kill the Iraqi army. Iraq's army might be on life support, but it wasn't dead, and in the aftermath of the cease-fire managed enough strength and firepower to destroy the fledgling opposition that had risen up among the Shiites in the south and the Kurdish minority in the north.

The accuracy of the mighty Patriot would be taken down a few pegs. The judgment to deliver chemical protection using pills still being tested would be questioned.

Even while the cease-fire was fresh, down in the ranks of the troops who were late to the battle there was a hollow feeling, which stories in this chapter explore. Climb into a Bradley, or walk up to a tank crew, and all it took was a quick question or a look to tap it.

Came all the way over here. Didn't get to fight.

Bunch of prisoners was all we saw.

The troops in some outfits, like the 1st Cav, took an obvious victory for their side as a lost opportunity to mix it up with live ammunition. Nearly 150 American troops and dozens of other allied troops had been killed. Sure, there were some soldiers, some units that seen some real fighting. Just not enough to go around, in their opinion.

Of course the big picture was a different story. Seen whole, wrapped in a headline, the war was a commander-in-chief's dream.

Massing more than a half-million troops on the front doorstep of the enemy, fine-tuning a highly-trained, well-motivated, expertly-led, multi-national coalition and sending it sweeping across the desert like a giant's forearm clad in chainmail, clearing everything in its path, was an accomplishment of some magnitude.

Some would say the cease-fire was called too soon, and the allies should have kept marching to Basra and Baghdad so Saddam Hussein could be toppled.

Some would say the allies shouldn't have let the Iraqis climb back into their military helicopters, which they used in the weeks following the cease-fire to put down an internal opposition the war helped produce.

Some would say Saddam was misled into believing that the United States wouldn't violently object if he took Kuwait and that once the allies responded, he tried earnestly to avoid a land war, yet the allies were determined to have one.

Some would say the brevity of the ground war proved that the Iraqi threat was never much to begin with.

Some would say the brief ground war proved an invading force really does need an overwhelming numerical advantage to succeed without getting mired down.

But ten years after the war, Saddam Hussein was still in power in Baghdad and allied pilots were still shooting missiles at radar sites in daily missions over the no-fly zones that covered much of northern and southern Iraq.

Every war has an aftermath. The aftermath of the Persian Gulf War arrived very suddenly, and promised to last a very long time.

Silent Battlefield Runs Out of Gas at the Cease-Fire; Republican Guard Makes a Run for It Through Basra

By Kevin Cooney

WEST OF BASRA, Iraq - The big guns of the last big battle of the Gulf War fell silent on Thursday morning, two hours before the time set by U.S. President George Bush for a cease-fire.

U.S. Army attack helicopters had run far ahead of their supply lines and when the cease-fire came, they were scattered at isolated bases throughout the desert west-southwest of Basra, fuel-less and useless.

They had entered the last stage of the battle on Wednesday afternoon, dozens of them chasing two Republican Guard armored and mechanised divisions and an artillery battalion fleeing Kuwait that was also pursued by the armor of the American VII Corps.

The Iraqis were moving with a swiftness that surprised American forces, senior U.S. officers said.

Apparently aware that they were outflanked to the west with a great marshland ahead of them to the north, the Iraqis raced to the northeast to try to break out through Basra, Iraq's second city, heavily damaged during the six weeks of air war.

The 24th Mechanized and the 101st and 82nd Airborne Divisions, on the western flank, made a sharp right turn at the Euphrates River and took off after them. "Like all soldiers we marched to the sound of the gun," said Col. Paul Murtha of Lansing, Kan., executive officer of the 18th Aviation Brigade.

Initial efforts to stop the Iraqis were described as a turkey shoot by Murtha.

Iraqi tanks had been placed on giant flatbed trucks to speed their journey north.

They were defenseless and easily picked off. Enough of them made it north to come under the protection of anti-aircraft fire, which was heavy as the final stages of the battle began, pilots said. A Blackhawk helicopter on a search-and-rescue mission to find a downed F-16 pilot was shot down and the eight men aboard lost their lives. An Apache attack helicopter escorting it was hit but managed to make it back to base.

Burning tanks littered the desert floor, returning pilots said. "It's a classic tank-air battle, from the textbooks, a tabletop battle," Murtha said.

For 16 hours, the desert was filled with fire and thunder as American tanks, artillery, helicopters and fixed-wing aircraft poured everything they had at the Iraqis.

As late as Thursday morning, Iraqi engineers were still trying to put a pontoon bridge across one of the waterways that stood in the way of reaching protection in the streets of Basra, said Lt. Col. Tony Jones of Washington, Ind., commander of the 3/227th Apache battalion. His pilots destroyed the Iraqis' final effort. Apache pilots bombing re-supply convoys north of Basra reported that not a single tank had made it to the city.

Through the dawn, American bombs continued to shake the desert.

By 6 a.m., it was over. The planes returned to their base and the helicopters and tanks, far ahead of the supply helicopters, gave up the battle.

The supply planes had been held back a day on Tuesday by rain, strong winds and fog. By 8 a.m. local time, the start of Bush's cease-fire, silence had once again taken over the desert.

1st Cav Soldiers Feel Cheated: "We Came All the Way Over Here. We Should Have Done Something"

By Charles Richards

It was the end of a long march for the 1st Cavalry Division.

Five months of physical discomfort and tedium in the Saudi desert, then a 30-hour route march (which they pronounced like the rout that was to be inflicted on Iraqi forces) deep into Iraq, that petered out some 100 kilometres (60 miles) south and west of Basra.

The 3rd Battalion of the 32nd Armoured Regiment (3-32) were to have been the lead force of the first brigade of the division. It was the sharpest battalion in the division.

You noticed its professionalism and sense of purpose the moment you approached its perimeter. Now, as the men grouped around a short wave radio listening to the languid tones of the BBC World Service newscaster announcing the cease-fire was in effect, they mused on the 100-hour war in which they had not fired a shot in anger.

Many of the tankers, as tankies are known in the U.S. military, were happy only that they would finally be going home—they hoped.

"I'll feel good when I'm back home with my wife and three kids," said one tank commander. His loader, Rick Severns of Springfield, Illinois, agreed: "I'd be satisfied if we got out of here without closing the breech."

Some of the tankers however were disappointed, cheated that they had spent all this time in the desert without actually having sent a few rounds down the range. On another tank in the same company (a company has 15 or 16 tanks), the men were all downcast.

"We came all the way over here. We should have done something," complained Specialist Edward Hawkins, of Detroit, Michigan. "I agree," said Staff Sergeant John Isaacs, from Fort Wayne, Indiana, his tank commander in the third platoon of Bravo Company. The commander of one of their neighbouring vehicles was of the same mind. "We should be kicking ass" said Staff Sergeant George Brock of Chattanooga, Tennessee. "I feel disappointed at not being able to do our job which these," he kicked the hull of the tank he was standing on, "are supposed to do. We need to be out there slinging. I want to go and shoot some."

"Here we were parked in the middle of the desert floor," Staff Sergeant Isaacs continued, "sitting here on our frigging haunches. We've got friendlies fighting. I wish in any way we could have supported some of them."

"We're going to go home with combat patches," Edward Hawkins added.

"We don't deserve it."

Theirs, however, was a minority view. For most, the fact that they had survived was reward enough. One such was the battalion intelligence officer, Capt. Robert Blevins, a great fan of the BBC World Service, who during this long stint in the desert had used its coverage of the Gulf crisis as the basis for his daily briefings. Capt. Blevins has lived in so many places he describes himself as a "citizen of the world." Even before the cease-fire was announced he was saying, "If we don't fire a single shot in anger we'll have done our job."

The 1st Cavalry Division's role during the past weeks had varied.

At the end of December, it was deployed north of the town of Hafr al Batin, to defend against any Iraqi pre-emptive attack down the Wadi al Batin, the watercourse to the east which was the only natural feature in the surrounding area.

Once hostilities began, the watercourse's importance was reversed.

1st Cav's mission was to take part in a deception operation—one of several in the theatre of operations—to lead the Iraqis to believe that the main thrust of the coalition assault was to come north east up that very same Wadi al Batin, which formed Kuwait's western border with Iraq. Then on G-Day, 1st Cav hived off from the operational control of VII Corps and was placed under direct control of Arcent (Army Central Command) as theater reserve. It was a backseat role which few in the 1st Cav relished, given their pride as Cavalry at the forward of any campaign.

Shortly before midmorning on Tuesday, the third day of the ground offensive, 1st Cavalry were given the order to march. Theirs was a unique mission: to engage the Republican Guard divisions they had been watching—the Faw, the Medina, the Hammurabi.

They were to move for 30 hours, then make contact with the Iraqi forces. Never before had the U.S. Army made such a long march to engage its enemy. Only the Russians in World War II had attempted such a feat. When General Patton marched up through Italy, it was fighting on the way, not with the deliberate intention of making contact 30 hours later.

It was a grey day to start the march to battle.

It had rained solidly the previous night. This helped keep the dust down. The swallows, which for the past week had been swooping low as they darted between the armoured vehicles on their own migration to the north, buzzed the fuelers before the final top up. 3-32 battalion headed southwest, leading the brigade.

Two hours on, it was hit by a fierce sandstorm that drove sand and rain almost horizontally across the column as it moved, blasting the paint off the sides of the vehicles. The fine sand covered the deep tracks left by the armour. It swirled in little eddies, quickly forming white drifts, like a snow scene on a Christmas card.

There was a slow refuel on the march, then the vehicles turned north towards the lanes cut in the earthwork berm that runs south of the Iraqi-Saudi border. Engineers had marked the lanes through the berm with giant signs marked A, B, C, D, E, with fluorescent chemical lights. At one point the column cut through a British supply train, with their Bed-ford trucks, Land Rovers and motorbikes—the only ones in the Saudi desert—and men in special-issue desert camouflage chequered scarves.

The Brits were popular with the Americans. Not only did they speak the same language, but the two armies were happy to trade items such as rations and clothing. Then they were through the berm and into Iraq, heading first north, then northeast. The move had an unexpected effect on the men. Like burglars, they wished to defile the place. Everywhere they went, once they crossed the unmarked border, they strewed about them the plastic containers of their rations which in Saudi Arabia they had been scrupulous in burning.

The march was long and slow, held up by the veteran M113 tracked vehicles. After a couple of hours there was the first sign of human presence: a line of power cables running east-west. They passed another U.S. Army unit, in dark green livery—a unit only recently arrived from Germany, which had not bothered with desert camouflage.

Scores of prisoners stood in a huddle.

Then as the scrub thickened, the battalion passed by a Bedouin camp.

It was a Biblical scene. Clothes aired on the guy ropes of the goat hair tent. Donkeys stood outside. Lambs, only days old, lay beside the entrance.

There were three trucks, one a water tender, outside.

A scrawny old Bedouin waved an empty blue plastic water can.

But the battalion was not stopping. This was no campaign of hearts and minds, but a Cavalry charge to cut off the Iraqi forces now reported to be in full retreat from in and around Kuwait. They passed a forward aviation unit, hiding in the folds in the terrain. Dark green Apache attack helicopters rose and landed in quick succession as they went off after their prey. A special electronic warfare Blackhawk chopper trailed an aerial for direction-finding intercepts or jamming.

As the battalion moved north, it spread out wider, for greater survivability. These sleek monsters of tanks passed over gentle undulating hillocks of fresh grass and scrub in a scene so pastoral it was easy to forget their lethal purpose.

After 30 hours on the move across the desert, and 306.4 kilometres (190 miles) from leaving their original battalion camp, the column started the final stretch, to fall upon the Iraqis like a wolf on the fold.

They were north of Kuwait, about 100 km (62 miles) south and west of Basra, and just 20 km short of the Rumallah oil field. In the 160 km (100 miles) or so it had traveled in Iraq, the only Iraqis it had passed were the Bedouin family.

There were no other signs of Iraqi military presence, of defences prepared or overrun, other than the spent artillery shells on an old range. The Iraqis, despite their much vaunted military machine, had left their southern flank exposed.

Before the last stretch, as the column moved forward to make the first hoped-for contact, the tank crews loosened up.

The turrets swung round as the tankers swiveled their shoulders in a final workout. The men gave the appearance of calm. One joked that he had to wait 45 minutes in line so as to order flowers for his wife for Valentine's Day. Another teased the platoon sergeant about his failure to deliver mail.

The tankers had their last cigarettes beside their machines. Then the tank engines started up with the whine like an aero engine, with which they are fitted. In Bravo Company's maintenance track, Sergeant Darrell Jolliff of Saint Mary's, Ohio, had his headset wired up to Led Zeppelin. The brigade—tank-heavy task forces and artillery—lined up in formation ready to move, like the knights in armour to which the cavalry are heirs.

On the flanks, helicopters provided the screen cover. All the practice, training and rehearsals were to be put to the test.

But the end of that 30-hour road march was an anticlimax. In the end, 3-32 were not to engage the other side.

The dangers were not over, however. As Bravo Company brought the tanks into a coil for the night, mortar rounds landed a hundred metres away. There was a sudden change of pressure in the air. The men leapt into the protection of their tanks. Almost immediately, a 25mm cannon mounted on a Bradley fighting vehicle sent tracers out in response. Later on that night, another Bradley started firing in a light show.

News came that night that the cease-fire had been agreed. Two hours before it came into effect, a huge barrage of MLRS rockets lit up the dawn sky, to give one last pounding to the Iraqi Republican Guard.

Even after the cease-fire at 8 a.m. local time, great thumps could be heard as the artillery engaged units. A Bradley fired on what was described as a bunker of Iraqis who either had not heard or ignored the cease-fire call.

American soldiers gathered round a destroyed Iraqi BMP armoured personnel carrier snapping pictures like so many tourists as nine black vultures circled overhead. Traces of blood had dried on the hull. It bore the marks of where it had been hit by 25mm cannon fire from a Bradley.

All around were the signs of war, and the men who waged it. In amongst the shattered rifles the unused rounds of ammunition and the rocket propelled grenades still in their plastic envelopes, was other evidence of the Iraqi soldiers for whom this box of steel had been home.

There were small cans of Kraft cheese, imported from Australia, Geisha brand mackerel from Japan, blankets and foam rubber mattresses; large loaves of brown bread, a pan of cooked rice, razors, a transistor radio, pieces of uniform, soap, a glasses case from Khalaf's store in Kuwait. The driver even had an Iraqi pin-up: a doe-eyed female face framed, in an Arabic veil. Inside the rear door, marked in yellow chalk, was the Arable word "Al-Hurriyah"— Freedom. On the other side was his name: Falah (The victorious). It was his epitaph: he was a victim of the attack.

The U.S. soldiers picked over the wreckage. Some were sobered by what they saw, conscious of their own mortality, "There but for the grace of God go we," said one captain.

For if every generation needs a war to be exposed to its true horrors, the Americans through their tactics of avoiding casualties were spared this awful experience.

They thus may be misled into believing that all war could be as easy and painless.

Some 25 km southeast, Steve Elfers, photographer with the Army Times, flew over another battlefield in a helicopter. It showed just how devastated the Iraqi army had been, routed by superior technology.

The Iraqis never even fought.

He saw the hulks of burnt out T-72 tanks with turrets blown off by air-launched missiles, "incredibly pinpoint-accurate hits, T-72s with no damage around them and the revetments just a burnout bloody mess.

"From the air it looked like one hit, one kill. It was modern warfare: there was nowhere to hide."

Thursday - February 28, 1991

"Maybe We Are the Good Guys"—U.S. Paratroopers Prepare to Return Home as Line in the Sand Fades

By Robert Dvorchak

IN SOUTHERN IRAQ - Word of the cease-fire in the 100-hour ground war came before dawn in the desert today, bringing a sleepy satisfaction to troops camped in Iraq.

"I'm elated. I consider Saddam's defeat a triumph of good over evil. We stood up to a tyrant," said Maj. Baxter Ennis, public affairs officer for the 82nd Airborne Division. "Hundreds of thousands of lives have been saved by standing up to Saddam Hussein. The world would have been a different place and millions of lives would have been saved if we would have stood up to Hitler in the 1930s," Ennis said.

He also said the quality of the U.S. military and its decisive performance, coupled with the overwhelming support of the American public, was a tonic for the leftover scars of another war a generation ago. "I think this war has healed the wounds of the Vietnam War. Our country really came together spiritually," Ennis said.

Other soldiers hoped that the support would continue when the conquering army returns after seven months of sacrifice in the Saudi Arabian desert.

"The military did its job. Now it's up to the American public to do its job and welcome these guys back home," said Capt. Clint Esarey.

"Definitely, there's a sense of letdown for some troopers. By going into combat, they thought they'd find glory. They'll find out the American public is so proud of them, they'll get everything they wanted just by going home," Esarey said.

There was a sense of pride among soldiers who took minimal casualties and captured thousands of prisoners in destroying Iraq's war machine. "When we took all those POWs and didn't mistreat them or gun them down, I wanted to cry. I was so proud to be a U.S. soldier. Maybe we are the good guys," said Spec. 4 Brannon Lamar, North Augusta, S.C.

Officers could sense a letdown in some troops who wanted to be more a part of the action. After all, these are soldiers who make their living jumping out of airplanes.

"It's kind of like a jump," said Col. Jack Nix, 43, of Atlanta, Ga., commander of the division's 1st Brigade. "No matter how many times you jump, there's always a little bit of fright. But if something happened to the plane and you couldn't go, you hear guys say, 'Boy, I wish I could have jumped today,'" said Nix, who parachuted into combat in Grenada and Panama. "Some guys say they wanted to see more action. But deep down inside they're glad they didn't. They know some of them might be killed or severely wounded," Nix said.

"Everybody feels left out some," said Pfc. Paul Jurgensen, 20, of Hicksville, N.Y. "But being left out is a lot better than going home injured or dead. I just want to go home alive." Other paratroopers, the first ground troops to arrive in August, said they accomplished what they were sent to do—deter Iraqi aggression.

"We drew the line in the sand," said Staff Sgt. Barry Kelly, 25, of Goodwater, Ala. "I'm not too thrilled at being shot at. People who want war scare me."

Spec. 4 David Brandt, 24, of Portland, Ore., hopes to get home to see a wife he hasn't seen in almost seven months. He got married nine days before being sent to Saudi Arabia. "I got mixed feelings. I've been here seven months and I wanted to see some action. But I've been to Panama and got shot at, and it's not a good feeling."

1st Sgt. Gregory Duhon, 38, of Eunice, La., agreed. "Once you get shot at, it's not something you want to jump out and do again," Duhon said. "I'm surprised Iraq held on as long as it did. Basically, it was a lot like the rest of the United States declaring war on Rhode Island," he added. "When you're playing in the big game and you're on the bench, you're going to have guys who feel let down. But I don't think you'll find too many guys who miss being shot at," said Lt. Robert Timm, 25, of New York City, executive officer of a company in 1st Brigade.

Still, there were some troopers who wanted to vent some of the frustration of sitting out in the desert for months—enduring the isolation, heat, cold, sand, flies, and other hardships. "I wanted to empty all my magazines," said Pfc. Robert Erculino, 20, of Elmira, N.Y. "It's kind of a letdown. I wanted to fire my weapon three or four times," said Spec. Timothy Marquez, 21, of Depeu, Ill.

"There was a lot of frustration built up, and we wanted to take it out on somebody. But we're going home safe. I'll get to see my wife and kids."

Cluster Bomb Deaths Infuriate Combat Engineers: "Remember What it Can Do if Something Goes Wrong"

By Laurence Jolidon

WITH THE U.S. ARMY - The accidental death of seven American soldiers while clearing unexploded bombs from an Iraqi airfield has puzzled and infuriated their fellow combat engineers.

Many find it difficult to believe that anyone schooled and drilled in the handling of mines and explosives, as the Army's combat engineers are, would handle the deadly cluster bombs that killed the seven recklessly.

But they also are aware how unpredictable mines and bombs can be, even in the hands of supposed veterans and experts. And they know even a minor slip can be fatal. "You can go to school after school and learn about these things," said Sgt. 1st Class Mike Panaranto, 36, of Terre Haute, Ind., "and they'll teach you exactly how each explosive is supposed to act and react. Then you go out and try it, and it'll do something different."

"You have to really respect this stuff, and remember what it can do if something goes wrong."

The seven soldiers were killed Tuesday (26 Feb.) afternoon while clearing the runways of an Iraqi military airbase of cluster bombs dropped by U.S. aircraft during the air campaign that preceded this week's ground offensive. The bombs are dropped in pod-like shells that split open on impact, releasing smaller canisters that also break open, scattering grenade-like charges in a circular cluster.

When the 27th Engineer Battalion (Combat Airborne) arrived at the As Salman airbase Tuesday morning, the French Foreign Legion troops that had seized it warned American officers that the base was littered with unexploded bombs, as well as other ordnance and possible mines and booby-traps left by Iraqi forces.

The American combat engineers, whose line platoons carry mine-clearing equipment and demolition charges as part of their "sapper" gear, volunteered to help clear the base of dangerous ordnance.

Panaranto said one team in his company set 75 separate charges during the day Tuesday. Beginning soon after the engineers arrived at the base about 8:30 a.m., loud explosions set by French and American demolition squads rocked the base every hour or so.

The last explosion heard that day, about 4:30 p.m., was the one in which the U.S. soldiers—including a company commander and platoon sergeant—were killed.

Accounts from soldiers in the battalion were incomplete, but many agreed on one main point: that one of the soldiers killed had picked up some of the unexploded bombs and was putting them in one place to destroy, perhaps to save demolition charges. One of the smaller bombs, the soldiers said, apparently went off or was dropped, setting off others. Some said that wind gusts might have set off one of the bombs.

During most of the day, the airfield was engulfed in a thick, brown haze caused by rain and windstorm that blew gusts strong enough to make walking across the runways and wide dirt median strip difficult. Visibility around the runway area was near zero for hours in the morning and early afternoon. By late afternoon, the wind and haze had diminished, but there were still strong gusts.

Textbook rules for handling unexploded cluster bombs, according to combat engineer NCOs in the battalion, teach a hands-off method of setting an explosive charge a few inches from the bomb, attaching a time fuse, then taking cover.

Another method mentioned during interviews preceding the ground offensive is to wash down a bomb-littered runway with a high-pressure hose.

"There's no need to actually touch any of those things," said Panaranto. "When you have rules, you go by what the rules say. When we have all day, and nobody's shooting at us, we take our time and make sure we do it right. You have to respect that stuff."

The Foreign Legion provided a helicopter to fly the bodies to a U.S. Army mortuary unit. Unconfirmed reports among the American engineers said one or two French soldiers were also killed by explosive charges in the seizing of the airbase. But reliable information about the French casualties is scarce on this fluid, mopped-up western flank of the coalition offensive.

French commanders interviewed in the field stated their forces had suffered no casualties. But American soldiers who were attached to French units in the initial phase of the offensive said French officers told them at least one Legionnaire was maimed or killed when a mine he was deactivating exploded, and that nine Legionnaires were killed and 20 wounded when a Foreign Legion infantry unit assaulted the town of As Salman (believed designated "Altamont" by the French) either late Monday (25 Feb.) or early Tuesday.

U.S. forces that entered Iraq west of Kuwait moved eastward Wednesday, their original mission of blocking and re-supplying for an extended ground war superseded by the incredibly speedy collapse of the Iraqi forces.

The Army engineers continued their construction role, however, scraping fresh roads through the desolate Iraqi desert so that convoys of American trucks, tanks, artillery, and vans can navigate toward a newly-liberated Kuwait.

The men of the 27th Engineer Battalion spent the last night before the cease-fire beside a paved highway, Main Supply Route Virginia. After their dinner meal, some worked under a bright, full moon repairing brakes and fixing flats.

Their long, six-month deployment in Saudi Arabia and hard, five-day drive through southern Iraq took a heavy toll on their aging vehicles. The 2½-ton dump trucks they have converted into minefield-breaching behemoths, carting soldiers who ride on top of crates of weapons, food, fuel, and explosive, date from the Vietnam War.

"They gave us new engines after we got over here," said Staff Sgt. Paul Sullivan, a line platoon squad leader from Irondequoit, N.Y. "And we've kept them running. But we've been told there are new trucks waiting for us when we get back to (Fort) Bragg."

Sullivan and his squad sat in the rocks and sand next to their "deuce and a half" for a field birthday party. Wednesday, Feb. 27th, was Sullivan's 30th birthday and Spec. Douglas Smith's 21st. Their birthday party fare was a dense, unfrosted blueberry cake and a pan of chocolate pudding, both from Army-issue rations.

"I've been holding onto these for the past five months," said Sullivan, "just waiting for the occasion. I've kept them wrapped up in my body bag."

Sullivan and Smith, of Hanover, Pa., reminisced about how they spent Feb. 27th last year, on deployment building an airfield in Honduras.

"This is fun tonight," said Smith. "Last year, the other guys tied us to the bumper of our truck and kept us that way for 45 minutes, dripping water on our heads like they were performing Chinese water torture."

To commemorate the occasion, and to remind Sullivan that he's getting pretty old, Smith and the rest of the 2nd squad, 2nd platoon of Charlie Company, gave Sullivan a squad "birthday card"—actually a flimsy party napkin with "Happy Birthday" printed on one side.

Inside was this note:

"Dear Paul. Happy Birthday. So today you are as old as dirt.

"You've seen many changes in your life. From the finding of fire to the invention of the wheel. Just think, years ago you were brought into this little game we call life. So on this special day, don't let the gray hair and age lines bring you down.

"We love you. God loves you."

When the cake and pudding were gone, the party broke up. Sullivan went to bed. Smith went on guard duty.

By morning, the war would be officially over. The engineers were still far from home, but they were building the roads that would take them back.

While "Twilight Zone" Plays, Kuwaitis Tell of Kidnappings by Iraqi Troops: Made-for-TV Liberation?

By George Rodrigue

KUWAIT CITY - After almost seven months of tomb-like occupation, Kuwait City came alive again Wednesday.

Allied troops rushed into the city as Saddam Hussein's shattered army rushed out, prompting a horn-honking, flag-waving celebration that was dampened only by new reports of Iraqi atrocities.

Free to walk the street without fear for the first time since Aug. 2, Kuwaitis sang, danced, fired machine guns into the air, and videotaped themselves with allied soldiers. Crowds, some in tears, swarmed the U.S. Embassy and bogged down a Marine convoy, showering the grunts with candy, cigarettes, and Kuwaiti flags, accompanied by shouts of "Thank you," "Welcome to Kuwait," and "We love you."

"I never expected that," said Lt. Gen. Walter Boomer, commander of Marine forces in the region. "I thought, what a great thing America has done to see the joy on their faces. I'll keep that memory forever."

Even grimy, flak-jacketed combat correspondents were pulled from vehicles and kissed on the cheeks by Kuwaiti men. "Bush is great! America is great! You tell them," said a man who identified himself only as Ahmed. It was a uniquely Kuwaiti celebration. Many of the cars were Mercedes or Japanese luxury models, which the Kuwaitis had been afraid to bring out of their garages while under Iraq's kleptomaniacal occupation.

At least one car's horn was programmed, eerily, to play the theme from the "Twilight Zone." Nearby, several men paraded a donkey whose rib cage bore the name "Saddam" in white paint. "You know, we never liberated a city like this in Vietnam," one veteran Marine reflected.

Another Marine watched a group of Kuwaitis watch the media, then hold aloft a burning Iraqi flag when the cameras were ready for it.

"Am I wrong to think this is a made-for-TV liberation?" he asked a print reporter.

If the visuals were sometimes stagy, the emotions were heartfelt. Crowds waved pictures of their exiled Emir, who is expected to return by the week's end.

When those ran out, they resorted to pictures of the nation's soccer team.

Saddam Hussein's portraits, which had been plastered all over the city, suffered from the newfound freedom. Stone-wielding children pecked the eyes out of Saddam wall murals. One trio tried to stone a Saddam poster taped to the second-floor window of an office building. When they missed, a Kuwaiti jumped out of a white Chevrolet and blasted the posters with an AK-47.

"What do you want me to tell you? It is my country coming back," said Mohammed Maer, 36, a Kuwaiti resistance fighter who was firing his own AK-47 assault rifle on the outskirts of town. "For seven months we could not go outside. If you went outside, the Iraqis might take you."

Others, however, said they were only beginning to grasp the scope of the Iraqis' last-minute wave of kidnappings from area mosques last Thursday and Friday.

Almost every Kuwaiti interviewed named several relatives or neighbors who had disappeared without a trace, presumably taken hostage and shipped to Baghdad.

One man estimated up to 14,000 citizens could have disappeared in all. Allied commanders have said they believe thousands of Kuwaitis, mostly young men, were plucked from the streets or from their own homes last week.

"They took my brother," said Faisal Al-Kandary, 22, a medical student. "He went to the mosque and they took him to prison, and after that we did not see him again. My father went to ask about him. 'What has he done? Why have you taken him?' And they said, 'If you do not keep quiet, we will take your other children.'"

Badria Al-Mufarej said she and her family lived "as hostages in our own house" under Iraqi occupation, except for trips to the mosque. On Friday, she said, her two brothers disappeared after such a trip. "We hope they will be coming back sometime, but nobody knows," she said. Some Kuwaitis said they had heard the disappeared were taken out of the city on buses. Others said that at least a few of them were found later, dead and horribly maimed. Neither report could be independently confirmed.

Other signs of the Iraqi occupation abounded Wednesday.

There was no wholesale destruction, but seashore luxury hotels, once symbols of the tiny emirate's immense oil wealth, were burned and gutted. So were many public buildings and, reportedly, many homes in the city's wealthier neighborhoods.

Downtown, storefront windows were broken or looted or both. Auto carcasses, stripped even of light bulbs and gearshift levers, littered streets and vacant lots.

There was no power, and residents said the city's water supply had failed.

Fires from scores of oil wells ignited by the Iraqis leapt at least 100 feet into the sky and gave the air a smudgy sting; a chilly rain felt greasy and foul.

In the Saudi Arabian capital of Riyadh, Gen. Norman Schwarzkopf accused the Iraqis of "unspeakable" atrocities. That brutality, he said, convinced allied commanders to step up their plans for the recapture of Kuwait City.

According to media reports, the drive to liberate the city began at 5 a.m. Tuesday. Troops from Saudi Arabia and other Gulf states rolled up from the south, along an almost-undefended coastal corridor. Marines accompanied by a massive American armored brigade raced in from the north and the west. A 33-ship amphibious task force, meanwhile, maneuvered to convince the Iraqis that the attack would come from the eastern seacoast.

The American armored column, 7.5 miles wide and more than 9 miles deep, covered roughly 31 miles in three and a half hours. Commanders said they "nudged" dug-in Iraqi troops into surrendering, by firing 50-cal. bullets into the Iraqis' positions. Smiling Iraqis would then emerge amidst a flutter of white flags.

Iraqi tank crews occasionally chose to fight, but were killed easily by the Americans' superior M1-A1 tanks and their TOW anti-tank missiles. Southwest of the city, about 20 Iraqi T-62 and T-72 tanks were on fire after a fierce battle with Marine tanks, said Lt. Col. Jan Huly, spokesman for the 2nd Marine Division.

The charred tanks "looked like a classy attraction at Disneyland," he said.

Citizens said most of the Iraqi army began fleeing the city by Sunday, leaving few soldiers to oppose the allied advance.

In effect, the city was liberated by the Iraqis themselves.

By Wednesday morning, Marines had squelched the last pocket of open resistance, at the Kuwait International Airport. One Marine officer said the Iraqis who fought there appeared to be trying to escape from the city, not pick a fight.

The American and Arab columns linked up Wednesday, for a brief triumphal parade through the city. The streets they passed spoke eloquently of the Iraqis' flight, as well as their occupation. Tanks and armored personnel carriers clogged major highways. Many seemed to be intact, but for their drivers' accidentally stranding them atop concrete median boundaries. Iraqi weapons, boots and uniforms also dotted many alleyways and parking lots, evidence that Saddam Hussein's occupation troops had changed to civilian clothes as the allies approached. "They even stole bicycles" to get away, one Kuwaiti said. "They ran like dogs."

Lt. Col. Huly said the 2nd Marine Division had destroyed at least 250 Iraqi tanks during the three-day war and captured numerous tanks, trucks, rocket launchers and other weapons. "It was once said that Saddam Hussein had the fourth largest army in the world," he told pool reporters. "I don't think he does anymore because we've got a good portion of it."

By Wednesday night, the Kuwaiti resistance—mostly civil servants with assault rifles—had begun to patrol the streets once more, searching in particular for any Iraqi soldiers who might become snipers. Among the Kuwaitis, the word was vengeance.

"We are not afraid of war," said engineering student Ahmen Nasser, 22. "We want it to go on until Saddam Hussein is killed. If there is a wolf on the street, do you leave him or kill him? Saddam Hussein is a wolf."

Mr. Hussein was not the only target of wrath. Habib Al-Dashti, 40, an engineer with the national airline, said the Palestinians who comprised a substantial portion of the nation's working population would have to pay for siding in large numbers with the Iraqis. "When the Iraqis were here, you would hear them say, 'You are finished, there is no Kuwait,'" he said. "Now they are different. You never see them. They stay in their homes. But we Kuwaiti people, we are not going to trust them anymore."

Most Kuwaitis however seemed to dwell on their good fortune on Wednesday.

"For the last seven months, it was horrible," said Nasser Busheri, 42, a civil servant. "But the people here were very close. There was no difference between families. Everyone was sharing food and everything. We hope to keep this union together forever, God willing."

March 1-6, 1991

"Ladies and gentlemen," Gen. Schwarzkopf said at his tour-de-force press briefing on the war in the closing hours of the campaign, "we were 150 miles from Baghdad and there was nothing between us and Baghdad."

Nothing was just another word for what was left of Saddam Hussein's once-feared military. The will of that "nothing" was never tested. The allied coalition fighting under Schwarzkopf's command had vanquished the Iraqi enemy with a 38-day air campaign and a 100-hour ground war and was then ordered to turn back before Baghdad.

The allied force had easily occupied a wide swath of Iraq, but they did not want to remain there as occupiers. As soon as they could safely be withdrawn, the great allied coalition scrubbed their weapons and vehicles, boarded planes and ships, and left.

In the week that followed the 100-hour land war, however, as this chapter shows, there were unexpected developments, unexpected consequences, and death.

One road connecting Iraq and Kuwait became known as the "Highway of Death" because so much carnage was visible there. Images from this stretch of road, played over and over on television back in the West, were said to have been a key factor in President Bush's decision to end the war when he did. He denied as much, but some of the Arab allies were reportedly very upset at the sight of so much destruction, and holding the coalition together was very high on Bush's agenda.

The rest of the world watching the war on TV had reacted, why shouldn't he?

This chapter gives an account of the place and of the events that took place there. Some military officials later commented that the "Highway of Death" name was undeserved since the tangle of wrecked and demolished military vehicles and civilian cars and trucks actually included few corpses. Many of the drivers and occupants actually escaped on foot, he argued. So it was their means of transportation that died. Either way, it was evident not much on that stretch of road was going anywhere.

The days immediately after the cease-fire were hectic around the Central Command offices. Gen. Schwarzkopf told in his memoirs of the hasty search for a site to hold the cease-fire talks where he would officially accept the surrender of the Iraqi commander. After ruling out the occupied airfield at Jalibah because too much unexploded ordnance remained on the ground there, he chose Safwan a village with an airfield in southeastern Iraq.

A map in his headquarters showed Safwan well within an area controlled by allied troops. The Iraqis would have to navigate an allied gantlet to attend. He told his staff the meeting with the Iraqi commanders would be on Sunday afternoon in three days, and to get the place ready.

But the next morning, the general's staff had bad news for him. Allied soldiers didn't really own Safwan. Even though it was an area Gen. Schwarzkopf had ordered his troops to take, Iraqi troops were still in control there and they weren't in a mood to clear out.

That instant, Gen. Schwarzkopf became a four-star general with two good reasons to be angry. First, he had enemy troops guarding the cease-fire site where he was supposed to be in charge. Secondly, there was a map in his headquarters that was lying to him.

By Sunday, the first problem was remedied. Sent on an urgent mission of military and diplomatic necessity, American tanks, troops, and helicopters from the 1st Infantry Division surrounded the Iraqis at Safwan and basically told them to take a hike or die right there.

The Iraqis retreated. The cease-fire meeting was held, on schedule and under the control of the allies. Stories in this chapter show the care with which the ceremonies were arranged, down to the location of the allied commander's diet soft drink.

Resolving the second problem involved a handwritten report from Gen. Fred Franks, VII Corps commander, whose troops had erroneously been shown in control of Safwan when apparently the closest any Americans had come was a flyby in a helicopter. In a post-war interview with PBS, Gen. Franks said he never could figure out how a map with such wrong information got posted in Schwarzkopf's command center. He did say, in part, ". . . if you talk about the scale of maps, on a large scale map distances show up as a very small space on a map, so I don't know how it happened . . ."

That's the way he described the problem, which of course puts the blame on the map—or, so to speak, shifts the rock to a different boot.

Schwarzkopf later described Gen. Franks' argument as "specious," but decided he had neither been "intentionally disobeyed nor deliberately deceived."

In a large-scale war like this one, even some major events show up as very small events at the time. An example in this chapter was the battle on Saturday, March 2nd, two days after the cease-fire, between the U.S. 24th Infantry Div., commanded by Gen. Barry McCaffrey, and an Iraqi force near the allied lines. Gen. McCaffrey and several of his commanders said the Iraqis fired on his forces first and he acted to defend his soldiers.

The 24th Division's reaction demolished the Iraqi force. Critics later accused McCaffrey of looking for a fight and attacking a retreating force trying to reach safety. But an Army investigation supported the general's version. The event was widely overlooked at the time, despite the pool report in this chapter.

The deaths of individual soldiers, too, were events that might have been overshadowed from a distance, but were clear as day in person.

In this chapter, a desert funeral service stands for much of the solemnity that followed the allied victory. The services celebrated life while on the ground beneath the soldiers' feet, and all around them, death lay in hiding.

In one of this chapter's most personal stories, a young, popular soldier loses his last race. In the end, being the fastest runner in his outfit was his undoing. His death, unfair at its heart, but no more unfair than many others, was one of the last—but not the last—endured by the soldiers who went to the desert.

American troops continued to fall in the desert, to helicopter accidents and mines and cluster bombs, for weeks after the enemy had stopped shooting.

Eventually the Saudis released many Iraqi prisoners. And the allied prisoners, all of those the Iraqis admitted holding, were returned.

The sand of the desert would shift in the wind, and hide many of the tracks made by this war. But even without the tracks, and without the shouts of soldiers, the whine of fighter planes or the roar of artillery, the place would forever be a battleground for those who were here.

War's Over: "Whether it Would Have Gotten Exciting Wonderful or Exciting Horrible, We Won't Know"

By Douglas Jehl

1 March

WITH U.S. FORCES, Iraq - And suddenly it was silent, the battlefield still smoldering from the final barrage of war.

Ahead lay scores of hulks of burning tanks, the remnants of an army trapped as it tried to flee Kuwait. Around them a border base had been reduced to chaos, the backs of bunkers broken by weeks of aerial bombardment, the sand strewn with scattered wreckage and littered with steel helmets Iraqi soldiers had left behind.

Yet at the forefront of an American advance, a division-wide row of armor remained unbroken, hundreds of main guns now pointed south and east toward a Kuwaiti border just two miles away on the brink of another battle.

It was 8 o'clock in the morning, and every soldier's radio had just come alive with the order to cease-fire. In a forward tank platoon, Sgt. Richard Smith of Sowego, Ill., cautiously lifted the heavy iron hatch that had been sealed tight over his head for war, unable to believe the fighting was really over. A deafening artillery barrage had just poured forth fire from every gun in the battalion on Iraqi positions just ahead, in a prelude to what commanders had warned could be the biggest battle of the war.

As the battalion radio urged the soldiers to stand by for attack, a 19-year-old ammunition-loader in the seat next to Smith read aloud from the Bible stowed behind his seat: "The war will rise up against me . . . my heart should not fear." But now politics had intervened; there would be no final battle. And after a lightning war that sent this armored division against Iraq's best forces in a 150-mile left hook, the soldiers in the Bradley fighting vehicle and across the American front lines began to breathe deep since crossing into Iraq.

"We wiped the sweat from our eyes and shook each other's hand," the 24-year-old Bradley gunner said. "And then we made some coffee." Next door along the line of armor, arrayed here on a rare patch of desert grass, a crew hoisted an American flag above its M1A1 tank to join others already flapping triumphantly over Iraqi territory: "You will never forget the last 100 hours," a weary commander, Col. James Riley told soldiers later as the permanence of the peace began somehow to sink in. "We were part of a movement that completely unhinged what the other guy had set up for months and months. And we came through just as unscathed as anyone thought was possible."

The end to war for this division came after its nearly 20,000 soldiers charged for nearly four days across the desert as part of a massive American flanking attack that turned to headlong pursuit as Iraqi forces sought to leave Kuwait.

In its closing drive, it clashed with elements of at least five Iraqi divisions, including the furious battle Wednesday afternoon against a Medinah Division force that sought to block the American advance while others continued to escape.

After four days and often sleepless nights, with a path of destruction from that fight and four smaller engagements spread for miles across the desert, the exact extent of the battle damage caused by the division remained difficult to assess.

But Maj. Gen. Ronald H. Griffith said reports indicated that the end-run attack, which brought the American unit crashing down on fleeing Iraqi forces, had wiped out three full Iraqi divisions, including the Medinah, as well as taking a heavy toll on another Republican Guard division. Only two Americans were killed in the attacks, and 36 were wounded. Early indications suggested that as many as 10,000 Iraqis had been killed.

"Look in the history books," Griffith urged officers gathered under the tent of a brigade command post erected after the battle. "This has never been done."

"You had a high school team playing in the Super Bowl against the New York Giants," said the forthright general, who directed much of the battle from aloft in a Blackhawk helicopter, "and they got their ass whipped."

With the division preparing before the cease-fire was announced to push further east to cut off fleeing Iraqi forces, the halt to battle nevertheless brought with it a measure of frustration.

Indeed even in the final minutes before the deadline, this division was moving toward an attack it hoped could wipe out at least a few more Iraqi tanks escaping from the bottle. "There is elation mixed with anger that we didn't go far enough," acknowledged Riley, the brigade commander, after the cease-fire order forced the division to abort the planned assault. "We needed to go another day. That son-of-a-bitch needed to be destroyed."

But as the commanders and other grime-faced soldiers stripped off the chemical-protection suits they had worn nonstop since war began, what was most palpable in this desert was a feeling of mass relief.

"If things kept going, probably it would have gotten exciting," said Sgt. 1st Class Roger Sturgiss, a 38-year-old senior non-commissioned officer from Port Hueneme, Calif. "Whether it would have gotten exciting wonderful or exciting horrible, we won't know, and that's just fine with us."

As silence replaced the din of war, an end to the roar and crash and rumble, the visual evidence of American destruction remained within easy reach.

Near a road that marked the center of the battlefield, T-72 tanks and BMP armored personnel (carriers) lay charred and broken, the parts strewn for hundreds of yards in explosions that had sent flames some 80 feet into the air.

Trucks had run off the roadway and now lay in battered heaps, some ripped apart by tank-sized rounds, others crashed head-on into poles and even one another amid what must have been the terror and confusion of the five-hour fight.

Some corpses lay atop the asphalt.

But other Iraqis appeared to have died in their vehicles as they burned, or were wounded and hauled away by others, their boots, gas masks, and helmets scattered at road's edge and deep into the desert, the legacy of American tanks that fired killing blows from two miles away.

In an eerie sign that others may have survived only by rapid flight, uneaten meals of rice and peas were still perched, spoons ready, inside some of the Iraqi armored vehicles.

The road, running through a sprawling military training area that served as a base for the Medinah, was but the center of fighting that extended for miles each side and began long before the ground offensive with what appeared to have been saturation bombing from the air.

But the freshest blows had been struck by the 45-minute-long artillery barrage that began promptly at 5:30, aimed at key sites across the compound in a softening-up attack Griffith called "one of the most devastating ever fired by a division in combat."

As armored vehicles rolled through the area only a few hours later, underground command bunkers lay exposed, roofs broken and collapsed, office chairs and tables and other unexpected contents askew and strewn across the sand.

And in what periodically interrupted the peacetime silence and turned the sky aglow, ammunition bunkers filled with rockets and artillery shells now burned in orange flame that periodically erupted in massive explosions.

Those Iraqi soldiers who emerged to surrender appeared almost shattered by the cumulative effects of war, suffering from what some said was weeks of exposure to the elements, some even in need of medical treatment for what doctors said was hypothermia.

Some American soldiers found time to patrol the battlefield in search of souvenirs, collecting helmets, patches and even the distinctive black berets worn by the Republican Guards. But with war having turned to peace so abruptly, many were still reliving the battle of their lives, the afternoon-long clash that pitted tank against tank in a remarkably one-sided fight. "It was like a movie out of World War II," said Spec. Jesse Sloan, the 19-year-old gunner from Sickenhoffen, West Germany. "You look to your left and to your right, and everybody's firing in line."

"You're superman," Lt. Eric Drake, a 23-year-old platoon leader from Wilsie, W.V., said of his taste of war. "You're invincible. You're rolling into battle and nothing can touch you." A few hours after the cease-fire, adrenaline was still clearly coursing through this 4th Battalion, 66th Tank Regiment, credited with at least 30 kills of tanks and armored vehicles. Soldiers spoke of turrets blown high into the sky, and of close calls from the mortar shells that landed too close or the artillery round that skipped across the sand.

But others spoke with a reflectiveness that had seemed lacking in pre-war bluster, a sober wisdom that made some suddenly appear old for their young years. "It was careful, controlled, deliberate chaos," concluded Drake, the tank platoon leader.

"Four days ago, your soldiers were sitting on the other side of the border not knowing what to expect," Riley, the brigade commander said of the transformation. "And now here we are 100 hours later, and every soldier is a combat veteran."

Only death remained still alien here, the product of a tightly-reined operation that, as the battle raged, could be seen to (be) marked with controls at every step to minimize American casualties.

Radio traffic monitored from within a Bradley command vehicle positioned just behind the American front lines was dominated by the cross-checks of commanders making sure that their soldiers did not fire on friendly forces. And where a soldier was killed, as a scout was in this unit late into the battle, all still seemed to grieve. "We're lucky in a way," said Maj. Scott Severson, the battalion executive officer. "We haven't had to become callous."

In the aftermath of battle, commanders said the head-to-head clash had validated their confidence in American stand-off tactics that rely on superior range and sighting capabilities to kill from safety beyond enemy reach. The more than 100 M1A1 tanks and Bradley fighting vehicles that fought within this 1st Brigade killed at least 100 targets virtually at will from ranges of two to three kilometers with Super Sabo armor-piercing rounds and TOW anti-tank missiles, commanders said.

At the same time, only one of the American armored vehicles in the brigade was hit by direct fire from an Iraqi side forced well beyond its range, with most rounds landing at least 300 meters short.

And with Iraqi units forced at last from the safety of their bunkers, soldiers and commanders alike described every battle as a feeding frenzy. "Our hope was we would get these guys out in the open," said

Severson, of Sierra Vista, Ariz. "And what you saw was the result of that happening. It was pretty much a one-way exchange."

Less than lessons, what soldiers wanted most to think of in the hours after war were the long-anticipated spoils: a speedy exit from the desert and a rapid flight back home. "It's going to be baby-making time when I get back to Germany," said Sgt. Ignatius Montgomery, 28, a squad leader from Mobile, Ala.

But while plans are being laid for a triumphant southward journey down the main Kuwaiti highway, commanders here believe the exodus from Iraq remains days if not weeks away. Nevertheless, there were clear indications by Thursday evening of peacetime mores returning as the Army begins what now appears likely to be a highly visible occupation here on Iraqi soil.

No longer, the Army command advised, would they be required to live under the rigid night-time blackout that sought to keep their location secret. In the Iraqi desert, war now turned to victorious cease-fire, white light would be just fine.

Smoke, Flames Etch a Hell Along Highway of Death; Gulf War's Cease-Fire Came Too Late for Many

By Tom Ferraro

1 March

ALONG HIGHWAY 8 - The cease-fire came too late Thursday for a stretch of Highway 8 transformed by bombs and rockets into a ghoulish scene from Hell.

Every couple of hundred yards or so, there was a charred or burning Iraqi military vehicle. In a few, bodies could be seen from the roadside. The remains of one Iraq soldier, his head thrown back, his mouth wide open, sat in the front seat of his flaming rig. Down the road, black smoke billowed from an armored personnel carrier possibly packed with up to a dozen dead.

Up ahead looking more like zombies than warriors, nine Iraqis walked in the moonlight along the side of the road and carried a white flag of surrender. U.S. forces cleared the highway Wednesday with attack planes, artillery fire, and M-1 tanks.

The heavy fire was conducted to prepare for a massive movement down the concrete pike by U.S. troops for what was to be a showdown with a unit of Saddam Hussein's elite Republican Guard. That battle was placed on hold, possibly permanently, by the cease-fire that went into effect at 8 a.m.

By then, though, much of Highway 8, at least a 20-mile stretch traveled in the pre-dawn hours by the 197th Infantry Brigade, was covered with death and destruction. A few dead Iraqi soldiers laid in the highway or on the sandy median strip, near their smoldering wrecks. A black dog sat still by one of the dead.

The stretch of highway is about 100 kilometers west of the city of Basra in eastern Iraq. In recent days with the ground war underway, few civilians have dared to travel it. Still, there appeared to be at least a few civilian vehicles, mostly cars, among the burning hulks. "Very sobering," said Maj. John Batiste, 38, of Jaffrey, N.H. "You never want to kill civilians, but in a war it happens."

At least two of the Iraqi trucks, both traveling from Kuwait, were packed with women's clothing, bicycles, and appliances, much of it in boxes marked as being from Kuwaiti department stores, suggesting the goods were looted from homes and shops in the tiny emirate. "That's evidence of some of their deeds," said Lt. Col. Wally Bunyea, 43, of Staten Island, N.Y. Bunyea said many of the vehicles headed southwest toward Kuwait carried ammunition, apparently for retreating Iraqi troops. "I'm glad that they didn't make it," Bunyea said. The dead Iraqis did receive roadside pity, though.

"We normally fire our artillery and don't see the damage. Today we did," said Sgt. Charles Collins, 31, of Benning, Ga. "Seeing them makes us see them as people," he said. "They have families too, too." Collins, head bowed, speaking softly, said: "I hope this cease-fire works so no one else dies and we can all go home."

Spec. 4 Michael Carter, 26, of Stockton, Calif., said although he had a camera on his ride down Highway 8, he wasn't tempted to take a picture. "My wife doesn't need to see this," said Carter.

"I took pictures," piped up Spec. Steve Campbell, 24, of Hartford, Conn., another artilleryman. "Why not? Who's going to stop me?" Campbell said, "They're the enemy and this is war. A man's got to do what he's got to do."

Col. Ted Reid, 47, of Newcastle, Pa., commander of the 197th and a veteran of Vietnam, spoke volumes after his trip down Highway 8 to a field command center. "Cease-fires are always too late for someone," said Reid, sipping a black cup of coffee.

War's Horrors Being Guarded: "It's Different When You See Their Faces, Blood Coming Out of Their Wounds"

By William Branigin

1 March

WITH U.S. FORCES IN IRAQ - Corporal David Richards looked on with distaste as American soldiers took advantage of a cease-fire to visit the grisly scene he was guarding.

By the side of a dirt road in Iraq's southeastern desert sat a truck belonging to President Saddam Hussein's elite Republican Guards. In and around it lay the bodies of eight Iraqi soldiers. The immediate area was cordoned off with white tape like some police crime scene. The headless corpse of one of the soldiers was on its back a short distance from the truck. Another body was wedged inside the engine compartment. Two more lay face up in the bed of the truck, their feet sticking grotesquely over the side.

This was the gruesome face of the Gulf War, a facet of the conflict not previously seen by many of the young American soldiers who took part in an allied ground offensive against Iraq this week. After weeks of a high-tech war waged largely from the sky, the horrors on the ground took some of the troops by surprise.

The truck, which soldiers say was struck by a missile from an Apache helicopter a couple of days before Thursday's cease-fire, represents just one example of the horrifying results of combat. Thousands of other potential horrors are littered across the southern Iraqi desert in the form of unexploded bombs dropped by American warplanes and mines left by Iraqi forces. Already units of the Army's 1st Cavalry Division that had suffered no combat casualties in their unopposed drive through southern Iraq have seen several of their number killed or wounded by bombs or mines in the area they are holding.

Not only have curious soldiers been tempted to pick up live ordnance, they also have been attracted to scenes like the one guarded by Richards, 21, of Huntsville,

Alabama, a member of the 545th Military Police Company based at the 1st Cavalry's home in Fort Hood, Texas. He said commanders have ordered U.S. forces not to disturb the truck or corpses, but many soldiers show up simply to look. "When we move out, we're just going to leave them here," Richards said. "I figure we should just dig a hole and bury them. It's kind of gross leaving them out here like this."

Specialist Daniel Rachell, a 20-year-old helicopter door gunner from Belleville, Ill., said that after seeing dead Iraqi soldiers for the first time the other day, he has admonished friends who boast about how many of the enemy have been killed by U.S. forces.

"I tell my friends it's different when you see their faces, with blood coming out of their wounds," Rachell said. "It shocked me, it really did."

Farther up the road from the truck guarded by Richards sat several other damaged or abandoned vehicles, halted in their tracks by apparent air strikes as they tried to flee a Republican Guard area. A Soviet-built BMD armored vehicle was slightly damaged in the rear, and an armor-piercing round had gone clear through its gun barrel. But still intact inside it were cannon rounds, sagger anti-tank rockets, grenades, and other munitions.

A child's lunch box, used to carry a soldier's shaving kit, sat pathetically atop the vehicle, whose occupants apparently escaped. Like the BMD, other military vehicles along the road bore the red triangle symbol denoting the Republican Guard. Documents found in the debris identified the vehicles as belonging to the Guard's Tawa Kalna ala Allah (Trust in God) Division.

Scattered by the bombs or rockets that halted the vehicles was an assortment of gear they had been hauling, ranging from communications equipment and office furniture to mattresses and bed frames.

Army intelligence officers said the division was decimated by the bombing and finally wiped out by allied armor in the ground offensive. A couple of miles away from the vehicles, a large expanse of desert that apparently had been a Republican Guard training area was devastated by aerial bombardment well before the U.S. armored units swept through.

In a wrecked command trailer bearing the logo of the Tokyu (cq) Car Corp. were three color TV sets, two video cassette recorders, a stereo, a refrigerator, an air conditioner, a sofa, a bed, carpets, executive chairs, and other signs of comfort in better times. One side of the trailer was riddled with shrapnel and bullet holes. Other trailers and vans sat tucked away in sand revetments in various stages of ruin. In one of them, apparently an officers' mess with an ornate wood-paneled ceiling, a teapot sat intact on a table amid debris of broken chairs, china, and other furnishings.

Well away from the trailers were shallow bunkers dug in the sand, including one whose roof was reinforced with part of a U.S. cluster bomb canister—evidence of an apparently vain attempt by the Republican Guards to remain there after the bombing began. The entire area was littered with pieces of ordnance, including hundreds of unexploded individual yellow cluster bombs sticking into the sand. Still attached to some of these "bomblets" were little parachutes used to delay their descent.

On one piece of cluster bomb canister someone had written, "To Saddam: From Who gives a f___." Another bore the words, "Love always, all ways. God, I love this bomb!" It was accompanied by a cartoon drawing of a skull-like head.

Life in Iraqi Desert Bunker Under Allied Bombing: Onion Skins, Orange Peels, Empty Tin of Cheese

By Mike Tharp

1 March

WITH U.S. FORCES IN SOUTHERN IRAQ - An Iraqi soldier lived in a semi underground bunker roofed with sandbags and walled with corrugated tin, ate onions, oranges, and rice, drank tea. He wore a jungle camouflage helmet, carried an AK-47 rifle, and lighted his cooking fire with cartridges from his ammunition pack. He also abandoned his tank without firing a shot and surrendered quickly.

These almost pitiful traces left by Iraqi defenders were strewn across the desert like detritus after a high tide. They showed why U.S. troops, in the words of one American soldier, "kicked ass and took names" in the 100-hour war.

Just how easy the coalition victory was could be seen at what could only be generously termed fighting positions manned by Iraqi soldiers before American aircraft, tanks, and troops cut a deadly swath through them in southern Iraq.

Dug in near the town of Al Busayyah, the bunkers held only one T-55 Russian-made tank that had been destroyed. A dozen other armored vehicles sat intact, green burlap and canvas sacks pulled over the barrels of their guns.

Littering the loamy sand around the emplacements were the remains of a defeated soldier's daily life. Damp tea leaves stuck to the bottom of a scorched kettle. Two-inch thick cotton pallets hung off rusted iron bed frames under the bunker's four-foot high ceiling.

Outside, a fire pit held onion skins, orange peels, and an empty can of Kraft processed cheddar cheese. Powder from red-tipped tracer cartridges had been used to ignite the fire. Several finger-long live rounds—machine gun ammunition—and empty brass casings were scattered around the bunker.

A helmet lay tipped on its green and black top. A dozen tanks and other armored vehicles sat half-submerged behind sandbagged walls. Only one bore the blackened vestiges of the American attack, a ragged hole gaping in its turret.

Less than two miles away, the town of Al Busayyah resembled a German village in the waning days of World War II. Apparently also serving as a division supply post, the town had been overrun by troops and tanks of several American combat units.

Military police from the 210th MP Group, a North Carolina National Guard unit, then secured the village. Combat engineers from the 37th Engineer Battalion blew up dozens of undetonated mines and other munitions, both U.S. and Iraqi, on the next day.

Al Busayyah's stone wall was jaggedly crenelated, its rusty water tower riddled with bullet holes. Low one-story buildings contained weapons and supplies: mortar rounds, anti-aircraft gun barrels, wooden crates of AK-47 rifles, uniforms, gas masks.

On one wall of a dusty room hung a 1991 calendar featuring Saddam Hussein's picture. Inside a warehouse were sacks of potatoes, rice, and onions and plastic containers of water. A pale green van, specially designed to decontaminate soldiers hit by gas or chemical weapons, stood nearby.

Apart from U.S. soldiers, the only signs of life were a donkey walking across a dusty plaza and three puppies yipping amid the rubble. The smell of burning rubber and cordite hung in the air.

March 1-6, 1991

Lt. Anthony Coggiola, an Asheville, N.C., National Guardsman and military policeman, had discovered five Iraqi soldiers cowering in a bunker inside the town. He fired a round into a sandbag and they surrendered.

"They kept saying, 'Inshallah!' (God wills it) and trying to kiss me," he said.

Coggiola, a deputy sheriff in North Carolina, joined the National Guard a month before Saddam Hussein invaded Kuwait. His unit was sent to Saudi Arabia last September.

"I joined the Guard because I wanted to work in the war against drugs," he said. "I guess I said 'war' too loud."

Added Coggiola: "If you write anything, tell my wife Sherrie and my daughter in Winston I'm OK."

He's OK.

Aftermath of Scud Strike on U.S. Barracks: Grief, Shock, Terror, Bullets Whizzing Through the Chaos

By Mark Mooney

2 March

KING FAHD MITLITARY CITY, Saudi Arabia - The Scud attack on an American barracks on the next-to-last day of the war was made worse because the GIs had been issued ammunition the day before and fires sent bullets whizzing through the chaos.

Victims of the blast said at least one person—someone trying to rescue the injured—was struck in the forehead by an M16 round.

In the first interviews with the injured since the Feb. 25 attack, they told of finding friends crushed to death right next to them and of watching the Scud warhead crash through the roof and explode on the floor in front of them.

One GI said 12 "best friends" were killed. Another, who had both legs broken, described how he dragged his buddy away from a fire. Sobbing, the soldier said his friend had both legs blown off, and he had been unable to find out what happened to him. The attack on a barracks killed 28 GIs and wounded 100.

Reporters were allowed into King Fahd Military Medical Complex because Kuwait's Crown Prince Saad Al-Abdullah Al-Salem Al-Sabah visited the wounded. The prince sent sprays of flowers and stopped briefly to ask a dozen wounded soldiers how they were feeling.

GIs were still dealing with the shock of being blasted out of their beds nearly 200 miles from the battlefield. "We're here a week and get blowed up," said Sgt. Robert Lessman, 24, of Mt. Pleasant, Pa., shaking his head.

"It seems so ironic because everyone started to take Scuds lightly. Nobody in 1,000 years thought a warhead would come right at us," he said.

Lessman, dressed in green hospital pajamas, sat propped in a bed. He had a large piece of shrapnel in his left thigh, a smaller chunk in his left shoulder, and his left eye was red and bruised from an operation to remove a sliver of metal from the eye. His face and neck were splattered with small burns from flying bits of fiberglass from the ceiling.

But Lessman is grateful to be alive. "The guy right next to me was killed by a beam from the building," he said. "He was in the bunk next to me in arms reach." Lessman said 13 members of his 14th Quartermaster Detachment died in the attack.

"Most of them were sitting on the floor playing Trivial Pursuit," he said.

But in a hellish twist, Lessman said each of the troops were issued 72 rounds of M16 ammo the previous day and fires from the explosion sent the bullets smashing around in the dark. "Some people were wounded from the bullets," he said. "One guy from our unit had two rounds in his hip. One guy went in to help rescue people and he was hit right in the forehead."

Lessman did not know if he survived.

Spec. Scott Edwards, 22, of Altoona, Pa., was in a different section of the building. "I could hear bullets flying, but I couldn't see anything," Edwards said. Edwards said the soldier on his left never got up from the blast, killed as he slept. "The guy on the other side of me, he was a mess when I saw him," Edwards said.

Edwards said he talked to the wounded soldier for a while and said his entire stomach was covered with blood. But the soldier was unconscious when he was taken away and Edwards did not know if he lived.

Spec. Neal Gowher, 20, of Greenburgh, Pa., said 12 of his friends died. "I knew every one of them like they were my best friends," said Gowker, who has lost the hearing in his left ear. "We'd see each other on weekends, and we'd talk a lot and party and stuff."

Spec. Brian Thompson said he was trying to organize a football game when the air raid alarm went off. He heard a bang and looked up in time to see the warhead crash through the roof and detonate on the floor. Thompson said that when he realized he survived, he told himself, "Thank God you're alive. You're alive, kid." At least one soldier has been scarred mentally as well as physically—although he displayed astonishing heroism. Pfc. Anthony Drees, 23, of Grand Forks, N.D., had one leg shattered by the blast and the other leg broken. "And it blew off part of my butt," he said, adding that he has shrapnel in his left forearm and has numerous small burns and cuts.

Drees was bending over his cot when the Scud crashed into the building. "I knew I'd been hit. I caught my breath for a second and looked up and the whole building was gone. My bed was against a wall and it was gone," he said, referring to the wall.

"I reached back and pieces of my leg were missing. My right shoe was off. I tried to chase it around and couldn't" move his leg, Drees said. "My friend next to me had both legs blown off," he continued, looking away. "I put my arm across his . . ."

Drees broke down crying, holding his face in his right hand. His left arm was immobilized in a cast and suspended with a sling attached to an overhead bar.

After a moment and a few deep breaths, he continued. "I put my arm across his chest and tried to crawl. I got him at least to the wall because the fire was after us. We were together since Day One of this s___," Drees said, now sobbing openly. "I don't know where he is. I can't find him." When Drees was able to compose himself, he added, "One more day and the damn war would have been over . . . God, I had a nice life, too."

Drees said he was studying aeronautics at the University of North Dakota when his reserve unit was activated. He was a member of ROTC, was treasurer of the Black Student Union and had a part-time job in a liquor store.

At least one of the units that suffered casualties in the blast held a memorial service at their headquarters yesterday. "I'll heal," said Lessman, who has not been able to sleep for the past two nights thinking of the GI who died next to him.

"But it's going to take a lot longer for families that lost someone," he said.

March 1-6, 1991

24th Infantry Commander Returns Iraqi Fire After Cease-Fire: Civilians, Children Among the Casualties

By Thomas Ferraro

2 March

EASTERN IRAQ - Army Lt. Col. Chuck Ware and his battalion fought in one of the biggest battles of the Gulf War on the third day of the cease-fire.

As smoke and flames rose from hundreds of pulverized Iraqi tanks and trucks, Ware stood beside his unscathed Bradley Fighting Vehicle and said: "They shot first. We won big."

"Maybe they didn't know there was a cease-fire. Maybe they care," said Ware, 41, of Starkville, Miss. "But we know that Saddam Hussein can't be trusted."

The Army said Saturday's shootout in rural eastern Iraq, about 50 kilometers west of the city of Basrah near the Rumallah oilfields, involved units of Saddam's once elite Republican Guard.

The battle carried the potential to be the final major offensive of the war. It occurred on the eve of Iraqi-allied talks Sunday aimed at bringing the war to a formal close.

Ware's battalion got into the thick of it shortly before 9 a.m., when one platoon reported that a massive Iraqi convoy, traveling northwest towards Baghdad, had just shot a couple of rockets at it. Ware promptly got permission from the chain-of-command of the Army's 24th Infantry Division to return fire. The fight promptly escalated with Ware's battalion receiving backup from Army artillery and 20 U.S. Cobra and Apache attack helicopters.

Together, in less than two hours, they destroyed 187 Iraqi armored vehicles, including 23 Soviet-made T-72 tanks, and more than 350 Iraqi military trucks, the Army said. One American tank and one U.S. Bradley were damaged.

There were no U.S. estimates on the number of Iraqi troops dead or injured. Ware said only one of his soldiers was hurt, having suffered a minor shrapnel wound.

Some Iraqi civilians were caught in the crossfire.

Cries of anguish from parents and loved ones could be heard on a rural road.

A projectile hit a truck, killing its driver. Nearby were remains of two children.

Army medics waded through a crowd of about 30 civilians, some tending wounds, others trying to provide comfort. Two old men embraced, sobbing. A woman wailed.

A reporter seeking to talk with the medics was promptly escorted away by two U.S. military officers. "No interviews," one said.

Ware said he had no knowledge of any casualties. But he said before his units fired, all targets were identified as Iraqi military. The U.S. and Iraqi tanks and armored vehicles exchanged fire while positioned from 1,000 to 2,000 yards away from each other. An Army spokesman said about 70 Iraqi soldiers were taken prisoner, many as they tried to flee, some on foot, others in vehicles.

Army Pfc. Jerry Brooks, 22, of Carlsbad, Calif., shouted, "Don't move!" as he searched an enemy soldier that he helped force to the ground. The Iraqi showed no emotion as Brooks checked him for weapons, tied his hands, and then placed him in a cattle car for transport to a nearby POW camp. "When we first heard about the cease-fire, we all started talking about going home," said Brooks, still winded. "But our platoon leader said it's not over yet."

"I won't believe the war is over now until we're on the plane going home."

Gen. Barry McCaffrey, commander of the Army's 24th Division, said many Iraqi soldiers may have been unaware of the cease-fire because U.S. forces destroyed their lines of communication. "Some might not even know we are here," he said. "But perhaps there are some out there just looking for a fight."

Several Army divisions, including McCaffrey's, crossed Iraq's southern border last Sunday, the first day of the ground war. In one of the biggest and swiftest military cavalry charges in history, they moved more than 240 miles into enemy territory in less than 48 hours to cut off supply routes from Baghdad to Kuwait and to box in more than 500,000 Iraqi soldiers.

Since the cease-fire went into effect Thursday, just as U.S.-led forces were ready to launch a major offensive in Iraq, there had been a number of reported violations by Saddam's forces. Several Army units reported receiving artillery or sporadic gunfire.

After Saturday's battle involving McCaffrey's 1st Brigade, Army Chaplain Jim Carter voiced thanks that no Americans were killed. In fact, the 24th Division, with more than 26,000 troops, reported as of Sunday no combat deaths.

"Let me shoot straight with you," Carter told a reporter. "I think it has a lot to do with prayer. I've been praying my guts out."

Setting of Ceremony at Safwan in Shadow of "Scud Mountain": Water, Coffee, and Diet Pepsi

By Richard Pyle

3 March

Three Iraqi officers led by unidentified Lt. Gen. arrived by back door of tent at 11:30 a.m. Pool (was) ushered in, found Iraqis seated at table facing Schwarzkopf and Prince Khalid.

Five Iraqi officers (were) seated behind their team. Allied leaders (were seated) behind theirs, (with) de la Billière (and) Roquejoffre in front row.

Table had bottles of water (one each), coffee cups, Diet Pepsi for H.N.S. (Schwarzkopf). They sat in black vinyl chairs (with) chrome hardware at (opposite) sides of brown wood table.

Eight Iraqis arrived in cars outside the base (and) were met by eight Humvees, two Bradleys, two M1 tanks, (and) two AH64s of the U.S. 1st Inf. Division. (They) were put in Humvees and brought to airstrip at Safwan, five klicks into Iraq above the Kuwait border. They drove to tent where (they) were) searched. (They were) met inside by Schwarzkopf, who then walked with them to meeting tent about 100 M away.

The meeting place is alongside the macadam airstrip. (The airstrip was empty and not bombed.) A nearby mountain is called "Scud Mountain" by GIs, and supposedly was a location for some Scud launches, according to Maj. Joseph Repya, Jr., of Minneapolis Minn., a 1st Inf Div officer.

There are four tents, as this (drawing).

No identification on Iraqis as yet. The leader is a Lt. Gen. Officer. On his left a B. Gen. (acts as) interpreter. One on right, could not tell.

Meeting still going on at 12:15 p.m.

-Richard Pyle

March 1-6, 1991

"Big Red One" Greets Grim-Faced Group from Baghdad

By Denholm Barnetson

Dateline: An airstrip in southern Iraq. Scene: Small Iraqi base in the desert occupied since Friday by 1st Infantry Division of U.S. 7th Corps—"The Big Red One."

Airstrip is lined by about 10 Apache helicopters and several M1A1 tanks, all with their crews inside.

Further back on either side of the airstrip on the sand are scores of tanks, armored vehicles, and green and sand colored tents.

To the south there is a line of hills. The area is otherwise flat. Black smoke lingers on the horizon in the direction of Kuwait, where oil fires are burning. Sky is clear.

Schwarzkopf arrived at 10 a.m. on a Blackhawk helicopter surrounded by several Apache helicopters and walked to the small green tent on the edge of the airstrip where the talks took place. (Please see story from Richard Pyle for scene inside the tent.)

Iraqi 8-man delegation (no names yet) arrived at 11:30 a.m. aboard an Iraqi vehicle with an M1 in front and behind, Bradleys to either side and two Apaches overhead.

They walked grim-faced with Schwarzkopf and other allied military leaders to the tent. Schwarzkopf told reporters before the talks "They've agreed to the terms of reference. This is not a negotiation, this is purely a discussion, I think it will be fairly routine."

Cease-Fire Signing at Safwan Iraq: "I'm Not Here to Give Them Anything," –Gen. Norman Schwarzkopf

3 March

Pool report on the cease-fire talks in southern Iraq between allied delegation led by Schwarzkopf, and Iraqis. Prepared by Ed Chen, Los Angeles Times; Steve Coll, Washington Post; John Fialka, Wall Street Journal; Phil Shenon, New York Times.

In SOUTHERN IRAQ - Allied commander in chief H. Norman Schwarzkopf said the Iraqi generals had agreed to all coalition demands during cease-fire talks held at an air-field here today, and that as a result, "We are well on our way to a lasting peace."

Schwarzkopf told reporters following about two hours of talks with a delegation of seven Iraqi generals that Iraq had agreed to release all prisoners of war soon in cooperation with the International Red Cross. Coalition generals requested a symbolic prisoner of war release immediately as a gesture of good faith, and Schwarzkopf said he was confident the Iraqis would comply.

Schwarzkopf and other allied generals who attended the talks said the discussions, held in an olive tent beneath a desert bluff, were cool, frank, and productive, with the Iraqis having apparently decided in advance to accede to all of the coalition conditions for a permanent cease-fire. These included disclosure of information about minefields in Kuwait and the Persian Gulf, the establishment of "control measures" to prevent accidental fighting between allied and Iraqi forces, and a pledge by the Iraqis to turn over all information about allied soldiers listed as missing in action.

On its side, the coalition generals agreed to arrange a complete withdrawal of allied troops from Iraqi territory once a formal cease-fire agreement is signed. It was not clear when such a document would be formalized, but Schwarzkopf indicated the signing might come within days.

On the subject of the thousands of Kuwait civilians thought to have been detained by Iraqi troops as they withdrew from the emirate, Schwarzkopf announced that both sides had agreed to treat all people held against their will as prisoners of war and to arrange for their release through the Red Cross. "I would say very candidly that the Iraqis came to discuss and to cooperate with a positive attitude," Schwarzkopf said.

The general said he was not sure if implementation of a formal cease-fire agreement would require a second meeting between allied and Iraqi generals, but he said the two sides had worked out details for holding such a meeting should the need arise.

Your sleep-deprived pool was out of the D.I.H. at 3:15 this morning en route to the Dhahran air base, en route by C-130 to Kuwait City. Arrived Kuwait's International airport at about 7:30 a.m. On the flight, it was possible to see more than a dozen well heads aflame, including several within a mile or two of the airport. Black smoke filled the skies.

Scene at the airport was of devastation. The Iraqis left little behind. The central terminal building and the nearby administration buildings had been torched, the windows blown out. The tarmac was littered with bits of metal from a British Airways 747 that had apparently been destroyed by the Iraqis in their flight from the city. All that remained intact was the tail—the B.A. logo could be easily made out—and four engine pods.

Departing Kuwait airport in a convoy of Chinook helicopters for an airfield in southern Iraq, just across Iraq-Kuwait border. The runway was the site of the cease-fire talks. En route, saw many more oil field fires. The heat from the fires was so intense that it could (be) felt from an open hatch along the side of the helicopter.

Schwarzkopf arrived at the airstrip at 9:57. His convoy was made up of three Blackhawk helicopters and six mean-looking Apaches armed with Hellfire missiles. The Schwarzkopf delegation had traveled from Riyadh to Kuwait in a Gulfstream and then connected to the Blackhawks at Kuwait.

Schwarzkopf looked confident, soldierly. Seemed to be in good humor. Wore full desert camouflage outfit. Walked from the Blackhawks down the runway to a group of tents set up on both sides of the runway.

Told reporter that he had not come here to negotiate with the Iraqis. "This isn't a negotiation," he said. "This is purely a discussion. I'm not here to give them anything. I'm here to tell them exactly what we expect of them."

Today's trip from Riyadh was Schwarzkopf's first visit to Kuwait since the war. Said he was startled to finally see oil field fires and damage to downtown. "I saw Kuwait many times before the war. I thought it was a beautiful place, full of nice people, and it's a tragedy to see that someone would set out to deliberately destroy a city the way the Iraqis have."

Also on both sides of the southern Iraqi runway was an arsenal of nasty American weaponry, including 50 U.S. armored vehicles, including M1-A1 tanks, Bradleys, and attack helicopters. Two Apaches were up, scanning the skies for trouble. The message to the Iraqis was clear.

The airfield was in an area of Iraq captured by the American First Infantry Division, "The Big Red One." Wooden sign posted at the airfield read: "WELCOME TO IRAQ, COURTESY THE BIG RED ONE."

By prior arrangement, the Iraqi delegation arrived by road at an allied checkpoint three miles from the airfield and was transported in a convoy of M1-A1 battle tanks and Bradley Fighting Vehicles.

Overhead, three Apache attack helicopters completed the massive show of American force. Seven generals representing the army, air force, and navy were in the Iraqi delegation, which was led by Lt. Gen. Sultan Hashim Ahmad and Lt. Gen. Salah Abbud Mahmud. At least one of them was believed to be an official of the Iraqi military's general staff.

Accompanied by General Schwarzkopf and Lt. General Khalid Bin Sultan Bin Abdul-Aziz, the Saudi commander who joined Gen. Schwarzkopf in the negotiations, the Iraqi generals entered an olive tent erected by the airfield runway at about 11:30 a.m.

Inside, they found a plain plywood floor and a small rectangular table with chairs for two participants from each side and their interpreters. Surrounding the table were seats for 40 coalition observers and 30 Iraqi observers, although there were only a total of eight officers in the Iraq delegation.

Water had been placed on the table for the participants, as well as a Diet Pepsi for Schwarzkopf. He indicated after the session that subsequent meetings to iron out the details would be handled by aides on either side at an undisclosed location.

During a brief moment before the negotiation, a small press pool was permitted inside the tent. The Iraqi negotiators appeared to be trying to be affable, while General Schwarzkopf and Lieut. General Khalid stared stiffly ahead.

The British commander, Sir Peter de la Billière, joined in the talks and described the tone as "cold but we did make progress."

Asked the timetable for the release of allied POWs from Iraq, he said of the Iraqis, "if they keep their word, it will be in days rather than weeks." He said he hoped the Iraqis were sincere. "The people round the table appeared to speak with the intention of deliberating. Whether that will materialize, we will have to wait and see."

Bugler Sounds Taps for a Fallen Scout: "Don't Worry, L.T., the Way is Clear and the Road is Safe"

By Douglas Jehl

4 March

WITH U.S. FORCES, Iraq - The rifle pointed nose-down into battle-trampled sand, a helmet perched atop it, a pair of empty boots behind.

A battalion of soldiers stood at stiff attention in a fierce desert wind, and a first sergeant yelled out the roll to his assembled scout platoon.

There was no answer when he shouted, then repeated, the name of Spec. Clarence "Johnny" Cash.

Then across the desert, to a backdrop of explosions from a demolished ammunition dump, the bugle strains of "Taps" began to sound in tribute to the soldier fallen just a few miles away, on Iraqi sands now occupied by the United States.

For Army forces who now sit in awkward limbo here, on a barren piece of enemy territory still littered with burned-out tanks and the unexploded remnants of American bombardment, this is a time of mixed emotions.

There is continued jubilation in this armored division over a victory whose swiftness still leaves commanders in a state of disbelief. But there is also great impatience to move beyond this war-scarred netherworld, and the transformation from the role of fighting force to occupying

Army has been one of unease and some discomfort. "I will tell you," said Maj. Gen. Ronald H. Griffith, commander of this 1st Armored Division, in an interview only hours after the cease-fire took effect, "there is no one I know wearing a uniform that has fallen in love with the Persian Gulf or wants to stay here any longer than he has to."

"We've got to get out of this minefield we're living in," he told commanders Sunday. And indeed, there were indications later Sunday right that the division might as early as Monday move into Kuwait.

But already in the four days since cease-fire brought this armored division to a sudden halt just shy of the Kuwaiti border, the accidental triggering of cluster-bombs the Air Force left behind has left at least three soldiers seriously wounded.

And with the future far from clear, soldiers and officers have struggled to adjust from war while occupying a battlefield marked at nearly every pace with other signs of the violent combat that preceded this uncertain peace. "Dead bombs, dead bodies, and scorched earth everywhere," observed Lt. Shawn Modula, a 27-year-old from Montpelier, Idaho, as he surveyed the land now held by what has become an American occupation force. "If this isn't hell, I don't know what is."

Griffith and other commanders here have made no secret of their desire to move to safer ground. But as long as the cease-fire remained impermanent, "they tell us we've got to stay in place until all this is worked out," said Maj. Roy Adams, operations officer of this division's 1st Brigade.

In some senses, peace has brought a sense of calm, a return to normality, even deep in Iraqi territory. At an outdoor service Sunday, a chalice of sacramental wine sat balanced on the hood of a Humvee jeep in the first Catholic mass performed since the shooting stopped. At division headquarters, helicopters began to ferry in the mail held back while the fighting raged.

Officers flew to Saudi Arabia to visit soldiers who had been wounded. And at dusk, a massive American armored tow truck could be seen hauling a still-intact Iraqi T-72 tank across the sands, an apparent battle trophy to be brought home to Germany. But there remains an eerie sense here—on what only days ago was an Iraqi military staging area—of living among the dead, with stretches of sand now dotted with hasty graves dug by Iraqis for their fellow soldiers killed during an American bombardment.

Every few hundred yards lies what is left of an Iraqi bunker, its roof sometimes reinforced with Air Force bomb casings apparently gathered in a last-ditch attempt at shelter. American soldiers, spelunkers of a sort, prowl beneath the surface, finding journals, clothing, furniture—but also some floors stained red with blood. And each time word has spread of another American grievously wounded as he stepped atop a U.S. cluster bomb, officers cringe and wonder aloud when they might leave this war zone behind.

"Look where you're walking," Lt. Col. Michael Leahy, an artillery battalion commander, urged one battery the other day, warning of the dangers in the soft sand. "Let's take every soldier home with everything he came with. Don't leave any hands or fingers behind."

Of the three soldiers in the division wounded in the accidental explosions, days after the war ended, two have lost parts of their feet. In a neighboring armored cavalry unit, one soldier was killed and another lost both hands.

Special explosive ordnance disposal teams have begun to clear sites near U.S. encampments. But with unexploded bombs and larger munitions of up to 2,000 pounds spread for miles across the desert, there is no expectation that the clean-up will be thorough. "There's so much stuff around here that if it's not directly interfering with operations, we're just going to leave it," one munitions expert said. "Hell, this is Iraq."

That recognition that this remains enemy territory has added to the apprehension, leaving some unnerved by the prospect of a retaliatory attack.

Officers urge soldiers to remain on guard, magazines of ammunition inserted into their weapons. But at least twice since the cease-fire took effect, units here have scrambled in pursuit of what turned out to be phantom Republican Guard tank battalions. Late Sunday, however, senior officers here were briefed on an arrangement apparently discussed—in the meeting earlier that day between American and Iraqi commanders, permitting free passage to non-hostile Iraqi units whose vehicles displayed an orange banner.

In another source of some unease, the very speed with which this Army division has come to sit so deep within Iraq has caused Griffith and some senior commanders to express concern that their victory might somehow be downgraded. "The press said this guy was eight feet tall; we took him down in four days," the two-star general said in the interview, voicing a theme he was to expand upon in after-action talks to his field commanders. "But I hope that we don't now say that this guy was a paper tiger because our guys steamrollered all over him," Griffith continued. "I hope somebody says that our guys were pretty good."

Perhaps more than anything else, however, it was the solemn battlefield service in memory of a soldier killed in action that has checked the sense of elation here, a moving reminder of the human cost of victory.

"We chose to do what soldiers do—dangerous, in a foreign country, with no prospect of going home," said Chaplain Timothy Kikkert, as the 4th Battalion, 36th Armored Regiment stood in honor of Cash, the "two-steppin' country-western kind of guy" his friends all called Johnny. The young specialist, a driver in a Bradley Fighting Vehicle, had been killed in the waning hours of battle last Wednesday as his scout platoon pushed forward, hoping to clear the way for a further advance by the battalion.

An Iraqi BMP armored vehicle caught the scouts by surprise, firing from point blank range with a main-gun round that tore Cash in two and severed the leg of the sergeant who stood in a turret behind him. With the rifle, helmet, and boots used to symbolize the fallen soldier, each soldier in the battalion, many fighting tears, would file past at the conclusion of the service to render one last slow salute.

"I can be sure that when my time comes, Cash—being the scout that he is—will be at Fiddler's Green before me," eulogized the dead soldier's platoon leader, Lt. Bob Michowicz, in a choked-voice allusion to an Irish poem memorized by every cavalryman. "And I will hear a voice saying, 'Don't worry, L.T., the way is clear, and the road is safe.'"

Quick Reflexes Lead Soldier Into Danger—"We'll Probably Lose More Guys Before We Get Out of Here"

By Mark Fritz

4 March

EASTERN IRAQ - He was the best runner in the battalion, the sharpest shooter in the company, a big kid with quick reflexes and a good eye.

When he heard the blast, he ran. Like everybody else, he thought it was incoming mortar fire. Nobody realized right away that a soldier had been hurt not by Iraqi artillery or an Iraqi mine, but by a dormant explosive from an allied cluster bomb.

Dave Wieczorek heard the blast less than 100 meters away and took off toward his Bradley fighting vehicle. His big boots came down on the sand and everybody heard a second explosion. Wieczorek flew up in the air. The blast blew the legs off the guy who finished first more often than anybody else. Later that night, after a helicopter plucked him from the desert floor and flew him to a hospital, he died.

Wieczorek, 20, of Gentry, Ark., was fatally wounded Thursday by friendly fire in an enemy field. The other soldier lost a leg but was expected to survive. A third who was near Wieczorek was wounded by flying shrapnel.

All three were members of the Wolfpack, otherwise known as Charlie Company of the 1st Battalion, 5th Calvary Regiment, an armored task force of the 1st Cavalry Division's 2nd Brigade. From Monday through Wednesday, the division staged a 340-kilometer trek through Iraq, the longest march of the land battle. It encountered light resistance and no U.S. deaths until Thursday, after the allied cease-fire froze it in place on a bomb-strewn Republican Guard position it was only meant to pass through.

The Republican Guard positions, just west of northwestern Kuwait, are covered with undetonated cluster bombs from .155mm artillery shells and unexploded allied missiles, along with bombed-out Iraqi bunkers and punctured vehicles. "Doctrine states that you do not use these types of munitions in places where you plan to put your ground troops," said Maj. Bob Bynum, 40, of South Fulton, Tenn. "A lot of these air munitions have a high dud rate. They're little mines when they're left on the field."

Lt. Col. Michael Parker, commander of the 1st Battalion, 5th Calvary, said it was "probably not" a good idea to stop in the area, but that the next area may have been worse. "We were only meant to pause here," said Parker, 42, of Dallas. "We don't know if there are booby traps, mines, or what. There could be pockets of resistance who don't know about the cease-fire. There could be eyes on this position where we're standing right now."

But he said any place in the Iraqi region around northern Kuwait, a Republican Guard stronghold heavily hit by allied artillery and aircraft and heavily mined by the Iraqis, could be as dangerous. Wieczorek's death and the injuries to the others was a somber reality check to the 1st Calvary soldiers who just completed the longest tactical march in military history. For a week before the land war began, the division pounded a line along southeastern Kuwait with artillery and sent in risky reconnaissance units in an effort to dupe the Iraqis into thinking the main thrust of the attack would come there.

On Monday, it made the last feint, pushing about 20 kilometers into Iraq, then abruptly turned around, traveled west along northern Saudi Arabia, and then moved through a breach already opened by other divisions.

Since arriving at the Republican Guard encampment, combat engineers have been blowing up Iraqi munitions dumps and clearing minefields. But they said they would not touch the unpredictable allied ordinance covering the area. "Anything that looks strange, we won't deal with," said Sgt. 1st Class David Marlow, 36, of Windsor, Mo. He said a special Explosives Ordnance Division team would be sent in to deal with the allied duds.

Soldiers reacted with dread to orders that they would begin walking the area on Saturday to begin marking places where the tiny bomblets were found. The same day, soldiers from Charlie Company's 14 Bradley platoons held a brief memorial service for Wieczorek. "We'll probably lose a couple more guys before we get out of here," said Bruce Brock, 21, whose family lives a couple of hours from Wieczorek's in Greenwood, Ark.

Brock and Wieczorek both manned the M-60 machine guns set up to defend the company whenever it wasn't moving. Soldiers in the platoon said they were inseparable. "He took care of me," Brock said. "He'd already been on the M-60 when they put me on it. He was a funny guy and pretty smart. We were going to get together again when we got back to the states."

Wieczorek joined the Army so he could get financial assistance for college. He almost never lost a race and won a Soldier Achievement medal after he finished first in his battalion after a 12-mile march with full gear. He was a crack shot and the Army wanted to send him to sniper school, his platoon mates said. "He was outgoing, gung-ho, really great physically," said Spec. 4 Rickey Weeks, 32, of Tupelo, Miss., who bunked with Wieczorek in basic training.

"He could really run."

Private Mike Jones, 20, of Dallas, saw Wieczorek's last run, saw the blast that ended it. Jones was the first man to reach him. "I kept talking to him, his eyes were really glassy," he said. "I started crying like a baby. His hands wanted to grip something. I put my hand down there and told him to grip it. I know he was in pain because he put me in pain."

Charlie Company gathered in an empty space under the hot sun for a memorial service. A color guard unfurled the battalion, regimental and American flags. Wieczorek's machine gun was stuck muzzle down in the sand, his helmet placed atop the weapon and his boots in front of it. Explosions sounded in the distance and smoke curled from several points on the horizon as engineers destroyed Iraqi ammunition.

The brief service drove home the fact that even in a war with low casualties, even one can be more than enough. "He was a great kid," said Staff Sgt. Bill Wilson, 34, of San Diego, Wieczorek's platoon leader. "It happened right after I told these guys to be careful." Wieczorek and the other two soldiers were hurt just hours after they got word of the cease-fire. "Everyone was happy and relaxed because of the good news," said Jones. "The Army teaches you to walk with head high. From now on, I look at the ground."

Jones now tucks a little yellow card printed with Psalm 91 in the elastic band of his helmet. The prayer, passed out by the chaplain after Wieczorek's death, is meant to ward off danger:

"You shall not be afraid of the terror by night," it says.

"Nor of the arrow that flies by day.

"Nor of the pestilence that walks in darkness.

"Nor of the destruction that lays waste at noonday.

"A thousand may fall at your side.

"And ten thousand at your right hand.

"But it shall not come near you."

---

10 Allied POWs Released in Bahrain: Few Details on Captivity but "Seem to be in Very Good Condition"

By Michael Hedges

5 March

MANAMA, Bahrain - Ten allied former prisoners of war showed no signs of having been mistreated by their captors, and some had received medical treatment in Iraq, according to an Air Force doctor who was part of a team which examined them on a flight here from Jordan.

"They seemed to be in very good condition," said Col. Wynn Mabry, an Air Force physician. "Some have had injuries related to their duties

... received during ejections," he said. But, "All are in good shape, good spirits, and during the flight were very talkative."

Among those who arrived at a coastal airfield aboard an Air Force C-141, and (were) quickly whisked to the nearby hospital ship USNS Mercy, were Navy Lt. Jeffrey Zaun, whose appearance on Iraqi television showing signs of injury prompted outrage at suspected Iraqi beating of prisoners. However, none of those examined by a team of six military surgeons and two psychiatrists reported being harmed during their captivity, said Col. Mabry. He said some of the prisoners did report feeling threatened during their capture and initial interrogation, but he declined to elaborate.

Col. Mabry said some of the former prisoners had received effective medical treatment from the Iraqis. "Their wounds were treated by Iraqi doctors promptly, they have no infections," he said. At least two of the former prisoners "have received orthopedic surgery," said Col. Mabry. "Those who have received treatment are doing well," he said.

Col. Mabry said a Navy and an Army psychiatrist examined the former American POWs. He said their scrutiny of the captives was preliminary, but, "both of the psychiatrists felt these people are in good mental health." Officials on the USNS Mercy said the freed prisoners would probably spend only three or four days on that hospital ship before returning to their home countries.

Col. Mabry said the ship had all the necessary medical facilities to serve as a care center for the nine men and one woman until they are released. The group arrived at the USNS Mercy at 4::6 (sic) a.m., walking up the ship's ramp to be greeted by about 30 members of the crew. Army Specialist Melissa Rathbun-Nealy, 20, of Grand Rapids, Mich., the lone American female captured during the war, walked aboard the ship wearing a gray sweatsuit and carrying an armful of cut flowers.

The nine male POWs, including five Americans, three British, and an Italian, wore olive green flight suits, the airmen with patches from their squadrons.

Senior medical officer of the Mercy, Capt. Paul Berry, said the released POWs requested hot showers and access to telephones to call home.

U.S. POWs "Cuffed Around" by Iraqis: "None Want to be Heroes. They Don't Want to Be in the Limelight"

By Carl Nolte and John Balzar

6 March

MOHRAQ, Bahrain – U.S. prisoners of war were "cuffed around" by their captors and suffered damage to their eardrums as a result, an attending physician says.

Other prisoners "complained about the way they were treated by the Iraqis," said Col. Richard Williams, who accompanied the second load of American and coalition prisoners released by Iraq.

These ex-POWs, including 15 Americans, arrived by bus and ambulance Wednesday night at the U.S. Navy Hospital ship Mercy. They joined six other Americans (three British) and one Italian who had arrived a day earlier.

Williams said he "could not verify" that the second arriving batch of POWs were treated in violation of the Geneva Convention. But physicians aboard the Mercy were not so hesitant when it came to the first group.

Their treatment was "not in complete accordance of the Geneva Convention," said Navy Capt. Richard Osborne, chief physician aboard the Mercy.

Lt. Gen. Lorenzo Girodo, vice chief of staff of the Italian Air Force, said he believed that at least one of two Italian prisoners were mistreated. "I think he was beaten."

In general, the POWs arriving Wednesday displayed good spirits. As they walked up the gangway of the Mercy, or in the case of two airmen, as they were carried on stretchers into the ship, they were asked, "How are you?"

"Great! . . . Good . . . Great . . . Great!" they answered, one by one. Some gave the thumbs-up sign and waved to hospital ship crew who cheered their arrival. At first a few looked surprised at the TV lights and VIP greeting, but seemed to break into smiles easily. The second woman POW to be released, Maj. Rhonda L. Cornum, of Freeville, N.Y., walked off a bus with both arms in casts and slings. Welcome home, she was told. She replied weakly, "Thank you."

She reportedly suffered two broken upper arms, a broken hand, facial injuries, and a knee injury as a result of the shooting down of her Blackhawk SH-60 helicopter, which was on a search-and-rescue mission to try and recover a missing pilot near Basra, Iraq. Two others survived the downing, and five were killed, military officials said.

Col. Williams described the second batch of patients as only in "fair condition" upon their release. They were thin for lack of food and "all" needed medical attention, he said. Williams said the Iraqis provided just "adequate" medical care to the coalition prisoners. At lower echelons, he said, some suffered a "general lack of medical care" but the treatment apparently improved as the prisoners were passed up the line. One, he said, was treated by the chief of orthopedics at a Baghdad hospital.

During their captivity, he continued, some of the Americans suffered injuries as the result of coalition air bombardment.

Williams said three of the arriving POWs were slapped around so severely by their captors they suffered eardrum perforation. But he said the injuries were or had healed. He did not identify which three, and said others may have similar stories of mistreatment.

The POWs were taken to the receiving ward of the hospital ship where they were to receive further attention. Naval officers said they expected the group to be sent back to the United States quite soon.

As for the first group of seven (Americans), who already received physical exams and treatment, medical officers declined to say if they had been physically or mentally mistreated. "They each have their story to tell. That is their story to tell," said Cmdr. Deborah Wear, chief psychiatrist aboard the Mercy. She said, however, the seven were suffering from a lack of sleep and "getting adjusted to walking free."

The question: "Were they abused by the Iraqis?"

Her answer: "They were in better condition than we expected. They are great people. They have all the characteristics of the American people. I'm proud of them. None of them wants to be considered heroes. They don't want to be in the limelight." As for lasting psychological damage, Ware gave a light-hearted answer: "For awhile, when loud noises occur they are apt to be a little jumpy."

"They were scared," Osborne said.

Capt. Paul Barry, commanding officer of the hospital unit aboard the ship, also declined a direct answer to the mistreatment question. "I don't feel very well qualified to answer whether they were mistreated. What struck me is their relief to be back home." Then he nodded to the ship on the sultry Gulf evening and said, "This is a little piece of the United States here."

Barry said the first POWs to be released were "doing very well."

In port in Bahrain, an island nation on the Persian Gulf near Saudi Arabia, the ship Mercy was geared up to treat 1,000 battle casualties per week. But they only had three patients from the ground war, two soldiers with broken legs and a third with serious injuries from a malfunction on a rocket launcher.

Meanwhile, your pool was treated to yet another tour of the Tripoli—the Helicopter Landing Platform ship that hit a mine Feb. 18 at 0435 hrs while on an anti-mine operation in the Gulf. Here we met and interviewed two brave sailors nominated for the Silver Star medal for valor. The Silver Star is the third-highest battlefield decoration.

The two are: Lt. Cmdr. Steve Senk, 42, of San Diego, chief engineer and damage control officer, and CWO3 Van Cavin, 38, of New Orleans, the assistant damage control officer. Both men were cited for valor by Capt. Bruce McEwen, of San Diego, after they survived the mine damage and supervised the damage control response that kept the ship afloat and operational.

The ship is now in dry dock near the hospital ship Mercy in Bahrain.

Both men rushed to shore up damaged bulkheads and vented the ship of dangerous paint fumes that posed risk of fire or explosion. The mine caused damage to the ship's paint locker.

"I don't think I was even nervous about it for the first three or four hours, until I stopped and had my first cup of coffee," said Senk. At that time, he said, he began to tremble. "Absolutely."

Senk said he recently called his father, a World War II veteran of naval service in the battle of the Philippine Sea, and said, "You can't imagine what it was like."

"Oh yes I can," said his father, who reminded him that in 1945 he served aboard the USS Houston, a cruiser that was torpedoed and suffered "almost exactly" the same kind of damage.

First Group of Iraqi POWs Released from "Brooklyn," Flown to Baghdad

By Ken Fireman

6 March

QAISUMAH, Saudi Arabia - The first group of Iraqi prisoners of war to be released by the allies since the end of the Persian Gulf conflict lifted off from this small desert airport Wednesday morning in two DC-9 commercial jets.

The planes were bound for Baghdad, where they were to unload the 294 freed Iraqi POWs and then return to Riyadh with 35 allied prisoners of war. The exchange was originally scheduled for Tuesday but was delayed because of bad weather.

The transfer of the Iraqis from a U.S.-run POW camp code-named "Brooklyn," located seven miles from the air strip, went smoothly and was completed without a hitch, according to officials of the International Committee of the Red Cross, which handled the transfer, and of the Red Crescent Society, which monitored the process.

As they arrived at the airfield in eight large buses, the Iraqi prisoners mostly did not look at or acknowledge the journalists and U.S. and British military personnel who had gathered on the edge of the tarmac to watch the transfer. But a few smiled and waved at the observers, two gave the V-for-victory sign, and one clasped his hands together and held them above his head like a triumphant boxer.

None of the POWs spoke to reporters during the transfer.

Most appeared in good health and walked steadily and without assistance from the buses to the planes and up the rear steps of the jets. But two were limping and one walked with the aid of a crutch. Most of the prisoners were garbed in orange or blue jump suits and many wore parkas or jackets to protect them against the cold desert wind. Several wore scarves. Most carried their personal belongings in sacks and carried bottles of water as well.

The captain of one of the jets, Pauli Rudolph, said he had no idea what he would find in Baghdad at the conclusion of the one-hour flight. He said there had been no contact with Iraqi authorities beforehand to determine the condition of runways at Baghdad's airport. He said he planned to fly to Baghdad and then circle the field and visually inspect conditions there. "The only thing we have is enough fuel to circle for a while and then come back if we have to," said Rudolph, a Swissair captain, who, like all the other crewmembers on the two flights had volunteered for the duty.

Another crewmember, Rene Herter, a cabin chief, said he was a veteran of similar flights to repatriate prisoners in 1988 at the close of the Iran-Iraq war.

"We had people on those flights who were prisoners for eight years," Herter said. "They were very quiet during the flight. But when the captain announced on the intercom that we had crossed the international border, they were very emotional."

Based on those experiences, Herter said, his expectation for Wednesday's flight was that "everybody's going to be glad." He said the crew planned to serve the released POWs cheese sandwiches, sweets, coffee or tea during the flight.

The planes used to fly the Iraqis bore the markings of Balair, a Swiss charter airline partially owned by Swissair, and carried insignia of the ICRC, which had chartered them for the flights. Each had seats for 149 passengers, according to Herter.

The prisoners were brought to the airfield in eight buses, seven of them colored beige and green and one blue and red. Each bus had an armed American MP seated front and rear. The buses formed two lines behind each plane and drove, one by one, up to the rear of the aircraft and disgorged its passengers. It took only 13 minutes (10:21 a.m. to 10:34 a.m. local time) for all the POWs to be transferred from buses to planes.

The planes then sat on the tarmac for a little more than an hour as ICRC representatives verified each POW's name against the passenger manifests, verified that all wished to be repatriated and completed the necessary paperwork with U.S. military officials to make the transfer official. Finally, at 11:37 a.m., the first plane began to taxi, followed three minutes later by the second. The first plane lifted off the runway at 11:41 a.m., the second at 11:46 a.m.

The release took place at a small airfield in northeastern Saudi Arabia 50 miles south of the Iraqi border and 120 miles southwest of Kuwait City. The site is a commercial airport, similar in size to those found in smaller American towns, but it apparently has been closed to commercial traffic for some time and is now being used exclusively by allied military forces.

On the edge of the tarmac is an American mobile air medical staging facility (MASF), the 1611th out of Tampa, Fla., nicknamed the Desert Dawgs, and a British medical unit. The British unit was being torn down and packed up Wednesday. The front of the American unit was decorated with a large signboard bearing a likeness of Bart Simpson wearing a Desert Storm T-shirt and telling passersby, "I was there, dudes."

The commander of the MASF unit, Air Force Capt. Karen Barnett, of Tampa, said her personnel had treated many Iraqi prisoners and felt some sympathy for them. "Some of these people, I know they're enemies, but they've been through so much," she said.

Another member of the unit, Air Force Sgt. Alacey Gilmore of Southampton, N.Y., joked about learning "the new dance step of the desert, the Iraqi shuffle." She then demonstrated by holding her hands above her head and shuffling her feet forward in imitation of a surrendering soldier.

Several members of the American and British medical units walked over and watched the transfer of the prisoners. One group of about 13 Americans climbed to the roof of the airport, planted an American flag and entertained themselves during the wait for the POWs by doing the wave, singing a lusty rendition of "Twist and Shout" and posing for photographs.

Other observers included U.S. military combat photographers and three Kuwaitis who have been serving with the British army as interpreters. One, Abdulah al Marzook, said he talked to many of the surrendering Iraqis during the recently concluded conflict. "Some of them were begging for forgiveness," Marzook said.

"They were telling me, 'Forgive us.' I said it wasn't my job to forgive them. Finally I said, 'Okay, I forgive you.' And one said, 'We don't deserve it.'"

Marzook said most of the Iraqis he met seemed to be unwilling conscripts. He said one, whose name he did not know, told him he had deserted from the army during the Iran-Iraq war and that the authorities had retaliated by killing his brother. He said the Iraqi told him he had wanted to desert again, but was afraid if he did so the rest of his family would be killed. Marzook said some of the POWs he spoke with were under 18 or over 50 years of age and that Iraqi authorities had altered the birth dates on their identification papers to make them appear eligible for military service.

Marzook, 20, said he was studying engineering in England when the Iraqi invasion took place. He said his immediate family was all in England on a vacation when Iraq invaded, but that several of his uncles were in Kuwait and had remained throughout the Iraqi occupation.

He has not spoken to any of them and doesn't know of their fate, but says he is proud of them because "they stayed in Kuwait."

PART II

Pencils in the Pool:
Bedouins of the Press

Press Will Live With the Troops; What do Troops Want? "They Would Like to Go Deep . . . to Go to Baghdad"

By Joseph Albright and David Lamb

7 January

WITH THE 82ND AIRBORNE DIVISION IN EASTERN SAUDI ARABIA - We watched units of the 82nd Airborne Division (4th Battalion of the 325th Airborne Infantry Regiment, which is part of the 2nd Brigade) as they "captured" mock buildings made of stacks of rubber tires.

We have also talked with troops and commanders about Jan. 15. There is no real news in this report but some interesting quotes. Here are some:

Col. Ron Rokosz, 45, of Chicago, commander of the 3rd Brigade of the 82nd Airborne Division (elements of whose brigade were the first ground forces in Saudi Arabia on Aug. 9). Asked about having press pools with his unit, he said he had sometime in the past attended a course on the military and the media at the Army War College. "I was amazed how many journalists came in (to speak to the course) being defensive, feeling every Army officer is down on the press. That we are still in the Vietnam syndrome. I don't feel that way at all. I am glad to see you people. It is good for the soldiers." Rokosz said he personally could not recall any "operational security" violations caused by the presence of the press during Desert Shield.

Maj. Baxter Ennis, public affairs officer of the 82nd Airborne Division, added this to the Rokosz comment: that he could recall one such violation, when Jane's Defense Weekly published what purported to be a list showing locations and types of aircraft in the Gulf. Ennis also said: "The thing we like best about the pool system as we understand it is currently planned is that the journalists are going to come out and live with us in the field. Your lives are going to be at stake just as much as our lives. And we really feel that a bond and a trust is going to develop between the units and the journalists. That will only work if the journalists are brought out to us and stay with us for long periods of time."

Lt. Col. John Vines, 41, of Bessemer, Ala., commander of the 4th Battalion, 325th Airborne Infantry, about what the troops want after Jan. 15: "I think they would like to go deep. I think they would like to go to Baghdad. They probably believe his center of gravity is in his government. And that he is willing to sacrifice untold thousands of Iraqis. He doesn't care. And that you have to neutralize him, not just his armed forces."

Q: Does your unit want to go?

A: Of course, everybody would like to go. Personally, to shoot him between the running lights."

Q: Your desire too?

A: I had a dream about shooting him with a large-caliber weapon right in the face. It was an interesting dream. He's caused a lot of death and destruction. This guy really needs to be brought to account. And I think we will do it. And these troops are ready to do it."

Spec. John Wall, 21, of Fayetteville, N.C. a TOW gunner, said he is apprehensive. "As long as nothing is going on, you got no reason to be scared. If combat starts, the thing about actually being scared is that you could never see your family again. When it comes down to the real deal, I should be able to do my job despite being scared."

Staff Sgt. David Shaffer, 25, Burlington, Iowa: "I am confident that if we do have to go to combat, we can do it. But there is an apprehension. It is the apprehension of dying and not being able to see your family again. I'm divorced, and before I left, I didn't get a chance to see my two kids. I'd just like to see them again." (Two daughters, Suraya, 6, and Sydnie, 4.)

Capt. Mark White, 32, of Pensacola, Fla., the 2nd Brigade assistant intelligence officer, was asked what he and other officers thought about having combat pools with the troops. He said: I think a lot of officers question whether we need the press over here. They are pretty concerned about operational security. They see a lot of things in the media which they feel are blatant opsec violations."

(He said officers have been particularly concerned about seeing maps and diagrams in newspapers showing where U.S. forces are purported to be deployed.)

Asked his own opinion, he said: "I understand that it is important for the public to have access to the story. I think it is a good thing that the military has sort of reached a compromise where there is access but it is controlled access. The press is not completely out and it is not completely given free rein."

Sgt. Thomas Gray, 27, of Omaha, Neb., a squad leader of an infantry platoon that had just finished a live-fire exercise in capturing a building, was asked about how he was dealing with the fear factor. Answer: "If you are not a little bit afraid, you are wrong, I guess. If you are not a little bit afraid, you could do something stupid."

Spec. Scott Schabacker, 22, of Hadley, Mass., who jumped with the 82nd into Panama and is now thinking about going into combat for the second time. "As far as going in, I don't worry about it. We've been training non-stop since we came here. I do worry some about getting out." Asked whether the troops will be upset if the troops don't see action, he said: "I don't think anybody will get upset if we don't go north."

On what he learned from Panama:

"In Panama, everyone was pretty excited to go down there and see what combat was like. But once you got there, it turned out it is not all that is cracked up to be and I will be just as glad if nothing happens."

Sgt. Adrian Saldivar, Corpus Christi, Tex.: "I figure if there's no war, we'll be going home about the end of January. If there's war, it'll be the end of March. Personally, I'm hoping for war. If we don't get rid of Saddam Hussein now, we're just going to have grief later. While we've got him by the nuts, we ought to squeeze."

Sgt. Wade Clare, 24, Madison, Wis.: "How would we feel if he suddenly withdrew? I think we'd feel relief but also a sense of letdown. We've been out here five months. Naturally we'd feel a little down if they said, 'Get on your birds and go home.' But just the same, I don't think anyone wants to go to war. A lot of us were in Panama, so we know there's not much glamorous about war. It's not all Rambo and gung-ho."

4 Enemy Choppers Defecting to a U.S. Base? A Story This Good (Still) Never Dropped in This Reporter's Lap

By Guy Gugliotta, Robert Jagodzinski, David Evans, and Jonathan Ferziger

7 January

The pool filed its report by fax from a medical facility on a Saudi military base in northeastern Saudi Arabia, then retired to a U.S. medical detachment where it spent the night in a tent.

At 11:42 p.m., Jan. 7, a base sentry entered the tent and told everyone (pool members and three U.S. Navy hospital corpsmen) to get up because the communications center reported "four incoming Iraqi aircraft."

Marine 1st Lt. Patrick Gibbons, the PAO attached to our portion of the Marine pool, visited the communications tent and reported that there were four Iraqi helicopters and that they wanted to defect. The sentry returned and repeated this information, adding that U.S. aircraft were escorting the helicopters in and that they were going to land "right here" at an airbase next to the detachment.

The corpsmen greeted this news with rumbles of disbelief. The hacks did also. This hack noted that in his entire career a story like this had never dropped in his lap and he was confident that it wouldn't happen this time either. And so it proved. Approximately 12:20 a.m., Jan. 8, this reporter and Lt. Gibbons left the tent in search of further information. They encountered the Navy Lt. (j.g.) who informed them that we could all "stand down" because the helos had landed at Khafji, about 20 miles north of the medical detachment.

During the 40 minutes the medical detachment was on alert, which consisted of little more than a bit of low-key milling around (sic). Hospitals do not see themselves as targets. (written by Guy Gugliotta.)

"Gentlemen, This is No Longer an Exercise"—Brit Hacks Learn "Operation Granby" Now "Desert Storm"

By Philip Jacobson

17 January

WITH THE 7TH ARMOURED BRIGADE - Our personal harbinger of war in the early hours of this morning was a genial major who stepped briskly into the crowded press tent to announce, "Gentlemen, this is no longer an exercise."

On his orders, we scrambled into our Nuclear, Biological, and Chemical Warfare suits, an exercise of some complexity with half-a-dozen reporters getting in each other's way. By the time we stumbled out, the rest of the camp was ticking over smoothly, the troops going about the business of real war with the same, much practiced, efficiency as during week after week of waiting.

As the sky gradually lightened, a full-scale CBW alert was sounded, camp siren blaring repeatedly as a signal to move to the heightened state of protection.

Twenty sticky, somewhat apprehensive minutes later, the stand down was announced and we went back to following BBC World Service accounts of what was supposed to be happening a few thousand kilometres away in Baghdad.

"Great stuff, sock it to them," said one of the young officers, who call themselves our escorts but actually look after us like surrogate mums.

It had been a night of more or less continuous troop movement in the desert around us, as thousands of British soldiers began redeploying to new positions on the jump off line near the front, ready for what we take to be the first, possibly decisive land battle of what we are still calling Operation Granby (no Desert Storm, or not yet, anyway).

While warplanes droned overhead, British armoured units and infantry and combat engineers streamed past towards the enemy, followed by the vast "tail" of their complex logistical operation. With the new movements came confirmation that the British divisional forces in Saudi Arabia were moving to battle positions: armchair strategists may make what they will of this, and although there is plenty of speculation here at the camp, we can only wait to find out—hopefully not the hard way.

According to the major, the record will show that he first received the war decoration from a colleague whose phone call awoke me in an adjacent tent.

Some urgent muttering could be heard, then the soft complaints of men aroused suddenly from their sleeping bags. The complaints had been rather more harsh earlier, when those braving the sharp chill of night discovered that the nearest "Desert Rose"—a contraption erected from plastic cups and stuck into the sand for purposes of urination—had been toppled over by some too-hasty user.

By the time our first-rate cooks had got breakfast underway, most of the soldiers around us had gathered their thoughts about the prospect, finally, of going in to fight. Nothing gung-ho, more a calm acceptance of what had changed and how it might affect them and their comrades.

For Sgt. Andy Mason, first thoughts were for the civilians of Iraq, on whom a terrible retribution for the miscalculations of their leader is now being visited.

For Cpl. Neil Newman, whose bottomless well of patience enables the press to learn survival in a hostile CBW climate, it was the signal to get a job that had lasted too long over as swiftly as possible. His own unit had been ready for weeks, now it was time to do it.

When the sun started to rise, we could see heavy dust clouds in the distance and the occasional thud of artillery carried on the desert air. Somewhere the gunners were doing their final preparations for what we assume will be a barrage as heavy as anything since the Second World War.

The Iraqi conscripts hunkered down in the front line in Kuwait must know it is coming, and must be terrified, as any sensible man would be. The aerial bombardment would be infinitely worse to endure: spare a thought for them, even if, like all of us with 7th Brigade, the wish is for a swift and crushing victory.

As for the rumour mill, working up to a peak of productivity, its first wartime contribution was news of a launch of five of Iraq's justly-feared Scud missiles. Four shot down, we were assured, the other got through to its target.

This turned out to be unfounded speculation, in the major's terse phrase. Bullshit is what the rest of us call it.

An Amiable but Uninformative Chat

By Philip Jacobson

A U.S. CH-53 helicopter clattered noisily in to drop off a passenger on a nearby ridge. Brigadier Patrick Cordingley, 7th's commander, arrived looking like a man whose day has begun particularly well.

While playing the straightest of bats to questions about the brigade's short-term operational plans, he certainly left the impression that his troops were getting closer and closer to fighting.

Escorted by several tough-looking soldiers, Brig. Cordingley accepted a red-hot "brew" and chatted amiably, if uninformatively, with BBC-TV's Martin Bell.

Earlier, we were given our first taste of an air attack warning: full CBW kit and steel helmets and down into the scrapes we had dug the day before.

Lying there until the all-clear was sounded, one realised that a five-foot-deep hole with sandbagged parapet is nothing much to write home about.

On the other hand, the sight of our cheerful young troops doubling over to air defence posts was profoundly reassuring, even if the battery of Hawk anti-aircraft missiles that had been perched on a nearby hillock would be guaranteed a warm welcome here. Listening to the BBC World Service in our foxhole, the news came that French forces would be engaged when the circumstances were suitable. A derisive cheer from a neighbouring scrape was clearly audible.

Round here, the assumption is that, Americans apart, the British are the ones who count.

Desert Rose, Blonde Annie Introduce the "Hackpack" to the Sandy Joys of Life in the Sweaty Trenches

By John Fullerton

18 January

WITH ALLIED FORCES - For war correspondents in the Saudi Arabian desert, winning bylines or prime time on television is the last thing to worry about.

Staying alive comes first.

Arriving at Britain's 7th Armoured Brigade on a lonely stretch of sand and scrub near Saudi Arabia's northern border, the first task of one group of correspondents and television crewmen was to dig their own trenches and fill sandbags by starlight.

Twenty-four hours later, the trenches were used - for real, during an air raid alarm.

The hackpack, as the soldiers affectionately call media people, were then introduced to Desert Rose, an improvised urinal made of empty water bottles glued together to form a pipe and protruding at a thirty-degree angle from a bed of sand and stones.

Desert Rose helps keep flies and rodents away by channeling fluid down from the surface of the desert. But navigating in pitch darkness from tent or trench to the device, and the business of unfastening cumbersome chemical clothing to relieve nature was not easy. The visitors quickly got used to the lack of privacy. They learned to use the "crappers" —lavatory bowls and seats beneath which polythene bags are suspended, and shrouded in scraps of sacking. Cleanliness is also vital in an area where dust and sand gets into the hair, between the teeth, and every crevice exposed to the chill winter wind.

Stripping off and dousing oneself with soapy water has become routine.

Survival training began in earnest on the second day with hours spent putting on and taking off gas masks and suits providing head-to-toe protection against nuclear radiation as well as chemical and biological weapons.

A stocky Scots corporal who specialises in chemical warfare soon had the hackpack marching briskly if awkwardly up and down in full protective gear, gasping for breath and streaming with sweat. The climax came when reporters and cameramen were ushered into a tent filled with clouds of anti-riot CS gas. They had to unscrew the filters on their gas masks and screw them back on again, all the while holding their breath and keeping their eyes shut.

Several hours of first aid training followed, with newsmen practicing mouth-to-mouth resuscitation on a dummy casualty, Blonde Annie. They were also briefed on the four "Bs"—breathing, bleeding, breaks, and burns—and how to punch a neat hole below a casualty's Adam's apple to keep oxygen flowing in to his lungs. And against the competitive instincts of the journalists, the "buddy-buddy" system came into being. This involves pairing off into twos, keeping an eye on a comrade's physical condition, and checking his equipment. For those veteran correspondents and photographers of civil war and guerrilla conflicts, wearing military-style clothing is anathema. Survival in many of the world's trouble-spots has meant wearing distinctively civilian dress.

The opposite holds true in the desert. Brightly-colored scarves, pullovers, or headgear are discarded, or else stewed in tea to help blend in with the beige sand dunes. The hackpack has also learned to live with the Gulf War alarm clock—that pre-dawn wakeup call that for three days in succession has taken the form of chemical and air-raid alerts. Journalists sleep with their gas masks on their makeshift pillows.

Free, Easy, Independent—That Was Before "Shrieking Klaxons and Fearsome Yell of 'Gas! Gas! Gas!'"

By Richard Kay

23 January

WITH THE DESERT RATS - There are few moments in war when it seems less enviable to be a correspondent than a soldier but this is one of them.

The infantrymen, of the Royal Scots and the cavalry of the 14th/20th Hussars in their tanks deployed across miles of empty sand, must take for granted their part in the great conflict that will surely soon begin. But for those of us who little more than a week ago found ourselves pitched into service alongside the British build-up at the front, it has at times meant a conscious effort of will.

Not only about transforming ourselves from, let's face it, a free, easy and independent civilian life into a soldier's routine of orders obeyed, but also about coming to terms with our own confusion of thoughts about what lies ahead. How shall WE cope with the fog of war? I hope we shall be permitted our apprehension.

For me these past ten days have been a revelation. While not in any way trying to diminish the role of the magnificent men who face long, hard, and certainly bloody battles ahead, we too have had to undergo intense self-examination a kind of battle-preparation, if you like. I suppose it was our Brigadier Christopher Hammerbeck who pulled it into sharp focus.

On my arrival, he looked me over in my newly pressed DPs, or desert pattern fatigues, helmet hanging with the strap undone for all the world like Audie Murphy, and asked if I had thought through what was going to happen.

Not to the troops but to me.

He didn't say it but he was talking about death. About a 7.62-calibre bullet round that comes out of the dark or a mist of poisoned chemicals that dusts the ground like a deadly crop spray. But surely, you think, you are a mere observer. That impressive white card in your tunic pocket bearing your picture and Ministry of Defence crest doesn't say soldier but war correspondent.

A day later, in the dead hours before dawn, the realisation that there is no distinction, no room for mere spectators, begins to sink in. The air is alive with the sound of shrieking klaxons and the fearsome yell of "Gas, gas, gas."

And the Iraqi special forces, said to be at large in our area, will surely show no such quarter with their piano wire and stealth.

It is a comfort to think of the sentries at night in their foxholes. Although how they distinguish between friend and foe when every piece of desert brush takes on the form of a man I can only guess.

For someone used to a great newspaper office where the lights of industry burn later into the night, life without so much as a candle is an extraordinary experience. There are, incidentally, enough perils in the shape of trenches, traps for the unwary, without worrying about Saddam's killer squads.

In a way these past days—and in the desert you have little concept of time or dates—have been something of an initiation. One of our number has left already, a victim of routine as much as anything, perhaps there will be others. In times of war, though, routine can be life-preserving. So let me tell you about a day with the Desert Rats.

We rise each morning at 6 a.m. when the flat half-light looks as I imagine the Western Front did in the First World War. The sand is wet and clammy and in the gloom you can see heads moving above the parapet of the guards' slit trenches.

My home has been the alcove of a tent, sleeping on a rickety old camp bed under sheets of pink CARM—chemical agent repellent material.

In the days to come, I think I shall long for such primitive comforts.

Squatting over a basin dug out of the sand with a jug of cold water in your hands may not be the most dignified way of starting the day but it does wake you up.

In the cookhouse at 7, the World Service News is listened to intently by men who at home would rarely tune their transistor dials to Radio 4.

The successes of Patriot, especially in knocking out the Scuds, are greeted with cheers. The losses of aircraft acknowledged in silence.

Scud has become the word of this war, in the same terrifying way as the name Exocet gripped every household with a sense of dread during the Falklands.

In this build-up to battle the day revolves around mealtimes. We eat on our feet off disposable plastic in full combat gear, helmets, flak jackets ready to move in an instant.

For us all, the respirator that could be the difference between living or dying a horrible death does not leave our side. It hangs in its green pouch like a six-gun ready for the quickest of quick draws. We have a ditty about getting it on in under ten seconds. "Be in time, do it in nine. Stay alive and make it five."

Shoulders once familiar with nothing heavier than the cut of a good flannel suit have grown used to a backpack of kit that would do credit to a sherpa. Chemical-proof charcoal-lined smock and trousers, clumsy rubber overshoes and water.

We have been accustomed to the stages of alert for donning the gear. Just the other night, I lay in my sleeping bag perspiring gently in the respirator for what seemed like hours as Scuds thundered out of hearing above our heads.

At a field casualty station, I lined up for an anthrax jab with our Scottish driver, Jock Johnson. "Better not turn us into badgers," he said suspiciously of the needle. If Saddam has his way, it could be the best unpleasant moment we have. To increase our resistance we are all taking NAPS, anti-nerve gas pills washed down three times a day with stewed Army tea.

Morning can mean "administration," the quaint army term for washing clothes or, if the water supply has got through, a cold, cold shower.

Being clean is just a distant memory. Sand permeates everything so like the soldiers I have my hair shorn to the scalp. While at night we turn our socks over the tops of our desert boots to keep out scorpions.

Orders to strike camp come abruptly and must be followed swiftly. Camouflage netting is packed away and trenches, over which we seemed to labour for so long, filled in. So we move on without showing sign of our presence.

Driving is another unforgettable experience. At night it is like navigating in a blind-fold. All the fuses that would show burning lamps must be removed. While in daylight hours every halt has to be accompanied by throwing a "scrim net" over the vehicle so it melts into the sand.

Night falls quickly like a great black curtain dropping across the skyline. By 8 p.m. the camp is silent, men sleeping or alone with their thoughts. Those hours alone are a time to reflect on the momentous days that lie ahead.

What will it really be like? We have spent long hours with battle groups to give us the tastes, sounds and sights of war—but then no one was firing at us.

To escape from those thoughts I have burrowed under my sleeping bag to write "blueys," the soldier's lifeline to loved ones, by torchlight. It brings memories of boarding school flooding back.

There have been lighter moments in these past days. Like a first aid class where my task was to heave Private Steve Smith into a fireman's lift.

All of 16 stones and as solid as a second row scrum international. He slammed over my shoulder with such force, I think we actually sank into the sand.

And good old Gunner Page, the Desert Rat who back home in Germany keeps in a cage a black rat called Arnold. None of us shall forget his crestfallen face after one chemical alert when he was ordered to carry out the dreaded sniff test. Or the afternoon of R&R spent playing with a miniature crossbow proudly outgunning the Army sharpshooters.

They will all be moments to treasure. Faces to remember, to sharpen the mind when we are baptised by battle.

Now it is dark, Allied planes are rumbling overhead on their nightly run to Baghdad. The last week with the Desert Rats has been a privilege, the next promises to be the most testing of our lives.

Battle of Red Tape Gets Off to a Blinding Start in a Windstorm and Ends in a Tent with a Few New Mates

By Gordon Airs

3 February

NORTHERN SAUDI ARABIA - At 1600 hours local army time, I at long last got to the Gulf front on behalf of the Scottish press after the Battle of the Red Tape.

The trip began at the coastal town of Dhahran when I was driven north by the army for several hours, passing long allied convoys moving south. After a transfer to a Land Rover from the 1st British Armoured Division, we drove for another couple of hours—this time struggling through blinding sandstorms.

The desert—when it can be seen—stretches flat and featureless to the distant horizon. Abandoned pre-war cars, now rusting wrecks, scar the landscape, including a bus sunk up to its axles.

Occasionally, small dusty petrol stations loom into view. Before the war they must hardly have done any business. Now it's big business for the small traders selling refreshments, food, small cookers and paraffin to the streams of U.S. and British forces.

Further up the road, at a station stop, half a dozen tanks hurtled north through the sand 100 yards from the road, watched by bored camels.

After the last spine-jolting lap over the bumpy tracks, I arrived at my base.

Just a small bunch of tents and Land Rovers, shrouded in camouflage netting somewhere in northern Saudi Arabia, near the Kuwaiti border.

Just north of here are the Royal Scots Dragoon Guards with their tanks, the Royal Scots with their armoured personnel carriers, and the Lowland Gunners of the 40th Field Regiment RA (Royal Artillery).

These gunners in fact will mark the start of any land battle—by firing the first salvos from their lethal 155mm self-propelled guns.

But for the moment it is all quiet on the Northern Front.

Home for me is a large tent, which just houses the 12 of us media representatives with our portable camp beds, and sleeping bags.

And having to share the tent sleeping quarters with 11 men is the girl described as the British Forces "pin-up"—intrepid BBC TV correspondent Kate Adie.

"Everybody has to muck in here together," I was told.

4 French Journalists Without Escorts Sent to Riyadh: Low on Fuel and "Unsure of Their Exact Location"

By Kirk Spitzer

8 February

NORTHEASTERN SAUDI ARABIA - A group of unescorted French journalists was ordered out of the northern Saudi desert after encountering elements of the 1st Marine Division at a remote outpost on the Kuwait-Saudi border.

The outpost is in an area of recent fighting between U.S. and Iraqi troops and is near the location a CBS News television crew disappeared more than three weeks ago.

The journalists were not members of the U.S. press pool covering combat activity in the Persian Gulf war and were not accompanied by a military escort.

According to a spokesman for the 1st Marine Division, four civilians who identified themselves as French journalists encountered Marines late Friday morning on the Saudi Arabian side of a border outpost southwest of the Umm Gudar oilfield in Kuwait.

The journalists, traveling in a privately owned vehicle, were low on fuel and "unsure of their exact location," said Chief Warrant Officer Eric Carlson, a spokesman for the division.

He said the Marines provided the journalists with fuel and directed them to Dhahran. Carlson said the journalists are not members of the U.S. press pool covering combat in Saudi Arabia and therefore are not allowed in combat areas. He said the Marines will ask the Saudi Arabian government to revoke the journalists' press credentials and Saudi visas.

He said the French journalists appeared to have "wandered into the area" and that they might have been killed by U.S. or Iraqi forces had they remained in the area after dark.

"It's a good thing it was daylight so we could identify them as civilians. Had the circumstances been less clear, they could very easily have been killed. This is an area where we have encountered the enemy," said Carlson.

He said the four journalists also represented a danger to the lives of Marines because they could have attracted attention to Marine positions.

He said the Marines also are concerned because the journalists had not agreed to press ground rules—including review of stories by military press officers prior to release—and could have revealed information of value to Iraqi forces.

The French journalists were identified as Albert Ripamonti, Alan Raffestine, Mark Savineau, and Philippe Brasquin.

They were not available for comment late Friday.

A CBS News television crew headed by correspondent Bob Simon disappeared in late January. The crew's vehicle and equipment were found abandoned along the Kuwait-Saudi border not far from the border outpost where the French journalists were encountered Friday. Simon and three others have not been seen or heard from since.

Copters Will Suddenly Materialize; "Not Told to Start Taking White Pills, Which Some Say Cause Nausea"

By Joseph Albright

17 February

WITH U.S. FORCES - We were told Saturday that in the event of a ground war, helicopters will suddenly materialize to take our copy and film back to Dhahran.

We hope you will do anything you can on your end to tighten down this arrangement. We were told of a particular American Army headquarters very close to the front lines where copy will be dropped by our escort officers to be picked up by the helicopter for the first day or so at least of the ground combat.

Maj. Doug Foster of 18th Airborne Corps is one officer who knows the details of this arrangement. I presume Col. Ned Longsworth, the chief PAO of the 18th Corps, was the one who set up the arrangement.

We don't know what is supposed to happen to the helos after they leave the front. Out here we have our equivalent of the

Sands Coffee Shop, where hacks gather in the morning to gab. It is a truck stop designated by the military as the media products pickup point for the hacks in their sector.

On my two or three outings from my artillery camp to the truck stop, a passerby stopping to gas up would be puzzled to see three or four un-Airborne-looking types, partly dressed in military duds, talking behind one Humvee.

Meanwhile, our escort officers, who run to the tall and lean and presentable looking, are caucusing behind another Humvee about how to deal with us and our copy.

We artillery-watchers number five: Scott Pelly, a CBS correspondent; Jim Helling, a CBS cameraman; Warren Arenstein, a CBS soundsman; Ken Jarecke, a Time magazine photographer; and me. We stay most of the time in a six-sided tent in the middle of the artillery headquarters, a circle of camouflaged tents several hundred yards in diameter located near the front but not exactly close to it.

The front.

We are free to walk around the camp without our escorts, but have no way of going anywhere outside the camp by ourselves. As in Dhahran, we have not run into much problem about the review process.

But we find that we cannot make our own decision about where we ought to be to cover the story. We have been taken on three forays to frontline artillery units within sight of Iraqi forward positions, including one overnight.

These trips were planned for the most part by the military. And we became willing onlookers for what they had scheduled. The one exception was a brief trip to a frontline unit Thursday because CBS needed to round out a story.

All day Saturday, troops in this headquarters camp went through chemical-biological refresher courses. The pressies willingly joined in and asked for a second private session with a chemical officer so that he could recheck the fit of our masks.

During the day, we were given two sets of pills. One is described as an antidote. One pill every 12 hours for a month is the prescribed dose.

We have enough pills for five days and are expecting more. The other pill is the nerve gas antidote enhancer that we learned about in our early January chem training. We and the rest of the camp have not (repeat not) been told to begin taking the pills, which some soldiers say cause nausea, gas and vomiting in some one percent of those taking them.

These are said to enhance the effect of atropine injections. We are also promised at some point a valium injector for use when suffering convulsions from nerve gas, to prevent damage to brain stem.

There are unconfirmed reports here that Iraqi forces may be equipped with generators capable of spreading anthrax spores over a wide area, perhaps as far as 200 kilometers from release. I am passing this along as something that you Dhahranites might be able to check out and use.

The reports come from one source here who is in a position to know what is being reported, but this doesn't mean I would be willing to go with it in print without some pretty good confirmation.

This morning hacks and some soldiers woke up to BBC reports about the Iraqi ambassador to the UN saying the conditions for Iraqi pullout aren't really conditions. We approached two soldiers on KP duty and wrote down quotes:

Pfc. Todd Connally, 21, of Rossville, Ga., said, "I don't believe it. We might just as well get it over with ourselves. He had plenty of time to get out."

Spec. Richard Powell, 25, of Orlando, Calif., said: "He shouldn't have been there in the first place. You don't go into somebody's country and then say you want to negotiate the conditions for wanting to get out."

While these two didn't put much stock in the reports, other soldiers seemed curious about how the diplomatic track was working. One woman soldier and one Montana National Guardsman approached a pool journalist to find out what they had heard.

As I am writing this, I am hearing muffled explosions from the north. It is now a little after 9 a.m. and I have heard about ten of the low thumps in a five-minute period.

I am also hearing planes but cannot see anything because it is overcast.

This is the first time I have heard the sounds of bombardment back in this camp, which is more than 25 kilometers back from the border.

The explosions paused while I typed the last three sentences, and I thought they were over, but then came another two whoomps.

And now I am hearing more planes. Cannot tell if they are going south or north. Officials here said the sounds we hear are not repeat not artillery. After 20 minutes explosions ceased. Heard maybe 20-30 booms.

Weather today is high overcast, good horizontal visibility because it is not windy and it rained last night, keeping the dust down.

Lower-Caste Bedouins? No, It's the Press: This is Your Shovel, These are Your Blisters

By Denis D. Gray

19 February

WITH THE 2ND MARINE DIVISION NEAR THE KUWAITI BORDER

While many criticize restrictive coverage and censorship clamped upon them by the U.S. military, few journalists with combat troops like the U.S. Marines have been heard to complain that they are not getting enough taste of life in the field.

"You guys live worse than officers, worse than a lot of enlisted men," said one surprised officer who likened reporters' living conditions to "a lower-caste Bedouin encampment."

Conditions vary. Rumors have wafted over the desert that the U.S. Army provides hot food and wind-proof tents. The Navy, by hallowed tradition, lives clean and well. And reporters returning from Air Force bases say some resemble those back in the United States, with nightly video entertainment and servicewomen running around in shorts.

Only a very small percentage of the 1,300 journalists in Saudi Arabia are assigned to so-called "combat pools"—and those who end up with the Marines here get more than they bargained for.

Organized by the military, small numbers of journalists are doled out to units in the Gulf zone. Critics say the system helps enforce guidelines laid down by the U.S. Department of Defense on what can and cannot be reported.

The nearly dozen journalists with the 2nd Marine Division, now poised near the Kuwaiti border, dig their own foxholes, fill sandbags, and help pitch their "fly tent," a tarpaulin shelter exposed on two sides to rain and the bitterly cold winter wind. Some prefer to sleep in surrounding holes rather than jammed cheek-by-jowl inside.

"The Marines have a certain attitude that we should be pulling our own weight out here. Sometimes they forget we are civilians and didn't go through Marine boot camp," said Linda Patillo, a correspondent for ABC television news who has been in the field since Jan. 15.

Since then she's averaged one hot shower a week, washes her hair with cold water out of a canteen and asks male tent-mates to close their eyes when she changes clothes.

"Today, I'm trying to file a story at the same time as filling sandbags in case there is incoming fire," the 34-year-old, Atlanta-based correspondent said.

More accustomed to wielding a camera than entrenching tool, Associated Press photographer Sadayuka Mikami sprouted blisters after filling in a chest-high foxhole that had been home for nearly a month. At the next location, he spent hours constructing a new hole only to have it flooded out by rain the first night.

The Public Affairs office, which handles the journalists, appears to be at the end of the already-spartan Marine supply line.

And some journalists are sent out from the Joint Information Bureau in Dhahran, which organizes the pools, lacking basic necessities like sleeping bags, canteens, ponchos, and even "flak jackets," which protect every Marine against shrapnel.

In a time-honored military practice, reporters scrounge and trade: a T-shirt for heating tablets; a news organization cap for a pair of warm gloves.

Some military escorts try their best to help and a natural camaraderie based on shared hardships develops with their charges. Others seem to resent that "babysitting" reporters deprives them of more Marine-like tasks, such as frontline action.

PAO officers in the field read media reports before they are sent to the rear and "flag" those deemed to have violated operational security or other press guidelines. Action, if any, is taken at higher military levels.

Journalists must normally be accompanied by escorts when interviewing troops, but this is not always done in practice. Some interviewed without an escort around are aware that their comments will be screened by the military; others are not and appear to talk frankly.

"The military is certainly an advocate of the pool system," said Capt. Scott Campbell, the 2nd Division's PAO. "It allows journalistic coverage of the battlefield while also allowing us to do the military job. It's the first time we have tried the pool concept on a large scale and I think we're learning what it takes to make it happen," he said. "We're going to have our ups and downs but I think it's workable."

While preferring open coverage to pools, Patillo said she saw some advantage to the latter. "By being forced to stay out in the field, we have gained valuable insight into the men who may have to fight this war. You don't get that living in a hotel and flying out here in a helicopter to spend a few hours on the ground."

Colin Nickerson of the Boston Globe said he felt only "vaguely uncomfortable" with reporting on troops upon which journalists must depend so intimately for their support and possibly survival. "Whenever you cover a war, you have to depend on the military force you happen to be with, whether it's guerrillas in Angola or the U.S. Marines in Saudi Arabia," he said. "You just hope the PAOs are greasing the wheels for the media and not running interference for the commanders."

Inventory for Combat: "It Would Mean a Soldier Was in Trouble and I Had the Nearest Pair of Helping Hands"

By Frank Bruni

21 February

WITH THE U.S. ARMY IN NORTHERN SAUDI ARABIA - Every day we did an inventory, both of our equipment and our knowledge.

Did we each have an unopened chemical suit in addition to an open one? Were we prepared to spend hour upon hour in it, so long that we might have to urinate and defecate in it and still move on? Every day we talked about what we might encounter, and how we would deal with it.

The correct response to sudden artillery fire was not to duck behind our truck. If hit, the truck, with its tank full of fuel, would become a secondary and perhaps more lethal bomb. We should find an open patch of sand and lie down low, even dig a hole so we could evade the sideways spray of shrapnel.

We talked about it in unemotional voices—Washington Post photographer Lucian Perkins, Army public affairs representative Sgt. Roy Caldwell, and I. The ground war, we sensed, would begin at any moment, and the frontline forces of the 3rd Armored Cavalry Regiment would breach and cross the two tall ridges of sand berms at the border.

The three of us would cross over with them, into an experience that, in the words of Maj. Shawn Tierney, "could be just as tough as driving across the desert with all these rocks—or could be your worst nightmare." Like him, like the roughly 7,000 soldiers in the regiment, like the entire military of our country, we had no idea precisely what waited on the other side, and there was no point in guessing. We would find out soon enough. We would know when we had to know, and perhaps not a moment sooner.

So where was the dread? I didn't see it in the soldiers.

I didn't see it in Lucian or Roy. And I didn't feel it in myself.

What I felt and sensed was an inexplicable serenity. Our course had been charted long ago and we had decided to follow it, setting aside misgivings and apprehensions. Now we were on our way. It was best to have it over and done with.

Lucian, Roy, and I talked about the journey ahead as if we were bound for a camping trip. Our approach to it was less emotional than methodical.

We should keep our canteens full at all times, for we might stray far from the supply train's water sources. We should keep our sleeping bags in waterproof shells for rain was sure to come. We should always wear our flak jackets, for shrapnel and bullets don't announce their arrival.

And we should be ready to pitch in. If someone yelled for me to grab one end of a litter and help carry a wounded soldier to the nearest transportation, I should do it.

The order would not mean anyone was forgetting I was only a journalist here. It would mean a soldier was in trouble, and I had the nearest pair of helping hands.

I nodded as I listened to Roy, a Montana National Guardsman called up to duty as a public affairs representative. He is 37, with a wife, three children, and a job with the phone company back in Helena. He has never been in battle before.

Among the three of us, he would be the only one to carry a rifle. We trusted he would never have to use it.

With all the M1-A1 tanks and Bradley fighting vehicles and howitzers traveling with us, we couldn't imagine a situation in which an Iraqi soldier would get close enough to us that Roy's rifle would be our only defense.

We made an agreement: if he had to fire, it meant it was time to get out. If he had to fire, it would be only once. After that, we wouldn't be around for him to fire again.

But we wouldn't make such a decision lightly, for it was important for us—for all the journalists traveling with and covering ground troops—to be here, to be this close.

We journalists spend our careers seeking and demanding access to places and situations most people never encounter. We stand at the bedside of a man dying of AIDS, because a society must know him before they can understand the tragedy of the disease. We knock on the door of the murder victim's widow, because a society must see her tears and hear her sob-muffled words before they can understand the full impact of crime.

Now our access meant personal danger. Could we suddenly say we didn't want it—thanks, but no thanks—when it was more important than ever before?

That would be the height of hypocrisy.

That would be wrong.

And so we were here, our heads scrunched into Kevlar helmets, our backpacks laden with chemical suits, doing no more than the half-a-million troops sent here by our government—marching into war.

Reporters May Have to Drive the Humvees for "The Doves of Warfare"

By Philip Davison

22 February

WITH THE U.S. MARINES NEAR IRAQI FRONT LINES - If Saddam Hussein manages to avoid a land war by means of the 11th hour Soviet plan, he may never know how close he came to destruction.

All last week, clocks were ticking away to G-Day as U.S. and allied forces assembled along the long front lines south of Kuwait and Iraq.

Throughout the week, days known as G minus-X have passed in the run-up to a final assault should President Bush say "Go."

Throughout the week, living on rocky terrain with the U.S. Marines, we have been increasingly briefed on the assault and the dangers we would face. Quietly, calmly, by a series of officers, we were told to expect something none of us, officers or newsmen, could scarcely conceive of.

It would be a war of dead, not wounded, we were told. If Iraqi weapons got in the first hit, we had little chance of survival. The Marines' battle plan was to get in the first shot whenever possible, or "waste" Iraqi artillery or aircraft as soon as they had surfaced.

We were told how to drive the Marines' jeep-like "Humvee" vehicles and warned we may be called upon to drive heavy lorries if we had to get casualties out of the combat zone. "You, the journalist, may be the only one in your vehicle to survive. You may have to drive your dead or wounded colleagues or Marine escorts out of the zone," a lieutenant quietly told us.

We were given increasing chemical weapons drills, warned that we would be advancing, writing our reports, taking our photographs in full chemical weapons suits and clumsy, hooded gas masks. Our first problems would be mines, particularly "state-of-the-art" Italian types, but hopefully they would be dealt with by the "breach teams" ahead.

If fired upon by artillery, we should keep moving. The same if we saw Iraqi helicopters swoop in. If forced to take cover, we should not stay in low bunkers for long in case chemical weapons were fired. The chemicals were likely to settle in low places, we were told.

All around, there was a quiet acceptance among Marine officers that the time was at hand. In conversations with them, the same theme recurred—that the object of the exercise was to get the job done, but to get as many of the young Marines, many of them teenagers, back to their families.

Senior officers also sounded the common theme that if the whole thing were called off, no one would complain. "Most military men are pacifists, we are the doves of warfare," Marine Col. Tom Donnelly told us in a quiet, philosophical briefing in his tent last week.

Donnelly is a Vietnam veteran, a jovial man with a penchant for joke-telling and a calm, reassuring manner. He was in Khe San during intensive bombardment of Marine positions during the Vietnam War but this, he warned us, could make that episode pale by comparison.

He noted our blood groups, assured us we could get out of the combat zone on any of the logistics helicopters or vehicles he controlled and wished us well.

PART III

Casualties of the Gulf War and Later Terrorist Acts

French - Desert Storm

Sgt. Yves Schmitt.   Cpl. Eric Cordier.

British - Desert Shield/Storm

Atkinson, P. P., Fusilier, RRF
Bolam, C. A. E., Corporal, RCT
Bunney, A., Fusilier, RRF
Burch, A. J., Major, REME
Cole, C. P., Fusilier, RRF
Collier, R. M., Flight Lieutenant, RAF
Collister, K., Flight Lieutenant, RAF
Consiglio, R. G., Cpl, PARA
Crofts, S. R., Lance Corporal, RCT
Denbury, D. E., Corporal, RE
Dent, N. T., Flight Lieutenant, RAF
Donald, N. W. D., Private, QOHldrs
Dowling, M. J., Sergeant, REME
Duffy, K. J., Flight Lieutenant, RAF
Elsdon, T. N. C., Wing Cmdr, RAF
Evans, F. C., Lance Corporal, REME
Ferguson, M., Private, QOHldrs
Fogerty, A. J., Private, RAOC
Foy, M. J., MM1, RFA
Gillespie, R. A, Fusilier, RRF
Going, R. H., Corporal, RAMC
Haggerty, T., Private, RS
Harris, P. J., MMl, RFA
Hicks, S. M., Flight Lieutenant, RFA

Hill, T. T. W., Lance Corporal, RCT
Keegan, P. P., Gunner, RA
Kinghan, J. S., Major, RE
Kinnear, D. B., Sergeant, RAPC
Lane, S. J., Corporal, RE
Lang, J. W., Private, QOHldrs
Leech, K., Fusilier, RRF
Lennox, G. K. S., Sq Lder, RAF
MacKinnon, D. A., Cmd Sgt, A&SH
McFadden, J. P., Dvr., RCT
Moult, C., Private, STAFFORDS
Napier, C. A., Guardsman, COLDM GDS
Phillips, V. D., Staff Sergeant, RAOC
Robins, R., Lance Corporal, RCT
Royle, R. A., Spartan, RE
Satchell, S. T., Fusilier, RRF
Taylor, S. P., Private, STAFFORDS
Thompson, L. J., Fusilier RRF
Tite, D. C., Staff Sergeant, RMP
Weeks, K. P., Squadron Leader, RAF
Wellington, L., Lance Cpl, RCT
Whitehead, E. A., Lieutenant, 16/5L
Wright, A. J., Lt Colonel, RE

British - Prisoners of War

Ankerson, Robert, Squadron Leader
Burgess, Simon, Flying Officer
Clark, Rupert, Flight Lieutenant
Peters, John, Flight Lieutenant

Nichol, Adrian, Flight Lieutenant
Stewart, Robert, Flight Lieutenant
Waddington, David, Flight Lieutenant

United States - Desert Shield/Storm

Adams, Thomas R., Jr., LCpl USMC
Alaniz, Andy, Spec USA
Allen, Frank C., Lance Cpl USMC
Allen, Michael R., Staff Sgt USA
Ames, David R., Staff Sgt USA
Anderson, Michael F., CWO 3USA
Applegate, Tony R., Staff Sgt USA

Arteaga, Jorge I., Capt USAF
Atherton, Steven E., Cpl USMC
Auger, Allen R., Cpl USMC
Avey, Hans C. R., Pfc USA
Awalt, Russell F., Staff Sgt USA
Bartusiak, Stanley W., Spec USA
Bates, Donald R., Staff Sgt USA

Bates, Tommie W., Capt USA
Beaudoin, Cindy M., Spec USA
Belas, Lee A., Sgt USA
Belliveau, Michael L., AE Mate3/cUSN
Benningfield, Alan H., BT2/cUSN
Bentzlin, Stephen E., Cpl USMC
Benz, Kurt A., Cpl USMC
Betz, Dennis W., Sgt USMC
Bianco, Scott F., Cpl USMC
Bland, Thomas C., Jr., Capt USAF
Blessinger, John P., Staff Sgt USAF
Blowe, James, Mr., Army/Cant
Blue, Tommy A., Sgt USA
Bnosky, Jeffrey J., Capt USA
Boliver, John A., Jr., Spec USA
Bongiorni, Joseph P., III, Sgt USA
Bowers, Tyrone, Pfc USA
Bowman, Charles L., Jr., Spec USA
Boxler, John T., Sgt USA
Brace, William C., Spec USA
Brant, Douglas L., Capt USAF
Bridges, Cindy D. J., Pfc USA
Brilinski, Roger P., Jr., Sgt USA
Brogdon, Tracy D., Sgt USA
Brooks, Tyrone M., BTech FUSN
Brown, Christopher B., Air App USN
Brown, Darrell K., Air App USN
Brown, James R., Spec USA
Budzian, Steven A., Air App USN
Buege, Paul G., Sr Mtr Sgt USAF
Bunch, Ricky L., Staff Sgt USA
Buege, Paul G., Sr Mtr Sgt USAF
Bunch, Ricky L, Staff Sgt USA
Burt, Paul L., Sgt USA
Bush, David, Spec USA
Butch, Michael R., ASMech2/cUSN
Butler, Tommy D., Spec USA
Butts, William T., Sgt1/cUSA
Caldwell, Thomas R., Capt USAF
Calloway, Kevin L., Pfc USA
Campisi, John F., Staff Sgt USAF
Carr, Jason C., Sgt USA
Carranza, Hector, Jr., LtCol USA
Carrington, Monray C., Seaman USN
Carter, Allen S., AMSAN/USN
Cash, Clarence A., Spec USA

Chapman, Christopher J., Sgt USA
Chinburg, Michael L., Capt USAF
Clark, Barry M., Sgt USAF
Clark, Beverly S., Spec USA
Clark, Larry M., Airman USN
Clark, Otto F., Master Sgt USA
Clark, Steven D., Spec USA
Clemente, Samuel J., Mr., Army/Cont
Codispodo, Edward M., LCpl USMC
Cohen, Gerald A., Pfc USA
Collins, Melford R., Pfc USA
Connelly, Mark A., Dr., Maj USA
Conner, Michael R., Sr., Staff Sgt USA
Connor, Patrick K., Lt USN
Cooke, Barry T., LtCmdr USN
Cooke, Michael D., Cpl USMC
Cooper, Ardon B., Pfc USA
Cooper, Charles W., Capt USA
Cormier, Dale T., Capt USAF
Costen, William T., Lt USN
Cotto, Ismael, Cpl USMC
Crask, Gary W., Spec USA
Craver, Alan B., Sgt USA
Crockford, James E., AS Mech3/cUSN
Cronin, William D., Jr., Capt USMC
Cronquist, Mark R., Spec USA
Cross, Shirley M., Aero. Mate1/c USN
Crumby, David R., Jr., Sgt USA
Cruz, George, Mr., Navy/Cont
Cunningham, James B., LCpl USMC
Curtin, John J., CWO3 USA
Dailey, Michael C., Jr., Pfc USA
Damian, Roy T., Jr., Spec USA
Daniel, Candace M., Pfc USA
Daniels, Michael D., Spec USA
Danielson, Donald C., Sgt USA
Daugherty, Robert L., Jr., Pfc, USA
Davila, Manuel M., Specialist, USA
Davis, Marty R., Pfc, USA
Dees, Tatiana, Staff Sergeant, USA
Delagneau, Rolando A., Spec USA
Delgado, Delwin, Sig 3/C USN
Delgado, Luis R., Sergeant, USA
Dierking, Ross A., Sergeant, USA
Diffenbaugh, Thomas M., WO1 USMC
Dillon, Gary S., Captain, USMC

Dillon, Young M., Sergeant, USA
Dolvin, Kevin R., Captain, USMC
Donaldson, Patrick A., CWO2 USA
Dougherty, Joseph D., III, LCpl USMC
Douthit, David A., Lt Colonel, USA
Douthit, David Q., Staff Sergeant, USA
Durrell, Robert L., Sergeant, USA
Dwyer, Robert J., Lieutenant, USN
Edwards, Jonathan R., Captain, USMC
Eichenlaub, Paul R., II, Captain, USAF
Fails, Dorothy L., Private, USA
Fajardo, Mario, Captain, USA
Farnen, Steven P., Specialist, USA
Felix, Eliseo C., Lance Cpl USMC
Fielder, Douglas L., Sergeant, USA
Finneral, George S., AM M 3/C USN
Fitz, Michael L., Pfc USA
Fleming, Anthony J., Av. Ord 3/C USN
Fleming, Joshua J., Private (E-2), USA
Fontaine, Gilbert A., A. Store Air USN
Foreman, Ira L., Sergeant, USA
Fowler, John C., Specialist, USA
Galvan, Arthur, Captain, USAF
Garrett, Mike A., Staff Sergeant, USA
Garvey, Philip H., Chief WO 4, USA
Garza, Arthur O., L Cpl, USMC
Gay, Pamela Y., Pfc USA
Gentry, Kenneth B., Staff Sgt USA
Gillespie, John H., Major, USA
Gilliland, David A., BTech3/CUSN
Godfrey, Robert G., CWO 3, USA
Gologram, Mark J., Sergeant, USA
Graybeal, Daniel E., Captain, USA
Gregory, Troy L., L Cpl USMC
Grimm, Walter D., Captain, USAF
Guerrero, Jorge L., Airman, USN
Haddad, Albert G., Jr., Cpl USMC
Haggerty, Thomas J., 1st Lt, USA
Hailey, Garland V., Staff Sergeant, USA
Hampton, Tracy, Sergeant, USA
Hancock, Joe H., Jr., Lieutenant Col., USA
Hansen, Steven M., Staff Sergeant, USA
Harris, Michael A., Jr., Staff Sergeant USA
Harrison, Timothy R., Staff Sgt, USAF
Hart, Adrian J., Specialist, USA
Hatcher, Raymond E., Jr., Staff Sgt, USA

Haws, Jimmy D., Staff Sergeant, USA
Hawthorne, James D., Sergeant, USMC
Hector, Wade E., Specialist, USA
Hedeen, Eric D., First Lieutenant, USAF
Hein, Kerry P., Chief WO 2, USA
Hein, Leroy E., Jr., Sergeant, USAF
Henderson, Barry K., Major, USAF
Henry-Garay, Luis A., Specialist, USA
Herr, David R., Jr., Captain, USMC
Heyden, James P., Specialist, USA
Heyman, David L., Specialist, USA
Hill, Timothy E., Specialist, USA
Hills, Kevin J., Av. El. Mate Airman, USN
Hoage, Adam T., Lance Corporal, USMC
Hodges, Robert K., Technical Sgt, USAF
Hogan, Larry G., Sergeant, USMC
Holland, Donnie R., Lt. Colonel, USAF
Hollen, Duane W., Jr., Specialist, USA
Hollenbeck, David C., Specialist, USA
Holt, William A., Av. Elec/Tech. 3/ C, USN
Holyfield, Ron R., Damage Cntr. 3/C, USN
Hook, Peter S., Major, USAF
Hopson, Trezzvant, Jr., Mr., Navy Contr.
Horwath, Raymond L., Jr., Cpl, USMC
Howard, Aaron W., Pfc, USA
Hughes, Robert J., Chief WO 3, USA
Hurley, Patrick R., Sergeant Major, USA
Hurley, William J., Captain, USMC
Hutchison, Mark E., Boiler Tech. 2/C, USN
Hutto, Earl, Civilian
Hutto, John W., Pfc, USA
Huyghue, Wilton L., Fireman, USN
Jackson, Arthur, Staff Sergeant, USA
Jackson, Kenneth J., Pfc, USA
Jackson, Mark D., Lieutenant, USN
Jackson, Timothy J., Fire Tech. 3/C, USN
James, Jimmy W., Specialist, USA
Jarrell, Thomas R., Specialist, USA
Jenkins, Thomas A., Lance Cpl, USMC
Jock, Dale W., Mach. Mate Fireman, USN
Joel, Daniel D., Cpl USMC
Jones, Alexander, AirAppr USN
Jones, Daniel M., ElMate3/c USN
Jones, Glen D., Spec USA
Jones, Phillip J., Cpl USMC
Kamm, Jonathan H., Staff Sgt USA

Kanuha, Damon V., Staff Sgt USAF
Keller, Kenneth T., Jr., Sgt USMC
Kelly, Shannon P., 2nd Lt USA
Kemp, Nathaniel H., MMSp/A USN
Keough, Frank S., Spec USA
Kidd, Anthony W., Spec USA
Kilkus, John R., Staff Sgt USMC
Kimbrell, Allen, Mr., Army Corps Engrs
Kime, Joseph G., III, Capt USA
King, Jerry L., Pfc USA
Kirk, Reuben G., III, Pfc USA
Koritz, Thomas F., Maj USAF
Kramer, David W., Pfc USA
Kutz, Edwin B., Sgt USA
LaMoureux, Dustin C., Pfc USA
Lake, Victor T., Jr., Cpl USMC
Lane, Brian L, LCpl USMC
Lang, James M., LCpl USMC
Larson, Thomas S., Lt USN
Lawton, Lorraine K., 2nd Lt USA
Lee, Richard R., CWO3 USA
Linderman, Michael Jr., LCpl USMC
Lindsey, J. Scott, Sgt USA
Long, William E., Maj USA
Love, James H., Lt USN
Lumpkins, James H., LCpl USMC
Lupatsky, Daniel, ElecMate2/cUSN
Madison, Anthony E., Spec USA
Mahan, Gary W., Spec USA
Maks, Joseph D., lstLt USA
Malak, George N., WO USA
Manns, Michael N., Jr., Fire USN
Martin, Christopher A., WO USA
Mason, Steven G., Spec USA
Matthews, Kelly L, Sgt USA
May, James M., II, Sr MSgt USAF
Mayes, Chrisine L., Spec USA
McCarthy, Eugene T., Maj USMC
McCoy, James R., Sgt USA
Mcreight, Brent A., Airman USN
McDougle, Melvin D., Sgt USA
McKinsey, Daniel C. BTFireA USN
McKnight, Bobby L., Spec USA
Middleton, Jeffrey T., Sgt USA
Miller, James R., Jr., Spec USA
Miller, Mark A., Pfc USA

Mills, Michael W., Spec USA
Mills, Randall C., Sgt USA
Mitchell, Adrienne L., Pvt USA
Mitchem, Earnest F., Jr., Sgt1/c USA
Mobley, Phillip D., Spec USA
Moller, Nels A., Sgt USA
Mongrella, Garett A., Sgt USMC
Monroe, Michael N., lstLt USMC
Monsen, Lance M., Staff Sgt USMC
Montalvo, Candelario, Jr., Sgt USMC
Moran, Thomas J., Staff Sgt USMC
Morgan, Donald W., Staff Sgt USA
Morgan, John K., WO USA
Mullin, Jeffrey E., StaffS USA
Murphy, Donald T., Sgt1/c USA
Murphy, Joe, First Sgt USA
Murray, James C., Jr., Spec USA
Myers, Donald R., Spec USA
Neberman, James F. Army/MatCmd
Neel, Randy L, AirApp USN
Nelson, Rocky J., Airman 1/c USAF
Noble, Shawnacee L., Pfc USA
Noline, Michael A., Pfc USMC
Noonan, Robert A., Spec USA
O'Brien, Cheryl L., Sgt USA
Oelschlager, John L. TSgt USAF
Oliver, Arthur D., LCpl USMC
Olson, Jeffery J., Capt USAF
Olson, Patrick B., Capt USAF
Ortiz, Patbouvier E., Staff Sgt USA
Pack, Aaron A., Sgt USMC
Paddock, John M., CWO4 USN
Palmer, William F., Spec USA
Parker, Fred R., Jr., BTec2/c USN
Patterson, Anthony T., Pvt USA
Paulson, Dale L., Spec USA
Perry, Kenneth J., Spec USA
Phillips, Kelly D., Spec USA
Phillis, Stephen R., Capt USAF
Plasch, David G., WO USA
Plummer, Marvin J. ABonMate2 USN
Plunk, Terry L., lstLt USA
Poole, Ramona L., SrAir USAF
Poremba, Kip A., LCpl USMC
Porter, Christian J., LCpl USMC
Poulet, James B. Capt USAF

Powell, Dodge R., Sgt USA
Rainwater, Norman R. Jr. Pfc USA
Randazzo, Ronald M., Sgt USA
Reel, Jeffrey D., Pfc USA
Reichle, Hal H., CWO2 USA
Reid, Fredrick A., Capt USAF
Rennison, Ronald D., Spec USA
Ritch, Todd C., Pfc USA
Rivera, Manuel, Jr. Capt USMC
Rivers, Ernest, Sgt USMC
Robinette, Stephen R. Sgt USA
Robson, Michael R., Staff Sgt USA
Rodriguez, Eloy A., Jr. MSgt USA
Rollins, Jeffrey A., Sgt USA
Romei, Timothy W., Cpl USMC
Rossi, Marie T., Maj USA
Rush, Scott A., Pfc USA
Russ, Leonard A., Sgt USA
San Juan, Archimedes P. LCpl USMC
Sanders, Henry J., Jr., 1st Sgt USA
Sapien, Manuel B., Jr., Spec USA
Satchell, Baldwin L., Sgt USA
Schiedler, Matthew J., DataSysT3 USN
Schmauss, Mark J., Staff Sgt USAF
Schmidt, Paul L., Mr., Navy/Cont
Scholand, Thomas J., LCpl USMC
Schramm, Stephen G., LtCol USAF
Schroeder, Scott A., LCpl USMC
Scott, Brian P., Sgt USA
Seay, Timothy B., DisbursClerk3 USN
Settimi, Jeffrey A., M/MSS/A USN
Shaw, David A., Staff Sgt USMC
Shaw, Timothy A., Pfc USA
Sherry, Kathleen M., 2nd Lt USA
Shukers, Jeffrey W., FiCtlTeCh USN
Siko, Stephen J., Spec USA
Simpson, Brian K., Spec USA
Smith, James A., Jr., MachMate3 USN
Smith, James M., Jr., Staff Sgt USA
Smith, Michael S., Sgt USA
Smith, Russell G., Jr., Sgt1/c USA
Snyder, David T., LCpl USMC
Snyder, John M., Lt USN
Speicher, Jeffrey W., Pfc USA
Speicher, Michael S., LtCmdr USN
   (redesignated Missing in Action)
Spellacy, David M., Capt USMC
Squires, Otha B., Jr., Spec USA
Stephens, Christopher H., Staff Sgt USA
Stephens, John B. Spec USA
Stephenson, Dion J. LCpl USMC
Stewart, Anthony D., LCpl USMC
Stewart, Roderick T., RadioSea USN
Stokes, Adrian L., Pfc USA
Stone, Thomas G., Spec USA
Streeter, Gary E., Sgt1/c USA
Strehlow, William A., Sgt USA
Stribling, Earl K., Maj USA
Sumerall, Roy J., StaffSgt USA
Swano, Peter L., Jr., Spec USA
Swanson, Richard P., AKC USN
Swartzendruber, George R. CWO2 USA
Sylvia, James H., Jr., Cpl USMC
Talley, Robert D., Pvt USA
Tapley, David L., S1/c USA
Tatum, James D., Spec USA
Thomas, Phillip J., AvMech2 USN
Thorp, James K., Capt USMC
Tillar, Donaldson P., III, 1stLt USA
Tormanen, Thomas R., LCpl USMC
Trautman, Steven R., Spec USA
Turner, Charles J., Lt USN
Underwood, Reginald C., Capt USMC
Valentine, Craig E., Lt(jg) USN
Valentine, Roger E., Pfc USA
Vega Velasquez, Mario, Sgt USA
Vigrass, Scott N., Pvt USA
Viquez, Carlos A., Dr. LtCol USA
Volden, Robert L., BTech1/c USN
Wade, Robert C., Pfc USA
Waldron, James E., LCpl USMC
Walker, Charles S., Pfc USA
Walker, Daniel B., LCpl USMC
Wallington, Michael C. LtCol USA
Walls, Frank J., Spec USA
Walrath, Thomas E., Spec USA
Walters, Dixon L., Jr., Capt USAF
Wanke, Patrick A., Pfc USA
Ware, Bobby M., Spec USA
**Warne, David A., Lt(j.g.) USN
Weaver, Brian P., AvElec2 USN
Weaver, Paul J., Maj USAF

Wedgewood, Troy M., Spec USA
Welch, Lawrence N., Sgt USA
West, John D. AvSM Airman USN
Whittenburg, Scotty L., Sgt USA
Wieczorek, David M., Pfc USA
Wilbourn, James N., III, Capt USMC
Wilcher, James, Sgt USA
Wilkinson, Philip L., MessSpc2 USN
Williams, Jonathan M., Cpl USA
Winkle, Corey L., Pfc USA
Winkley, Bernard S., CWO2 USMC
Witzke, Harold P., III, Sgt1/c USA
Wolverton, Richard V., Spec USA
Worthy, James E., Spec USA
Wright, Kevin E., Spec USA
Zabel, Carl W., Spec USA
Zeugner, Thomas C. M. Maj USA

United States - Prisoners of War - Desert Storm

Acree, Clifford M., LtCol USMC
Andrews, William F. Capt USAF
Berryman, Michael C., Capt USMC
Coleman, Melissa A., Spec USA
Cornum, Rhonda L., Maj USA
Dunlap, Troy A., Spec USA
Eberly, David W., Col USAF
Fox, Jeffrey D., LtCol USAF
Griffith, Thomas E., Jr. Maj USAF
Hunter, Guy L., Jr., CW04 USMC
Lockett, David, Spec USA
Roberts, Harry M., Capt USAF
Sanborn, Russell A. C., Capt USMC
Slade, Lawrence R., Lt USN
Small, Joseph J., III, Maj USMC
Stamaris, Daniel J., Jr., Staff Sgt USA
Storr, Richard D., Capt USAF
Sweet, Robert J., First Lt USAF
Tice, Jeffrey S., Maj USAF
Wetzel, Robert, Lt USN
Zaun, Jeffrey N., Lt USN

Americans Killed in Car Bombing, Saudi National Guard Headquarters, Riyadh, 13 Nov. 1995

Allen, James
Brozovsky, Alaric
Combs, William
Warrell, David, Sgt. 1/c
Wiley, Wayne

USAF Personnel Killed in Khobar Towers by Truck Bomb, 25 June 1996

Adams, Christopher J., Captain
Cafourek, Daniel, Staff Sgt.
Campbell, Millard D., Sgt
Cartrette, Earl Jr., Senior Airman
Fennig, Patrick P., Tech Sgt
Haun, Leland T., Captain
Heiser, Michael G., Master Sgt
Johnson, Kevin J., Staff Sgt
King, Ronald, Staff Sgt
Kitson, Kendall K. Jr., Master Sgt
Lester, Christopher, Airman 1stC
Marthaler, Brent, Airman 1stC
McVeigh, Brian, Airman 1stC
Morgera, Peter J., Airman 1stC
Nguyen, Thanh V., Technical Sergeant
Rimkus, Joseph, Airman 1stC
Taylor, Jeremy, Senior Airman
Wood, Justin R., Airman 1stC
Woody, Joshua E., Airman 1stC

U.S. Navy Personnel Killed aboard USS Cole, Aden, Yemen, 12 Oct. 2000

Clodfelter, Kenneth E. HullM.Tech3
Costelow, Richard, ElTech1/c
Francis, Lakeina Monique, MSpcSea
Gauna, Timothy Lee, InforSyTech
Gunn, Cherone Louis, SigSeaRec.
McDaniels, James Rodrick, Seaman
Nieto, Marc Ian, Engineman 2/c
Owens, Ronald Scott, EWarTech3
Palmer, Lakiba Nicole SeaRecrt

Parlett, Joshua Langdon, EngFire
Roy, Patrick Howard, FireAppr
Rux, Kevin Shawn, EWarTech2
Santiago, Ronchester MSpc3
Saunders, Timothy Lamont OpsSpec2
Swenchonis, Gary Graham, Fireman
Triplett, Andrew, Ensign
Wibberley, Craig Bryan, Seaman

Bibliography

Arabs: Journeys Beyond The Mirage, The. Lamb, David. Random House 1987.

At War in The Gulf. Blair, Colonel Arthur H. Texas A & M University Press, 1992.

Commandos, The. Waller, Douglas C. Bantam Doubleday Dell Inc., 1994.

Company C: The Real War in Iraq. Sack, John. Morrow, 1995.

Demonic Comedy, The. Roberts, Paul William. Farrar, Straus, and Giroux, 1997.

Gulf War Reader, The. Edited by Sifry and Christopher. Random House, 1991.

Hollow Victory. Record, Jeffrey. Brassey's, Inc., 1993.

Hotel Warriors. Fialka, John J. The Woodrow Wilson Center Press, 1992.

House of Saud, The. Holden, David, Richard Johns. Sidgwick and Jackson, 1981.

How To Defeat Saddam Hussein. Dupuy, Colonel Trevor N., Curt Johnson, David L. Bongard and Arnold C. Dupuy. Warner Books, Inc., 1991.

In The Eye of The Storm. Cohen, Roger, and Claudio Gatti. Farrar, Straus &: Giroux 1991.

It Doesn't Take A Hero. Gen. Norman Schwarzkopf, The Autobiography. Schwarzkopf, Gen. H. Norman. Bantam Doubleday Dell Inc., 1992.

Love and War. Hewitt, James. Blake Publishing, Ltd., 1999.

Military and The Media, The. Kennedy, William V. Praeger Publishers, 1993.

Persian Gulf TV War, The. Kellner, Douglas. Westview Press, 1992.

Saddam's Iraq: Revolution or Reaction? CARDRI: Committee Against Repression and for Democratic Rights in Iraq. Zed Books, Ltd., 1986.

Schwarzkopf in His Own Words. Pyle, Richard. Penguin Books, 1991.

Seeing Through the Media - The Persian Gulf War. Edited by Jeffords, Susan and Rabinovitz, Lauren. Rutgers University Press, 1994.

She Went To War. Cornum, Rhonda, with Peter Copeland. Presidio Press, 1992.

Triumph Without Victory - The History of the Persian Gulf War. Staff of U.S. News and World Report. Times Books, 1992.

Twilight Warriors. Arostegui, Martin C. St. Martin's Press, 1995.

Unholy Babylon - The Secret History of Saddam's War. Darwish, Adel and Alexander, Gregory. Victor Gollancz Ltd. 1991.

Members of Allied Coalition in Gulf War

Afghanistan - 300 Mujahadeen.
Argentina - Ships, 100 army engineers.
Australia - Numerous ships, photo interpreters, medical teams.
Bahrain - 36 aircraft.
Bangladesh - 6,000 troops.
Belgium - Warplanes, ships, transport planes, field hospital.
Canada - Ships, air tanker, field hospital, security troops.
Czechoslovakia - Medical team, anti-chemical warfare unit.
Denmark - Ship.
Egypt- 35,000 armored troops, aviation support.
France - 12,000 troops, 7 ships, helicopters, tanks, fighter planes
Germany - Minesweepers, ammo ship, NBC detection vehicles.
Greece.
Honduras - 200 troops.
Italy - Fighter planes, four warships.
Kuwait - 11,000 troops, aviation, ships.
Morocco - 1,500 troops.
Netherlands - Ships, field hospital, aviation personnel.
New Zealand - Airplanes and air support, medical team
Niger- 500 troops.
Norway - Ship.
Oman- 25,500 troops, aircraft, ships.
Pakistan - 5,000 troops.
Poland - Hospital ship.
Portugal - Logistics ship.
Qatar- Fighter planes, 40 tanks.
Romania - Field hospital, anti-chemical unit.
Saudi Arabia - Fighter planes, other aircraft.
Senegal - 500 troops.
South Korea - C-130.
Spain - Ships.
Syria - 20,000 troops,

Turkey - Airbases.
United Arab Emirates - 40,000 troops, 80 aircraft.
United Kingdom - armored division, ships, aircraft.
United States - 500,000-plus troops, six aircraft carrier battle groups, air wings, squadrons.

Acknowledgments

The first acknowledgement, of many owed, is that we should thank our lucky stars, because we—the 200 or so print reporters who made up the combat correspondents pool—truly had luck on our side.

It was very clear from the start that actual opportunities for seeing much at all beyond the sand dunes and the huge airfields and the silly guided bus tours arranged by our Saudi hosts were going to be limited. And while it may have been great duty to visit cute nurses on hospital ships or lanky, clear-eyed fighter pilots in ready rooms, the real shooting war was taking forever to get started.

The months necessary to bring more than a half-million troops to a state of war-readiness on the southern frontier of Iraq and Kuwait left far too much time for the type of unpleasantness, tedium and tension that accompanies a lengthy military buildup, including the un-newsworthy arguing and jockeying that goes into trying to get into and stay in position to cover a set-piece war like the one in the Persian Gulf.

There had to be a lot of luck—there were a hell of a lot of us there.

Hundreds of hacks from all over the world managed to navigate their way to the Gulf and snoop and troop around—some of us for the better part of a year. The drill that emerged over that fall and winter to deal with an evolving set of rules for covering the combat everyone knew was coming was a kind of rough democracy, among a group of men and women whose deepest instinct was to get the news first and let someone else preserve democracy.

Among those who kept their wits, and tried to inject reason into rules we all could accept, no one worked harder or more honorably than Joe Albright, a good man in many a bad situation.

From the first shots, some god of good fortune hovered while we went forth on foot, in Humvees, tanks, and armored personnel carriers, across the desert as bombs were falling and mines were exploding, convoys were speeding and bullets were flying, without losing a single soul to enemy or friendly fire.

Besides luck, one big reason we all lived to once again see the faces of families, friends, and editors was because we were usually riding amid or alongside one of the most fearsome and lethal assemblies of soldiers, sailors, Marines, ships, airmen, aircraft, and weapons ever assembled in the history of the world.

Especially in a war zone, none of us knows exactly how long we'll live. But you can count on living a damned sight longer if you ride with the likes of that able and well-armed crew.

Regardless of where any of us sit on the geopolitical spectrum that measures sympathy for the warrior class, not to acknowledge the obvious blood debt to that accidental privilege, and to the brave men and women who made up the allied coalition in the Persian Gulf War, would be churlish, if not wrong.

The dozens of names credited atop the stories in this collection illustrate another obvious debt. The long list makes it clear that this was a group effort, even before it was conceived as a book. Thanks go in equal measure to each and every one on that list for their diligence, energy and professionalism.

When we committed the writing collected here, we were all joined-up members—not only of the hated pool but of the fractious, combative, sometimes illustrious, and often selfish pursuit of digging for and writing the news.

Yet we agreed quickly and openly as a requirement of joining to let our work be seen and used by others. Shows you some stories are bigger than we are.

By all rights, there should have been more of us out there in the desert then, trying to cover the war. The conflict was brief, and the reasons for limiting access made sense from the perspective of security. But there was a lot of turf to cover in a short time, and we could have used some more help.

There were some on the military side of the media gulf who helped a great deal. Notable in this regard were Lt. Col. Pat Sivigny, USMC, and from the Army, Col. Bill Mulvey and Col. Larry Icenogle. For their steady, informed, and even-handed dealings with the press, and for their continued friendship and counsel, a special acknowledgement is in order.

In operating the public affairs desk of Joint Information Bureau in Dhahran, they conducted themselves in the highest traditions of trust, camaraderie, and fairness.

For his encouragement in the years that this collection gathered dust, his original vision that an archive of war writing could be turned into a book, and for his help in assembling the text and reading a long and rambling narrative, my thanks to Mike Hedges.

My sincere thanks also to Don North, for his support, advice, encouragement and wide knowledge of the Saudi side of the war, and to Ray Adler, who so ably assisted in the final design and generously provided office space for Ink-Slinger Press.

And finally, all of the errors, misspellings, knuckleheaded keystrokes, etc., found within are mine, except for those committed originally by the reporter who wrote the story and left intact in the interest of realism.

We'll all be better next time.

LJ

www.ingramcontent.com/pod-product-compliance
Lightning Source LLC
Chambersburg PA
CBHW071400230426
43669CB00010B/1398